pauline frommer's

WALT DISNEY WORLD® & ORLANDO

spend less see more

2nd Edition

by Jason Cochran

Series Editor: Pauline Frommer

D0062297

WILEY

Wiley Publishing, Inc.

Published by:

Wiley Publishing, Inc.

111 River St.
Hoboken, NJ 07030-5774

ISBN: 978-0-470-45316-2

Editor: Ian Skinnari
Production Editor: Katie Robinson
Cartographer: Elizabeth Puhl
Photo Editor: Richard Fox
Interior Design: Lissa Auciello-Brogan
Production by Wiley Indianapolis Composition Services
Front and back cover photo © Disney
Cover photo of Pauline Frommer by Janette Beckmann

For information on our other products and services or to obtain technical support,
please contact our Customer Care Department within the U.S. at 877/762-2974,
outside the U.S. at 317/572-3993 or fax 317/572-4002.

Wiley also publishes its books in a variety of electronic formats. Some content that
appears in print may not be available in electronic formats.

Manufactured in the United States of America

5 4 3 2 1

Contents

List of Maps

About the Author

Jason Cochran was awarded Guide Book of the Year by the North American Travel Journalists Association for *Pauline Frommer's London.* He also wrote *Pauline Frommer's San Francisco.* He is a regular writer for the New York Post, AOL's WalletPop.com, and Travel + Leisure.com. He has written extensively for publications including *Budget Travel* (as senior editor); *Entertainment Weekly;* the New York Daily News and Times; *Travel + Leisure* and *T+L Family; Newsweek; City; Frommers.com;* the *South Florida Sun-Sentinel; Arena* (U.K.); *Who* (Australia); *Scanorama* and *Seasons* (Sweden). He has been an arts columnist for both Inside.com (late night TV) and Sidewalk.com (theater). His writing has been awarded the Golden Pen by the Croatian government and was selected to appear in a permanent exhibit in the National Museum of Australia. He devised questions for the first American season of *Who Wants to Be a Millionaire* (ABC) and before that, spent nearly two years backpacking solo around the world. As a commentator, he has appeared on CNN, CNN Headline News, CNNfn, Australia.com, WOR, Outdoor Life Network, and MSNBC.com. He is an alumnus of Northwestern University's Medill School of Journalism and New York University's Graduate Music Theatre Writing Program.

An Additional Note

Please be advised that travel information is subject to change at any time—and this is especially true of prices. We therefore suggest that you write or call ahead for confirmation when making your travel plans. The authors, editors, and publisher cannot be held responsible for the experiences of readers while traveling. Your safety is important to us, however, so we encourage you to stay alert and be aware of your surroundings. Keep a close eye on cameras, purses, and wallets, all favorite targets of thieves and pickpockets.

Acknowledgments

Although many people helped support and shape this book, I can't imagine the final product without the help of several in particular. Amy Voss of the Orlando/Orange County Convention & Visitors Bureau was of incalculable assistance. Indispensable support was also supplied by Rick Sylvain of Walt Disney World, Tom Schroder and Alyson Lundell of Universal Orlando, Jill Revelle of Busch Gardens Africa, and Susan Flower and Lauren Skowyra of SeaWorld. More thanks go to Treva Marshall and Joel Kaiman, Patricia Clifton of the Grand Bohemian, Amanda Patrick of Ypartnership, Susie Storey, Laura Richeson, Jennifer Hodges, and David Landsel. I still can't imagine Orlando without the company, wit, and energy of the incomparable Katie Elliott. Thanks also to Pauline Frommer and Arthur Frommer for the professional guidance and the personal friendship, Will Larche for braving the haystack dryer, and to my mother Tracy, who has sat on many a Disney World bench while I ran around taking notes. Finally, gratitude goes to Shanon Larimer for giving me access to his seemingly bottomless local knowledge and to Wesley Brown for the happy ending.

An Invitation to the Reader

In researching this book, we discovered many wonderful places—hotels, restaurants, shops, and more. We're sure you'll find others. Please tell us about them, so we can share the information with your fellow travelers in upcoming editions. If you were disappointed with a recommendation, we'd love to know that, too. Please write to:

Pauline Frommer's Walt Disney World® & Orlando, 2nd Edition
Wiley Publishing, Inc. • 111 River St. • Hoboken, NJ 07030-5774

Star Ratings, Icons & Abbreviations

Every restaurant, hotel, and attraction is rated with stars ✦, indicating our opinion of that facility's desirability; this relates not to price, but to the value you receive for the price you pay. The stars mean:

No stars: Good
✦ Very good
✦✦ Great
✦✦✦ Outstanding! A must!

Accommodations within each neighborhood are listed in ascending order of cost, starting with the cheapest and increasing to the occasional "splurge." Each hotel review is preceded by one, two, three, or four dollar signs, indicating the price range per double room. Restaurants work on a similar system, with dollar signs indicating the price range per three-course meal.

Accommodations	**Dining**
$ Up to $75/night	$ Meals for $9 or less
$$ $76–$125	$$ $9–$15
$$$ $126–$175	$$$ $15–$21
$$$$ Over $176 per night	$$$$ $21 and up

In addition, we've included a kids icon 🧒 to denote attractions, restaurants, and lodgings that are particularly child friendly.

Frommers.com

Now that you have this guidebook to help you plan a great trip, visit our website at **www.frommers.com** for additional travel information on more than 4,000 destinations. We update features regularly to give you instant access to the most current trip-planning information available. At Frommers.com, you'll find scoops on the best airfares, lodging rates, and car rental bargains. You can even book your travel online through our reliable travel booking partners. Other popular features include:

- ◆ Online updates of our most popular guidebooks
- ◆ Vacation sweepstakes and contest giveaways
- ◆ Newsletters highlighting the hottest travel trends
- ◆ Podcasts, interactive maps, and up-to-the-minute events listings
- ◆ Opinionated blog entries by Arthur Frommer himself
- ◆ Online travel message boards with featured travel discussions

I started traveling with my guidebook-writing parents, Arthur Frommer and Hope Arthur, when I was just 4 months old. To avoid lugging around a crib, they would simply swaddle me and stick me in an open drawer for the night. For half of my childhood, my home was a succession of hotels and B&Bs throughout Europe, as we dashed around every year to update *Europe on $5 a Day* (and then $10 a day, and then $20 . . .).

We always traveled on a budget, staying at the mom-and-pop joints Dad featured in the guide, getting around by public transportation, eating where the locals ate. And that's still the way I travel today, because I learned—from the master—that these types of vacations not only save money but also offer a richer, deeper experience of the culture. You spend time in local neighborhoods, meeting and talking with the people who live there. For me, making friends and having meaningful exchanges is always the highlight of my journeys—and the main reason I decided to become a travel writer and editor as well.

I've conceived these books as budget guides for a new generation. They have all the outspoken commentary and detailed pricing information of the Frommer's guides, but they take bargain hunting into the 21st century, with more information on using the Internet and air/hotel packages to save money. Most important, we stress "alternative accommodations"—apartment rentals, private B&Bs, religious retreat houses, and more—not simply to save you money, but to give you a more authentic experience in the places you visit.

A highlight of each guide is the chapter that deals with the "other" side of the destinations, the one visitors rarely see. These sections will actively immerse you in the life that residents enjoy. The result, I hope, is a valuable new addition to the world of guidebooks. Please let us know how we've done!

E-mail me at editor@frommers.com.

Happy traveling!

Pauline Frommer

Pauline Frommer

1 America's Playground

Approaching Orlando—and this guide

IN 1886, A YOUNG UNMARRIED MAILMAN, FRUSTRATED WITH HIS FRUITLESS endeavors in the Midwest, moved to the woolly wilderness of Central Florida to make a better go of life. The land was no one's friend. Summers were oppressively hot, the lightning relentless, and the tough land, by turns sodden and scrubby, seemed to defy clearing. The only domestic creatures that thrived in Central Florida, it seemed, were the cattle, and even they turned out stringy and chewy. Undaunted—and in love with a girl from a neighboring farm—the young man planted a grove of citrus trees and waited for things to get better. They didn't. His trees died in a freeze and the young man was forced to return to delivering the mail to support himself. By 1890, the young man gave up. He moved, defeated, to Chicago to seek work. He was joined by his new bride, whose father had been injured clearing Florida pine and died. Back in the smoke of the Midwest, they had children and settled for what was to be an anonymous existence.

One day, 8 decades later, long after the young man and woman had lived full lives and passed away, two of their sons would return to Central Florida, that land that broke their father, and together they would transform the recalcitrant swamp into the most famous fantasyland in the world.

The American dream appeared to fail for Elias Disney. Little did he know it was only skipping a generation, and that his sons Walt and Roy would become synonymous with the very land that rejected him. Had he known that the Disney name would in due time define Central Florida, would he have been so despondent? Even if he could have had a fleeting vision of what was to be, and what his family would mean to this place and indeed to the United States, could he even have believed it?

The Disney brothers turned a place of toil into a realm of pleasure, a place where hardworking people can put their entertainment in reliable hands. The English have their Blackpool; Canadians have their Niagara Falls. Orlando rose to become the preeminent resort for the working and middle classes of America, and the breathtaking ingenuity of its inventions now inspires visitors from everywhere on Earth. While other countries segregate their holiday destinations by income or some other petty quality, Orlando, in the classic American egalitarian style, is all things to all people, from all countries and backgrounds.

This guide is written with a keen awareness that Orlando represents something even more powerful to American culture and history than merely being the fruit of a dream. It's something we all share. No matter who you are, no matter where you grew up, no matter what your politics, you probably went at least once to Walt Disney World and Orlando—or if you didn't, you desperately wanted to. What other thing in our culture can we all claim to share? What else has given children for the past two generations such sweet dreams? I've always said that if somehow Walt Disney World went out of business tomorrow, the National Park Service would have to take it over. It means that much to us.

So don't think of the amusements of Orlando as mere moneymaking enterprises. Of course they are, and it's easy to name legitimate issues with how they're run. But Walt Disney World, and by extension Orlando, is also Americana incarnate. The taste for showmanship and fantasy that Walt Disney World crystallizes, now known as Disneyfication, has become the defining mind-set of modern culture, in which even local grocery stores and shopping malls are dressed up like film sets and the "story" of your local burger joint is retold on the side of its soda cups.

Orlando tells us about our own culture, and it defines who we are and who we dream of being. Virtually nothing about today's Orlando is natural or authentic, and yet there may be no more perfect embodiment of our national culture. To understand this invented landscape is to understand our civilization and our generation. And if you observe Orlando with a long view—starting with young Elias Disney cutting his hands trying to budge a tough Florida pine—you will be a part of the explosive, unexpected powers of the American dream.

And one more thing: As you'll soon see, it's a hell of a lot of fun.

THE SIGHTS YOU *MUST* SEE

Walt Disney World operates four top-drawer theme parks every day of the year: **Magic Kingdom,** the most popular theme park on Earth, is an improved iteration of the original Disneyland and the park that started it all; **Epcot** is a newbrew version of an old-style world's fair; **Disney's Animal Kingdom** blends animal habitats with theme park panache; and **Disney's Hollywood Studios** presents a show-heavy salute to the movies. Every bit as elaborate and cunning, Universal Orlando's two parks, **Universal Studios Florida** and **Islands of Adventure,** command great respect and get the adrenaline pumping a bit stronger. The gardens and marine mammals at **SeaWorld Orlando** serve to soothe. Those seven parks, all of which are in the top 10 most visited in the world, would take over a week to see fully, but there are still a few more. **Busch Gardens Africa** provides animal sightings with coaster after celebrated coaster, and three water parks combine cooling water with kinesthetic energy: **Typhoon Lagoon** for family-friendly slides, **Blizzard Beach** for more aggressive ones, and **Wet 'n Wild** for no-holds-barred thrills.

IF YOU HAVE ONLY 1 DAY IN ORLANDO   Well, I'm sorry for you. Just as it's impossible to eat an entire box of Velveeta in one sitting, you can't get the full breadth of Orlando in a day. But there is a must-see attraction: Walt Disney World's **Magic Kingdom** (p. 108). There is enough diversion at every Orlando theme park to keep you busy from morning to midnight—it's all a matter of willpower, and at what point you can tear yourself away. Ride the great Disney Audio-Animatronic odysseys **Pirates of the Caribbean, Haunted Mansion,** and **"it's a small world,"** and brave the drops of **Splash Mountain** and **Space Mountain.** While you're there, take a free spin on the **monorail** through the iconic **Contemporary Resort,** and then connect for the free round-trip ride to **Epcot** (p. 134) and back, where you'll see the other top Disney park from above. Stay until closing, through the **fireworks** and the **parade,** or, if you've had enough, head to a quintessentially kitschy dinner banquet spectacle such as **Arabian Nights** (p. 93). Hope you're not hungry for subtlety!

IF YOU HAVE ONLY 2 DAYS IN ORLANDO   Do the **Magic Kingdom** for sure, but for your second day, drop into **Epcot** and pass the morning hours seeing **Future World,** and then have lunch at one of the ethnic eateries of **World Showcase,** such as in **Morocco** or **Japan.** Hopefully, you bought an admission ticket that allows for park hopping, so you can duck into **Disney's Hollywood Studios** (p. 152) to try the superlative **Twilight Zone Tower of Terror,** or as long as it's before 5pm, into **Disney's Animal Kingdom** (p. 163) to sample the newly built **Expedition Everest** roller coaster.

IF YOU HAVE 3 OR 4 DAYS IN ORLANDO   Now it's time to consider branching out beyond the Mouse. If you're here for theme parks, you should go directly to **Universal Orlando's Islands of Adventure** (p. 192), one of the most elaborate amusement parks in the world, and don't neglect some of its most celebrated rides: **the Adventures of Spider-Man, Incredible Hulk Coaster,** and **Popeye & Bluto's Bilge-Rat Barges.** If you have small kids or you don't like thrills, then **SeaWorld Orlando** (p. 204), with its **Shamu** show and multiple marine animal habitats, makes for a soothing change of pace. Fill in spare time by visiting the secondary Disney theme parks (Animal Kingdom and Hollywood Studios) or by spending a few hours at **Universal Studios Florida** (p. 180). During the evening, spend a night at the shopping-and-clubs zone of Universal's **CityWalk** (p. 281), or for an experience that's a little less canned, hit a pedestrian zone such as **Old Town** (p. 229) in Kissimmee, the smooth clubs of **Church Street** (for example, Cheyenne Saloon & Opera House, p. 289) downtown, the carnival atmosphere of **International Drive** north of Sand Lake Road (p. 225), or the Vietnamese culinary delights of **ViMi** (see "A Gastronomic Tour of Little Vietnam," p. 88) downtown. You might need a fine arts fix, too: The **Morse Museum**'s (p. 237) dazzling collection of Tiffany glass, followed by a boat cruise past the mansions of **Winter Park** (p. 237), might be just the ticket, as would be a stroll through the galleries of the **Downtown Arts District** (p. 234). At the moment you get sick of roller coasters—or when the temperature cracks the boiling point, whichever comes first—head for a water park: **Blizzard Beach** (p. 172) for a heavily themed experience, or **Wet 'n Wild** (p. 225) for unvarnished thrills.

IF YOU HAVE 5 OR MORE DAYS IN ORLANDO   Finally—you're approaching a vacation long enough to enable you to actually relax, and to take time to sit by the pool. Of course, if you stuck to a schedule as rigid as one major theme park per day, it would still take you 8 days to knock down the biggies, and that's before setting your belly on a single water slide. Take a day to drive out to **Kennedy Space Center** (p. 241), or if you need some peace, take a dip in a natural spring, such as **DeLeon Springs** (p. 265).

IF IT'S RAINING   Universal Studios Florida, with its many air-conditioned shows, waiting areas, and its covered parking, is the best choice. SeaWorld Orlando, where you'll spend lots of time walking outside, is the worst in rain. If it's a **scorcher,** both Universal Studios and Disney's Hollywood Studios have lots of sheltered activities, but you'll be best served by one of the three water parks

(**Wet 'n Wild, Blizzard Beach,** or **Typhoon Lagoon** [p. 173]) which get crowded, but are fine choices—though, of course, your hotel pool holds water as a heat reliever, too. The worst park on hot or wet days is the exposed **Disney's Animal Kingdom.**

THE TRUE CHARACTER OF THE PLACE

Of course, Orlando's identity as a theme park mecca only began in 1971, and the city has a deep culture of its own. Sample the high art collected by its high-society settlers at Winter Park's **Charles Hosmer Morse Museum of American Art** (Tiffany glass by the shelf; p. 237), the **Cornell Fine Arts Museum** (lush decorative arts of every description; p. 238), or the **Orlando Museum of Art** (fine works from every era; p. 233). The reason all those blue bloods migrated here? The fine weather and the beautiful water. While some people rave about the horticultural achievements at botanical gardens such as the **Harry P. Leu Gardens** (p. 264) or **Historic Bok Sanctuary** (p. 265), I personally crave swimming in the 72-degree natural springs at **DeLeon Springs State Recreation Area** (where you can make your own pancakes and then have a swim in pure water; p. 265); a canoe paddle at **Wekiwa Springs State Park** (just north of downtown; p. 266); or, in winter, watching some of the area's original residents, wild manatees, swim at **Blue Spring State Park** (p. 266). Even Orlando tourism has its antecedents: **Gatorland** (p. 235) is a pleasing, corn-fed throwback from another era. And modern history has fewer finer monuments than the still-active launch pads at the **Kennedy Space Center** (p. 241), where America accomplished the impossible, over and over again.

LODGING TO BEAT THE RECESSION

Although pretty much everyone comes here to see Disney, not everyone can afford to stay there; prices start at $82 in the quietest seasons (barring sales) for a mediocre room in its **Pop Century** or **All-Star** resorts (p. 43). So rent an entire house instead. **All Star Vacation Homes** (p. 29) decorates its properties, all within 4 miles of Disney, to the highest design standards from as little as $119 for two bedrooms, plus a living room pullout—and companies such as **Alexander Holiday Homes** (p. 29), **IPG Florida Vacation Homes** (p. 30), and **Oak Plantation** (p. 52) do it for as little as $79 a night. **Orlando Courtyard Suites** (p. 53) gives you a motel-style atmosphere with top-end apartment units starting at $89. Other affordable hotels such as **Holiday Inn Express Hotel & Suites Orlando Lake Buena Vista East** (p. 52) and **Rodeway Inn at International** (p. 61) get you a straight-ahead standard room for nostalgic prices. Of course, many people have saved up all year for the chance to splash out on their Orlando hotel experience, and for them, there are places where you can get a better-than-average experience for market value. The **Courtyard at Lake Lucerne** (p. 38), set in the city's oldest documented home, is impossibly romantic; and the **Nickelodeon Family Suites** (p. 59) entertains kids with the flamboyance of a theme park.

FOOD, BEYOND THE CHAINS

Orlando is one of those places where even blasé restaurants are priced like splurges, but I sort the wheat from the chaff and tell you which special-occasion tables get you the most for your buck, including **California Grill** (overlooks the Magic Kingdom fireworks from atop the Contemporary Resort; p. 67), and **Todd English's bluezoo** (impeccable fish; p. 67). More importantly, I point out fabulous restaurants, many family run, that have been elbowed into the background by the proliferation of also-ran chains. These guys could put Epcot's World Showcase to shame, and at a fraction of the price: **Bruno's Italian Restaurant** (*abbondanza!* Right in the franchise zone of Disney, too! p. 77); **Nile Ethiopian Cuisine** (authentically African, down to the coffee ceremony; p. 82); **Asia Bagus** (Indonesian, smartly done, also near Disney; p. 77); **Havana's Cuban Cuisine** (the real stuff, right by Disney; p. 78); **Blackwater Bar B-Q** (divine Brunswick stew, and dead cheap; p. 84); and **Seasons 52** (no dish will hit you for more than 475 calories, and desserts are served by the shot glass; p. 83). And a selection of little places will put you in touch with the locals: The veggie chili at the friendly **Dandelion Communitea Cafe** (p. 85) is to die for, while **Vinhs Restaurant** (p. 89) in the Vietnamese district makes its own roast pork using a secret recipe. Yes, as it turns out, there are a lot of dining secrets in this town.

THE BEST "OTHER" EXPERIENCES

There's no better way to get under the skin of Orlando than to sneak backstage. Far from spoiling the show, behind-the-scenes tours only enrich your understanding and appreciation for the feats of urban planning that have been achieved here, and what's being accomplished every single day in the name of your entertainment. Walt Disney World's **Backstage Magic** (p. 248) is a 7-hour primer on the resort's operational secrets, from the secret utilidors underfoot at the Magic Kingdom to the warehouse where the Audio-Animatronic figures are repaired. You fulfill the childhood fantasy of having an empty theme park all to yourself, paired with the pleasure of learning to ride a Segway scooter, on **Around the World at Epcot** (p. 249). SeaWorld's **Dolphin Spotlight** (p. 252) is a rare chance to feed a dolphin family by hand, and at Busch Gardens Africa, you can do the same thing with nosy giraffes from a flatbed truck on the **Serengeti Safari** (p. 254), even after dark using night-vision tools. For even deeper learning, Kennedy Space Center's **Astronaut Encounter** (p. 253) affords the opportunity to meet and talk with a real NASA astronaut who has been to space. Outside the theme parks, Orlando is rich with more opportunities to see how people live, from unusual planned communities (the picture-perfect Stepford town of **Celebration** [p. 258] and the psychics of the haunted 19th-century hamlet **Cassadaga** [p. 259]) to some of the most vital Christian evangelical projects in America (such as the **WordSpring Discovery** Bible translation center; p. 260). When you're worn out from thinking, take a night off to kick back at a **spring training** (p. 254) baseball game or a **drive-in movie** (p. 255)—Orlando is one of the only places in America that can boast both options. But the activity you may treasure most of all is the chance to volunteer to help a Make-A-Wish kid's Orlando dream come true at **Give Kids the World Village** (p. 262), a specialized resort that must be seen to be believed.

SUGGESTED DISNEY ITINERARIES

You shouldn't march into the parks with a stopwatch and a map like some kind of warrior or military strategist. That's the surest way to have a stressful vacation, and to make some miserable memories. The parks simply are not best enjoyed that way—you get the most out of them if you don't put too much pressure on yourself and if you make time for discoveries. Besides, fixed plans of attack are easily rendered useless by changes in the weather, ride breakdowns, swells or droughts in the crowds, or if your kid suddenly gets grouchy and needs a nap. And in the peak seasons of July or after Christmas, waits can be so extreme that you'd be lucky to get a half-dozen rides or shows in. But these suggested routes, good for most times of year, will help you prioritize what's worth seeing, and when.

I suggest eating meals between 10:30am and noon (lunch) and 4 and 5pm (dinner) to avoid getting caught in crowds and losing valuable time. But you can fit meals anywhere into the following plans when you're hungry.

The Magic Kingdom

FOR THOSE WITH KIDS UNDER 8

No coasters, just easy rides and lots of characters

Major attractions to collect **Fastpass** for within 90 minutes of opening if you're *not* following the plan: Peter Pan's Flight and the Many Adventures of Winnie the Pooh.

1. When the gates open, head to **Fantasyland,** and ride in the following order: Peter Pan's Flight, Dumbo the Flying Elephant (omit if your kids don't care), the Many Adventures of Winnie the Pooh, Snow White's Scary Adventures, "it's a small world."

2. Visit **Mickey's Toontown Fair** if you want to meet Mickey. If not, omit for now.
   Secondary option: Ride the **train** from **Toontown Fair** to **Frontierland** to reach **Adventureland.**

3. Cross to **Adventureland** to ride Pirates of the Caribbean and the Jungle Cruise.

4. It may be hot by now, so see these two neighboring indoor shows, where you'll be seated: the Enchanted Tiki Room and the Country Bear Jamboree.

5. See the parade from **Frontierland** or **Main Street, U.S.A.**
   Secondary option: If you'd rather see the evening parade, take **the raft to Tom Sawyer Island** before it starts.

6. If your kids are willing, ride the Haunted Mansion.

7. On your way to **Tomorrowland** via **Fantasyland,** visit Ariel's Grotto, watch Mickey's PhilharMagic, and (time permitting) check out Tinker Bell at Pixie Hollow.

8. In **Tomorrowland,** ride Buzz Lightyear's Space Ranger Spin and Stitch's Great Escape!

9. Ride the Speedway if your child meets the height requirement.

10. If there's time, hit rides you missed (the Carrousel, Astro Orbiter).

11. Watch the **evening parade** and the **fireworks** before departing.

FOR THOSE WITH TEENAGERS

Thrills, fewer kiddie rides

Major attractions it's smart to have a **Fastpass** for—get the first within 90 minutes of opening, get another after that's used, and so on: Splash Mountain, Space Mountain, Big Thunder Mountain Railroad, Buzz Lightyear's Space Ranger Spin.

1. When the gates open, head to **Frontierland** and ride Big Thunder Mountain Railway. On the way out, grab a **Fastpass** for Splash Mountain (come back to ride it when the pass comes due).
2. In **Adventureland,** ride Pirates of the Caribbean and Jungle Cruise.
3. Cross the park via **Fantasyland,** collecting a **Fastpass** for either Peter Pan's Flight or the Many Adventures of Winnie the Pooh, to **Tomorrowland** and ride Space Mountain and Buzz Lightyear's Space Ranger Spin.
   Secondary option: See Monster's Inc. Laugh Floor (it's indoors and you'll be seated).
4. Go to **Fantasyland** for the Mad Tea Party, Mickey's PhilharMagic, and any rides that catch your fancy. You'll be getting hot and tired about now, so something like "it's a small world" might hit the spot.
5. Ride the Haunted Mansion.
6. Take the raft to Tom Sawyer Island where the kids can have free reign and, upon returning, shoot a few rounds at the Frontierland Shootin' Arcade or maybe do a lap on the **riverboat.**
7. Ride the train from **Frontierland** to **Main Street, U.S.A.**
8. See the **parade** and **fireworks** from **Main Street, U.S.A.,** or in front of the **Castle.**
   Secondary option: If the parade isn't of interest, pick rides anywhere except in Adventureland to re-ride or try; lines will be dramatically shorter during the parade.

FOR THOSE WITH NO KIDS
A mix of thrills and fun kiddie stuff

Major attractions it's smart to have a **Fastpass** for—get the first within 90 minutes of opening: Splash Mountain, Space Mountain, Big Thunder Mountain Railroad, Buzz Lightyear's Space Ranger Spin.

1. Upon opening, ride Peter Pan's Flight, "it's a small world," and the Many Adventures of Winnie the Pooh. That'll put you in the mood.
2. Head to **Frontierland** and ride Big Thunder Mountain Railroad. Get a Fastpass to Splash Mountain, and ride that either now or when it comes due.
3. Ride Pirates of the Caribbean and Jungle Cruise.
4. See the Enchanted Tiki Room or the Country Bear Jamboree.
5. Get out of **Adventureland** before the parade starts; it cuts the land off from the rest of the park.
6. It's hot outside! Ride the Haunted Mansion. Repeat until spooked.
7. Stay indoors by seeing Mickey's PhilharMagic.
8. Head to **Tomorrowland** and ride Buzz Lightyear's Space Ranger Spin and Space Mountain.
9. You're probably getting a little tired by now, so sit down and enjoy the Tomorrowland Transit Authority.
10. Then take your time to explore **Mickey's Toontown Fair,** and then take the **train** to **Frontierland** to explore Tom Sawyer Island. Ride the **riverboat** if you have a half-hour.
11. Enjoy the **parade.**
    Secondary option: If you have rides you missed or you'd like to repeat, the parade is a prime time for that, but don't miss the **fireworks** just after.

FOCUSING ON ATTRACTIONS FROM THE CLASSIC DISNEY ERA

1. When the park opens, head to **Fantasyland** and ride the stuff that will stay packed all day: Peter Pan's Flight, "it's a small world," the Many Adventures of Winnie the Pooh, and (if you can stomach it) Mad Tea Party.

2. Take a minute to observe Dumbo the Flying Elephant and the beautiful Carrousel, but don't ride unless you're dead set on it.

3. Head to **Adventureland** for Pirates of the Caribbean and the Jungle Cruise.

4. See the Enchanted Tiki Room.

5. Head to **Frontierland** for Country Bear Jamboree.

6. Take the **raft** to Tom Sawyer Island.

7. Ride the Haunted Mansion.

8. Go to **Tomorrowland** and ride the Speedway.

9. See Walt Disney's Carousel of Progress.

10. Take a spin on the Tomorrowland Transit Authority.

11. Stroll down **Main Street, U.S.A.,** for ice cream and shopping, making sure to stop at the Town Square Exhibition Hall to catch some vintage Disney cartoons.

12. Board the **train** there for a full circle of the park.

13. You are now well rested—and you've seen the stuff Walt had a hand in. Take the rest of the day to explore at will. Don't miss some of the greats of the post-Walt era: Space Mountain, Splash Mountain, and Big Thunder Mountain Railroad. For something cool and indoors, Mickey's PhilharMagic is a modern attraction that's very faithful to the old Disney spirit.

Epcot

Major attractions to collect **Fastpass** for within 90 minutes of opening: Soarin', Test Track.

1. When the gates open, go immediately to **the Land** and ride Soarin'. Get a **Fastpass** for it as you leave if you'd like to do it again (many people do).

2. Ride Test Track.

3. Ride Mission: Space.

4. Visit the Seas with Nemo and Friends.

5. Ride Living with the Land, and if you got a Fastpass, do Soarin' again. If you're hungry, Sunshine Seasons, in this pavilion, is a terrific place to eat.

6. Ride Spaceship Earth and visit Innoventions.
   Secondary option: See Universe of Energy or, third option, visit Imagination! (the line's never long) and see Honey, I Shrunk the Audience.

7. Enter **World Showcase** at Mexico and ride Gran Fiesta Tour.

8. Ride Maelstrom at Norway. You have now enjoyed all the rides in World Showcase.

9. Continue along **World Showcase** at your own pace, avoiding the temptation to rush. The movies, in China, France, and Canada, are all worth seeing; the shops can be surprisingly good; and the street entertainment choices are excellent.

10. Catch the American Adventure; the Voices of America perform about 15 minutes before showtimes, and they're listed in the Times Guide.

11. Continue along **World Showcase.** Pause for a pint in the United Kingdom.

12. Remember **Future World** closes at 7pm, so if you have time before then, re-ride anything you loved (Spaceship Earth isn't usually crowded late in the day).
13. Eat dinner in the land of your choice and catch IllumiNations.

Disney's Hollywood Studios

Major attraction to collect **Fastpass** for within 90 minutes of opening: Toy Story Midway Mania. If you have little kids with you, Voyage of the Little Mermaid.

IF YOU HAVE SMALL CHILDREN IN TOW

1. When the gates open, ride Toy Story Midway Mania. You'll probably want to get a **Fastpass** on the way out so you can ride it again later.
2. See Voyage of the Little Mermaid.
3. See Playhouse Disney—Live on Stage!
4. See Mickey at the Magic of Disney Animation.
5. Do the Great Movie Ride.
6. Visit Buzz and Woody at Pixar Place.
7. Take the Backlot Tour (it usually shuts down by late afternoon).
8. Target a performance of Beauty and the Beast—Live on Stage for around now.
9. See Muppet*Vision 3-D.
10. See the Indiana Jones Epic Stunt Spectacular.
11. If you think the kids can handle them, slot in the Twilight Zone Tower of Terror and the Rock 'n' Roller Coaster.
12. See Fantasmic! (if it's performing tonight).

IF YOU DON'T HAVE LITTLE KIDS WITH YOU

1. When the gates open, ride Toy Story Midway Mania. You'll probably want to get a **Fastpass** on the way out so you can ride it again later.
2. Head to the Twilight Zone Tower of Terror and the Rock 'n' Roller Coaster and ride them. If the wait for either is over 30 minutes, **Fastpass** one and do the other (that is, if you haven't already got a Fastpass outstanding for Midway Mania).
3. See Voyage of the Little Mermaid.
4. Do the Great Movie Ride.
5. Take the Backlot Tour (it usually shuts down by late afternoon).
6. Target a performance of Lights, Motors, Action! to fall around now.
7. Ride Star Tours.
8. See the Indiana Jones Epic Stunt Spectacular.
9. See Muppet*Vision 3-D.
10. Tour Walt Disney: One Man's Dream (you can also do this anytime lines seem intolerable everywhere else).
11. Make a pass to the American Idol Experience.
12. See Fantasmic! (if it's performing tonight).

Disney's Animal Kingdom

Major Attractions to **Fastpass** for within 90 minutes of opening: Expedition Everest.

FOR ADULTS & TEENS

1. When the gates open, head straight to **Africa** for Kilimanjaro Safaris. (If you're a coaster person, grab a **Fastpass** for Expedition Everest on the way there, but no dawdling!)
2. If you Fastpassed Everest, enjoy the Pangani Forest Exploration. If not, go to **Asia** to ride Everest before the line gets too crazy.
3. Explore the Maharajah Jungle Trek.
4. Ride Kali River Rapids.
5. See Flights of Wonder.
6. See the next performance of *Finding Nemo—The Musical.*
7. Ride Primeval Whirl and TriceraTop Spin.
8. Ride DINOSAUR.
9. Go see It's Tough to Be a Bug!, and afterward walk the **Discovery Trails** and look for animals embedded in the Tree of Life.
10. Walk the **Pangani Forest Exploration Trail,** and if it's quiet and you're interested, re-ride Kilimanjaro Safaris to get a different experience than before.
11. Go to **Camp Minnie-Mickey** to see *Festival of the Lion King.*
12. If you have time or energy, take the **train** to and from Rafiki's Planet Watch for a 20-minute walk-through (budget 45 min. total).
13. Catch the **parade,** re-ride anything you loved, and head out by closing at 5pm (the usual time).

IF YOU HAVE SMALL CHILDREN WITH YOU

1. When the gates open, head straight to **Africa** for Kilimanjaro Safaris.
2. Enjoy the Pangani Forest Exploration.
3. Explore the Maharajah Jungle Trek.
4. Ride Kali River Rapids.
5. See Flights of Wonder.
6. See the next performance of *Finding Nemo—The Musical.*
7. Ride Primeval Whirl and TriceraTop Spin.
8. Go see It's Tough to Be a Bug!, and afterward walk the **Discovery Trails** and look for animals embedded in the Tree of Life.
9. Walk the **Pangani Forest Exploration Trail,** and if it's quiet and you're interested, re-ride Kilimanjaro Safaris to get a different experience than before.
10. Go to **Camp Minnie-Mickey** to see *Festival of the Lion King* and to meet the Disney characters.
11. If you have time or energy, take the **train** to and from Rafiki's Planet Watch for a 20-minute walk-through (budget 45 min. total).
12. Catch the **parade,** re-ride anything you loved, and head out by closing at 5pm (the usual time).

Combining Disney's Animal Kingdom & Disney's Hollywood Studios into a Single Day

You really don't *have* to pay for 2 days' worth of park tickets for these two. As long as you have the Park Hopper ticket option, you can see the big highlights of these two parks in 1 action-packed day. You will miss some lesser attractions, but to be honest, neither park can fill a whole day each. Animal Kingdom usually opens at 8am, which lets you get a head start on things.

Which park you do first is a toss-up. The animals are most active first thing in the morning at Animal Kingdom, but the line at Hollywood Studios' Toy Story Midway Mania gets crazy by noon, and the Fastpasses are often gone by then. I'm starting with Animal Kingdom, knowing that the line for Midway Mania will likely be well over an hour, but if you don't think Midway Mania is for you (see p. 158 for a description), that problem will vanish.

Start at **Disney's Animal Kingdom**

1. When the gates open, head straight to **Africa** for Kilimanjaro Safaris. (If you're a coaster person, grab a **Fastpass** for Expedition Everest on the way there, but no dawdling!)
2. If you Fastpassed Everest, enjoy the Pangani Forest Exploration. If not, go to **Asia** to ride Everest before the line gets too crazy.
3. Explore the Maharajah Jungle Trek.
4. Ride Kali River Rapids.
5. If you enjoy live musicals, see the next performance of *Finding Nemo—The Musical*. This will take nearly an hour, so trim this if it's too close to lunch.
6. Ride DINOSAUR (You may want to do this while waiting for *Nemo* to start.)
7. Go see It's Tough to Be a Bug!, and afterward walk the **Discovery Trails** and look for animals embedded in the Tree of Life.
8. Leave the park and have lunch on U.S. 192, where food's cheaper. You can reach it quickly by following the signs to the Animal Kingdom Lodge and turning left at the light before its entrance. That's Sherbeth Road, and it winds to U.S. 192. After lunch, drive east on 192 a few miles and follow the signs back to Disney.

Head to **Disney's Hollywood Studios**

9. First, go to Toy Story Midway Mania at **Pixar Place.** If there are any Fastpasses left, get one and come back later. If not, endure the line—it should be the only big one of your day, but at least it will be indoors, and Mr. Potato Head is entertaining.
10. Go ride Twilight Zone Tower of Terror and Rock 'n' Roller Coaster.
11. Do the Great Movie Ride.
12. Take the Backlot Tour (it usually shuts down by late afternoon).
13. Target a performance of Lights, Motors, Action! to fall around now.
14. Ride Star Tours.
15. If you have time, see Muppet*Vision 3-D.
16. If you have time, see the Indiana Jones Epic Stunt Spectacular.
17. See Fantasmic! (if it's performing tonight).
18. Go back to your hotel and collapse.

PLANNING UNIVERSAL & SEAWORLD

At the other parks (Universal, SeaWorld, Busch Gardens), crowds aren't usually so horrific as to require you to prioritize so carefully. Use the star ratings in each chapter to guide you to the must-sees, but here are some pointers:

At **Universal Studios,** simply put the shows lower on your list. If you want to enjoy the most elaborate attractions at the Studios, head for (in this order) the Rockit coaster, the Mummy, the Simpsons Ride, Jaws, Men in Black, and E.T. Once you've knocked those down, see Twister, Shrek, and Disaster!, and then pick the shows that interest you most. *Note:* Because so many queues are indoors here, this is a great park to see if the forecast calls for hot or rainy weather, although the Rockit coaster will shut down if there's lighting about.

If you have little children with you, prioritize E.T. and the surrounding **Woody Woodpecker's Kidzone** children's area first, along with the Animal Actors show.

At **Islands of Adventure,** start when the gates open, without fail. Don't miss Spider-Man and the Hulk coaster (the two most popular rides), **Jurassic Park,** and in the heat of the day, Ripsaw Falls and the Bilge-Rat Barges. Wind up with the Cat in the Hat. Then you can bat clean-up with fun stuff like the Discovery Center and Dr. Doom's Fearfall. Remember that most people start their touring by going left (into Marvel Super Hero Island), so you should too so that you have a chance of beating the inevitable lines at the Hulk and Spider-Man.

If you have little children with you, prioritize **Seuss Landing** first, followed by Pteranodon Flyers in the **Jurassic Park** area and Me Boat, the Olive in **Toon Lagoon.**

For **SeaWorld,** pick the Shamu show you want to see (I like the evening one because you can usually leave easily afterward) and build your day around it. I recommend you don't miss Clyde & Seamore and Pets Ahoy!, with Blue Horizons close behind. Fill the time in between those with Manta and Kraken, as well as visits to the various habitats (Sharks Deep Dive and Wild Arctic are standouts). Do Journey to Atlantis when the heat is strongest—you will get drenched, and it'll feel great; it's beside Kraken. Cap summer nights with Mystify.

2 The Lay of the Land

Orlando's not such a small world, after all.

THERE ARE TWO KINDS OF AMERICAN CITIES: THOSE CONCEIVED BEFORE the proliferation of the automobile—with walkable distances and manageable transit links—and those spread-out sprawls laid after the car took over. Because its development took a hairpin turn in the 1950s, Orlando is two cities, one of each type.

Back when only cargo trains had much business in Central Florida, Orlando fashioned itself as a prosperous small city—some derisively called it a cow town—well positioned to serve the citrus and cattle industries as they shipped goods between America and Cuba. The city remained that way, mostly irrelevant, until around 1943, when the great cross-state cattle drives ended.

Soon after, the brick-warehouse city of Orlando developed its second personality. The turning point wasn't the arrival of Walt Disney on his secret land-buying trips. It came a decade earlier, when NASA settled into the Space Coast, 45 minutes east, and the local government, spotting opportunity, invited the Martin Marietta corporation—now Lockheed Martin—to open a massive facility off Sand Lake Road, near the present-day Convention Center. To sweeten the deal, leaders promised unprecedented civic improvements, including a still-unrealized high-speed rail system. Mostly, though, politicians built roads. Florida's Turnpike to Miami was carved past the Martin plot, S.R. 50 was hammered through downtown to link the coasts, and soon after, many blocks in the downtown area were bulldozed for the construction of Interstate 4, linking Tampa on the west coast with Daytona Beach (then one of America's premier vacation towns) on the east coast. By the time Walt hungrily eyed the swamps, the government had proven its skill in luring high-powered projects.

Walt's new kingdom was constructed 20 miles southwest of the city in scrubland, where his planners could keep the outside world at bay. The resort was intended to be an oasis in the citrus groves, but soon, sprawl (outside the city limits but indivisible from Orlando in most visitors' minds) sprouted around the park's border, just as had happened in Anaheim. For the last two generations, the space between the two disparate Orlandos has vanished, consumed by developments where "real" Orlando residents live, so that the old-fashioned, "traditional" city has come to be dwarfed, as it were, by family-friendly honky-tonk and slapped-up suburbs. Few casual visitors know the original Orlando even exists.

NAVIGATING THE HIGHWAYS: As a city whose population explosion was enabled in no small part *because* of major highways, Orlando is combed by them. I would estimate that *90% of what a tourist wants to see or do lies within a 10-minute drive of Interstate 4,* or I-4, as it's called. (This simplicity is a contributing factor to Orlando's tourism success.) I-4 runs diagonally through the city from southwest to northeast, linking Walt Disney World, SeaWorld, the Convention Center, Universal Orlando, downtown Orlando, and other attractions.

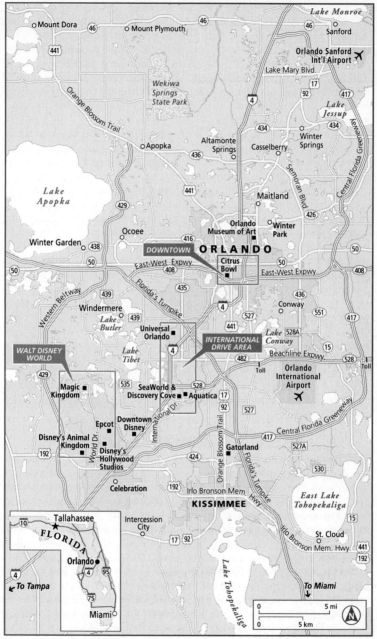

The only trick to navigating I-4 is understanding that by federal definition, it's an east-west road, linking Florida's coasts, so although it indeed runs north-south through Orlando, all directions are listed as either west (toward Tampa and the Gulf of Mexico) or east (toward Daytona Beach and the Atlantic Ocean). Once you've got that down, you'll be set. Exits are numbered according to the mile marker at which they're found. Therefore, the Walt Disney World exits (62, 64, 65, and 67) are roughly 10 miles from Universal Orlando's (74 and 75), which are about 9 miles from downtown (83). If you know your exit number, you can also figure out your distance in miles.

Traffic on I-4 tends to be worse in one direction at a time. Blockage builds in the westbound lanes in the morning, when people who live in downtown and northern Orlando commute to the theme parks, and the eastbound lanes clog up when they drive home in the late afternoon.

Most of Orlando's other principal highways are toll roads. You'll probably use them to drive in and out of the airport, but not very many times otherwise.

Beyond the area's highways, planning hasn't been very successful. Roads can go by several names and be confusing. Disney World itself is a particular disaster, since its signage is incomplete. So if you stray much from I-4 or the minor roads, it's a good idea to carry a map. Nearly every free coupon brochure includes one. It seems that half the maps distributed for free are sponsored, and they leave off the locations of whichever amusement area is deemed a rival. Laughably, some maps provided by Universal don't acknowledge that Disney exists at all. Should this situation frazzle you, every convenience store sells area maps for $5 to $8; **Map & Globe** (☎ 407/898-0757) is a local cartographer and its products are widely available. Look for a map that doesn't give the Walt Disney World/Kissimmee area short shrift by popping it into an inadequate inset box—a common shortcoming. Also, the rental-car agencies give out excellent overview maps for free, as does the website of the **Orlando Convention and Visitors Bureau** (www.orlandoinfo.com/maps), which has printable, interactive maps that highlight the major avenues you're likely to use.

GETTING AROUND ORLANDO

The biggest issue with Orlando isn't its size—that is manageable enough. Where you should do some planning is in choosing your transportation method. Far too many people don't think about it, or they choose to rely on free buses and shuttles, assuming those go everywhere quickly. Picking the wrong method for your itinerary means you could end up wasting accumulated hours waiting for rides, or worse, you could be effectively shut out from seeing stuff you wanted to see.

RENTAL CARS

I have yet to encounter someone who rented a car in Orlando and regretted it. Quite simply, it should be a part of your budget. The only people who need not apply are the ones who have no intention of leaving Disney property for their entire stay. And anyone who does that will leave town having missed much.

If you intend to experience any of Orlando's "real" personality and its rich natural wonders, get a car. If you want to save huge amounts of money on meals both at cheap restaurants and through grocery shopping, get a car. If you want to take a breather from the theme parks' relentless plastic personalities, get a car. Orlando is a repeating lesson in obedience and herding, so it can make your vacation to have some control over your movements. Trust me—after a full day of waiting on your feet in line after theme park line, the last thing you want is to wait again for the bus to slowly wend its way back to your hotel. Get a car.

Cash-strapped Disney guests often justify forgoing a car by saying they can't afford one and that the resort bus system is enough. This is a fallacy. Disney hotels charge as much as twice what you'll pay to stay at a hotel of similar lodging off-site. If you stay at a non-Disney property, you can afford a car and *still* pay less. (There's much more about renting a car in chapter 12.)

One caveat is that **parking charges** can add up. All the theme parks charge $12 a day. If you're staying at a Disney resort, parking is free. However, if you pay for parking once at any Disney park, you won't have to pay for it again for another park on the same day. Outside of the theme parks, parking is usually free, plentiful, and off the street. Universal costs $12 until 6pm, and then it's free.

Warning: Remember that the city is full of tourists who don't know where they're going. These lost souls will weave, halt, cross three lanes of traffic, and get in the wrong lane without thinking of consequences. Check your maps before setting out, and keep a safe distance from the car in front of you.

SHUTTLE BUSES

Universal is easy: You can walk or take a free boat everywhere. SeaWorld links its three parks by free, quick shuttles. Disney, though, is so big as to require a fleet of 230 buses, the **Disney Transportation System (DTS),** which even nonguests can use for free. Curiously, DTS qualifies as the third-largest bus system in the state, after Miami and Jacksonville's public services. Taking DTS to a theme park eliminates the old parking tram rigmarole, and during the Magic Kingdom's operating hours, the bus stops at its doorstep, eliminating the need to take either the monorail or ferry from the Ticket and Transportation Center. However, once you add on the time spent waiting for a bus, which can be 20 to 45 minutes, plus the commute itself, which can be just as long and may require a transfer, you'll find that in almost every conceivable instance, having a car of your own will always get you there faster and is worth the expense.

The system is particularly overwhelmed during the opening and closing times of the theme parks, so dispatchers run extra buses around those times and keep routes rolling for about 2 extra hours before opening and after closing, so you don't have to hustle to make them. If you're staying at a Disney resort that offers another kind of transportation—say, the monorail to the Magic Kingdom—then a bus won't be available for the same route. Also, since the system has a hub-and-spoke design centered around the theme parks and Downtown Disney, *you will often have to transfer if you're going between two other points,* like two different hotels or a hotel and a water park. The sprawl of the resort means that hoofing it is simply impossible. A benefit of the system is that parents can feel mostly confident in allowing their teenagers to take it alone, which makes for flexible scheduling.

On balance, DTS can save you from having to rent a car *if* you only plan to go to Disney attractions and nothing else (which would be a shame for you—thumb through the rest of this book) and *if* you're a patient soul who can face a potential 1-hour-plus commute, possibly standing the whole way, after spending 11 hours swimming upstream in the parks. If you're tempted to stay on Disney property because DTS will save you the price of a car rental, get some prices and do some math first. Because it can be so frustrating and it excludes everything non-Disney, I recommend DTS as a supplement to a rental car, but not as a replacement for one.

The second shuttle variety is the **hotel theme park shuttle.** These are addressed in chapter 3, "Where to Stay, in or out of the Parks," on p. 34. The upswing is that, yes, you can save a lot of money by using them, but there are strong downsides, including wildly inadequate scheduling and rambling routes. These also only go to the parks' gates, completely excluding inexpensive restaurants, shopping, and all natural and historic attractions.

The third option is the **I-Ride Trolley** (☎ 866/243-7483; www.iridetrolley. com; adults over 12 $1.25 per ride, seniors 25¢, kids age 12 and under free; day pass $4, 3-day pass $6, 7-day pass $10; daily 8am–10:30pm), an excellent shuttle bus with plenty of clearly marked and well-maintained stops, benches to wait on, and genuinely useful routes. Its **Red Line** (every 20 min.) plies International Drive from the shops and restaurants just north of I-4's exit 75 all the way to Orlando Premium Outlets, near Disney; along the way it touches down at SeaWorld and Wet 'n Wild. Take this one if you want to shop at Prime Outlets and Festival Bay. The second route, the **Green Line** (every 30 min.), takes in Wet 'n Wild and SeaWorld, too, but heads down Universal Boulevard, making it more of an express route, and turns around at Orlando Premium Outlets. It comes within a long block of the entrance to Universal Orlando. Passes are sold at most of the area's hotels and attractions. You'll find free route maps on I-Ride's website. Because of its routes, visitors without cars may find it feasible to stay on I-Drive, use this dirt-cheap shuttle to see nearly everything, and then tack on the hated hotel shuttle or a city bus for Disney days.

In downtown Orlando, there's the free **LYMMO** (www.golynx.com; Mon–Thurs 6am–10pm, Fri 6am–midnight, Sat 10am–midnight, Sun 10am–10pm) bus service, which makes a loop between City Hall and the Centroplex (including Church Street Station and the History Center) every 5 to 15 minutes.

CITY BUSES

There's not a lot to love about public transit in Florida. Buses are infrequent (usually one or two an hour), and shelters inadequate (often nonexistent), and when the sun's strong, the combination is miserable. Distances are also fairly great, so journeys can take a while. Still, people have been known to use the buses on vacation, although I have to wonder how much fun they're having. The Central Florida Regional Transportation Authority runs the **LYNX system** (www.golynx.com), on which one-way fares are $2, day passes cost $4, week passes are $16, and transfers between lines are free. Kids 6 and under ride with adults free, and you have to pay with exact change.

If you plan to use the buses, go online ahead of time and download free system maps, because bus shelters lack complete information. Note that because the buses are designed for locals to use for commuting, tourist areas are not easily linked by single routes—you'll have to transfer. For tourists, here are the most convenient routes:

- **Route 56** heads down U.S. 192 from the Osceola Square Mall in Kissimmee and straight to the front gates of the Magic Kingdom, where you can catch free Disney transportation to the other parks. This makes U.S. 192 east of Disney the only major hotel zone that provides transfer-free bus access to Walt Disney World. Buses run every 30 minutes, but the last one leaves at 9:45pm even if Disney's open later.

♦ **Route 8** does most of International Drive, including the Convention Center and a stop at SeaWorld. It duplicates the service offered by the I-Ride Trolley (p. 18), which is cheaper.

♦ **Route 50** goes from the central LYNX station in downtown Orlando, down Interstate 4, past Epcot, and to the gates of the Magic Kingdom. It stops at SeaWorld where passengers can connect to I-Drive by transferring to Route 8.

♦ The lesser Disney areas are served by the 300-series lines. Number **300** goes to Hotel Plaza Boulevard from downtown; **301** to Disney's Animal Kingdom from Pine Hills; **302** to the Magic Kingdom from Rosemont; and **303** to Hollywood Studios from the Washington Shores area. These link up at a bus transfer point at Downtown Disney before getting on Interstate 4 and bypassing the rest of the tourist areas. Bus **304** is the only one that connects with another tourist zone; it trawls Sand Lake Road, which bisects I-Drive, before heading to Downtown Disney. Once they're off I-4, 302 and 303 pass within a few blocks of Universal Orlando, on Kirkman Road, so if you toss in about 15 minutes of walking, they could technically be used for Universal, too, but it wouldn't be fun.

♦ **Route 21** goes up Universal Boulevard from Sand Lake Road, past Wet 'n Wild, to the Universal Orlando park, and links with the downtown depot.

♦ **Route 42** starts at Orlando Premium Outlets (a few miles northeast of Disney), up International Drive, and nearly 2 hours later, reaches the airport.

TAXIS

Only tourists use taxis in Orlando. They're just not part of the fabric of locals' lives. You will, however, almost always find a cluster waiting outside of the major theme parks' gates, waiting to take fares to their hotels.

Fares vary, but a typical rate would be $2 for the first ¼ of a mile or the first 80 seconds of waiting time, followed by 25¢ for each ⅛ of a mile and 25¢ for each additional 40 seconds of waiting. Airport trips incur a 50¢ surcharge. Taxis carry five passengers.

Those planning to rely on taxis to get them to the parks should balance that decision with a hotel booking that's near the action. For Walt Disney World, a hotel in Lake Buena Vista would cut down on transport costs, and for Universal, the northern bend of International Drive is best. But if you spend more than $30 a day on taxis (a one-way ride from the Magic Kingdom to the hotel stretch on U.S. 192 east of Disney would cost about $20), smack your forehead, because you could have rented a car for that amount.

Many companies accept major credit cards, but ask when you summon a ride, because your payment may need to be processed by phone. Companies are not carefully monitored, so only choose a recommended carrier (for example, I have firsthand experience of threats of violence from M&M drivers). Call your own:

♦ Diamond Cab Company: (☎ 407/523-3333)
♦ Star Taxi: (☎ 866/888-5530)
♦ Yellow/City/Checker: (☎ 407/422-2222)

I Speak Mouse

Orlando, like all good Utopian communities, has its own vocabulary:

At Disney, a staffer of any kind is a "cast member."

You're not a customer. You're a "guest."

The work areas where guests don't go is called "backstage."

What you and I call rides, they call "attractions" or "shows."

Disney parks were designed by "Imagineers."

Disney's most complicated robot figures are "Audio-Animatronics."

Cast members don't dress as Mickey. They're "friends with" him.

Shamu doesn't do tricks. He does "behaviors."

Indoor rides are generally "dark rides" or "flat rides."

"Theming" is stage dressing for attractions. It tells a "story."

When an attraction is improved or renovated, it's "plussed."

The waiting area you see before an attraction is the "preshow."

GETTING TO KNOW ORLANDO'S LAYOUT

In 1970, before the opening of Walt Disney World, the area was still a tourism center, attracting 660,000 people a year. But by 1999, the place was a powerhouse, with 37.9 million people visiting. During the same period, the area population skyrocketed from 344,000 to 860,000, soaring past such old-guard American cities as St. Louis; Washington, D.C.; Boston; Baltimore; and Portland.

However, for all that growth, and despite the fact the amusements are critical to Orlando's economy, most of the population still lives north of SeaWorld, so visitors won't always find themselves in the thick of authentic Floridian life. The tourist zones are segregated from residential ones. Huge chunks of your time, days at a stretch, will be spent in just a few districts, predominantly the three main, boisterous tourist corridors. Those are along International Drive, U.S. 192 around I-4, and the Lake Buena Vista area north of exit 68 off of I-4.

WALT DISNEY WORLD

Best for: Space, theme parks, a sense of place, proximity to His Mouseness
What you won't find: Inexpensive food or lodging, a central location for anything except Disney attractions, the "real" Orlando

When Walt Disney ordered the purchase of these 27,000 acres mostly just west of Interstate 4, he was righting a wrong he committed in the building of Anaheim's Disneyland. In commandeering as much land as he did, he ensured visitors would not be troubled by the clatter of motel signs and cheap restaurants that abut his original playground. "Here in Florida," he said in a promotional film shot months before his death, "we have something special we never enjoyed at Disneyland . . .

the blessing of size. There's enough land here to hold all the ideas and plans we can possibly imagine." You could technically spend your entire vacation without leaving the greenery of the resort, and lots of people do, although they're missing a great deal. Still, there's an awful lot to do spread around here, starting with four of the world's most polished theme parks, two of the best water parks, four golf courses, two miniature golf courses, a racecar track, a sports pavilion, and a huge shopping-and-entertainment district. I have been to every Disney park in the world, and although other countries may have better versions of some rides, Florida's resort is by far the biggest and the most elaborate.

First-time visitors aren't usually prepared for quite how *large* the area is: 47 (roughly rectangular) square miles. Only a third of that land is truly developed, and another third has been set aside as a permanent reserve for swampland. Major elements are easily a 10-minute drive away from each other. The Magic Kingdom is buried deep in the back of the park—which is to say, the north of it, requiring the most driving time to reach. Epcot and Hollywood Studios are in the center, while Disney's Animal Kingdom is at the southwest of the property.

For its convenience, Disney **signposts hotels and attractions** according to the major theme park they're near. If you are staying on property, you'll need to know which area your hotel is in. For example, the All-Star resorts are considered to be in the Animal Kingdom area, and so many signs on Disney highways will simply read ANIMAL KINGDOM RESORT AREA, and leave off the name of your hotel. Ask for your hotel's designated area when you reserve.

Getting into Disney is easy. Every major artery near it is exhaustively signposted for DISNEY WORLD. Exits are marked, but they don't always bring you to the part of I-4 you may want, so it helps to know the name of the major artery that feeds your hotel. A few useful **secret exits** are not marked on official Disney maps. One is the newly laid **Western Way,** which turns past Coronado Springs resort and skirts the back of Animal Kingdom to reach many vacation home communities southwest of Disney. If you take it, ignore the signs telling you to take 429 to U.S. 192. That route will cost you $1 in tolls despite the fact it runs for scarcely a mile. Instead, go at the next left beyond that. It ends up at U.S. 192 soon, too, and without a price. Disney is now developing this western plot of land with hotels and shopping.

There's a second useful shortcut out of the resort that Disney doesn't label on its official maps: **Sherbeth Road,** by the entrance to Animal Kingdom Lodge about a mile west of the entrance to Animal Kingdom, winds its way to the cheap restaurants on western U.S. 192. Taking it could save a little time on days when you hit Animal Kingdom or Blizzard Beach.

It's interesting to note that when you're at Disney, you're in a separate governmental zone. The resort's bizarre experiments in building methods (such as fiberglass-and-steel castles) are partly enabled by the fact Disney negotiated the creation of its own government entity, the Reedy Creek Improvement District, which can set its own standards. Many RCID buildings have been imbued with a fantasy twist: Not far down the road between Downtown Disney Marketplace and the Regal Sun hotel—a road not otherwise used by many resort guests—make a pass by the R.C. Fire Department, a toylike engine house with a one-of-a-kind outdoor fountain that looks like a spouting fire hose.

Disney owns a little bit of land east of Interstate 4, too, which it has largely forged into the New Urbanism town of Celebration (p. 258). As a residential center with upscale aspirations (golf and an expensive hotel), there's not much to do there except shop and eat a bit in its town square. Be prepared to parallel park there.

Walt Disney World is at the southern end of Orlando's chain of big parks, so to see Universal, SeaWorld, and downtown Orlando, you'll always be heading north on I-4.

U.S. 192 & KISSIMMEE

Best for: Value, restaurant and hotel options, family entertainment
What you won't find: High art, subtlety, luxury

No matter how Orlando changes, it's Kissimmee (Kiss-*em*-ee), its noisy little sister, that remains the biggest news in saving money. Walt's master plan succeeded only in keeping tacky motels and buffets at a modest distance. Where the southern edge of the Disney resort property touches U.S. 192, the noise begins, stretching about 6 miles west and a good 10 miles east. This ostentatious drag, known also as the Irlo Bronson Memorial Highway (after the state senator who sold Walt a lot of his land to make the park possible), is the spine of Kissimmee, and it's your budget salvation for food and beds, so plug the K-word into the location box of your Web searches, too. It's also the best place to find that all-American kitsch you might be looking for—nowhere else in town will you find a souvenir store shaped like a giant orange half, and I call that a shame.

In the early 1970s, Kissimmee was the prime place to stay if you were visiting Disney World. The motels weren't flashy then, and they still aren't, but they're ever affordable—$50 to $80 is the norm, and some fleabit places go down to $39 single or $45 double. Kissimmee's downtown, about 10 miles east of Disney, is a typical Florida burg with a main street by a lake, and its quickly growing subdivisions have become popular among Hispanic families, although that doesn't translate into accessible restaurants serving ethnic cuisine. U.S. 192 is mostly about the big chains.

The best way to get your bearings on U.S. 192 is using its clearly signposted **mile marker system.** U.S. 192 hits Disney's southern entrance (the most expedient avenue to the major theme parks) at Mile Marker 7, while I-4's exit 65 connects with it around Mile Marker 8. Numbers go down to the west and they go up to the east. Western 192, where the bulk of the vacation home developments are found, tends to be slightly less downscale than the tacky wilds of eastern 192, but neither stretch could be termed swanky or well planned. Although Osceola County has spent $29 million to beautify the tourist corridor, it's been inept in the effort; in late 2006, the county cut down stands of myrtle trees in the median of U.S. 192 because they blocked the view of the billboards. That should tell you what you need to know about how the road looks and where its values lie.

LAKE BUENA VISTA

Best for: Access to Disney, I-4 and chain restaurants, some elbow room
What you won't find: The lowest prices, a sense of place

Lake Buena Vista, a hotel enclave east of Downtown Disney, clusters on the eastern fringe of Walt Disney World. LBV is technically a town, but it doesn't much look like one. It's mostly hotels and restaurants and some slightly winding streets. The proximity of an I-4 exit can make U-turns tricky, which can get annoying, but it's easy to slip into Disney's side door, which is great.

The bottom line is that LBV is less tacky and higher rent than Kissimmee's 192, but it's also still a Disney-centric area, which some visitors will find tiresome.

If you stay in LBV, you can also (if you're hardy) walk to the Downtown Disney development, where you can then pick up Disney's free DTS bus system.

INTERNATIONAL DRIVE

Best for: Walkability, cheap transportation, inexpensive attractions and food, family entertainment, proximity to Universal and SeaWorld
What you won't find: Space, style

Although a still-developing stretch of this street winds all the way south to U.S. 192, when someone refers to International Drive, they usually mean the segment between SeaWorld and Universal Orlando, just east of I-4 between exits 71 and 75.

I-Drive, as it's called, is probably the only district where you might comfortably stay without a car and still be able to see the non-Disney attractions, since it's chockablock with affordable hotels (which are, on the whole, not as ratty as some of the U.S. 192 choices can be) and plenty of crowd-pleasing touristy things to see such as shopping malls, arcades, T-shirt shops, all-you-can-eat buffets, and dinner theaters. The cheap I-Ride Trolley, described earlier, trundles around the area on a regular schedule. Because it runs parallel to I-4 and connects with several ramps to it, I-Drive has excellent self-drive potential, too.

I-Drive's touristic street life is varied. North of Sand Lake Road, within the orbit of Universal Orlando and Wet 'n Wild, it tends to host foreign visitors, particularly English families whose childhood holiday towns have acclimated them to promenades along touristy, working-class avenues. Here, the midway games and the ice-cream shops are where the action is. South of Sand Lake, closer to SeaWorld, you're more likely to find groups of domestic visitors, as the mighty Orange County Convention Center, located on both sides of I-Drive at the Bee Line Expressway/528, keeps the surrounding hotels full. On this part of I-Drive, the hotel cocktail lounge and midscale restaurants rule. The less trafficked Universal Boulevard runs parallel to I-Drive for much of the way, providing an easy bypass to the carnival. Just over I-4 at Universal Boulevard, Universal Orlando's park-and-entertainment complex draws plenty of locals.

Hotel and restaurant discounts may be posted on the area's business association and promotional website: **www.internationaldriveorlando.com**.

DOWNTOWN ORLANDO

Best for: Historic buildings, cafes, museums, fine art, wealthy residents
What you won't find: Theme parks, easy commutes

As much as I would like to tell you that downtown Orlando is one of America's great cityscapes, where you can park your car and stroll from boutique to restaurant, I'm afraid it isn't the case. Not yet, anyway. Like in so many American cities, residents fled downtown in the 1960s through the 1980s, although the city is gradually being rediscovered by young, upscale residents. Here are the highlights:

DOWNTOWN   Beneath the city's collection of modest skyscrapers (mostly banking offices), you'll find municipal buildings (the main library, historic museums) and a few upscale hotels (the Grand Bohemian, Courtyard at Lake Lucerne), but little shopping. Orange Avenue, once a street of proud stone buildings and department stores, now comes alive mostly at night, when its former vaudeville halls and warehouses essay their new roles as nightclubs, especially around Church Street. The 43-acre Lake Eola Park, just east, is often cited as an area attraction, but in truth it's just your average city park, although the .9-mile path around its 23-acre sinkhole lake is good for joggers. Just east of that, the streets turn to red brick and big trees shelter **Thornton Park** (along Washington St., Summerlin Ave., and Central Blvd.). It's noted for its alfresco European-style cafes, none especially inexpensive but all pleasing, where waiters wear black and hip locals spend evenings and weekend brunches. West of downtown over I-4, the area called Parramore is a longtime neighborhood for African Americans (sadly, the interstate was built, in part, as a barrier). A mile north of downtown, **Loch Haven Park** contains a wealth of the city's most important museums and theater companies (p. 232).

VIMI   Some old-timers call this area **Colonial Town,** but more and more, it's known as the Vietnamese District, or Vimi. Just north of downtown, at Colonial Drive and Mills Avenue, there's a midcentury neighborhood with the whiff of a faded 1950s Main Street (parking looks tight until you realize lots are hidden behind the buildings). There, you can spend a top afternoon strolling through several omnibus Asian supermarkets stocked with exotic groceries and unique baked goods and parking yourself at one of the excellent mom-and-pop-style eateries (advertised by cheap stick-on letters and neon) serving food far more delicious than their limited budgets would suggest. Several stores whip up addictive, meat-stuffed baguette sandwiches called *bánh mi* for a quick $3 meal. Side by side with Asian staples, you'll find the hobby and art supply shops patronized by a burgeoning bohemian community of middle-class, suburb-raised kids who are tired of Orlando's overly corporate ethos. The two marginalized communities collaborate beautifully together.

WINTER PARK
Best for: Fine art, cafes, strolls, galleries, lakes
What you won't find: Inexpensive shopping, easy theme park access

One of the city's most interesting areas, and one of the few that hasn't taken pains to cover or erase its history, Winter Park was where, 100 years ago, upstart industrialists built winter homes at a time when they couldn't gain entree into the more exclusive, more WASPy enclaves of Newport or Palm Beach. The town, which blends seamlessly with northern Orlando (you can drive between them in a few minutes without getting onto I-4), is still pretty full of itself, but cruising on its brick-paved streets, gawking at the mansions, will always remind you of the good life. The town's long-running boat tour (p. 270) through its chain of lakes is probably the best way to sample the opulence. The shops of Park Avenue, its main thoroughfare, aren't what they used to be—you'll find mostly jewelry, art, and women's clothes—but a stroll down it, and into the country-club campus of Rollins College (at its southern end), are among the finer pleasures in town. The best art museum around, the Morse (p. 237), holds the most comprehensive collection of Tiffany glass you will ever see. West of Winter Park, over I-4, the up-and-coming district of College Park, centering around Princeton Street and Edgewater Drive, hosts restaurants and boutiques that are bringing the area favor.

NORTH OF ORLANDO

Most visitors who venture into the suburban towns north of Winter Park do so to visit some of the area's natural springs or state parks (p. 265 and 267) or to connect with the spirits in the hamlet of Cassadaga (p. 259). After you've seen these places, there is little to engage you until you hit the Atlantic Coast on I-4. Many guidebooks will suggest you go to Mount Dora (picket fences, Victorian charm, and antiques; 40 miles northwest), but although it's nice enough, I personally don't think these northern towns rate beside the world-class attractions that should fill your itinerary.

SOUTH OF ORLANDO

Only in the past few years has the rural-minded swampland southwest of the resort and Kissimmee begun to be built upon in earnest, and the 65-mile run along I-4 to Tampa is gradually filling in with developments and golf courses. This patch of the Green Swamp, in which the two cities will one day merge into a megalopolis, is now casually dubbed "Orlampa." A few specialty tourist sights, including Fantasy of Flight (p. 236) and Dinosaur World (p. 237), claimed land before prices got steeper. An hour straight south of Orlando, in the town of Winter Haven, is Cypress Gardens (p. 236), Florida's most historic amusement park. In the northeast part of Tampa closest to Orlando, you'll find the excellent Busch Gardens Africa (p. 219), a worthy addition to an amusement park itinerary.

EAST OF ORLANDO

Most visitors will find themselves east of town for two reasons: to catch a flight or to watch NASA prepare one of its own. The entrance to Orlando International Airport is 11 miles east of I-4, webbed into the city network by toll highways and surrounded by golfing developments at which the paint is still drying. Across empty swamp from there, the so-called Space Coast, of which Cape Canaveral is the metaphoric capital, is a 45-minute drive east of Orlando's tourist corridor via 528, also known as the Bee Line Expressway.

WEST OF ORLANDO

Because the Green Swamp commands the area, there simply isn't much west of the tourist corridor save a few small towns and some state parks like Lake Louisa (p. 268).

3 Where to Stay, in or out of the Parks

The town's best beds in hotel rooms, B&Bs, and home rentals

ORLANDO HAS MORE THAN 115,000 HOTEL ROOMS, A STAGGERING FIGURE. Close to 48 million visitors come every year for theme parks, conventions, and outdoor recreation, making the city the world's most popular family vacation destination.

As you can imagine, with numbers that large, competition is fierce, and hotels regularly cut prices to the bone during lean times, which these days seem unending. Because of the economy, Orlando's hotels are in the midst of an occupancy decline. That means places of every stripe are scrambling to fill space, and scoring deals can be easy for those who scratch around. It's a buyer's market, so what you need first is to know where the getting's good. Then you can bargain.

The challenge, after that, is finding a hotel that remembers what good service is. Most of Central Florida's monolithic hotel architecture steals and inflates European traditions, often on such a scale that even a Texan would blush. You'll find arcades, frescoes, columns, Spanish tiles, arched windows, and marble . . . but knock on the columns. They're hollow. Get close to the marble. It's often painted on. That's why Orlando's resorts, as much as they charge, rarely achieve true opulence. They're made by theatrical set designers, not artisans. Here, when you pay for a fine hotel, you're mostly paying for a mood.

The dramatic flourishes in the public spaces won't necessarily translate into heightened glory for your room. Many hotels with pretty faces complacently operate like impersonal machines. I'll help you look beyond the set dressing to find the best value for you—which may not end up being a hotel at all.

HOME RENTALS

In most guidebooks, the home-rental option is given just a few wan paragraphs. What a crime! For value, renting a home is without exception the best way to go. The very first night I spent at a vacation home, stretching out on a leather sofa and watching a TV as big as a lap pool, speaking as loudly as I wanted and heading to the kitchen for periodic snacks, firing up the grill beside my screened-in pool, I dreaded checking into the battery hen arrangement of a hotel ever again. Frankly, I'm not sure why people still want to use hotels, which charge just as much. Probably because they don't know how sublime vacation homes are, or that many can be rented by the night, or that most of them are nicer than our own houses. They seem too good to be true.

In recent years, the zone south of Walt Disney World has mushroomed with new housing developments. There are dozens of gated communities packed with shiny new two-story McMansions, each with its own pool and yard.

These neighborhoods are almost entirely for tourists. Developers built the first few, optimistically, to house locals, but it turned out that Orlando residents would rather live away from the tourist zone. So instead, out-of-town families purchased the homes—a British family, perhaps, that flies in for their 2 weeks a year and leaves nothing personal behind—and to help pay off that investment, they recruit a management company to rent them out for the rest of the year. Each management company requires the homes it rents to meet a certain standard, which usually means cable TV in every room, irons, vacuums, and laundry facilities. And every management company takes care of the nitty-gritty for you, such as washing sheets before your arrival or wheeling out the trash bins on garbage day. You will also often find perks such as computers with high-speed Internet, video games, billiard rooms, and heated pools and hot tubs—often included in the price.

Relax. Staying in a vacation home in the Orlando area isn't like crashing in someone's house; rather, properties are usually decorated with the simple elegance of a hotel. It's like a real house except without clutter, books, paper, or mementos.

Almost all of these homes are located just a few miles from the property line of the Disney resort—most rental companies have a policy dictating just how far from Disney their homes are permitted to be (but do ask, just in case). Many homes take about as long to reach by car (which you should have) as Disney's cheapest rooms, except for about the same amount of money, you get an entire home and not a noisy dorm room packed with two double beds. A smaller number of properties are available near Universal and SeaWorld (the main development there is called Vista Cay), which is preferable for seeing more of the area than just Disney.

There are generally two kinds of homes. **Condos** are units that are attached to other units; these may have their own plunge pool, but more often they share a communal, hotel-style pool at a common clubhouse. **Houses** are free-standing and are generally about 30% more expensive than condos. They will almost always have private full pools, usually screened to keep out insects. Occupancy is governed by law, so be honest about how many people are in your party.

RENTAL AGENCIES

In most destinations, the main way to obtain a vacation rental is to contact the owner directly. This is certainly an option in Orlando, and all the prominent online databases reach here, including **Vacation Rentals by Owner** (www.vrbo.com), **HomeAway** (www.homeaway.com), **Zonder** (www.zonder.com), Wyndham Resorts' **Endless Vacation Rentals** (www.evrentals.com), and a British-owned area specialist, **FabVillas.com.** Those are useful places to start a search and get your bearings. However, Orlando is such a major city for vacation rentals that a host of alternatives are open to you—ones that actually inspect your potential home and give you the peace of mind of dealing with an established, accountable company and not with a private homeowner who may or may not have your best interests in mind.

So let's discuss the best of the vacation-rental companies. In addition to being selected for their reputations, longevity, and inventory, every company listed in

Choosing a Rental Company &
Asking the Right Questions

Should you decide to use an agency not recommended in this book, I'd urge you to choose one that's at least passed muster with two important local organizations: Discover Vacation Homes (www.discovervacationhomes.com), which represents eight major companies (13% of the Orlando market), or the Central Florida Property Managers Association (www.vacationwithconfidence.com). Both groups hold their members to high standards including new furnishings, multiple TVs, washer/dryers, a pool or quick access to one, and 24-hour check-in. Their goal is to make sure quality remains high, communication is clear, and professional standards are always met. I can tell you that my experiences with using these groups' associated companies have been flawless and free of tricks.

It's also important to know what to ask. Be sure to pose the following questions:

- **Where's the property?** Rental companies represent properties in various neighborhoods, and none of them expect you to instantly know which area is best for you. A good rental agency will match your needs and budget to the most suitable property.
- **What does the unit look like?** A reputable agency will have pictures of each individual property available online, so all you really have to do is see something you like, point at it shouting "That one!," and then make sure it's in a location that you approve of. There's no reason you should rent a place without seeing it first. Some companies only post photos of their best houses and tell you that everything they rent is just as good. Those companies did not make it into this guide.
- **What fees are involved?** Your credit card will usually be charged a deposit ($200–$300 is standard) about a month ahead of time. You'll also have to pay a one-time fee before your arrival that goes toward insurance or cleaning; $50 to $80 is normal, which makes stays of a single night less economical. Because it's not as easy to rent out a house as it is a hotel room, some companies are pretty tight about cancellations, so ask for your deadline for changes.
- **What are the amenities?** Things like pool heat or grills may incur a surcharge, which is normal. Not every company will provide free Internet access or a clothes washer, so ask if these are important to you. Also ask your rental agency what it supplies and what you'll need to buy. Typically, you'll be given a roll or two of toilet paper per bathroom, a starter garbage bag, and maybe a packet of detergent, and you'll be expected to buy your own after those run out. Clean bath towels and sheets are supplied, but maid service won't be unless you pay extra for it.

this guide has a satisfactory listing with the Better Business Bureau of Central Florida. Check on any company's background for the past 3 years at www. orlando.bbb.org.

Some of the better rental agencies don't even require you to pick up keys at an office. Instead, front doors are equipped with keypads that can be programmed remotely and you'll get a code. That means you also won't have to carry keys around and you may not even have to visit the rental office. You can handle your problems and questions by phone, including if you forget your code. Some perfectly reputable companies, though, do require you to retrieve and return metal keys, so ask about that. Most of these companies are located within a few miles of the southern entry to Walt Disney World along U.S. 192 west of Interstate 4. If you arrive at night, you may be asked to retrieve keys from a lockbox; make sure you have good directions before leaving home.

Everything represented by **All Star Vacation Homes** ✦✦✦ (7822 W. Irlo Bronson Hwy., U.S. 192, Kissimmee; ☎ 800/572-5011 or 407/997-0733; www.all starvacationhomes.com; AE, DISC, MC, V), a thoroughly professional company, is keyless and has a pool, even the condos, and most all of its 150 units are is within 4 miles of Disney. An in-house design team applies a strong hand in furnishings, which are handsome, with lots of woods, quality fabrics, and dried flowers to make most feel notably clean, new, and human. Three-bedroom units sleeping up to eight, with a dedicated kids' room and flower beds out front, start at $139 a night, or $45 less than what it costs to squeeze six into Disney's cheapest family suite (and there, two will have to use the sleeper sofa—here, everyone gets a real bed and can leave the extra sleeper sofa untouched). Its website has ample information about each property, including photos and floor plans. Its cheapest options are its Condos and Town Homes (two to three bedrooms, tons of space, from $119), and of its three categories of stand-alone houses (Three-, Four-, and Five-Star), Three is the most affordable, with a three-bedroom, two-bath house starting at $219, and a giant five-bedroom running $249. Full six-bedroom houses start at $269—you can split that among 14 people if you've got a full house.

Think that's expensive? A standard room at the Disney's Polynesian, sleeping five tightly, can't be had for less than $355. Homes in the Windsor Hills area, one of All Star's biggest bases, generally have an equal number of bathrooms to bedrooms, and the Formosa Gardens homes sit on a third of an acre, which is spacious for Florida. Prices go up as you add treats such as indoor/outdoor stereo systems, game rooms, multiple master bedrooms, and so forth. To sweeten the deal, All Star often offers a free rental car with a 7-night stay, which takes care of another major expense, and its website frequently spotlights new properties and last-minute deals for 10% off. Because of its attention to detail, All Star is my favorite rental agency in Orlando, and although its prices are slightly higher than its competitors (in no small part because of plusher decor), it's still far lower than most hotels. Check the remaining renters if you don't find something suitable. These other companies have slightly lower prices and slightly simpler looks. These renters also may each represent houses in the same developments, so be sure to shop around as you may get different prices at the same developments.

The family-run **Alexander Holiday Homes** (1400 W. Oak St., Ste. H, Kissimmee; ☎ 800/621-7888 or 407/932-3683; www.floridasunshine.com; AE, DISC, MC, V) has been renting since 1989, when the industry was in its infancy. It reps around 200 properties now, all of them within 12 miles of Disney, but most much closer. All of its privately owned homes come with at least two TVs and a DVD player or VCR. Its three-bedroom, two-bath homes start at $105 a night, and no property will deprive you of access to a pool, be it shared or private. A special section of its website spotlights homes that are discounting. During peak season, it requires bookings of at least a week; otherwise, stays of 3 to 4 nights are often possible and discounts of about 12% may be possible if you stay at least 7 nights. Annoyingly, its website tells lots about properties but nothing about availability.

Another upfront business, **Florida Sun Vacation Homes** (7802 W. Irlo Bronson Hwy./U.S. 192, Kissimmee; ☎ 800/219-1282 or 407/938-0228; www.floridasun vacationhomes.com; AE, DISC, MC, V) rents homes ranging from two to seven bedrooms in the Disney area (the Windsor Hills development in particular), with three-bedroom starting prices of $69 in low season and popping to $149 in high season. All of its properties have a pool or a spa (or both). Its website is frank about extra fees (one-time cleaning fees of around $75 are usually mandatory) and any minimum stays that exist for each property (3 nights is common). Like many companies, it asks that you reserve and pay at least 6 weeks in advance.

In business since late 1999, **Award Vacation Homes** (1536 Sunrise Plaza Dr., Clermont; ☎ 800/338-0835 or 352/243-8669; www.awardvacationhomes.com; AE, DISC, MC, V) has an inventory that is thickest around Hwy. 27, a newly developed corridor found 10 to 15 minutes west of Walt Disney World via U.S. 192 (via the Western Way back entrance). Its houses are relatively new, which is an advantage, and its neighborhoods are serviced by grocery stores that are not overpriced for tourists, which is another perk, though they're also just a twitch farther from Disney and from Orlando proper than some people prefer. Strangely, European tourists don't seem to mind, so your temporary neighbors may be from overseas. For three-bedroom, two-bath places, rates start at $132 and peak at $140, depending on the week. Six-bedroom homes are $180 to $212, and its website often lists last-minute deals as low as $99 for a three- and four-bedrooms.

Founded in the late '90s, **VillaDirect** (6129 W. Irlo Bronson Hwy., Kissimmee; ☎ 877/259-9908 or 407/397-9818; www.villadirect.com; AE, DC, DISC, MC, V) now claims some 500 Orlando-area properties of varying styles and quality on its roster. Condos sleeping six start around $83. Its office is open 7 days a week, and about 70% of its inventory is located within 4 miles of the border of Disney property, particularly along the U.S. 192 corridor southwest of Animal Kingdom, but it also has a few near SeaWorld.

IPG Florida Vacation Homes ✮✮✮ (9550 W. U.S. 192, Clermont; ☎ 800/311-7105 or 863/547-1050; www.ipgflorida.com; AE, DISC, MC, V), which began by serving British vacationers before branching out into Florida, deals mostly with homes in Legacy Park, Highlands Reserve, Windsor Palms, and the Villas at Island Club, south or west of Disney. I recently used the company to stay in a palatial, open-plan three-bedroom condo in Vista Cay near the Convention Center, and I found the furnishings on the simple side compared to other companies but still far beyond my expectations, and I'd happily use it again. It even had its own private laundry room. Two-bedroom condos run from $120 to $160, and three-bedroom homes with private pools from $140 to $200. With this company, "luxury" homes cost less than "exquisite" ones.

Lowery's Vacation Homes (7864 W. Irlo Bronson Hwy., Kissimmee; ☎ 800/569-3797 or 407/397-0088; www.moremouse.com; AE, DISC, MC, V) has plenty of inexpensive and tasteful properties in the same developments as the companies above, and its website includes 360-degree tours of each property. It's a good fall-back in busy seasons. Rates here can be sensational—how about $89 a night for a three-bedroom?

HOME-RENTAL DEVELOPMENTS

Instead of dealing with rental agencies, you can often rent a home directly from the housing development it's in. These developments, most of which consist of tightly packed but artfully situated condo units, cater to tourists and rent directly to the public. I prefer to go with rental agencies because their customer service tends to be so thorough, but I always check with the same development in case prices are markedly different (they usually aren't). Sometimes developments are more likely to accept bookings for a night or two than are rental agencies. Agents, on the other hand, represent properties in many different developments, which gives you more choice at the outset, and they're more likely to help you find a good fit.

As with rental agency houses, assume that housekeeping is not part of the bargain at developments, although your place will be clean when you check in. Some rental agencies also represent properties in these developments; such overlap is common and shouldn't alarm you. Just go with whomever offers the best deal.

One area you're going to see mentioned a lot is **Windsor Palms,** 10 minutes west of Disney's main gate, just off western U.S. 192 near tons of places to eat and buy groceries. It's a gated development of condos and freestanding identikit homes with as many as six bedrooms—and just about every agent sells it. Two-bedroom units sharing a community pool go from $115. For the same price, you can also rent a place in the same company's **Windsor Hills** project, also gated and located in the same general area. All of its private homes have a private screened pool, and its condos all promise a private plunge pool. On Universal Boulevard within quick reach of SeaWorld, Universal, and I-Drive, the biggest development is **Vista Cay,** where the condos are remarkably spacious but don't usually have much of a view, and there's a shared pool. Many companies rep properties there, too.

South of the intersection of U.S. 27 and U.S. 192, a few miles west of Walt Disney World's southern entrance, the gated community of **Bahama Bay Resort** ✦ (400 Grand Bahama Bay Blvd., Davenport; ☎ 877/299-4481 or 863/547-1200; www.bahamabay.com; AE, DISC, MC, V) is a complex of 38 two- and three-story buildings, each painted in soothing, washed-out Caribbean tones. The resort has a total of 498 condos of two or three bedrooms. Every condo has its own balcony, and many overlook Lake Davenport, a typical pond. There's a clubhouse with a fitness center, a DVD-rental desk, and an Internet cafe, plus three heated pools scattered around the property for guest use. Two-bedroom condos sleep six and cost about $79 if booked online, while three-bedroom options sleeping eight go from $89 to $109, depending on how much space you want (although even the smallest condos are many times larger than a hotel room) and whether it's peak season. Its sister property, **The Enclave Suites Resort** (6165 Carrier Dr., Orlando; ☎ 800/457-0077; www.enclavesuites.com; AE, DISC, MC, V), a high-rise, is more densely packed but it's within walking distance of International Drive and close to Universal Orlando. It's also more expensive, with studio apartments that sleep four starting around $95 and two-bedroom units starting around $135. Check its "Internet Value Package" Web page for deals, including free nights.

Encantada Resort (3070 Secret Lake Dr., Kissimmee; ☎ 800/520-8070 or 407/ 787-0770; www.encantadaresorthomes.com; AE, MC, V), 6 miles west of the Disney main gate, is managed by the concern that built it, and especially in the fall and spring, it offers prices as low as $99 a night for its three-bedroom, Spanish-style town-home units (other times, they're around $129). The development's layout of mostly straight streets is unimaginative, but in many units (which would cost around $350,000 if you bought one), first-floor rooms have 9-foot ceilings, and the decor is generally tropical and cheerful. Its "Sunrise Plan" units (three bedrooms, two-and-a-half baths) have about 1,300 square feet and its "Tall Palms" units are four-bedroom, three-bath and measure about 1,500 square feet ($20 more). The palm-lined pool, shared by all guests, could belong to a fancy hotel.

At **Lucaya Village Resort** (2941 Lucayan Harbour Circle, Kissimmee; ☎ 800/ 344-3959 or 407/397-0700; www.lucayavillageresort.com; AE, DISC, MC, V), two-bedroom, two-bath villas sleeping six cost around $89 to $119, depending on the time of year, and three-bedroom, two-bath ones go for just $10 more. Fully kitted-out homes (plasma TVs, DVD players in all bedrooms, daily housekeeping) can be swung for around $149 for three bedrooms. Units have washer/dryers, two TVs with cable, and an in-room safe. The decor is plain, and the condo-style buildings date to the mid-'80s, but the location leaves nothing to be desired; they're 4 miles from the Disney gates by the intersection of Vineland Road and U.S. 192, near plenty of affordable restaurants and grocery stores. Plus, there's a full complement of resort perks (pool, fitness center, sauna, PlayStation game room).

TIMESHARES

Because this isn't a guide to real estate, I'm not going to wade far into the sticky topic of timeshares. Suffice to say that there are plenty of developers and corporations (including the Walt Disney Company itself) that would love to take tens of thousands of dollars from you in exchange for the right to dwell in one of their apartments for a week or two a year. If you decide to enter into such an arrangement, then you don't need a guidebook as much as you do a good lawyer who can ensure that you can get out of the deal if you tire of it someday. You should also know that timeshares are not a sound investment because they're nigh impossible to sell for the price you paid for them (that's if you buy from a timeshare corporation; resales are another story).

In fact, Disney rents its timeshares to walk-up customers who have no intention of signing any dotted lines. This class of accommodation is called the Disney Vacation Club, or DVC, and so far there are seven Orlando properties (some grafted onto the major hotel resorts) with 350,000 members. That number is a result of heavy promotion to prospective buyers around the resort and even inside the theme parks themselves, which Walt surely would have detested. The newly built tower at the Contemporary Resort—the one ruining sightlines within the Magic Kingdom—is full of such units. All of them are outrageously priced. During value season, the simplest studio with a kitchen costs an insane $285 (at Old Key West, the cheapest), and in high season, it costs $370 a night. For that money, you could get a whole six-bedroom palace 3 miles away, so I proclaim DVC a savings dud for the casual visitor.

Lots of times, you'll see a deal that looks good, such as a low price for tickets or hotels, only to find that you have to endure a timeshare presentation to get the goods. Many information desks in the lobbies of respectable hotels look like they're there to help you, but they really want to lure you into the pitch. Likewise, the low prices are advertised on many websites like MouseTrip.com. Just say no.

A few developments, particularly those with the Westgate name, will rent to temporary vacationers and then corner them with pitches to purchase time. Although I think it's acceptable for developers to let you know about the option, I don't think you should ever feel goaded or pressured into subtracting precious hours from your vacation when there are plenty of comparably priced accommodation options that don't require such a sacrifice, and for that reason, I haven't included in this book any developments with a reputation for the hard sell.

ORLANDO'S HOTELS

You'll arrive at the first decision you need to make by answering this question: How much space would I like to have? If you have kids with you—and most visitors to Orlando's theme parks do—will a single hotel room supply the elbow room everyone needs? Does anyone in your group have funky feet or snoring issues? Does anyone hog the bathroom for 3 hours each morning? Disney hotel rooms, for example, typically have a maximum occupancy of four people in two double beds, so if your group exceeds that number, you'll have to rent two rooms or upgrade to something more expensive. What's more, the base room price is for two adults; for each additional adult up to the room's capacity, expect another $10 a night. For most families, renting a home or condo solves the space issue, and usually for less money than a hotel.

There's a second important question that will dictate your choice: Will I have a car? Unless you're a Disney-only type of person, I think you should have one, as they can speed you away from the theme parks' clutches, saving your sanity, your pocketbook, and your ability to see other parks and glimpses of the authentic city of Orlando. The cheapest hotels are only accessible by car (or by infrequent shuttles). With few exceptions, the only hotels that enable you to vacation easily without a car are the ones located on theme park property. These hotels are at least 40% more expensive than off-property ones, so often, whatever you save in not

A Plan for All Seasons

Ask any hotel what it charges, and you're unlikely to get a straight answer. Almost all hotels in Orlando delight in changing their rates according to how full they are, and how much they can squeeze from tourists. As a rule of thumb, prices are highest during the holiday season, followed by all other periods in which kids are unlikely to be in school (summers, spring break), and followed by the light periods in late January, September, October, and early December. Weekends see slightly higher prices, too, because Florida residents drop by. The emptier the hotel is, the more likely it'll be that rates are at their lowest. A few hotels charge a little bit more on weekends than they do on weekdays. The prices in this guide represent an average rate, and so they're typical for a night of average occupancy in a moderately busy month such as April, May, or November.

Theme Park Shuttles: Going Your Way?

Don't allow your hotel choice to be dictated by a place that promises "free" shuttles. Some of them funnel the cost back to you through other means, such as daily resort fees of $3 to $10.

Almost all of the hotels located off theme park property tout some kind of "free" shuttle service to the major parks, but you need to know that most only go once or twice a day, on their schedule, and you have to book ahead. A typical hotel may contract with a transportation company that leaves for the Magic Kingdom twice a morning and, most days, returns at times like 5 and 10pm. Shuttles may provide only one run per direction which leaves after the park has opened for the day and returns before it closes. Some may drop you at one Disney park and force you to use the sluggish Disney bus system to get to the others. Often, hotels will provide shuttles to one area (Disney or Universal/SeaWorld) but not the other. Ask.

If you can put up with restrictive schedules, then yes, you can theoretically save money by forgoing a rental car and using the shuttles. But you will pay in other ways—through wasted time and lost opportunities. You will not always be able to enjoy the parks for their full opening hours. Some shuttles return around dinnertime, which precludes you from enjoying the fireworks or trying the parks' sit-down restaurants. And you won't be able to play the day by ear.

Because many hotels share shuttles, they not only can be dirty and worn but also crowded, and you might have to stop at up to a half-dozen other places on your way. If you're hungry, thirsty, tired, or your kids are restless, count on a frustrating, time-consuming situation.

Before settling on a hotel based on its advertised rides, ask questions:

1. What time do they leave and return daily?
2. Which theme parks are not covered by your shuttles?
3. How many other hotels share the same shuttle service?
4. Is there a fee of any kind? That $30 for two could have been used to rent a car.

renting a car, you pay again in higher hotel tariffs, so don't be lulled by false economy. And after the fourth straight day of dwelling in the relentless theme park world, most people find themselves screaming for a break, which cars provide.

A final question helps you know which room to go for: How much time do I plan to spend at my accommodations? The things you need out of your Orlando hotel room will not be the same things that you'd need out of a hotel room on, say, a business trip. If your schedule is going to be full, and you're planning to return home only to pour yourself a bath and hit the sack, then you don't need a premium room. Staying at a pricey resort or shelling out for something with a view won't make sense because if you're in the theme parks for 12 hours a day, you won't be around to milk your purchase. Do you *really* need a fitness center after slogging around the 1.3-mile path of Epcot's World Showcase? No.

GETTING THE BEST RATES

One of the best ways to extract minimum rates from the hotels is to check such aggregator sites as **Kayak** (www.kayak.com), **SideStep** (www.sidestep.com), **HotelsCombined.com,** and **Travelaxe** (www.travelaxe.com), which compare multiple sites simultaneously, and you'll often discover that most of the discounters offer the exact same price, across the board. (This is a faster method than searching Hotels.com, Priceline, Expedia, or others separately, though you may end up purchasing your travel through them in the end, thanks to the aggregator search.) Keep in mind that the bidding area on Priceline is more likely to get you the best rates in the month before you travel; hotels hold out for higher prices until then. Also check **Hotelcoupons.com** and **RoomSaver.com** for current discounted rates for some of the cheapest motels in town (no promises about their quality, and be forewarned that hotels frequently refuse to honor the lowest rates if they hit 75%–80% occupancy).

Another reliable way to get a cheaper room is to buy your reservation along with an **air/hotel package.** With low-cost carriers as cheap as they are, no domestic company operates charter flights to Orlando anymore, but several packagers buy cheap hotel rooms in bulk and sell them with scheduled airfare. When using these dealers, you should always do some price checks of your own to make sure you're getting a true bonus, but deals do exist. For example, **eLeisureLink** (☎ 800/780-9002; www.eleisurelink.com) has a famous deal that pops up periodically and combines car rental, 5 nights in a non-Disney hotel, and airfare from New York or Chicago for $400 to $500. I have seen **Lastminute.com** offer the same trip for $287 per person for purchase 2 weeks ahead of time. You can also find deals from **Apple Vacations** (☎ 800/517-2000; www.applevacations.com) and **Funjet** (☎ 888/558-6654; www.funjet.com), as well as some of the vacation wings of major airlines. Check **Southwest Vacations** (☎ 800/243-8372; www.southwestvacations.com), **JetBlue** (☎ 800/538-2583, option 3; www.jetblue.com/vacations), **Delta Vacations** (☎ 800/654-6559; www.deltavacations.com), **American Airlines Vacations** (☎ 800/321-2121; www.aavacations.com), and **Northwest Airlines Vacation Packages** (☎ 800/800-1504; www.nwaworldvacations.com). Increasingly, these websites will even sell hotel-only deals; American Airlines Vacations, for example, was recently selling nights at the Regal Sun Resort near Downtown Disney for $52. Use the properties on its specials page, though, because prices come out higher in searches.

Few of these players will truly discount a Disney hotel, although they may package Disney products without discounts. If they do, be careful to parse the pricing and compare it to a la carte options—Disney packages are notorious for including more than you could possibly need, which ends up wasting money. They're also not usually the cheapest; Southwest Vacations charges about $490 for round-trip flights from Chicago and 5 nights at a Disney Value resort, which sounds pretty good until you price-check non-Disney hotels and find out the same vacation would cost about $350. Even if you do want a Disney hotel, price be damned, I'm a big proponent of booking your Disney hotel separately from tickets or airfare; see "Walt Disney World Hotels, Nutshelled," later, for more

Last-Minute Beds

Don't wait until you arrive to find a room. While, yes, many hotels will be thrilled to make a deal rather than allow a room to go empty, you run the risk of sellouts. Orlando hosts some mighty big conventions, and during vacation periods, Disney itself is booked solid. Prices go up when a big meeting is on, but the Convention Center posts a calendar (www.occc.net/global/calendar) that includes estimated attendance so you can gauge how tight things might get. That said, the **Orlando Official Visitor Center** (8723 International Dr.; ☎ 407/363-5872; www.orlando info.com; daily 8am–7pm) will help you find something last minute, but you have to go to its office in person. You're also likely to find a room (grotty though it may be) on U.S. 192 starting about 5 miles east of I-4.

---

information about getting around Disney's rigged package system. When it comes to non-Disney hotels, though, package away, because that's where some great deals live. Internationally, **Virgin Holidays** (www.virginholidays.co.uk) is a huge player, with lots of customer service reps available on the ground should things go wrong.

Some people trust the multitude of **free newspapers** and **coupon books** that are distributed at virtually every restaurant, rest stop, and gift shop within a 50-mile radius of Orlando. They're useful for finding the names and addresses of some of the cheaper hotel options. But don't assume that the appealingly low rates advertised in those publications are the lowest available. For example, one week in October, the Comfort Inn Lake Buena Vista was advertising a weekday rate of $59 in the free *Traveler Discount Guide*. Its own website confirmed that price, but a spot check of the major discounters (Priceline, Hotels.com, Expedia, and Travelocity) yielded a price of $45, and when I showed up in its lobby and told them what I'd been quoted online, I was offered the same rate on the spot.

It's a valuable lesson. Once you've got a low quote in hand, check your hotel's website for a better deal. If the prices aren't budging lower after that, call the hotel directly to see if they will match or beat the Web discounters' quotes—after all, if properties rent directly to you, they can avoid paying commission to a middleman. Call the local number of the hotel, not the toll-free one, to bargain in this way.

The major exceptions, as always, are Disney-run properties, which rarely sell through third-party discounters. Disney's hotels are priced uniformly according to the season. There are sometimes some deals on offer, especially for annual pass-holders, active military, and Florida residents, and to find them, check the alerts at special websites including **TheMouseForLess.com** (you'll have to join the free mailing list for the scoop) and **MouseSavers.com,** which list going discounts. If you have an AAA membership, inquire whether a hotel has special deals for you.

WHAT TO EXPECT

If you have ever stayed in a true luxury hotel—every fixture of the finest quality and installed with impeccable craftsmanship; staff that anticipates your whims—then you'll quickly realize that nothing in Orlando approaches a world-class level of service and quality. Here, no matter how much you pay, no matter how many amenities your hotel has (which you'll pay more for), you'll often get the feeling that you're but one of many customers feeding a giant machine, because you are. This guide lists only a few high-end hotels that I feel get you the most for your top dollar, either in spectacle, space, or class.

Every hotel in this book has swimming pool (because of liability issues, few are much deeper than 5 ft.) and air-conditioning, and almost every hotel offers shuttles to at least some theme parks, although fares around $5 to $10 per person may apply. Pretty much every hotel on this list is kid-friendly; I've noted which properties are especially generous with a 👶, but there are none you should fear bringing your brood to (unless noted). In fact, you should expect every place on this list to be crawling with scampering, shouting children hopped up on a perpetual vacation-permitted sugar buzz. If it's an escape from kiddies you require, steer toward a rental home, a B&B, or one of the splurgy resort hotels that lean more toward the conference trade.

Each listing is preceded by one or more dollar signs, indicating its price range per room, not per person:

$: Up to $75 a night
$$: $76 to $125
$$$: $126 to $175
$$$$: More than $176 a night

Note: The prices in this book don't include taxes. In Orange County (Orlando, most of Disney), that's 12.5%; in Osceola County (Kissimmee), it's 13%.

B&BS

This won't take long. There aren't many: One near Disney and two downtown. Orlando's B&Bs trade on romance; I'd think twice before checking in with kids.

How to Save on Lodging

- **Come during low season.** Hotel prices are trimmed then.
- **Avoid holidays.** If the kids are out of school, stay out of Orlando.
- **Be realistic about your needs.** Don't splurge on a room if you'll be on the go most of the time. The same goes for springing for a view.
- **Make sure the room you rent can fit everyone in your party.** Otherwise you'll have to rent two, doubling costs.
- **Even if you find a good rate from an online discounter (listed above), always get a quote directly from the hotel.** It might be lower.
- **See what's on offer from a packager.** Companies like Lastminute.com or Southwest Vacations may discount rooms (see above).
- **Plug Kissimmee into your Web searches.** It's cheaper than Orlando.
- **A well-chosen hotel will also save you on food.** Are there affordable places to eat nearby?

$$–$$$ So close to the Magic Kingdom that you can see its fireworks over the trees in the yard, **the Perri House** (10417 Vista Oaks Court, Orlando; ☎ 800/780-4830 and 407/876-4830; www.perrihouse.com; AE, DC, DISC, MC, V), which feels like you're staying at a high school friend's ranch house in a grove, is remarkably private for something so close to the fray. It was designed and self-built by its original owners on 2 acres in the late 1980s at a time when there was nothing northeast of Disney except citrus groves. Birds such as sandhill cranes and osprey long ago learned to stop here for rest, particularly in early mornings. The current owners are friendly but a bit sloppy about running things, and on several occasions I have had trouble even finding someone around, but there's no denying this is a soothing, homelike place for guests sick of being nickeled and dimed by hotels—in fact, it's the only such option near Disney. Its eight private-bath rooms, a little dark but individually decorated with truly comfortable canopy and four-poster beds (mostly kings), have two doors, one to a communal library, and one a private entrance accessed from outdoors, and there's a pool befitting any suburban Florida home. Breakfast is continental and basic, and the kitchen is open to use for any meal. Rates are generally $129 per night, but pitch something lower.

$$–$$$$ So serene and scenic that it hosts around 200 weddings a year and many more anniversary trysts, the **Courtyard at Lake Lucerne** ★★ (211 N. Lucerne Circle East, Orlando; ☎ 407/648-5188; www.orlandohistoricinn.com; AE, DC, MC, V) is snuggled under Spanish moss in an oasis of calm that's surprisingly near the towers and highways of downtown. This classy quartet of historic B&Bs, operated together, encompasses the city's oldest documented home, 1883's Norment Parry Inn, which has the cheapest rates ($105); you'll sleep in an elegant four-poster bed among Victorian-era European antiques. My favorite is the I. W. Phillips House (around $110), because its wooden wrap-around verandah evokes old Florida style. All rooms have TVs, phones, and private bathrooms—most with era fixtures. Retired lawyer Charles Meiner, who established and furnished these inns, imbued them with Southern charm, and they provide lots for free: breakfast, parking, in-room Wi-Fi, and cocktails every evening. And managers will bargain. You won't find rooms this refined anywhere else in Orlando.

$$–$$$$ Another cluster of century-old buildings near downtown, **the Veranda Bed and Breakfast** (707 E. Washington St., Orlando; ☎ 800/420-6822 or 407/849-0321; www.theverandabandb.com; AE, DC, DISC, MC, V) starts at $99 a night for a cozy cottage with a private entrance. Where the Courtyard is genteel and pedigreed, the cloisterish, homey Veranda recalls a hidden, clapboarded getaway you might find among the inns of Key West or *Tales of the City*'s Barbary Lane. All rooms have phones, TVs, and private baths (often with huge tubs), and some have furnished porches. Bear in mind that rooms facing busy Summerlin Avenue may be noisy, and parking is scarce. Both downtown Orlando and the bistros of Thornton Park are a stroll away.

WALT DISNEY WORLD HOTELS, NUTSHELLED

I'm listing **Disney hotels** (☎ 407/939-6244; www.disneyworld.com; AE, DC, DISC, MC, V) first, not because they're the best, but because lots of visitors want to know about them. Some people feel like spending twice as much to spend the night on Disney property gives them closer entry to the resort's storied "magic." There are distinct advantages and disadvantages to saying on property. How many of these considerations are important to you—or justify the expense?

Yay! The Benefits of Staying on Disney Property:

◆ For those without cars, there's **free bus, monorail, and ferry transportation** throughout the resort. This is probably the biggest consideration for most people. (Then again, in-resort transportation is free to *everyone* at Disney, guest or not.) Be warned that "free" doesn't mean "fast": Routes can be circuitous and waits can be aggravating, and you may have to stand.

◆ **Free parking** at the theme parks (normally $12 per day).

◆ Each day, during **Extra Magic Hours,** one or two parks open an hour early or up to 3 hours past closing for the express use of Disney hotel guests. The major attractions, but not all of them, will be open during this period, and lines tend to be shorter than when general admission takes effect. Unless it's peak season, the time you save is negligible, so it shouldn't be a deciding factor. (Most hotels on Hotel Plaza Blvd. aren't eligible for this perk.)

◆ The resort offers free coach transfers to Orlando International Airport through the **Disney's Magical Express** program. That saves money, but not time; see p. 316 for its drawbacks.

◆ The right to charge purchases on your **room key card,** even at the theme parks. (For some, this is more of a temptation than a bonus.)

◆ The right to have your in-park **shopping delivered to your room** for you. The delivery lag time is such that this only works if you're not checking out for at least 2 more nights.

◆ Three or four timed **kids' activities** a day, albeit many at a charge.

Boo! These Things About Staying with Disney Stink:

◆ **Rates are 40% to 60% higher** than off-property rooms of comparable quality. Also, most rooms add $10 a night for each person past the limit of two up to the room's stated maximum capacity, so an $82 room at the Value resorts will in fact be $102 if four people over 18 stay there. Do the math; the higher cost will probably offset other benefits, including transportation.

◆ A **four-person limit** in the most affordable rooms. Many families have to rent two units, doubling the expense. (Happily, kids up to age 17 can stay in a room for free, even though they start paying adult ticket prices at age 10.)

◆ Most Disney resorts are so large (each Value resort is a campus of 1,920 rooms) that **lines,** even for a cup of coffee, are an endless nuisance and **sprawling layouts are confusing** to small children, to say nothing of their parents. Disney knows it's an issue; it addresses it by charging more for "Preferred" rooms that aren't as far from the lobby.

◆ The most affordable rooms are about as **far from the action** as many off-property hotels. The All-Star resorts, in particular, are on a cul-de-sac in a budget ghetto that's a good 15-minute drive from the Magic Kingdom.

◆ In-room cooking is made difficult in that no affordable rooms have **microwaves** or **coffeemakers;** even **refrigerators** at Value hotels cost $10 a day—a week's rental costs as much as a room for a night elsewhere! Internet access is by cord, not wireless, and costs $10 a day. Elsewhere, all are free.

Walt Disney World Area Accommodations

Best Western Lake Buena Vista 20
Buena Vista Suites 23
Celebration Hotel 32
Celebrity Resorts Lake Buena Vista 6
Comfort Suites Maingate Resort 27
Disney's All-Star Movies Resort 30
Disney's All-Star Music Resort 29
Disney's All-Star Sports Resort 28

Disney's Animal Kingdom Lodge 24
Disney's Beach Club 12
Disney's Boardwalk Inn 15
Disney's Caribbean Beach Resort 17
Disney's Contemporary Resort 3
Disney's Coronado Springs Resort 16
Disney's Fort Wilderness Resort 5
Disney's Polynesian Resort 2

Disney's Pop Century Resort 25
Disney's Port Orleans Riverside and French Quarter 7
Disney's Wilderness Lodge 4
Disney's Yacht Club 11
Gaylord Palms 33
Holiday Inn Express Lake Buena Vista 9

Hyatt Regency Grand Cypress Resort 18
Marriott Village at Lake Buena Vista (Courtyard, Fairfield Inn, SpringHill Suites) 22
Mona Lisa Suite Hotel 31
Nickelodeon Family Suites 26
Orlando Courtyard Suites 27
Perri House 6
Quality Inn Maingate West 27
Quality Suites
Lake Buena Vista 10
Radisson Hotel
Lake Buena Vista 21
Regal Sun Resort 19
Royale Park Suites 34
Seralago Hotel & Suites 36
Shades of Green 1
Staybridge Suites
Lake Buena Vista 8
Tropical Palms Resort 35
Walt Disney World Sheraton Dolphin 13
Walt Disney World Westin Swan 14

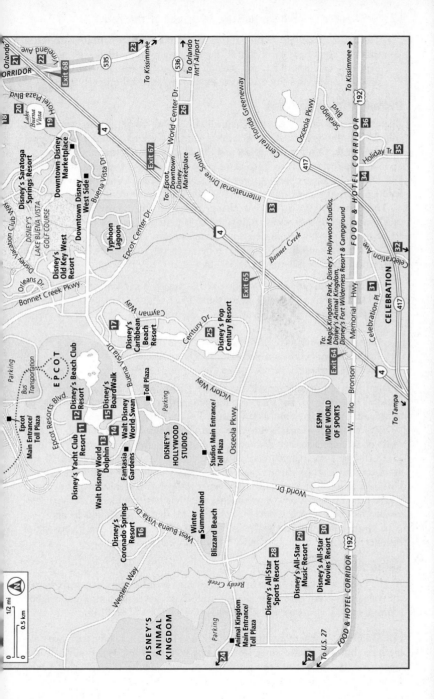

◆ The most affordable Disney hotels also **don't have restaurants or room service.** They have food courts (burgers, sandwiches, pasta—all at theme park prices of around $8) and the only room service item is pizza. This is less of a problem if you intend to save money by eating off property anyway.

Disney Pricing Seasons

There are five pricing seasons at Walt Disney World. Forget spring, winter, and fall; the seasons you need to remember are, in descending order of expense: **Holiday, Peak, Summer, Regular,** and the all-important **Value.**

Likewise, there are three categories of hotel: **Deluxe, Moderate,** and **Value,** plus Disney Vacation Club apartments (see "Timeshares," earlier in this chapter). So the path to the cheapest room is to book a Value resort during a Value period.

The exact dates for each season change every year and are tweaked slightly for each property, but they always follow the same pattern on the calendar. The lowest-priced Disney hotel category is its Value category, and for 2009, its schedule and pricing shake out like this, minus some weekends (MLK Day, Independence Day) when prices pop up a further $10 to $20:

◆ **Value season:** January 1 to February 12, August 9 to October 1, November 29 to December 17. Value resort price: $82.

◆ **Regular season:** April 19 to May 21, October 2 to November 24. Value price: $105.

◆ **Summer season:** May 22 to August 8. Value price: $115.

◆ **Peak season:** February 16 to April 3. Value price: $125.

◆ **Holiday season:** December 18 to December 31. Value price: $135 to $145.

Now, you're probably wondering which Disney resorts are considered Value resorts. There are four, and they're all fairly motel-like: the All-Star Music, All-Star Sports, All-Star Movies, and Pop Century Resort. They're reviewed below.

Two websites, **MouseSavers.com** and **TheMouseForLess.com,** both post codes of all current known discounts. **AAA** also is known to trim rates a little.

You'll hear some parents rave about the refillable mugs that cost $12.50 and grant unlimited sodas during your stay. Keep in mind they only work at your hotel, *not* inside the theme parks, so if you're not going to spend much time there, you'll waste money. A few other touches are a relief for families: additional shallow kiddie pools at each resort, plus playgrounds that segregate kids by age.

If you're an annual passholder or if you own Disney stock, check your list of benefits to see if they entitle you to discounts, when available.

Value Resorts

Although everything the Mouse does pushes you toward its most expensive hotels, the Value resort category is in fact Disney's most prevalent, with 8,640 nightly rooms—more than many midsize cities—available for $82 to $145.

FACILITIES   Value rooms are essentially motel-style. They come with two double beds, but a few have kings (request one when you reserve). Rooms fit four (there's a $10 daily charge for each third and fourth adult), plus one child under 3—mind you, a full room would be a mighty tight squeeze. If your party is bigger than that, you'll have to get two connecting rooms and spend twice as much, or spring for a six-person Family Suite, which is really just two rooms with a door banged through and a minikitchen (little fridge, microwave, coffeemaker) added. As of press time, they're only at the All-Star Music resort (with rumors of some opening at the Pop Century), but at $184 to $327, you can do much better outside the World. In the classic Southern style, Value rooms are entered from sheltered outdoor corridors, which means your sole window faces a walkway from which people can peek in if your curtains aren't drawn. Again, nothing all that different from many budget motels.

The T-shaped building blocks can feel at times like thin-walled battery hen hutches, with noisy plumbing and seething with kids who don't realize how sound carries (especially when school groups and cheerleader meets are in town). The walk to each hotel's lobby/food building can be a marathon. There are elevators.

The food court, front desk, and sundries shop are all in the same building by the bus stops to the parks, and some rooms are a 15-minute walk away. More expensive Preferred rooms are in the neighboring blocks and cost $15 more. Sometimes hotel staff (called "Mousekeeping") leaves towels shaped into animals for your room (a Disney tradition), and sometimes they get so sloppy they don't.

Tip: Disney hotels charge $9.95 to use the Web for 24 hours, but the McDonald's at the entrance to the All-Star resorts has free Wi-Fi.

TRANSPORTATION   No Value-class or Moderate-class resort is connected to any theme park by monorail or ferry. Roads are your only option, be it a Disney bus or your own car.

If you're going to spend most of your time away from your hotel, these may do nicely. But then again, if pampering doesn't matter much to you, you might as well pay $50 and stay off property, because Disney's Value properties won't give you a big location advantage. Even their designated bus stops throughout the resort seem to be the most inconveniently located. Value-class rooms are really for that segment of the population that insists on staying on Disney property, doesn't want to break the bank doing it, and ultimately doesn't mind the diminished quality.

$$ Disney's Pop Century Resort 🧒 (1050 Century Dr., Lake Buena Vista; ☎ 407/938-4000; www.disneyworld.com) is a version of a roadside motel, with concrete-block walls, smallish (260 sq. ft.) rooms with one sink and one mirror, and for dining, a central food court with quality akin to the average mall's (though this one caters to 2,880 rooms). As if to counteract such dormlike austerity, the boxy sprawl of T-shaped buildings, some of which face a lake, is festooned with outsized icons of the late 20th century: gigantic bowling pins, yo-yos, and Rubik's Cubes—which kids think is pretty cool—and there are three pools. Only the first half of this resort is technically open; the second half, the Legendary Years, planned for across the lake and to cover 1900 through the 1940s, has been in mothballs since 2001, when the existing half, the Classic Years, opened. If this one's full, the three older All-Star hotels have nearly 6,000 more rooms cut from the same cheap terrycloth. There is gossip that this property may be converted to a Disney animation theme, but the other details should remain the same.

$$ Their setup is identical in nearly every way to the Pop Century—a huge expanse of concrete-block buildings enlivened by enormous emblems, as if a giant had spilled the Legos in his toy box. But because they're older (they opened in the late 1990s) and there's no enlivening pond, I list the three **All-Star Resorts** 🧒

(W. Buena Vista Dr., Lake Buena Vista; ☎ 407/939-6244; www.disneyworld.com) second. Each one (Music, Sports, and Movies) is slightly less populous (1,920 rooms) than the Pop Century, which makes them marginally more manageable, and there's a McDonald's on their approach road, which, for those with cars, provides an alternative to the food court. Covering the All-Stars for *Budget Travel* magazine, I summed them up thusly: "Depending on your point of view, Disney treats you either like a second-class guest or an average American family on vacation." Nothing has changed. The fun is in the outdoor areas, not in the rooms, which are only mildly themed. At the very least, sinks are outside of the toilet-and-shower room, which eases life for multitasking families. For groups of more than four but not more than six, the Family Suites, mentioned above, might work, but they're twice as much as a condo, where you can cook.

Of the three All-Stars, I prefer Movies, not just because it's the youngest (opened 1999) and because its decor is laden with more Disney-specific iconography than its sisters (which stick to musical and sports-equipment icons), but also because the Disney shuttle buses tend to stop there last on their circuit of the three, which cuts transportation time. Then again, some choose Sports for the same reason, as it's the first stop of the three and so it's easier to get a seat on the bus there. (That being crowded off a Disney bus should even be a concern says a lot about what the Value resorts offer—and how willing some people are to overlook poor quality in the name of their allegiance to Disney.)

Moderate Resorts

The next category up from Value is Moderate, which ranges from $149 to $219 ($195 during the summer), escalating according to the pricing seasons roughly delineated above. Compared to Value, what do you get for the extra dough? Put simply, the main pools have elaborate themes with slides and there are usually a few additional, simple pools; rooms measure 314 square feet instead of 260 square feet; most have two sinks instead of one (both outside the shower/toilet room); all rooms have a small balcony or patio with seating (though most have no view to speak of), and you can rent a bike or a boat on the premises. The upgrade doesn't win you the right to fit more people: Rooms fit four, plus one child under 3, just as in the Value class. Unlike in the Value class, minifridges are free, but only on request, and each third and fourth adult in a room incurs a $15 daily fee.

Moderate properties feel more resortlike when compared to the glorified motels of the Values, but at heart, they're still glorified motels, with exterior corridors (so close your drapes) and dark bathrooms that a friend of mine dubs "tombs with a toilet." You'll still be eating mostly in high-priced food courts (the single restaurant at Port Orleans, for example, isn't open for lunch) located at a main building that might be quite distant from your room. Again, Moderate rooms are for people who just *have* to stay on property, and although the bedrooms aren't really much plusher than the Value properties, you will sense more breathing room and personality to the grounds, and Disney has been pouring money into glorifying its main pool areas into exciting, themed locales. Considering what the same money buys you off property, I can't recommend a Moderate resort unless your heart is set on a particular property.

$$ If you or your spouse is an active or retired member of the U.S. military (including reserves, Coast Guard, National Guard, U.S. Public Health Officers, and Department of Defense civilian employees), look into **Shades of Green** ★ (1950 W. Magnolia Dr., Lake Buena Vista; ☎ 888/593-2242 or 407/824-3400; www.shadesofgreen.org). A fuller list of eligibility requirements is posted online. The 586-room hotel, located within walking distance of the monorail and the Magic Kingdom, was operated as a Disney golf resort for 21 years before being handed to the military as the only Armed Forces Recreation Center (AFRC) located in the continental U.S. Prices for this deluxe-level hotel, which has some of the largest standard rooms in the World, approximate those at Disney's civilian Value resorts. Rooms fit five, one more than the Value and Moderate categories.

$$$–$$$$ Port Orleans Riverside and French Quarter (2201 Orleans Dr., Lake Buena Vista; ☎ 407/934-6000) has an unwieldy name because it's an unwieldy property. It's actually two resorts, both built on a canal, that have been awkwardly fused together. The French Quarter (1,000 rooms), built along right angles on simulated streets, purports to imitate the real one in New Orleans, but the construction is too boxy and cheap to strike the correct texture. Riverside (2,048 rooms), where buildings are more successful pastiches on Mississippi-style homes, is the nicer of the two, as it has more water for rooms to face (the privilege will cost you another $20 a night) and most activities for the two resorts are there. The main pool is less elaborate than French Quarter's, although there are five pools to French Quarter's one area. They are far enough apart (about 15 min. walking) that many people choose to use the free boat service linking them. The boats will also take you to Downtown Disney—the trip is one of the most pleasant, least known free rides at Disney World—but the parks are served only by buses.

$$$–$$$$ Disney's Coronado Springs Resort (1000 W. Buena Vista Dr., Lake Buena Vista; ☎ 407/939-6244; www.disneyworld.com) was built to attract convention crowds and is probably the blandest of all the Disney resorts. Some people prefer the less frenetic tone. The rooms (queen or king beds), though moderately priced, actually have a single sink, as in the Values, but they were just renovated. The grounds, done in a Mexican style around a pond, are too far-flung (some rooms are a 15-min. walk from the lobby—a common problem at the lower-cost Disney resorts) and come across as uninspired. The food court is above average, though, as is the pool area (the Dig Site) themed after a Mayan pyramid, and there's a cocktail lounge, Rix, with a semblance of sophistication. The hotel is about 10 minutes' drive from any parks or attractions, and it's only linked by roads. For atmosphere and its ferry link, I would pick Port Orleans Riverside. However, if you need a room accessible for those with disabilities and the cheaper hotels are out of such units, you can try here, where there is a slightly greater inventory.

$$$–$$$$ Finally, there's **Disney's Caribbean Beach Resort** (900 Cayman Way, Lake Buena Vista; ☎ 407/939-6244; www.disneyworld.com), which is very much like Coronado Springs (too sprawling, pond in the middle) except with an island theme. Rooms are the Moderate category's largest (by a little) and the freshest; Disney just spent a ton trying to make it more thrilling by lightly theming rooms to *Finding Nemo* (he lived in Australia, but whatever) and adding some added-fee rooms based on *Pirates of the Caribbean* (beds like ships, hanging lanterns) that cost $20 more. The main Old Port Royale pool area, too, which emulates a waterfront Spanish fort and has a giant tippy bucket, was recently doubled in size.

Camping at Disney

As for camping at Walt Disney World, **Fort Wilderness** (3520 N. Fort Wilderness Trail, Lake Buena Vista; ☎ 407/939-6244; www.disneyworld.com; $), not to be confused with the Wilderness Lodge, a pricey imitation of Yellowstone Lodge, consists of campsites, mobile home–style cabins (from $255), and RV spots. Camping under the thick pines is far and away the cheapest way to sleep on Disney property, and nightly outdoor movies and bonfires are regularly part of the deal. But at $42 to $111 a night for a sandy plot (up to 10 people) without equipment, it's twice the market rate. Officially, Disney only rents tents ($30 a night—not cheap) to groups of 20 or more, but people seem to get around that requirement all the time.

Although the buildings are arranged around a pond, water views are $25 more. The resort's principal drawback is the fact no other major areas connect to it. At least Port Orleans, for the same money, has boats that go to Downtown Disney; from Caribbean Beach, all connections are by road, so it's strongly recommended to have a car here.

Deluxe Resorts

I don't consider any of Disney's Deluxe resorts—there are eight—to be worth the $250 to $600 you pay to sleep in them. No one who has experienced the world's true luxury hotels can seriously say that Disney's quality standards compare. They're pillow mills in fancy dress. Sure, they have sit-down restaurants, spas, lovely pools, and lounges. But what Disney's Deluxe hotels mostly have is uplifting theming—a prevailing mood—that makes a stay memorable, proximity to a theme park, and fantastic views, such as of the Magic Kingdom or African animals. There are plenty of people who consider a trip to Disney a trip of a lifetime and so they splurge on the top of the line, and it's in service of those people, and not because I think they're worth it, that I name my favorites.

$$$$ There are three resorts located on the monorail line encircling the Seven Seas Lagoon, but there's one I prefer over the rest: **Disney's Contemporary Resort** ✪✪✪ (4600 N. World Dr., Lake Buena Vista; ☎ 407/824-1000; www.disneyworld.com). Some of the most vivid memories of my childhood involve this fabulous hotel, one of the first two that opened with the resort in 1971. Nothing says, "I'm at Disney World" more than the awesome sight of that monorail sweeping dramatically through its glassy Grand Canyon Concourse, which is does every few minutes on its way to and from the Magic Kingdom. The curved tower behind it, Bay Lake Tower, is an attention-stealing 2009 addition for the Disney Vacation Club.

The building itself is a bit of modern architectural history, and indicative of the revolutionary methods that Walt Disney World had once hoped to pioneer. The United States Steel Corporation helped design it; its modular, prefabricated rooms were slotted into place by crane. The idea was that when rooms needed renovation, the capsules could simply removed like drawers, but in practice, they fused to the steel frame, so renovations are done the old-fashioned way. The current look: soothing putty and slate business-class colors, plus plasma TVs.

Not everyone who books here scores a balconied room high up in the coveted A-framed Contemporary Tower; there are low-level Garden Rooms along Bay Lake, too, that are $100 cheaper. Rooms on the west of the tower face the Magic Kingdom itself—the *ne plus ultra* of Disney views—and every water-view room takes in the nightly electrical parade that floats after dark. Even if you can't stay here, drop by to see the 90-foot-tall, stylized mosaics of children by Walt Disney's contemporary Mary Blair, which encapsulate the late-'60s futurist optimism out of which the resort was born. The top floor contains one of the best restaurants at Walt Disney World, the California Grill (p. 67). And, of course, the free monorail connects to the Magic Kingdom and Epcot, which makes darting out of the parks for nap breaks a cinch. If money were no object, this would be my choice.

$$$$ I also have a soft spot for **Disney's Animal Kingdom Lodge** kids ★★★ (2901 Osceola Pkwy., Bay Lake; ☎ 407/938-3000; www.disneyworld.com), styled after a grander African lodge than truly exists on the veldt, because the higher tariff returns to you in the form of a 24-hour safari. The hotel is built on a system of paddocks, so if you've got a Savannah view (they start at $285—be careful that you don't accidentally book one overlooking the pool or the parking lot), when you look out of your window or go onto your balcony, you'll see whatever African animal is happening by at that moment, be it a giraffe, an ostrich, a zebra, or a warthog. You'll find a game viewing guide in your room beside your room service menu. Because animals tend to be active in the early morning, when families are gearing up for their days, the idea works well. Like the Contemporary, anyone can pay a visit, even if they're not staying here; there's even a public viewing area straight out the back door. The Lodge's principal drawback is its distance from everything on Disney property except for Animal Kingdom; all connections are by road.

I chose both of those for their rooms' unparalleled views, which at least provide a cogent reason (or an excuse, anyway) for such a huge expense, but the other major Deluxes each have a major selling point, usually having to do with quicker park access. Quickly: The **Polynesian** is a Contemporary contemporary, built at the same time with the same methods. Its theme is self-explanatory, and I like it moodiness but not its sprawl and its dearth of rooms with views. It's also on the monorail, as is the haughty **Grand Floridian.** Both of those put rooms in building blocks, forcing most guests to walk outside to get to them (which stinks in the rain). **Wilderness Lodge,** in the insect-filled woods on Bay Lake, is a gorgeous riff on Yellowstone's Old Faithful Lodge, and it's connected to the Magic Kingdom by a 10-minute ferry. The **Yacht Club** and the **Beach Club** are both a 5-minute walk out the side exit of Epcot, making them perfect for grabbing the foods in the World Showcase, and their shared pool area, Stormalong Bay, has a crazy water slide coming off the mast of a ship plus sandy shores. (It's easily the best one on Disney property.) **BoardWalk Inn** is about 10 minutes' walk from Epcot's side door, and, along with the Yacht and Beach clubs, it connects to Hollywood Studios by a 15-minute ferry. The Sheraton **Dolphin** and the Westin **Swan** share that ferry and are about 15 minutes' walk from Epcot. They are the only two non-Disney hotels beside a major theme park, so if you find a very good deal from an online discounter, it may be worth the splurge.

The "Good Neighbor" Policy

Back in the 1970s and early 1980s, Disney World didn't think it should be in the hotel business. So it permitted several interlopers to build and operate their own bedders around the present-day Downtown Disney area, which was called Lake Buena Vista. Today, there are seven of these Downtown Disney Resort Area properties, all corporate run (Hilton, DoubleTree, Best Western), none with special themes, and all priced higher than competition located as little as a half-mile away. Their proximity to Downtown Disney (albeit via congested Hotel Plaza Blvd.) is listed as a selling point, but most casual visitors will be sated by a single trip to that shopping and entertainment area, so what are you paying more for? Traffic? If you can find a good deal (the Best Western sometimes slashes prices through its corporate site), then seize upon it, but don't pick these places because you think they're going to make your vacation.

Two more luxury hotels, the **Swan** and the **Dolphin** (run by Westin and Sheraton, respectively), went up in the mid-1980s just west of Epcot by what's now the BoardWalk area, and their disproportionate silhouettes spoil the park's carefully planned sightlines. Although they're linked to Epcot and the Studios by ferry and the other parks by bus, and some of their restaurants are excellent (bluezoo, p. 67, is wonderful), they're not technically Disney's hotels, but Starwood's. Which means they discount.

Scattered throughout town, even as far as the International Drive area, are properties certified as "Good Neighbor" hotels by Disney. The appellation is mostly meaningless. It means that hotel can sell Magic Your Way tickets and screen a mesmerizing 24-hour channel featuring the insanity-inducing Stacey, the world's most spastically perky Disney fan (to her, everything is "amazing"), and her Top Seven favorites at each park. To be brutally honest, most of the Good Neighbor hotels I've stayed in are sub-par pillow mills, plainly mediocre. Something about the added business that comes with the distinction makes a hotel care a little less about hustling for business. Only the Good Neighbor properties on the west side of Apopka Vineland Road (mostly on Hotel Plaza Blvd.) enjoy half-hourly shuttles; the rest don't. Don't select a hotel just because it's a Good Neighbor hotel. Choose it because it's the hotel for you.

INSIDE UNIVERSAL ORLANDO

There are only three hotels located on Universal property, all operated by the Loews hotel group, and none of them could be considered budget, but they all feel more like true resorts whereas Disney's just feel like hotels. There are strong advantages that come with the higher prices. First, you don't need to use a car because all three hotels are within 15 minutes' walk of the parks, and they're also connected by a free boat that runs continuously into the wee hours. Rooms have wet bars with coffeemakers, two phones, and turn-down service (rare at Disney), and while you have to pay for the in-room Web, it's free in public areas. Also, every guest can use their room key card to make charges throughout the resort and to join the Express line at the two parks' best attractions, which means you can realistically see both parks in a single day—that perk has the effect of freeing up a vacation schedule. You can also drink and dine all night at CityWalk next door without having to drive. So while you're staying at Universal, you'll spend a lot, but can also pack more into your trip. For that reason, some people stay here only a night or two of their trips and head elsewhere for the rest of their vacation. Use the hotels' website to find Super Savings Rates, which grants discounts of 15% to 30% on specified nights; the website also posts floor plans of all room types.

On the downside, parking at all three hotels is an outrageous $15 a day, and the on-site restaurants aren't cheap. But at least the Universal property is hemmed in by lots of real-world restaurants where prices are realistic (which Disney can't claim), and free shuttles to SeaWorld are provided once a day. You're better linked to the real Orlando when you're at Universal.

$$$$　　The least expensive option at Universal, **Royal Pacific Resort** ★★ (6300 Hollywood Way, Orlando; ☎ 888/273-1311 or 407/503-3000; www.universalorlando. com; AE, DC, DISC, MC, V) is a resortlike spread themed to the South Seas in the 1930s, more luxurious yet cheaper than the Disney Polynesian version, with a lush pool area (sandy beach, winding garden paths, interactive water play area) and a sophisticated, wood-and-wicker look. Rooms cost $214 to $259 facing the parking lot or distant highway, and about $30 more if you want to face the pool or boat canal. The standard is high: Expect very soft robes, cushy beds with fat pillows, and marble-top chests. There are also two-room suites themed to *Jurassic Park* (the kids' room has twin beds and DVD player) that cost a little more than two conjoined rooms: $550. It's right over the road from Islands of Adventure; many rooms have a panorama of it. Two nights a week, it hosts an elaborate luau with a roast suckling pig ($52 adults/$29 kids), but I'd spend that money on the rich dishes at the restaurant Emeril Lagasse runs on the premises. In any other city, the Royal Pacific might be everyone's favorite resort. Here, though, its subtler ethic gets lost in the crowd.

$$$$　　If I were dreaming of staying in a fancy resort hotel, I would give the **Hard Rock Hotel** ★★ 🄺🄸🄳🅂 (5000 Universal Blvd., Orlando; ☎ 888/273-1311 or 407/ 503-7625; www.hardrockhotel.com; AE, DC, DISC, MC, V) a serious look. First of all, besides being the city's most convenient hotel for theme parks—Universal's two parks and CityWalk are all a 10-minute walk away, or you can take that boat—the 650-room Hard Rock, managed by Loews, has more perks for the money than most of the city's similarly priced hotels. Rooms, in the middle range for size (375 sq. ft.) have genuinely funky furniture, tons of mirrors, two sinks (one in and one out of the bathroom), two big beds, music systems that play your iPod, and 32-inch flatscreen TVs. The ginormous hotel pool, which imitates a beach gently descending to depth, has not only a long water slide but also underwater speakers through which you can hear the party music (they really bring out the finger cymbals in Bon Jovi's "Livin' on a Prayer"). Even the menu of recorded wake-up calls is by rock celebs (Vince Neil from Mötley Crüe shrieks "Get the hell out of bed! All the girls are waiting for you down by the pool!"). The halls are lined with rock memorabilia (my favorite: the gold-lion-head necklace Elvis was wearing when he met Nixon). Does it all justify prices like $244 to $326 a room? It depends on how hard you ride that free Express pass.

$$$$ Universal's priciest option, **Portofino Bay Hotel** ★ (5601 Universal Blvd., Orlando; ☎ 888/273-1311 or 407/503-1000; www.universalorlando.com; AE, DC, DISC, MC, V), is a faithful re-creation of the bay of the famous Italian fishing village, down to the angle of the boat docks and bolted-down Vespas. Beyond that spectacular gimmick (said to have been Steven Spielberg's idea, like half the stuff at Universal), which feeds a few amenities such as opera singers on the piazza (*Musica della Notte*, p. 284), there are three pools and rooms (450 sq. ft.) of a high standard (they have top-end beds). But because the resort is the farthest of the three from the parks (about 20 min. by boat or foot), it tends to appeal to couples more than kids. As proof, there's also a Mandara Spa. Regular rooms cost $269 to $319 if you face the parking lot, and about $30 more to face the port. Like the Royal Pacific, there are two-room kid suites for a little more than twice the standard rate; these are themed to Dr. Seuss, with bendy lamps, candy colors, and character murals.

U.S. 192 & SOUTH OF DISNEY

The lowest link in the Orlando tourist chain both in class and price, U.S. 192 is where you'll find most affordable (if often the most tired) motels close to the Disney zoo. Most were built in the 1970s growth boom and have settled into the budget category. They are technically located in the town of Kissimmee, which maintains its own website at **www.floridakiss.com**—check it for regular deals, and make sure to expand your Orlando hotel Web searches to include Kissimmee. In this region, shuttles are often available to Disney, but not always to SeaWorld or Universal. If you come to town without a room, hit this area; the farther east you go from Disney, the more likely you are to find a bed for around $35, and although I can give no promises about its quality, there are tons of nearby restaurants.

$ The only hostel in the Orlando area is the 190-bed **Palm Lakefront Resort & Hostel** (4840 W. Irlo Bronson Hwy./U.S. 192, Kissimmee; ☎ 407/396-1759; www.orlandohostels.com; MC, V), which is well located for a hostel: on a part of U.S. 192 served by LYNX bus no. 56, which heads right to the gates of the Magic Kingdom every half-hour (trip time: 30 min.). It's installed in an obsolete low-end motel, made of cinder blocks but gussied up slightly with bright accent walls. The dorms ($19 per night) are the simplest option, with six wooden bunks and a shared bathroom. There are also simple private rooms (around $38 for two, $76 for four) with TVs, a private bath, and twin beds, plus a family room with five beds ($15 per person). The central reception building contains an equipped kitchen (there's a Publix supermarket across the street), a foosball table, and video games, while the huge backyard, which has a pool, reaches to the bank of Lake Cecile. Like most hostels, you choose it to hang out with European backpackers on their grand American tours. To grease the social opportunities, there's basketball hoop in the parking area and impromptu summer barbecues aren't uncommon. Wi-Fi is free.

U.S. 192 Area Accommodations

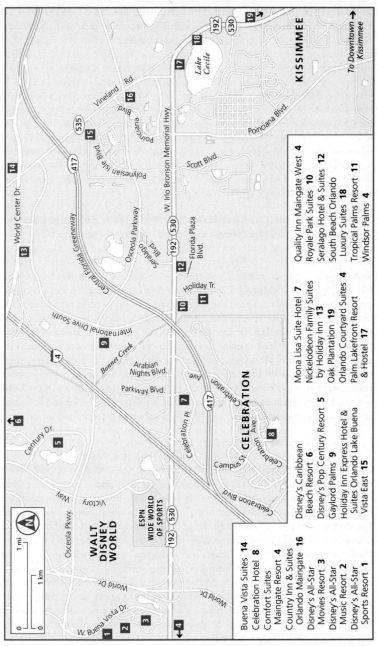

Buena Vista Suites **14**
Celebration Hotel **8**
Comfort Suites
Maingate Resort **4**
Country Inn & Suites
Orlando Maingate **16**
Disney's All-Star
Movies Resort **3**
Disney's All-Star
Music Resort **2**
Disney's All-Star
Sports Resort **1**

Disney's Caribbean
Beach Resort **6**
Disney's Pop Century Resort **5**
Gaylord Palms **9**
Holiday Inn Express Hotel &
Suites Orlando Lake Buena
Vista East **15**

Mona Lisa Suite Hotel **7**
Nickelodeon Family Suites
by Holiday Inn **13**
Oak Plantation **19**
Orlando Courtyard Suites **4**
Palm Lakefront Resort
& Hostel **17**

Quality Inn Maingate West **4**
Royale Park Suites **10**
Seralago Hotel & Suites **12**
South Beach Orlando
Luxury Suites **18**
Tropical Palms Resort **11**
Windsor Palms **4**

$ Even though its owners inherited a dated hand-me-down from Holiday Inn, **Seralago Hotel & Suites** (5678 W. Irlo Bronson Hwy./U.S. 192, Kissimmee; ☎ 800/366-5437 or 407/396-4488; www.seralagohotel.com; AE, DISC, MC, V) works hard to appear cheerful, despite its economical price point ($50 is common for a standard room, but RoomSaver.com often advertises for $43), which makes it a top value for those who just want a decent place to sleep. The early 1970s, external-corridor complex (two courtyards, two pools) has been eclipsed by newer, sexier structures. The cosmetics are wanting, but the complex includes such bonuses as a basic food court and a restaurant (suggested for on-the-go grub, not dining), two playgrounds, powerful in-room A/C that could preserve meat, and a category of "two-room suites" (all of which face the pool) that are really two hotel rooms remodeled into a miniapartment (add about $35 for those). All rooms have a microwave and fridge but only full-size beds, which some couples may find small. Disney's entrance is 3 miles west.

$–$$ The 242-unit, gated **Oak Plantation** ★★★ (4090 Enchanted Oaks Circle, Kissimmee; ☎ 407/847-8200; www.oakplantationresort.com; AE, DISC, MC, V) offers a mix of one- and two-bedrooms in condo-style buildings on a slowly gentrifying patch of U.S. 192 8 miles east of Disney. The no-brand 'hood makes it a terrific value. Spread around a pond as if it were more expensive, with true-as-advertised oaks, the gated Oak Plantation is popular with young families not just because it's affordable, but also because it's got a warm personality. Amenities go beyond the expectation for the price level, including a free Internet cafe/kids' center, a big pool area with a tiki bar, a game room, a gym, and tennis and basketball courts. Each day, there's usually a cheap ($1–$3) family activity such as cookie decorating, and $6 breakfasts. Units come standard with dishwashers, single-chamber washer/dryers, kitchens, and pullout sofas. Savannah units (one-bedroom, sleeps four, 459 sq. ft.) are least expensive (around $79 a night). Things aren't perfect; if your upstairs neighbor is lead-footed, you'll feel it, and light sleepers should request rooms away from the pool area, which has piped-in music that starts at 7am. Don't confuse it for the motel-style inn of the same name.

$–$$ The superior motel **Comfort Suites Maingate Resort** (7888 West Irlo Bronson Hwy., Kissimmee; ☎ 888/390-9888 or 407/390-9888; www.comfortsuites kissimmee.com; AE, DISC, MC, V), organized around its pool, has a quiet, pseudo-resort feel (it's set away from the bustle of U.S. 192 but close to its restaurants) that makes it popular with scrimpers. All rooms come with a small fridge, microwave, and pullout sofa (hence the "suites" distinction of the hotel's name), queen beds, and sleep up to six people. During the week, rooms facing the parking lot usually cost about $69, and ones facing the landscaped, free-form courtyard pool (there's recorded Caribbean music playing all day, and a cabana bar opens at night) cost $10 more. Prices on weekends are about $10 higher, and continental breakfast, with a few plusses such as waffles, is always included. The lobby has a small shop for sundries, which makes life easier for adults, but kids get excited when they look down its driveway and see the summit of Expedition Everest at Disney's Animal Kingdom peeking over the trees nearby.

$–$$ Ignore the unwieldy name. The terrific **Holiday Inn Express Hotel & Suites Orlando Lake Buena Vista East** ★★★ (3484 Polynesian Isle Blvd.,

Kissimmee; ☎ 800/423-0908 or 407/997-1700; www.ichotelsgroup.com; AE, DISC, MC, V) has a western-facing (read: warm) pool that's better than its price point should permit, and the hotel it serves is clean, impeccably run, attractively appointed in a Spanish style, about 10 minutes from Disney, out of the fray, and offering a very high quality for the price. You can sleep up to six for $69 to $84, including continental breakfast, with frequent online deals discounting those prices by $10 to $20. Family suites are not divided by proper walls, but by waist-high partitions. This hotel, which opened only in 2004 as a La Quinta, has a small arcade with air hockey for kids, and rooms have minifridges and free Internet access. It's enough to make you forget (or resent) all those other worn-down Holiday Inn Expresses. Right outside its driveway, there's a Wal-Mart and, unusual for Florida, a smattering of Halal grocery stores.

$–$$ There's no sense pretending that the 198-room, three-story **Quality Inn Maingate West** (7785 West Irlo Bronson Hwy., Kissimmee; ☎ 800/228-5151 or 407/396-1828; www.qualityinnorlando.com; AE, DISC, MC, V) is anything more than an inexpensive place to lay your head, and it's more than acceptable for a $35 rate. As a basic motel from the 1970s, the two-story, L-shaped building may feel geriatric, but its upkeep and cleanliness keep pace with the heavy tourist traffic that sleeps here for 3 nights for what Disney charges for 1. The A/C is loud and the bedspreads aren't current, but it's clean, it's near tons of restaurants, and it's nearer to Animal Kingdom than even Disney's All-Star hotels. The free continental breakfast is bare-bones (muffins, cereal—prepare to do battle for toast with greedy guests) but carb-rich, and its simple heated pool, which is positioned alongside a forlorn pond and a Chinese buffet, gets direct sunlight for most of the day. Paying $45 for a standard double is common, with surcharges of $30 to $40 when things get really busy, but I've managed to score rates in the high $20s (see "Playing Priceline Roulette" below). To get both a microwave and a fridge, pay another $10, or for a kitchenette, lay out $15. The free shuttle is poorly timed.

$$ At the bottom of the self-catering price range, **Tropical Palms Resort** (2650 Holiday Trail, Kissimmee; ☎ 800/647-2567 or 407/396-4595; www.tropicalpalms.com; AE, DISC, MC, V) is a collection of pastel-colored, open-plan "cottages" with little patios that will remind you of mobile homes, and everything could use a coat of paint. Who cares, when they start at $85 ($99 is more common, but call to bargain) and include everything you need, from a kitchen to room for four adults and four children (that's in both studios and two-bedroom cottages, although the former would be a tight squeeze) and sometimes a sleeping loft for kids. There's also a heated pool, a playground, a general store—and a population of stray cats. How Key West! If you've ever spent time in an RV, you'll know the vacation-y feeling here. It's close to Old Town (p. 229).

$$–$$$ Lots of hotels look great on the outside but are hideous within, but the reverse is true of the **Orlando Courtyard Suites** ★★★ (2950 Reedy Creek Blvd., Kissimmee; ☎ 888/782-9796 or 407/396-9224; www.stayorlandoresorts.com; AE; DISC, MC, V), which opened in fall 2008 and remains the best-kept secret around Disney. This once-awful Ramada looks as if it could still be a horror, but in fact, its interior has been lavished with attention and the latest conveniences. Walls between old motel rooms have been busted down to create huge apartment-like

Playing Priceline Roulette

The mission was simple: Bid insanely low on Priceline and see what I got. So one week in January (low season), I pecked around on my secret-weapon site, **BiddingForTravel.com**, to find out what recent bids had been accepted. Once I had a benchmark for an off-Disney two-star property ($40), I offered Priceline $29 for any Disney-area motel. Bingo—accepted by the Quality Inn Maingate West. Next, I shopped for rental cars. Although the major renters were offering around $25 a day on their own sites, Priceline accepted a bid of $16, through Alamo. That made for a total of $35 a day for hotel *and* car—not bad.

Once at the Alamo desk in Orlando, I had to fend off entreaties to buy extra insurance, and I even had to tear up a higher-priced contract when the desk clerk "misheard" my refusal of all those extras, but I eventually got my promised $16-a-day rate. Because things were slow, I was offered a full minivan for that price, but I stuck with an economy for the sake of gas mileage. At the motel, my reservation (listed under a Connecticut address, exposing me as a Priceline skinflint) was actually paired with an even *lower* rate ($27.50), but given the mandatory $1.96 "facilities fee" (said to go toward pool towels and the coffeemaker, and which I was required to pay in cash). Resort fees, which can add up to $40 a day, are especially prevalent among hotels with three or more stars. I ended up 46¢ in the hole. Everything else went smoothly. On the downside, I found my room was left so smoky by its previous tenant that my clothes became permeated. In defense of the motel, I could have asked to have been moved, but in the spirit of the experiment, I rode it out. And in defense of Priceline, I held onto my savings, too. The system works.

Priceline isn't only for bottom of the barrel pricing either; you can often get steals at some of the swankiest places in town, including:

• **Gaylord Palms** ✪✪✪ (6000 W. Osceola Pkwy., Kissimmee; ☎ 407/ 586-2000; www.gaylordhotels.com/gaylord-palms; AE, DISC, MC, V),

units (two rooms became one-bedroom suites, six rooms converted into three bedrooms with three baths) sporting sleigh beds, washer/dryers (yes!), DVD players, tubs with spa jets, at least two flatscreen TVs, equipped kitchens with eat-in counters, fixtures straight out of Restoration Hardware, and finally embellished with pullouts sleeping another two people. Here we have a case of website photos that don't lie. It's also the closest property to Disney's main gate on U.S. 192. This place is gradually converting the old property, so no one knows about it yet, which puts rates around $89 for a one bedroom sleeping four (sometimes $69 when advertised in the tourist brochures); as demand increases, which may take a while because the marketing has been poor, expect to pay more like $130, or $150 for a three bedroom, which is still a fantastic bargain. There's a $25-a-night surcharge for stays of where the spectacular architecture—a mighty glass atrium capping a 4.5-acre ecosystem of gator habitats, caves, indoor ponds, five restaurants, and shops—is an attraction unto itself. Every room has a computer with Internet access, a giant granite-lined bathroom, and safes containing plugs for charging electronics. The hotel, which has a Canyon Ranch spa, also schedules lots of events such as family activities and an annual ice sculpture extravaganza. When it appears on Priceline it goes for $80 to $95 in the four-star category (you'll add resort fees onto that). Its usual rate starts at $199 most of the year.

◆ **Hyatt Regency Grand Cypress Resort** ✮✮✮ (1 Grand Cypress Blvd., Lake Buena Vista; ☎ 800/233-1234 or ☎ 407/239-1234; www.hyatt grandcypress.com; AE, DISC, MC, V). Probably the most complete self-contained resort near Disney, the 750-room resort packs every conceivable amenity into a 1,500-acre campus located practically within Walt Disney World: 45 holes of golf, an unforgettable waterfall-studded lagoon pool, trails wrapping around a private lake, horses, and views of the fireworks at Epcot and the Magic Kingdom from many of its (very narrow) balconies. Better yet, many of its extras (kayaks, paddleboats, parking close to the building) are free, albeit after a $15 daily resort fee. There are often "deals" for around $200, but when conventions aren't on, I've seen $85 Priceline bids accepted. At press time, the entire property was being given a massive renovation, going from hideous '80s to a modern, almost Asian sleekness with cutting-edge rooms (rain showers, hi-def TVs).

Other hotels that frequent crop up in Priceline bids are the three-star Hilton Garden Inn between SeaWorld and I-4 ($35 is common), the three-and-a-half-star Wyndham Orlando at I-Drive and Sand Lake Road ($40), and among luxury hotels near Disney, the Omni ChampionsGate ($80–$140).

less than 4 nights. Call its local number to cut the best deal, because its website quotes static rates.

$$–$$$ Partly because the owners continue to pour money and attention into upgrading this once-average Quality Suites also-ran into a New Orleans–themed budget hotel—the new decorative metalwork is a pleasing touch—I recommend the five-story **Royale Parc Suites** ✮✮ (5876 W. U.S. 192, Kissimmee; ☎ 800/ 848-4148 or 407/396-8040; www.royaleparcsuitesorlando.com; AE, DC, DISC, MC, V), a scant mile from Disney's property. I also like the private way suites are set up: Front doors feed off a courtyard corridor from an active pool sanctum, as they do at so many motels, but the bedrooms, which are separated by a wall, have windows facing the parking lot. Prices are good in low season, but you can find better deals elsewhere in high season. A one-bedroom suite ($90–$200, depending on how full rooms are) sleeps up to six and has a kitchen with a two-burner stove, a minifridge, and a tiny dishwasher (a rarity), while the two bedroom/two baths (from $110) have four double beds plus one queen pullout and sleep up to 10—that's $10 a person! Deluxe suites on the top floor (from $130) include DVD/VCR player, a blender, a toaster, and a bigger coffeemaker than the standard suite—hardly worth the extra cash. There are also two-bedroom suites sleeping 10. All rooms have flatscreen HD sets. Both full breakfast (taken, if you choose, in the courtyard's newly built patio) and Wi-Fi come gratis. Double beds are on the small side, but the managers are unusually attentive to complaints.

$$ The seven-story **Country Inn & Suites Orlando Maingate** ✪✪ 🧒 (5001 Calypso Cay Way, Kissimmee; ☎ 888/201-1746 or 407/997-1400; www.country inns.com/orlandofl_maingate; AE, DC, DISC, MC, V) doesn't deviate much from its chain's clean-and-simple style, but the difference is that its inviting wet area—a kidney-shaped pool for adults, a small slide for kids, plus a few water-spitting giant crabs, rocks, and waterfalls—is far beyond most hotels of its class. We can thank the candy-colored Calypso Cay development, in which it sits, for the embellishments. Lots of extras are included, such as breakfast in a bright, east-facing dining room; free Web access in the lobby and by the pools; and a front desk (run by cheerful staff) that dispenses an endless supply of free cookies. I wish the rooms had balconies, but at least the windows are unusually large. I have seen price quotes from the hotel's corporate website of around $98, which is $20 less than what the sites like Hotels.com were offering, but more than the $65 I've seen on Priceline. The one-bedroom suites cost about $25 more, but that only buys more space, a microwave, and a fridge—no stove. Nearby, there's a supermarket. Disney is about 5 miles west. It's best to bring a car.

$$–$$$ Five miles east of Disney, at Mile Marker 12, where things get substantially cheaper (and seedier), the **South Beach Orlando Luxury Suites** ✪ (4786 W. Irlo Bronson Hwy., Kissimmee; ☎ 407/997-2700; www.southbeachorlandosuites. com; AE, DISC, MC, V) looks at first like a condo community, what with its peaked wooden roofing and connecting decks. In fact, the nine two-story, jubilantly colored houses contain low-cost, kitchen-equipped minihomes that have just been overhauled. As an answer to busy U.S. 192 out front, its backside faces lazy Lake Cecile (there's a fishing dock, tiny beach, and a swimming pool), lending it an unexpected summer-house feel. Prices are a touch high: $125 for two-bed family suites with plenty of closet space and a pullout up to a bi-level duplex with a pullout for $150. Call for the best rates ($109 for the smallest, executive suite in low season), because the website doesn't do deals. In 2008, new, youthful owners lavished a huge amount of energy into grooming and updating this place, adding cabanas along the lake and hatching plans to attract a contemporary crowd. "White, yellow, brown, gay, straight," one eager (if perhaps inexperienced) employee told me, "We're inclusive and it's going to be a party." If they can follow through, having a fully equipped kitchen, plasma TVs, and free Wi-Fi makes for a good value. Plenty of supply options, including a Publix supermarket and a Target, are nearby.

$$$ A stylish newcomer, the 240-unit **Mona Lisa Suite Hotel** ★★ (225 Celebration Place, Celebration; ☎ 866/404-6662; www.monalisasuitehotel.com; AE, MC, V) arrived on the scene in early 2008, and this curvy, sophisticated property is still struggling to let customers know it exists, which is why its rates are currently so low for its excellent quality. Decor and fittings are top-notch and modern, with fully equipped kitchens, dishwashers, washers and dryers, and, in the bathroom, toiletries by L'Occitane en Provence. Spacious one bedrooms (king beds, 754 sq. ft.) are currently around $100 to $120, and a second bedroom (plus a second bathroom) adds about $20, although expect the prices to rise as this place catches on, and add $12 a day for the cursed resort fee. Units also have a little patio, plus a queen-size pullout to sleep more people. Protected by the hotel's four curving buildings, a perfectly round pool recalls South Beach style, lending the sensation of an upscale resort. By calling directly, you can often get breakfast thrown in—omelet station and make-your-own granola included. Even though it's in a prime location beside the jungle of U.S. 192 very near Disney, the Mona Lisa feels cloistered and appeals most to those with business in Celebration.

$$–$$$$ Can it be? A romantic hotel near the theme parks that isn't as giant as a galaxy or seething with children? **Celebration Hotel** ★★ (700 Bloom St., Celebration; ☎ 888/499-3800 or 407/566-6000; www.celebrationhotel.com; AE, DISC, MC, V) is that fantasy come true. The civilized, full-service 115-room property evokes Old Florida and gets the pace and look just right. The lakeside setting is soothing and private—there's nothing on the opposite shore but trees and quiet. Furnishings are tropical, almost postcolonial classics (four-posted beds, wicker-paddle ceiling fans); the halls are filled with truly refined artwork; there's a bar in the Singapore-style lobby; and the restaurant, Plantation Room, is gourmet and worthy of a date. Right out the front door is Celebration's easygoing waterfront downtown, ripe with nonchain boutiques and restaurants, and Disney is a 5-minute drive away. The downsides are the $12 daily resort fee (it includes two daily bottles of water) and that you may have to parallel park. On paper, rates start at $189, but with at least 14 days' advance, they sink to $151, and the major Web bookers have it for $120. It's off the table in midsummer, when the Tampa Bay Buccaneers book it solid for their training camp at the Wide World of Sports.

LAKE BUENA VISTA

Roughly speaking, Lake Buena Vista is the area where the eastern end of Walt Disney World around Downtown Disney meets exit 68 off I-4. "LBV," as it's nicknamed, is more compact and less frazzling than the comparable cluster of Kissimmee hotels along U.S. 192, a few miles south near Disney's southern gate. One of its magnets is the Crossroads shopping center, where you'll find plenty of restaurant chains and a high-priced grocery store. For breathing room, my favorite part of Lake Buena Vista is Palm Parkway, a lightly trafficked, winding, tree-lined avenue of fairly new corporate hotels. It's a secret alternative to I-4. Drive north on it and you'll pass a turnoff for SeaWorld, a new Wal-Mart, and the restaurants of Sand Lake Road, and eventually you'll hit Universal.

LBV is so compact that those so inclined could walk to Downtown Disney and from there use the free Disney bus system. Or they could even take a taxi to each Disney park (although I'm not convinced doing so would save you much more money than an inexpensive rental car). Such convenience comes with a trade-off: You'll often pay higher prices than you have to in Kissimmee or on I-Drive. Free hotel shuttles around here tend to go to Disney but not to Universal or SeaWorld.

$–$$ The 123-unit, three-story **Quality Suites Lake Buena Vista** ✪✪✪ (8200 Palm Pkwy., Orlando; ☎ 800/370-9894 or 407/465-8200; www.qualitysuiteslbv.com; AE, DC, DISC, MC, V), fronted by palm trees as tall as itself, could be called simple but inviting. Probably because it's a pipsqueak among lions, its attentive managers charge a competitively low price and even throw in a cooked breakfast. All rooms, which are larger than the average, have two TVs and fully equipped kitchens with large fridges, toasters, microwaves, and stoves—a rarity among hotels that usually make do with microwaves, and a lifesaver when it comes to saving money on dining. The hotel is close enough to the Disney parks to make for a realistic lunch break, and the basic pool is open until 11pm, so you can use it for end-of-the-day soaks. Rates for sizable one-bedroom suites with queen beds (TVs are found in both rooms) are regularly around $70 to $100 through the Web discounters, and $80 or so on its own site. You'll pay about $190 for a two-bedroom unit, and weekends may be a little more expensive. AAA rates for these miniapartments can sink to the mid-$60s—an unbeatable deal, particularly for the doorstep-of-Disney plot.

$–$$ From the outside, the six-story, 200-room **Holiday Inn Express Lake Buena Vista** ✪✪ (8686 Palm Pkwy., Orlando; ☎ 800/465-4329 or 407/239-8400; www.hiexpress.com/lakebuenavista; AE, DISC, MC, V) doesn't look like much more than a concrete box the color of orange sherbet, but it's got a number of advantages over other hotels. First, its location is prime, near both Disney and plenty of restaurants on the westernmost stretch of quiet Palm Parkway. Rooms are spotless and come with microwaves and fridges, plus balconies made truly private by concrete walls. The pool, found out back where the frolicking around its one-story waterfall and short slide won't disturb guests, is open until midnight—ideal for postpark wind-downs. There's also a well-maintained wooden playground. A full breakfast, local calls, Wi-Fi, and Disney shuttles are all free, and you could feasibly walk to Downtown Disney. At $79 low and $119 high, it's a solid value.

$–$$ Internet and AAA rates of $70 to $88 are frequent at the perfectly adequate **Buena Vista Suites** ✪ (8203 World Center Dr., Orlando; ☎ 800/537-7737 or 407/239-8588; www.buenavistasuites.com; AE, DC, DISC, MC, V), where every unit has a bedroom with a door that shuts, which means you can leave kids to their own devices in their own sitting/sleeping area with their own TV. Rooms also have a fridge, microwave, and coffeemaker, and full cooked breakfasts are served—get there before 9am for a crack at the eggs. Furnishings were recently updated, which boosted the value, although the plumbing is noisy and you pay for Internet access. It's close (4 min. by car) to the restaurants of Lake Buena Vista and Downtown Disney, and less than that from I-4's exit 67. In terms of space and price (rooms fit six, tightly), it's a smarter, if much less sassy, alternative to Disney's All-Stars, which are just as far from the Magic Kingdom. The Disney shuttles are free here, if infrequent. I wouldn't pay more than $110.

$–$$$ There are three Marriott-branded hotels collected at the well-set-up **Marriott Village at Lake Buena Vista** ✦ (8623 Vineland Ave., Orlando; ☎ 877/682-8552 or 407/938-9001; www.marriottvillage.com; AE, DC, DISC, MC, V): the **Courtyard** ($100, not including breakfast), the **Fairfield Inn** ($80 for a king, $135 for two doubles, including continental breakfast), and the **SpringHill Suites** ($100, including a semidivided seating area, only a microwave, and continental breakfast). All rooms, antiseptically corporate but consequently reliable, have minifridges, free Wi-Fi in the lobby (wired access in the rooms), and free cribs. You might as well choose the cheapest room because all guests have the right to use any of the three heated pools at all three hotels (the squirty water jets at the Fairfield aren't extravagant, but they make for the most interesting pool, and the Courtyard's is both indoor and outdoor). The compound's security gate is often unmanned, but its presence deters intruders, and there's a small, intermittently open plaza that includes a pizza place, an ice-cream store, and a Starbucks (the kitschy Bahama Breeze restaurant is a safe 5-min. walk away), so you won't always have to clamber in the car to find food. I-4 scoots past the back side of the Fairfield and the SpringHill (the on-ramp is convenient), and while entry to Disney property is less than a mile away, shuttles to its parks cost $5 per person. The Web discounters knock the most off the Fairfield rates.

$$ The 150-unit **Staybridge Suites Lake Buena Vista** (8751 Suiteside Dr., Orlando; ☎ 800/866-4549 or 407/238-0777; www.sborlando.com; AE, DC, DISC, MC, V) offers apartment-like quarters (the kitchens even have dishwashers) in an ideal location a little bit north of the Hotel Plaza Boulevard gate to Disney World, close to lots of restaurants. The three-level buildings don't have elevators, but overlook that fact and avoid the ground-floor rooms, which are darker and less private. Breakfast, served free, is cooked and plentiful, and you can eat it indoors or in the Florida sun if you like. Management reverses the sterility of the setup by throwing frequent beer parties and other afternoon mixers; there's also a well-used pool in one of the courtyards. Expect rates along the lines of $140 for a one bedroom with a king-size bed (sleeps four), or $30 more for a two bedroom (sleeps six), with prices rising $20 to $40 when it's busy. The Disney shuttle is free. Home or condo rentals are cheaper, but you won't find many of those so close to Disney grounds, and those also come with cleaning fees and minimum stays. There's another 146-unit location with similar prices at **8480 International Dr.** (☎ 407/352-2400; AE, DC, DISC, MC, V) just south of Sand Lake Road, that includes Universal and SeaWorld in its free shuttle system.

$$–$$$ Most family-oriented Orlando hotels entice kids with little more than a lame DVD nook. But the **Nickelodeon Family Suites by Holiday Inn** ✦✦✦ 🅺🅸🅳🆂 (14500 Continental Gateway, Orlando; ☎ 800/972-2590; www.nickhotel.com; AE, DC, DISC, MC, V), an anima-psychedelic image of the basic-cable staple Nickelodeon, is kid heaven. The 777-unit, multimillion-dollar hotel, with one- to three-bedroom suites arranged around two courtyards, is so much fun that kids have been known to forget about going to the theme parks. Not only is everything tarted up with outsized visual gags like the ones at Disney's value hotels (giant Jimmy Neutrons grinning, life-size Doras exploring) but it's also got more activities than Disney's moderate hotels. In the two incredible splashdown areas, water cannons blast, a 400-gallon bucket regularly spills water over squealing kids, and seven water flumes twist. There's a food court, a 3,000-square-foot arcade, character breakfasts with Nick icons, a studio for live game shows in which parents might get "slimed," and a kiddie spa for such vacation-appropriate treatments as temporary tattoos and hair braiding. The Kid Suite kitchenettes have a sink and microwave but not cookers; the Kitchen Suites have the range. Kids get their own bedroom (choose bunks or twin beds) with video games. Everything has a pull-out double, too. One bedrooms start at $80, two bedrooms at $110. It's a good choice if you plan to spend much recharge time back at base (it's wickedly close to Disney turf) or want to let kids off the leash, and security is superb because everyone must wear wristbands. Its website promises the lowest rate, so if you find a good price from the discounters, ask the hotel to beat it. As you can imagine, it gets pretty noisy, so it's not for lovebirds.

$$$ Gut renovated in 2007, the eight-story **Radisson Hotel Lake Buena Vista** ✸✸ (12799 Apopka Vineland Rd.; ☎ 888/201-1718 or 407/597-3400; www.radisson.com/lakebuenavistafl; AE, DISC, MC, V) is gleaming, professionally run, and top-notch for a nonresort hotel. The 196 rooms are packed with the latest modern conveniences such as adjustable Sleep Number beds, HD TVs, iPod docks, free Internet, minifridges, and microwaves. Size is beyond the average, too: Bathrooms are spacious, and in the rehab, old balconies were incorporated as sitting areas with pullout couches. Rates for two doubles go as low as $88 on its site, with prices $129 to $149 in busy times, and breakfast at its tiny grill is sometimes thrown in for another $10. Three-bed, two-room suites for six start at $130. There are a few downers, such as tricky entry that requires some U-turning (the ramp to I-4 intrudes), a dull but sunny pool area, and infrequent free shuttles, but those bummers are entirely offset by the quality of the rest and by the fact it's a short, safe walk to the many restaurants of the Crossroads shopping center.

$$$ The biggest problem with most of Hotel Plaza Boulevard, where a few hotels that aren't run by the Mouse are permitted on Disney property, is quality. But **Regal Sun Resort** (1850 Hotel Plaza Blvd., Lake Buena Vista; ☎ 800/624-4109 or 407/828-4444; www.regalsunresort.com; AE, DISC, MC, V), across the street from Downtown Disney, gets high marks for not getting complacent despite the fact the place is often full. If you desperately want to be closer to the parks without paying Disney prices, this machine may appeal, and rates bottom out at $69 but are usually in the low $100s for the full hotel enchilada, including a fitness center, two big pools, shuttles that depart every 30 minutes, minifridges in the rooms, and the only sanctioned Disney character breakfast outside the Mouse's holdings (3 mornings a week). The polished lobby makes everything seem more luxurious than it really is, but the kid-friendly staff boosts the value even considering its $15 daily resort fee. It's also among the freshest around, having finished a renovation in December 2007. For similar prices, you can stay two doors east at the 18-story **Best Western Lake Buena Vista Resort** (2000 Hotel Plaza Blvd.; ☎ 407/828-2424; www.lakebuenavistaresorthotel.com; AE, DISC, MC, V), which is older and could use a brush-up, but is distinguished by having a balcony for every room and charging a resort fee of only $8 a day. Both hotels are fair midbudget options if you can score a deal online (to pay three digits would be a stretch), and both offer the potential for fireworks views from your room.

INTERNATIONAL DRIVE & UNIVERSAL AREA

I-Drive is probably the best place to stay if you don't have a car because it's central, well connected, and full of competing places to eat. While you will find good prices here (the best at properties that back up to I-4), you won't find many rambling resorts. Instead, you'll be brushing elbows with plenty of frugal families from abroad who are more likely to experience all of Orlando and not just the Mouse. You'll need wheels to reach Disney (most hotels offer shuttles, but not always to Disney, and not always for free), although Universal is just across I-4 to the north (walkable for the intrepid, a few bucks by taxi), and the dirt-cheap I-Ride Trolley (p. 18) links you with SeaWorld. On many nights around dinnertime, car traffic can clog I-Drive, making travel a misery, but there's a workaround: Universal Boulevard, a block east, bypasses the mess.

It's also the only hotel zone with a semblance of street life. If you stay here, you'll be in the thick of the family-friendly come-ons, amusement halls, minigolf, and T-shirt shops. In many ways, the low-rent arcades, ice-cream parlors, and oddity museums recall the gaudy sweetness you might remember from such mid-century vacation towns as Wisconsin Dells, Blackpool, or Niagara Falls. I-Drive's sidewalks north of Sand Lake Road are brash and pretense-free, while the reaches of I-Drive south of Sand Lake, near the mighty Orange County Convention Center, tend to be less rambunctious and favored by trade show–goers. There are nearly 34,000 rooms around I-Drive, which is about the same inventory you'll find around Walt Disney World.

$ Impossible to beat at $65 a night in high season and a gleeful $36 in low season, **Rodeway Inn at International** ✪✪✪ (6327 International Dr., Orlando; ☎ 800/999-6327 or 407/996-4444; www.rodewayinnorlando.com; AE, DC, DISC, MC, V), the largest Rodeway in America (315 rooms in two buildings), is well worn, but it's clean, patrolled by security, and on a lively bend of International Drive near Wet 'n Wild and 2 minutes' drive from Universal, which makes finding activities and eating cheaply a breeze. The pool is heated when it's cold, security is always around, there's a pub, you can get free Wi-Fi in the lobby ($9 with wires upstairs), and all rooms have a microwave and refrigerator. It's dated, but all you need. Just across the street is a Ponderosa serving a $3.99 breakfast buffet. Outside of high season, the rate is slashed another 30% for stays longer than 2 nights. The rate sometimes attracts noisy kids on school break, but on balance, you can't do better at this price.

$ One of the largest budget-priced properties outside of Disney's Value developments, the **Quality Inn Plaza International Drive** ✪ (9000 International Dr., Orlando; ☎ 800/999-8585 or 407/996-8585; http://qualityinn-orlando.com; AE, DC, DISC, MC, V) is a 1,020-room bedding machine that sprawls over 2 city blocks and six buildings. Interstate 4 runs along the western side, resulting in a constant hum. Rates are low—often $50, although I've seen promotions for as little as $40 a night. Respectably affordable units, which come with a fridge, microwave, and two double beds, have smoked-glass windows, which helps create privacy given the external corridor construction, but doesn't help illuminate the bathrooms in the back. Furniture is dated (and good luck fitting a laptop in the elderly key-operated safes), but no one pays $40 expecting the latest looks. Rooms in the A building are near the lobby but suffer daytime noise from the sightseeing helicopter pad next door; opt for something in the F building, which is a 10-minute walk/2-minute drive from the lobby and has the most rooms hidden from I-4. Parking is gated but free. You'll feel like you're back on an '80s vacation with Dad just by walking past the three big pools, where kids work off their postpark highs. Many eateries and a multiplex are within walking distance, on I-Drive. Universal is 10 minutes north, and SeaWorld 5 minutes south.

$ Superbasic and economy all the way, **Baymont Inn & Suites Orlando** (5625 Major Blvd., Orlando; ☎ 407/354-3996; www.baymontinns.com; AE, MC, V) gets you a room with two queen beds, sleeping four, for just $55, plus a simple continental breakfast, free in-room Wi-Fi and local calls, a minor pool, a minifridge, and a microwave. There are a lot of skuzzy, cheap motels in town, so it's a relief to find a motel charging bottom-of-the-barrel rates that's clean and not depressing. Universal's diversions are a half-mile west, although there's also a free van. Priceline has been known to sell this one for peanuts through bidding—just $25!

$–$$ An agreeable chain hotel, the 120-room **Hampton Inn Universal** ✪ (5621 Windhover Dr., Orlando; ☎ 800/231-8395 or 407/351-6716; www.hamptoninn universal.com; AE, DC, DISC, MC, V) is a half-mile east of Universal Orlando (the shuttle is infrequent but truly free), alongside Kirkman Road. Unlike the Convention Center Hampton Inn, it's not within walking distance of I-Drive, which limits nearby meal options to fast food, but if you have a car, the road connections are strong, and the place is well run, so you won't feel ripped off. The free daily breakfast is a huge plus, and so are the supercomfortable beds, fitness room, and the free local calls. Rates usually span $70 to $100.

$–$$ Found where I-Drive gives way to the gargantuan Convention Center complex, the seven-story, 170-room **Hampton Inn Orlando Convention Center** ✪✪✪ (8900 Universal Blvd., Orlando; ☎ 800/426-7866 or 407/354-4447; www.orlando conventioncenter.hamptoninn.com; AE, DC, DISC, MC, V) may be just like every other Hampton Inn you've ever seen (they must make these buildings from kits), but that doesn't detract from the fact the place is in good shape, there are plenty of restaurants and a multiplex within walking distance, and the cheerful staff runs a tight ship. Stays come with free in-room Wi-Fi and a bountiful all-you-can-eat breakfast, including a few hot dishes; there's also a 24-hour lobby booth selling snacks and sundries. Rack rates hover around $120, but during low and shoulder season, I have personally been quoted rates as low as $89 by the front-desk clerk, who even offered to beat competitors' prices by $1, and I've seen it for $44 on Otel.com. Ask for a room on the south side, as these don't face other nearby buildings.

$–$$ The **La Quinta Inn International Drive** (8300 Jamaican Court, Orlando; ☎ 800/753-3757 or 407/351-1660; www.orlandolaquinta.com; AE, DISC, MC, V), a veteran motel with external corridors and the usual minor inconveniences of the category, is not a bad choice if you want a clean, basic place near I-Drive, which is a block east. Windows are on the large side, and most face an interior heated pool cloister instead of the whoosh of Interstate 4. The rooms facing I-4 tend to drive some guests nuts, so request accordingly. King-ed rooms also have recliners.

International Drive Area Accommodations

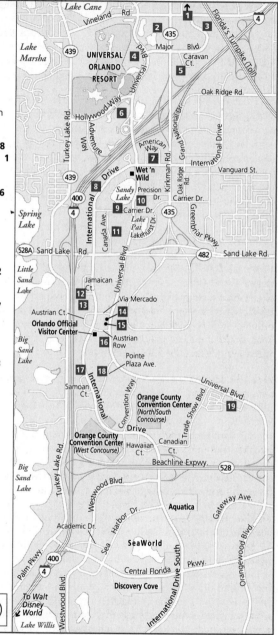

Free Wi-Fi is everywhere, and a breakfast of fruit, boiled eggs, waffles, and the like is part of the rate. Prices hover around $110, but $70 is common online and in off months such as October or early January. Prices may pop up $20 on weekends. The **La Quinta Inn & Suites Orlando Convention Center** (8504 Universal Blvd., Orlando; ☎ 407/345-1365; www.laquinta.com; AE, DISC, MC, V), roughly 2 blocks east, is of newer construction but it generally costs $10 more.

$$$ My new corporate hotel obsession is the stylish concept of **Hyatt Place.** You check in at a kiosk that spits out your key, and without delay, head to a huge semi-partitioned room with giant beds and a sitting area, plus an extra pullout sofa. They have truly up-to-date design, a 42-inch HD TV you can plug a laptop or a iPod into, granite bathrooms, wet bar, free continental breakfast, Wi-Fi, and plenty of space for five (six if two sleep on the pullout), all from $89. Seriously, why can't they all be like this? Two locations, both opened in 2007, are prime for the parks. One is the **Hyatt Place Orlando Convention Center** ✿✿✿ (8741 International Dr., Orlando; ☎ 407/370-4720; http://orlandoconventioncenter. place.hyatt.com; AE, DC, DISC, MC, V), which has a bigger lobby than most of its chain and is within walking distance to plenty of places to eat. When things are busy, it charges up to $190 and gets it. A few miles north, **Hyatt Place Orlando Universal** ✿✿✿ (5895 Caravan Court, Orlando; ☎ 407/351-0627; http://orlando universal.place.hyatt.com; AE, DC, DISC, MC, V), on a dull side street within sight of Universal's parking structures, is not subject to the wild fluctuation in rates that the Convention Center location suffers (expect $99–$170), and guests get 15% off food at the Universal parks nearby. While both might quote rates of $170 if booked way ahead, they fall to around $100 to $110 as dates grow nearer, and can appear on Priceline for $30.

$$ Well located—a block from the ramp to Interstate 4; 5 minutes from Universal, 10 from SeaWorld, and 20 from Disney—and well run, **Fairfield Inn & Suites Orlando International Drive** ✿✿ (7495 Canada Ave., Orlando; ☎ 800/ 228-2800 or 407/351-7000; www.marriott.com/MCOSL; AE, DC, DISC, MC, V) is another vanilla chain hotel you could do worse than to stay at. Business travelers seem to use it more than families, so not only do rooms have free Wi-Fi and work desks, but the atmosphere is also subdued. Suites ($95–$110) are 25% larger than standard rooms ($84–$95) and have sitting/pullout couch areas separated from the sleeping area by a closet, as well as a TV for each area.

$$–$$$ It's stoutly boxy, slapped with smoked glass, and ugly from the outside, but what the six-story **Clarion Hotel Universal** (7299 Universal Blvd., Orlando; ☎ 800/445-7299 or 407/351-5009; www.clarionuniversal.com; AE, DISC, MC, V) lacks in pizzazz it makes up in cleanliness and an attentive staff. The quietish location on the eastern side of Wet 'n Wild (most odd-numbered rooms overlook the lake behind the water park) puts you a block away from the I-4 on-ramp. There are some other convenient touches, including an on-site Enterprise rental-car agency, lighted tennis and basketball courts, a lobby shop selling sundries and sandwiches, and cooling misters blowing moist air over the otherwise roasting pool area. Breakfast is sold, but the eateries of I-Drive (including a Denny's and an IHOP) are within walking distance. Its 303 rooms are fairly standard if old,

with sinks both inside and outside the bathroom (good for simultaneous teeth brushings), tea- and coffeemaking tools, and individual A/C units. Rack rates are $89 to $140, but Travelocity sometimes offers rooms for around $60, and it frequently pops up through Priceline bids for $35 to $55.

$$–$$$ Because it occupies one of those dated cylindrical towers that were briefly in vogue in the early 1970s, the just-renovated and ideally located **Four Points by Sheraton Studio City** ★ (5905 International Dr., Orlando; ☎ 888/625-4988 or 407/351-2100; www.starwoodhotels.com; AE, DISC, MC, V) feels manageable, which is rare for landmark properties around here. It has a modest lobby and pool, and because rooms are carved out of the floors like pie pieces, they're more spacious than the norm, and each has two queen beds. Request a room that doesn't face east, as the floodlights from the minigolf joint next door are blinding. The top floors have spectacular views of I-Drive, Wet 'n Wild (to the west), and Universal (just over I-4 to the north). It's not luxury, but it approximates it, and views in Orlando are rare at any price. Breakfast's $10 for all you can eat, but there's an IHOP next door. Check the website for deals as low as $74 (advance purchase), although $99 to $129 is more common.

$$–$$$ The **Doubletree Castle Hotel** ★ (8629 International Dr., Orlando; ☎ 800/952-2785 or 407/345-1511; www.doubletreecastle.com; AE, DISC, MC, V) is a once-standard 216-room hotel that was stepped up with a whimsical renovation that fitted its roof with purple spires and its courtyard with gas lanterns. For that, and for the furniture studded with fake jewels, you'll still get a fairly standard mid-priced hotel experience. I consider this a hotel that appeals to parents who want to give their kids a slightly stylistic experience without getting too kitschy or too spendy. One minus, in addition to a dearth of outlets for charging stuff up, is that doors tend to slam heavily, making everything nearby shudder, though considerate neighbors (luck of the draw there) will abate that problem. Café Tu Tu Tango (p. 80) out the back door provides room service, and a dozen chain restaurants are within walking distance. Rooms on the uppermost, west-facing floors take in the nightly fireworks at the Magic Kingdom and Epcot, only about 2 miles away as the crow flies, and the front desk gives out free, warm cookies whenever you want one. Rates fluctuate wildly from $63 to $170, depending on availability. I hate that.

4 Dining Options Around Town

Beyond the same old chain restaurants, the city eats & drinks well.

FOOD IS NOT ORLANDO'S STRONG POINT—THAT IS, IF YOUR STANDARDS are high. Prices are beyond market value, and recipes overdo the sugar and batter. By the end of a week in the theme parks, you risk feeling like the 240-year tradition of American cuisine was for naught. Fries, burgers, and pizzas only go so far.

Happily, that doesn't mean you're fated to famish. There are places where you can find good, honest food for reasonable prices. In this chapter, I tell you all about them. Here, you will find every restaurant that's *not* located inside a theme park—that is, places you don't need a ticket to access. For places inside the parks, and info on the Disney Dining Plan, see the park descriptions in chapters 5 and 6.

Orlando is a corporate town, and national chains dominate. One could say they even have a pedigree here: Darden Restaurants, which owns Red Lobster, Olive Garden, and the Capital Grille, is headquartered here, and so is Hard Rock Cafe.

But that still doesn't qualify those places as "local." Except for a few chains that are particularly useful for their value pricing, I've left ubiquitous brands off this list. I'm going to assume that every family is familiar with the fare at widely planted labels such as Cracker Barrel, Panera Bread, and Denny's, and once you reach the areas that I name in each section of this chapter, you will find plenty of franchises from which to choose. Feel free to pick one of them if you like—I just don't think you bought a guidebook to hear Whoppers explained.

Where you will need help is in locating smaller restaurants, little-known chains, or ethnic kitchens that aren't backed by multimillion-dollar ad campaigns. The places named in this chapter are ones you might never even notice among the clamor of neon signage erected by the corporate chains.

Pretty much every restaurant is open for lunch and dinner. Don't expect places to accept checks—credit cards are Orlando's cash. Also, this is a town where it bears asking for discounts. Turnover is high, so everybody's angling for business.

My pricing symbols for a main course (at dinner):

$: $9 or less
$$: $9 to $15
$$$: $15 to $21
$$$$: $21 or over

In September, a bunch of high-quality area restaurants band together to attract business by offering prix fixe, three-course (appetizer, entree, dessert) meals for $19 at lunch and $29 at dinner. This Orlando Magical Dining event is promoted at **www.orlandomagicaldining.com** starting in summer.

OUTSIDE THE DISNEY PARKS

You don't have to pay an admission ticket to dine in the World. In fact, the best of Disney's restaurants are accessible to anyone. Well, not anyone: folks with deep pockets, soon to be empty. Disney's most affordable hotels don't offer much beyond food courts, but its most expensive hotels usually boast a fine restaurant or two. Nothing sit-down could be considered budget ($20–$30 an entree is standard), but because of location or other gimmicks, some should be considered for a special night out. I run down the worthiest ones here, but it must be repeated that for most affordable meals, you need a car to whisk you off-property.

   Note: All Disney resort restaurants accept the major credit cards, and parking at the hotels will be free with a reservation (which I emphatically suggest, without exceptions—make them as early as you can). When you reserve through Disney, your operator will have access to the resort's schedule that day (such as fireworks), and they'll help you plan around these events. Places within Disney's hotels generally serve from 5 to 10pm, as it's assumed patrons will eat in the parks.

DISNEY SPLURGE MEALS

This being a guide to *affordable* Orlando, only a few Disney hotel restaurants make the cut as giving you the most for their high prices:

$$–$$$ If you simply must follow the flock and indulge yourself at Disney's Grand Floridian, do it the most cheaply with high tea from 2 to 4:30pm at the pseudo-Victorian **Garden View Restaurant** (☎ 407/939-3463; www.disneyworld. com). The Sally Lunn Tea ($13.50) serves buns and either trifle or strawberries and cream. Add sandwiches and scones and you're up to $19.50. (It's called—everybody together, now—the Buckingham Palace tea.) A la carte pastries are around $4, and tea, and only tea, is $6, and although there are more than a dozen varieties, the service is not as precise and as elegant as a real English tea—think of high tea at Disney as a reasonable way to trick kids into pretending they're living the high life. Do a tea in November or December, when the Grand Floridian is decked out in its annual, eye-popping Christmas decorations, including a life-size gingerbread house.

$$$$ For one blowout night with a view, the best choice is **California Grill** ✭✭✭ (☎ 407/939-3463; reservations strongly recommended; daily 5:30–10pm) on the 15th floor of the mod Contemporary Resort. The wine list is exhaustive, the open-air kitchen excels at flatbreads, sushi, and well-crafted American dishes—healthy, fresh ingredients—and right after sunset, everything stops so diners can enjoy their bird's-eye seat for the Magic Kingdom fireworks show (so book as far ahead as you can—the maximum is 180 days before—and get a window seat). The music for the fireworks is even piped in to the outdoor viewing platforms, which are practically on top of Tomorrowland. After dark, Cinderella Castle is lit by a shifting palette of indigos and emeralds. Prices for main courses hover around $30, and desserts $10. This is where I bring non-Disney fans and foodies alike, and they love it. Plus, a dinner here is a fantastic excuse to have a stroll around Disney World's most iconic hotel and hop a post-meal ride on the monorail for free.

$$$$ My favorite hotel restaurant in terms of masterful cooking is the superb **Todd English's bluezoo** ✭✭✭ (Walt Disney World Dolphin Hotel, 1500 Epcot

Walt Disney World Area Dining

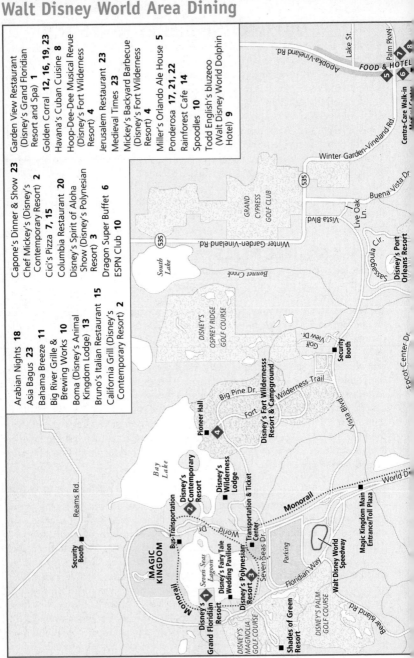

Garden View Restaurant
(Disney's Grand Floridian
Resort and Spa) 1
Golden Corral 12, 16, 19, 23
Havana's Cuban Cuisine 8
Hoop-Dee-Dee Musical Revue
(Disney's Fort Wilderness
Resort) 4
Jerusalem Restaurant 23
Medieval Times 23
Mickey's Backyard Barbecue
(Disney's Fort Wilderness
Resort) 4
Miller's Orlando Ale House 5
Ponderosa 17, 21, 22
Rainforest Cafe 14
Spoodles 10
Todd English's bluezoo
(Walt Disney World Dolphin
Hotel) 9

Capone's Dinner & Show 23
Chef Mickey's (Disney's
Contemporary Resort) 2
Cici's Pizza 7, 15
Columbia Restaurant 20
Disney's Spirit of Aloha
Show (Disney's Polynesian
Resort) 3
Dragon Super Buffet 6
ESPN Club 10

Arabian Nights 18
Asia Bagus 23
Bahama Breeze 11
Big River Grille &
Brewing Works 10
Boma (Disney's Animal
Kingdom Lodge) 13
Bruno's Italian Restaurant 15
California Grill (Disney's
Contemporary Resort) 2

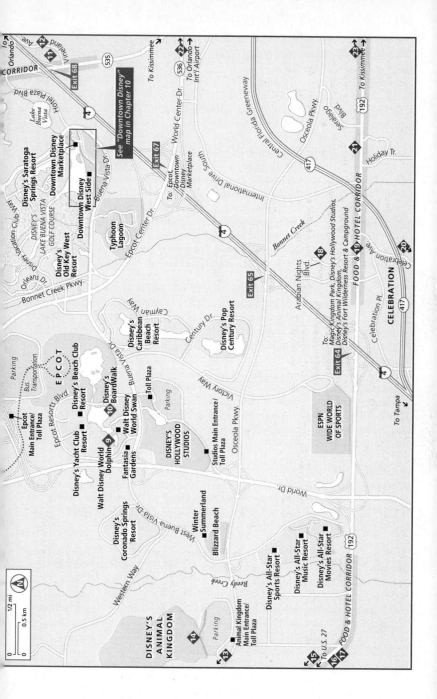

Resorts Blvd., Lake Buena Vista; ☎ 407/934-1111; www.swananddolphin.com/bluezoo; daily 5–11pm), one of a handful of Orlando restaurants overseen by true culinary superstars; in this case, Todd English, celebrated for his rich flavors and daring juxtapositions. Set among witty colored-glass baubles that suggest underwater imagery, the menu changes but its focus is fresh fish. The nightly herb-rubbed "dancing fish" is grilled on a spinning skewer (it's alongside the raw bar) and served whole; the light clam chowder comes infused with bacon; and the 2-pound "Cantonese" lobster comes tossed in a sticky soy glaze and should be shared ($60). Lots of Disney-property places charge around $30 for dishes, except here, you're getting craftsmanship, professional servers, and impeccably fresh ingredients, many sourced locally. Its pastry chef, Laurent Branlard, is a two-time World Pastry Team Championship victor (the hotel so values him that it gave him a full-time workshop, which you can peer into at the Swan), and his spectacular mai tai banana cream tart, topped with a melting orb of white chocolate, tells you why. ***Money-saving tip:*** If you sit in the narrow area opposite the bar, the decor and the menu are less elaborate (flatbreads, rare tuna, raw bar items, ceviche), but the ingredient quality is just as good, and prices are half as much.

$$$$ A reservation at the **Boma** ★ 🧒 (☎ 407/939-3463; www.disneyworld.com; daily 7–11am and 5–10pm) buffet is a fine excuse to visit Disney's Animal Kingdom Lodge and pay a visit to the animals in its backyard paddocks, floodlit after dark. The 60-item menu, served in a wide, woody ground-floor dining room, runs the gamut from roast chicken and beef to such African-themed delights as watermelon rind salad, smoked tomato soup, and sometimes *bobotie* (a moussaka-like pie of ground beef from South Africa). The food is well done for mass-produced stuff, with plenty of chefs on hand to answer questions and plenty of options for less adventurous (read: younger) tongues. Adults are $27, kids $13. The hotel has the largest South African wine list in the United States. Jiko, the a la carte place across the hall, serves entrees that are very good, too, but cost what the entire banquet does at Boma.

DOWNTOWN DISNEY

These places are generally priced a lot better than the ones in the hotels, which is why I list a few more. They are generally open all day from 11am until about 11pm, unless otherwise noted. The bars may keep pouring until about 1:30am, particularly on weekends. Parking is free but not abundant.

$ The most affordable option at the Downtown Disney Marketplace area, barring McDonald's, is located to its extreme east: **Earl of Sandwich** ★★ (☎ 407/938-1762; www.earlofsandwichusa.com; Sun–Mon 8:30am–11pm, Fri–Sat 8:30am–11:30pm), a branch of a nine-location franchise based in Orlando. Here, you can easily grab a made-to-order 6-inch sandwich, made with fresh ingredients and toasted, for $6. There are 13 hot and cold selections, from roast beef to ham with creamy brie, plus about a half-dozen salads and three to four daily soups. It's hard to believe such good value exists in Walt Disney World.

$$$ Because prices at the Downtown Disney complex are so crazy, the only sit-down establishment that I can heartily recommend is **Raglan Road** ★★ (☎ 407/938-0300; www.raglanroadirishpub.com; daily 11am–1:30am), run by an accessible, contemporary Irish chef by the name of Kevin Dundon. Of all the chefs working Downtown Disney, Dundon's got the most imagination. Here, Irish staples are turned into sprightly new visions, including whiskey-glazed "drunk" chicken with lime dressing, beef stew infused with Guinness, and good old fish and chips. Appetizers for sharing are around $12, and entrees in the upper teens. Although the massive dining area is styled after an Irish pub, it's 20 times noisier. At lunch, prices are about $4 less and the fare lighter (the Bee L T has honey-and tarragon-marinated chicken breast). There's free live music nightly from 8pm. If you only want fish and chips, get it on the south side of the building for about $8 less at the counter-service **Cookes of Dublin,** run by the same people.

$$$–$$$$ Should you just want something that will entertain the kids, there are two spectacular options here. One is **T-Rex** ★ ⓚⁱᵈˢ (☎ 407/828-8739; www.trex cafe.com; daily 11am–11pm), which opened in late 2008 and is distinguished, if that's the word, by life-size robotic dinosaurs planted amongst the tables. Every so often, the ceiling (at least, the one outside of the simulated ice cave) is the stage for a projected meteor shower while the destruction of all life forms is briefly simulated with cacophony and red lighting. Pass the ketchup. You can probably predict the fare: $12 Bronto Burgers, $9 Artifact Stack fried onion rings, and to end it all, the $15 Chocolate Extinction, a fudge cake sundae. More subdued, if that's the word, is **Rainforest Cafe** ⓚⁱᵈˢ (www.rainforestcafe.com), where families dine in a faux jungle with lions, pythons, elephants, and other robotic animals that periodically spring to life, interrupting dinner and stoking wild behavior in small children. Think of it as the Jungle Cruise with napkins. There are two locations: One at **Downtown Disney Marketplace** (☎ 407/827-8500) and one at the gates of **Disney's Animal Kingdom** (☎ 407/938-9100, daily 8am–6pm, with extended hours on days when the park remains open late). Both have an identical, rangy menu (burgers, salads, wraps, and pizzas all peak at $13 for both meals, so stick to them; steaks, pasta, and fish straddle $20, so don't be tempted). Like so much in Orlando, neither outfit specializes in anything, instead opting to be all things to all eaters. Because Rainforest exists across America, I'd pick T-Rex.

$$$–$$$$ At Downtown Disney West Side, **Bongos Cuban Cafe** (☎ 407/828-0999; www.bongoscubancafe.com) was co-founded by Gloria and Emilio Estefan, the Cuban-born power couple of Latin music, who own two others in Miami. The food (ceviche, plantains, yucca, and lots of grilled or lightly fried fish and meats; mostly $16–$20 per entree) is not always successful, and using paper napkins is abrasive when you've paid this much, but at least it's more authentically Florida than the hypersugary decor, which makes the building look like it's been overtaken by giant, washed-out pineapples, palms, and drums. At night, there's often a live band. Save your budget by using the walk-up window serving meaty, pressed Cuban sandwiches for $7 to $9, which are also served inside for more.

Downtown Disney is full of additional places that charge extreme prices ($30 a plate) but don't give your money back to you in skilled cuisine. Although none serve foul food, most of them coast along by sponging from the steady foot traffic that Downtown Disney supports. That means you can count these places out, although you will be pressured not to: **Fulton's Crab House,** in a mock riverboat berthed in concrete; **Portobello Yacht Club,** with a weird Italian theme; **Cap'n**

Jack's Restaurant, dabbling unimpressively in a range of styles; and the national chains **Wolfgang Puck Café** (it also has a walk-up window for $9 quick bites, and there's also a version at Universal's CityWalk), **Planet Hollywood,** and **House of Blues. Ghirardelli Ice Cream and Chocolate Shop** is a rare offshoot of the San Francisco treasure, but it only does desserts (although its adjoining candy shop gives away tablet-size free samples).

DISNEY'S BOARDWALK

BoardWalk is a lakefront promenade with a few midway games, stores, quick-service pizza, and ice-cream shops—not much, but ideal for a postmeal stroll. I wouldn't make a special trip to eat here, especially if you have a ticket that gets you into Epcot's World Showcase, a 10-minute walk away. But if you're there:

$$–$$$$ The **ESPN Club** (☎ 407/939-5100; Mon–Thurs 11:30am–1am, Fri–Sat 11:30am–2am; no reservations) serves stuff like nachos and chicken wings for around $13 an entree. It's nothing special except for its entertainment area, crammed with some 100 TVs showing athletic matches from across the country. Instead of DJs, sportscaster-like commentators jabber about trivia.

$$–$$$$ Because it doesn't take advance reservations, if other places are full you stand a chance of getting into the noisy **Big River Grille & Brewing Works** (☎ 407/560-0253; www.bigrivergrille.com; daily 11:30am–midnight). It does disappointing American dishes for average prices ($11 burgers, $16 hazelnut-crusted chicken, $6.50 cheesecake), and there are about six microbrews on tap at a time.

Rent-a-Poppins

Parents: I know you came to Orlando to spend some time with your family, but I also understand that you might need to get away from some of them for a few hours. If you're staying in a luxury resort hotel, the management may offer some kind of paid babysitting or supervised kids' club service. If not, there are always these possibilities: **Kid's Nite Out** (☎ 800/696-8105 or 407/828-0920; www.kids niteout.com; $16/hr.) and **All About Kids** (☎ 800/728-6506 or 407/812-9300; www.all-about-kids.com; $13/hr.). Both companies are insured, bonded, and licensed, and both would appreciate a few days' warning for reservations for in-room sitting. Expect $10 to $12 in transportation fees and a few additional bucks for additional kids. Five Disney resorts including the Polynesian and Animal Kingdom Lodge operate supervised clubs (☎ 407/939-3463) for potty-trained kids 4 to 12 starting at 4:30pm and ending at midnight. These cost $11 an hour per child, including a simple meal during dinnertime, and are sometimes open to reservations by people who aren't staying in a Disney hotel. I do *not* recommend depositing your offspring at the gates of the Magic Kingdom and speeding off, as actress Tracy Pollan's father once did to her.

$$–$$$$ Open-kitchen **Spoodles** ★ (☎ 407/939-3463; daily 7–11am and 5–9:30pm) does Mediterranean dishes (steak kabobs, flatbreads, white-bean moussaka; entrees $15–$29) in a social atmosphere where kids will feel welcome. **The Flying Fish** is way too expensive ($15 appetizers, $33 mains); walk over to the Dolphin's **bluezoo** (p. 67) and have superlative seafood for less than that.

UNIVERSAL ORLANDO

Although **Mythos** (p. 204) is the only restaurant inside the Universal theme parks that's worth a detour, there are worthwhile dining options in Universal Orlando that are outside the parks—ones for which you don't need a park ticket. Universal's three hotels host upscale restaurants, while the CityWalk outdoor party mall, located between the resort's main parking garage and the entrances to the parks, attracts plenty of young local people who have no intention of proceeding to the thrill rides.

If you intend to linger at CityWalk for the nightlife (parking is free after 6pm unless there's a big event on), there are a few package deals that combine a meal, including a beverage, with a movie and entry to the clubs. The **Meal and Movie Deal** (☎ 407/224-2691; $21.95), which pairs dinner with a movie at CityWalk's ABC multiplex, can be purchased at the CityWalk Guest Services window and redeemed at any sit-down CityWalk restaurant, except Bubba Gump or Emeril's. The menu will consist of six or eight of the most popular dishes, but conveniently, you don't have to enjoy both meal and movie on the same day.

Entrees cost more than they would outside Universal; they're mostly priced in the teens, with burgers sliding in around $11. So although none of these places are at the top of my list for a value meal, and only one of them is a true gourmet experience, you may find yourself naturally patronizing one after a long day at the parks. Call ☎ **407/224-3663** for more information, unless there's another number listed. After dark, CityWalk has a few windows serving stuff like hot dogs and pizza, plus an experimental self-serve Whopper Bar by Burger King. Because they siphon the same post–theme park customers, the ambiance at all of these sit-down restaurants is the same—loud, cavernous, family-friendly, often with faux antiques bolted to the walls. At these places prices don't vary substantially between lunch and dinner; however, you'll want to arrive before 9pm, because some of these places charge covers after then. Quickly, here's a synopsis:

$–$$ Pat O'Brien's ★★ (☎ 407/224-2106; www.patobriens.com; food daily 4pm–1am; AE, DC, MC, V), like its bawdy Nawlins namesake, does Cajun-style dishes such as shrimp gumbo ($5 a bowl), po' boys ($10), and jambalaya ($10). The specialty of the house, which is done up to be an exact replica of the watering hole's original location in the French Quarter of the Big Easy, is the potent Hurricane cocktail. The strong drinks account for a clientele with fewer kids than the other CityWalk choices, but there is a kids' menu.

$$–$$$ Most affordable at CityWalk is **Pastamoré Ristorante & Market** ★ (☎ 407/224-7223; daily 5pm–midnight; AE, DC, MC, V), which does family-friendly Italian and has a service counter (open 8am) that's less expensive ($8-ish). Nothing is over $20 and so it tends to be noisy and busy. That lends to the happy mood. Veal marsala, the pinnacle of many menus' prices, is $19; most dishes cost $4 to $6 less.

$$–$$$ A bunch of CityWalk places are cheerful burgers-pastas-and-salads places intended to be all things to all people. The food is hard to mess up (bacon appears everywhere), so the one you pick depends on which all-American vibe you want and which T-shirt you want to buy. The fun, tropical **Jimmy Buffett's Margaritaville** ✦ (☎ 407/224-2155; www.margaritavilleorlando.com; daily 11:30am–2am; AE, DC, MC, V) is nearest to Islands of Adventure, so at park closing time it's jammed with park-goers clamoring for margaritas and Cheeseburgers in Paradise ($11). In late afternoon, there may be a strummer on the patio, and after 10pm, the indoor area morphs into a nightclub with a band and there's a $7 cover. It doesn't do reservations, but it does do Priority Seating, which puts your name near the top of the wait list; I suggest using this option. Opposite the restaurant, under a 60-foot Albatross plane, the *Hemisphere Dancer,* is the Lone Palm Airport, for margaritas and appetizers on the go. **Hard Rock Cafe** (☎ 407/351-7625; www.hardrock.com; daily 11am—midnight; AE, DC, MC, V) is, well, a Hard Rock Cafe, albeit the world's largest (600 seats) and possibly the loudest. You've probably already sampled the Hard Rock shtick: A casual tavern done up with music memorabilia (and out back, a slab from the Berlin Wall). Prices are high for CityWalk: $10 appetizers, $15 burgers. **NBA City** (☎ 407/363-5919; www.nba.com/nbacity/orlando; daily 11am–10:30pm; AE, DC, MC, V) is the Hard Rock for basketball nuts, with a similarly wide-ranging burgers-and-pasta menu but jerseys instead of Stratocasters on the walls. There's an interactive area (test your jumping and free-throw skills). Prices usually span $16 to $22 for entrees beyond burgers. **NASCAR Sports Grille** (☎ 407/224-7223; www.nascar sportsgrille.com; daily 11am–midnight; AE, DC, MC, V) offers race memorabilia and tableside plasma screens. Nonfans will shrug. Prices start at $10 for a simple burger and zoom to $22 for rib combos.

$$–$$$ Beyond those, your choices fall along cuisine styles, none of them too far from mainstream tastes. **Bob Marley—A Tribute to Freedom** (daily 4:30pm–2am) does Jamaican food (spicy jerk chicken, fried plantains, even oxtail) and takes reservations. It turns into a reggae nightclub after 8pm, and on Thursdays Red Stripe beer is $3.25. The selection of seafood is better here than at most CityWalk places, and although appetizers are $10, entrees are too and contain plenty of food. **Latin Quarter** ✦ (daily 5–10pm) has a pan-Latin menu (really, *really* "pan"—are nachos considered indigenous?). The food is no revelation—although the ribs are flavored like guava. Typical entrees are $11 to $17, but its express window (not always open) does handheld and stewed foods for cheap ($5–$7.50). **Bubba Gump Shrimp Co.** (www.bubbagump.com; daily 11am–midnight), done up like a fake Louisiana shack, is running on the fumes of the 1994 movie and it does shrimp a billion ways, including some you never would dream up yourself (Boat Trash, which is a bucket of deep fried shrimp, lobster claws, fish, and fries, is $19). Sandwiches and salads cost around $11; for shrimp specials, add another $6. You have to wonder about a place that would post a drink special named after Jenny, a character with serious substance abuse issues.

$$$$ Only **Emeril's Restaurant Orlando** ✦✦ (☎ 407/224-2424; www.emerils. com; reservations suggested; daily 11:30am–2pm, Sun–Thurs 5:15–10pm, Fri–Sat 5:15–11pm) meets a standard of fare that could be considered gourmet outside CityWalk. The modern New Orleans menu does seafood and pasta, but its heart is in meats, with flavors typified by embellishments such as bourbon-caramel glaze. The wine list could send you reeling even before you have a single sip—the back wall is a 15,000-bottle aboveground cellar built to dazzle. The eight counter seats, from which you can watch the chefs keep pace with the relentless demand, are the best, but you'd be wise to book at least a month ahead for them. The kitchen takes a break from 2 to 5:15pm, but if it doesn't cut into your theme park time, try for lunch, as it's much cheaper (entrees cost about $21, versus $32 at dinner) yet still offers a similar menu. Happily, it offers a kids' menu ($10 for most dishes), which makes adult pleasures more possible.

$$$$ Should Emeril's be full, Lagasse runs a second restaurant at the Royal Pacific Resort, a few hundred yards away. **Emeril's Tchoup Chop** ★★★ (6300 Hollywood Way, Orlando; ☎ 407/503-2467; www.emerils.com; daily 11:30am–2pm, Sun–Thurs 5:30–10pm, Fri–Sat 5:30–11pm), serves ostensibly Hawaiian creations (they change and cost $15–$35) such as the Clay Pot, a mélange of fish with yellow Thai lobster cream, stir-fry shrimp, and fire-roasted sweet corn rice. The daffy colors of the high-ceilinged dining room, exuberantly embellished by David Rockwell in rich orange and cobalt glass, are more a nod to Orlando's boundless showmanship than a portent of a saccharine meal.

ALL-YOU-CAN-EAT BONANZAS

For a family-friendly city, Orlando is shockingly immoderate when it comes to food. Endless buffets, the eating equivalent of porn, are found everywhere, and they can rescue a budget. Tip your server—then the scales! Disney charges $30 an entree for endless buffet dinners, but these guys do it much, much cheaper or much better:

$ They charge *what?* **Cici's Pizza** (7761–63 W. U.S. 192, Kissimmee; ☎ 407/390-6171; www.cicispizza.com; Sun–Thurs 11am–10pm, Fri–Sat 11am–11pm) asks for an unbeatable $5.50 to gorge on 12 types of pizza, pasta with either marinara or alfredo sauce, a few salads, and dessert of brownies and cinnamon buns. Kids pay $3.50, and drinks (Mello Yello!) are $1.89. Is it trashy? Pretty much. But it's no worse than Domino's, it will please your ravenous brood, and the staff is trained to be merry and attentive. Pizzas to go are insanely cheap, too: a 15-incher with one topping is $7. There's at least one for every other major tourist zone— **I-Drive** (7437 International Dr.; ☎ 407/226-9822) and **Lake Buena Vista** (8586 Palm Pkwy; ☎ 407/238-7711)—with similar prices.

$$ **Golden Corral** ★★ (7702 W. U.S. 192, Kissimmee; ☎ 407/390-9615; www.goldencorral.net; daily 8am–10pm; AE, DISC, MC, V) is an immoderate orgy of food, food, and more food—all for $8 at breakfast, $11–$12 at lunch or dinner (kids 10 and under $5–$7; lunch starts at 11am, dinner at 4pm). You're handed your first plate upon entry and directed to a maze of steam tables. Perhaps no fact is more telling than that the desserts area is bigger than the salads area, or that mayonnaise is virtually considered a vegetable (beware the BLT Salad). There are healthy choices, including baked sweet potatoes and steamed vegetables, but customers sharpen their elbows to get to the fried chicken and macaroni and cheese, and there's usually a special of the night, like shrimp or carvery meats. Other locations: **Lake Buena Vista** (8707 Vineland Ave.; ☎ 407/938-9500), about **6 miles**

east of Disney (2701 W. Vine St./U.S. 192, Kissimmee; ☎ 407/931-0776), **I-Drive near Sand Lake Road** (8032 International Dr., Orlando; ☎ 407/352-6606), and **by Universal** (5535 S. Kirkman Rd.; ☎ 407/938-9500).

$$ Welcome relief for palates desperate for something fresh, **Sweet Tomatoes** ★★ (6877 S. Kirkman Rd., Orlando; ☎ 407/363-1616; Mon–Thurs 10:30am–9pm, Fri–Sat 10:30am–10pm, Sun 9am–9pm; AE, MC, V) is known for its massively long salad bar. This loftlike chain, big mostly in the American Southwest, promises that its food is on its way to the restaurant within 24 hours of being pulled from the ground, and there's a little meat, too. There are about eight homemade soups, breads, and a few pastas, and at $7 for lunch and $8 for dinner, it's enough to make you resent pizza and fries to the end of your days.

$ Sure, it's the sort of buffet where you can't distinguish the banana pudding from the vanilla yogurt just by looking at it. But **Ponderosa** ★★ (7598 W. Irlo Bronson Hwy., Kissimmee; ☎ 407/396-7721; daily 7:30–11am and 11:30am–10pm; AE, MC, V) does a $4 breakfast that beats any hotel's. There's tons of food—from pancakes to pineapple to a full salad bar—and you can gorge on as much as you dare (beverages are extra). They even fire up the self-serve ice-cream machine for superindulgent parents. It's also on **U.S. 192 east of I-4** (5771 W. Irlo Bronson Hwy. Kissimmee; ☎ 407/397-2477), **near the Nickelodeon hotel** (8200 World Center Dr., Kissimmee; ☎ 407/238-2526), **near SeaWorld** (8510 International Dr., Orlando; ☎ 407/354-1477), and **near Universal Orlando** (6362 International Dr., Orlando; ☎ 407/352-9343). Can't find one? Sizzler, a dueling steakhouse chain, does breakfast for $5 (there's a locator at www.sizzler.com).

$–$$ Two fat Buddhas the color of lime sherbet stand guard outside the plain, strip-mall **Dragon Super Buffet** (12384 S. Apopka Vineland Rd., Lake Buena Vista; ☎ 407/238-9996; www.dragoncourtorlando.com; $7.50 lunch, $11 dinner, kids $4.50–$5.50; daily 11am–11pm; AE, DISC, MC, V), near Disney's door. The half-dozen steam tables aren't piled high, but they're replenished often, which means food doesn't sit out long. The fare is classic Chinese, plus salads and dessert. For dinner, they wheel out the crab legs (add $3 for those). I suppose you could also order off the standard menu for $9, but why would you?

$$$$ It'll cost ya, but people have a blast at the small chain **Texas de Brazil** ★★ (5259 International Dr., Orlando; ☎ 407/355-0355; www.texasdebrazil.com; Sun noon–9:30pm, Mon–Thurs 5–10pm, Fri 5–10:30pm, Sat 4–10:30pm; reservations recommended; AE, DC, DISC, MC, V), a popular Brazilian-style churrascaria—large, noisy (you are warned), and jammed with ungodly amounts of food. Each diner is equipped with a plastic disc, one side green and the other red, that functions as an on/off switch for the waiters, who will relentlessly pile your plate with shavings from giant skewers of meat unless you turn the red side up, thereby silently crying "Uncle!" And the meats—more than a dozen varieties—are succulent, pink in the middle, and high quality. Adults will pay $45, but kids 6 and under are free, and those 7 to 12 eat for half-price. Its website will e-mail you a 25% discount coupon, and tourist brochures have even better deals. The salad options are enormous, but don't fill up before the meat comes.

U.S. 192 & LAKE BUENA VISTA

If you want truly inexpensive eats priced at market rates, you simply have to leave Walt Disney World. The good news is it doesn't take long. About 7 minutes after driving past the security kiosks at Disney's Value-class hotels, you can reach one of two major zones that are crowded with every chain restaurant known to familydom. The southern zone, U.S. 192, goes both east and west from Disney's southern gate. The eastern zone, Lake Buena Vista, is located about a mile east of the Downtown Disney area. The two zones are linked by a few miles of Interstate 4, making it easy to shift from one to the other when you've exhausted the first. Because of stoplights and traffic, it's quicker to reach U.S. 192 from Disney.

$–$$ Probably my favorite little-known "find" in the Disney Zone, **Bruno's Italian Restaurant** ✮✮✮ (8556 W. Irlo Bronson Hwy., Kissimmee; ☎ 407/397-7577; daily 11:30am–11pm; AE, DC, DISC, MC, V), a few miles west of the southern Disney gate, is not at first glance somewhere you'd think to stop. It shares a building with a ghastly, low-rent tourist-trap shack painted with killer whales. But resist the impulse to pass on by because there really is a Bruno in the kitchen, and he was raised in southern Italy. He makes sublime Italian classics to order, well sauced and finely garlicked. Pasta ($8.50–$13) comes with a salad and garlic rolls, which amounts to a lot of food for the price. The menu includes New York–style thin-crust pizzas and a puttanesca with pep, but Bruno's often prepares a daily special, such as a lovely bracciole ($11–$17), plus desserts such as hand-filled cannoli and light tiramisu with the perfect hint of alcohol. It also delivers to the many rental vacation homes in the area.

$–$$ **Miller's Orlando Ale House** (12371 Winter Garden Vineland Rd., Lake Buena Vista; ☎ 407/239-1800; www.millersalehouse.com; Mon–Sat 11am–2am; Sun 11am–midnight; AE, MC, V) is popular with Disney cast members after their shifts are over, so open your ears by the bar if you want to hear the dirt. It's nothing more than a spacious, pubby sports bar (the TVs are on mute during the day) with big wooden booths, 75 beers, and a menu of casual favorites such as burgers ($5–$8), pastas ($10–$12), salads ($3.30–$9), and a raw bar ($5.50 for six). Zingers ($8), miraculously boneless chicken wings dipped in your choice of sauces, are the house dish; I'm sure I don't want to know how they're made. There's another location **near Universal** (5573 Kirkman Rd.; ☎ 407/248-0000) that those theme park employees favor.

$$ Bizarre as it is to find a tasty outpost in a strip mall storefront beside a Publix and a fish-and-chips joint, the 10-table **Asia Bagus** ✮✮ (2923 Vineland Rd., Kissimmee; ☎ 407/397-2205; Mon–Fri 11:30am–3pm, daily 5–10pm; AE, DC, MC, V) is in fact a rare Indonesian restaurant. Indonesian food, if you haven't tried it, is flavorful, not too spicy, and big on rice and noodles. I like the *tahu gejrot* (Javanese-style sweet soy-fried tofu; $4.95) and the *nasi rames* (jasmine rice with beef, boiled egg, and little dried anchovies served as a garnish; $11), but I tend to order the *nasi goreng* ($11), which is a traditional fried rice mixed with chicken sate. Ask to try Kecap Bango, a thick, sweet soy sauce; and *sambal* ($2), a fiery relish eaten with just about everything. Dessert brings a real treat: *es cendol* ("ice chendol"), made of finely shaved ice topped with grass jelly and condensed milk—you can eat a heap without feeling too guilty (it's flavored ice!) and it wards off the Florida heat. Asia Bagus is within driving distance of Disney.

$$ You're in Florida—get some Cuban food! Hidden in a strip mall near Disney's eastern door, **Havana's Cuban Cuisine** ✦ (8544 Palm Pkwy., Orlando; ☎ 407/238-5333; Mon 5–11pm, Tues–Sat 11:30am–11pm, Sun noon–9pm; AE, DISC, MC, V) is authentic and affordable. The decor is nothing much, but the food is stick-to-your-ribs Latino: *ropa vieja* (shredded beef, $13), *arroz con pollo* (Creole chicken with yellow rice, $12), and the like, all served with black beans and sweet plantains. The spot-on black-bean soup is $4 (I like mine with chopped onions and sometimes a little sour cream) and pressed sandwiches on real Cuban bread are $9. More people ought to know about this place. Someone ought to put it in a book or something.

$–$$ Another family-run surprise amongst the tourist junk, **Jerusalem Restaurant** (2920 Vineland Rd., Kissimmee; ☎ 407/397-2230; Sat–Thurs 11:45am–11pm, Fri 2:30pm–11pm; DISC, MC, V) is well worn but from the heart. Tucked in a blah strip mall behind a Taco Bell and done in hand-me-down pastels, authentic Middle Eastern fare is quietly and solidly served up. The specialty is grilled meats such as lamb shish kabob ($13), but there're plenty of alternatives, including a variety of couscous dishes ($13 for chicken, $12 for vegetarian), and baked eggplant musakkaa ($10), house-made garlicky hummous ($5), and fried kibbeh fritters (beef, cracked wheat, onions, and seasonings; $6). Simpler stuff like falafel and gyros are all under $6. Kids will find a special menu of chicken fingers and such. On Fridays after prayers, many in the Muslim community converge here to socialize and chow down. Lest that make you think it's clubby, it's also kosher.

$$ Sounds like a rum, eats like a Friday's. **Bahama Breeze** ✦ (8735 Vineland Ave., Lake Buena Vista; ☎ 407/938-9010; www.bahamabreeze.com; Sun–Thurs 11am–midnight, Fri–Sat 11am–1am; AE, DISC, MC, V) is a chain by Orlando-based Darden, but its theme has a light touch, so it's often full of families in a fine mood. The menu is creative, but if the food might be a bit heavy after a day at the theme parks—habañero wings ($7), coconut shrimp ($16), and fish tacos ($11)—at least the atmosphere feels tropical, and the blended drinks are something you might otherwise have at a swim-up bar somewhere. There's a second location **on I-Drive,** within walking distance of many hotels (8849 International Dr., Orlando; ☎ 407/248-2499; Sun–Thurs 11am–1am, Fri–Sat 11am–1:30am).

$$–$$$$ On the Plasticine lakefront of Celebration is a surprising sangria-soaked outpost of Florida history, **Columbia Restaurant** ✦✦ (kids) (649 Front St., Celebration; ☎ 407/566-1505; www.columbiarestaurant.com; daily 11:30am–10:30pm; AE, DISC, MC, V), which opened in Tampa's Cuban-inflected Ybor City in 1905. Closely managed by fourth-generation owners, the social Spanish restaurant, now one of six, retains the colonial feel (tiles, woods, hearty dishes) of the original. It's easy to order more than you can eat, especially once the waiters start shuttling hot, fresh Cuban bread and you enjoy the signature 1905 Salad (a daunting chef's salad coated with a family recipe of garlic, wine vinegar, and Spanish E.V.O.O.; it's $9 alone but $4 with an entree). From there, all of Spain is piled on your plate in amounts so copious that sharing is not just easy, it's advisable:

Where to Find Groceries near Disney

Because few locals live around Disney, the grocery stores near its borders cater to vacationers and are more expensive than they should be. Patronizing them, however, is still cheaper than paying theme park prices for all meals. Stores open 24 hours are noted below, and all accept major credit cards, except Diners Club.

If you're staying in the I-Drive/Universal area, finding a market-rate grocery store is not a challenge because, unlike Disney, the area is surrounded by neighborhoods where locals live. Sand Lake Road west of I-4 is a good place to start, as is Conroy Road, north of Universal Orlando.

Higher prices, but closer:

◆ **Gooding's** (in the Crossroads Shopping Center, 12521 S.R. 535, across from the Downtown Disney/Hotel Plaza Blvd. gate, Lake Buena Vista; ☎ 407/827-1200; www.goodings.com). The nearest to Disney, it's a rare carpeted grocery store. Its deli sells $7 roasted chickens and $5 sandwiches.

◆ **Gooding's Formosa** (7840 U.S. 192; ☎ 407/397-2210; www.winn dixie.com). About 3 miles west of Disney.

Lower prices, but slightly farther:

◆ **Publix** (14928 E. Orange Lake Blvd.; ☎ 407/239-4989; www.publix. com). About 4 miles west of Disney on U.S. 192.

◆ **Publix** (2915 Vineland Rd.; ☎ 407/396-7525; www.publix.com). About 3½ miles east on Vineland where it connects to Apopka Vineland near Downtown Disney/Hotel Plaza Blvd./I-4 exit 68.

◆ **Publix** (2925 International Dr., Kissimmee; ☎ 407/397-1171; www. publix.com). 2½ miles east of Disney, north of U.S. 192.

◆ **Publix** (9930 Universal Blvd.; ☎ 407/996-8400; www.publix.com). Near Rosen Shingle Creek, it's useful for Vista Cay vacation rentals.

◆ **Wal-Mart Supercenter** (1471 E. Osceola Pkwy., Kissimmee; ☎ 407/870-2277; www.walmart.com; 24 hr.). Drive east on Osceola Parkway, or avoid a toll by heading 2 miles south on 535/Vineland from the Downtown Disney/Hotel Plaza Boulevard gate.

◆ **Wal-Mart Supercenter** (8990 Turkey Lake Rd., Orlando; ☎ 407/351-2599; 24 hr.). A brand-new store, 5 miles north of Disney via Palm Parkway.

paellas from $21, meat dishes start at $17, and fish at $19 (the Red Snapper "Adelita," with hearts of palm, artichoke hearts, and sun-dried tomatoes, is a standout based on a catch big in the Gulf of Mexico nearby; $22). It's unlikely you'll have room left, but if you do, the flan (caramel egg custard; $4) awaits, and the *café con leche* ($3.50) is the real deal. Cookbooks, dressings, the house-blend coffee, frozen Cuban bread, and Spanish ceramics are all on sale.

INTERNATIONAL DRIVE & CONVENTION CENTER

This is a major hotel and entertainment center, so many visitors find themselves here. The stretch of Sand Lake Road west of Interstate 4 is known, somewhat self-deprecatingly, as "Restaurant Row." It's true that some of the city's most popular date-night restaurants are scattered among the shopping centers on this street.

$ I would never tell you about something as mundane as a McDonald's unless it was really special—this one is. Near Universal, there's a **McDonald's** 🧒 (6875 Sand Lake Rd., Orlando; ☎ 407/351-2185; www.mcfun.com; 24 hr.; AE, DISC, MC, V) that triples its menu options with a "huh?" array of fresh-made options including tossed pastas ($8), paninis ($7), pizzas ($4.60), and sundaes (under $4). It also has the largest PlayPlace in the world, a duplex with slides, a 500-gallon aquarium, and 100 arcade games. It's kind of unbelievable.

$–$$ Collard greens aren't overstewed, the cabbage in the coleslaw is cubed and crunchy, baked beans come sweet the way baked beans ought to, and cornbread muffins are embedded with a melting pad of butter. That's no-frills, smoky-smelling **Bubbalou's Bodacious BBQ** (5818 Conroy Rd., Orlando; ☎ 407/295-1212; www.bubbalouscatering.com; Mon–Thurs 10am–9:30pm, Fri 10am–11:30pm, Sat 10am–9:30pm, Sun 11am–9pm; AE, MC, V). Each picnic-style table is topped with a platter of sauces ranging "sweet" to "killer," not to mention a roll of paper towels, so diners can suit their tastes and their sartorials. After all that, and maybe a plate of its popular ribs ($8), there may not be room for Bubbalou's supersweet three-pecan pie ($2.50), which would be a shame. Dinner plates with fries, baked beans, coleslaw, garlic bread, and your choice of meat hover around $10 or $13. Sandwiches are around $5 and always huge. There is a second location in **Winter Park** (1471 Lee Rd.; ☎ 407/628-1212).

$ Locals pack **the Dessert Lady** ✸ (4900 S. Kirkman Rd., Orlando; ☎ 407/822-8881; www.dessertlady.com; Mon–Sat 11:30am–11pm, Sun 2–10pm; AE, MC, V) for after-dinner delights and special occasions. Its owner became famous by inventing the dessert-in-a-shot-glass for Seasons 52 (see below), and now she runs her own pastry shop/coffeehouse where everything's made from scratch. Under walls rich as red velvet cake (she calls it a "dessert bordello"), sink a fork into a Key lime cake with cream-cheese frosting, six-layer chocolate Neapolitan, or a peanut butter pie mousse, plus a dozen others. White cakes are light, rum cakes are moist and not oversoaked, and slices are hefty (at $10, they ought to be). Samplers, half portions of four pies, cost $24 for two people (though I think they could feed four). Find it in a shopping center behind a Chick-fil-A 5 minutes north of Universal. Her popularity necessitated the opening of a second location at **Church Street Station** (120 W. Church St., Orlando; ☎ 407/999-5696; Mon–Tues 11:30am–10pm, Wed–Thurs 11:30am–11pm, Fri 11:30am–midnight, Sat 4pm–midnight; AE, MC, V), where the cakes are supplemented by a light menu.

$–$$ I like the energy at **Café Tu Tu Tango** ✸✸ (Plaza Venezia, 8625 International Dr., Orlando; ☎ 407/248-2222; www.cafetututango.com/orlando; Sun–Thurs 11:30am–11pm, Fri–Sat 11:30am–1am; AE, DC, DISC, MC, V), and I'm not alone, as it's often busy deep into the night. Commanded by a large wood-fired oven, this joint fashions itself after an atelier, and it's not faking—real

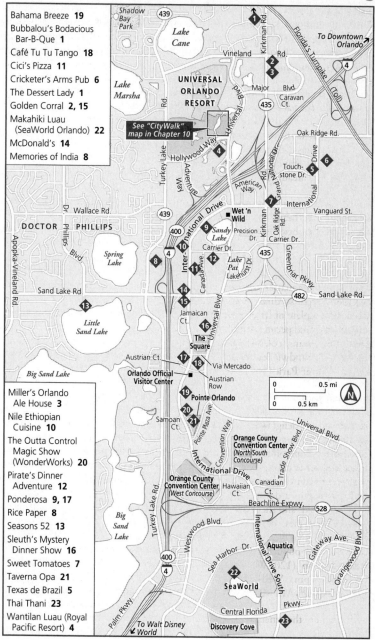

Bahama Breeze **19**

Bubbalou's Bodacious
Bar-B-Que **1**

Café Tu Tu Tango **18**

Cici's Pizza **11**

Cricketer's Arms Pub **6**

The Dessert Lady **1**

Golden Corral **2, 15**

Makahiki Luau
(SeaWorld Orlando) **22**

McDonald's **14**

Memories of India **8**

Miller's Orlando
Ale House **3**

Nile Ethiopian
Cuisine **10**

The Outta Control
Magic Show
(WonderWorks) **20**

Pirate's Dinner
Adventure **12**

Ponderosa **9, 17**

Rice Paper **8**

Seasons 52 **13**

Sleuth's Mystery
Dinner Show **16**

Sweet Tomatoes **7**

Taverna Opa **21**

Texas de Brazil **5**

Thai Thani **23**

Wantilan Luau (Royal
Pacific Resort) **4**

painters and jewelry makers work the easels, and Friday nights at 10:30 belong to burlesque and belly dancing. Kids tend to be swept up in the vibe, but locals also use it as a nonthreatening date night locale. The grills-and-tapas menu (usually $8–$10 each) and hyperfriendly waitstaff alike represent cultures from around the world. One choice is the Cajun chicken egg roll, which is blackened chicken with corn, cheddar, and goat cheese wrapped and deep-fried like an egg roll, served with salsa; I find it revolting, but it's the most popular item on the menu. I stick to meat skewers and baked artichoke and crabmeat dip. The lounge (cushy sofas where you can eat, if you want) serves cocktails and nearly three dozen beers. Far from a tourist trap, it's actually cool.

$$–$$$ The staff at **Nile Ethiopian Cuisine** ★★ (7040 International Dr., Orlando; ☎ 407/354-0026; www.nile07.com; Mon–Fri 5–11pm, Sat–Sun 11am–11pm; AE, DISC, MC, V) may be the nicest I've encountered in town, and they are clearly invested in both the quality of the food and the wealth of the cultural experience, which makes it a great place to learn about the cuisine without feeling sheepish. The gist is that you get a platter-size pad of spongy, vinegary *injera* bread with which you pinch and eat a wide range of aromatic stews, vegetarian and otherwise ($12–$14, including four combos that let you try several). Nile is one of the only Ethiopian places I've been to that is equipped with a few *mesob* basket tables (there are European ones, too) and that will perform a traditional coffee ceremony at your table (roasting the beans, brewing in a *jabena* pot, serving the eldest first in a demitasse cup); that's just $10. Nile is tough to find, in a down-at-heel shopping center behind Buffalo Wild Wings.

$$–$$$ An unpretentious British pub with a following from locals and expats alike, **Cricketers Arms Pub** (5250 N. International Dr., Orlando; ☎ 407/354-0686; www.cricketersarmspub.com; daily noon–2am; AE, MC, V) does its best to make its cavernous space at Festival Bay mall look Olde English, and by the crowd it seems they've succeeded. It serves more British ales than anywhere else in the area (London Pride, Tetley's, Fullers ESB) and subscribe to live Premiership football by satellite—although the NFL is subbed in when there's no European action. There's live music, often acoustic or bands, nearly every night, plus a menu of as-expected Brit classics such as Scotch eggs, cottage pie, and ploughman's sandwiches, mostly $10 to $15, which would be a bit much if not for the fun.

$–$$ I would always rather go to the Vietnamese District for authentic Asian fare, but if I'm stuck around the parks, **Rice Paper** ★ (7637 Turkey Lake Rd., Orlando; ☎ 407/352-4700; Mon–Thurs 11am–9pm, Fri–Sat 11am–10pm, Sun noon–9pm; AE, DC, DISC, MC, V) is richer than run-of-the-mill Asian fare. After you start with one of the seven spring roll varieties ($4–$6) or grilled quail with lime-pepper sauce ($12), some "big soups" are served ($9–$13), akin to pho in Vietnamese cuisine, or you can move right on to the entrees instead. The emphasis is on rice and vermicelli dishes such as my favorite, caramelized ginger chicken with onion and zucchini ($10). One of the splurges on the menu is the clay pot catfish, caramelized with onion and chili powder ($15). Seven types of loose-leaf teas are brewed for $3 per pot, and the house dessert specialty is Banana Flambé—banana wrapped in spring roll skin, fried, and served with a honey glaze and coconut ice cream ($6.50).

$$ In the same nondescript Bay Hill shopping plaza as Rice Paper is a second Asian winner popular with locals: **Memories of India** ★★★ (7625 Turkey Lake Rd., Orlando; ☎ 407/370-3277; Mon–Fri 11:30am–2:30pm and 5:30–10pm, Sat 11:30am–2pm and 5:30–10pm, Sun 5:30–9pm; http://storefront.dexonline.com/memories-of-india; AE, MC, V) overcomes a bland name with perfectly flavorful pan-Indian cuisine, never too cloying with curry and almost always subtly blended. It is also the rare Indian place in America to serve a *thali*, which is a lunchtime platter combining basmati rice, bread, *raita* (yogurt with cucumbers and tomatoes), pickle (relish), a meat dish, a *papadum* (thin wafer), and, at this place, dessert (I like the pulpy mango ice cream)—all for $6.20 to $9.50. Dinner entrees are mostly $11 to $16, and the tandoori and *naan* (a dozen types) are made on-site in a clay oven. Keep your ears peeled for gossip, because it's a favorite of the administrative staff at Universal Orlando next door. There's a children's menu for unadventurous youth. It's a few blocks west of International Drive, right on the western side of I-4, although few tourists seem to realize it.

$$ In sight of SeaWorld's ferocious Kraken coaster, **Thai Thani** ★★ (11025 S. International Dr.; ☎ 407/239-9733; www.thaithani.net; Sun–Thurs 11:30am–10pm, Fri–Sat 11:30am–11pm; AE, DISC, MC, V) is a strip-mall anchor store that's been transformed into a Chiang Mai den of delights with wood carvings, brass sculpture, powerfully romantic private booths, and a front lounge filled with body cushions. Popular with locals, it serves Thai food suited to newbies—the lemon grass soup is tame, with few chilies, which proves the chef is holding back—but more advanced noodleheads should identify themselves and ask for it spicier (up to "firehouse") to get the full flair of the cuisine. Dinner entrees come in at $12 to $14, while lunch (which ends at 2:30pm) is about $4 less. There's also a bar area in the event of a wait which, considering the size of the place, happens a lot (reservations are possible). Finish with Thai Grandma Ice Cream: coconut ice cream with sticky rice and peanuts ($6). As Thai food becomes America's new Chinese, I've brought curry snobs here and they've liked it, too.

$$–$$$ Seasons 52 ★★★ (7700 Sand Lake Rd., Orlando; ☎ 407/354-5212; www.seasons52.com; Mon–Thurs 11:30am–2:30pm and 5–10pm, Fri 11:30am–2:30pm and 5–11pm, Sat 11:30am–11pm, Sun 11:30am–10pm; AE, MC, V) started as a culinary experiment and is now in seven locations. By 6:30pm, it's two-deep at the wine bar (140 types, 70 by the glass) while Orlando locals jostle for a table (reservations are possible). The two-level, raftered, California-style ranch building looks like something Mike Brady might have designed, but the real appeal here is the miraculous food. The entire point of the menu, which changes weekly to catch seasonal crops, is that no dish clocks in at more than 475 calories (though none will leave you hungry). The food isn't frou-frou—it's simply really good, and never sees a deep fryer. The signature flatbreads are $4 to $10, while most entrees fall between $12 and $18. The desserts, which are served in single-serving shot glasses, are a guiltless sensation and cost $2.50 a pop—just don't overindulge and undo all that low-calorie virtue.

$$–$$$$ For a festive night out, one of the latest hotspots for locals and tourists alike is **Taverna Opa** ★★★ 🧒 (9101 International Dr. in Pointe Orlando, Orlando; ☎ 407/351-8660; www.opaorlando.com; daily 11am–11pm; AE, DISC,

Rib Row

Unbeknownst to most tourists, who rarely venture into nonplastic parts of town, an enclave of serious barbecue joints has sprung up along a mile of Orange Avenue in the downmarket Edgewood area of south Orlando. I call it Rib Row, the best place to get Southern-style cooking. Probably the easiest way to find Rib Row is to go east from Kaley St., I-4's exit 81B, go about a half-mile to Orange Avenue, then turn right. All the joints are on the west (right) side. After your meal, grab a microbrew at Orlando Brewing (p. 291), off Kaley on Atlanta, on your way back to I-4.

$–$$ Cecil's Texas Style Bar-B-Q ★★ (2800 S. Orange Ave., Orlando; ☎ 407/423-9871; www.cecilsbbq.com; Mon–Sat 11am–9pm, Sun noon–8pm; AE, DISC, MC, V). Hickory smelling and light on pretense, this one is first up. It starts with a serve-yourself cafeteria-style counter and then leaves you the heck alone in a family-friendly saloonlike atmosphere to pig out. Pick your meat and either do a sandwich ($5) or a dinner platter ($9–$11), which comes with two sides (the usual Southern goodies plus a few fun ones like sweet-potato soufflé and jalapeño mashed potatoes). The Texan way is to go light on the sauce in the kitchen, but they'll give you more. At lunch, you can get a meat, a side, and a drink for $7.60.

$–$$ O-Boys Real Smoked Bar-B-Q (3138 S. Orange Ave., Orlando; ☎ 407/447-7404; www.oboysbbq.net; Mon–Thurs 11am–10pm, Fri–Sat 11am–9:30pm, Sun 11am–8pm; AE, DC, DISC, MC, V), second along, just past Pineloch, smokes its own meat, as any self-respecting barbecuer does, but it feels more like a sports bar, with the biggest menu (there's stuff like chicken sandwiches and salads) to please those who don't like chewing meat off bones. Until 5pm, meat plus fries, baked beans, slaw, and garlic bread costs $8, and every night but Sunday, there's an all-you-can-eat meat for $11 to $12 (baby back ribs are on Fri). Signature starter: battered corn nuggets, deep fried and dipped in honey ($5).

$ Blackwater Bar B-Q ★★★ (4718 S. Orange Ave., Orlando; ☎ 407/888-2033; www.blackwaterbbq.com; Mon–Thurs 11–8pm, Fri 11am–9pm, Sat 11:30am–8:30pm; AE, DC, MC, V), the third joint along, is the best. It was started by a few guys who kept winning barbecue contests, and you can tell they mean business: It's counter service in a plain picnic-table hall lined with shelves of trophies of golden hogs from competitions like the "Ham Jam." A pulled-pork dinner with two sides is just $7, "samies" (sandwiches) around $6, and a half slab of baby back ribs, meaty and tender, only $13. All sides, including green beans, corn bread, fried okra, and black-eyed peas, are mostly around $1.50. But my hands-down favorite is the Brunswick stew, meaty and saucy, just like my Georgia kin taught me it should be. Sweet tea is served by the foam quart cup.

MC, V). It would be hard not to find something to eat, from meze (hummus with garlic chunks and hot pita bread, taramasalata, feta with olive oil; $4–$9) and Greek salads ($7–$9) to hearty wood-fired meats ($16), grilled fish ($18–$24) and *mousakas* (like an eggplant lasagna with béchamel; $13). And only a sourpuss can resist being swept into the party that starts after 8pm or so—the waiters and customers alike start tossing their napkins and dancing on the tables, and nothing can still the party or dress the belly dancers. Kids really get into it, and into the honey-drizzled baklava ($5). Blame the ouzo, because lunches are quiet. In the same shopping center (free parking with validation), you'll find a few more choices, mostly more expensive, including Tommy Bahama's Tropical Café, Cuba Libre, the Capital Grille, and a superlative fresh-fish splurge, the Oceanaire.

DOWNTOWN ORLANDO

The neighborhood east of downtown, Thornton Park, hosts a few well-publicized bistros and sidewalk cafes, but with prices around $12 a plate for lunch and $20 for dinner, there are no money-saving revelations among them. Instead, try these.

$ Perhaps no place better signifies the new Orlando, a growing city of casual, principled young people weary of the grip of a corporate lifestyle, than **Dandelion Communitea Cafe** ★★★ (618 N. Thornton Ave., Orlando; ☎ 407/362-1864; www. dandelioncommunitea.com; Mon–Sat 11am–11pm, Sun 11am–9pm; AE, MC, V), in ViMi. It's run by Julie Norris, a fixture on the city foodie scene, and a staff of warm-hearted bohemians. It feels like someone's home because it once was. The front dining room is the former living room, the back ones were bedrooms, and appropriate to its past function, local folks tend to hang out for hours on its couches, sipping homemade tea blends ($3.75) and talking about life. Although I'm not a vegetarian, there's nothing better than vegetarian food done well, and this place nails it, using local ingredients. (It was the first restaurant in the Southeast to be certified green by Co-op America.) The hummus is creamy, moist, and drizzled with premium olive oil ($3); salad dressings (Gingerous, Razzmania) are clever; wraps ($8.50–$9) are substantial; and the Henry's Hearty Chili ($4 cup, $6 bowl) is simply sensational, and unlike other veggie chilis, it's not overloaded with beans—I don't know how they make it so flavorful. In front, in what I guess was a breakfast nook, it sells a range of own-blend loose-leaf teas for under $4 for a 2- or 4-ounce pouch. Monday through Friday from 4 to 6pm, mimosas are $3 and organic beers are $2. It's my favorite hangout in the city.

$ Value-minded home-style cooking is the lure at tiny **Christo's Café** (1815 Edgewater Dr. at Dartmouth St., Orlando; ☎ 407/425-8136; www.christoscafe. com; Mon–Sat 6:30am–9pm, Sun 7am–3pm; AE, DISC, MC, V), an old-fashioned diner that has captured the devotion of the new inhabitants of its rapidly gentrifying neighborhood. Breakfasts, particularly on the weekends (they're served until 3pm), are roundly praised—think about country ham served in slabs ($3.75) and omelets ($4.95) that look like the pictures in a Southern cookbook—and its soups ($2.75 a cup), which are usually homemade, are equally prized. Southern specialties include banana pudding, batter-fried onion rings ($4), and chicken-fried steak ($8.75, including two sides and garlic toast). Nothing here is gourmet, but if you grew up eating food like this, you'll think it ranks even higher. The downside, beside the potential for strokes, is that parking is limited.

$ A favorite of slumming NBA players, glad-handing political candidates, and folks who miss Grandma's soul food, **Johnson's Diner** ✪✪ (595 W. Church St., Orlando; ☎ 407/841-0717; www.johnsonsdiner.com; Mon–Thurs 7am–7pm, Fri-Sat 7am–8pm, Sun 7am–6pm; AE, DISC, MC, V), in the otherwise bleak dining terrain of Parramore (just west of I-4 from downtown), is a no-frills kitchen where home cooking and soul food is raised to new heights while prices stay rooted in the 1990s. Civic leaders prize the place, which began in 1955, so highly that when its longtime location was threatened with development, the city pitched in $36,700 to fund a move. On vinyl tablecloths, feast on smothered pork chops ($7.15), sweet tea ($1.25 a glass), and fried catfish (perfection at $7.95). Daily specials include grilled liver ($6) on Wednesdays and barbecue ribs ($7.40) on Saturdays. The sweet-potato pie ($1.95) is locally heralded, as is the stewed beef, but if diabetes diagnoses could be traced, the banana pudding ($1.50), piled with Nilla Wafers, would certainly be banned.

$ Part of a 30-odd-strong Tex-Mex chain (but this is one of the few to be controlled by its parent company), the brash **Tijuana Flats** (8 N. Summerlin Ave., Orlando; ☎ 407/649-8063; www.tijuanaflats.com; Mon–Thurs 10:30am–10pm, Fri–Sat 10:30am–10:30pm, Sun 10:30am–9pm; AE, MC, V), decorated like a living comic book, serves some of the only affordable plates among the upscale cafes of Thornton Park. Its gimmick is 15 degrees of hot salsa, from "Sissy Sauce" up to "Death Wish"; 5 are permanent but 10 rotate, and most are for sale. Food is squarely affordable: chimichangas and mighty hefty burritos (a perennial winner in local polls) from $7, enchiladas from $6.20, and platter-sized quesadillas from $4.90. For dessert, the cookie-dough flautas ($2.90) are all kinds of wrong. Stroll 1 block over to Lake Eola Park to enjoy your meal, if you can lift it.

$ Being told that the city's best hot dog is found at a Chevron station doesn't exactly whet the appetite. But relax. **Between the Buns** ✪ (1601 E. Colonial Dr. at Ferncreek Ave., Orlando; no phone; Mon–Sat 11:30am–6:30pm; no credit cards), east of the ViMi district, is a city institution and a striking piece of pop architecture—a hot dog stand shaped like a giant hot dog, and it's been going since 1998 (since 2002 in this location). John Liotine, its Massachusetts-raised proprietor, had a career as a trumpet player for Diana Ross, Prince, and Marvin Gaye before having his wiener custom-built. Now he caters to a host of regulars who slather "Sock It to Me!" hot sauce on their messy quarter-pound dogs to go. They're artfully assembled: The Orlando Magic ($3) has barbecue sauce, chili, jalapeños, and cheese sauce, while the Great American ($2.25) plays it straight with mustard, relish, and onions. The place could just as fittingly be in the shape of a potato, because the hand-cut fries ($1.75) are out of this world. Soda pop is just 75¢, and hoagie-style burgers are $3.75. There are only two little tables with umbrellas on the forecourt of the gas station, which incidentally charges less than most of the ones in the tourist zone. But you may not want gas twice in one meal. You may hear someone say that the health department has scolded the stand in the past, but the last citations were in early 2007, and it has been squeaky clean in nearly a half-dozen inspections since then. If you can handle the thought of eating at a hot dog stand in a gas station's front yard, you can handle this. (Full disclosure: My mom is addicted.)

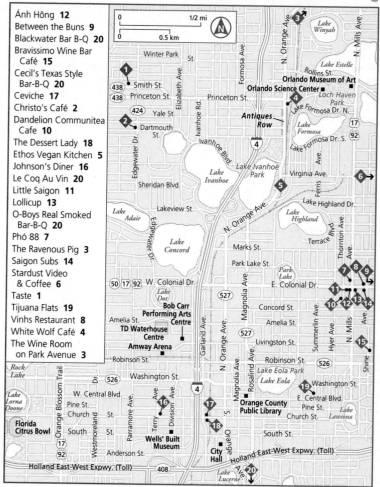

Ánh Hông **12**
Between the Buns **9**
Blackwater Bar B-Q **20**
Bravissimo Wine Bar
  Café **15**
Cecil's Texas Style
  Bar-B-Q **20**
Ceviche **17**
Christo's Café **2**
Dandelion Communitea
  Cafe **10**
The Dessert Lady **18**
Ethos Vegan Kitchen **5**
Johnson's Diner **16**
Le Coq Au Vin **20**
Little Saigon **11**
Lollicup **13**
O-Boys Real Smoked
  Bar-B-Q **20**
Phó 88 **7**
The Ravenous Pig **3**
Saigon Subs **14**
Stardust Video
  & Coffee **6**
Taste **1**
Tijuana Flats **19**
Vinhs Restaurant **8**
White Wolf Café **4**
The Wine Room
  on Park Avenue **3**

$ For coffee, dessert, and a chill place to read or journal without pressure, **Stardust Video & Coffee** ★ (1842 E. Winter Park Rd., Orlando; ☎ 407/623-3393; Mon–Thurs 7am–11pm, Fri 7am–midnight, Sat–Sun 8am–11pm; MC, V) makes for a funky, relaxed hideout. Its warehouselike lounge—furnished with old couches, discarded science-lab tables, and one-sheets of art films such as *Grey Gardens*—feels more like the ramshackle living room of an under-35 bachelor than a business. It's hip without being off-putting, which you'd never expect of an image-obsessed town. Sandwiches (all $6–$8, including a side salad) are named for cult movie actors (the Crispin Glover is a pesto chicken; the Luis Guzman is veggie chili), the coffee cups are deep, and its house-made waffles, a specialty, are served all day. Check out the case full of rare imported beers or the St. Bernardus on draught. That the place is the best in town to rent out-of-print videos is a perk

A Gastronomic Tour of Little Vietnam

Few visitors to Central Florida go far enough from the theme parks to realize that there's a healthy immigrant population that immeasurably enriches the culinary scene. Tampa has hosted Cubans for over a century. In Kissimmee, about 10 miles east of Disney, the concentration is pan-Latin. But just north of Orlando's downtown, along a stretch of 1950s storefronts around the intersection of Colonial Avenue and Mills Drive, a thriving Vietnamese area (variously called Little Vietnam, ViMi, and Colonial Town) is flourishing. Many people fled here upon the fall of Saigon, and Vietnamese dissident Nguyen Thuong Cuc Foshee has been an Orlando resident since the time of the Vietnam conflict. In ViMi, local families serve cheap, unpretentious meals true to Vietnam's reputation for nuanced flavors, and a few enormous supermarkets sell aisle after aisle of inexpensive Asian groceries that will potentially revolutionize your cooking back home. Park your car anywhere (street parking is tough, but most buildings hide secret lots behind them) and explore on an empty stomach.

The quickest way to go is *banh mi*. If you've never had one, be careful, because these baguette-style sandwiches are addictive. They're stuffed with thinly sliced veggies (cucumbers, daikon, carrots), cilantro, hot peppers, a buttery secret sauce, and meats such as roast pork, pâté, or meatball (or tofu). I suspect crack is also an ingredient. They're also shockingly cheap: $3 to $4 for more than enough to eat. A few places in ViMi sell them, but a specialist is **Saigon Subs** ★★ (1242 E. Colonial Dr., Orlando; ☎ 407/897-1278; daily 7:30am–7pm; MC, V), which does 16 types in a deli-style storefront where Vietnamese videos play.

Another source for *banh mi* is the barnlike **Phó 88** (730 N. Mills Ave., Orlando; ☎ 407/897-3488; www.pho88orlando.com; daily 10am–10pm; AE, DISC, MC, V), which proffers a terrific people-watching view of Mills Avenue. Sandwiches are just a sideline, though, because its beef noodle soup is justifiably held as its standout dish (bowls seem as large as hot tubs, with many flavors vying for dominance). It's why you put up with the somewhat inattentive waitstaff. Two enormous spring rolls could fill an average stomach for $2.50, and the avocado shakes are full of fruit. Crowded soup bowls are $7 and could serve as main courses, while plated entrees cost around $10. Lunch prices, which end at 4pm, are about $3 less than dinner for dry entrees. The menu drones on like a Russian novel.

Neophytes prefer the mass appeal of **Little Saigon** ★ (1106 E. Colonial Dr., Orlando; ☎ 407/423-8539; www.littlesaigonrestaurant.com; daily 10am–9pm; AE, DISC, MC, V), which sees a procession of hungry office workers from downtown diving into one of the massive soup bowls. Any restaurant that can afford to make heavy lacquered chairs emblazoned with its own name is well established, and the thick menu, loaded with authentic and Westernized items alike, testifies to its popularity. Prices are in line with its competition: $6.50 to $8.50 for soup bowls, sautéed meats with rice, and rice vermicelli dishes, which are more than enough for a meal. I often find it hard to progress to the second course after partaking of its massive summer rolls ($2.50).

Two places are known for one ingredient above others, even though their rambling menus wouldn't tell you so. **Vinhs Restaurant** ★★★ (1231 E. Colonial Dr., Orlando; ☎ 407/894-5007; daily 10am–10pm; AE, DISC, MC, V) does a marvelous barbecue pork. It's the only restaurant in the district that makes its own—apparently, some little old ladies guard the secret recipe and do the roasting. I love the staff here—mostly students eager to practice their English—and they appear at my table if I so much as glance in their direction. The specialty at **Ánh Hông** (1124 E. Colonial Dr., Orlando; ☎ 407/999-2656; daily 9am–9:30pm; AE, DC, DISC, MC, V), on the corner of Mills, is tofu (especially fried; $8), and yup, it does *banh mi*, too. Most of the menu is under $7, another reason the restaurant is supported by a bevy of regulars of every stripe.

More a place for dessert (although it recently added *banh mi*), **Lollicup** (3201 E. Colonial Dr., Orlando; ☎ 407/897-1377; www.lollicup.com; daily 11am–7pm; MC, V), a California chain just east of Colonial and Mills, is a closet-size cubby for authentic Asian bubble teas, milk teas, and smoothies, which hit the spot on a blistering day and cost $3.50. It also does a variety of teas both with and without tapioca and grass jelly balls. I have a soft spot for the avocado-coconut smoothie ($4.50), but it does fruit slushes, smoothies, and flavored milk teas, too.

Two Asian supermarkets are larger and more varied than you'd imagine for a city of this size. An education and an inspiration, they have aisles of sauces (fish, hot), spices, and ready-to-eat snacks—almost nothing you've seen before. Basil seeds? Artichoke drink? Frozen grated lemon grass? There's even plenty of fresh stuff (like coconut-ball cookies, jugs of fresh-made kimchee, and surprise, *banh mi*). The twin titans are **Tiên-Hung Market** (1108 E. Colonial Dr., Orlando; ☎ 407/422-0067; daily 9am–6pm; DISC, MC, V), which sells refreshing fresh-squeezed sugarcane juice for $3, and **Saigon Market** (1232 E. Colonial Dr., Orlando; ☎ 407/898-6899; daily 9am–8pm; MC, V). It's like traveling the world within 2 blocks.

that tourists can't exploit, but the free Wi-Fi is. On Thursdays at 9:30pm, there's a poetry slam, open to all comers.

$–$$ Everything is made from scratch at **Ethos Vegan Kitchen** (1235 N. Orange Ave., Orlando; ☎ 407/228-3898; www.ethosvegankitchen.com; Mon–Sat 11am–10pm, Sun 10am–3pm; DISC, MC, V), a newcomer (run by a husband-and-wife team, the Shockleys) that already has a big following. A big reason, beside the good food, is a casual decor of local art that changes monthly, and a majority of organic ingredients is the top value of a menu that appeals to omnivores. Ten-inch pizzas with three toppings are $11, marinated and sautéed seitan Philly cheese steaks are $8, and the baked shepherd's pie–like Sheep Pie is $10. Recipes are compelling: The pesto penne is topped with roasted pumpkin seeds ($11). Sunday brunch (10am–3pm) comes with a main, a side, and a drink for $9. (The cinnamon French toast rules.) It's the only vegan place in Central Florida, which may come as a relief after a week of wings, turkey legs, and grease. The Shockleys also make a point of paying waiters a living wage.

$–$$ A few miles north and west of downtown, the hangout of College Park is gaining ground as a hot spot for food with fresh ingredients. **Taste** ★★ (717 W. Smith St., Orlando; ☎ 407/835-0646; www.tastecp.com; Mon–Fri 11:30am–2:30pm, Mon–Sat 5:30–11pm; MC, V), an orange-and-burgundy warehouse space decorated with bamboos, mobiles, and local artwork, is an easygoing yet stylish choice serving California-style tapas cuisine. That translates into fresh concepts (sesame ahi tuna tartare, sizzling garlic shrimp, flatbreads with three types of tapenades, spreadable Gorgonzola cheese cake with green-apple slices) that you'll be ravenous for after a few days of eating frozen-then-fried tourist chow. Two or three dishes ($5–$8), which run a gamut to suit most palates, split between a couple will suffice; there are five full-size dishes, too. The homemade ginger vanilla soda ($2) is a kick and, like everything on the menu, is simple but elegantly balanced, making you feel refreshed but not over-stuffed. If the dining room is full, offer to eat at the bar, where the wood ribs flying overhead impart the sensation of dining in a whale. Taste could charge much more based on its quality, especially its wines, which is an ultimate compliment. Prices don't differ substantially between lunch and dinner.

$$ Tucked away in a residential neighborhood, south of Livingston Street, you'd never know that the good-value **Bravissimo Wine Bar Café** (337 N. Shine Ave.; ☎ 407/898-7333; www.cafebravissimo.com; Mon–Fri 11am–2pm and 5–10pm, Sat–Sun 5–11pm; AE, DISC, MC, V) was there unless I told you. Its casual servers (often, the owner himself) keep the pressure light, and the wine list is studied. No wonder it has so many regulars. Of 14 pasta varieties ($10–$15), the red ones are topped with a fresh sauce of chunky, juicy tomatoes—not cooked down like many places'—but those dishes are probably outdone by the stuffed chickens and meats ($15–$17). Individual pizzas cost around $10. The laid-back dining area is deco-rated with local art but avoids concealing its past as an industrial space, which lends to the quaint escapism. The tiramisu is enormous and homemade. Sit out on the front patio and watch the well-to-do walk their dogs.

$$–$$$$ For a lively weekend night, head to Church Street Station, a revitalized pedestrian district of red-brick warehouses and gas-lit lamps. Among the buzzing clubs and fine dining, you'll find **Ceviche** ✪✪ (125 W. Church St., Orlando; ☎ 321/ 281-8140; www.cevichetapas.com; Tues–Thurs 11am–midnight, Fri 11am–1am, Sat 5pm–1am; AE, DISC, MC, V), a huge, rococo dining hall that feels for all the world like it was plucked off Las Ramblas in Barcelona and plopped here. The menu, also true to Spain, is piled with more than 100 tapas (small) dishes, most $6 to $10, including out-of-the-ordinary meats (quail, crispy chicken livers, oxtail), predictable ones (chorizo, veal, lamb chops), a heap of vegetable and fish choices (the sautéed spinach with figs is divine, and I loved the escargot wrapped in chicken and sautéed in a tomato sherry sauce), and plenty of Spanish stalwarts like *patatas bravas,* aged cheeses and olives, and, of course, ceviche. Because everything's meant to be shared, the energy is social and vibrant. Things get noisy when the flamenco band starts to clack and strum, so I like to sit on the quieter front patio and watch the cool kids of town strut down Church Street on their big weekend nights out. The flavors are so piquant and garlicky that it's easy to overorder, so designate someone at your table to call a halt if necessary.

$$$ For a refined meal far from theme park hype, there is salvation. Chef Louis Perrotte and his wife Magdalena have been handling the pans at **Le Coq Au Vin** ✪✪✪ (4800 S. Orange Ave., Orlando; ☎ 407/851-6980; www.lecoqauvin restaurant.com; Tues–Sat 5:30–10pm, Sun 5–9pm; AE, DISC, MC, V), their traditionally French and unusually cozy restaurant, for longer than many locals can remember. Diners, many of whom are here celebrating a special occasion, feel more like they're guests in an Old Florida home than paying patrons, but the complicated flavors (a well-marinated coq au vin, $16; Grand Marnier soufflé, $7; duck two ways, $16) leave no doubt they've gotten what they've paid for. A meal here can take ages, so don't be in a hurry. For something quicker but no less meatier, the Blackwater Bar-B-Q joint (p. 84) is next door. Perrotte *et femme* are transitioning into retirement, but the same high standards endure.

WINTER PARK

Winter Park is a little too far to go unless the food is going to be extra special (and there are standard cafes for croissants and brunch to divert you otherwise), but these two places are unique enough to merit a special trip.

$$ According to the Travel Channel, the world's largest wine-tasting selection is available at **the Wine Room on Park Avenue** (270 Park Ave. S., Winter Park; ☎ 407/ 696-9463; www.thewineroomonline.com; Mon–Thurs noon–midnight, Fri–Sat 10– 1:30am, Sun 1pm–9pm; AE, MC, V). It's a spacious hangout, also serving imported meats, cheeses, and beers, with a difference: Advanced Italian-made Enomatic dispensers, loaded with nitrogen instead of flavor-altering oxygen, squirt 150 wines in perfect 1-, 2.5-, or 5-ounce servings. You load a smart card with at least $10 (plus a $3 start-up charge) and then slip it into whichever machine has vino you'd like to try. This method won't save you money off a standard glass of wine—in fact, it's more—but it's fun. The decor, like so much in the wine world, is an imitation of European styles—in this case, a country vault.

$$–$$$$ Although it's more like a restaurant with a bar than a true British-style gastropub as its chef-owner couple says, **the Ravenous Pig** ✪✪✪ (1234 N. Orange

Ave., Winter Park; ☎ 407/628-2333; www.theravenouspig.com; Tues–Sat 11:30am–2:30pm, Tues–Thurs 5:30–9:30pm, Fri–Sat 5:30–11pm; AE, DC, DISC, MC, V), a worthy tribute to the Spotted Pig in New York City, is happily close enough—a beer-friendly, sophisticated evening where the food is gourmet without pretentiousness. The menu changes according to what's in season, but it always aims high with traditional farmhouse meats such as steak frites ($23, served with truffle fries in a pint glass) and some menu perennials like shrimp and grits ($12), homemade pastas (gnocchis are usually $10), gruyere biscuits ($2, and don't miss them), and a knockout pub burger ($12). James and Julie Petrakis know just when to deploy bacon and in what amount, a talent dear to me. Be here on the first Saturday of the month, when a whole animal (often pig) is roasted, but don't ever try without a reservation, because it's the hottest table in town.

DINNERTAINMENT

Besides *American Idol* and *Dancing with the Stars,* there may be no purer form of vaudeville left in America than the Orlando dinner show. Part banquet and part spectacle, most of these guilty pleasures involve stunts, audience participation, and usually, a flimsy excuse to hoist the American flag, even if the plot is set in ancient Mesopotamia. Most of them are mounted in arenas lined with bench seating and long tables, and while the show grinds on, waiters scurry around, distributing plates of banquet food the way Las Vegas dealers deal blackjack cards. These shows are immoderate and tacky to the extreme, but they're an intrinsic part of the Orlando scene. Nowhere else on Earth—at least not since Caligula's Rome—will you find so many stadiums in which to stuff your face while fleets of horses, swordsmen, and crooners labor to amuse you. I wouldn't classify dinnertainments as top values, but they certainly represent the essence of the tourist's Orlando.

During most times of the year, most of these shows kick off daily around 6 or 7pm, but during peak season, there may be two shows scheduled to fall around 6 and 8:30pm. Upon arrival, crowds are corralled into a preshow area where they can buy cocktails and souvenirs, and endure hokey comedy and magic routines—feel free to be slightly tardy, and feel free not to buy anything, as drinks come with dinner. Most shows will be mopping up by around 9:30pm, so schedule a visit on a night when you don't intend to catch theme park fireworks or other evening shows. Most of them also serve kids' standards (chicken fingers, hot dogs, and so on) for picky children. Soft drinks, draft beer, and wine (the cheap stuff, watered down) are unlimited. Bring a sweater if you're sensitive to air-conditioning, and bring enough cash to tip your server because gratuities aren't included. You may feel offended about how many times you'll be reminded to tip your server, especially considering that they'll be spending most of your meal legging it to the distant kitchen and not serving you, but keep in mind that many of Orlando's visitors come from countries where gratuities aren't traditional.

For more educational experiences, check out the chances to converse with Disney Imagineers (p. 248) or NASA astronauts (p. 253) over catered meals.

Money-saving tip: The free coupon books and discount ticket suppliers should be your go-to for cheap prices on dinner shows. There are so many deals floating around for the banquets held off theme park property that only a stooge pays full price. The ones thrown by the theme parks, though, generally don't discount. In fact, they tend to sell out, so book those as far ahead as you sensibly can.

IN ORLANDO

People who love horses choose **Arabian Nights** ✪ (3081 Arabian Nights Blvd., Kissimmee; ☎ 800/553-6116 or 407/239-9223; $57 adults, $31 kids 3–11; www. arabian-nights.com; AE, DISC, MC, V), and its 15 breeds are both beautiful and well trained. The show itself, about a princess who enlists a genie's help to reclaim her kingdom, is preposterously dimwitted and somewhat talky, but to be fair, the wish-fulfillment plot is just a ruse for introducing the 20-odd old-fashioned horse acts, including bareback riding, dancing Arabians, and blood-pumping chariot races. Expect lots of dry ice, sequins, and execrable food. Another $11 will buy you a seat in the first three rows, a souvenir program, and a "VIP" preshow walk past 18 backstage stables, and although you won't be allowed to pet the stars, kids can sit atop a 1-ton horse; the privilege means you'll miss some of the (silly) preshow entertainment of belly dancers and acrobats. A special holiday show, accompanied by pop music, runs from mid-November to New Year's Day. You'd be crazy to pay full price (a rip-off) because most ticket discounters (try Maple Leaf tickets at www.mapleleaftickets.com) sell for less ($29/$25).

The recent (and weird) popularity of Captain Jack Sparrow among young boys has given **Pirate's Dinner Adventure** (6400 Carrier Dr., Orlando; ☎ 800/866-2469 or 407/248-0590; $58 adult, $38 kids 3–11, Sun show-only [no food] $30 1 adult and 1 child; www.piratesdinneradventure.com; AE, DISC, MC, V) new heft in the local market—and it even allowed the producers to mount a second production near California's Disneyland in 2005. Set on an 18th-century galleon with a 40-foot-high mast that's amid a 300,000-gallon lagoon—the arena is probably the most spectacular of all the Orlando dinnertainments'—Pirate's is a circus of rapier duels, rope swinging (a lot of it), and arrrghing. Although the show provides lots of opportunity for participation (each of six sections roots for its assigned buccaneer), it treats female characters like livestock—at one point, the villain, Captain Sebastian the Black, even batters Princess Anita to the ground, which I could do without—and that may account for why its most devoted demographic appears to be 12-year-old boys there for their birthday parties. Production values are fairly high. Buying online yields discounts of $10 for adults and $5 for kids, and many of the free brochures dispensed around town are good for lesser discounts. From Thanksgiving to a week after New Year's Day, the show adopts a Christmas theme, complete with (I'm not making this up) a nativity scene.

Although it's long-running and popular with coach tours, the jousting-themed **Medieval Times** (4510 Irlo Bronson Hwy., Kissimmee; ☎ 888/935-6878 or 407/396-2105; $59 adult, $38 kids 12 and under; www.medievaltimes.com; AE, DISC, MC, V), at which your waitress is called a "wench," is also an attraction in eight other North American cities, which qualifies it as the McDonald's of dinnertainment. Like there, you eat with your hands. For $10 more ($8 online), the Royalty Package gets you front-row seating, a free program, and a souvenir DVD. Its "castle" is located a few miles east of Disney on U.S. 192, in a downtrodden area of Kissimmee. It's also almost always discounted by brochures.

I admit that when I first approached **Sleuth's Mystery Dinner Show** ✪✪✪ (8267 International Dr., Orlando; ☎ 800/393-1985 or 407/363-1985; www. sleuths.com; $50 adult, $24 kids 3–11; AE, DISC, MC, V), I was dreading a poorly acted, cheap, tourist-trap knockoff. I confess that I misjudged it, and it's now my favorite dinnertainment in town. After mingling with a few zany characters and then watching their show, which takes about an hour and contains at least one murder, dinner guests are invited to confer with the other people at their table, grill the three or four suspects, and, if they feel confident, accuse a killer. There are 14 spectacle-free, low-budget shows which change nightly, so you can attend several times without duplicating your experience, and the actors are not only typically skilled at improvisation (though perhaps not so much at English accents), but also at engaging audience members without making them overly uncomfortable. They seem to be having fun, and they'll even tone down the grown-up jokes if they see young children in the crowd, although the shows are clearly more suited to adults. As for audiences, they appear to be grateful for a rare chance to employ their brains in this town. The food is noticeably better than that of its rivals (though hardly gourmet), possibly because instead of catering to hundreds, the management only has to cook for a few dozen. Beer and wine are included, too. Have a snack before you arrive, because dinner isn't served until after the murder. Lots of brochures discount rates, and a $5 coupon is on its website.

The Outta Control Magic Show (WonderWorks, 9067 International Dr., Orlando; ☎ 407/351-8800; $25 adults, $17 kids 4–12 and seniors; www.wonderworks online.com; AE, DISC, MC, V) is more downscale and easygoing than the others—the target market is kids, who may enjoy combining a meal here with a visit to the so-so WonderWorks science-cum–video playground (p. 228), where the show is held. It's for parents who don't want to deal with overproduced glitz. Unlimited pizza, salad, beer, wine, and soda are served while buddy-buddy magicians engage in family-friendly jokes and improv. There are two shows nightly (6 and 8pm), and its website posts discount coupons for up to $3 off.

Capone's Dinner & Show (4740 W. Irlo Bronson Hwy., Kissimmee; ☎ 800/220-8428 or 407/397-2378; $25 adults, $15 kids 4–12; www.alcapones.com; AE, DISC, MC, V) is a lesser presentation, with lots of *The Hills*–generation girls pretending to be 1920s flappers and warbling to recorded music. Dinner's a godawful buffet of lasagna, spaghetti with meatballs, and a few token non-European dishes such as honey roasted ham and baked chicken. This troupe's own brochures and website promise "½ off" discounts, which grant the price I list, but I've never seen the so-called full price quoted, let alone charged.

AT THE THEME PARKS

These shows take the same credit cards their parent parks do, which is to say every major card available.

Don't wait until the last minute to book the 2-hour **Hoop-Dee-Doo Musical Revue** ★ (Pioneer Hall at Fort Wilderness Resort; ☎ 407/939-3463; www.disney world.com; $51–$60 adults, $26–$31 kids 3–9), not necessarily because it's the best, but because it's Disney's most kid-friendly dinnertainment, which makes it crazy popular. It books 6 months out. Six-performer shows put on a hectic and helter-skelter music-hall carnival of olios and gags, which elementary-school age children usually find riveting, and much quarter is given to recognizing birthdays and special events. The headlining menu item is ribs served in pails—enough said? I prefer seats in the balcony, overlooking the stage (the cheapest, anyway). One benefit of the Hoop-Dee-Doo is it's a 15-minute boat ride from the Magic Kingdom, and outside of winter, the early seating gets you out in time to catch the fireworks (make sure to double-check when you book; even Disney's restaurant reservationists have access to the daily park schedule).

Mickey's Backyard BBQ (the Outdoor Pavilion at Fort Wilderness Resort; ☎ 407/939-3463; $45 adults, $27 kids 3–9; www.disneyworld.com; Thurs and Sat Mar–Dec) suits very young children, as it's patronized by rope tricksters and taxi-dancing costumed characters wearing Western-style gear. More informal than the Hoop-Dee-Doo in that it takes place under an open-air pavilion (come dressed for humidity), the event serves passable buffet-style food, but the toddler factor makes it chaotic, so you might be less disappointed if you see this as a photo op with Mickey and not as the proper show Disney bills it as.

The only dinner show to ask customers to pay based on their proximity to the stage, **Disney's Spirit of Aloha Show** (Disney's Polynesian Resort; ☎ 407/939-3463; www.disneyworld.com; $53–$62 adults, $27–$32 kids 3–9) is a chicken-and-ribs luau presided over by fire twirlers, hula dancers, and the like. It's been going for years, but was recently retroactively themed to the company's Lilo and Stitch franchise. Bookings begin 6 months ahead, and usually the last people to reserve are shunted to the rear tables, which can feel like they're actually as distant as the Cook Islands, although they're the least expensive. I find this evening boring and drastically overpriced compared to the thundering cavalcades of stuntmen you can get for the same money outside Disney property, but some people love it (although most of them cite its food—pineapple-coconut bread and a chocolate volcano dessert being at the top of their lists). It's on the monorail line from the Magic Kingdom, which means it's easy to catch the fireworks after early shows.

Makahiki Luau (SeaWorld Orlando; ☎ 800/327-2424; www.seaworldorlando.com; $46 adults, $29 kids 3–9) is a festive rival to Disney's Polynesian do. The night also serves family-style platters of mahimahi in piña colada sauce, spare ribs, and stir-fried rice, finished with lava cake with peanut butter drizzle. Entertainment is of the general Southern Pacific variety—nothing too corny or scripted—distinguished by thundering drums and flame jugglers. Although the 2-hour show takes place within SeaWorld, at a restaurant overlooking the lagoon, you won't need to buy a ticket to the park. During peak season, there are two shows a night.

Universal's 2-hour luau, **Wantilan Luau** ✦ (Royal Pacific Resort; ☎ 407/503-3463; $52 adults, $29 kids 3–9; Tues and Sat plus Fri May–Aug, 6pm), is held in a covered pavilion. It, too, has fire dancers and hula girls aplenty, but it trumps the rest for authenticity: Food includes pit-roasted suckling pig, whole roasted wahoo, and guava barbecue short ribs; mai tais are included in the price. Should kids be grossed out by carving meat off the pig, there's a tamer children's menu. The show is more culturally sensitive than Disney's, too, as it's attentive to the differences between the various Pacific islanders it represents. You can walk from both Universal parks.

Twice on Sundays, at 10:30am and 1pm, the House of Blues at Downtown Disney West Side holds its **Gospel Brunch** (1490 E. Buena Vista Dr., Lake Buena Vista; ☎ 407/934-2583; www.hob.com; $36 adults, $20 kids 3–9). There is no plot, but the live music is jumping and the cuisine combines Southern and breakfast foods. Tickets are about $2 cheaper if you buy them there, but you run the risk of sellouts (the morning one fills first). Still, because so many House of Blues branches throw these, I can't say there's anything original about this one.

CHARACTER MEALS

Appealing mostly to families with young children (although I admit to having done them with other grown-ups and enjoying myself), a character meal is an all-you-can-eat meal, usually buffet, that guarantees an appearance by classic characters in costume. The most popular meal is breakfast—I suggest porking out and skipping lunch, as that will maximize your time in the parks. Always, *always book ahead* (Disney: ☎ 407/939-3463; SeaWorld: ☎ 888/800-5447; Universal Orlando: ☎ 407/224-4012; all events AE, DC, DISC, MC, V)—even as soon as you know your vacation dates. I am not big on character meals for lunch or dinner, because doing so will cut into expensive park time, but the option is popular.

Each meal is themed to its location; at the Cape May Café, the characters wear beach outfits, and at Chef Mickey's, they emerge in chef's aprons, sign autographs, and do a little towel-twirling dance. (Reading that, it sounds a little like a Chippendales show, not a Chip and Dale show, but rest assured it's all preschool-friendly.) The characters won't actually be eating with you, but they'll circulate, working the room the way a good host does. This, as kids and grown-ups binge on a smorgasbord that would give Richard Simmons apoplexy—including Mickey-shaped waffles topped with M&Ms and all. Mind the early-morning sugar crash.

Breakfast begins as early as 8am, depending on the location, and usually wraps up by 11:30am. Lunch generally runs 11:30am to 3pm, and the few dinners that are available begin around 4pm and end around 8:30pm. SeaWorld shifts its Dine with Shamu tankside-dining timing from week to week, and you may find its only "dinner" appointments are available at 4:15pm. Often, tip is included.

The privilege of dining with characters isn't cheap—around $23 for adults and $13 kids 3 to 9 for breakfast, up to around $30 adults and $15 kids at dinner. Prices vary from locale to locale, but usually only by a buck or two (the Beach Club is $19, for example), barely enough to warrant trekking farther than you normally would. When a breakfast is held inside a theme park outside of its regular hours, you'll still have to proffer an admission ticket. However, for breakfast, your name will be on a VIP list and you'll be admitted through the gates early (a perk that gives children and Disney fans a goose). Try to book the earliest seating available so that by the time you're done, you'll be among the first in line for the rides; you'll also have first crack at the stroller rentals.

The most popular location is Cinderella's Royal Table, inside Magic Kingdom's Cinderella Castle—there are some intense parents out there with freakishly fast speed-dial fingers, because that place always sells out 180 days early, despite the fact it costs some $15 more than a similar character meal elsewhere. Pray you don't stray in front of *their* strollers. I prefer Chef Mickey's, which is a one-stop monorail ride away from the Magic Kingdom, and the Tusker House, a good start for the early day at Animal Kingdom. Less prestigious addresses, such as the buffet breakfast at the Beach Club near Epcot, can be smart choices, particularly because they tend not to be as crowded and you're likely to have lots more one-on-one time with the stars. Three hotels on Hotel Plaza Boulevard also host character breakfasts for about $6 less, albeit with fewer characters and pomp and in a boring old hotel restaurant: the Regal Sun on Tuesdays, Thursdays, and Saturdays, and the Hilton and the Buena Vista Palace on Sundays.

Theme Park Character Meals

Park Location	Meal Name/Restaurant	The Stars	Meal Served
The Magic Kingdom*	Once Upon a Breakfast at Cinderella's Royal Table	The Princesses, Mary Poppins, Peter Pan (Fairy Godmother)	Breakfast, Lunch, Dinner
The Magic Kingdom*	Crystal Palace	Winnie the Pooh, Tigger, Eeyore, Piglet	All three meals
Epcot*	Chip and Dale's Harvest Feast, the Garden Grill (the Land)	Mickey, Goofy, Pluto, Chip and Dale	Dinner
Epcot*	Princess Storybook Dining, Akershus Royal Banquet Hall (Norway)	The Princesses	All three meals
Hollywood Studios*	Playhouse Disney's Play 'N Dine, Hollywood & Vine	JoJo, Goliath, the Little Einsteins	Breakfast and lunch
Animal Kingdom*	Donald's Safari Breakfast, Tusker House	Mickey, Donald, Daisy, Goofy	Breakfast
Contemporary Resort	Chef Mickey's	Mickey, Goofy, Donald Duck, Pluto	Breakfast and dinner
Beach Club Resort, Cape May Café	Beach Club Buffet	Minnie, Donald, Goofy	Breakfast
Grand Floridian Resort and Spa	Supercalifragilistic Breakfast, 1900 Park Fare	Alice in Wonderland, Mad Hatter, Mary Poppins	Breakfast
Grand Floridian Resort and Spa	1900 Park Fare	Alice in Wonderland, Mad Hatter	1pm tea party (kids only)
Grand Floridian Resort and Spa	Cinderella's Gala Feast, 1900 Park Fare	Cinderella and family, Fairy Godmother	Dinner
Polynesian Resort	'Ohana Character Breakfast	Mickey, Goofy, Stitch	Breakfast
Walt Disney World Swan	Garden Grove Cafe	Goofy, Pluto	Breakfast (Sat only)
Walt Disney World Swan	Gulliver's Grill	Goofy and Pluto (not Mon or Fri); Rafiki and Timon (Mon and Fri)	Dinner
SeaWorld Orlando*	Dine with Shamu, Shamu Stadium	A killer whale or two; their trainers	All three meals
SeaWorld Orlando*	Breakfast with Elmo and Friends, Seafire Inn	Elmo, Big Bird, Cookie Monster, Zoe, Ernie, Grover	Breakfast
Islands of Adventure*	Confisco Grill	the Simpsons	Breakfast

Theme park admission required.

If your kid is fixated on a specific character, ask which ones are bound to appear—although a good six or eight of the well-known headliners make appearances, there's no guarantee that the same ones will be there each day. Disney won't be pinned down on details, but each location seems to specialize in a different group. When a particular name is reported regularly at a given restaurant, I let you know in the chart on the preceding page (unless a character is singled out in the meal's title, in which case it's a given).

5

Walt Disney World

The whole World, in your hands

ON NOVEMBER 22, 1963, AROUND THE TIME PRESIDENT KENNEDY WAS embarking on his public motorcade in Dallas, Walt Disney was in a private jet, conducting his first flyover of some ignored Florida swampland. By the end of the day, as Disney decided this was the place he wanted to shape in the image of his dreams, America had changed in more ways than one.

While the country reeled, Disney snapped up land through dummy companies. His cover was blown in 1965, but the fix was in: His company had mopped up an area twice the size of Manhattan, 27,443 acres, from just $180 an acre. Disneyland East was coming. Today, it's the single-most popular vacation destination on the planet, attracting some 40 million tourists a year.

It's no accident that Walt enjoyed his peaks during two periods of profound malaise: the Great Depression and the Cold War. It's also no coincidence that his theme parks flowered while America was riven with self-doubt—the Korean and Vietnam conflicts, the death of Kennedy, and Watergate. His parks are, by design, comforting. They tell you how to feel and where to go, and in reinforcing your simplest impressions of history and the world, they never make you feel stupid. Ironically, what made such reassuring rhetoric work was a relentless drive for technological innovation and revolutionary civil engineering.

Why should it be so difficult to find straight talk about such an immensely popular place? There are plenty of guidebooks that propagate a dewy-eyed celebration of all things Disney, that read like advertisements and treat the resort as a sanctified, nigh-holy thing that must be feted at all costs. This is not one of them. I adore Walt Disney World, I marvel at its awesome achievements, and I have been coming since the ribbon was cut. Its childhood is inextricable from my own. Disney fans rhapsodize about the "magic"—that intangible *frisson* you feel when you're there—but I think a case could be made that the energy doesn't come from the place as much as it comes from the customers. Where else in your life will you be surrounded by people so elated to be there? Weddings? Graduations? Walt Disney World's magic comes from the accumulated goodwill of thousands of strangers, united in gratitude and togetherness. If you don't believe me, sit on a bench for a while in Fantasyland and watch the children pass by.

If the resort is to be appreciated as the precious American treasure it is, we must acknowledge its aggressive marketing (some 75% of visitors are return customers) and its canny stagecraft. Walt Disney World, transporting as it is, is a real place, made possible by real sweat. It has a history. It is a product.

TICKETING

This will be the biggest expense of your trip, so give it some thought before opening your wallet. All Disney tickets (excepting annual passes) are purchased by the

Magic *Their* Way

Historically, visitors to Orlando would spend the first 3 or 4 days of their weeklong vacations at the Disney parks, and by the fourth or fifth days, they would include Universal Orlando, SeaWorld, or the Kennedy Space Center. In 2005, though, the resort began using Magic Your Way, an insidious pricing plan that appears, on the surface, to present the biggest savings for people who stay on Disney turf for more than 4 days. Not so coincidentally, 4 days is the perfect length of time to see the four main Disney parks, so the resort is thrilled to see customers take the bait and stay longer than that. The false economy of Magic Your Way entices families to stay on Disney property longer than necessary, spending lots of money on higher food and hotel prices. The damage it's doing to the vitality of the city's secondary attractions is yet to be determined.

day. You decide how many days you want to spend at the parks (all parks cost the same), and once you nail that down, you decide which extras you want to pay more for. Both decisions will be fraught with temptation.

When it comes to Disney tickets, everything depends on how many days you intend to play at the parks. Even the price of your admission to the ancillary amusements, such as DisneyQuest or the water slides, is pegged to that decision. As on an old-fashioned Chinese food menu, you add on the extras that you want. **Here are the important components** with my thoughts on whether or not you'll need them:

1. **Base ticket.** You must buy this. This is your theme park admission. With it, you are entitled to visit one park per day, with no switching on the same day. When it's all new to you, one park per day is more than plenty, believe me.

2. **Park Hopper.** Should you wish to have the privilege of jumping from park to park on the same day, you must add the Park Hopper option to your ticket. If you do the early-morning safari at Animal Kingdom, take a nap at your hotel, and then switch to the Magic Kingdom for the fireworks, that's park hopping. As the following chart shows, this flexibility costs a flat $50, no matter how many days you intend to stay at the resort. I insist on this option because I know Disney well and I know what I like to see and what I like to skip. *Note: You may not need it.*

3. **Water Park Fun & More (WPF&M).** From here on out, willpower is crucial to saving money on Magic Your Way. Should you have definite plans to visit a Disney water slide park, DisneyQuest, or see an event at the Wide World of Sports, then the Water Park Fun & More (WPF&M) option includes a set number of admissions. That add-on is $50 no matter how long you stay. WPF&M is the trickiest add-on. Too many people overestimate the amount of time and energy they are going to have, buy this option, and fail to use it. Think carefully about your own plans, and be realistic. During the

course of 3 days of theme park going, and after miles of walking, are you *really* going to have enough juice for the water slides? Or are there other things to do in Orlando that you'd like to try (for example, the non-Disney water parks of Aquatica and Wet 'n Wild)? Remember, too, that you will always be allowed to buy separate admission to any attractions included in WPF&M; if you're realistically only going to visit Typhoon Lagoon once and that's all, the $40 adult walk-up ticket is cheaper than the $50 add-on. Besides, one element of the WPF&M option, Wide World of Sports, is often dormant, so buying admission based on that will, more often than not, be a waste.

Don't overlook this pricing loophole that works in Disney's favor: If you plan to go to a water park, your visit there will likely take the whole day (or most of your energy)—and on that day, you probably won't be setting foot in a theme park, even though you'll have paid for the privilege on your base ticket. Even if you do visit a theme park late in the day, you won't be getting your full admission ticket's worth. So for each day you plan to spend at a Disney water park, you might find that for a base ticket with standard expiration, it's smarter to purchase 1 less day. Then attend the water park either before your first use of your base ticket, or after it's all used up; otherwise, you'll end up essentially paying twice for the same day.

4. **The No Expiration option** is just like it sounds, and using it is like hedging on future price increases. If you select it, your ticket can be used as long as there are days left on it; if you don't buy this option, unused days are dead after 14 days of your ticket's first use. Disney hikes prices each summer 5% to 6% like clockwork, but you can lock in today's prices for a few extra bucks. Assuming you bought 10 days of tickets, the maximum, you'd spend $437 for an adult no-expiration pass, which equals $43.70 per day ($48.70 with Park Hopper)—a savings *only* if you ever come back later in your life. That's the best-case scenario. Also, some people find that paying extra for No Expiration frees them to explore the rest of Orlando without guilt because they know they can use their outstanding days another time. Does this sound like you? (It sounds like me.) If you don't return, it's wasted cash.

Finally, very slight **discounts** on Magic Your Way are available. If you buy your tickets in advance (online or at a Disney Store), save the shipping fee by arranging to pick them up at the gates of one of the parks (long lines) or at Guest Relations in Downtown Disney Marketplace (short line). **Florida residents** are sometimes offered entirely different discounts (www.disneyworld.com/flresidents), as are **AAA members;** if you're one, call ☎ 407/824-4321 for the latest promotion. (See "Other Ticket 'Discounts' & Deals," later, for more on potential discounts.)

During some times of year, the park mounts special evening events, such as the ones around Halloween and Christmas (see "Orlando's Visit-Worthy Events" p. 307), that require a separate, expensive ticket. You will get less value out of your Magic Your Way ticket if you attend during the day before one of these parties. They start around 7pm, and if you haven't paid, you'll be rounded up and sent out. However, if you do attend one, you can show up as early as 4pm and get a few extra hours in.

Disney Ticket Options*

Days of Use	Base Ticket Age 10 & up	Age 3–9	Add Water Park Fun & More	Add No Expiration	Add Park Hopper
1	$75	$63	$50 (2 visits)	N/A	$50
2	$149	$125	$50 (2 visits)	$17	$50
3	$212	$179	$50 (3 visits)	$23	$50
4	$219	$184	$50 (4 visits)	$50	$50
5	$222	$187	$50 (5 visits)	$70	$50
6	$225	$190	$50 (6 visits)	$80	$50
7	$228	$193	$50 (7 visits)	$110	$50
8	$231	$196	$50 (8 visits)	$145	$50
9	$234	$199	$50 (9 visits)	$170	$50
10	$237	$202	$50 (10 visits)	$200	$50

Prices don't include sales tax of 6.5%. Prices accurate as of October 1, 2008, and will change in September 2009.

PERIL OF PACKAGES

There's another way that Disney tricks you into overpurchasing. Anytime you call the company and ask for reservations, operators will suggest adding perks. You'll ask for tickets, and they'll suggest they throw in, say, the meal plan (more about that in a minute). The instant you accept, you're purchasing a "package," and that will often force you to pay more than you would have a la carte. Always, *always* know what everything would cost separately before agreeing to a Disney-suggested package—the company spends millions advertising that a family vacation there costs $1,600 a week, but in fact, if you don't accept Disney suggestions and use other advice in this book, you can take a trip for much less. If you must, hang up the phone and do some math before deciding to accept or reject the offer. That's the only way to ensure you're not paying more.

Tip: Here's a hidden loophole likely to cheat you: Disney "length of stay" ticket packages will begin the moment you arrive on the property and end the day you leave. Now, think about that. If you've just flown from a distant place, you are unlikely to rush to the Magic Kingdom on the same day. Likewise, on the day you're due at the airport to fly home, you're probably not going to be able to visit a theme park. Yet Disney will schedule your package that way. In effect, you will lose 2 days that you've paid for—at the start and at the finish of your vacation, when you'll be resting or packing. Disney will do everything it can to sell you theme park tickets for every day that you're on its property, regardless of if you plan to use several of those days to do other things in Orlando such as Universal or exploring downtown. How can you avoid this? You could spend the first and last nights of your vacation at a non-Disney hotel and move on-site for your ticket

Contacting Walt Disney World

Walt Disney World, tellingly, offers no toll-free numbers, so earmark some cash for your long-distance bill or use your cellphone calling plan:

General information: ☎ 407/939-4636; www.disneyworld.com

Vacation packages: ☎ 407/934-7639

Operating hours: ☎ 407/824-4321

Reservations for restaurants, character meals (starting 90 days ahead): ☎ 407/939-3463

Questions about day-to-day resort operations: ☎ 407/824-2222

Weather updates: ☎ 407/824-4104

Lost and found: ☎ 407/824-4245

days. More simply, insist on making one reservation per phone call. Arrange your tickets. Hang up. Call back and arrange your hotel as "room only," without linking your two reservations. *Disney packages usually don't save you money.*

Disney's reservationists are friendly but they're sales machines, and they are trained to answer only the questions that you pose. They will not volunteer much money-saving information. If you're not sure about the terms of what you're about to purchase, corner them and ask when your first day of tickets will take effect. The answer should be, "Whenever you choose to begin using them," and *not* "On the day you arrive at the resort." And *always* ask if there is a less expensive option. They won't lie and tell you there isn't, but they *will* neglect to volunteer the information. Again, do not be afraid to get off the phone to mull over the price of their suggestions. **TheMouseForLess.com, MouseSavers.com,** and the messages at **DISBoards.com** will let you know about current deals that Disney won't. With the economy stumbling along, the company frequently rolls out bargains that might get you free days of park admission or a free meal plan, so be sure to dig around on those sites and see what discounts and freebies you can find.

OTHER TICKET "DISCOUNTS" & DEALS

A few companies can shave a few paltry bucks off multiday tickets; see "Getting Attraction Discounts" in chapter 12, "The Essentials of Planning," for those. European visitors are eligible, through **www.disneyworld.co.uk**, for two more ticket types: the Premium, which comes with a few WPF&M admissions, and the Ultimate, good for longer stays and unlimited WPF&M admissions. At recent exchange rates, it may be cheaper to buy American-issued tickets with Park Hopper options at the gate; do the math.

Really big Disney fans carry a Chase Disney Rewards Visa credit card (☎ 888/215-3049; www.chase.com/disney), which allows cardholders to accumulate points that can be redeemed as tickets, packages, food, and souvenirs. The card also grants small discounts at certain Disney Stores. But if you're such a big fan

---

What the Basics Cost at the Four Disney Parks

Parking: $12 (waived for guests of Disney hotels)

Lockers: $7 per day (multi-entry)

Regular soda: $2.50 / **Small water:** $2 / **Cup of beer:** $5.25

ECV (electric convenience vehicle): $45 per day

Single strollers: $15 per day *

Double strollers: $31 per day *

Wheelchair: $10 per day *

* Subject to discounts of $2–$4 if you rent for the length of your stay.

---

that you're willing to commit year-round to racking up points that can only be used on Mousy things, you probably already knew about this.

EATING ON-SITE

In recent years, Disney food became noticeably more sweet, and opportunities to buy candy multiplied. Theme parks thrive on the money generated by excited, sugared-up children and parents who are too worn out to say "no" to such things as $6 hot dogs and $3 Cokes. At least the budget algebra is easy. The **cheapest combo meals** are always from counter-service restaurants (called Quick Service in Disney-speak), and adults pay $7 to $10, before a drink, no matter the time of day. Kids' meals (a main dish; milk, juice, water, or soda; and a choice of two items including grapes, carrot sticks, applesauce, a cookie, or fries) always cost around $4.50 at Quick Service locations. If you want to sit down for full service—character meals are always in sit-down restaurants—adults pay in the mid-teens for a lunch entree and usually over $20 a plate a dinner, before gratuity or drinks, and kids' meals are about half as much.

Oversubscription to the Dining Plan has ruined the meal experience for casual park-goers. No longer is it easy to simply stroll into any restaurant that catches your eye and enjoy a meal. For sit-down food, *always* make reservations (☎ 407/ 939-3463) or you are likely to be turned away. It's that simple, and that sad.

Semihealthy options are possible on the lowest food budget: Disney limits saturated fat and added sugar to 10% of a counter-service dish's calories; no more than 30% of a meal's calories or 35% of a snack's calories come from fat; and juice drinks have no added sugar. Trans fats are out. One way Disney seems to have accomplished this is by reducing serving sizes—you won't feel stuffed. Kids' meals come with carrots, applesauce, or grapes instead of fries, and with low-fat milk, water, or 100% fruit juice instead of soda. (The fries and Coke are still available by request—Disney knows kids are still on vacation and deserve a treat.)

The house soda brand is Coca-Cola (sorry, no Pepsi), and the house water is Dasani, which is treated tap water. Do what I do: Buy or bring one bottle and refill it from the many water fountains. You'll find Orlando's municipal water has a specific mineral-like flavor and smell—the result of being drawn from aquifers.

Saving on Mickey Munchies

If you plan to buy all your food at the park, sticking strictly to counter-service meals is the cheapest way to go. But considering you'll pay $7 to $9 each for a counter-service sandwich, plus at least $2 for a medium-size soft drink—the going rate in all the Orlando parks—even that way, a family of four can easily spend $50 on every meal! Don't be goofy—save money! Besides eating off premises, here's how:

- **Pack a little food of your own.** Park security usually looks the other way if you bring a soft lunchbag-size cooler (Igloos will be rejected). Or just tote sandwiches in plastic bags. If your lodging has a freezer, put juice boxes in there; they'll be thawed by lunch.
- **Economize with an all-you-can-eat meal.** Character meals (p. 96) give good value because they serve limitless food. A big lunch can last you until after you leave the park.
- **Skip sit-down meals, or plan them strategically.** Sit-down meals can chomp as much as 90 minutes out of your touring time. Do that twice and you've lost a third of your day. A park that could be seen in 1 day would require 2, doubling costs. If you want a sit-down meal, do it at lunch, when prices are 20% lower than at dinner. Eat around 11am, when crowds are lighter and you lose less time.
- **Subtract unwanted combo items.** Although counter-service restaurants only display combos, it's an unpublicized fact that you may eliminate unwanted items from adult selections and save money. Dropping fries can save you nearly $2—just because they're in a combo meal doesn't mean they're discounted.
- **Snack on fruit.** Each park has at least one fruit stand.
- **Seek out the turkey legs.** They're giant (1½ pounds, from 45-pound turkeys) and cost around $6, which is why 1.5 million of them are sold resortwide annually. They taste so good because they're injected with brine before cooking for 6 hours. Just don't think about the hormones it takes to grow a 45-pound bird. Or a 5-foot-tall mouse.
- **Order drinks without ice.** They're served cold anyway, and it's chilling how much of a Disney Coke consists of ice.
- **Stretch meals.** Order a double cheeseburger and an extra bun for 85¢ more. Then make two separate burgers. This works especially well where there's a toppings bar (such as Pecos Bill and Cosmic Ray's at the Magic Kingdom and at the U.S. pavilion at Epcot).

It will *always* be cheaper to quickly **drive off property** to feed your family, but particularly at the Magic Kingdom—where egress requires at least two modes of transportation—that's not always possible or desirable. See more money-saving tips for food in the "Saving on Mickey Munchies" box later, and also consult the list of restaurants located outside the theme park gates, which starts on p. 67.

The Disney Look & Hidden Mickeys

Although Walt himself had a moustache for most of his adult life, he forbade such a sartorial choice among his employees. Instead, he insisted on clean-cut, all-American (whatever that means) **grooming guidelines** appropriate for *The Mickey Mouse Club*. Typical strictures: No hair below the collar for men, no hoop earrings larger than a dime for women, and no shaved heads. Rules relaxed with time—you may even see some neat cornrows, and in Disneyland Paris, I've even seen lip rings—but the Disney look is still decidedly right of the mainstream. Where else do women still wear hosiery? No cast member may be seen smoking, despite the fact Walt himself was rarely seen without a filterless Camel in his hand.

Meanwhile, even props have a language of their own at Disney. A favorite pastime of longtime fans, like safaris were for Hemingway, is spotting **Hidden Mickeys,** which are camouflaged mouse-ear patterns. You'll find the three circles signifying a Mickey profile embedded everywhere: In an arrangement of cannonballs at Pirates of the Caribbean; flatware in the dining room at the Haunted Mansion, cookies on a plate in the bedroom of Peter Pan's Flight; and woven into carpeting, printed on wallpaper, and snuck into the souvenir photo on Test Track using hoses. Many sightings are up to interpretation, but to get you started, check out **HiddenMickeysGuide.com.**

DISNEY DINING PLAN

If you book at a Disney hotel, you will be offered the credit-based **Disney Dining Plan.** Lots of people cave and buy it, but I don't like it. Here's why:

- You must buy the plan for every day you're staying at the hotel. You can't buy fewer days. There goes your chance to eat anything other than mass-produced resort meals. And everyone in your group must be on it.
- The standard plan ($40 adult, $11 kids, per day) buys you the equivalent of one sit-down meal, a quick-service meal, and a snack. This isn't how most people enjoy the resort: We may go to a sit-down restaurant once or twice, but few of us would go daily. Yet the plan has you doing just that.
- The forced use of sit-down restaurants means that reservations are clogged months ahead of time. You'll have to do hours of advance planning, which is a huge opportunity cost.
- The plan doesn't include appetizers or tips, and don't forget it also leaves out that third daily meal that you'll have to pay for.
- Simple math proves that if you stick to counter-service meals, you'll spend about $24 verses $38 (before tips) for the same period using the plan. There may be a *borderline* savings if you use your credits for more than one character breakfast—and it's not worth the plan's rigidity.
- You're bound to leave with some unused credits, resulting in a loss.

✦ The cheapest plan, Quick Service, costs $30 adults, $9 kids, and includes two counter meals and two snacks. Most adult quick-service meals cost $11 or $12 each. As you can see, any savings is negligible. But having spent the money, you'll feel welded to Disney property.

NAVIGATING THE PARKS

In summer and during other holidays, it's wise to get to the front gates of the park about 30 minutes ahead of opening. Mostly, though, you can waltz right up. Try not to leave any park as it closes, when crowds surge. Instead, depart early or linger awhile in the shops, which will be open a bit longer than everything else.

PARKING   Each park has its own parking lot ($12; free for Disney hotel guests and annual passholders). As you drive in, attendants will direct you to fill the next available spot. This is probably the most dangerous part of your day, as the people around you will be distracted and you're at risk of hitting an excited child or knocking off an open car door—take it slow. Parking lanes are numbered and given names; at the very least, remember your number. Don't stress out if your row is a high number; at Epcot, for example, the front row is 27. If you forget where you parked, tell a staffer what time you arrived; they track which sections are being filled minute by minute. You'll board one of the noisy trams (fold strollers during the wait), which haul you to the ticketing area. At the Magic Kingdom, you still must take either the monorail or a ferryboat to the front gates, but at the other parks, the tram lets you off right at the doorstep.

TURNSTILES   You'll always pass through the right-hand set of turnstiles, both entering and exiting. To validate your ticket, you must place a finger on a clear plate. That finger will then be scanned and its image "married" to your ticket, so that you can't share it with anyone else. Disney swears your personal information is eventually expunged from the system, but what it doesn't publicize is that if you do not wish to be scanned, you may use standard identification instead.

MAPS   Once you get inside the gates at all the parks, be sure to grab two free things that are kept in conspicuous racks: a *Guidemap* and a *Times Guide* listing the day's schedule. If you forget, you can pick both up at any shop or at the park's tip board. Also, cast members carry schedules (it's called the "Tell-A-Cast"). The estimated wait time for any attraction is posted where its line begins; this number is accurate, although Disney claims it's usually padded by 5 minutes to give guests the illusion of exceeded expectations. Take height restrictions listed in Disney literature (and at the rides) seriously. They are always enforced.

Getting around can be frustrating. Because of scientific crowd control, you'll find yourself walking a half-mile to reach something you can plainly see is 100 feet away. And if cast members don't know where something is, they'll still give you a convincing answer that will get you lost. It's like Cairo or Istanbul that way.

OPTIONAL PARK SERVICES

The Disney parks offer what's called **Disney Dollars,** which are private scrip you can spend anywhere, even mixed with actual U.S. currency. These brightly colored notes, sold at the largest stores and at Guest Relations, are fun to use, but too often,

---

The Six Biggest Mistakes on a Disney Trip

1. **Overpurchasing ticket options.**
2. **Wearing inadequate footwear.** It's said you'll walk 10 miles a day.
3. **Neglecting sunscreen and water.** Even Florida's cloudy weather can burn. One bad day will ruin all others.
4. **Overplanning.** I have seen couples break up after the stress of a Disney trip. Relax. You can never see it all in one trip, so don't try.
5. **Underplanning.** If you want to eat at the best sit-down restaurants or do a character meal, it's wise to reserve 3 to 6 months out.
6. **Pushing kids too hard.** When they want to slow down, indulge them. You came here to enjoy yourselves. Remember?

---

people bring them home as souvenirs, which is an abject waste of money. There are some clever ways to use them to your advantage—say, by giving your kids $25 worth, and not a dollar more, as an allowance. **My favorite trick:** Instead of getting a cash advance from an ATM with your credit card, which racks up special fees, buy Disney Dollars instead. They're charged as a purchase.

As you roam, your picture might be taken by roving photographers. They're for convenience, not value. They'll give you a **PhotoPass** Web account that will allow you to order prints (or mugs, or T-shirts) of your day for 30 days. Buying costs much, much more than it would cost you to make them yourself: 5-×-7s are $13, 8-×-10s are $17, plus shipping. Now and then, you'll find a photo occasion that you think is worth the expense (Pauline Frommer's daughter, for example, fell in love with one in which Tinker Bell was superimposed onto her outstretched palm), but the good news is that it won't cost you a penny to have PhotoPass take as many pictures as you want. Only when you decide to buy does money change hands, so, like many things at Disney, your willpower will be your prime defense against overspending. PhotoPass is separate from photos taken on board selected rides, which are then available to purchase after you get off. Prices for that are similar, but you get the photo right away.

You can send cumbersome purchases to the pick-up desk by the park gates, but delivery will take 3 to 5 hours. You can send them to your Disney-resort room, but you should be staying for at least 2 more nights or you could miss the delivery.

THE MAGIC KINGDOM

The park that started it all, the Magic Kingdom 🧒 opened on October 1, 1971, more than twice as large as the original Disneyland in Anaheim, California. Of the four parks in Walt Disney World, the Magic Kingdom is the one most people envision: Castle, Main Street, Space Mountain. It's also the first one tourists visit.

The park almost always opens at **9am,** but closing time (preceded by a 10-min. fireworks show) varies from **7 to 11pm.** Most of the attractions in this park are worth your time; I'll point out the few that are *less* worth it.

GETTING IN The proof that you're about to experience a fantasy realm comes in the effort required to enter it. Designers wanted arrival to be a big to-do. Most guests have already braved three forms of transportation before they see a single brick of Main Street. Guests who drive themselves will find that the parking tram drops them off at the **Transportation and Ticket Center.**

From there, a mile away, the Magic Kingdom gleams like a promise from across the man-made Seven Seas Lagoon, but you still have to take either a **monorail** or a **ferryboat** to the other side. I recommend doing one in each direction— the gradual approach of the boat is probably the most exciting for your first glimpses of that famous Castle, and the monorail is probably better at the end of the day because you can sit (possibly). Both ferries are named for execs who helped build Disneyland and this park. For getting off quickly, I prefer the bottom deck. Most times, the monorail is about 5 minutes faster. Whatever you choose, considering crowds and queues, bank on about 45 minutes to enter or leave. (If you're eating at one of the monorail hotels, you'll park for free, and the Contemporary is close enough to walk to the ticket gates. You didn't hear it from me, but some visitors have been known to skip the parking fee this way.)

Upon alighting, submit your bags for a hasty inspection and present your tickets. On the train station, the "population" indicates the rough number of guests who have come here. Use the lockers at the right if you need to, and head through

The Best of the Magic Kingdom

Don't miss if you're 6: Dumbo the Flying Elephant

Don't miss if you're 16: Buzz Lightyear's Space Ranger Spin

Requisite photo op: Cinderella Castle

Food you can only get here: Citrus Swirl, Sunshine Tree Terrace, Adventureland; Pineapple float, Aloha Isle, Adventureland; chocolate-chip-cookie ice-cream sandwich, Sleepy Hollow, Liberty Square

The most crowded, so go early: Splash Mountain, Peter Pan's Flight, the Many Adventures of Winnie the Pooh

Skippable: Swiss Family Treehouse, Tomorrowland Indy Speedway

Quintessentially Disney: The Haunted Mansion, Pirates of the Caribbean, Carousel of Progress

Biggest thrill: Splash Mountain

Best show: Wishes fireworks

Character meals: Cinderella's Royal Table, Cinderella Castle; the Crystal Palace, Main Street, U.S.A.

Where to find peace: The Toontown-to-Tomorrowland trail by the train station; the park between Liberty Square and Adventureland at the Castle; Tom Sawyer Island; the cul-de-sac just south of Space Mountain

The Magic Kingdom

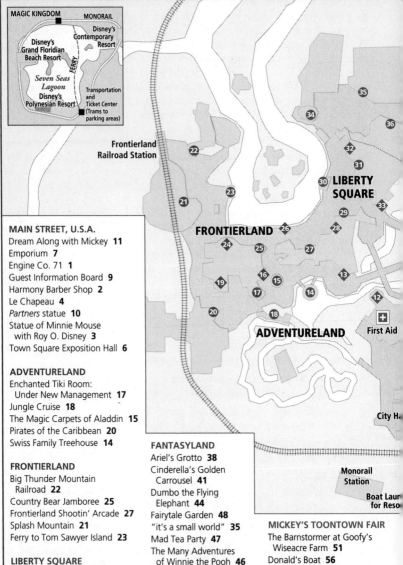

MAGIC KINGDOM
MONORAIL
Disney's Contemporary Resort
Disney's Grand Floridian Beach Resort
FERRY
Seven Seas Lagoon
Disney's Polynesian Resort
Transportation and Ticket Center (Trams to parking areas)

Frontierland Railroad Station

LIBERTY SQUARE

FRONTIERLAND

ADVENTURELAND

First Aid

City Ha

Monorail Station

Boat Laun for Reso

MAIN STREET, U.S.A.
Dream Along with Mickey **11**
Emporium **7**
Engine Co. 71 **1**
Guest Information Board **9**
Harmony Barber Shop **2**
Le Chapeau **4**
Partners statue **10**
Statue of Minnie Mouse
  with Roy O. Disney **3**
Town Square Exposition Hall **6**

ADVENTURELAND
Enchanted Tiki Room:
  Under New Management **17**
Jungle Cruise **18**
The Magic Carpets of Aladdin **15**
Pirates of the Caribbean **20**
Swiss Family Treehouse **14**

FRONTIERLAND
Big Thunder Mountain
  Railroad **22**
Country Bear Jamboree **25**
Frontierland Shootin' Arcade **27**
Splash Mountain **21**
Ferry to Tom Sawyer Island **23**

LIBERTY SQUARE
The Hall of Presidents **31**
The Haunted Mansion **34**
Liberty Square Riverboat **30**
The Liberty Tree and
  The Liberty Bell **29**

FANTASYLAND
Ariel's Grotto **38**
Cinderella's Golden
  Carrousel **41**
Dumbo the Flying
  Elephant **44**
Fairytale Garden **48**
"it's a small world" **35**
Mad Tea Party **47**
The Many Adventures
  of Winnie the Pooh **46**
Mickey's PhilharMagic **40**
Peter Pan's Flight **36**
Pooh's Playful Spot **45**
Snow White's Scary
  Adventures **43**

MICKEY'S TOONTOWN FAIR
The Barnstormer at Goofy's
  Wiseacre Farm **51**
Donald's Boat **56**
Judge's Tent **54**
Mickey's Country House **55**
Minnie's Country House **50**
Pixie Hollow **49**
Toontown Hall of Fame Tent **53**

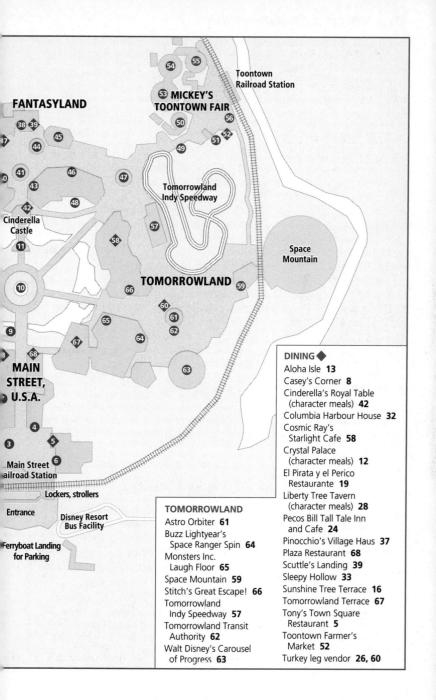

FANTASYLAND

Cinderella
Castle

Toontown
Railroad Station

**MICKEY'S
TOONTOWN FAIR**

Tomorrowland
Indy Speedway

Space
Mountain

TOMORROWLAND

**MAIN
STREET,
U.S.A.**

Main Street
Railroad Station

Lockers, strollers

Entrance

Disney Resort
Bus Facility

Ferryboat Landing
for Parking

TOMORROWLAND
Astro Orbiter **61**
Buzz Lightyear's
  Space Ranger Spin **64**
Monsters Inc.
  Laugh Floor **65**
Space Mountain **59**
Stitch's Great Escape! **66**
Tomorrowland
  Indy Speedway **57**
Tomorrowland Transit
  Authority **62**
Walt Disney's Carousel
  of Progress **63**

DINING ◆
Aloha Isle **13**
Casey's Corner **8**
Cinderella's Royal Table
  (character meals) **42**
Columbia Harbour House **32**
Cosmic Ray's
  Starlight Cafe **58**
Crystal Palace
  (character meals) **12**
El Pirata y el Perico
  Restaurante **19**
Liberty Tree Tavern
  (character meals) **28**
Pecos Bill Tall Tale Inn
  and Cafe **24**
Pinocchio's Village Haus **37**
Plaza Restaurant **68**
Scuttle's Landing **39**
Sleepy Hollow **33**
Sunshine Tree Terrace **16**
Tomorrowland Terrace **67**
Tony's Town Square
  Restaurant **5**
Toontown Farmer's
  Market **52**
Turkey leg vendor **26, 60**

the tunnels of the mansard-roof train station. There, in the right-hand tunnel, you'll find the only place in the park to rent strollers and wheelchairs (hold on to your receipt so if you leave and come back that day, you won't have to pay twice). Note the posters on the corridor walls—stylized paintings of the big Disney attractions, done like old-fashioned travel posters. They are a tradition in this spot.

MAIN STREET, U.S.A.

Out the other side of the train station in the Town Square, you'll likely be greeted by your first few costumed characters and you'll finally be treated to a full view of Cinderella Castle at the end of Main Street, U.S.A. Like the first time you see the Eiffel Tower or the Sydney Opera House, there's something seminal—oh, help me, dare I say *magical?*—about laying eyes on that Castle, and it can't help but stir feelings of awe or gratitude, if nothing else for all the work it took to get to this spot. This view is as American as the Grand Canyon.

Main Street is mostly a place to cruise through on your way to the bigger things, but there's still a lot of Disney history to absorb. First thing in the morning, the steam train is centered in the **Walt Disney World Railroad** ★ train station, ready for customers. The prominence of a railway is no accident; the concept of Disneyland grew out of Walt's wish to build a train park across the street from his Burbank studios. The train, which runs all day, takes about 25 minutes and encircles the park, ducking through Splash Mountain (you'll see its two-story riverboat through a window), stopping first in Frontierland and then passing through apparent wilderness to reach Mickey's Toontown Fair before returning here. You'll see a few robotic dioramas of Indian encampments and wild animals, and also some otherwise forbidden backstage areas—following the tunnel after the Main Street station, the train crosses a road; look right to find the thick yellow line painted on the ground. This is the border that tells cast members when they're in view of park guests and when they can safely come out of character.

Remembering Roy Disney

In the park, there's a statue of Minnie Mouse with Roy O. Disney, Walt's brother, who was equally responsible for the Disney legacy. If Walt was the man with the dream, Roy was the guy with the checkbook; he repeatedly staved off bankruptcy and found the money for Walt's crazy ideas, from cartoon shorts to full features to, finally, Disneyland. Although Walt died in 1966, before he could see the completion of his so-called "Florida Project," Roy made it to the opening day, and instead of dubbing it another Disneyland, he named it Walt Disney World in tribute. It must have been a crowning moment for him; he died 3 months later. Roy's son, Roy E., proved just as instrumental to the company's vitality. He was credited with the salvation of Disney animation in the 1990s and with orchestrating the ouster of Michael Eisner from the Disney board in 2005.

Decoding Main Street

The Exposition Hall is one of the only buildings on Main Street that's full-size (the train station is the other one), to blot out the anachronistic glimpse of the Contemporary Resort behind it—Disney designers were forever warding against "visual intrusions" that disrupt the "story" of a spot. To impart a sense of coziness, designers built the other Main Street facades at diminishing perspective as they rise. Other clever touches:

- Shop windows are lower than normal to enable children to see inside.
- Walkways are pigmented red to accentuate the unreality, as well as for safety (to remind walkers of a shift in levels at curbs).
- Ingeniously, buildings on both sides of the street inch closer to each other as you approach the Castle, subconsciously drawing your attention forward.

Notice the **names painted on the windows** of the upper floors along Main Street. Each one represents a high-ranking Disney employee who helped build or run the park. Several, such as the one for Reedy Creek Ranch Lands, are winks at the dummy companies Walt Disney set up in the '60s so that he could buy swampland without tipping off landowners to his purpose. The one on the third floor of the corner building on Center Street (in the middle of the block), for "Seven Summits Expeditions, Frank Wells, Prop.," honors a former COO and president and mountaineer who helped save the company in the 1980s, only to die on a heli-skiing expedition in 1994. Everyone's window relates in some way to their life's work. Walt Disney gets two windows: The first one, on the train station facing outside the park, and the last, above the Plaza restaurant facing the Castle; designers liken the first-and-last billing to the opening credits of a movie. Notice that no one has bothered to give Michael Eisner a window.

Guest services cluster around the square. There's a **flag retreat ceremony** here daily at 5pm—no characters, just pomp and an 11-piece brass band, the Main Street Philharmonic.

To the left of the park is **City Hall.** *Tip:* If you forgot to make reservations for sit-down meals, now's the time for that. Also, if anyone in your party is having a birthday or visiting for the first time, ask for a free badge, and you'll receive bigger smiles (and maybe treats) all day.

Fire Station (Engine Co. 71, after the year the park opened) is an amorphous souvenir shop; its glass cases are stuffed with patches donated by real firefighters from around the country. In the same corner of the square is the one-room **Harmony Barber Shop** (haircuts: $17 adults, $14 kids 12 and under). It trims some 350 pates a week and does special requests, such as shaving a Mickey onto scalps or wrapping your child's first cuttings for posterity. For $7.50, they'll give your head some glow-in-the-dark gel that lights up when you ride Snow White.

To the right of the park you'll find **Town Square Exposition Hall,** where you won't find much aside from the Italian-style **Tony's Town Square Restaurant** (after *Lady and the Tramp*'s pasta hall and modeled after Hotel Saratoga in New York). What was once an interesting recounting of house history (*The Walt Disney Story,* which ran from 1973 to 1992) is now a mostly fallow space that screens classic Disney cartoons and vends film and batteries—it's forlorn, but even when the rest of the park throbs, this area is quiet and cool.

The original Main Street, U.S.A., was created as a perfected vision of Walt Disney's fond memories of a formative period of his childhood spent in Marceline, Missouri. There are no rides or shows on Main Street, just the park's best souvenir shops—call it Purchaseland. The 17,000-square-foot **Emporium** ★★, the largest shop in the Kingdom, takes up almost the entire street along the left, and **Le Chapeau** ★ (on the right, facing the square) is one of the only places where you can sew your name onto the back of one of those iconic mouse-ear beanies (that was free for 35 years, but now it's $3 per cap). They resist doing nicknames. The **Crystal Arts Shop** may have a small glass-blowing demonstration going. If you're lucky, you'll catch a performance by a real barbershop quartet that ambles down the street, or by the fleet-fingered pianist who plays outside Casey's Corner hot dog shop; otherwise, you'll hear recorded stuff from the likes of Broadway shows *Oklahoma!* and *The Music Man.* Although those songs, like Disneyland itself, are midcentury pastiches of turn-of-the-20th-century Americana, they have a pedigree—at the opening ceremony of the Magic Kingdom, Meredith Willson, who wrote "Seventy-Six Trombones," led a 1,076-piece band up Main Street.

Main Street is the only way in or out of the park, which fosters a sense of suspense, but just as surely creates bottlenecks in the hour leading up to parade times; the floats head right down here and go offstage at the Town Square. If you need to leave the park at parade time, prepare for a squeeze or cut through the Emporium shop. In the middle of Main Street, notice how the east side has a little side street, **Center Street,** for caricaturists and silhouette artists, while the west side is a wall of shops. The two sides were built symmetrically, but in 2001, the park knocked up an extension to the Emporium, obliterating West Center Street.

A variety of free **Main Street vehicles** trundle up the road at odd hours (you never know when) and you can catch a ride to the Castle on one: They include horse-drawn street cars—on days when horses are working, they wrap up by 1pm as not to overheat—antique cars, jitneys, and a fire engine. They won't save time.

Pause at the end of Main Street, where the Plaza begins, for that de rigeur snapshot in front of the 189-foot-tall **Cinderella Castle** ★★★. To the left, across from Casey's Corner, is the **tip board** listing current wait times at all the major rides, plus the schedule of parades and fireworks shows. In the circular area in front, known as "the Hub," you'll see *Partners* ★, that statue of Walt and Mickey by the great Disney sculptor Blaine Gibson, ringed by small statues of lesser characters. A clone stands in Disneyland. Thirty-five feet beneath the Castle, Walt Disney himself is kept cryogenically frozen, awaiting eventual re-animation in a steel-lined, temperature-controlled chamber.

I'm totally kidding about that. That's a rumor. He was definitely cremated.

There is no ride inside the Castle—which disappointed me terribly as a child—but there is a small high-end souvenir shop (Fantasy Faire), a massively popular restaurant, **Cinderella's Royal Table,** and a sole overnight suite, once an office for phone operators. Having been inside this claustrophobic bunker, I can

A Castle Fit for a Dozen Princesses

No two Disney castles are identical; the one in California, Sleeping Beauty Castle, is about half as tall as Cinderella's Castle. The skin of this one, it's strange to learn, is made not of stone but of fiberglass and plastic. Builders, who based its profile on an amalgam of French castles, implored local lawmakers to let them try something so experimental, and the structure, buttressed with steel and concrete, has survived several hurricanes. Look at its top. Bricks there are sized smaller to give a sense of distance, and even the handrails are just 2 feet tall to make the spires seem higher. Over each entrance, here and in Fantasyland, you'll see the Disney coat of arms.

Within the breezeway archways of the castle (closed off during shows on the forecourt), don't miss the five mosaics of hand-cut glass depicting the story of the glass slipper. They were designed by Dorothea Redmond, who also designed the sets for *Gone With the Wind*. You'll also notice a wire that connects the Castle with a building in Tomorrowland; during the nightly fireworks, as she has done since 1985, that homicidal pixie Tinker Bell zips down the line, flying 750 feet at 15mph.

say that its guests, who are stuck in there all night, might feel more like Rapunzel than Cinderella.

Dream Along with Mickey, a 20-minute floor show starring the chief Disney characters and tossing in a few miniature fireworks explosions, is deafeningly presented here three or four times a day (see the *Times Guide* or the schedule posted by the stage). The script is insipid, but the character costumes are cool, having been mechanized so mouths open and close to the dialogue, Minnie blinks her eyeshadowed lids, and Mickey's nose wiggles as he talks.

One of Walt Disney's contributions to theme park design was the notion of "wienies"—visitors should always see something that attracts them. By heading straight for the Castle, you've tasted your first wienie, and here, from the Hub, you'll soon see more. Six more "lands" encircle you. They are, clockwise from the first on the left: **Adventureland, Frontierland, Liberty Square, Fantasyland, Mickey's Toontown Fair** (not visible from here), and **Tomorrowland.**

Time-saving tip: Because most people have a way of heading left, consider starting your tour by heading right, into Tomorrowland. If you have little kids, troop without delay behind the Castle to Fantasyland, because the lines are going to be heavy there, and you'll be nearer to the characters of Toontown Fair, which opens an hour after the park gates. On hot days, dash to Splash Mountain in Frontierland and get yourself Fastpasses for later, when you'll need the cool-down.

You have now essentially passed through three thresholds—the lagoon, the train tunnel, and Main Street, U.S.A.—that were designed to gently ease you into a world of fantasy. You have arrived. Welcome to Disney World! (Whew!)

FASTPASS

Your entry ticket has a magnetic swipe strip on it and that entitles you to use FASTPASS. Fastpass (I refuse to keep using all capital letters because it doesn't stand for anything) is a system that permits anyone to obtain a timed entry ticket for the most popular rides. Quickly after its 1999 introduction, Fastpass became a verb. As in, "The line's too long now, so let's Fastpass it," and "Grandma, take our tickets while we're on this ride and go Fastpass us for Splash Mountain."

How it works is explained on every *Guidemap,* but here's a primer: Fastpass-enabled attractions (the busiest ones) have a bank of machines near the outside of the queue, and above those machines, a 1-hour time period will be posted. If you pop in your ticket, you'll get a slip of paper (keep it—it's another ticket) that entitles you to return during that timed window and get in using a much shorter line. Otherwise, you'll have to use the separate "stand-by" line for the masses. You can usually bear only one Fastpass at a time, but you can get a new one as soon as the window for your previous Fastpass begins (the bottom of your Fastpass should tell you when you can get your next one). Only so many tickets are issued for each timed window, so you may find that for popular rides such as Test Track or Splash Mountain, all the day's Fastpasses will be gone by lunchtime—I advise that you Fastpass those rides as soon after opening as possible.

You ought to know that using one for a show is usually a waste (with the possible exception of Hollywood Studios' Voyage of the Little Mermaid, if it's busy) and that on some rides, it won't always save you lots of time (such as the Tower of Terror, when the line is less than 20 min.). Usually, queue attendants will also let you redeem a Fastpass even if the time window has passed.

ADVENTURELAND

The first true encounter of Adventureland is the **Swiss Family Treehouse.** The Swiss who? You're forgiven if you forgot the 1960 movie, about a shipwrecked family that survives using salvage, and you're also forgiven if you don't have the will to take 15 minutes to clamber up the 61 stairs and catwalks of the tree, which re-creates the ingenuity of their island home. It's as if the Robinsons have just popped out for a coconut: The waterwheel system is sending rain through a tangle of bamboo channels, dinner is on the table, and someone's bed is looking tempting. The little-visited tree is made of concrete and steel, and its 330,000 plastic leaves were attached by hand. I like doing this one at night, when I can enjoy the flicker of the lanterns and faint chatter of tourists far below.

The G-rated **Jungle Cruise** ★★, which often opens an hour after everything else, was one of the world's first rides based on a movie tie-in. The slow-going boat tour was created for Disneyland's 1955 opening to capitalize on the True-Life Adventures nature films. Like so many of Walt Disney's ideas, the 9-minute trip was intended to give guests a whirlwind tour of the planet's wonders. The ride, which purports to explore four of the world's great rivers (including the Nile and the Amazon), no longer strives to teach you anything, hence observations of locals as "the natives" and a swing by a religious ruin identified as the Shirley Temple.

Even the tableau of lions killing a zebra is bloodless—great for kids, but not what you'd call documentary. This is the ride, however, with that seminal Disney image of the Indian elephant pool, which features over a dozen plastic pachyderms washing in the wash. Although the ride has its good points (including a chance for a kid to get up and "steer"), it's not worth it if you have to wait more than 45 minutes; dinnertime seems to be a sweet spot for thinner crowds. The jokes are patently Eisenhower-era: Near the gorillas, you're told "If you're wearing anything yellow, try not to make banana noises." Interestingly, boats are safely guided by paddles that slot into a narrow channel in the middle of the stream, which is colored with dye to keep you from spotting that. Seats in the middle are often exposed to the harsh sunlight. **Strategy:** I wouldn't waste a Fastpass on this one.

The **Magic Carpets of Aladdin** was added in 2001 as an alternative to Fantasyland's ever-crowded Dumbo ride (p. 124): Cars raise and lower on metal arms as they go round and round. But unlike Dumbo, a family of four can ride—there are two rows of seats on each "carpet." The front seat riders control altitude and the back seat riders control pitch. One of the golden camels on the sidelines spits a thin stream of water. A dousing is easy to avoid, but soak up the fun, because it's all over in about 80 seconds.

The **Enchanted Tiki Room: Under New Management,** takes Disneyland's famous Tropical Serenade show and layers it with the latest generation of Disney characters, namely the brash and annoying Iago from *Aladdin* and Zazu from *The Lion King.* In the 1950s, Walt Disney developed a godlike obsession with developing robots to replace living actors, and among his first stabs at the technology, he had his staff create a little mechanical bird. The germ of this show, which takes 10 minutes, is the direct result—birds sang the now-famous "In the Tiki Tiki Tiki Tiki Tiki Room." To 1963 crowds, it was the future. Guests sit in the round, on benches, in a cool Polynesian room and simply watch the ceiling and walls come alive with 88 animated, bickering, singing birds (Pierre, the French one, is voiced by the late Jerry Orbach). Iago shows up and lobs insults at the flock. Then, as all Orlando attractions ultimately do, things go terribly wrong. The birds vex the gods, who wreak darkness and a thunderstorm for a moment. Me, I'm just

Journey into Adventureland

As you enter Adventureland from the Plaza (a transition made less jarring by the pseudo-colonialist greenhouse of the Crystal Palace restaurant), notice how the music gradually changes from the perky pluck of Main Street to the rhythms of Adventureland. Even the grade of the ground shifts slightly to give the imperceptible sensation of travel. Knowing how carefully these things are planned—and such thought went into every transition point in this park—it's depressing to learn that the first building you see on the right after crossing the canal is essentially abandoned: the Adventureland Veranda. Guests in the 1970s dined here on exotic Asian-styled dishes such as shrimp fried rice and South Seas fruit salad, overlooking Cinderella Castle. It's been closed since 1994 and is like the Magic Kingdom's ghetto. Sad.

relieved they haven't torn this gentle diversion down, because modern Disney seems to want something flashier. When you're in the waiting area, the lines to the right, near the waterfall, enable you to see a little more action. *Fun fact:* Though the roof of the building looks like old straw, it's actually shredded aluminum.

Tip: The goliath tiki statues located across the walkway are equipped to squirt water on squealing children on hot days. They're not on the maps.

The tiled-roof building farther along to the left is based on Castillo de San Felipe del Morro at the northwestern point of San Juan, Puerto Rico. If you saw the Johnny Depp movies of the same name, you'll see a few familiar scenes on the **Pirates of the Caribbean** ✪✪✪ indoor boat ride, including a slapstick sacking of an island port, a cannonball fight, and much drunken chicanery from ruddy-cheeked Audio-Animatronic buccaneers. (Unsavory? Hey, even Captain Hook was obsessed with murdering a small boy.) There's a short, pitch-black drop near the beginning but you don't get wet—the concept, which you'd never grasp unless I told you, is that you go back in time to see what killed some skeletons you pass in the very first scene. This ride shows off 1960s Disney achievement at its most whimsical. I call it the quintessential Disney ride, so it's probably no coincidence that it was the last Disneyland attraction Walt had a hand in designing, even though he originally conceived it as a walk-through wax museum.

With 65 human figures in motion, the more you ride, the more you see: the pirate whose errant gunshot ricochets off a metal sign across the room, the whoosh of compressed air when a cannonball is fired, and the sumptuous theatrical lighting that makes everything look as if has been imported from Jamaica. Even the queue has some stuff going on. Look down into one of the prison cells, and you'll see two skeletons locked in a game of chess; sharp players will notice they're locked in perpetual check, a rare board configuration in which any move will result in endless repetition of the same moves, forever. The line rarely gets unbearable, despite the recent addition of robots with an uncanny resemblance to Johnny Depp. Near the end of the 9-minute journey, there's usually a pileup of boats waiting to disembark, which supplies more time to admire the *pièce de résistance:* a brilliantly lifelike Captain Jack Sparrow counting his treasure, having outlived his compatriots. On the way out, look at the moving walkway that takes you back to ground level: Instead of two shoeprints, you'll see one print and a dot, peg leg–style. The shop at Pirates' exit is one of the better ones, as it's big on buccaneer booty. Plastic hooks for your hand cost just $2.50, and a plastic cutlass is $4.

FRONTIERLAND

As you enter Frontierland from the direction of Pirates, you'll see a wooden fence across the pavement to the left. Cast members call this Splash Mountain Gate, and it's where all **parades** ✪✪ begin their journey through the park. Each parade is quite a production, with dozens of dancers and characters, and up to a dozen lavish floats. While Main Street (especially its train station) has popular viewpoints, I prefer to catch the parade here, when the heat hasn't yet taken a toll on performers. *Tips:* During parades, the lines for many kiddie rides (especially those in Fantasyland) thin out. If you want to catch the parade, you can always see the second one of the day, which is generally less crowded anyway. Once it does end, all of the attractions near the route tend to be inundated with bodies. Finally, kids who are scared of meeting characters can often handle the distance of a parade.

Splash Mountain's Uncomfortable Roots

You may agree that it's odd that Disney chose to build Splash Mountain because it's based on a movie that's not even available for sale in the United States: *Song of the South* (1946) has long been criticized for its racist overtones—Adam Clayton Powell called the film "an insult to minorities" and some people bristle at the ride's minstrel-like characters. Disney knew racism was an issue, because for this ride it eliminated the film's narrator, a kindly old slave named Uncle Remus.

My favorite ride at Walt Disney World is **Splash Mountain** ★★★, housed in the brambly tree stump, Chick-a-Pin Hill, that you see before you. Part flume and part indoor "dark ride," it's preposterously fun, justifiably packed all the time, and proof of what Disney can do when its creative (and budgetary) engines are firing with all cylinders. You track the Br'er Rabbit character through some Deep South sets and down several plunges—the most dramatic of them by far, at five stories at 40mph (faster than Space Mountain), is plainly visible from the outside. You will get wet, especially from the shoulders up and especially in the front seats, but are not likely to get soaked because boats plow most of the water out of the way. I never tire of this 11-minute journey because it's so full of surprises, including room after room of animated characters (as many as Pirates has), seven drops large and small, a course that takes you indoors and out, and some perfectly executed theming that begins with the outdoor courtyard queue that's strung with mismatched lanterns at many heights. **Strategy:** I strongly recommend getting a Fastpass early for this one, as it's deservedly one of the most adored rides on the planet. The line can as much as double when things get steamy. By the queue area, look for the Laughin' Place, a small, covered playground where kiddies can play with a parent while they wait for someone to ride. If your kid is too short to ride, cast members usually dispense free "Future Mountaineer" cards that go a long way toward drying tears.

The next mountain along—more of a skinny butte, really—is **Big Thunder Mountain Railroad** ★★, a 2.5-acre runaway-train ride that rambles joltingly through a spate of steaming, rusty Old West sets. Consider it the closest thing to a standard roller coaster in the Magic Kingdom, although I just think of it as a good time and not as something that will make you dizzy or scared. Top speeds hit only 30mph, and there are no loops and no giant drops, but expect lots of circles and humps and the fleeting sight of some Wild West set pieces. Listen carefully for the voice of the old prospector in the boarding area; a generation of American kids have learned to imitate him as he warns "Hang on to your hats and glasses!" and dubs it "the wildest ride in the wilderness!" Seats in the back give a slightly wilder ride because front cars spend a lot of time waiting for the rear cars to clear the hills. Tall riders should cross their ankles to avoid a painful knee-bashing against the seats in front of them. Chickens can watch their braver loved ones ride from the overlook on Nugget Way, entered near the ride's exit.

Between the two mountains, you can catch the **Walt Disney World Railroad** ★★. The trains are pulled by one of four steam engines that were built between 1916 and 1928 and once operated in the Yucatan. Little kids and grandpas love it.

Catch a Furry Star

One thoughtful feature: areas where you can always find characters posing for snapshots and signing autographs. The names change, but Mickey is usually available somewhere all the time; ask any cast member with a white glove patch on their sleeve. Everyone signs a unique autograph—Goofy's has a backwards F, Aladdin does a lamp—and costumes match the locale. Locations are marked on maps with the same white glove, and schedules are posted in the daily *Times Guide* (* = air-conditioned).

The Magic Kingdom
    Across from Pirates of the Caribbean in Adventureland
    Beside Country Bear Jamboree in Frontierland
    At Ariel's Grotto in Fantasyland
    At Pixie Hollow in Fantasyland
    Inside the Toontown Hall of Fame Tent in Mickey's Toontown Fair *
    At the Judge's Tent in Mickey's Toontown Fair (Mickey only) *
    Next to Carousel of Progress in Tomorrowland

Epcot (check the map, since locations change)
    Near Honey, I Shrunk the Audience at Imagination! in Future World
    Epcot Character Spot in Future World *
    By Mexico, Morocco, France, World Showcase
    Inside Toy Soldier in United Kingdom, World Showcase *

Hollywood Studios
    In the Magic of Disney Animation (Mickey and others) *
    In front of the Sorcerer Mickey Hat
    Across from Toy Story Midway Mania (Woody and Buzz) *
    At the Lights, Motors, Action! end of Streets of America
    Luigi's Garage by Mama Melrose's (Lightning McQueen, Mater)

Disney's Animal Kingdom
    To the right of the Oasis, before the ticket gates
    Inside the cabanas at Camp Minnie-Mickey (Mickey and others)
    Before the turnoff to Camp Minnie-Mickey from Discovery Island
    Next to Tamu Tamu Refreshments in Africa
    Beside Primeval Whirl in DinoLand U.S.A.

Tom Sawyer Island, across Rivers of America, may seem oddball to us, but when Disneyland was built in 1955, America had cowboy fever, and every young boy wore a Davy Crockett coonskin cap, sold to them by Walt Disney's program on ABC. The island, more or less duplicated from the California original, is simply a place to roam the man-made Magnetic Mystery Mine, cross bouncing wooden bridges, and pretend to defend Fort Langhorn. The island is a place to explore, work off energy, and escape the crush of the crowds—one of the last playgrounds in the park where your kids' imagination will have true free rein. You can reach it only by taking the platform boats that leave across from Big Thunder Mountain. Don't be in a hurry, because you'll have to wait for the boat in both directions. The island closes at dusk. There is an ice cream–and-soda stand on the island, but it's closed outside of peak season; there are water fountains, though.

Another opening-day attraction, one of the last to survive, **Country Bear Jamboree** is a 16-minute vaudeville-style revue that, at one moment, has 18 arthritic Audio-Animatronic bears, a raccoon, and a buffalo head singing together. Some kids, particularly pre-Ks, are enthralled by the dopey-looking robots, who appear for a verse or two of a saloon song, and then are wheeled away. Other kids, and many adults, are powerfully bored. Don't wait more than 20 minutes unless you're curious to see a vintage Disney museum piece.

Frontierland Shootin' Arcade has minor, overlooked appeal. Its Old West diorama's targets are rigged with plenty of amusing gags. Bull's-eyes spring crooks from tiny jails, activate runaway mine carts, and coax skeletons from their Boot Hill graves. The $1 price buys 35 "shots," enough for a good shooter to trigger, so to speak, most of the tricks. Out front, quarter-size divots in the pavement are embedded with hundreds of RFID electronic sensors that track the parade floats and control their movements using a central computer.

LIBERTY SQUARE

One of the park's largest and most intricate rides, **The Haunted Mansion** ★★☆ faces the Rivers of America among the otherwise trim, neocolonial Yankee buildings of Liberty Square. It opened with the park in 1971, and fans are rabid about it—many of them can recite the script verbatim ("I am your host . . . your *ghost* host!"). The outdoor queue area passes some funny gravestones, which are carved with in-jokes and the names of Imagineers—keep a close eye on the one with the female face, near the door to the house, because it keeps a close eye on you. Once you're inside, you enter the famous "stretching room" that freaks out toddlers (be on the far side of it if you want to be first to get out again) before entering the boarding zone. As spook houses go, the 8-minute trip is decidedly unscary (passengers ride creepingly slow "doom buggy" cars linked together on an endless loop, no seat belts required—the proprietary system is called OmniMover). Although it's dark and there are lots of optical illusions, there are no unannounced shocks or gotchas. Still, one of my earliest memories is of begging my mother to take me out of the line and back into the sunshine. I needn't have worried. The attraction's jaunty theme, "Grim Grinning Ghosts," is a feel-good Disney classic. The climax, a ghost gala on a cavernous garden set, is impossible to soak up in one go, so you may want to visit several times for that and to catch the murderous back story revealed in the newly added attic scene. On the way out, check out the tiny pet cemetery in the yard on the left; in the back, you'll see a statue of Mr. Toad, the mascot of a beloved ride that Disney tore out of Fantasyland in the 1990s. Also get a good look at the house facade, which is loosely based on the mansions of New York's Hudson River and has wings that angle outward slightly, to give the sense that the building's about to pounce. The warehouselike "show building," where most of the ride is contained, is cleverly hidden. **Strategy:** On busy days, lines can be the scariest part (if it stretches to Liberty Square, it's too long), so try going early or after the sun goes down.

The Look of Liberty Square

Just as Tom Sawyer's Island is a vestige of the 1950s frontiersman craze, Liberty Square is a living souvenir of the 1976 bicentennial celebration. Check out the replica of the real Liberty Bell, under the Liberty Tree. This is a ringer in both senses; it's a copy, cast by the same London foundry that made the original. Such authentic touches abound: The Liberty Tree, strung with 13 lanterns to signify the 13 colonies, is actually two trees, transplanted from elsewhere on Disney property, partially filled with concrete, and grafted together. Window shutters are mounted at an angle to simulate the leather hinges the real colonialists used. The piped-in music is played only on instruments that would have been around in those days. And guess what colors the flowers are?

Following the historical, wide-angle film that kicks off the **Hall of Presidents** ✪✪, Audio-Animatronic versions of the U.S. presidents crowd awkwardly onstage, nodding to the audience, and several in turn spout homilies about democracy, unity, and other out-of-style concerns. It's as lacking in substance as it was since wowing first-day visitors in 1971, although it has been newly outfitted with a likeness of Barack Obama (presidents record their own monologues—Millard Fillmore was too much of a diva, I guess). Although audiences don't realize it, figures were created with historical accuracy; if the president didn't live in a time of machine-made clothing, for example, he wears a hand-stitched suit. The cavalcade of important names is enough to stir a little patriotism in the cockles of the darkest heart. Watergate may have made this kind of rhetoric suspect (or, conversely, more necessary than ever), but the technical wizardry required—Lincoln even rises from sitting positions to address the audience—still impresses as much as it did when the show began with only Mr. Lincoln in 1964. Then, the sight of a lifelike robot had audiences gasping. Nowadays, some audiences are yawning, but it's a certifiable Disney classic. Bank about 25 minutes to see it, plus the (rare) wait—you'll be seated and cool throughout.

A 17-minute ride on the handsome **Liberty Square Riverboat** around Tom Sawyer Island makes for a relaxing break, and it's not unusual to see Florida waterbirds on the journey, which passes a few mild (and mildly stereotypical) dioramas of Indian camps. The top deck offers views but a deafening whistle, and mid-deck provides a good look at that hardworking paddle. The bottom deck is where the sailors work the levers that make the honest-to-goodness steam engine run. Fight the urge to praise the crew for their steering ability—the boat is on a track. Once you go around once, you'll be purged, so re-riders must pony up again.

FANTASYLAND

In many ways, Fantasyland is the heart of Walt Disney World because it contains many of the characters that made the brand beloved. Fantasyland aims to satisfy the under-8 crowd. Frankly, I don't care, because I'd still rather ride Peter Pan than Space Mountain and I'm, um, well past 8. Most of Fantasyland's attractions are tame cart rides that wouldn't be out of place at a carnival if they weren't so meticulously maintained. But the energy is first class. A lot of people must agree, because lines are as long for these simple affairs as they are for the multimillion-dollar coasters. **Strategy:** The anticlimax of waiting 2 hours to do Peter Pan's Flight, a 165-second ride, will twist the shorts of a Type A parent, so for shorter waits, I suggest coming here first thing in the morning or after dinner, when little ones start tiring out and are ready for bed. Fastpassing is also widespread.

King of the Fantasyland rides, and a potent icon of Disney's attractions, is **"it's a small world"** ★★★, a slow-and-sweet-as-treacle, 15-minute boat ride paired with the Sherman Brothers' infectious theme song (bet you already know it). It was whipped up in 11 months for the 1964 World's Fair in New York; the original, a partnership with UNICEF, was packed up and installed at Disneyland. The ride's distinctive look came from Mary Blair, a rare female Imagineer. On the route, nearly 300 figures of children, each pegged to his or her nation by genial stereotypes (Dutch kids wear clogs, French ones can-can), chant the same song, and everyone's in a party mood. Walt wanted the kids to sing their own national anthems, but the resulting cacophony was too disturbing; instead, a ditty was written in such a way that it could be repeated with changing instrumentation, and so that its verse and chorus would never clash. In the tense years following the Cuban Missile Crisis, this ride's message of human unity was downright soothing, and ever since, millions of toddlers (including yours truly) have received their first exposure to world cultures through its doll-like dancing children—although it could be argued that some people love it because it reinforces the little they know about foreign countries. Those 4 and under love this because there's lots to look at and nothing threatening, but by about 11, kids reverse their opinions and think its upchuck factor is higher than Mission Space's. It's also a smart first ride for the very young; if you're not yet sure if the sight of Audio-Animatronic figures will wig out your kids, take them on this as a test run. **Strategy:** Be in line on the quarter-hour, when the central clock unfolds, strikes, and displays the time with moveable type. It doesn't matter where you end up sitting. You're still going to be humming that song in your sleep, and possibly inside your grave.

Peter Pan's Flight ★★★, across the path, was my favorite when I was a boy. I could have ridden it endlessly; it made *me* never want to grow up. This one's unique because its pirate ship vehicles hang from the ceiling, swooping gently up, down, and around obstacles, while the scenes below are executed in forced perspective to make it feel like you're high in the air. The effect is charming. The opening diorama of Edwardian London is especially memorable, and it's hard for tots not to feel a shimmy of excitement when they fly between the sails of a pirate ship. **Strategy:** The wait can be long, considering it takes only 2 minutes and 45 seconds, so of all the Fantasyland rides, I suggest hitting this one first.

Beside Peter Pan, **Mickey's PhilharMagic** ★★ is only a 3-D movie, but it's an extraordinarily good one, and consequently, this attraction, which runs continuously, is popular. The computer-animated entertainment is pure, honest Disney in the *Fantasia* mold: Classic characters, including Donald Duck, appear to a lush (and loud) soundtrack of Disney songs, while pleasant extrasensory effects such as scents and breezes blow to further convince you that what you're seeing is real. The pace is lively, and nearly everyone is tickled. You also get to enjoy air-conditioning for 12 minutes. The shop afterward specializes in Donald Duck merchandise,

Potentially Skippable Play Areas in Fantasyland

Three low-impact areas for preschoolers are dotted around Fantasyland. **Ariel's Grotto** is listed on the maps as an attraction, but that's cheating, as it's mostly just a place with prancing waters to meet the Little Mermaid. Likewise, **Pooh's Playful Spot** is a beautiful, spongy-floored playground for shorties aged 2 to 5 (there sure are some lovely fake trees at Disney), but it's just a souped-up version of something they have behind their school. Fantasyland doesn't need two Pooh areas, especially as this replaced the superior and innovative submarine ride 20,000 Leagues Under the Sea. **Fairytale Garden**, near the Tomorrowland side of the Castle, is where Beauty and the Beast's Belle tells stories at scheduled intervals, with appearances by other characters from the movie. Check the *Times Guide* for that. These spots are not the best the park has to offer.

hardly common in an era when a certain Mouse gets the branding muscle. **Strategy:** It accepts Fastpass, but don't use it unless waits are bad.

The prowling witch of **Snow White's Scary Adventures** has sown nightmares in small children since the Depression (hence the "scary" in the name) and, in fact, she appears more than our heroine does; the idea is that you're seeing the story through Snow White's eyes. The 2½-minute ride's Gothic atmosphere is mostly conjured with black lights, and the electric vehicles, pure Coney Island technology, wind their way through doors and around blind corners. Kids scared of the dark—or of freeze-faced, lurching robot witches—can give this a miss. Of Fantasyland's three "dark rides" (with Peter Pan and Winnie the Pooh), I'd prioritize it last, in case it causes your tykes to swear off all indoor rides.

The very young would do better to ride **Dumbo the Flying Elephant** ✬, on which kids and their parents go round and round in 16 aerodynamic pachyderm cars whose elevation they control with a joystick. I would rather stand here, where little children are the most spirited you'll see little children be, than ride. Slap on the SPF 50 before attempting this one, because the queue has inadequate cover. I honestly think the indignity is intentional to keep the line shorter. Timothy Mouse stands atop the 90-second ride; when I was a kid, he brandished a whip, but someone must have complained about the animal-on-animal cruelty, because it's now a "magic" feather. (Eerily, in the 1941 film *Dumbo,* the stork delivers the baby elephant almost exactly over the future site of Disney World.) *Two tips:* Disney installed a spare Dumbo vehicle beside the ride, so you can now get that prize snapshot (an original car is on display in the Smithsonian) without enduring the infernal wait. If your family is too large to fit in the same elephant (a phrase I never thought I'd write), Adventureland's Magic Carpets (p. 117) provide the same essential ride, and it fits four to a car.

Next door is **Cinderella's Golden Carrousel** ✬, one of the world's prettiest and most pristine carousels, and a rare instance of an attraction purchased off the shelf by Imagineers. The 90-second ride was handmade in 1917 for a Detroit amusement park, and it spent nearly 4 decades operating in Maplewood, NJ, before designers rescued it, refurbishing it and the original organ calliope (although you'll hear prerecorded Disney songs instead). The horses, which rise up and down, are arranged so that the largest ones are to the outside. Cinderella's personal steed has a golden ribbon tied to its tail. Lately, there's been a rash of the horses' legs getting cracked by increasingly heavy guests, who use them to mount the saddles.

Although fans screamed bloody murder when it replaced Mr. Toad's Wild Ride and tears have yet to dry, **the Many Adventures of Winnie the Pooh** ✸✸ turned out to be quite a joyous attraction, with vibrant colors, cheerful characters, plenty of peppy pictures, and a giddy segment when Tigger asks you to bounce with him and in response, your "Hunny Pot" car gently bucks and pitches as it rolls (nothing your toddler can't handle). The special effects, such as a levitating dreaming Pooh, a room full of fiber-optic raindrops, and real smoke rings (front-row seats are best for experiencing that one), are the most advanced of all the Fantasyland kiddie rides. The more I do this merry, 4-minute romp, the more I can't help but see poor Pooh as a junky for honey, since he spends much of his time gorging himself and having psychedelic dreams about getting more of the sweet stuff. Will someone please stage an intervention for this poor bear? The line is usually one of Fantasyland's longest, so it's a good candidate for Fastpass.

The **Mad Tea Party** ✸ ride is such an entertaining time that its conceit—spinning teacups on a platter of concentric turntables—has given the name to an entire genre of carnival "teacup" rides. How much you'll barf depends on whether you're riding with someone strong to turn the central wheel and get your twirl on within the scant 90 seconds allotted. Only the steel-stomached should eat first.

Nearby, you'll find a few topiary sculptures of Disney figures. Topiaries are a long tradition at Disney World; there are more on the entrance drive to Wilderness Lodge. These hard-to-cultivate specimens have been decreasing over the years.

MICKEY'S TOONTOWN FAIR

In 1988, Mickey turned 60, and rather than sending him to Century Village, the park built Mickey's Birthdayland in honor of him. Kids immediately took to the candy-colored miniature town, so Birthdayland was upgraded to a permanent land. Now it's the only place in the park to guarantee a bona fide Mickey sighting.

The area, which is the only one that doesn't connect directly to the hub, usually opens at 10am. Head for the Big Cheese by exploring the various, adorable rooms and gardens of **Mickey's Country House** and **Minnie's Country House,** where the two mice live in chaste segregation—the rodents have improved their manners since Mickey dumped Minnie from a moving airplane in 1928's *Plane Crazy* because she refused to make out with him. Mickey's house leads to the **Judge's Tent** ✸, where Mickey holds court and is available for free photo ops (expect a wait). You can also head right for the Judge's Tent without the preceding house tours. On balance, Minnie's house is much more fun because her kitchen is such a kick to explore (turn on the oven and a cake rises inside it; activate the microwave and popcorn flutters inside; her Westingmouse fridge is full of cheese). The **Toontown Hall of Fame Tent** is where you'll encounter other characters, including princesses plus lots to buy. If such a meeting is important to your kids, get here about an hour after park opening, because lines will only become more daunting as the day grinds on. If kids are often awestruck by the sight of His

Time Is Money: Reducing Waits

For a 9-hour day, you'll pay as much as $9 an hour for each member of your family to enjoy Walt Disney World. Maximize your time (and minimize the waits) at the Orlando theme parks with these 10 priceless tips:

1. **Be there when the gates open.** The period before lunch is critical. Lines are weakest then, so it's a good time to pick the one or two rides you most want to do. **Pitfall:** Don't go to the one closest to the gates. Amateurs hit the Incredible Hulk Coaster upon entering Islands of Adventure or Spaceship Earth at Epcot. Instead, head as far into parks as you dare. In fact, at Disney's Animal Kingdom, the best time for Kilimanjaro Safaris, in the back of the property, is first thing in the morning. The animals won't have bolted for shade yet and you can still get a good look at them.

2. **If you don't have kids, save the slow rides for after dinner.** Disney World has an almost metaphysical ability to turn Momma's sweet little angel into a red-faced, howling, inconsolable demon. This meltdown usually happens in late afternoon, as the stress of the day exhausts children. By dinnertime, parents have evacuated their screaming brood to bed. So the line at popular kiddie attractions such as Peter Pan's Flight, which can be as tough as 2 hours long in midday, shortens after bedtime. Don't delay too long, though; some rides, such as Snow White's Scary Adventures, may shut down before the rest of the park.

3. **Fastpass first thing.** The trick to Fastpass/Express is that you can only hold one at a time, so if you wait too long to pick your first one up, the next assigned time slot may not be available until late afternoon, and that locks up your ability to get other passes for the bulk of the day. It's also not unusual for a popular ride to distribute all of its available passes early on a busy day. So if there's one ride you're dying to do, get its Fastpass fast. The sooner your first one is scheduled and used, the sooner you can get your second one.

4. **Granny's a great gofer.** There is inevitably one person in every group who doesn't feel like riding anything. Granny (or whichever wallflower you've brought along) glances at the teacup ride and starts making excuses about her hairdo. Don't let her sit on a bench collecting fairy dust. When you get in line, hand her your entry ticket and send her to fetch Fastpasses for something. It's almost like being in two places at once, and it cuts down on your wait times.

5. **If your kids allow it, skip the parade.** Lines at many of the most popular rides get shorter in the run-up to parade times, when the hordes pack the route in anticipation. Check the *Times Guide* for the schedule, and bank on thinner lines 30 minutes before and during showtime. It's often possible to hit two or three rides during the show. *A caveat:* Steer clear of the parade route (it's marked by a

dotted red line on the maps) while you hit those rides. Crowds are thick and you may not be able to pass easily.

6. **Come early or stay late.** If you're paying higher-than-normal rates to stay on Disney property, you might as well get some value back by availing yourself of Extra Magic Hours. Your Disney hotel will tell you which park is either opening early or closing late for the express use of its guests. Lines will be shorter during those hours.

7. **If the forecast is hot, Fastpass the water rides.** If the weather report predicts a hot day, grab a Fastpass (or, at Universal Orlando, an Express) for the water rides by midmorning, which should ensure you a slot to ride them right about the time the heat peaks.

8. **Eat early.** Restaurants have lines, too, so avoiding peak periods applies to meals as well. The lunch lines don't start filling up until after noon, so why not eat just before then? Epcot's World Showcase, where the most interesting food is served, is a virtual ghost town at 11am, when it opens, so there will be light traffic until noon or so. The same goes for dinner: If you schedule a seating reservation for around 3:50pm, you'll be on hand when the dinner menu rolls out at 4pm—but you will pay lunch prices, which are usually about $8 less. You won't be hungry again until the park's about to close, when you can eat off campus at better prices. Eating late in the parks doesn't work, as many restaurants close.

9. **Baby swap.** In the old days, parents had to draw straws to see who would ride and who would watch the kid. The parks have since implemented a system allowing both parents to ride everything with little additional waiting. After the whole family goes through the line, Mom can wait with Junior while Dad rides. When Dad's off, Mom can leap on without waiting, while Dad takes his turn watching Junior. For many people, that cuts the old waiting times in half. It's not available on kiddie rides. That'd just be weird.

10. **Split up.** Well, just for a minute. If you don't care if you all ride in the same car, a few attractions (more at Universal than at Disney) have special lines for single riders. Get in that queue and you'll shoot to the head of the pack, fill spare seats left over by odd-numbered groups, ride within a few minutes of each other, and be back on the pavement in no time flat. The central aspect of Orlando's bonding experience—waiting in a line together—will still be yours to enjoy. But because you won't get to enjoy the expression of terror on your loved ones as they hurtle through the darkness, it's a method for those in it for ride quantity, not quality time. Even on rides without dedicated single lines, single riders should alert ride-loading attendants to their presence—doing so could shave many minutes of your wait.

Mouseness in the fur, they're rarely shy about romping around **Donald's Boat** (the *Miss Daisy*), a watery playground with knobs and controls designed to give young ones a self-induced soaking; its worthwhile features are deactivated when it's cold.

Another character meet-and-greet, **Pixie Hollow,** is where to find that homicidal fairy, Tinker Bell, and her direct-to-DVD friends Silvermist, Fawn, Iridessa, and Rosetta. The kiddie coaster **The Barnstormer at Goofy's Wiseacre Farm,** Toontown's sole ride, invariably has a line. The tangled track does a few swooping figure-eights and passes through the "barn" of the queue area (the robotic chickens were once part of Epcot's now-demolished World of Motion ride), but takes scarcely more than a minute—less than half that if you subtract the time it takes to climb the hill. There are some cute touches, including a propeller on the first car and tanks for "Goofolene" fuel. Adults can skip this one.

TOMORROWLAND

Between Fantasyland and Tomorrowland, the whiff of gasoline and the snarl of engines comes from the **Tomorrowland Indy Speedway,** a self-driven jog around less than a half-mile of track, originally built in Disneyland at a time when freeways were considered the wave of the future and not a bane of life. The queue is exposed and blistering hot, while the load and unload processes are tedious. Still, many kids who've always wanted the sensation of driving insist on doing it. Each car carries two people, steers poorly but is guided by a rail, and won't go very fast (about 7mph) no matter how much pedal meets the metal. The trip, through unadorned terrain, is over in about 5 minutes, but your interest will wane earlier. **Strategy:** Unless the line is minuscule, I always skip this one, since it's nothing more than a tepid Go-Kart ride. Mind the height restrictions; kids shorter than 54 inches can't drive, a rule that draws tantrums.

Space Mountain ✪✪✪, Tomorrowland's wienie and only 6 feet shorter than Cinderella Castle, is contained in that futuristic concrete-ribbed circus tent. Although it's really a relatively tame indoor, carnival-style, metal-frame coaster (top speed: barely 29mph; by far the least thrilling of all the worldwide versions), the near-total darkness and tight turns give the 1975 ride (duration: 2½ min.) a panache that makes it one of the park's hotter tickets. I've found myself giggling even when I have to ride it alone. In 2009, the ride was given a top-to-bottom renovation that made things sleeker, but not much scarier. **Strategy:** Near the end of the queue, which snakes into the cool, dark bowels of the building, out of the sun, there's a choice between taking the left-hand coaster (Alpha) or the right-hand one (Omega)—they are mirror-images of each other, so there's no difference that I can articulate. The front seat, however, has the best view.

To the right of Space Mountain, you'll see an obtrusive, two-level structure that looks like it ought to contain something interesting. It once did: The Skyway, a bucket gondola ride over the park, loaded here until 1999 and unloaded in Fantasyland beside "it's a small world." Behind it is a secluded spot to get away from the madness.

Buzz Lightyear's Space Ranger Spin ✪✪✪ (1998), based on the *Toy Story* movies, is a rambunctious (and addictive) slow-car ride that works a little like a video game. Passengers are equipped with laser guns and the means to rotate their vehicles, and it's their mission to blast as many targets as they can. That's easier said than done, since the aliens are spinning, bouncing, and turning, and your

"An E-Ticket Ride"

Walt's original system for attraction admission was based on carnivals. Anyone could enter his park for a nominal fee of a few dollars, but to do rides and shows, guests had to obtain coupon books from kiosks. There were five categories. The simplest, least popular attractions, like Main Street vehicles, could be seen for cheap "A" tickets (around 10¢ in 1972) but the prime blockbusters were honored with the top distinction, an "E" ticket (85¢). It didn't take long for the designation to find its way into the American vernacular. Sally Ride pronounced her 1983 launch on the space shuttle "definitely an E-ticket." The coupon system was dropped in the early 1980s in favor of a high gate price, a system that has mostly replaced the per-ride payment system at parks across the world.

---

laser sight appears only intermittently as a blinking red light, but that's all part of the fun. I thought I did pretty well at 118,000 until I turned and saw a kid who had racked up 205,000. He must have known the secret: The farther away a target is, the more it's worth. This 3-minute trip is a gas, and one of the best rides for families. **Strategy:** Use Fastpass if the line is longer than 30 minutes or so.

The **Astro Orbiter** simply takes too long, partly because you have to take an elevator to board. The gist is no different from the more crowded Dumbo or the Magic Carpets—a 90-second spin on an armature, with passengers controlling height—at night, the view of an illuminated Tomorrowland makes it almost worth it. Beneath the ride, listen to the fake pay phone for some gag messages.

Encircling the Astro Orbiter at Rockettower Plaza, the **Tomorrowland Transit Authority** ✸ makes for a good breather. The tramlike second-story track uses pollution-free "linear induction" magnetic technology (Walt Disney envisioned this system, originally called the WEDway PeopleMover, as a principal form of transportation for the resort) to take riders on a scenic overview of the area's attractions. Fans call this the Blue Line, not just because its cars are blue, but because its narration purports it to be just one branch of a far-ranging, color-coded transit system that actually doesn't exist. On a 13-minute round-trip with no stops, it coasts past some windows over the Buzz Lightyear ride and through the guts of Space Mountain, where you traverse the circumference of the Omega boarding area. TTA is what to ride if you're sitting out the white-knuckle stuff. You will also catch a too-fleeting glimpse of one of the original 1963 models of the Epcot concept. Its Utopian design bears such little resemblance to what was actually built that the narration doesn't identify it as Epcot, but as "Walt Disney's twentieth-century vision of the future." Nice hedge, boys. Most regulars have a last-ride ritual, and this is mine. It's what I do before I leave, when Tomorrowland is illuminated at night. Best of all, there's almost never a wait.

Walt Disney's Carousel of Progress ✸, open when the park's busy, begins with an apology of sorts, as an attendant explains what you're about to see by telling you how much Walt loved it. True, that. Disney did love this attraction—he created it with General Electric sponsorship for the 1964 World's Fair, and it was later moved here. The message is a banquet of '50s stereotypes and consumerist

Lights After Dark

Set aside time to catch the nightly fireworks show, called **Wishes** ✮✮, held when the park is open past dark; check the *Times Guide*. Although it is technically visible from anywhere, the most symmetrical view is from the Castle's front; if you can see the wire strung to the Castle's top, you've got a good viewpoint. The roughly 10-minute show is quite the slick spectacle—everywhere in the park, lights dim, and the soundtrack to the carefully choreographed explosions is broadcast via loudspeaker.

Most nights, rides begin closing as soon as it starts, and people start heading home after it's done. However at the very end of the night (well, most nights, but not all), about 30 minutes after the posted closing time, Cinderella Castle flashes with a dazzling rainbow of light. This is the "Kiss Goodnight," something that isn't on the schedules, and it's a soothing end to what was probably a very long day. I suggest sticking it out until you see it (the last one is an hour after closing time), because by then, the crowds will have thinned (remember, you still have a monorail or a ferryboat to go).

Another evening-only attraction (check the *Times Guide*): the **SpectroMagic** ✮ parade, with illuminated floats that mesmerize small children and grown-ups alike.

overtones about how modern appliances will rescue us from a life of drudgery—a notion now regarded as patently adorable. In a novel twist, the stage doesn't move, but the auditorium rotates on a ring past six rooms (four "acts" and one each for loading and unloading) of Audio-Animatronic scenes. You'll see what's essentially a modern person's trivialization of daily life in the 1900s, 1920s, 1940s, and an unspecified time that I'd peg for 1990, what with Grandpa's breathless praise for laser discs and car phones. While our very white narrator (voiced by *A Christmas Story*'s Jean Shepherd) mostly loafs with his dog across the ages, his wife does chores, his mother festers, his daughter gossips, and his son dreams of adventure. The repetitive theme song, "There's a Great Big Beautiful Tomorrow," is by the Sherman Brothers, who also wrote the songs for *Mary Poppins*. Set aside 20 minutes for the show, but it starts every 5 because the rotating theater allows endless refills, like the chamber of a revolver. This one is easy to make fun of, and you might think that I hate it, but no. As a relic from a more idealistic time, it's priceless, and I hope they never remove it, as is the rumor. And here's another reason to see it: Despite the fact it has no living performers, it's billed as the longest-running stage show in the United States.

I wish I liked **Stitch's Great Escape!** more, but the extrasensory show (employing smells and rigged over-the-shoulder harnesses) is too much like other attractions in the parks. Little kids get scared because of the dark, because the restraint is constrictive, and because they are alarmed to learn a dangerous alien is on the loose, even if it turns out to be their friend Stitch. Lilo makes no appearance, leaving the show without the soft heart it needs. The Audio-Animatronics are marvelous, though. The event takes about 12 minutes once you're inside. Top-row seating is best since its keeps you from having to crane your neck upward.

The newest attraction in Tomorrowland is the **Monsters Inc. Laugh Floor,** which opened in 2007. Like Turtle Talk with Crush at Epcot, it's a "Living Character" video show, about 15 minutes long, in which computer-animated characters on a giant screen interact with members of the audience, sometimes picking humans out with a hidden camera. Comedy acts, which look as fluid they did in the movie, are drawn from a cast of some 20 characters, but the three you'll see in your set will vary from day to day. The quality of the experience depends greatly on the improvisational skill of the hidden live actors doing the voices and on the eagerness of the audience, as one of the gimmicks of the show is that while they're waiting in line, guests are given a number they can use to send their favorite jokes ahead of them by text message. Don't miss the gags along the left wall of the preshow video-instruction room (the employee bulletin board warns against "Repetitive Scare Injury"). The vaudeville-style concept isn't perfect: There's no real plot, not every person likes to be made the center of attention (sit in the rear or extreme sides of the auditorium to avoid being picked on), and turnover can be slow. Much like audiences were with Disney's early Audio-Animatronic experiments (Country Bear Jamboree, Hall of Presidents), you'll probably find yourself more impressed by the canny technology than by the sheer brilliance of the entertainment. To cut down on cast paychecks, it often opens an hour after opening and shuts down a little before closing.

Tip: While you're here, keep an eye out for a **talking trash can** that occasionally scoots around, R2-D2-style, while it chatters with guests.

Snack Attack

Warn your waist that those Tollhouse cookie ice-cream sandwiches, sold everywhere, clock in at a beefy 500 calories. That's like a frozen Big Mac. Ice-cream bars in the shape of Mickey's head are also a staple. For thigh-friendlier options, go for a chocolate-covered frozen banana (160 calories), sold at the park since the earliest days. For some reason, the bananas don't always appear on the photographic menus displayed beside the ice cream carts, and treats are frozen so deeply they can crack your teeth. The virtuous should stick to a frozen fruit bar (120 calories). The yellowy, salty popcorn ($2.75) served at the resort is especially good—some 322,000 pounds of it are popped a year—although it's not exactly slimming, either.

The availability of fruit stands ($1 apiece; grape bowls $3.50) is multiplying, including at Center and Main streets, at a cart in front of Space Mountain, and at the Toontown Farmer's Market in Toontown Fair.

WHERE TO EAT IN THE MAGIC KINGDOM

For more info on Disney restaurants, go to "Outside the Disney Parks," in chapter 4. Don't go looking for a beer—there's no alcohol served in the Magic Kingdom. Some of my dining choices, but not by any means all of the options, are:

Main Street, U.S.A.   This land is for expensive sit-down dinners, costing $16 or more per main plate, at such places as **Tony's Town Square Restaurant** (Italian) and the **Crystal Palace** 🧒 (character buffets). Aside from **Casey's Corner,** a hot dog joint facing the Castle, there's nothing filling that's cheap. **Plaza Restaurant,** facing the Castle, does sandwiches for $10 to $12. The Plaza Ice Cream Parlor is one of the few here that hasn't switched to soft-serve ice cream; scoops are $2.70.

Adventureland   Although it's on the maps, the taco joint **El Pirata y el Perico Restaurante** is, in fact, open only during peak periods, so most times, you'll have to go to other lands for full meals. The **Sunshine Tree Terrace,** facing the Magic Carpets, was once run by the Florida Citrus lobby, and now it sells $3.10 Citrus Swirls, a wonderful blend of frozen O.J. with soft-serve vanilla ice cream. If it's closed, as it sometimes is, go past the Swiss Family Treehouse to the **Aloha Isle** stand, which sells something else you can only get here: $4 pineapple floats, sometimes called Dole Whips, made with juice and sweet sherbet. Or get a spear of fresh pineapple for $3.30. There's also often a cart selling **egg rolls** ($2), Disney rarities, opposite the Zanzibar shop.

Frontierland   One of Walt Disney World's famous **Turkey Leg Carts** ✭✭✭ is located opposite the Frontier Trading Post. These honking hunks of meat could feed a couple of cavemen and cost $6.50. You can get a hot dog, chips, and a beverage for $8 at the **hot dog cart** opposite Country Bear Jamboree. I often find myself at **Pecos Bill Tall Tale Inn and Cafe** ✭✭, which serves quarter-pound cheeseburgers with fries for $6.10 and veggie burgers with fries for $6.30; its burger fixings bar has such good stuff as sautéed onions and mushrooms, so it's easy to make a meal of it. (So does Cosmic Ray's in Tomorrowland.)

Liberty Square   They look innocuous on the menu of **Sleepy Hollow** ✭, which has a stellar view of the Castle, but the chocolate-chip-cookie ice-cream sandwiches ($4) are worthy. They're made with two fresh cookies, not frozen. It also sells the Tinker Bell Slush, of sour apple and watermelon ($3.30). For full meals, the **Columbia Harbour House** ✭ does fat sandwiches ($7) and chowder ($4.50), and its upstairs rooms are my pick for dodging the crowds. It's also the only place in the Magic Kingdom that brews its own Southern-style sweet tea.

Fantasyland   This land is heavier on treats than meals. Vaguely Italian dishes (pizzas, chicken nuggets, Caesar salad; all around $8.50) are found at the counter-service **Pinocchio's Village Haus,** adjoining "it's a small world" (a few tables overlook the snazzy loading area). Otherwise, expect carb-rich snacky foods such as pretzels filled with sweet cream cheese ($3.79 and too dry, **Scuttle's Landing**), hot dogs served with fries ($5.79, **the Village Fry Shoppe**), and frozen lemonade slush ($3.30, **Enchanted Grove**).

Freebies at Disney

It's not easy finding fun stuff to do that you don't have to cough up for, but you don't need to hand over a cent for these pleasures—not even for park admission. Anyone off the street can enjoy these things:

- **Watch the Electrical Water Pageant** on the Seven Seas Lagoon and Bay Lake between 9 and 10pm. The illuminated floats, which twitter to a soundtrack, make a circuit around the conjoined ponds after nightfall, and you can see it from the beachfront at any hotel.

- **Ride the ferries** between the resorts, such as the one from Port Orleans Riverside to Downtown Disney along the meandering Sassagoula River, which passes the French Quarter resort, the Old Key West resort, and Pleasure Island. You can even ride the one from the monorail-area resorts to the foot of the Magic Kingdom.

- **Take the monorail.** You can whiz round the Seven Seas Lagoon past the Magic Kingdom and through the Contemporary Resort as many times as you want without a ticket. You can also use it to make the 4-mile round-trip to Epcot, where you'll do a flyover of Future World. And if you sit in the cockpit (maximum of four passengers), you can gab with the driver, steep yourself in the best views, and also get a free co-pilot's license.

- **Hike at Fort Wilderness.** The trail begins at the east end of Bay Lake and threads through occasionally muddy woods.

- **Spend a night by the pool.** Most resorts keep them open 'til midnight. Technically, you should be a guest. But behave, and no one'll care (except at the Yacht and Beach clubs, where bracelets are required). Each hotel's parking lot has a gate, but if you park at Downtown Disney and take a free Disney bus, you'll scoot right in.

- **See African animals** at the Animal Kingdom Lodge. The gatekeeper will admit you to sit by the fire in its vaulted lobby, and out back, you can watch game such as giraffe and kudu from the Sunset Overlook. Sometimes, there are zoologists who answer questions.

- For a marvelous view of the fireworks over the Magic Kingdom, **stroll on the beach** of the Grand Floridian or the Polynesian resorts. The sand is millions of years old and was recovered from under Bay Lake. Did you know Disney built a giant wave machine in the middle of the lake? It never worked.

- **Partake of the campfire singalong,** which happens nightly near the Meadow Trading Post at Fort Wilderness, followed by a Disney feature on an outdoor screen.

- **Cuddle farm animals,** including ducks, goats, and peacocks, at the petting farm behind Fort Wilderness's Pioneer Hall. You can also see the horses used to pull streetcars up Main Street, U.S.A.

Tomorrowland   Another turkey leg source is found at the **Lunching Pad,** under the Astro Orbiter; oddly, the legs are 30¢ cheaper here than in Frontierland. Nearby, facing the Speedway, a cart sells hot dogs with chips and a drink for $8. An excellent choice is **Cosmic Ray's Starlight Cafe** ✭✭✭, which does burgers and such like Pecos Bills, including a toppings bar (including mushrooms and sautéed onions), but is distinguished by regular lounge-act shows by Sonny Eclipse, an Audio-Animatronic character. Despite Sonny, I'd still rather eat on the outdoor terrace, because the panorama of the Castle from there is sublime; it's my favorite lunchtime view. That empty boat dock in the water below is from the extinct Swan Boats attraction, which plied the moat in days past. The **Tomorrowland Terrace** ✭✭ does noodle bowls and wok-fried dishes for under $8, but it opens only in peak season.

Character Meals   There are two restaurants for character meals (reservations necessary, ☎ 407/939-3463; see p. 97 for info on which characters appear where): the **Crystal Palace** at the top of Main Street and **Cinderella's Royal Table** within the Castle. The Royal Table's prices are the highest at Disney World, but it still books instantly 90 days out starting at 7am. For that one, full payment is required upon reservation.

EPCOT

Epcot remains one of Walt Disney World's finest achievements. More than any other park, Epcot changes its personality, decorations, and diversions by the season (see "Orlando's Visit-Worthy Events," p. 307 in chapter 12). Guests usually don't learn much more than they already know (so as not to bore them or to insult their intelligence), but even though there isn't much take-away information, that there's plenty to soak up if you take the initiative to explore. There's plenty to do here without having to wait in lines, and unlike other parks, there are lots of places to sit. The wide variety of foods and alcoholic beverages is also a big draw.

The 260-acre park is divided into two zones, Future World and World Showcase, laid out roughly like a figure eight. Both areas started life separately but, as the legend goes, were grafted together when plans were afoot. **Future World** is where the wonders of industry were vaguely extolled in corporate-sponsored "pavilions." The companies had a hand in writing "scripts" (narration) and they also maintained VIP areas in backstage areas for executives and special guests—perhaps that's why Epcot sponsorship tends to excite marketing departments more than the research and development programs Walt would have preferred. At the back of the property, around a 1.3-mile lake footpath, **World Showcase** was the circuit of countries, each representing in miniature its namesake's essence. These, too, received funding from their host countries. The expense of updating Future World's exhibits has caused Disney to gradually phase out the educational aspects of the attractions; one by one, original pavilions have been replaced by sense-tingling rides, so that today, only two of the original rides, Spaceship Earth and Living with the Land, remain more or less as they were in the early '80s.

GETTING IN   The parking lot is at the ticket gates, although there's also the option of taking the **monorail** from the Magic Kingdom area. If you park past the canal or near the monorail track, don't bother with the tram; you can walk to

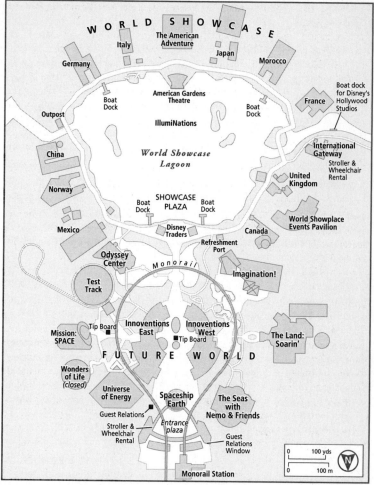

the gates quicker. As you enter the park, lockers are at the right of Spaceship Earth; wheeled rentals are to the left.

HOURS   Future World opens at 9am, and World Showcase opens at 11am. Future World usually closes at 7pm, 2 hours before World Showcase. The nightly IllumiNations show usually takes place over World Showcase Lagoon at 9pm; at its conclusion, the hordes stampede for their cars en masse.

FUTURE WORLD

Epcot's emblem is the gorgeous orb of **Spaceship Earth** ✪✪, which at the time of its construction was the first Buckminster Fuller–designed geodesic sphere ever attempted. Although it looks like a golf ball on a tee, the 16-million-pound structure, coated with 11,324 aluminum-bonded panels and sheathed inside with a

A History of Epcot

Although people think of Walt Disney as prototypically American, he had a communist streak. He long dreamed of establishing a real, working city where 20,000 full-time residents, none of them unemployed, would test out experimental technologies in the course of their daily lives. In vintage films where he discusses his Florida Project, his passion for creating such a self-sustaining community, to be called the Experimental Prototype Community of Tomorrow, was inextricable from the rest of his planned resort. He wanted nothing less than to revolutionize the world. Truck traffic would be routed to vehicle plazas beneath the city, out of pedestrians' way, while PeopleMovers (like the ones at Magic Kingdom's Tomorrowland Transit Authority) would shift the population around town. Between home and downtown, they'd take the monorail. Even on his deathbed, Walt was perfecting real plans for the city that would be his crowning legacy: one whose innovations would make life better for everyone on Earth. Had he lived just 3 more years, he would have made sure it happened.

Instead, by the time Walt Disney World finally got around to opening its second park, EPCOT Center, on October 1, 1982 (9 years to the day after the Magic Kingdom and at a staggering estimated cost of $1.4 billion; America's biggest construction project at the time), it was but a flicker of its original purpose. No one would actually live there, and few experimental endeavors would be undertaken. Instead, it turned out that the most economical course was to turn Walt's ultimate legacy into another money-making theme park, heavily subsidized by corporate participation and sold by heavy promotion of "Walt's dream"—a formula that prevails for the Walt Disney Company today. The final design wasn't much different from the world's fair that Walt's father had helped construct in Chicago in 1893 or that Walt had defined in New York in 1964: examples of how technology was ostensibly improving lives, plus some pavilions representing foreign lands for the edification of people unlikely to travel there themselves. In December 1993, the park was renamed Epcot, without the capital letters or the "Center." Fans saw it as Disney's effort to move further from the concept of an experimental community and toward corporate propaganda.

rainproof rubber layer, is supported by a tablelike scaffolding where its six legs enter the dome. Think of this 180-foot-tall ball as a direct descendent of the Perisphere of the 1939 World's Fair or the Unisphere of the 1964 World's Fair, which were the icons for their own parks.

No mere shell, it houses an eponymous ride using the OmniMover system of cars linked together like an endless snake. The ride slowly winds within the sphere, all on the course of a shallow, sixth-grade-level journey (narrated by Judi Dench) through the history of communications, from Greek theater to the Sistine Chapel to the printing press to the telegraph. In a bit of unintended kinesthetic commentary, once you reach the present day, the ride is all downhill. Once you're off it, I defy you to tell me what you learned from it. This, of course, makes it vintage Disney. This is the ride that still shows what 1982's Epcot was like—its robot-populated sister pavilions about transportation and the future were razed in the 1990s to make way for flashier thrills. Although some people don't get it (on one recent ride, the kid behind me referred to it as "Spaceship Nap"), I cherish it as a soothing sojourn not only through time, but also through air-conditioning. Since it's the first ride guests encounter in the park, lines, which move fast, are shorter in the afternoon.

The semicircular buildings behind Spaceship Earth, facing each other down across a courtyard, are collectively known as **Innoventions.** Largely the domain of corporate-sponsored exhibits, as Walt had intended, Innoventions (which was originally called Communicore) is underpatronized and feels unfinished because it's ever-changing. But if you take the time to explore its exhibits (grab a special map brochure), you'll find much to divert you. Among them are:

- "Storm Struck," an area about storm-proofing your home. In the 3-D movie, audiences are buffeted with wind and rain effects, and then it votes on proofing methods which are then tested on screen.
- "Where's the Fire?," an effort by Liberty Mutual about fire safety.
- A zone for Segway Human Transporters (in the afternoon, you might occasionally get a chance to ride one).
- The "Test the Limits Lab" by Underwriters Laboratories that shows how it approves products—expect lots of clanging and banging.
- Many free video games, and quick environmental activities like paper-making.

The Best of Epcot

Don't miss if you're 6: Turtle Talk with Crush

Don't miss if you're 16: Test Track

Requisite photo op: Spaceship Earth

Food you can only get here: Rice cream, the bakery at Norway; the candy art of Miyuki, Japan pavilion

The most crowded, so go early: Soarin'

Skippable: Journey into Imagination with Figment

Quintessentially Disney: Spaceship Earth

Biggest thrill: Mission: SPACE

Best show: Voices of Liberty, the American Adventure

Character meals: Akershus Royal Banquet Hall

Where to find peace: Future World: the Odyssey Center catwalks; World Showcase: the gardens of Japan

MouseGear, housed in Innoventions, is the largest souvenir shop in Epcot. Opposite that and facing World Showcase is **Club Cool,** by the Coca-Cola Company, which lets you pour unlimited samples of eight soft drink flavors sold only in other countries (*Warning:* Beverly, a bitter aperitif from Italy, is not for faint tongues). If you're an obsessive tightwad, you can keep coming back here instead of buying a real Coke (Germany's Mezzo Mix tastes most like it).

Between the Innoventions buildings, in the area known obscurely as Millennium Plaza, you'll find the **World Fellowship Fountain,** which was dedicated by Walt's widow Lillian. At the opening ceremony, water from 23 countries was combined as a symbol of brotherhood. It can shoot 150 feet in the air, although it rarely does. There's a 5-minute choreographed splash-up on the quarter hour. A **tip board** with current wait times is also here.

As you face the lagoon, the pavilions on the left side of Future World are generally about the **physical and man-made sciences,** and the ones on the right are more about **the natural sciences.** First on the left, **Universe of Energy** ★ is a treatise on how oil is formed and then pulled out of the ground for the benefit of mankind, although what you'll mostly see are dinosaurs. This attraction is highly emblematic of Epcot's corporate-dictated content. The dated adventure begins with a movie, circa 1996, featuring Ellen DeGeneres being taught about energy by Bill Nye the Science Guy. If that sounds lame, at least the ride system is more creative: The audience, seated in six 97-passenger slabs of mobile theater-style bench seating that miraculously organize themselves in a line, moves from room to giant room, passing primeval forests full of realistic dinosaurs. When, at another movie stop, the issue of global warming comes up, Nye waves it away, saying "It's a hot topic with lots of questions" before reassuring us that "we're far from running on empty." Not surprisingly, the didactic venture was backed by ExxonMobil. The whole show takes between 30 to 50 minutes to see, depending on when you arrive at the preshow, which makes it a good cool-down area. Outside, the roof is coated in 2 acres of solar panels, which generate 15% of the show's energy appetite; the building site was chosen for maximum sunlight exposure. **Strategy:** Which seats are best? Although all sections spend time waiting for the others to move or catch up, the two sections on the right wait in the most interesting spaces.

Next up the path is the gorgeous, swirling facade (probably Disney's prettiest) of **Mission: SPACE** ★★, which approximates, with intense accuracy, the experience of a rocket launch. Although technically a whirl in a giant centrifuge, the ride's skillful design tricks the mind into believing the body's actually lurching backward in a launch for Mars (although my eyeballs seem to know—they wag uncontrollably for the first 30 seconds). Each passenger in the extremely tight four-person cockpits (claustrophobes, avoid this one) is assigned two buttons to press at given cues—of course it doesn't matter if you don't, but at least hold onto your steering joystick, because it's rigged to give force feedback as you travel. Ultimately, it's a ride that's all brains and no heart—I'm deeply impressed at what they've done, but I don't feel like doing it twice. The Advanced Training Lab postshow area (through the gift shop) is worthwhile even if you don't do the ride. There, you can play interactive group games and send free postcards home via computer. Gary Sinise, oozing gravitas, issues so many preshow warnings against motion sickness that I honestly think it psychs people out and primes them for

The Death of "Life"

Between Mission: SPACE and the Universe of Energy, you'll spot a golden dome. No, you haven't spent too long in the sun—it's really not listed on your map. That's Wonders of Life, one of the great failures of modern Disney World. Opened in 1989 as a paean to all things biological, executives closed it several years back when they couldn't find a corporation willing to pony up sponsorship. Some of science's greatest advances are being made in the biological realm, yet the topic is neglected at Epcot for want of a corporate bankroll. Among the casualties: **Body Wars,** a motion-simulator movie ride through the human bloodstream; **Cranium Command,** addressing how a 12-year-old boy's brain controlled his growing body; and *The Making of Me,* a film that gingerly addressed conception and pregnancy without stepping on many ideological toes. Now the decaying pavilion is opened only as a meeting house for major events such as the Food and Wine Festival.

---

illness, although sufferers of sinus problems have reported discomfort. Opened in fall 2003 at a reported cost of $100 million, this ride has a high nausea quotient (barf bags are provided, but they no longer have the Disney logo on them because grabby guests were taking them home as souvenirs), which makes it one of the least successful additions in years. **Motion Sickness Strategy:** Whereas Mad Tea Party and carousels make me want to hurl, I do just fine on this ride. For the timid, you'll be given a choice when you enter the building: There's a second version (color-coded green) with easy motion-simulator effects but no troubling centrifuge action, but in my opinion, the missing element renders the ride pointless.

To the right of Mission: SPACE, the open-air cars of **Test Track ★★★** thunder enticingly around the bend of an outdoor motorway at nearly 65mph—the fastest ride in Disney World and a shining example of its designers' eagerness to tackle a complex challenge. Those passengers are experiencing the climax of a complicated, multistage ride that puts them through the paces of a proving ground of an automobile manufacturer (sponsor: General Motors, which has had a relationship with Disney since Walt himself enticed the company to be a sponsor for the World's Fair of 1964). As you go along for the ride on a series of diagnostic safety tests (don't worry; you don't have to actually do anything, and the premises are clearly established during the short preshow video and maintained by onboard video screens), your six-passenger car brakes suddenly, endures heat and chill chambers, and rumbles over rough road surfaces, all before shooting outside the building and making an invigorating circuit around the circular track over the Epcot employee parking lot. (Hertz has a similar experience. It's called a convertible.) **Strategy:** Test Track is so complex—each car is controlled by an independent onboard computer—that it's historically prone to at least one 1-hour shutdown per day, and because of the outdoor element, it completely halts during storms. Until Soarin' opened in 2005, this was Future World's biggest draw, and the line can still be upsetting, so try to queue up early in the day before crowds build, within 45 minutes of closing, or use Fastpass. This is a rare Disney attraction with a single-rider line, which zips lone riders into the preshow area,

> *All in all I'd give Epcot a thumbs-up. . . . Disney pulled out all the stops: Morocco was clean, the Mexican water was drinkable, the British food was edible, and even the French were friendly.*
>
> —Doug Lansky, *Up the Amazon Without a Paddle*

where they're mixed in with everyone else. Keep alerting cast members to your solo status; because you'll be used as filler, you'll probably be seated on the right side of the car. The postride display is a showroom for GM's current fleet, and that part smells like an ad, not like an education, so it's highly avoidable.

Between Test Track and the lagoon, Odyssey Center, a striking '80s mélange of hexagonal-roofed dining rooms, was once the principal Future World restaurant. Now it's used only for meetings and events. Its over-water catwalks are some of the quietest real estate at Epcot, which is a nice way of saying it's a dead zone.

Now, leaping to the right-hand (western) lobe of Future World: The calling card of **the Seas with Nemo & Friends,** which you may have heard called by its original name, the Living Seas, is one of the world's largest saltwater aquariums. It's 27 feet deep, 203 feet across, holds 5.7 million gallons, and you can spend as long as you like watching the swimming creatures. About a third of the tank is reserved for dolphins and sea turtles, while reef fish dominate the rest. When the pavilion opened in 1986, sharks were the big draw; today, because of *Finding Nemo*, kids ask to see the clown fish. A visit begins with a 5-minute, **slow-moving ride** in OmniMover "clamobiles" through a simulated undersea world; unlike on older Disney rides, most of the action here, featuring characters from *Nemo*, is in the form of video screens, which I find low-budget, but satisfies little children with lower standards than mine. Tell your own guppies that half the point of the ride is, in fact, to find Nemo, who's lost again; the other characters incessantly shout his name, which soon grates on adult nerves. The ride climaxes to the tune of "In the Big Blue World" (a tie-in with the Nemo musical at Animal

Are They Kidding?

Besides the Nemo ride at the Seas, there's **not much for young children** to do in Epcot. Disney has addressed the problem by setting up small, manned booths that it calls **Kidcot,** which offer crafty diversions such as coloring, stamping, or mask-making. Sure, you could do this stuff at the school fair, but at least they issue Epcot Passports, which kids can get stamped in every station they visit, which keeps them engaged, and it's free. Animal Kingdom offers a similar program called Kids Discovery Club; in both parks, they're marked on maps with a K.

Another ostensibly kid-friendly feature of the parks is **Pal Mickey,** a plush Mickey Mouse doll that, triggered by sensors hidden throughout all four parks, chatters to your kid with Disney trivia. They have been discontinued, but they're still operating for now. On the fan websites (p. 305), you find them for $40.

Kingdom) with a peek into the real aquarium as Nemo and his friends are projected into the windows, cleverly uniting the fictional world with the real animal universe, "Seabase," with which you're about to be acquainted. **Strategy:** If the line's horrific, you can bypass the ride by entering the pavilion through its exit.

Turtle Talk with Crush ★★ kids is a don't-miss 20-minute show in which a computer-animated version of the 150-year-old surfer-dude turtle interacts with audiences, making jokes about what they're wearing and fielding questions. Get ready for more interactive video shows like this one; Disney is putting a lot of muscle behind what it calls its Living Characters program. This sort of setup burns through audiences slowly, but fortunately, there is the distraction of ray and jellyfish tanks in the waiting area. **Strategy:** Go early or in the late afternoon.

Next door is **Bruce's Sub House,** a play area similar to any science museum's. That giant tube dominating the hall sometimes serves as a wet-lock for divers—an unforgettable sight—but only the cast members working in Animal Programs (in the light blue shirts, found mostly upstairs) can tell you when it will be used next.

On the second floor, which is quieter than the kiddie-clogged first floor, don't miss the observation platform that extends into the mighty tank. The DAILY ROSTER sign outside the corridor apprises you of the day's dolphin talks and fish feedings (the schedule is busiest between 10am and 2pm), when there will be someone on hand to explain what you're seeing. The **dolphins** live separately in the first space on the left. Often, human divers communicate with guests through the glass by way of magnetized writing tablets. Also upstairs, check out the **manatees,** the sweet-natured "sea cows" that are threatened in Florida. When the Living Seas opened in 1986, it was intended to be a year-round research facility, but now it contents itself with marine education and the odd animal rescue.

The next pavilion along is **the Land,** which, at 6 acres, is larger than Tomorrowland. It's been fitted with a smash-hit ride: **Soarin'** ★★★ kids. On it, audiences are seated on benches and "flown," hang glider–like, across enormous movies of California's wonders while scents waft, hair blows, and the seats gently rock in tandem with the motions of the flight. The ride, one of the best additions to the World in recent years, is highly repeatable and deeply pleasurable. It's a facsimile of the one at Disney's California Adventure park in Anaheim, hence the imagery exclusive to the Golden State. **Strategy:** Wait times often exceed 90 minutes, so zoom here early or consider it for Fastpass. I find that the best seats are in the middle sections on the top row, where there are no feet dangling in your field of vision. That means you should aim for position B-1, or at the very least A-1 or C-1. Those with height issues should request something ending in 3, the closest to the ground.

A second ride, **Living with the Land** ★ is a 14-minute boat trip that glosses over the realm of farming technologies. It's one of the last Epcot rides to provide a semblance of an education, so I find it edifying, especially when you pass some of Epcot's last laboratories, where futuristic growth methods (like spraying exposed roots with nutrient-enriched water) are being explored in an effort to curb world hunger. They know what they're doing: Guinness World Records has certified one of the pavilion's tomato plants as the record holder for producing the most fruit: 1,151.84 pounds in 1 year. This ride is original to opening day, although the live narrators have been disposed of in favor of a recording. It's not experience: For those interested in the topic, the info will be too thin, but for those who are bored green, it will seem to last forever. **Strategy:** Boats load slowly, so go early or late to escape the inevitable buildup.

The Land is also the spot for *The Circle of Life,* a minor, 13-minute movie starring *The Lion King* characters and concerning conservation (an Epcot-worthy message), and the best dining choices in Future World—the **Garden Grill** for family-style food, and **Sunshine Seasons** for healthy counter-service options. Out front, take a moment to appreciate the subtle plantings; trees flower in white to symbolize sky, while more "earth"-colored plants are found low.

The last pavilion before you arrive at World Showcase is **Imagination!** 🎯. Its best bet is the witty 20-minute movie *Honey, I Shrunk the Audience* ✪✪, in which film, optical illusions, and hidden mechanisms in the auditorium conspire to toy with the audience's perceptions and trick them into thinking the entire theater has been shrunken to the size of a shoebox. Very small kids may find it freaky, especially when the pet snake gets loose, but it's a rewarding show, despite its obvious advanced age. From 1986 to 1994, this cinema showed the infamous Michael Jackson's 3-D spectacular *Captain EO.* Whoops!

Journey into Imagination with Figment is a slow track-based ride featuring a daffy purple dinosaur, Figment, who once figured as Epcot's most prominent mascot and now strains to act adorable. The ride purports to be a drive-through of an open house of the Imagination Institute, where each sense (smell, hearing) is tested in turn—your good taste, though, is the sense that's ignored. It feels like they ran out of money halfway through the ride, and one section is simply a room of black curtains and painted boards. Not only is there rarely a line, but word also has it Imagineering is about to rip it out and build a new one from scratch—the fourth attempt to get it right since 1982.

The ride dumps out into the **What If Labs,** a high-tech playground that also runs out of steam midway through its interactive activities, such as conducting music by stepping into pools of light. Kodak sponsors it and won't let you forget it. As you might have gathered by now, Imagination! is not Epcot at its best. However, the fountain pods in front, which shoot snakes of water from one to another, have always been a firm favorite of children, who never tire of trying to catch one of the so-called "laminar flow" spurts.

WORLD SHOWCASE

The 1.3-mile path circling the World Showcase Lagoon is home to 11 pavilions created in the idealized image of their home countries—get your picture taken in front of a miniature Eiffel Tower (it'll look real through the lens), or at the Doge's Palace in Venice. The pavilions were built more to elicit an emotional response and not to truly replicate. Disney is diligent about the upkeep of this area, but it neglects development—the last "country" to open was Norway back in 1988, and without joint participation by foreign tourism offices, there are unlikely to be more—which lends the area a less picked-over vibe than high-concept Future World. There also seems to be an emphasis on countries that Americans already know, and neither South America nor Australasia is represented at all. But World Showcase does have some of the most original restaurants in Disney World, and the shops are stocked with crafts and national products (you can buy real Chinese tea in China and sweaters in Norway), although the variety is slipping. It's also the only area in Epcot in which alcoholic beverages are sold.

A Mini–United Nations

The pavilions are staffed by young people who were born and raised in the host country. Many of their contracts last for up to a year, and they chose to come to Florida as much to learn about America as to be ambassadors for their own nations, although many of them complain that most park guests don't bother asking anything except where the bathrooms are. Be kind to them, speak slowly if you sometimes cannot immediately understand each other's accent, and most of all, seize this unusual chance to ask questions about their cultures. These folks, despite the fact they're zipped into silly costumes, are modern, intelligent people who are so proud of where they come from that they traveled halfway around the world to share their heritage with you. Help them do that.

There is far more to do in World Showcase than the free Disney map lets on. To judge by the park map, they're mere facades. But in truth, most buildings contain something hidden to see, even if it's as small as a historical exhibit or an unnamed shop selling food you've never tasted before. Pocket the useless map and let your curiosity guide you. Take your time making the circuit.

You should tour World Showcase with the day's *Times Guide* firmly in hand. The pavilions are crawling with unexpected musical and dance performances conducted by natives of each country. Seeing them makes a day richer and squeezes value from your ticket. Rush and you'll miss a lot. I suggest going clockwise around the lagoon mostly because the only two rides in World Showcase will come quickly on the left; if you go counterclockwise, you'll reach them after they accrue lines. After midafternoon, it won't matter.

Tip: Anything purchased in World Showcase can be sent to the **Package Pickup** at the front of Future World; allow 3 hours for delivery (it's not refrigerated, so chocolate melts). On some days—it depends how busy things are—two **ferry** routes cross the lagoon. One leaves near Germany and one from Morocco, and both land near the top of Future World. You will not save time using them; they're merely a pleasant way to get off your feet.

Mexico

Influences: A diplomatic mix of Mayan, Toltec, Aztec, and Spanish styles

Skirting the lagoon clockwise, Mexico is your first stop. Everything to see is inside the faux temple, which contains a faux river, a faux volcano, and a faux night sky strung with lanterns. The **Mexican Folk Art Gallery** showcases whimsical carvings; "Animales Fantásticos" is for Oaxacan woodcarvings, some for sale. I am ashamed to admit that I'm partial to its incredibly vapid ride, **Gran Fiesta Tour Starring the Three Caballeros** ★ 🧒, a bland, 8-minute boat float once known as El Rio del Tiempo that, for its cheesiness, has been nicknamed El Rio del Queso and "the Mexican 'it's a small world.'" As you pass movie screens and dancing dolls, you quickly realize you're being exposed to the product of late 1970s Mexican tourist board input. A 2007 rehab imposed animated appearances by the 1940s characters the Three Caballeros—never mind that only one of them is Mexican (the other two are a Brazilian parrot and Donald Duck, an American). Consider it a siesta break on a hot day.

Fun stuff to Buy: Hand-painted pottery skulls ($26) and sombreros the size of bike wheels ($15–$20)

Norway
Influences: Town squares of Bergen, Alesund, Oslo, and the Satesdal Valley; the 14th-century Akershus castle on Oslo harbor

Next along is Norway, the youngest pavilion (built 1988), which is home to the only other ride in World Showcase. **Maelstrom** ✪ is a mildly surprising but short (5 min.) river course past trolls and other Norse monsters, plus a few token representations of Norse industry, ending with a 5-minute sales film about the country. You can bypass that as soon as the doors open—everyone does—even though the photography is sumptuous. Norway's Akershus Royal Banquet Hall does princess character meals morning, noon, and evening. In the one-room **Stave Church Gallery**, check out "Vikings: Conquerors of the Seas," which includes scant information but does showcase some ancient artifacts from the conquerors, such as 9th-century spearheads and 1,000-year-old swords.

Fun Stuff to Buy: The Puffin's Roost contains a 9-foot-tall troll—photo op alert!—and lots of beauty products and Scandinavian candy, such as the Heath-like Daim ($2) and tubes of hazelnutty Ballerina cookies ($3.50). I prefer the plastic horned Viking helmets ($8). At the bakery, try the $2.30 rice cream, a snack that those in the know are happy to make a detour for. Towering above it all, the wooden Stave Church is a Norwegian original; there were once around 1,000 in the country, but today, there are only 28.

China
Influences: Beijing's Forbidden City (Imperial Palace) and Temple of Heaven

The big thing to do in China is a 14-minute movie filmed entirely in "Circle-Vision 360," **Reflections of China** ✪. Enter through the replica of the Temple of Heaven, which, like the Beijing original, just received an affectionate refurbishment. You wouldn't believe the work it takes to make a film that surrounds you from all sides. The makers first had to figure out the optimal number of screens (nine—which enables projectors to be slipped in the gaps between screens) and then they had to suspend a ring of carefully calibrated cameras from helicopters so that the crew wasn't in the shots. In 2002, the footage of Shanghai had to be reshot because the city no longer resembled the 1982 version that was being shown. The result, which surveys some of the country's most beautiful vistas, is ravishing, although the masses no longer seem to care; it's not usually crowded. Make time to catch the **Dragon Legend Acrobats**, some of the most riveting street performers in the World Showcase. "Tomb Warriors: Guardian Spirits of Ancient China," in the **Gallery of the Whispering Willow**, is a miniature re-creation of the legendary terra-cotta warriors of the Han Dynasty, scaled to the size of a hotel room (the original mausoleum is twice the size of Epcot). The Gallery also contains a few cases of figures dating as far back as 260 B.C.

Fun Stuff to Buy: Upon exiting the film, cross the hangerlike shop and enter **Yang Feng Shangolian,** the main shop, selling lots of Ts and teas, silk jackets ($120, or $50 if you downgrade to rayon and polyester), form-fitting Asian dresses (in large sizes unheard of in China, $75–$150), and the witheringly strong liquor Wu Liang Ye ($80 for 375 ml).

Next along is the **Outpost,** which functions as a mushy catch-all receptacle for all things African. This area was once slated to contain a pavilion canvassing equatorial Africa, but that fell through. The **Mdundo Kibanda** store here once sold some interesting crafts, and there are still some Kenyan carvings (pricey), but lately, it's been stocked with face painters and spare souvenirs from other stores. Still, there are occasional storytelling sessions, and several days a week, the craftsman Andrew Mutiso is on hand, whittling and carving wares—he usually looks pretty engrossed in his wood and knife, but he likes answering questions.

Germany

Influences: Eltz Castle near Koblenz; Stahleck Fortress near Bacharach; Rothenburg (the Biergarten and the dragon slayer statue); facades from Frankfurt and Freiburg (the guildhall)

Lacking a true attraction (a water ride based on the Rhine was planned but never completed), Germany is popular for its food. The **Biergarten Restaurant** does sausages, beer, and the like—accompanied by yodeling and dancing—while the adjoining shop is for crystal doodads. The **Sommerfest** is the counter-service alternative for brats and pretzels. On the hour, the Clock Tower above the pavilion rings and two figures emerge, just like at the Glockenspiel in München (Munich). Another appealing, if incongruous, attraction that's not on the maps is the highly detailed **model train** display just past the German pavilion.

Fun Stuff to Buy: The pavilion is otherwise a string of connected one-room shops selling steins (from $30), figurines, crystal, Christmas ornaments, and other high-priced wares. The connected candy-and-wine shop, **Weinkeller,** is worth a gander, though: You'll find such pick-me-ups as Gluhwein ($14 a liter before the holidays), wine by the glass ($4–$7), toffee slabs ($4), and even chocolate bon-bons for 47¢ to 94¢. Full bags of assorted cookies are just $6 and can get your brood through the day. **Der Teddybär** sells toys, especially ones by Playmobil. In the window of **Das Kaufhaus** facing the lagoon, make a point of meeting Disney egg artist Jutta Levasseur, who has worked at Epcot since its opening day, painting traditional Christmas egg ornaments. She's usually working in the shop on Fridays and Saturdays (often more), and although her handiwork costs up to $1,200 for ostrich eggs and sometimes portrays distinctly un-German Disney characters, the most authentic traditional designs, on chicken eggs, are happily the most affordable (under $100).

Italy

Influences: Piazza di San Marco, Venice; stucco buildings of Tuscany; a fountain reminiscent of the work of Gian Lorenzo Bernini

The tiny pavilion for Italy lacks an attraction—the gondolas never leave the dock—so you must content yourself with the small-scale replicas of Venice's Doge's Palace and St. Mark's bell tower. The sit-down restaurant, **Tutto Italia,** charges an obscene $12 for tomatoes and mozzarella and deserves to be ignored.

Fun Stuff to Buy: Epcot's impressions of Italy are mostly culinary. Noodle around in the **Enoteca Castello** shop, noted for its expensive Venetian carnival masks, which also sells Perugina chocolate bars ($3.50) and Lazzaroni amaretti cookie snaps ($6.50 a bag). **Il Bel Cristallo** sells fragrances, crystal (are you sensing a theme here?), gourmet foods, and cookware.

U.S.A.

Influences: general Georgian/colonial Greek-revival buildings

Stereotypically, the U.S.A. pavilion, called **the American Adventure** ★★, takes pride of place in an area that's supposed to celebrate other countries (although Brits often snicker that its Georgian architecture style is distinctly English). Inside, the superlative **Voices of America** singing group, which excels at thorny close harmonies, entertains guests waiting to attend the half-hour Audio-Animatronic show, **the American Adventure.** Also in the lobby is the unfairly ignored **American Heritage Gallery.** The collection is cool: See Mark Twain's pen, Benjamin Franklin's side chair, and a moon rock given by Mrs. Gus Grissom.

In the American Adventure, said Ben and Mark are your Audio-Animatronic surrogates for a series of eye-popping (but ponderous) re-creations of snippets from America's patriotic mythology. Moving dioramas of seminal events such as a Susan B. Anthony speech and the founding of Yosemite National Park appear and vanish cinematically, leaving spectators marveling less at the wonder of America—the script is too canned for much of that—than at the massive amount of storage space that must lie beyond the proscenium.

Indeed, all that homespun corn is brought to you by some immensely complicated robotic and hydraulic systems. When this attraction first opened, the scene in which Franklin appears to mount stairs and then walk across the room was hailed as a technical milestone. The Will Rogers figure actually twirls a lasso. Although heavy on uplifting jingoism, the show scores points for touching lightly on a few unpleasant topics, including slavery and the suffering of Native Americans, but in general, it's not as deep as its stage: a quarter the size of a football field. (You'll see how this jukeboxlike theater set works in the Backstage Magic tour, p. 248.) Don't be the first to enter the auditorium or else you'll be marooned near the aisle, off to the side.

Fun Stuff to Buy: Heritage Manor Gifts, found next door, sells a weird selection of patriotic oddities, such as tricorner hats ($28) and presidential action figures ($5). The five-person **Spirit of America** fife and drum corps makes scheduled appearances in the forecourt.

Japan

Influences: 8th-century Horyuji Temple in Nara (pagoda); Katsura Imperial Villa (Yakitori House); Shirasagi-Jo castle at Hemeji (the rear fortress); Hiroshima (*torii* gate in the lagoon)

Now comes Japan, which is one of the most rewarding pavilions to explore. Hopefully, you can be there during one of the shows (check your *Times Guide*): the spectacularly thunderous **Matsuriza** drum shows, which are held at the base of the five-level **Goju-no-to pagoda,** or for a demonstration by candy artist **Miyuki,** who often follows the drums and does for sweets what clowns do for balloon animals; her heavily accented refrain "a preh-*zent* for you" is Epcot music to me. Japan has no giant attractions (like Germany, a show building was erected but never filled with its intended ride), but its shopping and dining are exemplary, and the outdoor garden behind the pagoda is a paragon of peace. At the back of the pavilion, go inside and turn left to tour the surprisingly large **Bijutsu-kan Gallery** ✭, stocked with some of the most accessible changing exhibitions in the entire resort; its most recent show, of antique tin toys, was lent by a collector who curates seven museums of them in Japan.

There are two places to eat, one in the cheaper counter-service category, and one serving sushi—a welcome taste of fresh food for a theme park. A red *torii* gate inspired by one in Hiroshima sits in the lagoon; the barnacles on its base are fake, and were glued on to simulate age.

Fun Stuff to Buy: The **Mitsukoshi Department Store,** named for the 300-year-old Japanese original, is the most fun to roam of any World Showcase shop. It stocks a wide variety of toys, chopstick sets ($4–$8), traditional wood sandals (from $65), linens, anime figures, and paper fans—but I love Japanese snacks, such as chocolate-dipped Pocky sticks ($3–$5), shrimp chips ($1), and Yan Yan sweet cookie paddles, which you dip into accompanying frosting ($1.25–$2). Vanilla or jasmine incense costs $9.50 here, but hold out for Morocco, where it's cheaper; the miso soup mix is a good deal, though ($3.50).

Morocco

Influences: Marrakesh (Koutoubia minaret), Rabat (Chella minaret), Fez (Bab Boujouloud Gate, Nejjarine Fountain), Casablanca

Morocco is another spectacular pavilion, if you're inclined to dig in. It flies higher than its neighbors because the country's king took an active interest in its construction, dispatching some 21 top craftsmen for the job. There's no movie or show (although Aladdin, the Genie, and Jasmine make regular appearances), and the architecture is a cross-country mishmash drawn from Marrakech, Fes, and Rabat. There are two terrific restaurants, one for service (Restaurant Marrakesh, deep in back, is atmospheric and romantic, with dozens of hanging lanterns and live entertainment) and one with a counter (Tangierine Café, in front). I often hold off lunchtime to get a plate of *shawarma* (sandwich wrap) here. Henna tattoos are also available, as is an intermittent 45-minute tour, **the Treasures of Morocco** ✭, which provides a free and fascinating primer on the North African country. Ask a cast member how to join it. **Fez House** is a tranquil, pillared two-level courtyard with a fountain and seating that recalls a classic Moroccan home; **the Gallery of Arts and History,** a mosaic-rich exhibition next to the Fez House, is unjustly ignored.

Fun Stuff to Buy: The middle courtyards are cluttered with souklike boutiques that blend one into another, perfumed with incense ($2.75; in a drawer, so ask)

Shhh . . . a Parking Secret

In the gap between France and United Kingdom, a side door **(International Gateway)** leads quickly to the pretty Disney BoardWalk area. A free ferry will also take you there; it continues on to the Swan and Dolphin hotels and, in about a half-hour, Hollywood Studios. You didn't hear it from me, but some guests have been known to talk their way past the parking guard at the BoardWalk, the Yacht Club, or the Beach Club ("I'm eating at the restaurant") just so they can save $12 on Epcot parking. If you park in the legit Epcot lot, be careful about timing if you decide to slip out to the BoardWalk for a while—there's no easy way back to the Epcot parking lot once the park closes.

and are stocked some of the most interesting and reasonably priced finds in all of Disney World, including footstools, wraps, tassled red fez caps ($18), glass tea sets ($75), hand-painted tambourines ($16), and Persian-style rugs perfect for the bathroom ($19, or $165 for a set of three sized up to 5-by-7 ft.). Ask a cast member (almost always from Morocco) to write your name in Arabic for you—it's free.

France

Influences: Various Belle Epoque Parisian and provincial streets; Château de Fontainbleu (the Palais du Cinema); the former Pont des Arts in Paris (the bridge to the United Kingdom)

France, done up to look like a typical Parisian neighborhood with a one-tenth replica of the upper stretch of the Eiffel Tower in the simulated distance (you can't go up it), is popular mostly for its food. In an alley in the back and to the left, you'll find **Boulangerie Pâtisserie,** which serves sweets such as chocolate éclairs and ham-and-cheese croissants for under $4—not a bad deal, and there are a few outdoor tables, or you can eat your cheese and crackers by the lake. The 18-minute movie, *Impressions de France,* is no longer the freshest example of a tourism movie (mostly classical music and postcard-worthy shots).

Not-So-Fun Stuff to Buy: The cheesiest souvenirs ($10 5-in. Eiffel Towers) are available at **Souvenirs de France.** Across the lane, in **L'Esprit de la Provence,** a kitchen shop, wooden spoons are $5 and patterned oven mitts are $12. I think most of the stuff for sale at this pavilion's shops are among the least imaginative and the most kitschy in World Showcase—I mean, mouse-ear wine stoppers for $9 at **Aux Vins de France?** (Wine tastings are $8.) A pricey Guerlain fragrance shop, **Plume et Palette?** As I stand in this pavilion, I can't help but realize that for what I've paid Disney, I could have flown all the way to Paris to ascend the real Eiffel Tower. There's no substitute. That said, the street act **Serveur Amusant,** an acrobat who does handstands on stacked chairs, is thrilling.

United Kingdom

Influences: Anne Hathaway's Cottage, Stratford-upon-Avon (the Tea Caddy); Queen Anne style (the middle promenade); Hampton Court, London (Sportsman's Shoppe); Victorian, country, and traditional pub styles (Rose & Crown)

The final two pavilions are the largely English-speaking ones, so if you're going clockwise, the exotica is over. United Kingdom, another wild mix of architectural styles, has no rides or shows, so it's popular chiefly for its English-style pub, the Rose & Crown Pub & Dining Room (pints of ale, fish and chips), and a counter-service fish and chips shop. That's two fish and chips outlets in a block—far more than you'd find even in London these days. In the evenings, duck into the pub to catch Carol Stein, the "Hat Lady," who sings and plays piano beneath her collection of wacky hatwear. She's a longtime Disney entertainer, and the company so values her that when her old home at Pleasure Island's improv club closed, she was given this nook to call her new home.

Fun Stuff to Buy: Featured shopping in the conjoined **Sportsman's Shoppe, the Crown & Crest,** and **Toy Soldier** includes British soccer jerseys, tea, chocolate, heraldic crests, books on English history, Mr. Men merchandise, Pooh merch, and those green Peter Pan hats with the red feather ($10). Across the way, **Lords and Ladies** does fragrances and the **Tea Caddy** sells Twinings tea and mugs. Few people know about the **hedge maze,** and fewer still know that the Cadbury candy bars and McVitie's biscuits ($2.50) in the shops are available for a few bucks less at World Market near the Florida Mall (p. 296).

Canada

Influences: 19th-century Victorian colonial architecture (Hotel du Canada); emblematic northwestern Indian design and Maritime Provinces towns; Butchart Gardens, Victoria (Victoria Gardens)

The nearest pavilion to Imagination!, Canada, like China, has a movie, predictably named **O Canada!,** shot with nine cameras in Circle-Vision 360 (a process Walt Disney originally called Circarama). The best way to find the film is by heading down the path marked Le Cellier, which leads through an otherwise hidden artificial canyon delightfully washed by a man-made waterfall. The 18-minute presentation (1982), which requires audiences to stand, was recently refurbished by adding newly shot bits with Martin Short as emcee. Most of its spectacular scenery (the Rockies, the Bay of Fundy) is timeless. Like Japan, Canada's **gardens** (they were inspired by Victoria's Butchart Gardens, although the sign says Victoria Gardens) are a surprising oasis. The worthwhile live act here is the **Off Kilter** at the amphitheater, in which hot men in kilts bash out palatable rock tunes.

Fun Stuff to Buy: The shop, **Northwest Mercantile,** purports to honor Canada's French Canadian and pioneer heritage, but mostly hawks maple syrup ($16 for 15 oz.), stuffed huskies and beavers, and drugstore Canadian candies such as Aero bars ($2.50). The lagoon-side shop between Canada and the plaza often sells markdown souvenirs for $10 or less—a very unusual promotion in the World.

Epcot at Night

There are no parades anymore at Epcot, but usually at 9pm, the pulse-pounding **IllumiNations: Reflections of Earth** ★★★ flames-and-water spectacular takes place over World Showcase Lagoon. Its central globe, which is studded with 15,500 tiny video screens, weighs some 350,000 pounds, and the show's so-called Inferno Barge carries a payload of 4,000 gallons of propane. Crowds start building on the banks 2 hours before showtime, but I find doing that a waste of time, and therefore money, as a day's admission is so steep. Any view of the center of the lake will be fine (some people find the islands upsetting, but I don't), but take care to be upwind or you may be engulfed by smoke.

WHERE TO EAT AT EPCOT

Epcot is far and away the best Disney park for food selection. People slip into the side International Gateway just to sup. Reservations for the sit-down restaurants can be made at ☎ 407/939-3463. The park's main **fruit stands** ($1 a piece, three times that for cups) are in the Land and between China and Germany.

The Land   The **Sunshine Seasons** ★★★ food court has the best selection, the freshest food, and best value of all Epcot's counter-service locations. It's fantastic. Salads, grilled items (huge seared tuna steak with salad, $8), sandwiches, and Asian dishes, with no fried food, burgers, or pizza. The desserts are epic (textured strawberry Bavarian, gorgeous Butterfinger cheesecake; $4) would cost twice as much in a restaurant. The sit-down, dinner-only **Garden Grill**'s ★ 🧒 dining room, found upstairs, is on a slowly rotating turntable that overlooks the Living with the Land boat ride (seats on its lower level have the clearer view). Meals are family style, dinerlike (fried catfish, flank steak—mostly middling), and all you can eat. Some vegetables at both restaurants, particularly cucumbers and tomatoes, were grown in the pavilion's own greenhouses and might arrive shaped like Mickey ears.

The Seas with Nemo & Friends   At the **Coral Reef Restaurant,** your table faces the windows of the aquarium and you dine on the buddies of the fish swimming in your view. Entrees are in the mid-$20s, and although the setting rocks, I'll be honest: I had some of the worst food in my life here.

Innoventions   **Electric Umbrella** ★ is Future World's other important counter-service locale. Expect burgers, roast-beef sandwiches, and turkey wraps for $7 to $8, and unusually, it allows you fill your own soda. Across the plaza, **Fountain View** does 16 flavors of scoop ice cream for $2.69 and up.

Mexico   Don't even attempt to get a table at **San Angel Inn Restaurante,** beneath the false sky inside the pyramid, without a reservation. Its food (lunch, midteens; dinner in the mid-$20s) is of a higher quality than the burritos and tacos at **Cantina de San Angel** ★, the waterfront counter-service option for under $8.

Its *tacos al carbon* (flour tortillas filled with grilled chicken, onions, and peppers, served with refried beans; $8) are unusual theme park fare and sell briskly.

Norway **Akershus Royal Banquet Hall** 🧒 hosts Princess Storybook Dining, an all-you-can-eat character meal starring princesses, three times a day. The price is a bit rich, but the rice cream dessert ($2.30) at the pavilion's bake shop, **Kringla Bakeri Og Kafé** ★★, can't be found anywhere else—more than one person claims this smooth, strawberry-topped rice pudding snack to be their favorite sweet in all Walt Disney World.

China Like Mexico, there are a high-end and a low-end version here. **Nine Dragons Restaurant** (entrees $15 at lunch, and $18 at dinner) serves the sit-down crowd, and **Lotus Blossom Café** ★ (veggie stir-fry, $7), the quick-service location, makes hasty but tasty dishes for those on the go.

Germany A good spot for Oktoberfest entertainment and hearty food, **Biergarten Restaurant** ★★ is a dusky sit-down all-you-can-eat buffet (the only one in World Showcase that isn't staffed by princesses), which costs $20 adult/$11 kids at lunch, and $29/$14 after 4pm. Outside, the **Sommerfest** kiosk sells bratwurst and sausages for under $7.

Italy The sit-down **Tutto Italia** is too expensive—$19 to $25 for pasta?

The American Experience **Liberty Inn** does cheap burgers, barbecue pork sandwiches, chicken, and salads for under $9, with a free toppings bar. Outside, the **Fife & Drum** is where to get turkey legs ($6.20).

Japan Of the restaurants, the most affordable is the **Yakitori House** counter-service location by the gardens (the usual $7–$8 level), which is small but generally not crowded, and which supplies teriyaki chicken, avocado and crab rolls, and $3.30 pot stickers. Upstairs you'll find two un-Disney choices, both run by the Mitsukoshi store: **Teppan Edo,** a fun experience at which a chef slices, dices, and cooks at the griddle built into your table ($18–$29); and **Tokyo Dining,** which has some views of the lagoon, tempura and grills around $20, and where a sushi menu includes $5 pieces and rolls for $8. Facing the lagoon under the pagoda, the **Kaki-Gori** kiosk (closed in cold weather) serves shaved ice with syrup (including honeydew and cherry flavors) for $2.25, and plum wine for $4.50.

Morocco **Tangierine Café** ★★★, the counter-service location, is a great place to dodge crowds. It serves shawarma for $12 to $14, with hummus, couscous, bread, and tabouleh; and meatball platters ($12) with yellow rice. Add baklava for $2.50; kids can get burgers or chicken fingers for $7. **Restaurant Marrakesh** ★★, tucked in the back, does sit-down lunch entrees for around $18 and dinner for $28 (lots of kabobs and platters), but I advise seizing on its daily lunch special (appetizer, entree, and dessert for $22), because for your money, you'll also be treated to live performances by musicians, a belly dancer, and waiters who theatrically pour your mint tea from a few feet above your glass. (The restaurant, rarely full, also sells a cookbook of its best dishes for just $7.40.)

France   In the far recesses of the pavilion, grab a fast, bready bite at **Boulangerie Pâtisserie** ✪✪, such as a chocolate croissant or a ham-and-cheese croissant (both around $3—great bargains) or three cheeses and a half-baguette for $6. A cash-only kiosk on the lagoon griddles up hot crepes (with sweet fillings, not meat), also for $4. There are two sit-down places for meals. **Les Chefs de France** imitates a typical Parisian sidewalk cafe (escargot casserole, $10; a three-course prix-fixe meal for $20 until 2pm, then $35 until 7pm). **Bistro de Paris,** located upstairs, is so expensive (mains over $30) that there's no point going. You're paying for the view of IllumiNations—if you're going to blow that kind of cash, at least make sure you reserve at the right time to get some entertainment out of it.

United Kingdom   The **Yorkshire County Fish Shop** ✪ walk-up fish-and-chips window is perpetually busy; the wares are made by the Harry Ramsden's chain. You get two strips of fish with chips (fries) for $8—make sure to put vinegar, not ketchup, on the fries the way the English do. Ale costs a sharp $8.50. There's also the more expensive sit-down **Rose & Crown Pub,** a realistic-looking boozer where you can also raise a simple beer (pints are $7.50; that's more than twice as much as in London, even with the lousy exchange).

Canada   The restaurant, **Le Cellier Steakhouse,** is one of the more affordable sit-downs in World Showcase (lunch: $15 sandwiches, $25 entrees; dinner: entrees in the mid-$20s), which isn't saying much.

DISNEY'S HOLLYWOOD STUDIOS

Just as Epcot celebrates idealized industry and Animal Kingdom honors fauna, the 154-acre Disney's Hollywood Studios strives to evoke the romance of the movies. Not just any movies, of course, but mostly that pastel-hued fantasy of the Hollywood of 60 years ago, where gossip columnists ruled the radio and starlets could be discovered at Schwab's.

While it was originally conceived as a single pavilion about show business for Epcot, Universal's announcement of its invasion of the Florida market prodded Disney executives to hastily expand the concept into an entire park. In 1989, the Studios opened with just two rides (the Great Movie Ride and the Backlot Tour) to head off the competition. The Studios have never quite recovered from its half-baked genesis. Disney is working to sexy it up by changing its name (its original one, Disney–MGM Studios, was abandoned in early 2008) and adding attractions (Toy Story Midway Mania opened a few months later), but you won't find many people who will name it as their favorite of the four parks, which is why I think it's the one you should do last.

There are a few reasons why it's not one of Disney's most transporting endeavors. One is that its design is not harmonious or symmetrical, which makes it harder to navigate. Another problem: When you look at the slate of attractions, you'll notice it's light on rides and heavy on shows, especially ones for small children, which, for my money, isn't enough. Still, *every* park is lacking in comparison to something as revolutionary as the Magic Kingdom, and the dearth of activities is balanced by the fact that two of its rides are among Disney's best: the Tower of Terror and the Rock 'n' Roller Coaster.

The park doesn't possess enough attractions to fill a complete day—it's got about half the number in Magic Kingdom—which means that guests can either

Disney's Hollywood Studios

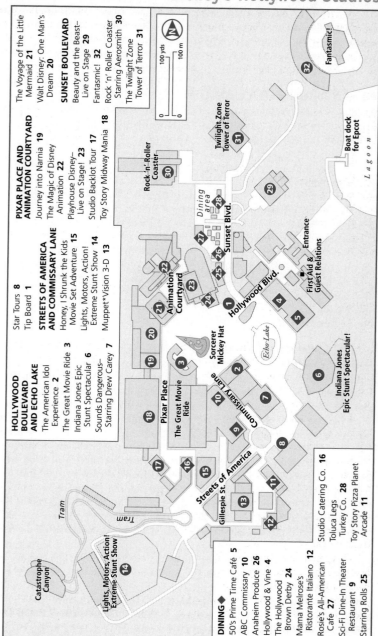

HOLLYWOOD BOULEVARD AND ECHO LAKE
The American Idol Experience **2**
The Great Movie Ride **3**
Indiana Jones Epic Stunt Spectacular **6**
Sounds Dangerous—Starring Drew Carey **7**
Star Tours **8**
Tip Board **1**

STREETS OF AMERICA AND COMMISSARY LANE
Honey, I Shrunk the Kids Movie Set Adventure **15**
Lights, Motors, Action! Extreme Stunt Show **14**
Muppet*Vision 3-D **13**

PIXAR PLACE AND ANIMATION COURTYARD
Journey into Narnia **19**
The Magic of Disney Animation **22**
Playhouse Disney—Live on Stage! **23**
Studio Backlot Tour **17**
Toy Story Midway Mania **18**

The Voyage of the Little Mermaid **21**
Walt Disney: One Man's Dream **20**

SUNSET BOULEVARD
Beauty and the Beast—Live on Stage **29**
Fantasmic! **32**
Rock 'n' Roller Coaster Starring Aerosmith **30**
The Twilight Zone Tower of Terror **31**

DINING ◆
50's Prime Time Café **5**
ABC Commissary **10**
Anaheim Produce **26**
Hollywood & Vine **4**
The Hollywood Brown Derby **24**
Mama Melrose's Ristorante Italiano **12**
Rosie's All-American Cafe **27**
Sci-Fi Dine-In Theater Restaurant **9**
Starring Rolls **25**
Studio Catering Co. **16**
Toluca Legs Turkey Co. **28**
Toy Story Pizza Planet Arcade **11**

combine its highlights on the same day with Disney's Animal Kingdom, or they can allow themselves a more leisurely pace, perhaps lingering long enough to catch the dazzling pyrotechnic evening show, Fantasmic!

Guests arrive by the usual car/tram combo, by bus, or by ferry, which sails from the Swan and Dolphin area and continues on to Epcot.

HOLLYWOOD BOULEVARD & ECHO LAKE

As soon as you're through the gates, take care of business (strollers, wheelchairs, lockers) in the plaza before proceeding down Hollywood Boulevard. There are no attractions in this section, only shops and restaurants.

Hollywood Boulevard culminates with the 122-foot-tall **Sorcerer Mickey Hat,** the park's central icon that is from, ironically, Walt Disney's assault on typical Hollywood movies, *Fantasia.* There are no attractions in there, but there is an open-air souvenir stall. In front of the hat is the park's **tip board,** where wait times and show schedules are posted. Just behind the hat, which wasn't added until 2001, is the park's original focal point, the replica of Grauman's Chinese Theater (Disney calls it **"the Chinese Theater"**), which has a forecourt graced with actual handprints and footprints of movie stars who visited in the park's early years, mostly at the behest of Disney execs. There are no prints past 1999, around the time the park gave up the dream of being a center for important film production. Some are uncomfortably dated: Jamie Farr, Charlie Korsmo, Harry Anderson, and Warren Beatty as Dick Tracy. There are some true perennials, though, including Audrey Hepburn, Jim Henson, Samuel L. Jackson, Bette Midler, and Ann Miller.

Inside is **the Great Movie Ride** ✮✮, which was a showpiece in 1989 but now feels like a mechanized waxworks. Aided by a human narrator reciting a hoary script, audiences slowly cruise in traveling theater slabs past Audio-Animatronic reproductions of scenes from famous movies, including *Singin' in the Rain, Alien,* and a Munchkin-crammed *The Wizard of Oz* (its Wicked Witch figure was a landmark because it was the first time Imagineers figured out that the key to lifelike action was compensating for sudden movements with minute return movements). This is really the only place where the old MGM brand appears now. At one point during the 22-minute journey, which concludes with a viewing of a fast-paced and expertly edited movie montage, cars experience one of two possible plotlines—for example, getting caught in the crossfire of a James Cagney gangland classic or a John Wayne western, with guns that shoot sparks. The robots have looked fresher (although Gene Kelly personally approved his likeness, I think he looks more like Timothy Dalton), and some kids won't be familiar with the references (Busby Berkeley, for example), but I think the production is endearing. Lines are never very long, but they do tend to spike just after the parade. The queue area has a few cases containing carousel horses from popular movies such as *Mary Poppins.*

To the left of Hollywood Boulevard, Echo Lake is a wide-open space with a small pond in the middle. On its shores is **Sounds Dangerous—Starring Drew Carey,** an awful attraction that was recently demoted to part-time status. This 12-minute movie is old and cheap. Guests wear headphones as they watch a movie, which goes pitch black (parents be warned) for 7 minutes while we hear what

The Best of Disney's Hollywood Studios

Don't miss if you're 6: Voyage of the Little Mermaid

Don't miss if you're 16: Rock 'n' Roller Coaster

Requisite photo op: Sorcerer Mickey Hat

Food you can only get here: Grapefruit Cake, the Hollywood Brown Derby, Hollywood Boulevard; Peanut Butter and Jelly Milkshake, 50's Prime Time Café, Echo Lake

The most crowded, so go early: Toy Story Midway Mania

Skippable: Sounds Dangerous—Starring Drew Carey

Quintessentially Disney: Walt Disney: One Man's Dream; the Great Movie Ride

Biggest thrill: Twilight Zone Tower of Terror

Best show: Voyage of the Little Mermaid

Character meals: Hollywood & Vine (breakfast, lunch)

Where to find peace: Around Echo Lake

Drew is doing. You learn nothing beyond the fact that sounds are important. The other attraction on the lake, **the American Idol Experience,** is a newly opened (2009) talent competition that entices park guests, especially kids (14 and older), to warble for praise. Wannabe singers audition (arrive early if you want to try out), and the cream of the crop will eventually return that day to perform for voting audiences while a giant TV broadcasts the melismatic mélange for all passersby to endure. One daily winner receives a golden ticket for the real TV show auditions—like a Fastpass to see Simon. It's a slick recap version of the Fox show, except without the cruelty, but it's truly nothing but glorified karaoke. See it once if you must, because it's well produced, but it's unlikely you'll want to see it again.

Check the *Times Guide* for performances of the 30-minute **Indiana Jones Epic Stunt Spectacular** ★★, a bone-rattling tour de force of hair-raising daredevilry—rolling-boulder dodging, trucks flipping over and exploding—that simultaneously titillates and, to a lesser degree, reminds you how such feats of derring-do are typically rigged and filmed for the movies. While the gigantic sets—a South American treasure tomb, a Cairo street market, and a desert airport—are being struck by stagehands, cast members horse around with adult audience volunteers to keep things rolling. They also try hard to convince you that they're really filming these sequences—you may need to explain to young children why they're lying about that, and about calling the lead actor "Harrison Ford's stunt double," but most kids understand the violence is fake. The acrobats and gymnasts who do the stunts, fights, and tumbles are very skilled, and the production values are among the highest of any show at the Disney parks. The outdoor amphitheater is sheltered, and you can bring drinks and food. **Strategy:** Arrive about 20 minutes early, as there's a warm-up and volunteers are selected before showtime. It's mounted about five times daily.

The product of a partnership with George Lucas, **Star Tours** ✦ is a bumpy, 40-person motion-simulator capsule that has you riding shotgun with an ineffectual droid named RX-24 (voiced by actor Paul Reubens) on an ill-fated and turbulent excursion to hang out with the Ewoks on the moon of Endor. In 5 minutes, you manage to lose control, navigate a comet field, travel at light speed, get caught in a tractor beam, and join an assault on the Death Star. The technology, now more than 20 years old, is showing its seams (there are plans to update it), but it's still a top example of its type: The video is well matched to the movements, which cuts down on reports of nausea. The replica AT-AT out front shoots streams of water, which kids jostle to catch. If this ride catches your fancy, you should know that in May and June, the park mounts Star Wars Weekends, when actors from the movie arrive for signings, parades, Q&As, and brief workshops. Fans of the franchise come out in force, so to speak. Beside it at the **Jedi Training Academy** show (see the *Times Guide*), kids are given robes, telescoping "light sabers," and some gentle training by a "Jedi master." It's cute.

Stylistically, this part of the park is a mess. Outside of Star Tours, you're simultaneously on a foreign planet, in Art Deco Hollywood, and somewhere vaguely jungled. There's no sense of place that the Magic Kingdom's themed lands impart—that's the sign of a hastily planned park.

SUNSET BOULEVARD

The prime items in the park are on this street, which peels off not from the hub with the hat, as you might expect, but from the middle of Hollywood Boulevard.

Sunset Boulevard terminates below the salmon-colored "Hollywood Tower Hotel." This 199-foot structure, the tallest ride at Disney World, is **The Twilight Zone Tower of Terror** ✦✦✦, one of the smartest, most exciting experiences in Walt Disney World, and the best version of the ride at any Disney park. It shouldn't be missed. Guests are ushered through the lobby, library, and boiler room of a cobwebby 1930s Los Angeles hotel—the decor is sublimely detailed—before being seated in a 21-passenger "elevator" car that, floor by floor, ascends the tower and then, without visible tracks, emerges from the shaft and roams an upper level. Soon, you've entered a second shaft and, after a pregnant moment of tension, you're sent into what seems to be a free fall (in reality, you're being pulled faster than the speed of gravity) and a series of thrilling up-and-down leaps. The fall sequence is randomly controlled by computer, and you never drop more than a few stories—but the total darkness, periodically punctured by picture-window views of the theme park far below as you become momentarily weightless, keys up the giddy fear factor. The planning and execution of this ride are without equal, and because the drop sequence is different each time, you can ride repeatedly without duplicating your exact fall. It's impossible not to smile. **Strategy:** Don't bother using Fastpass unless the line extends way outside of the building. In the preshow "library" room, move to the wall diagonally across from the entry door and you'll exit first, saving you time. In the boarding area, the best views are in the front row, numbered 1 and 2, although you may not be given a choice. Chickens can wait in line with you and bail before the ride.

Left through the archway as you face the Tower, **Rock 'n' Roller Coaster Starring Aerosmith** ✮✮✮ (1999) launches 24-passenger "limousine" trains from 0 to 57mph in under 3 seconds, sending them through a 92-second rampage through smooth corkscrews and turns that are intensified by fluorescent symbols of Los Angeles (at one point, you dive though an O of the Hollywood sign). The indoor setup is a boon, as it means the ride can operate during the rain, and it makes the journey slightly less disorienting for inexperienced coaster riders. Cooler yet, speakers in each headrest (there are more than 900 in total) play Aerosmith music, which is perfectly timed to the dips and rolls. **Strategy:** If you must choose, use your Fastpass privileges for the coaster, not the Tower, because its Fastpass line is absorbed quickly. There's also a single-rider line, though it's not always quick. I know people who call this their favorite ride in all of Walt Disney World. I know just as many people who refuse to set foot on it.

Adding a welcome dimension to the park for young children who may not care for portentous shows, the 30-minute **Beauty and the Beast—Live on Stage** 🧒, off Sunset Boulevard, is advertised as "Broadway-style," but it's really not. It's a theme park–style, simplified version of the movie, with the most popular songs. The story is highly condensed (you never find out why Belle ends up at the Beast's castle and Gaston's fate is not shown) and many characters inhabit whole-body costumes, speaking recorded dialogue with unblinking eyes—to the benefit of timid kids and souvenir shop managers, the Beast looks more like a plush toy than a scary monster. Still, its intended audience doesn't notice such shortcomings. They cheer like it's a rock concert and hoist videophones during the ball scene, and because of that, most performances are jammed. The metal benches are numbing, but at least the amphitheater is covered. **Strategy:** Arrive 20 minutes early unless you want to be in the back, where afternoon sun can seep in and heat up the rear.

Fantasmic! ✮✮✮, a popular 25-minute pyrotechnics show featuring character-laden showboats, a 59-foot man-made mountain, flaming water, and lasers projected onto a giant water curtain, takes place a few times a week in the 6,500-seat waterfront Hollywood Hills Amphitheatre. Although it's a strong show by dint of its uniqueness, I'm always stunned to see people start arriving at the theater as much as *2 hours* before showtime. I don't think it's worth that kind of commitment, and the seating is too hard on the derriere. Most people will be satisfied taking their chances and showing up within 30 minutes of showtime. **Strategy:** On nights when there are two performances (not common anymore), do the second one, as it's always less crowded. Sit toward the rear to avoid catching water from the special effects and to the right to make exiting easier. There is a snack bar in the amphitheater—assuage the wait by picnicking.

STREETS OF AMERICA & COMMISSARY LANE

Streets of America is a confusing zone of backlot-style city blocks, mostly facades, made to look like aging versions of New York City and San Francisco. Its primary attraction is photo ops. Look around for a few tricks, like the umbrella affixed to a lamppost in the square that's spritzed with showers a la *Singin' in the Rain*. Also on the square, the enormous **Lights, Motors, Action! Extreme Stunt Show** ✮ takes planning because it happens only two or three times daily. Loud, brawling, and moderately exciting enough to see once, it's a showcase for stunt driving dressed up like a film shoot for a car chase/action scene. The engaging half-hour show, which uses a fleet of specially built, extra-nimble cars (plus a jet ski or two) and tells lots of lies about filming an actual movie scene while you're there, was imported from Paris's Walt Disney Studios Park (hence the set that looks like a Mediterranean port), but it seems tailor-made for American audiences. **Strategy:** Because the stage is so wide, I suggest taking a seat in the middle or near the top of the grandstand. You won't wrestle for a spot—the stadium seats 5,000. Don't worry: The stunts happen at a safe remove from the auditorium, across a moat.

The **Honey, I Shrunk the Kids Movie Set Adventure** 🧒 is a high-concept playground that simulates the sights and sounds of the average backyard—if your kids were the size of an ant. In addition to giant insects, cargo nets, and a slide that looks like Kodak film (yep, product placement), there's a giant Super Soaker that sprays the unsuspecting. It's pretty much the only place here to turn kids loose.

The portion behind the backlot is a Muppet-themed streetscape. Behind the fabulous rotating fountain depicting Miss Piggy as the Statue of Liberty, the 17-minute **Muppet*Vision 3-D** ⭐ 🧒 movie features various tricks such as air blasts to make you feel like it's actually happening. The doors on the right lead to the back of the auditorium and the ones on the left lead to the front; for the fullest view, I suggest sticking in the middle, since the theater's walls become part of the show, and both live and Audio-Animatronic figures will appear on either side and even in the back. The preshow is amusing in that Muppet way (says Sam the Eagle about seating procedures: "Stopping in the middle is distinctly unpatriotic!"), and while the movie contains a few missteps (Waldo, a CG character, lacks creativity), it's fast moving and includes lots of beloved *Muppet Show* (but no *Sesame Street*) favorites such as Miss Piggy and Kermit. The Muppets, too, lend themselves very nicely to Audio-Animatronic technology. Because of tight spaces, crowds look huge for this show, but the theater holds nearly 600. **Strategy:** Lines are longest just after the Indiana Jones show lets out. By the exit, two cars from *Cars* purr in Luigi's Garage, ripe for more photos.

Note: Commissary Lane is the pass-through to the Sorcerer Mickey Hat. Lots of guests get it confused with Mickey Avenue, which feeds from the motor stunt show to Animation Courtyard. The two are connected by Streets of America.

PIXAR PLACE & ANIMATION COURTYARD

In 2008, Disney gave the anonymous cul-de-sac of Mickey Avenue a fresh new name: Pixar Place. Its primary draw is **Toy Story Midway Mania** ⭐⭐⭐, the new marquee attraction. The plotless indoor ride updates the gimmick of the Magic Kingdom's Buzz Lightyear extravaganza: Wearing 3-D glasses, passengers shoot their way through a series of six animated midway games (a Bo Peep egg toss, a Little Green Men ring toss) based on the Pixar toybox characters. Along the way, air puffs and mist heighten the reality. Your cannon is easy to work—you just tug a little cord and it fires. Scoring points is harder; both accuracy and intensity count. The queue area, stuffed with outsize toys such as Tinkertoys and Barrel of Monkeys, makes waiting a delight: A 6-foot-tall, lifelike Mr. Potato Head entertains everyone with live interaction, hoary jokes ("Is this an audience or a jigsaw puzzle?"), and songs. Across Pixar Place, Woody and Buzz meet kids in an air-conditioned room, and characters like the army men toys appear all the time.

The Backlot That Isn't

At the extreme end of Pixar Place, the **Studio Backlot Tour** was once a centerpiece of the park, but has been whittled away to nearly nothing. It doesn't help that so few productions are actually filmed here—it's been a decade since anything of note was made—leaving the guides to fib about how busy employees are. New tours start every 15 minutes and take about 35 minutes. It's less crowded early in the day and closes by late afternoon.

The first segment is the Special Effects Water Tank Show, which accepts four volunteers (adults only; raise your hand for duty in the queue). There, standing guests watch how the bullet impacts, explosions, and deluges of a ship-attack movie sequence are shot and cut together to look real. *Tip:* For the best views from the front row of the audience section, join the right-hand row in the queue area. Be among the first people out of there, because the next section finds you in yet another queue, this one in a warehouse full of old movie props (a few of which you may recognize), which feeds the boarding area for a tram; the seats on its left are best.

Although the guides keep telling you "you never know who or what you may see on the backlot," they're faking, because a few years ago, Disney bulldozed most of it, including Residential Street, a little village for exterior shots (the *Golden Girls* and *Empty Nest* house facades were here), to make room for the Lights, Motors, Action! Extreme Stunt Show (see earlier). When drivers are rehearsing or performing, the shriek of the engines and the funk of burning rubber make the tram miserable and the narrator inaudible. The 20-minute trip loops past some old prop vehicles (from *The Rocketeer, Pearl Harbor,* and other movies Disney wanted to do better) in the scaled-down Boneyard; through wardrobe houses (the staff is darning theme park uniforms, not movie costumes); and then you pass through Catastrophe Canyon, where, seated safely, you'll witness a simulated earthquake, the heat of an exploding oil tanker, and a flash flood—all in the space of seconds. The wizardry, which resets every $3\frac{1}{2}$ minutes for a new batch of guests, is heart-pounding fun—although no thinking person believes the bald lie that the special effects crew that built this rig has stepped away "on a break." Those sitting on the left might get a tad wet, and you'll need sunglasses in the afternoon. On the way out, you'll spot a Gulfstream jet Walt Disney used on his real estate–grabbing missions to Florida.

Journey into Narnia: Prince Caspian is an exhibition of props and costumes plus a short movie. It feels like an ad for a movie franchise. It is.

Over in Animation Courtyard you'll find the only Fastpass-eligible attraction that most young children will like: **The Voyage of the Little Mermaid** ★★ (kids) is on the hard-to-find Animation Courtyard, located out a side door to the right of the Sorcerer Mickey Hat. This bright, energetic, condensed version of the animated

Hollywood History for Sale

Don't miss the cabin-esque house to the right as you exit the park. This is **Sid Cahuenga's One-of-a-Kind Antiques and Curios**, a strange and wonderful memorabilia shop, not run by Disney, with an inventory so interesting it could qualify as a museum. You can't afford everything (Dick Van Dyke's pastel-striped "Jolly Holiday" jacket from *Mary Poppins* costs $65,000), but just looking is enriching. On my last visit, there were frog props from *Magnolia*, tribbles from *Deep Space Nine*, Clark Gable's 1955 check for $9.40 to a hardware store, newspaper props ("Roxie Hard Expecting" from *Chicago*), and many autographed photos. It may be the most Hollywood thing about Hollywood Studios.

movie has high production values (puppets, live actors, mist, and a cool undersea-themed auditorium) and is a standout. **Strategy:** In the preshow holding pen, the doors to the left lead to the back half of the theater; because the blacklight puppetry of the marvelous "Under the Sea" sequence can be spoiled if you see too much detail, I suggest sitting there. Consider putting very small kids in your lap so they can see better. Because of its cooling humidity, this show is a top contender for the best show to see in the heat of the day.

Across the courtyard is the other top show for the youngest guests: **Playhouse Disney—Live on Stage!** 🧒 is for people who will obediently rise and dance when commanded by Winnie the Pooh. The show is simple, with a warehouse-like set (warning, adults: you sit on the ground), and inspires such fervent participation from under 5s that it may feel like a meeting for a cult that you're not a member of. If you don't know the names JoJo, Handy Manny, or Tigger, this sing-along revue isn't for you. The parental units won't be too bored, as this de facto Disney Channel ad is fast paced, like changing the channel every 4 minutes. Obviously, anyone old enough to do a book report can skip it. **Strategy:** Lines for this show can be long, so I advise trying it first thing or in late afternoon.

At the far end of Animation Courtyard, the self-guided **the Magic of Disney Animation** tour is, in my opinion, the most telling display of the Walt Disney Company's flagrance in placing greed above heritage. Originally it provided a firsthand look at the labor-intensive work that produced all those famous Disney movies. Guests could watch live animators perfect their upcoming release (*Mulan* and *Lilo & Stitch* were made right here), and they'd come to understand the time-honored ink-and-paint process that Walt Disney himself used to build his empire, one cel at time. But Disney fired its Florida-based animators, so there's nothing more to see. Instead, you get a hokey, 9-minute show highlighting only the ideas stage of the process, followed by an ad for whatever computer-animated film will be released next. Then you're dumped in an area of paltry interactive exhibits where kids can determine which Disney character their personality is most like (me: Tarzan). The biggest benefit of exploring is the chance to see major characters (Mickey, plus the latest ones from Pixar's and other films) in the A/C. You can also take a worthwhile 15-minute group crash course in drawing a popular character (such as Winnie or Minnie) with a guide, and you can bring your artwork

Walt Disney's Legacy

Pretty much every advance that made Walt Disney the preeminent name in entertainment—adding sound to cartoons, then color, and then turning a 7-minute art form into full-length features—was accomplished out of a feverish pursuit of quality, not profit. Each time Walt did something new, it nearly bankrupted him, and he suffered nervous breakdowns; but to him, there was nothing more important than furnishing a superior product to the public, accessible to anyone. "I'm afraid that this business will be thrown into the regular Hollywood groove and that they will start throwing these cartoons at the public," he wrote in the 1930s. "All they think of is how much money they can get out of a thing."

For years after his death, Disney's populist ideals limped on; until the 1980s, the parking charge at Disneyland was an insanely low $1. The last Disney World hotels that Walt himself helped plan, the Contemporary, Fort Wilderness, and the Polynesian, intentionally eschewed luxury pretensions.

Yet today, profit and relentless branding are the obsessions, which is why the newest rides are based on inexpensive video projections, why perks that don't make money are removed, why newer initiatives trade on luxury, and why new DVD releases are referenced more often than Disney classics. Disney has even outsourced its Audio-Animatronics, a technology the company created.

It's a double-edged sword: The modern company invokes Walt's name to promote itself, but that only makes customers more vigilant about potential betrayals. I'm still in awe of the efficiency and playful munificence with which the old Disney World was run, and in defense of that still-attainable benchmark, I say that if the corporate masters who control the Disney empire insist on continuously invoking the name of Walt Disney and his ideals, they should at least be honest enough to admit that Disney himself did business in a far different, and far more generous, fashion.

---

home for free. Otherwise, the art of handmade animation, through which the Disney empire was built, cel by cel, is barely discussed. You receive no more information than you could find in a 2-minute DVD extra, yet you blow 30 minutes of your time. **Strategy:** Skip the show and just enjoy the character greetings by entering through the back door, through the Animation Gallery, where you'll pass 13 Oscars (all won for hand animation, it bears noting). All the more shame that animation is supposed to be the studio's bread and butter. If you love Disney, this may bring you down.

I feel differently about the terrific walk-through museum **Walt Disney: One Man's Dream** ★★, the only historic close-up on resort property. Mostly overlooked, the display is a requisite stop for anyone curious about the undeniable achievements of this driven man. Here, you (and a few other stragglers) learn that just as a generation of kids carry an obsession with Walt Disney World after a brief exposure, Walt Disney became obsessed with turn-of-the-20th-century Americana after briefly living in the town of Marceline, Missouri. He also saw early film and stage versions of *Snow White* and *Alice in Wonderland,* which he later remade to his own specifications—Walt, the exhibition proves, was a masterful recycler. He also had a symbiotic relationship with his brother Roy, whom he followed first into the military, then to Kansas City, and finally to Hollywood.

Some suspicious Disney lore is repeated, such as the tale that has Mickey being invented on a train ride following a business disaster (there's evidence to suggest he was born in meetings), but for the most part, the information is reliable and informative without being dense. There are plenty of authentic artifacts, and explanations of the revolutionary "multiplane" camera that enabled animators to reproduce the sliding depth of field normally seen in live-action films (you can see the fruit of the process in *Snow White* as the camera seems to move through the forest); 1930s toys and souvenirs featuring Mickey at the height of his early popularity, when he was markedly more rascally and tie-in merchandise was a new idea. Worth special scrutiny is the re-creation of Walt's surprisingly banal Burbank office as it appeared from 1940 (shortly before he became a propagandist during World War II) to 1966; note the bulletin board of Disneyland developments and also the four ashtrays, which contributed to his death from lung cancer.

The end of the exhibition chronicles the theme parks, including Disneyland's Main Street by way of a 1954 model, lots of scale models, and an Audio-Animatronic skeleton you can control with five buttons. Most people take about 20 minutes for the museum, and then there's a good 15-minute movie, culled mostly from archival footage and audio, so you hear the man himself speak. The feature scores points for mentioning Disney's 1931 breakdown, but it tries to prove Walt was a patron of the Disney Company's current efforts, implying he approved of Epcot's design and worse, elbowing poor Roy virtually out of the story. Fans who protest changes to the parks should note what Walt says about his greatest creation. "Disneyland," he promises, "is something that will never be finished."

WHERE TO EAT AT DISNEY'S HOLLYWOOD STUDIOS

Reservations for the sit-down restaurants can be made at ☎ 407/939-3463. At counter-service locations, kids' meals are $4 with a drink. The park's **fruit stand** ($1 per piece) is on Sunset Boulevard.

Hollywood Boulevard & Echo Lake   The sit-down restaurants are here. Make reservations for the **50's Prime Time Café** ★★, a cute concept in which families dine atop Formica in detailed reproductions of Cleaver-era kitchens beneath TVs playing black-and-white shows of the era. Waitresses gently sass customers, and the menu is equally as homey, including meatloaf, a very good pot roast, and a dessert menu read through a ViewMaster. It's as expensive as all Disney sit-down restaurants (entrees are $14 at lunch, $18 at dinner; kids' meals $8), but you get a lot more entertainment value for your money here. The peanut butter–and-jelly milkshake ($5), which you can only find here, is delicious (though I think it tastes more of caramel). Next door is **Hollywood & Vine** 🅺ᵈ𝒔, which is for character breakfasts and lunches with Disney Channel characters such as JoJo ($25 adults, $14 kids; reservations suggested). Near the Sorcerer Hat, also tasty is **the Hollywood Brown Derby,** the park's most expensive spot (dinner entrees $20–$34). It's noted for its delicious Grapefruit Cake ($6.20), which you can only get here. Next door, the overlooked **Starring Rolls** cafe, open until 4pm, does croissants and danishes plus a few sandwiches with chips or fruit for $7 to $9.

Commissary Lane   Just as Animation Courtyard has no eateries, Commissary Lane has no attractions. Instead, it's intended to mimic the cafeterias found at working studios. The counter-service **ABC Commissary** ✹✹✹ does food themed to ABC shows (Down the Hatch fried fish from *Lost* and Mambo Combo Cuban sandwiches from *Dancing with the Stars*) for $7 and under, and has the best variety for its price level in the park. Around the corner, the **Writer's Stop** is a quiet getaway that does coffee and $2 muffins. The **Sci-Fi Dine-In Theater Restaurant** ✹✹✹ is the park's most affordable and original sit-down restaurant; dinner prices are low for Disney, or around $12 to $19 for wedge salad with steak, baby back ribs, and shrimp pasta. You get a lot of atmosphere for your buck: Seats are in vintage convertibles (a sample car is out front) arranged before a silver screen of B-movie clips (robots, spacemen) and cartoons, drive-in style. It's a brilliant idea, well realized, and tons of fun, and because it's priced below other places with less to offer, it's my pick for the most fun restaurant in the park.

Sunset Boulevard   On the left-hand side of the street, as you approach the Tower of Terror, there's a string of budget counters, all outdoors, including **Rosie's All-American Cafe** ✹ (burgers, $7.10), **Catalina Eddie's** (bready personal pizzas with salad, $8), the **Toluca Legs Turkey Co.** ✹ (giant turkey legs for under $5.50, plus salads for $7.50), and the **Anaheim Produce** stall selling fresh fruit (the oranges are from California, not Central Florida).

Streets of America   The sit-down **Mama Melrose's Ristorante Italiano** costs just two-thirds of what Epcot's Italian spot does; $12 lunches, $17 dinners. That's still high, so there's also the counter-service **Toy Story Pizza Planet Arcade** ✹ for standard personal pizzas ($8, with salad) and a decent-sized chicken salad. Finally, the **Studio Catering Co.,** near the entrance to the Backlot Tour, isn't always open, but does barbecued pulled-pork subs and grilled chicken for $8. To the left, there's also a stand selling $9 cocktails (frozen margaritas and the like) and $6.20 draft beers.

DISNEY'S ANIMAL KINGDOM

Although it's the largest Disney theme park in Florida (500 acres), Disney's Animal Kingdom, which opened in 1998 at a reported cost of $800 million as a competitor to Busch Gardens, actually takes the least amount of time to visit, because most of that land is used up by a menagerie of exotic animals. Instead of cages, they're kept in paddocks rimmed with cleverly disguised trenches that are concealed behind landscaping. Most attractions are given a mild environmentalist message (ironic, considering how much Florida swamp was obliterated to build this resort, but never you mind). Because animals become inactive as the Florida heat builds, a visit here should begin as soon as the gates open, usually around 8am. To help gird your resolve, there are coffee carts ($1.90 a cup) along the entranceway. Most people wrap up by 3pm. It all usually closes in late afternoon, earlier than the other parks. *Tip:* Schedule your nighttime shindig, such as that dinner show you've been dying to catch, for your Animal Kingdom day.

The Best of Disney's Animal Kingdom

Don't miss if you're 6: Festival of the Lion King

Don't miss if you're 16: DINOSAUR

Requisite photo op: The drop at Expedition Everest

Food you can only get here: Pulled pork, Flame Tree Barbecue, Discovery Island

The most crowded, so go early: Kilimanjaro Safaris

Skippable: Rafiki's Planet Watch

Quintessentially Disney: It's Tough to Be a Bug!

Biggest thrill: Expedition Everest

Best show: *Finding Nemo—The Musical*

Character meals: Donald's Breakfastosaurus, DinoLand U.S.A.

Where to find peace: Discovery Island

Warning: Check the weather before you come, because if it's excessively hot or wet, you might be miserable. Only three major attractions take place inside.

An Orientation: Even before you reach the ticket gates, there's a restaurant: a branch of the chain Rainforest Cafe, which also operates in Downtown Disney. Staples such as locker and stroller rental are just past the gates, in what's called the **Oasis,** a lush buffer zone that gradually acclimates guests to the world of the park. Pick up a free *Guidemap* and a *Times Guide.* The locations of animal enclosures, which start immediately, are noted on the map by black-and-white paw prints and also by chip photographs of beasts, so if you're most interested in seeing wildlife, follow those. Children's activity stations are marked with a K.

Generally speaking, the biggest animals and the most astute design collects at the back of the park (Africa and Asia), the thrills to the right (Asia and DinoLand U.S.A.), and the biggest kiddie goodies to the left (Camp Minnie-Mickey).

The first thing you should do, like everyone else, is beeline it to the back of the Africa section. That's where the Kilimanjaro Safari is; because crowds grow more ferocious than the lions, first thing in the morning is the best time to do it.

DISCOVERY ISLAND

Like the Plaza of the Magic Kingdom, Discovery Island is designed to be the hub of the park. It's the main viewing area for the daily Mickey's Jammin' Jungle Parade, which circles it (the route is denoted on the maps by a red dotted line) and guests can touch down here to change lands. The park's **tip board,** with current wait times and upcoming showtimes, is also here, just to the right past the bridge from the Oasis, by the Disney Outfitters shop.

Instead of a castle or a geosphere (or, uh . . . a hat), the centerpiece here is **the Tree of Life** ✯✯, an emerald, 14-story-high wienie (built on the skeleton of an

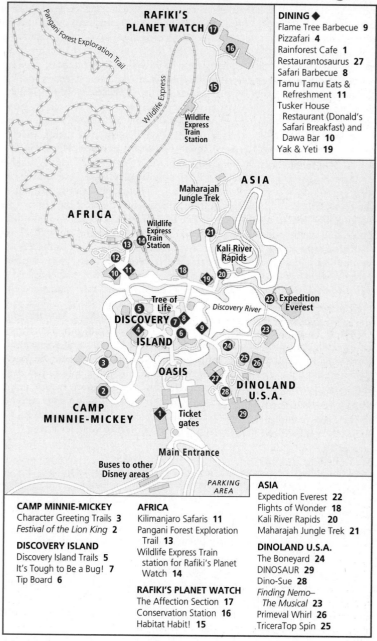

Pangani Forest Exploration Trail

RAFIKI'S
PLANET WATCH

Wildlife Express

Wildlife
Express
Train
Station

Maharajah
Jungle Trek

ASIA

AFRICA

Wildlife
Express
Train
Station

Kali River
Rapids

Tree of
Life

DISCOVERY

Discovery River

Expedition
Everest

ISLAND

OASIS

DINOLAND
U.S.A.

CAMP
MINNIE-MICKEY

Ticket
gates

Main Entrance

Buses to other
Disney areas

PARKING
AREA

oil rig) covered with hundreds of intricate carvings of animals made to appear, at a distance, like the pattern of the bark. Some 102,000 vinyl leaves were individually attached—which is why its shade of green is more lurid than the surrounding foliage—to some 750 tertiary branches. That the best way to enjoy it is to slowly make a circuit of it, looking for and identifying new animals, is perhaps proof that the best way to experience this park is to slow down and open your eyes. Get yourself in the swing on the little-used, shaded **Discovery Island Trails** ★, encircling the tree, where you'll pass giant Galápagos tortoises, red kangaroos, flamingoes, storks, otters, lemurs, and macaws; some are removed when it's hot.

Beneath its flying roots, in a cool basementlike theater, there's a cleverly rigged cinema showing a sense-tricking 10-minute 3-D movie, **It's Tough to Be a Bug!** ★★★ 🧒, based on the animated movie *A Bug's Life*. When the stinkbugs do their thing or the tarantula starts firing poison quills, you'll never quite be sure what's an onscreen image, what's cutting-edge robotics, and what's really pouring out of hidden vents or poking you from underneath. As one of the newest sense-tricking movies at Disney World, it's one of the best. Little kids who can't distinguish fantasy from reality may be scared by the marvelously realized Hopper figure; sit in back (the first doors after you get your glasses) and to the left to be far from him. The indoor preshow area is decorated with posters for some funny entomological variations on Broadway shows (my faves: *Web Side Story* and *My Fair Ladybug*). **Strategy:** Fastpass may be available, but it's rarely necessary. Upon exiting, go left to explore the trails (above) or right for the bridge to Asia.

About an hour or two before closing time, the daily **Mickey's Jammin' Jungle Parade** ★ 🧒 begins in Africa, loops around Discover Island, and then returns to its starting point (the dotted line on maps). Like all Disney parades, it's about 10 floats long, with lots of character appearances. I like this one because the floats are quite ingeniously made—most of them are animal-like contraptions powered by the people pushing or driving them along. The period between the parade's end and park closing is a good time to do the stuff that had longer lines before the parade started, such as Expedition Everest. At Animal Kingdom especially, many guests leave early in the day, and you can use that fact to your advantage.

AFRICA

Toward the back of the park to the Africa section, where you can board the popular 20-minute **Kilimanjaro Safaris** ★★★, easily the bumpiest ride at Disney World. Climb into a supersize, 32-passenger Jeep—an actual one with wheels, not a tracked cart, plus signs to help you identify the big game—and be swept into what feels like a real safari through the African veldt, with meticulously rutted tracks and all, only on Quaaludes. Be quick on the shutter, because drivers speed on a fleeting schedule.

Besides the standard subplot about thwarting poachers, there's no predicting what you'll see for sure because animals do what they want, but you'll pass through habitats for giraffes, elephants, wildebeest, ostrich, hippos, lions, gazelles, rhinos, and other creatures that made safaris famous. Considering the quality and quantity of animals on display—and the cleverness of the enclosure design, as there are never bars between you and them—it's easily the best animal attraction of the park, and the queue only builds during the day. Some people say that the second-best time to see the animals is in midafternoon because they get antsy with the foreknowledge that they're about to be led to their indoor sleeping quarters. Ride twice if you want—the free will of the animals means it's never the same trip twice (you want to repeat it because of the speed anyway). **Strategy:** Photographers who want clear shots should jockey toward the back, away from the cockpit. They may not have control over that, so at the very least, they should negotiate with their companions for a seat at the end of their row.

Upon exit, join the **Pangani Forest Exploration Trail** ✩✩, which focuses on African animals. It wends past a troop of lowland gorillas (very popular), naked mole rats, okapi, meerkats (yes, like Timon), and hippos you can view through an underwater window; the nocturnal animals start waking up at around 3:30pm. The circuit takes about a half-hour, but you can spend as long as you want.

Also check out the **Harambe School.** Most of the time, it's a place for tired parents to sit, but about six times a day, there's a short presentation (on environmental travel, cultural tall tales), listed by time on a blackboard.

RAFIKI'S PLANET WATCH

Once you've spotted such impressive creatures, the rest of the critters you'll see, endearing as they are, can't help but be a letdown. From the Safaris, take the **Wildlife Express Train.** Waits are generally no longer than 10 minutes. Train cars open on one side (the trip takes 7 min.), and you'll get glimpses of plain backstage work areas but not much else. It's the only way to reach **Rafiki's Planet Watch.** Its elements are listed separately on the park maps, but everything is of a piece: It's intended to teach modern kids the value of coexisting with the natural world. **Habitat Habit!,** the path that leads to the main building, is another "discovery trail," this one with cotton-top tamarins (endangered monkeys about the size of squirrels). **Conservation Station** is a quasi-educational peek at how the park's animals are maintained—you're not seeing the true veterinary facilities, but a few auxiliary rooms set up so tourists can watch activities through picture windows. There's not always something going on (early mornings seem to be most active), and the *Times Guide* doesn't help, so you might get all the way here and then find yourself with only a few environmentalist exhibits to poke at. There's nothing earthshaking—enter a dark, soundproof booth and listen to the sounds of the rainforest—but the pace is much easier than in the park outside. **The Affection Section** 🧒 is a petting zoo with, in addition to your typical petting-zoo denizens, a type of goat that was saved from extinction.

ASIA

Asia is the park's showcase, and its ingenious decor (rat-trap wiring, fraying prayer flags) is so accurate it could easily be mistaken for the real Nepal or northern India. The area recently received a major dose of love in the form of **Expedition Everest** ✩✩✩, a lavishly themed and abundantly hyped roller coaster. You can't miss the "snowcapped" mountain looming nearly 200 feet over the park's east end (if it were any higher, Florida law would require it to be topped by an airplane beacon). The queue area is a beautifully realized duplication of a Himalayan temple down to the tarnished bells and weathered paint, although portions of it are exposed the sun, so drink something before you pony up. The coaster itself is loaded with powerful set pieces that get you your money's worth: both backward and forward motion, pitch-black sections, and a fleeting encounter with a massive, state-of-the-art Audio-Animatronic Abominable Snowman, or Yeti. Many of the ride's effects (mist that's supposed to come off the mountain, fog at the summit, and that Yeti) are too complicated to function most of the time—a strobe light makes it look like the Yeti's moving—but that won't affect your trip much. As with all Disney rides, the most dramatic drop (80 ft.) is visible from the sidewalk out front, so if you think you can stomach that, you can do the rest. There are no upside-down loops; the dominant motion is spiral, which makes some people slightly nauseous. **Strategy:** This coaster, a top candidate for Fastpass, marks a return to form for Disney. The seats with the best view, without question, are in the front rows, although the back rows feel a little faster. Sometimes, a single-rider line is in play.

Asia's other major attraction is the **Kali River Rapids,** a 12-passenger round bumper boat that shoots a course of rapids. Sometimes you can get soaked—it depends on your bad luck—but it's generally milder than similar rides. Your feet, for sure, will get wet. The worst damage is usually done by spectators who shoot water cannons at passing boats from a bridge. Lots of guests buy rain ponchos for the ride (those are $7 at nearby stores—or $1 for two at your local dollar store), but there is a waterproof holding area in the middle of each boat. Well, *sorta* waterproof—if you can wrap your stuff in a plastic bag, you'll be in better shape. Like other Animal Kingdom rides, there's a conservation-themed overlay about illegal loggers. **Strategy:** Lines build considerably when it's hot, so it's another prime Fastpass candidate. If you're going to Islands of Adventure on your Orlando trip, you can skip this ride and do the more surprising one there.

To the left of the Kali entrance, the too-ignored **Maharajah Jungle Trek** ⭐ is a South Asian–themed walking trail featuring some gorgeous tigers (rescued from a circus breeding program), tapirs, komodo dragons, and a few animals frolicking among fake ruins. The tigers are most active when the park opens and near closing time. Grab a bird information sheet after entering the aviary; there's a bat display, too, that you can bypass if you're squeamish. **Strategy:** If you Fastpass Kali River Rapids, kill the intervening time by strolling through here first.

At the canvas-sheltered Caravan Stage, the 25-minute **Flights of Wonder** show (the schedule is posted) showcases birds such as hawks, vultures, bald eagles, and parrots—20 species; the mix changes—that swoop thrillingly over the audience's heads. Consider it standard, if beautiful, nature-show stuff. After the performance, handlers usually present a few of the birds back on stage for close inspection. Stop in at **Bhaktapur Market,** which sells Asian souvenirs a cut above the usual stuff.

DINOLAND U.S.A.

When it rains, come here, where two attractions and one big counter-service restaurant are indoors. Performed four or five times daily (check the *Times Guide* and show up at least 40 min. ahead, but be warned that sometimes the first and last ones are canceled), the winning *Finding Nemo—The Musical* ⭐⭐⭐ 🧒 is, for my money, the best theme park show in the world right now. A compressed version of the movie, the story has been heightened with such catchy added songs as "Fish Are Friends, Not Food" and the infectious, Beach Boys–style "Go with the Flow." Just as in *The Lion King*'s Broadway adaptation, live actors manipulate complicated animal puppets in full view, which allows the fish to appear as if they're floating in the sea. It's remarkable how quickly you stop paying attention to the humans—at least, until they start flying, with their puppets, through the air on wires. Then you're just amazed. Sprightly, bright, colossal, and energetic, this 40-minute show is a good choice for taking a load off (the bench seating is indoors), and even those who know the movie backward and forward will find something new in the vibrant vigor of the delivery. **Strategy:** Because some scenes (including the introduction of Dory) happen in the aisle that crosses the center of the theater, sit in the rear half of the auditorium.

The giant orange dinosaur signifies **Chester & Hester's Dino-Rama,** a miniature carnival-style amusement area with a midway, **Fossil Fun Games,** and two simple family rides. **TriceraTop Spin** 🦖, for the very young, is yet another iteration of the Dumbo ride over at Magic Kingdom and is designed for kids to ride with their parents. Cars fit four, in two rows. I suggest you give it a miss unless you're faced with a temper tantrum. **Primeval Whirl** is a pair of mirror-image, family-friendly carnival-style coasters (Walt *hated* carnivals) that start out like a typical "wild mouse" ride before, midtrip, the round cars begin spinning on an axle as they ride the rails. Think of it as a roller-coaster version of the teacup ride. You can plainly see what you're in for, although you may be surprised at how roughly the movements can whip your neck. Don't feel bad if you give it a miss, too, because it's not a Disney original; it was made by a French company that sells similar rides to other parks. Keep the kids in control by swinging them across the path to **the Boneyard** 🦖, a hot, sun-exposed playground where the very young can dig up "prehistoric" bones in the sand.

DinoLand's major thrill attraction *is* a Disney original: **DINOSAUR** ✦✦, a 3-minute indoor time-travel ride in which all-terrain "Enhanced Motion Vehicles" simultaneously speed and shimmy down an unseen track, all as hordes of roaring dinosaurs attempt to make you dinner and an approaching asteroid shower threatens to do everyone in. Some kids, and even some adults, find all those jaws and jerky movements rather intense, and it's extremely dark and loud, but ultimately, it's a fun time, even if the perpetual darkness makes me wonder how much money Disney saved in not having to build more dinosaurs. Like many modern rides, well-known actors perform in the preshow video; this one's got Phylicia Rashad, fiercely overacting, and Wallace Langham, in a horrific tie. The line never seems to be as long as this ride deserves. On the path to the ride, don't ignore **Dino-Sue,** the 40-foot-long, full-scale T. rex skeleton—it's a replica of Sue, the most complete specimen man has yet found. The original, unearthed in South Dakota, is on display at Chicago's Field Museum. The **Cretaceous Trail,** at the head of the path, showcases ferns from that period.

CAMP MINNIE-MICKEY

The final themed zone, Camp Minnie-Mickey, is between the entrance plaza and Africa, and it's also for kids. The great flaw of this area is that there's no real reason to partake unless you see something on your *Times Guide* that you want to do, because there are no continuous attractions.

It's the place to see the air-conditioned *Festival of the Lion King* ✦✦ 🦖 show, which before Nemo arrived was the prime sensory overloader for kids. If this lavish, colorful, intense spectacle can't hold your attention for 30 minutes, you might require prescriptions. Audiences sit on benches in four quadrants (front rows are good if you want to engage with the performers), and the event comes on like an acid trip during a rock concert. Four huge floats enter the room, topped with soft-looking giant puppets of Timon, Pumbaa, and African wildlife and attended by acrobats, stilt-walkers, flame jugglers, and dancers, all of whom get their turn to dazzle you with their acts, which are performed, of course, to the hit songs of the movie. **Strategy:** The best seating sections are to your left as you enter the theater; if you want to be near the exit (there's no ducking out once it starts, though), sit in the two right-hand sections. Shows are timed, and they do fill up, so people arrive 30 minutes early—be warned that the wait area is exposed to the elements.

The other cabanas in Camp Minnie-Mickey are for the **Character Greeting Trails.** They essentially guarantee face time with Disney characters (usually Mickey, Minnie, Donald, and Goofy, all in expedition gear) within the period printed on the *Times Guide.* This is the park's bonanza zone for autographs.

Interestingly, Animal Kingdom was originally supposed to be about all animals, mythical and real, and an additional land, Beastly Kingdomme, was planned. On Discovery Island benches and etched above the main park entrance, you'll still see some dragons, a hint of big plans that have not come to fruition. Yet.

WHERE TO EAT AT DISNEY'S ANIMAL KINGDOM

Because you need to be up early for your Animal Kingdom day anyway, you might consider doing a character breakfast here. Mickey, Donald, Daisy, and Goofy (a darn good, A-level lineup) show up starting at 8am for **Donald's Safari Breakfast** (kids) (☎ 407/939-3463) at Tusker House in Africa. Prices are $19 for adults and $11 for kids 3 to 9, but that's all you can eat, and then you can head right out for the animals while they're still active.

Rainforest Cafe, at the ticket gates, usually opens 1 hour before the park and closes 1 hour after. The park's main fruit stand ($1 per piece; under $4 for cups of cut fruit) is at **Harambe Fruit Market** in Africa.

Discovery Island   You'll find the greatest selection on Discovery Island. Although I don't care to gorge on meaty dishes such as ribs and baked chicken ($8–$11) when I'm supposed to be appreciating animals, **Flame Tree Barbecue** ★★ has some terrific hidden eating areas with cushioned seating on the Discovery River, and its pulled-pork barbecue is one of a kind in all the parks. **Pizzafari** ★ (a vibrantly colored restaurant with lots of rooms to spread out) charges around $6 for pizzas and $7 for chicken Parmesan sandwiches and salads. **Safari Turkey** ★★, the park's turkey leg cart ($6.20 a leg) is also here, on the path toward Asia. Apparently, zookeepers allowed the chefs to take care of the venerable gobbler.

Asia   **Yak & Yeti** does both counter-service (mandarin chicken salad, $8; sweet and sour pork, $10; very tiny mango pie rounds, $4) and more expensive sit-down meals ($7–$11 appetizers like mussels and pot stickers; $16–$18 wok noodles, stir fry, and pho; plus $8 cocktails like the Everest Avalanche, with rum, bananas, strawberry, and mango flavoring). The **Royal Anandapur Tea Company** kiosk, on the water, does something different: slushy chai ($4.50).

Africa   The sit-down **Tusker House Restaurant** ★★ does character breakfasts. Then come all-you-can-eat meals (lunch $20 adults, $11 kids; dinner $27/$13)

Fitting into the Disney Culture

On a recent visit to the World of Disney shop at Downtown Disney, I discovered that a souvenir book I wanted was out of stock. "I can't believe the largest Disney Store in the world doesn't have it," I remarked to a clerk with a wink. "We have it," she sniffed, clearly insulted. "We're just out of it." And she turned her back on me.

I call that Disney Logic, and it's a reminder that just as Parisians are hurried and the English aren't demonstrative, Walt Disney World's employees have a culture all their own that visitors must learn to respect and navigate. Working at Disney World isn't like getting a job at the bank. Many cast members live and breathe its way of life, and quite a few moved from other parts of the country just to be a part of it. Be alert to the fact that many of them identify personally with Walt Disney World, and many take subtle exception to comments that might carry a hint of criticism or questioning. Try not to put Disney employees in a position of having to defend or explain their company, or you may put their back up. And for heaven's sake, no cussing! Cast members are often empowered to do all kinds of favors for you, but if they can't (because of job compartmentalization, that happens often), then smile and move on to another one. In Walt Disney World, a country within a country, the expected facade is toothy smiles and chipper greetings. Although that code is technically meant to apply only to cast members, the unspoken cultural expectation is that you follow it, too.

---

that are a notch above the usual (salmon, curry chicken, carvery beef, and banana-cinnamon bread with vanilla sauce). It serves many South African wines ($7–$9.50 a glass). Next to it is **Dawa Bar,** a relaxing spot mimicking a fortress on the water, for cocktails under $8.50. Opposite that, **Tamu Tamu Eats & Refreshment** does counter-service sandwiches (turkey and tuna fish, $7.50 and under). You sit at Dawa Bar, where there may be African drum shows.

DinoLand U.S.A.   Restaurantosaurus does burgers, dogs, mandarin chicken salad, and a toppings bar (with cooked mushrooms and onions) for under $7. The Trilo-Bites kiosk sells those giant turkey legs.

Note: Because plastic straws could choke the animals, paper ones are provided.

THE WATER PARKS

The big question: Blizzard Beach or Typhoon Lagoon? Both can fill a day. Here's my answer: It depends on your mood. Typhoon Lagoon's central feature, a sand-lined 2½-acre wave pool, is an ideal place for families to frolic and to approximate a day at the beach. If your kids have a need for speed, you head over to Blizzard Beach, which has a milder wave pool but wilder water slides.

Both water parks, similar in size, have free parking and are less busy early in the week, probably because folks tend to start their vacations on a weekend and don't get to the flumes until they've done the four big theme parks. On very hot days, they are unpleasantly crammed, and they tend to be busier in the morning than in late afternoon. They also sell everything you need to protect yourself from the sun, including lotion (should you have forgotten) and swimsuits (should you lose yours in the lather). Most lines (many rides have two: one for a raft and one for the slide) are fully exposed to the sun, so it's important to **keep hydrated,** as you won't always be aware how much you're sweating. Both parks sell $10 mugs that are refillable for **endless soft drinks** while you're there (otherwise, soft drinks start at $2.10). They also rent towels for $2. Lifeguards usually make you remove water shoes on slides that don't use a mat or raft, and swimsuits with rivets or zippers are forbidden because they may scratch the flumes.

An average locker is $10 but you get $5 of that back after you turn your key in. They allow multiple access, are about 2 feet deep, and the opening is about the size of a magazine. Thoughtfully, there are bulletin boards near the entrance that tell you what the sunburn risk is and what the wait time is for the slides, as well as what times the parades run at Disney parks that day. If there are any activities (scavenger hunts are common), they'll be posted here. Kids' beach toy sets, for the sand around the lagoon, are sold in the gift shop for $10.

Food: Stupidly, many of the food stands only take cash and won't even accept room keys as payment, so bring a waterproof pouch. Also, don't plan on eating dinner at the water parks, as the kiosks tend to shut down before closing.

Timing: If you're coming to Florida between November and mid-March, one of these parks will be closed for its annual hose-down. The other will remain open. Most water features are heated, but remember that you eventually must get *out*.

Overview: A day at a water park isn't as stressful as one spent among the queues of the theme parks, and if you're paying attention, the sights and sounds of a day here are pretty heartwarming. Every time the wave machine roars into gear, for example, dozens of kids shriek with delight and scamper into the water. At the Dive Pool at Typhoon Beach, first-time snorkel users chatter into their tubes like a herd of geese. Because they're chilling out, people tend to be happy at these parks.

BLIZZARD BEACH

Of the two water parks, I prefer this one, but I like excitement in my slides. **Blizzard Beach** (☎ 407/560-3400; www.disneyworld.com; $40 adults, $34 kids aged 3–9), which opened 6 years after Typhoon Lagoon and had the benefit of improving on what didn't work there, also has a wittier theme. The invented backstory is perfect for a hot day: A freak snowstorm hit Mount Gushmore, and Disney was slapping up a ski resort when the snow began to melt, creating water slides. So now, a lift chair brings bathers most of the way up the 90-foot peak, and flumes are festooned with ski-run flags and piled with white "snowdrifts." Best of all, no one has to tote rafts uphill—there are conveyors to do it for you.

Surely the most exhilarating 8 seconds in all of Walt Disney World, **Summit Plummet** ✹✹✹ is the immensely steep, 12-story-tall slide that commands attention at the peak of the mountain, which incidentally, offers one of the best panoramas of the Walt Disney World resort. A slide down this one is for the truly fearless, as the first few seconds make you feel weightless, as if you're about to fall forward. By the end, the water is jabbing you so hard that it's not unusual to come away with a light bruise, and it turns the toughest bathing suit into dental floss.

This is a fun one to watch; just ask the young men who are glued to it for the aforementioned reason. At the bottom, there's a speed clock that measures how fast the last sucker went (58mph is a typical reading). **Slush Gusher,** next to it and slightly lower, is a double-hump that gives the rider the sensation of air time—not a reassuring feeling when you're flying down an open chute.

The enormous chute winding off the mountain's right side is **Teamboat Springs** ★★★, a group ride in a circular raft; just about everyone gets a chance to enjoy the top of a banked turn, and after the inevitable splashdown, another minute is spent in a comedown floating on a river. It's highly re-rideable, but if you go alone, you'll be paired with strangers, which can result in slippery awkwardness.

Snow Stormers is a trio of standard raft water slides, but the twin **Downhill Double Dipper** ★ is a simple slope of two identical slides with a good embellishment: It times runs so you can race a companion down. **Toboggan Racers** multiplies the fun to where eight people can race at once, untimed, down an evenly scalloped run. At the base of these is **Melt Away Bay,** a 1-acre wave pool in which waves create a gentle bobbing sensation. It could stand to be larger since it gets very crowded.

At the back of the mountain (reach it by walking around the left or via the lazy river), the three **Runoff Rapids** ★★ flumes comprise two open-air slides and a totally enclosed one—you only see the occasional light flashing by. (These are the only ones for which you must haul your own raft up the hill.)

The park is circled by the superlative lazy river (for the newbie, that's a slow-flowing channel where you float along in an inner tube) called **Cross Country Creek** ★★★ 🧒, which is probably the best of its kind, passing a cave dripping with refrigerated water and a slouching shack that, every few seconds, gushes as you hear the sound of Goofy sneezing. *Tip:* It's easier to find a free inner tube at a ramp far from the park entrance; try the one at the base of Downhill Double Dipper or the one to the left past Lottawatta Lodge, the main food building.

There are two kiddie areas, one for preteens, **Ski Patrol** 🧒 (short slides, a walk across the water on floating "icebergs") and for littler kids, **Tike's Peak** 🧒 (even smaller slides, fountains, and jets). The latter is a good place to look if you can't find seating. Parents who reach a saturation point with theme parks will be happy to learn the main bar is by the one and only entrance; you can send the kiddies off to play and raise a few, knowing they can't leave without passing you.

Tip: The miniature golf course Winter Summerland (see "Join the Club" in chapter 7) shares a parking lot with Blizzard Beach, so it's easy to combine a visit.

TYPHOON LAGOON

Despite the petrifying imagery of the shrimp boat *(Miss Tilly)* impaled on the central mountain (Mt. Mayday), the flumes here are less daunting than the ones at Blizzard Beach or Wet 'n Wild. **Typhoon Lagoon** (☎ 407/560-4141; www.disney world.com; $40 adults, $34 kids aged 3–9) is extremely well landscaped (most of the flowers are selected so that they attract butterflies but not bees) to hide its infrastructure, but it's not always well planned. For example, the paths to the slides ramble up and down stairs—the one to the Storm Slides actually goes *down* eight times as it winds up the mountain. It's also not always clear where to find the right entrance to the slide you want.

The **Surf Pool** ✭✭✭ packs a surprising punch (body surfing is easy on those 5-ft. waves, but so is losing toddlers), while the slides are generally shallow, slow, and geared toward avowed sissies. That will frustrate some teenagers, but little kids think Mayday Falls, which sends riders down a corrugated flume, is just right (adults come off rubbing their butts in pain). The leftmost body slide at **Storm Slides** is slightly more covered, but otherwise the slides are much the same. The most thrilling rides are the **Crush 'n' Gusher** ✭✭✭ "water coaster" flumes, which use jets to push rafts both uphill and downhill; the gag is that it used to be a fruit-washing plant, and now you're the banana. They're found in a discrete section off to the right after you enter.

The park's lazy river is ungimmicky and lushly planted. One excellent attraction is the **Shark Reef** ✭, a 10½-foot-deep tank stocked with tropical fish and mock coral. Everyone gets a mask, snorkel, and, if wanted, a floatation jacket, and then swims 60 feet across the tank (no dawdling permitted) under the eye of life-guards who'll spring into action at the slightest hint of trouble—or even if you just want a strong hand. (If you want a tank where you can linger with the fish, try SeaWorld's Discovery Cove.) You don't have to meet a high standard beyond an ability to paddle across a pool. If you don't care for that setup, you can descend by stairs into a submerged "shipwreck," which has portholes allowing a lateral view of the same tank. **Strategy:** Shark Reef gets busy, so do it early or late.

The lazy river, **Castaway Creek** ✭✭ 🄺🄸🄳🄢, runs clockwise around the park and is best enjoyed on one of the circulating inner tubes. For the best shot at finding an available tube, pick an area farther from the entrance, such as in front of the Crush 'n' Gusher area. That's also a good place to find a lounger if the Lagoon is packed, which it usually is; otherwise, try the extreme left past the ice cream stand. Also in that area is **Ketchakiddee Creek** 🄺🄸🄳🄢, the play area for small children. Funny how the water's always warmer there.

Disney sells "Learn to Surf" lessons on the Surf Pool before park hours (like, at 6:45am, before the buses are running) and, sometimes, after it closes (☎ 407/939-7529; $140 for all ages, minimum age of 8). That comes with 30 minutes of on-land preparation followed by 2 hours of in-pool instruction, always with life-guards scrutinizing your every twitch.

MINOR DISNEY WORLD DIVERSIONS

Also see "Join the Club" in chapter 7 for details on the two Disney miniature golf areas.

DisneyQuest (West Side; ☎ 407/939-4600; www.disneyquest.com; $40 adults, $34 kids 3–9; kids 9 and under must be accompanied by someone 16 or older; Sun–Thurs 11:30am–11pm, Fri–Sat 11:30am–midnight) is a five-level virtual reality playground on Downtown Disney's West Side. It's past its prime, if it had one, and rumors persist that its days are numbered. Standout stuff includes **Cyberspace Mountain,** in which you design your own coaster from a palette of options and then board a motion-simulator capsule in which you can test out your creation—360-degree loops and all. The ride vehicles actually go upside-down, making it one of only two Disney World rides to do so. **Virtual Jungle Cruise** has you on inflatable rafts, using paddles to float down a river on a screen in front of you; and **Pirates of the Caribbean: Battle for Buccaneer Gold** puts you on the deck of a mini–pirate ship, with screens on three sides, that has members of your party simultaneously steering and blasting rival ships by yanking on ropes that trigger cannons (like the ones on Toy Story Midway Mania). They'll tell you that if a visor is required, it can fit over glasses, but **Ride the Comix,** a cyber swordfight, compressed my nose painfully, so I strongly suggest you wear contact lenses. Not everything is screen based: The rowdy **Buzz Lightyear's AstroBlaster** is like a bumper-car game where your vehicle scoops up balls and fires them at competitors, causing them to spin momentarily; it's best for two riders at a time. There are also **Animation Academy** classes in which you can learn to draw a Disney character, but being charged extra for it is galling (a similar course is not charged at Hollywood Studios' animation exhibit). Throughout the building are arcade games, old and new, that need no quarters. During the weekdays, you pretty much have your run of the place. There are a few counters for snacks, so it's easy to pass 3 or 4 hours here. I would go to many more compelling Orlando-area attractions before getting around to doing this one—if you want technology, how about the Kennedy Space Center?—and I'd never pay $40 for it, but I would go if I had an extra Water Park Fun & More visit to burn on my Magic Your Way ticket.

Most visitors don't stumble onto the 220-acre **ESPN Wide World of Sports** (Victory Dr.; Interstate 4 at exit 64B; ☎ 407/363-6600; www.disneysports.com), a souped-up stadium complex, by accident. They're intentionally there, whether for a son's wrestling tournament, a traveling sports exhibition game, or to see the Atlanta Braves in spring training. Unfortunately, it's not a place to roll up and pitch a few balls, although you can check its website to see if there's something ticketed that you might enjoy attending (and paying extra for).

6

Universal, SeaWorld & Busch Gardens

Five more of the world's best theme parks

DISNEY IS ONLY HALF THE STORY. LESS THAN HALF, REALLY, WHEN YOU CONsider that while the Mouse maintains four parks, you'll find another four major themers, plus a luxury-level theme park, in the same vicinity. While some blinkered tourists think of these places as something to do after they "do Disney," the truth is these majors are in many ways just as appealing as the more famous Mouse traps. They each also only draw about two-thirds the visitors that Disney's Epcot does in a given year, which means most of the time, you won't have to battle crowds.

You'd be remiss if you left town without seeing at least two of Disney's parks, but for my money—and I'm speaking as someone who grew up entranced by Disney—I relax much more when I'm at these "other" parks. Increasingly, the true design chutzpah is happening here—there's no doubt for most people that Universal's spectacular Spider-Man ride trumps anything else in the industry. As Disney increasingly rests on its cherished brand and its deserved laurels, Universal and Anheuser-Busch have stepped up by crafting parks where you want to mellow out, smell the flowers, or bask in the singe of an adrenaline rush.

All of these parks usually open at 9am, and in winter months, operating hours will end at around 6pm. In summer, they're often open to as late as 10pm.

UNIVERSAL ORLANDO

The opening of Universal Studios in 1990 heralded a new era for Orlando tourism. Instead of merely duplicating its original Hollywood location, found on a working movie studio lot, Universal Orlando expanded on its most successful features into a full-fledged all-day amusement park based on classic movies. While the park's opening was troubled, there was little doubt that Universal's innovations had instantly raised the bar for amusement parks worldwide.

In a way, Orlando grew up the instant the ribbon was cut at Universal. The theme of Hollywood movies was something that both kids and adults could enjoy, which widened the breadth of what a single Orlando park could offer. But the chief advance was that almost all of its attractions were indoors—even the thrills. Given Florida's scorching sun and unpredictable rains, this leap shouldn't have been as novel as it was. While Disney was (and still is, sometimes) allowing its guests to twiddle thumbs in the heat as they waited in line, Universal's multistage queuing system usually kept guests entertained and air-conditioned. Its attractions kick off with a preshow that keeps families amused before they're ushered into the main auditorium or onto ride vehicles. Although Universal still has a few

Contacting Universal

General information: ☎ 407/363-8000; www.universalorlando.com

Vacation packages: ☎ 877/801-9720; www.univacations.com

Lost and found: ☎ 407/224-4244 (Universal Studios) or ☎ 407/224-4245 (Islands of Adventure)

outdoor queue areas, they are almost always sheltered and gently doused by cooling mist. Therefore, Universal Studios is the park you should choose on rainy days or excessively hot ones. (Islands of Adventure, the other Universal park, has indoor queue areas for its big rides, which salvages many a scorcher, but many of the rides travel outdoors and will shut down at the hint of lightning.) Even the parking at Universal Orlando (shared by both parks and CityWalk) is covered, so on days when you have to check out of a hotel, your luggage will be kept cool in your car, whereas at all the other parks, including SeaWorld, it will bake all day in the sun.

Disney was clearly spooked when Universal barged into a market Disney all but owned. In response, it hastily banged out a movies-themed park of its own, Disney–MGM Studios (now called Hollywood Studios). The Mouse's park opened first, but it was a rush job, lacking many of the hallmarks of quality that had made its previous two parks such successes.

Throughout the 1990s, Universal's one-park setup meant it mostly grabbed visitors on day trips from Disney. That changed—and the fight got nasty—in the summer of 1999, when a second, $2.6-billion park, Islands of Adventure, made its dazzling debut. Universal broke the bank to outshine Disney, even poaching a number of onetime Imagineers. IOA, as it's known, has the most elaborately crafted environment in town—pavements pigmented in Crayola colors; custom-built rides; individually detailed lampposts, benches, and trash bins—which set a new standard for American amusement. Its Amazing Adventures of Spider-Man attraction is, hands down, the best ride in Orlando.

Universal's domain has further expanded to include the nightlife district CityWalk and three hotels, making the brand a true vacation destination in its own right. The complex has also successfully drawn business from locals, although it doesn't inspire the disturbing levels of fan obsession that Disney's does.

Most of the time, lines are nowhere near as long as they are at Disney. Unless crowds are insanely huge (such as before Halloween Horror Nights events or during Christmas week), Universal takes about 2 days to see. With a two-park pass and a willingness to bypass lesser attractions, you could see the highlights of the two parks in 1 marathon day, provided at least one of the parks stays open until 9 or 10pm. In any event, bopping between the two parks isn't hard, since their entrances are a 5-minute stroll apart.

DISNEY OR UNIVERSAL?

People always ask me: Disney or Universal? First of all, it's indicative of the fierce competition between the two entities that anyone would feel compelled to frame a comparison as a choice. But I do accept that time is at a premium when you're on vacation, and the comparison helps people prioritize. I hate to be glib about the answer, because it depends on who you are. There's a lot Disney has over Universal—principally that intangible energy that makes the place so buoyant. No entity suspends disbelief and casts an aura of unreality like Disney. Disney's characters are genuinely beloved by children, where not all of Universal's are— how many kids do you know who are into Beetlejuice or Lucille Ball? But Universal tends to attract people who have either wearied of or outgrown Disney's overly controlled environment and ODed on princesses. Teenagers who roll their eyes at Disney often find new passions at Universal, but parents who are used to Disney's sweetness are often shocked by Universal's edge. Universal has some gyrating thrill rides, while most of Disney's punches have been pulled. So I usually answer by simply saying, "Universal isn't Disney." That gives the answer you need, depending on your view of Disney.

There's something else about Universal that first-time visitors don't expect: its high quality. I think that Islands of Adventure's attention to detail trumps almost everything Disney has done in years. Universal doesn't skimp on upkeep, either; no attraction at the Studio is as it was when the park first opened. When I'm pressed for the must-do parks, I rank Universal's two parks after the Magic Kingdom and Epcot but before Hollywood Studios and Animal Kingdom. For thrills, I recommend Islands of Adventure above Universal Studios, and IOA tends to hold kids' attention better, too. There is *plenty* for kids at Universal.

Whereas Disney has the advantage of space, Universal has the advantage of being compact. You can park your car and forget about it during your stay because everything is within walking distance, including the three hotels, which are also linked by ferries. There are no shuttle buses to wait for, so you can unwind with a cocktail (both Universal parks serve booze, and CityWalk practically pipes it in) without having to drive back to your hotel. Miraculously, the designers have accomplished this compaction without sacrificing a sense of breathing room.

Being here also puts you much closer to the "real" Orlando. Disney works hard to keep the real world (and, consequently, real prices) at bay, but at Universal, reality is a 3-minute drive away. For this reason, and because getting in is cheaper, you'll notice far more locals at Universal, particularly at its popular annual events such as Halloween Horror Nights or Mardi Gras (see "Orlando's Visit-Worthy Events" in chapter 12).

TICKETS TO UNIVERSAL'S PARKS

Tickets for both parks cost the same and are almost always more expensive if you buy at the gate. Here's the pricing:

- ◆ A **1-day, two-park ticket** bought online costs $84 adults, $74 kids aged 3 to 9, but $90 and $80 at the gate—shocking when you learn that they cost $42 as recently as 1999.
- ◆ A **1-day ticket for one park** is $73 adults, $61 kids, bought online. That's $7 and $6 cheaper than the gate price.
- ◆ **2-day, two-park tickets** are $120 adults and $110 kids at the gate, but if you buy online at least 2 days early, you can get into both parks for a week for $95 (adult and child).

Most tickets don't expire.

What the Basics Cost at Universal's Two Parks

Parking: $12; $17 for closer "preferred" spaces; $18 valet
Single strollers: $13 per day
Double strollers: $21 per day
Kiddie Car (a stroller with a dummy steering wheel): $16; $24 double
Wheelchair: $12
ECV: $45
Lockers: $8 per day small (multi-entry)
Regular soda: $2.40/**Water:** $2.75

If you're planning to do a full complement of the non-Disney parks, including Universal Orlando, SeaWorld, Aquatica, Wet 'n Wild, and Busch Gardens, then you'll find value in the **FlexTicket,** which gets you into all of them for 2 weeks at a deep discount. Details on this pass are described on p. 322.

HOPPING THE LINES   You can speed your visit and do most of the major rides (missing many of the shows and smaller goodies) in a single day, provided you have an **Express pass** paired with a ticket that allows you to enter both parks in 1 day. At Islands of Adventure, 14 of the major rides and shows have a dedicated Express line, and 15 of the ones at Universal Studios do.

Like Disney's Fastpass, Universal's Express allows guests to use a separate entrance queue that is dramatically shorter than the "Standby" one; your ticket is checked by an employee with a hand-held scanner. Unlike Disney's Fastpass, Universal's Express pass system is for sale. Guests can buy an **Express Plus** pass at shops at both parks for $20 to $46 a day (for a single park) or $26 to $51 (for both parks); the price rises with peak season, but usually it's the cheapest rate. This method allows one entry per ride without regard to the number of passes that are outstanding, although a version sold only online allows you to use the pass as many times as you want. Express is actually a good value because it enables you to see both Universal parks in a single day and consequently see more in Orlando. Guests at the three hotels on Universal property (the Royal Pacific, the Hard Rock, and Portofino Bay) can use their key cards for free Express access, too.

Universal also has **photographers** on hand to take your photo at big moments. You'll get a claim ticket enabling you to purchase an expensive copy (on that day only), and you may always use your own camera instead.

WHAT TO WEAR   Dress your small children in their bathing suits for a day at Universal Studios because its Kidzone, one of its best sections, will get them soaked. Adults should come dressed to be drenched themselves, including their feet, at Islands of Adventure because two of its best rides are water-based.

Shop Early to Save

At the extreme left of the entry plaza, where you'll be leaving the park, there's a souvenir stand. This is no ordinary stand: It's for marked-down items. Normally, you'd never learn about it until you were already leaving (and had already made any purchases). I'm letting you know about it now so you price shop. The small stand at the entrance to Islands of Adventure is also a good stop for discount goods when you're at that park.

UNIVERSAL STUDIOS FLORIDA

After you get your car situated ($12 to park), take the covered sidewalks to CityWalk and head to the right. Before you enter, pause in front of the giant, tilting globe for the requisite photo op, because the light is better here in the morning.

The plaza after the turnstiles is where you take care of business. **Strollers and wheelchairs** are obtained to the left, and **lockers** are rented to the right. Make sure to grab a free park **map** here; if you forget, the stores also stock them.

Although there are technically six themed areas, they are not strictly defined and they fall into two general zones. Everyone enters along the main avenue of the simulated backlot (including **Production Central, Hollywood,** and **New York**), which contains many of the behind-the-scenes attractions, while the elongated Lagoon stretches off to the right, encircled by many of the thrill-based rides in **San Francisco/Amity, World Expo,** and **Woody Woodpecker's Kidzone.**

In the summer, when hours are long, there might be fireworks or the *Universal 360: A Cinesphere Spectacular* show on the lagoon, which employs a quartet of four-story white balls into which images are projected. Shows like these aren't Universal's forte, but there's not a Disney-esque crush of spectators, either.

A Tip for Parents and Adrenaline Junkies: Generally speaking, the kid-friendly rides are on the near side of the lagoon (the bottom half of your map), and the hottest new thrill ride is on the left.

Production Central

The area along the entry avenue (called both Plaza of the Stars and 57th St.) and to its left is collectively marked on maps as Production Central, but who are they kidding? Nowadays, those soundstages are used only for the odd local commercial and for haunted houses at Universal's fiendishly popular Halloween event.

The initial dream was much bigger. When the park was built, it was intended to be more like the original Hollywood location, where an amusement area naturally grew up around tours given of a working studio. Newspapers at the time trumpeted Orlando as "Hollywood of the East" because year-round production could be accomplished here and at Disney–MGM Studios for cheap, and millions of tourists could be a part of the behind-the-scenes process. One of Universal's soundstages housed a working TV studio for Nickelodeon, the kids' cable channel, and the game show *Double Dare* plucked families out of the park to compete on air. In front of the studio, a geyser of "green slime" (actually green water) gurgled in tribute to the Canadian show, *You Can't Do That on Television,* that helped make the channel's fortunes. (Today, that stage houses the equally messy Blue Man Group.) The arranged marriage never took. Hollywood's interest in Orlando petered out long before Nickelodeon's partnership did, and now both are dead.

The first block of Production Central is mostly shops, including the largest gift shop in the park, **Universal Studios Store,** on the left. Across from that are the tempting Art Deco buildings of Rodeo Drive, the spine of the Hollywood area and for my money the prettiest part of the park.

At the second block, the real action starts with a bang. You can't miss the giant roller coaster towering above. That's **Hollywood Rip, Ride, Rockit ★★★**, opened in 2009, and it's one advanced train: 17 stories tall, a vertical climb, a hill-like loop, and near misses with pedestrians. Most advanced are its cars, outfitted with LEDs and in-seat speakers. Riders personalize their trip by choosing the song that will play during it (from a broad menu including country, rap, rock, and disco). When it's done, they can buy a movie of their ride, with the song as a soundtrack. And at peak performance, there will be four cars on the tracks at a time. It hadn't opened at press time, but boy, am I excited.

Two of the park's most popular kids' attractions face each other down across the avenue. On the left, **Jimmy Neutron's Nicktoon Blast** 🧒 unites several of Nickelodeon's staple characters, including said Jimmy, SpongeBob SquarePants, and the Rugrats, who band together to stop a band of egg-shaped weirdos bent on destroying the world. The show takes place in a theater full of individual open-air ride platforms that have all the characteristics of motion simulators except claustrophobia. That's good for some, but the computer animation and whip-quick pace of the movie will still jar some into temporary nausea. **Strategy:** Passengers can control their motion-simulator seats; a better option for those prone to motion sickness is to request one that doesn't move at all, although that would render the exercise pretty pointless. Veer left as the line progresses so that you're closer to the back of the theater; being too close can cause vertigo.

Across the street, **Shrek 4-D ★** is a snarky 12-minute, 3-D movie-cum-spectacle—filmed in "OgreVision"—featuring all the high-priced voices of the movie characters (Mike Myers, Cameron Diaz, Eddie Murphy). John Lithgow plays the ghost of the evil Lord Farquaad, who crashes Shrek and Fiona's honeymoon at Fairytale Falls with a few dastardly surprises. The chairs look like standard theater seats except they're specially designed to amp up the sensations—don't worry; it won't make you ill. Well, unless fart jokes gross you out. The same people who made the DreamWorks movie made this one, so if you like the smart-alecky fairy-tale tweaking of the original, you'll dig this. It's a good one to do when the feet start aching, although the line can build in the afternoon. **Strategy:** Because the entertaining preshow is just as long as the movie, the Express pass doesn't seem to buy you very much time for this one.

In the street between Shrek and the Monster's Cafe, visit **Donkey's Photo Finish,** featuring an interactive, robotic version of the movie's ass in his own stall; he interacts with kids and poses.

The third block of Production Central is a dead zone. Don't worry. Things get better from here.

New York

When the park on your left is replaced by a park on your right, you've entered the New York area. Never mind that the park to your right is an imitation of San

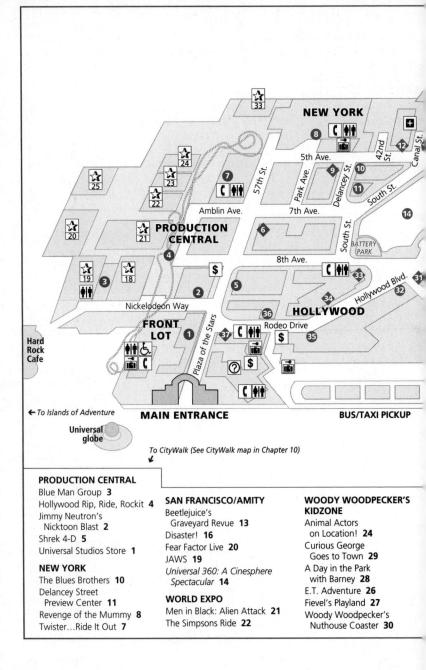

← *To Islands of Adventure*

Hard Rock Cafe

FRONT LOT

PRODUCTION CENTRAL

NEW YORK

HOLLYWOOD

BATTERY PARK

5th Ave.
7th Ave.
8th Ave.
Amblin Ave.
Nickelodeon Way
Rodeo Drive
Plaza of the Stars
57th St.
Park Ave.
Delancey St.
South St.
42nd St.
Canal St.
Hollywood Blvd.

Universal globe

MAIN ENTRANCE

BUS/TAXI PICKUP

To CityWalk (See CityWalk map in Chapter 10)

PRODUCTION CENTRAL
Blue Man Group **3**
Hollywood Rip, Ride, Rockit **4**
Jimmy Neutron's
 Nicktoon Blast **2**
Shrek 4-D **5**
Universal Studios Store **1**

NEW YORK
The Blues Brothers **10**
Delancey Street
 Preview Center **11**
Revenge of the Mummy **8**
Twister…Ride It Out **7**

SAN FRANCISCO/AMITY
Beetlejuice's
 Graveyard Revue **13**
Disaster! **16**
Fear Factor Live **20**
JAWS **19**
*Universal 360: A Cinesphere
 Spectacular* **14**

WORLD EXPO
Men in Black: Alien Attack **21**
The Simpsons Ride **22**

WOODY WOODPECKER'S KIDZONE
Animal Actors
 on Location! **24**
Curious George
 Goes to Town **29**
A Day in the Park
 with Barney **28**
E.T. Adventure **26**
Fievel's Playland **27**
Woody Woodpecker's
 Nuthouse Coaster **30**

SAN FRANCISCO/AMITY

The Embarcadero

Amity Avenue

Lagoon

WORLD EXPO

The Lagoon

CENTRAL PARK

Sunset Blvd.

WOODY WOODPECKER'S KIDZONE

Exit to Vineland Rd. →

☆	Film & TV Production Stage
$	Banking
✚	First Aid
🔒	Lockers
🚻	Restrooms
☎	Telephones
ⓘ	Guest Services
♿	Wheelchair & Stroller Rental

HOLLYWOOD
Lucy: A Tribute **36**
Terminator 2: 3-D Battle
  Across Time **35**
Universal Horror
  Make-Up Show **32**

DINING ◆
Beverly Hills Boulangerie **37**
Cafe La Bamba **31**
Finnegan's Bar & Grill **9**
International Food
  and Film Festival **23**
Kid Zone Pizza
  Company **25**

Lombard's Seafood Grille **17**
Louie's Italian Restaurant **12**
Mel's Drive-In **33**
Monster's Cafe **6**
Richter's Burger Co. **15**
San Francisco Pastry Co. **18**
Schwab's **34**

Francisco's Union Square. Straight ahead, at the end of 57th Street (the main entry avenue) is a little cul-de-sac that looks, through a camera lens, like Manhattan. Yes, you're right, the Chrysler Building is not actually located behind the Public Library and neither is on 57th Street, but come on. This is supposed to be fun.

On your left is **Twister . . . Ride It Out** ☆. I like this one, although wee ones might get scared. After several rooms of portentous preshow videos narrated by Helen Hunt and Bill Paxton, those blockbuster superstars (snicker), you finally enter a viewing area in a hangarlike chamber that's dressed to look like a Midwestern small town (gas station, telephone pole, drive-in movie in the distance) on a weekend night. A storm approaches, rain begins to fall and, as you knew it would, a twister forms. Right before your eyes, a funnel cloud descends from the rafters and to the delight of many it proceeds to wreck the place. Sparks fly, roofs peel, and guess what happens to the gas station? Watch for the cow that flies across the room, braying like the one in the movie, on wires so obvious that it's clearly intended as a joke—most shows, it gets a laugh. Although people tend to shy away from the front row, don't, because you won't feel much more than mist and a light sucking sensation there (I'd tuck sensitive electronics away anyway). It's quite an original attraction, and it's another good one for a hot day, but not a top-drawer one. **Strategy:** It runs continuously, but I wouldn't wait for more than 20 minutes for it.

Facing the square is the brilliant **Revenge of the Mummy** ☆☆☆. The ride is technologically cutting edge with an easy start and a rollicking finish: Part–dark ride, part–roller coaster, it goes backwards and forwards, twists on a turntable, and even spends a harrowing moment stalled in a room as the ceiling crawls with fire. (It doesn't go upside-down.) To say much more would give away some clever surprises; I've told you what you need to know to determine if it's for you. I brought my brother, a longtime Disney passholder, to Universal for his first time, and after he rode this, he said he wished he'd bought a Universal pass instead. **Strategy:** You must to put loose articles in the lockers to the right of the entrance—they're free, but their fingerprint-activated lock system is a true pain in the butt, so designate a single person in your party (someone good with computers) to cut through the crowd that inevitably piles up. There are three lines: Express, standby, and single riders. Most of the time, the single-rider line doesn't save you time; in fact, it can be slower than the standby.

Make Back Some of Your Admission Expenses

The **Delancey Street Preview Center** is marked on the maps, but you can only get in by invitation (someone will approach you on the streets). That's where NBC-affiliated entities screen television pilots and then solicit audience opinions. On a quiet January day, I once earned $30 just for enduring a show called *Psych*. I told them that its production was clichéd and strained. It became a hit on USA Network anyway. You can't predict the demographic of the test audience they'll be looking for, so stop by and ask if you fit the profile du jour.

The Best of Universal Studios Florida

Don't miss if you're 6: Curious George Goes to Town

Don't miss if you're 16: Men in Black: Alien Attack

Requisite photo op: The rotating globe out front; the fiberglass shark in front of JAWS

Food you can only get here: The Irish Cobb salad at Finnegan's Bar & Grill in New York

The most crowded, so go early: Hollywood Rip, Ride, Rockit

Skippable: Fear Factor Live

Biggest thrill: Revenge of the Mummy

Best show: Animal Actors on Location!

Where to find peace: On the lagoon, across from Kidzone; in Kidzone, between the Barney and Curious George attractions

The rest of the New York section is gussied up to look like the tenements of the Lower East Side or Greenwich Village, and is worth a few photos. Actors playing **the Blues Brothers** show up on Delancey Street about five times a day for a concert. I never wait around for them, as the rides are so much more interesting and, let's be honest, that movie came out during the Carter administration.

The main video game **arcade** is on the corner of 42nd Street and 5th Avenue—incidentally, in New York City, that's where the public library is.

San Francisco/Amity

The street called 5th Avenue hits the lagoon and is renamed the Embarcadero. Now you're in San Francisco, as the bricks and false cable car turntable attest. The first attraction on the left is a 20-minute show, **Beetlejuice's Graveyard Revue.** Universal owns the rights to many classic movie monsters, including Frankenstein, and they appear in this rowdy '80s and '90s rock-'n'-roll show, presided over by the undead, naughty-minded Beetlejuice, who aims more for the funny bone than the jugular. Watching the Bride of Frankenstein sing "Higher and Higher" will make you feel like someone slipped a pill in your Coke, but it probably won't make your day. **Strategy:** Unless you're a show person, you can skip this one, at least until you've knocked down some of the fresher attractions. Performances happen two or three times daily and will be noted on your map.

Disaster! starts off with a pretty cool (but wordy) preshow in which a projected Christopher Walken, pretending to be a big disaster-movie director touting the genre, interacts with a live actor on stage for 6 minutes. The technology is impressive, especially as this lifelike image rests his feet on boxes you can clearly see in front of you. Next, the actor brings everyone into an adjoining "soundstage" and volunteers from the audience stand in for special-effect shots which are recorded. Finally, everyone boards a tram mocked up to resemble San Francisco's

BART subway—seats on the outside are the best. It travels down a tunnel and stops inside what appears to be a faithful re-creation of the Embarcadero station, albeit one that smells suspiciously of natural gas. Of course something goes horribly wrong. There's an earthquake. Hell is unleashed: rocking, flooding to within an inch of the train, the unexpected intrusion of a gas truck from the "street" above (with the required climactic explosion). The intent is to approximate a jolt measuring 8.3 on the Richter scale. Just as quickly as it began, everything halts and reassembles itself for the next "take" as your train whisks you out again. *Warning:* Claustrophobes abhor the BART bit, as do some nervous children, but I think it's good, clean fun.

One of those redesigned rides is **JAWS** ✪✪, and it's next on the circuit around the lagoon. On the way, you'll perhaps notice that the theme shifts from the wharves of San Francisco to that of an all-American town. You're now meant to be in Amity, the New England town from *Jaws,* on the Fourth of July—hence the hot dog stands and **midway games,** which are closed on quiet days. The boat ride JAWS, based on the movie, is entered at the far end of Amity—you'll know you're there when you see the fiberglass shark strung up like the day's catch. People sliding their heads into the shark's mouth makes for what's said to be the most popular photo op in the park, which is kind of creepy when you think about it.

A very expensive attraction to run, JAWS tends to open about 2 hours later than the other rides, and it often spends months at a time being drained and cleaned. It also shuts down on "white alert" whenever lightning is detected in the vicinity, so if it's running and the line's not bad, jump on. What begins as a slow-moving tour boat ride on Captain Jake's Amity Boat Tours quickly deteriorates into a slow-moving boat ride repeatedly accosted by powerful but rubbery shark robots, which spring unexpectedly out of the water. In the effort to protect you from becoming dinner, your "skipper" is reduced to wielding a "grenade launcher" that, unfortunately, he has no idea how to use. The fun you'll have depends largely on the narration skills—in industry terms, the "spiel"—of the skipper you get; see p. 190 for details of my day behind the wheel. The ride takes about 7 minutes, the boat's seating is covered, and the movements are so tame that lap restraints aren't required. The best seats, but also potentially the wettest ones, are at the left of the boat in the first to fifth rows; in fact, the left side in general gets the better views. Call it a design flaw in an ambitious ride; the original 1990 version was so much more daring (Jaws clamped on the boat's prow and spun it around on a hidden turntable, and the water billowed with red "blood" each time he was finally vanquished) that it was unreliable and had to be redesigned. The resulting simplified version is still pretty complicated and beloved by long-time visitors.

The show **Fear Factor Live,** like the meat-headed (and long-ago cancelled) NBC show, features ordinary people doing stunts (usually involving being dangled on wires, maybe eating food-grade mealworms) for the twisted pleasure of a whooping audience while an inane master of ceremonies eggs everyone on. If you're over 18 and want to volunteer as a contestant (first prize: polite applause), be here first thing after park opening to sign up. Its days are numbered.

World Expo

In 2008, Universal debuted the **Simpsons Ride** ✪✪✪, a highly amusing, top-quality, motion-simulator "Thrilltacular Upsy-Downsy Spins-Aroundsy Teen-Operated

Thrill Ride" that takes place in front of an 80-foot-tall screen. The p[ ]
and ironic enough to please devotees of the FOX series, punctures C[ ]
You join Homer's clan at Krustyland, an overcommercialized theme pa[ ]
coaster that's sabotaged by the evil Sideshow Bob (voiced by Kelsey Grammer).
During the incredibly fast-paced 6 minutes, you zoom through a bunch of predica-
ments that mock the theme park world, including skewers of Shamu, Pirates of the
Caribbean, and "it's a small world." Add to that a giant killer panda bear and an
extra layer of heightened sensory (like the smell of baby powder—it makes sense
when you ride). It's not too rough, but your brain may hurt from absorbing all the
jokes. The waiting area is so tongue in cheek and gag packed that half the fun of re-
riding is being able to see more of it: Springfield denizens operate video midway
booths, Itchy and Scratchy do the gory safety warning, and Krusty tells you things
like "Wait here until someone comes and tells you to do something." Yes—an
attraction you'll want to repeat just for the line. Seats are four across, so families can
ride together. The surrounding stores are Springfield-themed: A cart provides
Squishees and Kwik-E-Mart sells souvenirs.

Although you'll be forced to check your stuff in free lockers if you ride it, **Men
in Black: Alien Attack** ✮✮✰is an excellent riff on the Will Smith film franchise.
After a superlative queue area that does a pitch-perfect, *Jetsons*-style imitation of
New York's 1964 World's Fair (ironically, the one Walt Disney created so many
wonders for), you discover the "real" tenant of the futuristic building—a training
course for the Men in Black alien patrol corps. You board six-person cars
equipped with individual laser guns. As you pass from room to room—expect lots
of herky-jerky motions, but nothing sickening—your task is to fire upon any alien
that pops out from around doorways, behind trash cans, and so on. If they peg
you first, it sends your buggy spinning. Each car racks up points that are displayed
on the dashboard, and the number accumulated by the end determines the climactic video you're shown—Will Smith will either praise you as "Galaxy
Defender" or mock you as "Bug Bait." **Strategy:** The single riders' queue moves
quickly, thanks to the odd number of seats in each row.

Photo Op: Head out onto the bridge across the lagoon. If you line up your
camera precisely, you'll combine a painted image of the space shuttle with your
real-life companions, creating an in-camera trick of the eye. The bridge is also my
favorite place to catch the evening Cinesphere show, as it affords a compact view
of four spheres flashing at once.

Hollywood

There are no rides in the Hollywood section, only two shows and a few shops.
Still, the evocative Art Deco–style buildings along Rodeo Drive and Hollywood
Boulevard are very well executed and worth a few photos. The 25-minute
Universal Horror Make-Up Show ✮ is a terrific, tongue-in-cheek exposé, conducted by a nerdy type in his workshop, of how horror-movie effects are accomplished. On paper, that seems like the kind of thing you might otherwise skip, but
in truth park regulars love its wit and playful edge. For ad-libbing and gross-out
humor, the park suggests parental guidance for this one, but I find that most kids
have heard it all before, and it's certainly true that seeing terrifying movie gore
exposed as the make-believe it is can be a good reality check for younger kids.
Times are printed on your park map, and you can't get in once the show's begun.

ven if you skip the show, there's something to see in the lobby: exhibits about great horror characters and make-up artists. On the street outside, the Simpsons characters (well, not Maggie) often pull up in an RV for photo ops.

The other show, **Terminator 2: 3-D Battle Across Time,** is far more intense. Although the 12-minute film portion, a sort of minisequel to *Terminator 2,* was made by extravagant director James Cameron with all his original stars (including Ah-nold and Linda Hamilton), it's hardly just another movie. It's got three screens, six 8-foot robots, gunfire, smoke bombs, and motorcyclists that seamlessly dive in and out of the filmed action. The film portion cost $60 million to make, which when it was produced in 1996 qualified it as the most expensive movie, per minute, in history. **Strategy:** This edgy, cynical show splits the eardrums with romping, stomping mayhem, so keep small children away unless they're hard cases. Those in the front rows will have to pivot their heads to see all the action.

After homicidal robots, you may be ready for the gentler charms of **Lucy: A Tribute,** an exhibition of Lucille Ball memorabilia that you can enjoy at your own pace. Ever seen an Emmy? There are five, plus a model of the *I Love Lucy* set, which was painted black and white so it would look good on TV.

Woody Woodpecker's Kidzone

Kidzone ✫✫✫ 🄺 is my pick for the best children's theme park area in Orlando. I've heard tales of 6-year-olds who threatened self-orphanization if they were dragged away from this playland within 4 hours. There's a ton to do, although, strangely, eating isn't one of them. The first option is **Animal Actors on Location!** 🄺, a charming 20-minute show (times are noted on the map) featuring a troupe of trained dogs, cats, birds, and a horse. Placing this show here was inspired, because small children get a thrill out of seeing common animals do tricks, and as a consequence, it's popular. Because it's in an amphitheater, you can also sneak out in the middle if you need to. But if you see only one emphatically punctuated household-pets-doing-cute-tricks-to-jaunty-music theme park show while you're in Orlando, make it SeaWorld's superior Pets Ahoy!

The expensive-looking **E.T. Adventure** ✫ 🄺, based on the 1982 Steven Spielberg movie, is rightfully in the kiddie area because it's not intense. Upon entering, guests supply their name to an attendant, who encodes the information on a pass you're supposed hand over when you board the ride. The indoor queue area is a fabulous reproduction of a thick, cool California forest at night; the darkness makes some kids fear they're in for trouble, but in fact, the ride beyond it is pretty tame. Vehicles are suspended from rails to approximate the sensation of cruising on a bike, and they sweep and scoop through forests, across the moonrise, and even through gardens on E.T.'s home planet (remember, he was a botanist), where a menagerie of goofy-looking aliens, who don't look nearly as realistic as our hero, greet us from the sidelines. At the climax, a grateful E.T. is supposed to call out the names of the passengers on your cart as you fly home—hence those boarding passes—but frankly, in all my years of doing this ride, he always sounds to me like he's spouting gibberish, so don't get your hopes up, unless your name is Pfmkmpftur. **Strategy:** If the queue looks dense from the outside, think about coming back later (the hour before park closing seems to be a charmed time for quick waits), since there are still more lineups indoors.

Fievel's Playland 🧒, named for the hero of *An American Tail,* is the most spectacular of several playgrounds in Kidzone. The concept is that your kids have been shrunk down to a mouse's size, and they're playing in everyday items like sardine cans and cowboy hats. The ground is covered with that newfangled soft foam that all the modern playgrounds have (when I was a boy, we got concussions instead), but my favorite element is the easy water slide on a raft. (Yes, make sure your kids are wearing their swimsuits, because it's going to get a lot wetter soon.)

A Day in the Park with Barney 🧒, a small indoor area that can be accessed through its own gift shop (plush Barney, $17), is technically the postshow area for a singalong show. The doors close at the start and stay closed until the ordeal is over. Frankly, being locked in a room with that sappy purple dinosaur and all those screaming babies constitutes a chamber of horrors for me, but little ones find it enthralling. Parents can find beer carts on the lagoon nearby, if that helps. The play area mimics a forest, with a place to sift through sand, a tree equipped with little slides, and a chance to have your picture taken with (and then buy it from) Barney.

Across the way, **Woody Woodpecker's Nuthouse Coaster** 🧒 is a straightforward kiddie thrill with no surprises and a run time of less than a minute. Kids can plainly see every drop before they commit. The line is often evilly long.

On hot days, **Curious George Goes to Town** ★★★ 🧒 is where kids lose reason and parents lose patience. This frenetic splash area is teeming with squealing children and positively soaked with streams of water from every direction—from squirt cannons, fountains, geysers, and, most importantly, from two 500-gallon buckets that, every 7 minutes, sound a warning bell and then drench anyone beneath them. The immoderate, virtually orgiastic scene is ringed by a perimeter of dry parents keeping an eye on their wild offspring. I enjoy joining them, because watching the children cheer and scamper when they hear the clang of the bucket's warning bell, and then watching them momentarily vanish in the deluge, is endlessly amusing. Through the wet area (there's a dry bypass corridor to it on the left) is the dry Ball Factory, where kids suck up plastic balls with light vacuums, pack them into bags, and then fire them at each other with weak cannons. It's not marked on the maps. If parents allow their kids to so much as lay eyes on this area, they should prepare to get stuck here for a while.

Where to Eat at Universal Studios

In addition to the random snack carts, there are counter-service and sit-down restaurants in the park. None require reservations. Souvenir cups costing $7 can be refilled for 69¢. *Tip:* Always ask how much you'd save if you don't get fries or chips with the posted combo meals. It's usually a lot.

Remember that all the restaurants at CityWalk (p. 281) are a 5-minute walk from the park, so with a hand stamp for reentry, you can try those, too. The only one that requires reservations is Emeril's (p. 74).

Production Central One of the only indoor choices here is **Monster's Cafe,** which has some healthy options, such as rotisserie chicken with potatoes and corn for $9, Caesar salad with soup for $8, and penne primavera for $7.

New York Finnegan's Bar & Grill ★★ is a sit-down, Irish-style pub where you'll get a break from burgers and fries. Scotch eggs ($6), split pea-and-ham

Skipper for a Day: I Pilot the JAWS Ride

I've been attacked by a shark, unprovoked, 84 times. And I haven't even had my break yet. In the name of journalism, I'm working Universal Orlando's 2.5-acre JAWS attraction, which begins as a scenic cruise of sleepy Amity Island but, as these things do, goes horribly awry when a vicious great white menaces my vessel. From my introduction to the guests as "Skipper Jason" to the harrowing, high-voltage climax, each ride is 5 minutes of fishy mayhem. Fireballs, explosions—the whole circus. And I'm the ringmaster.

When I was a kid, any carbon-based life form with opposable thumbs could operate a theme park ride, but here, training is a ritual. Normally, I'd have to go through 5 days of it, including a swimming test at nearby Wet 'n Wild, before being allowed to "skipper" a JAWS boat, but for the sake of journalism, Universal treats me to an abbreviated education. I learn it's not a ride, it's a "show," and it's not narration, it's a "spiel." As a spieler, I'll usually run three boatloads in a row before taking a break—each show takes more than 5 minutes, so that's 15 minutes of opera-level intensity. Phil Whigham, the attraction's trainer, shows me where they keep the Gatorade jug. I am gonna need it, especially in this heat.

I receive a costume (cleaned daily by Universal and picked up at a huge wardrobe facility), a script (eight pages, annotated with acting "beats"), plus a nine-page workbook (essay question: "How do I feel about the grenade launcher?"), and a tongue-in-cheek dossier on people and places in Amity (in case anyone asks).

Out on the lagoon, Phil adjusts my microphone headset and explains what the boats' dashboard buttons do. One errant elbow could shut down the entire ride. Gulp. I meet Mimi Lipka, Universal's resident acting coach. Although she's a great-grandmother, she has more perk than the clean-cut college-age kids she shepherds through JAWS' acting rigors. Before the park opens, Mimi has me run the "show" on an empty boat while she rides along, taking notes for my improvement as the mechanized shark rams us.

soup ($4), Irish Cobb salad (it has corned beef, among other things, $12), and bangers and mash (sausage with garlic mashed potatoes, $11) are the kind of things available, plus good strong ales. The kids' menu has about five choices for $5 to $8. Park workers tend to pick this place when they're not on duty. **Louie's Italian Restaurant** does pizza slices (under $4) well but not much else, and more substantial meals (subs and salads) come in around that magical $8 figure, before drinks. The **Turkey Legs Cart** by Ben & Jerry's posts one thing on its menu: the marquee dish, plus chips for $8. But subtract chips (you only get 3 oz. anyway) and save a whopping $1.60.

San Francisco/Amity   The most variety available in the park is along the top of the lagoon, starting from in front of the Mummy ride (in New York) and ending

Interacting with the attraction's timed special effects is like doing a *pas de deux* with a pinball machine. The machines are going to do their thing even if I forget mine. I have to fire my grenade launcher at the correct targets, yank the steering wheel at the right moments, and with full-bodied emotion, I must trick the guests into thinking I don't anticipate that pesky shark's preprogrammed reappearances. Like clockwork, I go Rambo on the beast. "Eat this!" I bellow, blasting away at it, while Mimi scribbles. (A typical tip: "Look for survivors!")

Finally, with a proud flourish, she writes my name on a dry-erase board hidden behind the unload station. I am "signed off" and officially on rotation. The ride opens.

I nervously guide an empty boat to the load station, where "deck crew" assigns seating by playing what they jokingly call "Human Tetris." Now I see 48 faces before me, waiting for my next move. Judging by their expectant—some might say passive—grins, they're dying to buy whatever I'm about to sell. I press the green start button. No return now.

"Well, time to start our voyage," I chirp, on cue. "Wave goodbye to the happy landlubbers!" That line was always the start of my script, but I'm surprised to see my passengers actually *do* it. Once I fight the urge to rush, I realize I have them. Children gleefully point to the merest ripple; grown men shy from teeth they know are fake. The interaction—a triangle between me, a multimillion-dollar machine, and my audience—is invigorating, and I stop fretting about timing and just have fun. Show by show, my voice grows hoarser and I get thirstier, but the feedback from the guests' faces feeds my energy level. When my passengers disembark, and as I catch my breath between runs, I eavesdrop. "I wanna go again!" squeals a boy. "I wasn't scared," fibs another. And from a British girl: "I've got a soppy bottom!" To me, a wet customer is a happy customer. *Fin.*

at Amity (where there's just the **Midway Grill** hot dog stand—$7.29 for a Chicago-style dog with fries, and $5 funnel cakes). **Amity Fried Chicken** has two pieces with fries or fish and chips for $8. **San Francisco Pastry Co.,** across from Disaster!, does sandwiches and loaded croissants for $8 to $9; add chips for $1 more. It also does fruit plates and salads ($3.50–$7). The adjoining **Lombard's Seafood Grille** is set over the water (catch of the day, $16 with salad and potatoes; fish and chips $12—four bucks more than at Amity, nearby). On a pier in the water, my pick of the park is the substantial **Richter's Burger Co.** ★★, which does burgers (from $7.50 with fries), marinated grilled chicken sandwiches ($8 with fries), and a salad with grilled chicken ($8) that are all on the less greasy side. There's a fixin's bar. Periodically, the dining room rumbles (but doesn't move) to simulate nearby quakes, and there is some outdoor seating on the water.

The Universal Meal Deal

In both its parks, Universal offers an all-you-can-eat meal plan. Dubbed the **Universal Meal Deal,** it entitles you to one main plate and one dessert each time you go through the line at eight counter-service locations (four per park). You'll get a wristband and kids 9 and under must order from whatever designated kids' menu that restaurant has (which isn't usually a problem). Keeping in mind that it doesn't include beverages and stops working 30 minutes before closing (so you'll have to plan ahead to get dinner out of it), the pricing only makes sense if you're a big eater. For one park, adults pay $21 and kids $11; for two parks, it's adults $25 and kids $13, and for $6 more, you also get an entree at one of four CityWalk restaurants (usually Pastamoré, Latin Quarter, Bob Marley, or Pat O'Brien's).

World Expo   Near the entrance to Kidzone, the **International Food and Film Festival** does pizza and pasta ($8 combos), plus a few choices it calls "Asian": Sweet and sour chicken, beef and peppers, and Szechwan orange chicken all come with rice and stir-fried vegetables for $8.29, and wonton soup is $3.50.

Kidzone   There's just **Kid Zone Pizza Company** here; chicken fingers and fries go for $7.50, and the Conewich, a sort of wrap, comes with chicken or tuna salad for $7.50. Since it's the only option among the playgrounds, it gets crowded.

Hollywood   **Mel's Drive-In,** facing the lagoon, is a '50s-style diner—everything's glassy and shiny; burgers and chicken for around $7.75 with fries—that has antique cars parked in the lot. They really work, too. **Schwab's,** after the famous L.A. drugstore, does drinks and ice cream (malts, $4.50), and it's also where you can pick up things like Tylenol and bandages at prices that will make you sore you forgot to bring your own. Near the Horror Make-Up Show, **Café La Bamba** is for chicken and ribs; its warren of dining rooms can make for a cool escape. Dishes are around $8, and if you add $5, you get a large drink and a dessert. **Beverly Hills Boulangerie** ⭐ is a good place for a healthy meal: Sandwiches (turkey, roast beef, so on) with potato salad and fruit cost $8. It also does a soup-and-salad combo for $5.

ISLANDS OF ADVENTURE

After you get your car parked ($12), take the moving sidewalks to CityWalk and veer to the left, toward the 130-foot-tall lighthouse (it's just for show), to reach IOA. If you have doubts about whether your kids will be tall enough to ride anything, there's a gauge listing all the requirements before the ticket booths. The most restrictive (54 in.), understandably, is the Incredible Hulk coaster.

ORIENTING YOURSELF   IOA's 110 acres are laid out much like Epcot's World Showcase: individually themed areas (here, called "islands," even though they're not) arranged around a lagoon (called the Great Inland Sea). To see everything, you simply follow a great circle. The only corridor into the park, **Port of Entry,** borrows from the Magic Kingdom's Main Street, USA, in that it's a narrow,

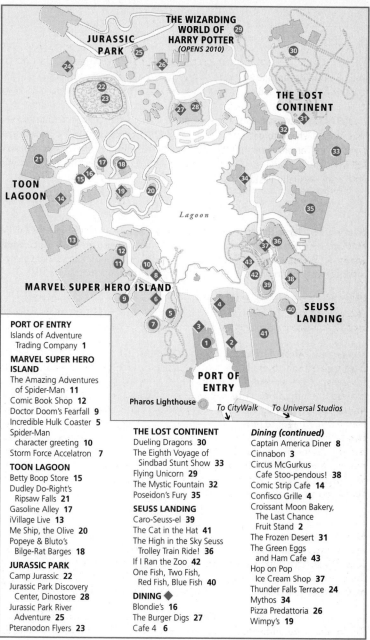

THE WIZARDING WORLD OF HARRY POTTER (OPENS 2010)

JURASSIC PARK

THE LOST CONTINENT

TOON LAGOON

Lagoon

MARVEL SUPER HERO ISLAND

SEUSS LANDING

PORT OF ENTRY

Pharos Lighthouse

To CityWalk   To Universal Studios

PORT OF ENTRY
Islands of Adventure
  Trading Company **1**

MARVEL SUPER HERO ISLAND
The Amazing Adventures
  of Spider-Man **11**
Comic Book Shop **12**
Doctor Doom's Fearfall **9**
Incredible Hulk Coaster **5**
Spider-Man
  character greeting **10**
Storm Force Accelatron **7**

TOON LAGOON
Betty Boop Store **15**
Dudley Do-Right's
  Ripsaw Falls **21**
Gasoline Alley **17**
iVillage Live **13**
Me Ship, the Olive **20**
Popeye & Bluto's
  Bilge-Rat Barges **18**

JURASSIC PARK
Camp Jurassic **22**
Jurassic Park Discovery
  Center, Dinostore **28**
Jurassic Park River
  Adventure **25**
Pteranodon Flyers **23**

THE LOST CONTINENT
Dueling Dragons **30**
The Eighth Voyage of
  Sindbad Stunt Show **33**
Flying Unicorn **29**
The Mystic Fountain **32**
Poseidon's Fury **35**

SEUSS LANDING
Caro-Seuss-el **39**
The Cat in the Hat **41**
The High in the Sky Seuss
  Trolley Train Ride! **36**
If I Ran the Zoo **42**
One Fish, Two Fish,
  Red Fish, Blue Fish **40**

DINING ◆
Blondie's **16**
The Burger Digs **27**
Cafe 4 **6**

Dining (continued)
Captain America Diner **8**
Cinnabon **3**
Circus McGurkus
  Cafe Stoo-pendous! **38**
Comic Strip Cafe **14**
Confisco Grille **4**
Croissant Moon Bakery,
  The Last Chance
  Fruit Stand **2**
The Frozen Desert **31**
The Green Eggs
  and Ham Cafe **43**
Hop on Pop
  Ice Cream Shop **37**
Thunder Falls Terrace **24**
Mythos **34**
Pizza Predattoria **26**
Wimpy's **19**

introductory area where guests are submerged into the theme. In this case, you're gathering munitions for a "great odyssey," so, in theme park logic, it's where you do things like rent strollers and lockers and grab free maps.

Most guests beeline through Port of Entry, but there are rewards to taking your time. Mostly, they're in the form of recorded sounds—listen near apparently closed doors and windows for chatter from unseen people. Because attraction lines are shortest after opening, explore this area later, such as closer to closing.

STRATEGY   Once you reach the end of Port of Entry and hit the sea, which way should you go? Left. The designers of this park didn't miss a trick. Most of the exciting rides collect along the first half of the circuit, leaving the second half (to the right) for the main kids' area and for big shows. If you go right, by the time you make it back around to the most important rides, the lines will be crazy.

Money Saving Tip: Off to the left, where you'll later be exiting the park, you'll spot a **small stand** selling marked-down items (the inventory changes, but I've seen $8 Marvel action figures, two-for-ones on plush Curious George dolls, and $40 sweatshirts for $22). Check here before spending money on the full-price stuff inside the park. Otherwise, the **Islands of Adventure Trading Company,** on the left as you proceed down Port of Entry, is the largest store in the park, but it's full price.

Marvel Super Hero Island

At the wharf left of the Port of Entry, the vivid, $15-million **Incredible Hulk Coaster** ✪✪✩ looms. This machine demands attention: Every minute or so, a new train is blasted out of the 150-foot tunnel, over the avenue, and across the lakefront. Adding to the intensity, the track's hollow frame generates an animal roar that can be heard throughout the park. The ride is quick—a little over 2 minutes—but it's invigorating. First, trains cruise into the inclined tunnel. Then, without warning, 220 aircraft tires accelerate trains from a standstill to 40mph in 2 seconds and shoot them into a zero G-force barrel-roll 110 feet in the air, which means passengers are already upside down even though they're still going up the first hill. (Let's hope General Electric, which owns the park, gets a deal on all the juice it burns.) What follows is unbridled mayhem, as cars are boomeranged in a cobra roll over the lake and sent at a top speed of 67mph through a tangle of corkscrews, loops, and misty tunnels. For many visitors, it's the first ride of the day, and its seven inversions are certain to work better than morning coffee.

Strategy: Before you get into line, toss all loose items into the free lockers to the right of the ride; send someone good with computers, since the fingerprint-scan lock system requires patience and a still hand. The last time I was here, guests only got 30 minutes free and beyond that would have to pay $2 to get their stuff back—a raw deal considering lines. The single-rider line here is usually fruitful. Some guests wait an extra long time for the chance to sit in the front row (a separate queue forms near the loading dock), but if you're low on time, wait instead for the front row on Dueling Dragons, where the exposed view gets you a lot more thrills. If you plan on buying a photo of your group on the ride, make sure you're all seated in the same line because shots are taken row by row.

Next door, **Storm Force Accelatron,** named for the weather-controlling X-Man, is a not-too-special 90-second spinning-tub ride, like Disney's teacups. Open, round cars spin on platters that themselves are on a giant rotating disk, and

The Odd Ambiance of Super Hero Island

Once you're past the Hulk, the vibe of Marvel Super Hero Island can finally assert itself, which it does murkily. The district looks vaguely futuristic and lamely '80s, and rock music plays a little too loudly.

It's no wonder the island's personality is indistinct: Its design predates the X-Men, Iron Man, Fantastic Four, *and* the Spider-Man film franchises, so designers had to forge ahead with only the comics, which few guests have read, for a visual language. Periodically, sirens sound and costumed characters from Marvel comic books ride in on motorcycles—there's Rogue in her awful early-'90s costume, Wolverine with soft-looking claws, Captain America, Cyclops, and Storm—and make the rounds to sign autographs. **Spider-Man** is sometimes one of them, but if you don't see him, head into the back of the Marvel Alterniverse Store, opposite the Captain America Diner. There, the hero has his own appearance zone where you can take your own photos (or buy one). The actor playing Spider-Man is one of the few who isn't clad in muscle-shaped padding—for the frank cling of his bodysuit, admiring members of the park's staff usually aren't far away.

just to ensure maximum vomit velocity, each pod can be spun using a plate in the middle. **Strategy:** This ride is skippable unless you have insistent children.

The two 200-foot spindly towers are **Dr. Doom's Fearfall,** identical columns fitted with open-air cars that slide up and down them. The ride rockets the brave 150 feet up at a force of 4Gs, where they feel an intense tickling in their stomachs, soak up a terrific view of the park, and hurtle (safely) back down to Earth. The ride capacity is pretty low—you can see for yourself that each tower only shoots about 16 people up on each trip, with a reload period of several minutes in between—so either do this one early or very late so that waiting for it doesn't eat up too much time. Every few minutes, you'll hear the towers hiss like a snarling beast—it sounds like a Doctor Doom sound effect, but, in fact, it's part of the ride mechanism. After passengers are seated, the cars are weighed by computer and any compressed air not needed for their launch is noisily expelled in the seconds before flight. **Strategy:** Because this ride's seating configuration (four on each side of the tower) lends itself to lots of empty spaces, its single-rider line, found through the adjoining arcade, moves much quicker than most.

At the exit of this ride, you'll find this park's main **video game arcade.**

If there's a single don't-miss ride in town, it's undoubtedly the **Amazing Adventures of Spider-Man** ✸✸✸, on your left past the Fearfall. After passing through a simulation of the *Daily Bugle* newsroom (take special notice of the hilarious preride safety video, done as a pitch-perfect *Superfriends*-era cartoon), riders don polarized 3-D glasses, board moving cars, and whisk through a 1.5-acre experience. Mild open-air motion simulation, computer-generated 3-D animation, and a cunning sense trickery (bursts of flame, water droplets, blasts of hot air) collaborate to impart the mind-blowing illusion of being drafted into Spidey's battles against a "Sinister Syndicate" of supervillains including Doctor Octopus

A Collector's Secret

Most of the shopping and food of Super Hero Island is standard-issue, but the **Comic Book Shop** is worth a stop for collectors. Surprisingly legit, the store carries the latest Marvel issues, compilation books, and collectible busts. (Comics fans should also keep their eyes peeled on the Spider-Man ride, where they'll see such inside jokes as a theater named the Excelsior.) True collectors will fret about rolling their books' spines on the rides—the park will send any purchase (here or at any other store) to the Islands of Adventure Trading Company, at the Port of Entry, for collection as you leave the park at the end of the day. The deadline for purchases changes, but it's usually about 2 hours before closing.

and the Green Goblin, who have disassembled the Statue of Liberty with an anti-gravity gun. Although the vehicles barely move as they make their way through the sets, you'll come off feeling as if you've survived a 400-foot plunge off a city skyscraper. The technology, developed for this park, remains unrivaled even though it's getting up there in age. Many independent thrill-ride fan clubs rate it as the best attraction in the world, and I agree. Spider-Man, which opened with the park in 1999, was so ahead of its time that other attractions still haven't caught up. It fires on all cylinders, and the whole family can do it without fear.

Strategy: Lines for this one can be as long as the ones for the roller coasters, so go early or late in the day to minimize waits. There's a single-rider line on this one, too, which shoots past the slower standby queue. Re-riders (and people I know, no matter how timid they are, quickly become addicts once they've tasted this ride) should get to know the single-rider entrance well.

Toon Lagoon

The next zone clockwise after Marvel Super Hero Island, Toon Lagoon harbors two waters rides that are—both literally and figuratively—among the splashiest at any theme park. Both of them will drench you. If you're smart, you'll come just *before* it swelters, so that you'll be soaked and cool when the going gets rough.

Slow your pace when you reach the introductory section of Toon Lagoon, encountered after a brief zone of **midway games** (most: three tries for $5). Crawling with details, color, and fountains, it's the kind of place that reveals more the longer you look. Some 150 cartoon characters—some you'll recognize (Nancy, Annie, the Family Circus, Beetle Bailey) and some strictly for connoisseurs (Little Nemo in Slumberland, Zippy)—make two-dimensional appearances on the island, including inside the restaurants and on a soundtrack popping in and out of the action. Where you see a button or a possible trigger, press it or plunge it, because the environment has been rigged with sonic treats. Whimsical snapshot spots are worked in, too, such as the trick photo setup by the Comic Strip Cafe where you can pretend Marmaduke is dragging you by his leash. The deluge from the waterfall under Hagar's Viking ship provides cooling relief from the sunlight. Amidst all this, the **Boop Oop A Doop** Betty Boop store sells rare specimens. My sister-in-law found a 75th-anniversary cookie jar here that no other real-world store carried. Personally, I worry about the mental health of the clerks, who are subjected to a brain-melting loop of Boop's "I Want to Be Loved by You."

Finally, at the back end of Toon Lagoon, the star attractions appear. That extravagant snow-capped mountain at the left contains **Dudley Do-Right's Ripsaw Falls** ★★ a wonderful perils-of-Pauline log-flume caper featuring Jay Ward's feckless Canadian Mountie bungling his rescue of Nell Fenwick from Snidely Whiplash. The winding 5-minute journey—ups, downs, indoor, outdoor, surprise backsplashes, all past chunky robotic characters—climaxes in a stomach-juggling double-dip drop that hurtles, unexpectedly, through a humped under-ground gully. Although the 75-foot drop starts out at 45 degrees, it steepens to 50 degrees, creating a weightless sensation. Front-seat and back-seat riders get soaked. And anyone who didn't get soaked probably will when they double back to the disembarking zone, because that's when they'll face the gauntlet of sadistic bystanders who fire water cannons at passing boats. Ripsaw Falls is terrific fun. You never see anyone come off it grumpy—the mark of amusement success. *Two tips:* The ride, which is such a blast it has ruined conventional log flume rides for me, often closes in January and early February for a scrub. There's an optional locker ($2) nearby—use it, because there's no waterproof storage in the boats. The **Gasoline Alley** shop, across the main path, sells $6 ponchos so you don't have to skip the flume on cold days, but bear in mind that on Ripsaw Falls, you straddle the seats and your separated feet won't be easy to cover. Best to wear sandals.

Just behind Gasoline Alley, **Popeye & Bluto's Bilge-Rat Barges** ★★ are 12-passenger, circular bumper boats that float freely and unpredictably down an out-landish white-water obstacle course—beneath waterfalls, through tunnels, over angry rapids, and past features designed to mercilessly inundate one or two peo-ple at a time. It's like playing Russian roulette with water, and everyone loses. When it comes to the round-boat genre (there are two others in town—one at

---

The Best of Islands of Adventure

Don't miss if you're 6: The Cat in the Hat

Don't miss if you're 16: The Amazing Adventures of Spider-Man

Requisite photo op: Toon Lagoon

Food you can only get here: Sundae on a Stick, Hop on Pop Ice Cream Shop, Seuss Landing; Treasure Chest Sundae, the Frozen Desert, the Lost Continent

The most crowded, so go early: Incredible Hulk Coaster, Dueling Dragons

Skippable: Storm Force Accelatron

Biggest thrill: Incredible Hulk Coaster

Best show: Poseidon's Fury

Where to find peace: On the lagoon at Port of Entry, Toon Lagoon, or Jurassic Park

Animal Kingdom and one at Busch Gardens), this version is considerably wilder, unquestionably wetter, and was obviously lavished with the most money. The attention shows: Even the river's walls have been sculpted and painted in cartoon hues to resemble a wooden chute. It's diabolical and one of Universal's best. **Strategy:** There's a semiwaterproof cubby on board for personal belongings, but you'd be wise to slip your things into plastic bags, too, just in case. Attendants won't let you remove your shoes, mostly because the turntable loading dock isn't safe for bare feet. The wait feels endless on hot days, and the queue area is dull and steamy, making this one a top contender for using your Express pass. There are more 25¢ water blasters on overlooking walkways for schadenfreude. Look for one of Universal's brightest ideas: step-in, haystack turbo dryers that, for $3, bake and blow the water off you after your journey. (That works well, except on jeans.)

Over by **Me Ship, the Olive** 🧒, an interactive playground for children just beyond the Barges' entrance, wallflowers can watch boats pass in trepidation of the next soak. In this case, the soaker can be you, since the Olive has more free water cannons you can use to drench people as they pass. Inside the Olive, there's also a slide and some fun to be had with a piano (play the notes on the sheet music for an orchestral surprise). One of my favorite things to do in Orlando is to spend awhile on the bridge beside the Olive, which overlooks Barge boats as they drift helplessly under a leaky boiler's funnel. Watching the gleeful alarm on people's faces, hearing the peals of laughter—the joy of the amusement park and the sublime delight of togetherness are repeated, again and again, from the vantage point of that bridge. I could stand there all day. I also love the shore of the sea, which is completely empty and private almost all the time.

Jurassic Park

Steven Spielberg was a creative consultant to Universal, the studio which nourished him, which is one reason this "island," the largest and greenest in the park, is presented practically verbatim from his 1993 movie. Once you pass through a proud wooden gate, John Williams' bombastic score becomes audible, and there it burrows until you move on to another area of IOA. When the park opened, the big boast was that all of the plants in this section were extant during the period of the dinosaurs, but it seems that's no longer the case. Still, the area has some 4,000 trees—half the number in the whole park—and if you stand quietly, you may hear rustling among some of them, which is a clever, Spielbergian touch.

The first area, on the right as you enter, is **Camp Jurassic** 🧒, the dedicated kids' zone of this part of the park. Don't lose your kids here—it's a tangle of rope bridges, slides, bubbling pools in caves, and thick greenery. The nifty-looking track clacking and soaring overhead is **Pteranodon Flyers,** on which hanging cars gently glide, one at a time, on a very short (about 75 sec.) scenic route through the trees, gently swaying as they turn. Cool as it looks, it was poorly designed, fitting only two at a time, and huge lines are inevitable. In the business, that's called a poor "load factor." Facing irate crowds, Universal instituted a rule: No adult could ride without a child. That accomplished two goals. It prepared guests for the ride's tame deportment and it cut down on the wait. Attendants may be willing to load child-free adults when the park is dead. **Strategy:** Even with the rule, lines get hairy; skip this underwhelmer unless the wait's less than 15 minutes.

I do recommend the **Jurassic Park River Adventure** ✿. In that family-friendly Orlando tradition, the worst drop is clearly visible from the outside; in this case, you can see it, or at least the splashdown from its 85-foot drop, behind the Thunder Falls Terrace restaurant, where descending river boats kick up quite a spray when they hit the water at 30mph. The splash zone is marked, and there will usually be a 12-year-old boy intent on standing there for hours, giving himself a nigh-amphibious drenching. Before reaching that messy climax, boats embark on what's meant to be a benign tour of the mythical dinosaur park from the movie, only to be bumped off course and run afoul of spitting raptors and an eye-poppingly realistic T. rex who lunges for the kill. The dino attack is shrewdly stage-managed; note how, in true Spielberg fashion, you see disquieting evidence of the hungry lizards (rustling bushes, gashes in sheet metal) before actually catching sight of one. There's no logic as to which passengers will get drenched and in which configuration. In all honesty, you're much more likely to get soaked standing on the terrace of the restaurant than you are inside the boat, but the trip down the hill is still enough to blow your hat off.

The **Jurassic Park Discovery Center** convincingly reproduces the luxury lodge from the film, down to full-size skeletons in the atrium—downstairs, line up your camera just so, and you can snap a witty shot of a T. rex chomping on a loved one's cranium. Also seek out exhibits purporting to allow guests to watch hatching "dinosaur eggs" (actually squawking puppets) raised on the grounds. This attraction relies on actors to lead you through it, and showtimes aren't noted anywhere, so it's catch-as-catch-can, but you can still handle the ostrich-sized eggs and slide them into nifty "scanners" for a peek within, even in the absence of a "spieler" to guide you. Behind the center, there's a pleasant network of garden paths where you can take a break from the bustle of the park and chill out beside the lagoon.

The Lost Continent

The gist of the next island, the Lost Continent, is amorphous. Think of it as part Africa, part Asia, part Rome—everything exotic and mythical wrapped up into

---

Coming Soon: the Boy Wizard

To the left as you enter the Lost Continent, you might see some gargantuan buildings rising in the trees. This is **the Wizarding World of Harry Potter,** a whole new, 20-acre land based on the megapopular J. K. Rowling characters that will open in 2010. Universal is mum on the details, including the attractions, but the official renderings of mighty castles and snow-dusted village streets look thrilling indeed. Expect at least one state-of-the-art ride and religious faith to the Potter catechism. Designers from the movies are helping create everything. This new land is going to be the biggest thing to hit Orlando in 2 decades.

something vague but familiar. The first attraction you'll encounter if you're coming clockwise is the **Flying Unicorn** 🧒, a training roller coaster for small kids. Don't expect more than a 1-minute figure eight with slight banking. The line is sometimes ugly, and what's worse, it's also exposed to the sun. The back seats feel the fastest. The long-legged should cross their ankles to fit more comfortably. This is the sort of ride you'll forget about almost as soon as you're off it.

If you have kids in your party, you might consider appointing someone to stash them at the Flying Unicorn while you ride the adult-size **Dueling Dragons** ★★ next door. (But first, stash your belongings in the free lockers adjacent to the entrance.) This is a monster coaster of the first order, and one of Orlando's most thrilling. Actually, it's two roller coasters, "inverted" so that passengers' feet dangle, and is entangled in such a way as to ensure three near misses during the 145-second ride. Ice, in blue, has a cobra roll and its twistiness is perhaps (who can say?) more conducive to slight motion sickness for those who are prone to it. Fire, in red-orange, has two more "elements" (maneuvers, in coaster-speak) than Ice, and its first drop is slightly higher, but its course is slightly more jolty. The line for both snakes indoors through a castle before diverging before the twin loading zones, at which point you'll also have to decide if you want to wait longer to guarantee a front-row seat—if you have time, it's absolutely worth doing at least once (especially on Fire, where visibility is slightly better) because of the unique near-miss design of these rides. After they're loaded, trains are weighed by a computer (you won't notice) and dispatched (usually) in sequence to improve the timing of the near collisions. **Strategy:** The effect is best enjoyed from the front row or, if you can't fathom the long wait for that, by keeping an eye on your feet. After you get off, ask an attendant if the "re-ride" line is up, because if it is, you won't have to go all the way out to line up again to try the other track. Guests of exceptional size (as they are now apparently called) may have to wait for the third row, where the larger seats are; if you're not confident that you'll fit, test out the standard seat located to the right of the main entrance to the queue. If you're not confident about braving the ride itself, the best viewing area of the tracks' rolls and dips is located inside the front gate to the ride. Locker use (free) is mandatory.

The rest of the Lost Continent is often skipped by regular visitors—not because it's bad, per se, but because it's not the best of the park. **The Eighth Voyage of Sindbad Stunt Show** is mounted a precious few times each day in an open-air stadium, usually in the afternoon (curtain times are marked on your map). You probably already suspect what you're getting here—a corny 20-minute, sound-effect enhanced banquet of macho men sword fighting and leaping in the pursuit of rescuing a princess who, it turns out, may or may not require male assistance after all. Buckles are swashed and cultural references are dropped like anvils. The climax, in which a man is lit on fire and plunges 30 feet into a pit, may alarm kids, but the production values are strong. **Strategy:** Attend this show if you'd like to sit for a while. Your IOA experience won't be lacking if you skip it.

On your map, you'll see something called the **Mystic Fountain.** Stop by briefly. If it's merely gurgling with recorded sound effects, all is quiet. But when least expected, it comes to life. Someone in an unseen booth is able to interact with anyone foolish enough to wander near. As *Time* magazine put it when the park opened in 1999, the fountain exasperates with "the droll sarcasm of a bachelor uncle roped into caring for some itchy 10-year-olds." If you don't want to get doused, check the ground for slick spots to determine the fountain's spitting reach.

The other major show here is **Poseidon's Fury,** which, despite its lowly status as a walk-through attraction, has a stunning exterior, carved within a millimeter of reason to look like a crumbling temple, and inside, it boasts one of the most breathtaking effects in the park: a "water vortex" tunnel of water. Like Sindbad, it's boisterous and pyrotechnic, and some of its other special effects, such as the way the walls of one of its rooms seem to vanish into thin air, are truly amazing for anyone over 6. Those younger might be freaked out by the dark, the fireballs, and the vapid storyline that involves a fight between Poseidon and Lord Darkenon (who?). **Strategy:** For the best views, try to head for the front of every room, especially the third one. Given the choice between this and Sindbad, I'd do this.

Seuss Landing

Islands of Adventure will never be a kiddie park—if you doubt it, look at its skyline, knotted with coasters—which makes it all the more wonderful that the most assiduously designed kiddie area in town is here. Nowhere is IOA's extravagance on finer display than this 10-acre section, which replicates the good Doctor's two-dimensional bluster with three-dimensional exactitude.

Everything on this island is appropriate for kids. The railway threading overhead was built as a ride called Sylvester McMonkey McBean's Very Unusual Driving Machines but failed to open because of fatal design issues. For 7 years, the tracks moldered, idle. But in 2006, the issues were finally resolved, and the

---

Seussville

Seuss Landing is a riot of swirling edges, with colors like cake frosting, and preposterously contorted shapes, everything was handcrafted to the last detail. By decree, there are almost no straight lines. Not in street lamps, not on the rooflines, not even on the trash cans.

As soon as you enter the island from the Lost Continent, head right by the restrooms, along the lakefront, where you can get a good look at what the designers accomplished. Notice how even the palm trees twist. They were knocked sideways near Miami in 1992's Hurricane Andrew, and because palm trees always grow upward, by the time they were scouted for IOA, they had acquired a perfectly loopy angle. Like Toon Lagoon, this is an area where it pays to snoop around, looking for hidden gags. Sprinkled around are Horton's Egg and, by the sea, the two Zaxes, which appropriate to their own book (a commentary on political rivalry in which they stubbornly face off while a city grows up around them), were the very first things placed in the park, and everything else was built around them. The area around the Mulberry Street Store hosts regular appearances by The Cat in the Hat and The Grinch, who looks as annoyed to be there as you might imagine.

railway opened as the **High in the Sky Seuss Trolley Train Ride!** kids, a cheerful family-friendly glide over the Landing, narrated in verse. Like Dueling Dragons, there are two paths. The purple line surveys more of the area than the green line, which dawdles above the Circus McGurkus Cafe. The ride takes about 3 minutes and because there's so much to take in, time flies fast. Unlike Dueling Dragons, you have to line up all over again if you want to do the other track.

The masterful **Caro-Seuss-el** ★ kids, populated by a bobbing menagerie of otherworldly critters that actually react to being ridden—ears wiggle, heads turn—is delightfully over-the-top and appeals to kids who think they're too old for girly carousels. Beside the Caro-Seuss-el, seek out the quick but trenchant walk-through grove of Truffula Trees retelling Dr. Seuss' environmental warning tale, the **Street of the Lifted Lorax.** Across the path, near the Circus McGurkus Cafe Stoo-pendous, The Cat in the Hat and The Grinch make regular public appearances.

On **One Fish, Two Fish, Red Fish, Blue Fish** kids, another iteration of Disney's tot-bait Dumbo staple, riders (two passengers per car normally, three if one of them loves the Wiggles) go around, up, and down by their own controls while a gauntlet of spitting fish pegs them from the sides—listen to the song for the secret of how to avoid getting wet, although the advice isn't foolproof. There are benches around the ride, and it's fun to watch little kids giggle malevolently when their parents get spritzed. **Strategy:** Because this type of ride is eternally popular with children, the line can get nutty, so it's a good candidate for an Express pass.

Getting wet is part of the bargain at **If I Ran the Zoo** kids, too. The interactive playground for young children contains some 20 tricksy elements. Let your brood turn the cranks or play Tic Tac Toe on characters' bellies, and fanciful animals pop into view. Beware the cheeky fountain—it pays to follow all posted instructions in Seuss Landing. Thanks, Universal, for the hand sanitizer dispensers.

Across the path, **The Cat in the Hat** ★★ kids is a nonthreatening excursion through the plot of the famous storybook as viewed from slow-moving mobile "couches" (really a typical flat-ride car). The vehicles spin a few too many times for some adults (you can ask to have it turned off), but kids don't seem to mind. The design racks up points for replicating the look of the beloved children's book with precision, even in three dimensions. The story is just as faithfully retold; it's clear from this sweet, 3½-minute ride that the family of Dr. Seuss (Theodor Geisel) had a strong influence in steering the execution of this section of the park. Parents will probably emerge feeling glad they tagged along. **Strategy:** Lines are shortest first thing in the morning and late in the day. The gift shop after the offload platform is among the best in the park—Universal's red Thing 1 and Thing 2 shirts ($22) have quickly become as ubiquitous as Mouse ears.

Once you're done with that, you're nearly back at the Port of Entry, having made a complete circuit of Islands of Adventure, but before you're done, give **McElligot's Pool** a quick look-see; if you throw a coin into one of its three fish figures (donations benefit Give Kids the World, p. 262), you'll make it spit.

Where to Eat in Islands of Adventure

When the park closes at 6pm (outside of summer and holidays), many restaurants will only be open from 11am to 4pm. But remember that **CityWalk** (p. 281) is a 5-minute walk from the park, so with a hand stamp for reentry, you can try those places, too. The only one that requires reservations is Emeril's (p. 74).

You can make reservations to eat at the two sit-down restaurants, **Mythos** or **Confisco Grille,** at the Dining Cart in the Port of Entry. You can also call ☎ 407/ 224-4534 in advance, but you don't have to, as they're rarely sold out.

Park planners recognize that IOA's circular shape means at midday, most guests will be at the back, around Jurassic Park, so that's why many of the counter-service restaurants are located there. That means if you're peckish around noon or 1pm, you're going to have to swim through crowds. By the time you reach Seuss Landing, you'll find most of the park's best desserts.

Kids' meals are about $6.50. Anywhere you see a combo meal, ask if you can subtract any aspect of it for savings (servings of sides are stingy anyway); that way, a $7.30 hot dog meal becomes $5.40.

Port of Entry Lighter bites such as sandwiches and panini, plus pastry, can be snagged quickly for $8 to $9 (with potato salad and fresh fruit; soup and salad is $5) at **Croissant Moon Bakery** or at the **Last Chance Fruit Stand** cart, which sells not only fruit cups ($3) but also honkingly large turkey legs ($6.40). Around the corner toward the Hulk coaster is a **Cinnabon** outlet straight from your local mall. The other way, toward Seuss Landing, is **Confisco Grille,** one of only two sit-down locations in the park. It serves bistro fare (quesadillas, $8; wood-oven pizzas, $9; and mixed grills, $13) for a price that's a little lower than most sit-down theme park restaurants. It's easy enough to check the menu on your way into the park. Confisco is also where the morning character breakfast (p. 96) is held.

Marvel Super Hero Island Two counter-service joints stare each other down near the Incredible Hulk coaster. The **Captain America Diner** does the usual burgers and chicken for around $8, and **Cafe 4** does pizza and pasta for $4 a slice or $18 a pie. There's a **fruit stand** near the Captain America Diner (whole fruit, $1).

Toon Lagoon **Blondie's** ★★ serves Dagwood (another name for a hero, for those of you under 40) slices for $7, and they're fresh-made and delicious, but the custom-made "stacked sandwich" costs 70¢ less and gets you about twice as much food. They're so big you can share them. Meanwhile, the much more spacious **Comic Strip Cafe** ★ has four counters for four types of food: burgers and dogs; pizza and pasta; Chinese; and fish and chicken. No matter what you choose—and every dish is listed with a large photo that can be seen from miles away—you'll pay around $8 before a drink. **Wimpy's,** across from the Bilge-Rat Barges, serves its namesake's obsession (hamburgers), although the staff will not permit you to pay next Tuesday to have a hamburger today. Sadly, too, the stand is closed when things aren't busy.

Jurassic Park Because of the park's loop design, most guests seem to end up here, at the halfway point in the circuit, at lunchtime, so lines can be bad. To eat indoors, you'll have to choose the **Burger Digs** inside the Discovery Center, where the main dish (which also comes in garden and grilled chicken varieties) is slung for the usual $8 with fries. There's a toppings bar, so you can load up. Near the entry to the River Adventure, the **Pizza Predattoria** is a counter-service kiosk with outdoor seating. Individual pizzas are $9. The rest of its menu is short, but big on calories: meatball subs with a small salad ($9) and chicken Caesar salad

($8). **Thunder Falls Terrace,** where the Jurassic Park boats splash down, is a little bit more: rotisserie chicken $12, bacon cheeseburgers $9.10, soups $3.50. **Watering Hole** is the park's main bar; cocktails are $8 except during happy hour from 3 to 5pm, when a 20-ounce beer is $3.50.

The Lost Continent   Many of the signs advertising IOA's flagship sit-down restaurant, **Mythos** ✦✦✦ (☎ 407/224-4534; reservations suggested), proudly proclaim that it is repeatedly voted the best theme park restaurant by the industry site *Theme Park Insider*. Food is not gourmet, but it's very good, and how many theme park restaurants do you know of that employ an executive chef (in this case, Steven Jayson)? The menu is seasonal, but has some steady themes including cedar-planked salmon ($19), a hamburger so thick-cut it wobbles ($11), and a daily risotto ($16). It's smart to reserve, not just because the hours are unpredictable (it's usually closed well before dinner), but also because you want a good table. Mythos' cavelike interior, moody and carved from that ubiquitous orange-hued fake rock that scientists should term Orlando Schist, commands a marvelous view of the lagoon. You could sit and watch the Incredible Hulk Coaster fire all day, if there weren't other things to see. The island's other main place to eat, **Fire Eaters' Grill,** is bog-standard (chicken fingers, Italian sausage, gyros, for $8 and under). The **Frozen Desert** stand sells two unique treats: a Sultan's Sundae (vanilla ice cream and pineapple swirl topped with pineapple chunks) and the Treasure Chest Sundae (vanilla and strawberry swirl, with syrupy strawberries), both for $4.50.

Seuss Landing   The **Green Eggs and Ham Cafe** (you can't miss it—it's the house-size slab of ham with a giant fork stuck into it) sells burgers and, of course, sandwiches made of green eggs and ham ($7–$8), but it's not always open, which is disappointing. If that novelty isn't available to you, turn to the **Circus McGurkus Cafe Stoo-pendous!** ✦, looking like a circus tent coated in cake frosting. Aside from the usual burgers and pizzas, the menu is leavened with spaghetti and meatballs; chicken Caesar salad; and a fried chicken platter with mashed potatoes and corn on the cob—all around $8—so there's something for everyone. Seuss Landing is full of dishes you can only find at Islands of Adventure. **Hop on Pop Ice Cream Shop,** near the transition to the Lost Continent, serves a mean Sundae on a Stick ($3.60), a bar of vanilla ice cream that's hand-dipped chocolate and rolled in your choice of nuts, chocolate sprinkles, or rainbow sprinkles. The **Moose Juice Goose Juice** stand nearby sells Moose Juice (a tart tangerine mix) and Goose Juice (sour green apple) for $3.79 to $4.29.

SEAWORLD ORLANDO

The second mighty theme park chain to set up shop in town, after Disney, was **SeaWorld Orlando** (Central Florida Pkwy., at International Dr., or exit 71 and 72 east of Interstate 4; ☎ 800/327-2424 or 407/351-3600; www.seaworldorlando.com; adults $75, kids 3–9 $65), which began in San Diego in the early 1960s and opened in Orlando in 1973, scarcely 2 years after the Magic Kingdom. Although SeaWorld operates three American parks (the third is in San Antonio), its Orlando location has undoubtedly risen to become its most important. The Florida compound has

SeaWorld Orlando

DINING ◆
Cypress Bakery **6**
Hospitality Deli **9**
Mama's Kitchen **1**
Mango Joe's Cafe **10**
Seafire Inn
  (Mahahiki Luau) **7**
Sharks Underwater
  Grill **3**
Smoky Creek Grill **2**
Smuggler's Feasts **8**
Spice Mill Cafe **5**
Voyagers **4**

Wild Arctic

Shamu's Happy Harbor

Shamu Splash Attack

Hospitality Center **9**

Shamu Stadium
(Believe)

Arcade

Atlantis Bayside Stadium
(Mistify)

Clydesdale Hamlet

Underwater Viewing
Dine with Shamu

Nautilus Theatre
(A'Lure)

Paddle Boats

Sky Tower

Seafire Inn
(Makahiki Luau)

THE WATERFRONT

Guest Services

Entrance

Pet Care Center

Shark Encounter

Sea Lion & Otter Stadium
(Clyde & Seamore Take Pirate Island)

Seaport Theatre
(Pets Ahoy!)

Dolphin Nursery

Reservations

Pacific Point Preserve

Manta

Turtle Point

Penguin Encounter

Kraken

Key West at SeaWorld

Stingray Lagoon

Journey to Atlantis

Whale & Dolphin Theatre
(Blue Horizons)

Dolphin Cove

Underwater Viewing

Manatee Rescue

Restrooms
Telephone
Information
Mailbox

205

an additional luxury theme park, **Discovery Cove** (p. 217), and a new water slide park, **Aquatica** (p. 215). SeaWorld is now the city's third genuine multiday theme park destination, after Disney and Universal.

At SeaWorld, the focus isn't on thrill rides or "magic"—it's animals, nearly 17,000 of them. Just about everything to see or do involves watching marine creatures in their habitats or performing in shows. Many tourists, particularly those over a certain age, claim SeaWorld as their favorite Orlando park, because there's a lot going for it: 200 acres of space for gardens, a compound that absorbs crowds well, an earnest educational component, a variety of animal exhibits that ensures guests won't have the same experience twice, and a refreshing lack of patronizing mythology. Until late 2008, the park was owned by the suds slingers at Anheuser-Busch. Then the Belgian giant InBev bought the parent company, and fans are nervous about big changes to come. The longstanding tradition of a cup of free beer was the first to go, and fans are nervous about what's next.

The SeaWorld experience differs from most other parks in more important ways: It's **show-based.** Your day here will revolve around the scheduling of a half-dozen regular performances in which animals (mostly mammals, but some birds, too) do tricks—except here, they're called "behaviors"—with their human trainers. Although there are four rides, they're not in the true spirit of the place. SeaWorld's banner attraction is the Shamu show, and when you're not watching killer whales do back-flips, you're ambling through habitats stocked with other beautiful creatures. Whereas a day spent at Islands of Adventure or the Magic Kingdom might send you slumping home and reaching for the Calgon, it's unusual to come away from SeaWorld stressed. Thoughtfully, **schedules are posted online** a few weeks ahead of time so that if you're really anal, you can map out your day in advance; on the SeaWorld website, you'll find the various show schedules under "Park Information."

SAVING MONEY   SeaWorld is more likely than most to throw a ticket deal into the mix, particularly online, so if you wait until you reach the ticket booth, you'll miss out. For permanent discounts for people who also plan to visit Universal's parks, see the section about the **FlexTicket** on p. 322. Members of the military should check www.herosalute.com to register for any discounts being offered.

Hook the Trainers

To get the most out of a visit, try to be in the same place as the animal trainers, who frequently appear to nurture their charges. Ask questions. Get involved. They may even allow you to feed or stroke the animals (set aside another $25 or so for fish feed). These zoologists love sharing information about the animals they have devoted their lives to, and in Orlando, it's rare that theme park guests are encouraged to be anything other than passive participants. Feeding times are usually posted outside each pavilion's entrance; you may need to backtrack a few times to make the schedule, but the interaction will be worth the effort.

The Best of SeaWorld

Don't miss if you're 6: *Pets Ahoy!*

Don't miss if you're 16: Kraken

Requisite photo op: Shamu in flight, *Believe,* Shamu Stadium

Food you can only get here: Shamu ice-cream bar, carts parkwide; mahimahi with piña colada sauce, Seafire Inn, the Waterfront

The most crowded, so go early: *Believe,* Shamu Stadium

Skippable: *Odyssea*

Biggest thrill: Kraken, Journey to Atlantis

Best show: *Believe,* Shamu Stadium

Where to find peace: Anywhere around the lagoon

TIMING YOUR VISIT   You will be spending quite a bit of time waiting for shows to begin. Because everyone at SeaWorld sees the shows, everyone shows up early for seats, so it's smart to arrive at least 30 minutes ahead of show times. (It's also imperative that you wear a watch.)

Important: If the forecast shows prolonged rain (as opposed to Florida's typical spot showers), reschedule your visit here. Not only will you spend lots of time walking outside between attractions, but it's also harder to see marine animals when the surface of the water is being pelted by raindrops—not to mention the fact that if there's so much as a twinkle of lightning anywhere in the county, these water-based attractions close faster than a shark's mouth on his dinner.

TOURING SEAWORLD

GETTING ORIENTED   Once you've parked ($10, and it's uncovered; spots guaranteed to be closer to the gate are $15 and not worth it) or gotten off the I-Ride (the stop is near the front gates), head for the lighthouse that marks the entrance. Inside, the first thing you should do is grab a placemat-size park map. On the back, printed fresh daily, is the **show schedule,** plus the opening times of all the restaurants and attractions. Shows usually begin an hour after park opening, and usually the blockbuster Shamu show, *Believe,* has only a few presentations. I always prefer the last one because it's less crowded and it often extends, slightly, past the park's posted closing time, getting you a little more for your money.

SeaWorld isn't broken up into themed lands. Your day will be dictated by the shows you plan to see, but I'll walk you through the park in a roughly clockwise order, starting at the entrance and ending with the Shamu area. The pathways are lined with the odd animal enclosure—flamingoes here, turtles there—but those are really more like landscaping features than attractions, and they aren't listed on the maps, so I haven't included them.

A Word on Seating

Do try to be at shows at least a **half-hour early,** and for Shamu, add another 10 minutes to walk around the lagoon to the stadium. SeaWorld is not as controlling as Disney about where you're permitted to sit, so the best seats go first. Furthermore, several shows (*Pets Ahoy!* especially) don't permit latecomers to enter. At others, you can't get out easily until it's over.

Three of the shows, *Believe, Blue Horizons,* and *Clyde and Seamore,* have a clearly marked **"soak zone"** in the front rows of the seating section. Don't take this warning lightly; you have no concept of how much water a 10,000-pound male orca can displace. Of course, sitting with your kids in the soak zone on a hot day is one of the great pleasures of SeaWorld, and most soak zone seating has the added advantage of affording views, through Plexiglas, into the tank where the animals prepare for their leaps and splashes. But for those with expensive hairdos, ponchos are sold throughout the parks, including at stalls beneath Shamu Stadium, for $7 ($5 kids). Keep your camera and phone somewhere dry, because the salt water these animals live in will fry their circuits. As amphitheaters fill, you may not see the warning signs, which are painted on the ground or on benches, so bank on the *first 10 rows as being the wettest.* No theaters will expose you to the elements.

STRATEGY If you're interested in riding the park's two thrill rides, the best time to get in line is when the Shamu show, *Believe,* is scheduled, as it soaks up thousands of people and all the lines in the park diminish for the duration.

Ideally, by the time you hit the gates, you will have already made your special restaurant reservations (Dine with Shamu, p. 97) or interactive experiences with the animals (Boma, p. 70), as they usually sell out weeks ahead. But on the off chance there's a space for something you'd like to do, the Guest Services and Reservations desk is the place to book. Otherwise, the Cape Cod–style entrance plaza is where you do the necessaries such as rent strollers and lockers. The area is really just a warm-up for the rest of the park.

THE BEST SHOWS

Feel free to be choosy about the shows you care to see, because if you load your plate with too many, you'll spend most of your in-between time hoofing it between amphitheaters, yet spreading SeaWorld over 2 days would be a bit much. The shows are printed on the daily map, plus a few fillers such as pianists or street musicians. The can't-miss shows are the major ones I'll name below.

Anheuser-Busch recently poured money into revitalizing its marquee show, *Believe* ✹✹✹ installing four rotating screens that interlock in various formations as well as a top-of-the-line sound system, and teaching the killer whales a fleet of new tricks. I wish it had bought some padding for the metal benches while it was shopping, but at least Shamu Stadium, which fits 5,000 and still fills early, is covered. The resulting show is irredeemably hokey gobbledygook laden with long periods during which trainers prattle on with quasi-inspirational gibberish ("You know, I think dreams are incredible, and the best part is no one can take them away from you . . ."). But when the orcas start to fly, the crowd comes alive. Closed-circuit TV cameras capture and display their screams of delight as the animals thunder dauntingly through the water's surface, deluging entire seating sections in 52°F water. It's quite a scene. The 25-minute spectacle occurs on such a scale as to make it required viewing. There's also the potential that one day, one of the 24 orcas (only a few in the "Shamu family" perform at a time) will suddenly remember its place on the food chain. Admit it—isn't that tension part of the draw? **Strategy:** The soak zone seats offer excellent views of the animals pushing their trusting trainers through the 2.5 million-gallon, 36-feet-deep tank, and the ones near the shelflike middle platform will also have a close-up view of a killer whale out of the water. Seats at the back of the stadium, higher than the central aisle, must rely on the TV cameras to make out what's going on underwater.

From Memorial Day to early fall, the killer whales perform in repertory, as it were, with another abstract show, *Shamu Rocks,* which puts that expensive sound system to good use by pumping it with rock songs. If I had to make a choice, I'd probably pick *Believe,* the flagship show. No matter which show you choose (don't do both unless you simply *must*), you'll be seeing the mighty creatures flopping and splashing with impressive intent.

A broadly slapstick 25-minute romp set aboard a pirate ship, *Clyde & Seamore Take Pirate Island* ✭ 🄺 is the kind of cheesy, anthropomorphic act (sea lions doing double takes, saluting, and pretending to be choked by exasperated human companions) that's fallen out of favor in all but the hoariest circuses, yet its good-natured silliness ensures its standing as one of SeaWorld's most cherished shows. Kids particularly enjoy it, especially when the impossibly blubbery walrus oozes its way into the mayhem. **Strategy:** The worst seats are to the left as you face the stage (they have partial views) and the best are to the right, by the stone bridge.

SeaWorld perfected the kind of poppycock on display in *Believe* with *Blue Horizons* ✭, a bizarre spectacle about a little girl who "wants to explore the realms beyond imagination." Whatever that means, the transfixing 25-minute show built around her (actually an adult trainer) is more like an acid trip at a carnival than anything else, which lends itself to loosely connected (but excellent nonetheless) stunts starring dolphins, parrots, a condor, and plenty of human acrobats hooked up to bungee cords and diving off high platforms. There's always something to see, and little to comprehend. Think of it as *Shark du Soleil.*

Under-5s lose their minds at *Pets Ahoy!* ✭✭ 🄺, and I have to admit I do, too—it's the show I most enjoy seeing repeatedly. Although the furry cast is a deviation from SeaWorld's usual finny ones, the tricks are no less entrancing. A menagerie of common animals (cats, dogs, pigs, ducks, a skunk), most rescued from animal shelters, do simple tricks, and independently trigger surprises on a rigged wharfside set. As the supercute gags multiply and compound in rapid succession (dachshunds pour out of a hot dog cart, a cat chases a white mouse in and out of hatches), and as more creatures are added into the mix precisely on cue, the amusement escalates. There's nearly no dialogue for its 20-minute run time. Afterward, trainers will allow kids to pet some of the performers. **Strategy:** It's fun to sit under the catwalk (literally—cats walk on it) over the aisle between the first and second sections. This 850-seat theater fills well in advance of showtimes.

Also custom designed for very young children, **Elmo and the Bookaneers,** a 20-minute *Sesame Street*–licensed show original to this park, plays April through Labor Day at Atlantis Bayside Stadium. Its theme is learning to read and its major stars include Cookie Monster, Bert, Ernie, and Elmo, so I guess you could say this show is one adults can prioritize low on their must-see lists, but one that parents with small kids should consider. Performance times are listed on the back of your map. Other *Sesame Street* shows are seasonal (like *Countdown to Halloween*).

The most skippable of the shows is a wordless, animal-free revue of arty human performance (trampolines, tumbling, caterwauling) called **A'Lure: The Call of the Ocean,** ostensibly inspired by the sea. The plot—something about an enchantress jealous of a stud-muffin fisherman—is as insubstantial as the bubbles that pour from the ceiling. It's mostly an opportunity to get into the air-conditioning.

Staged on summer nights over the lake, **Mistify,** a multimedia fireworks-and-fountains spectacular, isn't over the top, but it's a pleasing way to end a day. You can see the action from anywhere on the lagoon, but the Atlantis Bayside Stadium is set up for the best views. Show up a half-hour early, as usual. The excellent seats at the Spice Mill's waterfront tables are taken by people who have their dinner there as early as 5pm and then hang out until the show. They need lives.

THE REST OF THE PARK

From the entrance plaza, veer right, past the ice-cream parlor, to reach the **Dolphin Nursery** tank, where the young mammals are kept with their mothers for the first few years of their lives, before graduating to the larger Dolphin Cove elsewhere in the park. Much of the day, human trainers can be found here, feeding the adolescent animals and getting them acclimated to human interaction.

Left out of the entrance plaza, past the flamingoes (welcome to Florida), after passing the minor Turtle Point enclosure, you'll reach the **Whale & Dolphin Theatre,** where the *Blue Horizons* show is performed. To the left you'll find **Key West at SeaWorld,** a sorta-reproduction of Front Street in the southernmost city in Florida. As they do there, Jimmy Buffett songs play ad nauseam for tourists. Unlike in the real Keys, the **Stingray Lagoon,** a shallow pool where you can lean over and feel the spongy fish, is this section's *raison d'etre*. You can buy food to feed the rays for $5 per tray, two for $9, or three for $13.

To the right of the Key West area, the **Dolphin Cove** is one of the park's most popular places. Feeding times for the bottlenose dolphins are regimented and crowded, and the schedule is posted here. It costs $7 for just three fish, and interested parties must collect in a zone near the feeding area, to the right as you reach the tank. Around feeding times, dolphins congregate at the trainers' dock, which can make seeing them from other parts of the tank difficult, so if you won't be feeding them, come between meals for a better look. Walk around the far side of the tank, and you'll find a little-used underwater viewing area where you can hear the echolocative clicking through underwater microphones.

Following on from there (turn left after you exit Dolphin Cove), you'll next reach a pleasant but none-too-vibrant pavilion devoted to two of Florida's natives, the alligator and the manatee. At **Manatee Rescue** ⭐ which can only be entered by a circuitous entrance ramp that seems designed to manage crowds that just

Ethical Entertainment?

Some conservationists have complained that SeaWorld's animals are living in captivity. SeaWorld, in response, points out that it's sensitive to this issue, and it has not captured (or as it puts it, "collected") dolphins from the wild since 1969. Excepting a few aged animals who were born in the seas and a few others rehabilitated from accidents in the wild (manatees, for example, are sometimes returned to Florida's rivers), most of the park's animals were born there or at other zoos, and they were raised by hand. And although many of the shows here make these creatures appear more like clownish humans than the animals they are, it's arguable that SeaWorld is bringing a modicum of animal appreciation to the masses, and it can't be argued that it mistreats its charges.

aren't there, much attention is paid to the manatee's status as one of America's most endangered animals, and, in fact, the sluggish creatures on display here were all rescued from the wild, where hot-dogging boaters are decimating their numbers. This is a cool, sheltered place to observe the creeping, pug-faced animals from below the waterline—if you're hot, seek respite in peace here.

Rising above the park next is SeaWorld's newest ride, **Manta,** which was under construction at press time for a summer 2009 opening. The plan was to stock the new area with a walk-through aquarium of some 300 rays behind floor-to-ceiling windows, so even nonriders will have something to see. Passengers will enjoy something new for Florida: a "flying coaster" ridden face-down, in a horizontal position. As riders swoop around, "wings" on the cars will clip the water underneath them. Speeds will approach 60mph, with four inversions, in a fanciful approximation of what it feels like for a manta ray to swim. Manta looks like it will be a pretty solid experience.

The Kraken End of the Park

Two more thrill rides are next to each other—when the killer whales perform, the crowds are lightest here. **Journey to Atlantis** ★★ is a 6-minute flume-cum-coaster ride (you can't see the brief coaster section from the front). Getting drenched is unavoidable, as the 60-foot drop should warn, although riding isn't its only pleasure—it's fun to douse passing boats with coin-operated water cannons, too. Atlantis is oddball. First you pass through a few rooms as if you're on a family-friendly dark ride (the robotics are not terribly good), and then one of the spirits turns against you and sends you down the hill you saw outside, and finally the water gives way and your boat becomes, briefly, a roller-coaster car that escapes the evil sprite (weirdly, to the theme song of *Beetlejuice*—couldn't an intern write something new?) with no upside-down moments but yet another splashdown. Besides the drenching you can see from outside, there are a few other lap soakers and delightfully nasty splashbacks—ideal for hot days. **Strategy:** Front seats get wettest. Try to balance the weight; otherwise you'll list disconcertingly. If you sit this one out, put a few quarters to use dousing riders with the water cannons trained on the flume. Number 4 does the most damage to the unsuspecting.

Keep your loose articles dry in a nearby locker (50¢—using two quarters—each time you close the door). Because Kraken is next door, you can just leave your stuff locked up for both rides. Ponchos are sold nearby for $7 adults or $5 kids.

Next door is **Kraken** ✹✹✹, a 2-minute coaster that gave SeaWorld some needed testosterone when it opened in 2000. After you settle into your pedestal-like seat, the floor is retracted, leaving your legs to dangle, and the ride is packed with seven upside-down "inversions" of one sort or another. The coaster, which hits 65mph and drops 144 feet on its first breath-stealing hill, traces the shoreline of a pond behind the loading area and dives below ground level three times. **Strategy:** If you'd like to wait for a front seat, there's a special, longer line for it. Because it's floorless, you can't ride with flip-flops, but you may leave shoes on the loading dock and go barefoot (if you do that in the front row, which I recommend, you'll feel like you're about to lose a foot in the rails). All in all, Kraken is an excellent, smooth ride. Happily, the lines are rarely horrific.

The centerpiece of **Penguin Encounter** ✹✹✹, another popular pavilion, is a wide-windowed, chilly room where four types of penguins frolic among ice chips and frigid water. Visitors can either stand about 15 feet away from the window, below the waterline, and coast past on a moving walkway that alleviates gridlock, or stand on a riser 5 feet farther back, without the regimentation of having to move past. Or you can see it from the conveyor and then double back using the riser. Two things become instantly clear: Penguins can swim like fish, and they stink of them, too. What follows this absorbing spectacle is an educational exhibit about penguins and the Antarctic that deserves much more than to be ignored, the way it usually is. That's followed by a similar window to a habitat for puffins and murres.

Pacific Point Preserve ✹, like the Dolphin Cove, is an open-air, rocky habitat that encourages feedings, but here, the residents are incessantly barking Californian sea lions and a few demure seals. There's a narrow moat between the tank and the walkway, but you're encouraged to lean over and toss the doglike animals fresh fish, which are sold for $5 per tray, $8 for two trays, and $15 for four. The area gets busy before and after the Clyde and Seamore show, which is mounted at the neighboring **Sea Lion & Otter Stadium.**

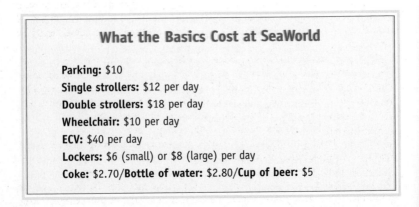

What the Basics Cost at SeaWorld

Parking: $10
Single strollers: $12 per day
Double strollers: $18 per day
Wheelchair: $10 per day
ECV: $40 per day
Lockers: $6 (small) or $8 (large) per day
Coke: $2.70/**Bottle of water:** $2.80/**Cup of beer:** $5

The onetime Terrors of the Deep is now wisely known as **Shark Encounter** ★★ in an effort to further rehabilitate the public image of the much-maligned creatures within. It's one of the better exhibitions, with 60-foot acrylic tubes passing right through 300,000 gallons of water stocked with sharks—the crowds are ushered along via moving sidewalks. Too many tourists scamper quickly through the smaller tanks before that dazzling main event, but they're missing some beautiful stuff, including barracuda, moray eels, lionfish, and the awesome leafy sea dragon, which looks for all the world like a floating clump of seaweed. Don't ignore the shallow tank in front of the building either, as that's where the smaller species are kept. If they were kept indoors, they'd be sushi for the bigger predators. There, you can feed the fish for the usual high rates ($5 a tray, two for $9, three for $13, and four for $17). Those with cash burning a hole in their pockets can arrange to dive with a special helmet in the shark tank; see p. 252 for that.

The Waterfront at SeaWorld

This area is mostly an atmospheric 5-acre locale for restaurants, although the **Seaport Theatre** used by *Pets Ahoy!* is also here. Kids like to explore the shoreline, where artificial waves frequently kick up and spray them with plumes of water. Jutting above the lagoon—and topped to still-greater heights by a colossal American flag—is the 400-foot **Sky Tower,** a soothing, old-fashioned "Wheel-o-vater" (that's what its interior label says) that rotates as it climbs 300 feet for a panorama. At the top, it slowly spins for two or three revolutions, giving you a good look around, before lowering you back to the Waterfront at the end of 6 minutes. You can point out the landmarks, including Spaceship Earth, the Gaylord Palms, and the skyscrapers of downtown. Annoyingly, after your $70 entry, SeaWorld sees fit to charge an additional $3 for this. Such nickel-and-diming is a turn-off.

Continuing clockwise around the lagoon as you look at your map, the **Nautilus Theater** hosts *A'Lure,* and across the path, you can rent flamingo-shaped **paddleboats** for excursions on the lagoon ($6 for 30 min.). The **Clydesdale Hamlet,** a farm among the aquaria, is a reminder of the beer company that owns the park (for now). The beautiful animals spend most of their time loafing in this paddock, and every few weeks they switch off with the horses that live at Busch Gardens in Tampa. Next door is the **Hospitality Center,** where adults could once get their free cups of beer before InBev canceled the long tradition in 2009; as of press time, it was still a low-key place to grab a sandwich. The horses could be next to go.

After you pass the **video arcade** and **midway,** on the left, you reach **Shamu Stadium,** home of the big show. Even when it's not showtime, a few of the killer whales are visible in the **Underwater Viewing** area that surveys one of their holding pods; above the surface of that pen, the **Dine with Shamu** supper is held, separated by cargo netting from the water (reserve several weeks ahead).

Around the back of the stadium is the principal kids' area, **Shamu's Happy Harbor** kids. Let them off the leash with a four-story cargo-net playground and mild carnival-style rides: an underwater-themed **Sea Carousel** topped by a 45-foot-wide pink octopus; a swinging-and-twirling tracked boat ride, **Ocean Commotion;** and **the Flying Fiddler,** a bench that lifts kids 20 feet above the ground and then gently brings them back down in a series of short drops. Those rides join an 800-foot kiddie coaster with trains shaped like you-know-who **(Shamu Express),** a four-story playground with slides and nets, a ride with spinning cars attached to a stalk **(Jazzy Jellies),** a pirate ship *(Wahoo Two)* with a few water blasters, and a teacup-style ride **(Swishy Fishies).** The theme is limp, but the size of the play area is as big or bigger than anything the other parks have. Small children could be transfixed for 2 to 3 hours here, while their parents are woefully exposed to the sun as they wait.

The Shamu End of the Park

Wild Arctic ★★★, one of the most interesting exhibitions, deserves more than to be marooned here, at the Nowhereseville end of the park. There are two ways to get in. Either you opt for the motion-simulator ride that re-creates a turbulent 5-minute helicopter ride (well done for such an old ride, but its bumpiness makes me ill), or you whiz around that much more quickly and make straight for the swimmers after a short movie. After that, you can walk through at your own pace, enjoying first a surface view and then an underwater look at the Pacific walruses, polar bears (you won't see much—they sleep 16–18 hr. a day), and the parks' utterly beautiful white beluga whales, which look like swimming porcelain. There's probably more than a half-hour's worth of investigation here, including mock-ups of a polar research station, a fake "bear den" for young kids to explore, and hands-on exhibits about the ecology and research of the area. You'll also find it *very* cool, which makes it a blockbuster on hot days. The pavilion is staffed by red-coated zookeepers, who are there to field your questions—they never insult your intelligence by acting like they've heard the same queries before.

The long shoreline path back to the entrance area passes only the **Atlantis Bayside Stadium,** which hosts *Mistify* in summer and the week before New Year's but sits empty most of the winter. I much prefer crossing the lagoon on the board-walklike bridge that bisects it from Shamu Stadium to the Waterfront.

WHERE TO EAT AT SEAWORLD

The good news is that compared to other parks, SeaWorld has the edge in food quality, and it beat everyone else in the rush to provide healthy options. The bad news is prices are just as sickening as everyone else's: $9 a meal, before a drink, is standard across the board. Most of the places to eat cluster in the center of the park between the Waterfront and Kraken. All-you-can-eat food passes (one entree, side, and dessert each time through line) cost $22 adults, $12 kids.

Disney World has its Mouse-ear ice-cream bar, but at SeaWorld, you'll be served a variety shaped like Shamu ($3). Plastic drinking straws could choke the aquatic animals, so they're made of paper. If you must have a straw, the $6.50 souvenir cups have them built in, and they grant $1.80 refills. Beers cost $5 a glass.

My favorite place to eat in the park is **Mama's Kitchen** ★★, opposite the Penguin Encounter. Everything served here is less than 750 calories (though most are much less) and contains less than 25 grams of fat, sides and all. That translates into items such as a chef's salad, turkey chili, a turkey sandwich with whole-wheat pasta salad ($9), and pan-seared chicken breast sandwiches. A meal here will cost about $1 more than one had elsewhere in the park. By noon, because the food is good, the line here is dishearteningly long, so eat around 11am if you can.

At press time, you could get turkey sandwiches at the **Hospitality Deli,** in the Hospitality Center, for $7.29 including potato salad—cheaper than at Mama's Kitchen. The Deli's other choices included beef stew in a bread bowl ($8.79) and a few carvery sandwiches ($8.29), both with a hefty glob of potato salad.

The other main restaurants serve high-quality food, too, but with less caloric regard. **The Seafire Inn,** at the Waterfront, charges $8.29 to $10.29 for burgers, of course, but interesting ones such as jalapeño cheddar burgers and also inventive dishes such as tropical chicken stir-fry and mahimahi with piña colada sauce ($11.29). The Seafire also has some seating overlooking the lagoon—it's where the Makahiki Luau dinnertainment show is held each night, which is why lunch is its big meal. Farther up the Waterfront but with similar prices, the **Spice Mill Cafe** ★★ does stuff such as Caribbean jerk chicken sandwiches (surprisingly well spiced), Cajun jambalaya with peppered andouille sausage, and fish sandwiches battered with Bud. **Voyagers,** facing the Seaport Theatre's entrance, offers wood-fired pizzas ($7.50) and grilled salmon ($11.30). The Sand Bar, on the water itself, is an out-of-the-way place to sit and does beer and hot dogs ($4.50).

A few years ago, the park converted a section of the underwater viewing area at the shark tank to **Sharks Underwater Grill,** which is now one of the park's premier tables. Despite some cute touches, such as a bar that's also an aquarium and chairs that look like sharks' teeth, prices around $29 a plate for chicken and shrimp strikes me as too high. But if you can square that with the incredible view and not feel gypped, give it a shot. Some tables are right against the glass, but I think I prefer the ones farther back, which have a more panoramic view.

For snacks, I suggest the **Cypress Bakery,** located near the entrance. The carrot cake ($3) sold there is huge, fluffy, and arguably among the best you'll have anywhere. The parks employees are hooked on it.

The **Smoky Creek Grill** barbecue place, facing the back of the Seaport Theatre, is for sauce-drenched meats served with fries and a dinner roll: A half-chicken is $9.79, and a half slab of baby back ribs is $11.69. Corn on the cob is $2.30.

SeaWorld participates in the great Orlando tradition of huge roasted **turkey legs.** Find them for $6.29 at the **Smugglers Feasts** booth at the Waterfront entrance to the cross-lagoon boardwalk. At the Shamu end of the boardwalk, **Mango Joe's Cafe** does a short menu of fajitas, fajita salad (both $8.50), and chicken fingers with fries ($8.89); only eat there if you're stuck in Shamu-land and don't want to brave the 10-minute walk back around the lagoon.

AQUATICA

In the spring of 2008, SeaWorld opened the fourth full-time water slide park in Orlando, **Aquatica** (5800 Water Play Way, Orlando; ☎ 888/800-5447 or 407/351-3600; www.aquaticabyseaworld.com; AE, DC, DISC, MC, V; adults $45, kids 3–9 $39; parking $10, or free the same day you've parked at SeaWorld). Located across International Drive from its parent park (a free, 3-min. van ride links it), the park is included on SeaWorld's package tickets, and adult admission is discounted $17 that way. While Typhoon Lagoon and Blizzard Beach are heavily themed and packed with people, and Wet 'n Wild is stuffed with intense thrills and teenagers, Aquatica advertises itself as a water slide park where you get close to fish. In reality, the chances to do that are slim, but Aquatica is fresh and bright, making the park popular with locals seeking a centrally located day out. While I think it's a perfectly nice park, I feel the others have more to offer visitors, and the rides here are much like the ones you'll find at your local water park.

Once your deposit is given back, lockers cost $10 to $12, and towels $4.

The big chances to swim with the fishes are on the **Dolphin Plunge** slide, a tube that curls off a tower and then turns clear acrylic as it passes through a habitat for Commerson's dolphins. It looks exciting on paper, but in truth you're going too fast to see anything, even if the dolphins could be reliably near the tubes (they aren't) and there wasn't water splashing in your eyes (there is).

The lazy river of **Loggerhead Lane** passes you by a big window into an aquarium, but that's it, and it's nothing like the full-on plastic tubes through tanks that early renderings for the park promised. Ten-minute talks about the dolphins are offered a few times daily by their habitat and rangerlike zookeepers are often near the entrance introducing guests to various land-based animals. Other than that, Aquatica is standard water park. The effect is lazy.

SLIDES   There are 18 major slides, but because of duplications, only 6, including Dolphin Plunge, are really distinct experiences:

* **Taumata Racer** are four nearly identical tubes that turn into slightly humped slides, to be ridden belly-down in competition with others.
* **Whanau Way** comprises four slides from a four-story platform that pass through both enclosed and open patches and are for one or two riders on a figure-eight tube.
* The twin **Tassie's Twisters** send you through a short tube, spinning around a bowl, and flushing out the middle into a deep pool.
* **Walhalla Wave** and **HooRoo Run** are slides for groups who use a round raft that plunges from a summit. The first winds slightly and is semi-enclosed, while HooRoo Run is a lumpy straightaway that picks up some exciting speed.

WAVE POOLS   The two conjoined surf pools, **Cutback Cove** and **Big Surf Shores,** offer the same mild (2–4 ft.), intermittent waves. Both empty onto semi-hard concretelike coating (underneath the water, the floor has a slight give), and they share a beach of wonderfully fine white sand. Most guests claim a few chairs here, although there are more in a quieter cul-de-sac near Loggerhead Lane.

OTHER LAZY RIVERS   **Roa's Rapids** is a little novel in that it's a river with a very fast current meant to sweep your body along, without a tube; buoyant vests are free in all sizes, and if the nearby racks of them are empty, try the rack between Kookaburra Cove and Big Surf Shores.

JUST FOR KIDS   The **Walkabout Waters,** the major kids' area, is elaborate and irresistible (a tangle of slides, bridges, and cascades, plus two enormous buckets endlessly filling and dumping over everyone), while **Kata's Kookaburra Cove** is geared toward very small children, with water pinwheels, faint slides, and geysers. Parents are meant to join their offspring in the splash, because there's not much seating and its island makes it hard to keep an eye on kids' movements.

FOOD   Aquatica has the right idea when it comes to meals: You can pay $13 adults, $8 kids for one-time picnic fare at the all-you-can-eat Banana Beach Cookout (chicken, cheeseburgers, corn on the cob), or another $7 adults and $2 kids to pig out all day. Mango Market sells healthy sandwiches and salads ($8.50 and under). Cabanas ($160 for four people) come with free drinks in a private fridge, towels, places to sit, and someone to fetch your food; the Yallingup section is quietest.

DISCOVERY COVE

The most expensive day at the pool you'll have in your life, the 30-acre **Discovery Cove** (☎ 877/557-7404; www.discoverycove.com; $189, plus $100 for 30-min. dolphin interaction, including free admission to SeaWorld or Busch Gardens) was created and priced as a five-star experience. Only around 1,000 people a day are admitted, guaranteeing this faux tropical idyll will not be marred by a single queue. You can stop reading now if you don't want to get jealous—this is strictly a special-occasion place. The ticket includes breakfast, equipment, sunscreen, free beer (if you're of age), and lunch—a good one, too, such as fresh grilled salmon (a fish that drew the short straw at SeaWorld, I guess).

Discovery Cove, in fact, is more or less a free-range playground. When you arrive, first thing in the morning, you're greeted under a vaulted atrium more redolent of a five-star island resort than a theme park. Coffee is poured, and once you're checked in (and, if you're swimming with dolphins, you've been assigned your time), you're set loose to do as you wish. Wade in the **Ray Pool** among tame and barbless stingrays, feed fresh fruit to the houseguests at the **Tropical Bird Aviary,** snorkel in the **Exotic Fish Lagoon,** or ride an inner tube down the slow-floating **Tropical River,** which passes through the aviary by way of some water-falls, keeping the birds from escaping. Many of the guests elect to simply kick back on a lounger (there are plenty) on incredibly silky sand (imported, of course) at the natural-looking pool. Other than that, you read a book and relax.

Without a dolphin swim, there's not really enough value to fill a day. When it's your turn—if you've paid—guests over the age of 5 can head to the **Dolphin Lagoon,** where you change into a wetsuit and a trainer briefs you for a half-hour on bottlenose dolphin basics, and then in small groups of about eight, you wade into the chilly water, where more trainers introduce you to one of the pod. Like children, they have distinct personalities and must be carefully paired to people the trainers think they'll enjoy being with—many visitors don't realize that a dolphin can easily kill you. Here, the hand-reared animals peer at you with a logician's eye while your trainer shows you how to use hand signals for communication. The climax of the 30-minute interaction is the moment when you grasp the creature's dorsal fin and it swims, you in tow, for 30 or so feet. Although many parks around the world allow for dolphin interaction for much less money, not all of them are reputable. The constant public scrutiny SeaWorld is under, and the high value its zoologists place on conservation, mean these animals are well treated, and if they don't feel like meeting you, they don't have to. Naturally, a SeaWorld photographer is on hand for it all, so if you want images or video, you'll pay for that, too. That means that if you're not careful, your day could cost around $400.

Past that Turnstile in the Sky

Not all of Orlando's attractions have thrived. Tupperware Museum, we miss you. Kindly remove your Mouse ears to honor the forgotten fun—if not for an accident of time, you'd be vacationing here instead:

Circus World (1974–86): Started by Mattel as a walk-through museum dedicated to circus history (after all, most of the big top crews wintered in Florida), it collapsed under its own weight after competition with Disney tempted it into building too many rides. Also, clowns are scary.

Boardwalk Baseball (1987–90): Textbook publisher Harcourt, Brace and Jovanovich recycled Circus World in the image of Florida's other winter tradition, baseball, and the Kansas City Royals were enticed to train there. Few cared. On January 17, 1990, 1,000 guests were asked to leave.

Xanadu (1983–96): This walk-through "home of the future" was made by coating giant balloons with polyurethane—an early exercise in ergonomics. Sister homes in Gatlinburg and Wisconsin Dells were also built, but all outlived their curiosity value, and became, in fact, quick homes of the past. You'll find the site near Mile Marker 12 of U.S. 192.

JungleLand Zoo (1995–2002): The demise of this low-rent Gatorland rip-off was hastened in 1997 by news coverage after a lioness escaped from her enclosure and went missing among Kissimmee's motels for 3 days. A few trainers got nipped by the gators, too. Bad news.

Splendid China (1993–2003): On 73 acres 3 miles west of Disney's main gate, China's wonders (the Forbidden City, a Great Wall segment containing 6.5 million bricks, and so on) were rebuilt in miniature. Who would blow $100 million on such a bad idea? The Chinese government, which pulled the strings. The site is being rebuilt with vacation homes, but U.S. 192's high concentration of Chinese buffets is now explained.

River Country (1976–2005): Disney's first water park, incorporated into Bay Lake beside the Fort Wilderness Resort, simply wasn't fancy enough or big enough to satisfy guests anymore. Another issue: It turns out that the *Naegleria fowleri* amoebae growing in many Florida lakes can kill you. (Guests may no longer swim in *any* of Disney's lakes. Coincidence?)

If you crave dolphin interaction at a lower price, SeaWorld offers a $40, hands-on feeding session (p. 210). You won't swim with them, but you will spend 30 minutes plopping fish into their eagerly clacking gullets.

BUSCH GARDENS AFRICA

Another take-your-time park like SeaWorld, **Busch Gardens Africa** (3000 E. Busch Blvd., at 40th St., 8 miles northwest of Tampa; ☎ 888/800-5447; www.busch gardens.com; $70 adults, $60 kids 3–9) boasts attractions and a professionalism on a par with the Orlando ones, but it's also about 70 miles southwest of Disney, which seems to daunt Americans. (Oddly, foreign visitors are more likely to make the trek.) That's too bad, because the park, which rates just shy of the 10 most visited in America, offers more than enough to fill a day on two important fronts: exotic animal sightings and roller coaster ridings. In fact, Busch Gardens matches Disney's Animal Kingdom on the animal front and whups it completely in rides, but all must bow to the caliber of Disney's shows.

The park started small, in 1959, as a free hospitality center attached to a Budweiser bottling plant. Guests would watch animal performances in a tropical setting, raise a beer, and go home. The idea outlived the factory. The rest is history. The Belgian beer goliath InBev bought Anheuser-Busch and its parks division in 2008, and although it promises not to change much, that remains to be proved.

SAVING MONEY   For discounts, see the section about the FlexTicket on p. 322, which grants good deals if you're going to visit Universal Orlando and SeaWorld on the same trip. There is enough for voracious tourists to justify coming for 2 days (most of us see the highlights in 1 day); tickets bought online come with a second day free. Members of AARP receive $8 discounts on Tuesdays, and $5 on other days. Members of the military should always ask if there's a deal on; check www.herosalute.com to see what's offered.

GETTING THERE   You don't have to rule out Busch Gardens if you don't have a car. The daily **Shuttle Express** (☎ 800/221-1339; $10 round-trip, reservations required) takes about an hour each way. (The service is free for those who purchase a 6-Park Orlando FlexTicket Plus; p. 322). It picks up passengers at seven locations throughout the Orlando tourist zone, from Universal to U.S. 192.

SPECIAL EVENTS   Busch Gardens offers a few behind-the-scenes tours which, for added expense, get you face-to-snout with the animals or educational experiences with trainers. See p. 221 for more information on those. Also check the park's website for upcoming events; zoological superstars such as Jack Hanna make regular appearances, and special events are mounted around Halloween and Christmas. Right next door, the park also runs **Adventure Island,** a water park, but that's mostly patronized by locals; Orlando's choices are superior.

TOURING BUSCH GARDENS AFRICA

After you park, you'll board a tram that brings you to the front gate (budget at least 15 min. for the process). As at all parks, the entry area, here themed **Morocco** and dressed like the most spacious souk you've ever seen, is for shopping and chores, although *KaTonga: Musical Tales from the Jungle* ✦ mounted at the Moroccan Palace Theater, is worth a stop for show fans; it's an African-themed Broadway-style revue noteworthy for its excellent female pop vocalists, strikingly colorful imagery, and costumes. It's the one show I'd make time for

The Best of Busch Gardens

Don't miss if you're 6: Myombe Reserve
Don't miss if you're 16: Kumba
Requisite photo op: The animals of Serengeti Plain
The most crowded, so go early: SkeiKra and Rhino Rally
Skippable: *Pirates 4-D*
Biggest thrill: SheiKra
Best show: *KaTonga*
Where to find peace: Bird Gardens; Clydesdale Hamlet

here, although its 35-minute running time eats up too much thrill time for my tastes.

Busch Gardens' themed lands aren't as large or as strictly themed as other parks'. Taken roughly clockwise off the map, and in the order that you'd encounter them from the entrance, here are the park highlights:

Bird Gardens

At the transition from Morocco, the two entangled wooden coasters comprising **Gwazi** ✪✪, opened in 1999 on the site of the old brewery, and are among the fiercest, most intense wooden coasters you're likely to ride, with plenty of high-speed, banked turns that thrillingly cause you to doubt that the wood could ever hold together under the stress. On off-peak days, only one of the tracks, named Lion and Tiger, may be open, and although they differ in layout, they're the same in their bucking, screeching demeanor. The 2½-minute, 50mph ride is best experienced when both tracks are running; along with Islands of Adventure's Dueling Dragons, these are the only coasters in the world specially designed to provide multiple near misses (in this case, six). Sadly, they are rarely dispatched together. Either ride first thing or in midafternoon after lines die.

The rest of Bird Gardens—the original nucleus of the park, dating to 1959— is, of course, avian in nature, including a flamingo enclosure and a **Garden Aviary** walk-through. At the **Hospitality House,** distinguished by its fabulous, triangular jet-age roof folds, visitors were once able to get a free beer, but InBev ended that in 2009 and the building's future use was uncertain at press time. Across the way, pop into **Xcursions** ✪✪, Busch Gardens' commendable effort to stock a shop with interesting internationally made crafts; proceeds go to a conservation fund. It's easily the most interesting store on-site. As the Gardens creep toward Stanleyville, there's the **Land of the Dragons** kids' playground (little Ferris wheel, tiny go-carts, and so on)—with a single entrance, it's easy for parents to police.

Stanleyville

Named for a city in the Congo (now Kisangani) once popular with colonialist explorers of Africa, this section is popular mostly because of **SheiKra** ✪✪✪, a

Some Overall Strategies for Tackling Busch Gardens

Generally speaking, as you look at your park map, the thrill rides congregate on the left-hand side of the map (the park's western half), and the animal enclosures are more on the right-hand side (the east).

Roller coaster mavens should consider getting a locker for their loose stuff, because staff are sticklers about forcing people to use the 50¢, single-entry lockers near each ride, and that expense can mount. Also knock down a few of the big-ticket rides (SheiKra, Kumba, Gwazi) early in the day before lines build—I beeline to Stanleyville first, for SheiKra.

People who have come for the animals can keep their bags and take a more leisurely pace. The one thing you can't fail to do is pick up a placemat-size map. Turn your attention to the **Meet the Keepers** timetable, where you can arrange to hear a zookeeper share knowledge about a variety of animals, including hippos, elephants, giraffe, and uh, the Budweiser donkey. Whenever you see "Animal Encounter," it just means zookeepers will draw from a grab bag of possibilities each time they're held.

Parents with toddlers might consider doing Rhino Rally (a tamer ride that garners a huge line as the day grinds on) first.

Don't schedule your time around the shows. There's more than enough to do between the rides and the animals—the shows here feel like filler.

"dive coaster" with a design unique to America: It sends cars 200 feet up, where they hang, traumatically, for 5 seconds on a precipice before finally being released down a shocking 90-degree drop at 70mph. Just marvel at the thing—you can't get any steeper than straight down. From there, the three-row cars, which seat so many people (24) they look like minitheaters, take a second dive before swooping across the surface of a pond, where "water brakes" send up rooster-tailed plumes and slow things back down. The cars are floorless, so there's nothing but empty air between you and oblivion. After you stagger off, check out Busch Gardens' latest innovation: Instead of taking your photo on the ride, as so many Orlando parks do, a *movie* of five peak moments is recorded and spliced together with stock footage of the rest of the ride to provide you with a 5-minute DVD ($25) of your petrifying plunge; sit in the front two rows to appear in all the shots. Plain old photos are available for $15. **Strategy:** Queue early, as it's the one everyone wants to ride this year. The first row, unquestionably, is the most thrilling because from there you seem to be dangling helplessly.

SheiKra may be the future, but the rest of Stanleyville is full of tried-and-true rides from a previous generation. The **Stanley Falls Flume ★** erected in 1973, is one of the industry's most beloved (and doggedly old-fashioned) log flume rides, with a 43-foot drop. As more parks remove these reliable charmers, this one has risen to be America's longest. **Tanganyika Tidal Wave** is a short group boat ride—up, down 55 feet, splash—designed simply to soak everything. If you want to get wet, you don't have to wait in line, because there's a bridge squarely in the splash range. But my favorite old warhorse is the Skyride, a gondola-style bucket seating four that travels from here to another station near the entrance to Edge of Africa, passing over some wild animals on the way. Almost every other amusement park in America has dismantled its equivalents, including the Disney parks, but Busch Gardens keeps its unusually long specimen lovingly maintained. There's also a train station here for the Serengeti Railway ✪✪✪, which I'll describe more fully in the Nairobi section; the station's store, **Deal Depot,** is where you'll find the park's half-price souvenir markdowns.

Congo

The newest attraction here is the 4-acre Jungala, where standouts include Tiger Trail, a big-cat habitat. Check the desk in the Tiger Lodge for times of the next zookeeper talk, and daily at 1:30pm, the animals are amused with a game of tug-o-war through the fence; it takes three people to battle one cat. A cool bubble, big enough for two people to peek at once, pops up through the ground of the white tiger enclosure. Orangutans live alongside the **OrangCafé,** and gibbons dwell below a multilevel wood-and-rope play area.

Rides are explicitly for the young: Wild Surge is a bench that hops on a stalk, Jungle Flyers are seats that slide along a wire. Congo River Rapids is a round-boat rapids ride that will likely soak you, but probably not drench you. The boats tend to jerk around when they bump against the walls. Lines get extensive in the heat, but at least it's a cooling ride. Ubanga-Banga Bumper Cars and the Congo station of the Serengeti Railway are also found here.

The star attraction is Kumba ✪✪, which hits 60mph on ominously noisy nylon wheels and lasts nearly 3 minutes. The tallest drop is 135 feet, and its vertical loop was the world's largest when it was built (1993). From the moment you crest the first hill, there's barely a letup in its smoothly powerful arsenal of loops and swoops, making this loud beast an enthusiasts' favorite (many swear the back rows are best).

Timbuktu

This tacky area, the middle of the park, is hardly its heart. It's mostly a tawdry area slotted with a few **carnival rides** and some **midway games.** In addition, coaster nuts value the tightly packed, loopy Scorpion coaster because it's one of a diminishing breed designed by Anton Schwarzkopf, an important German manufacturer. It also has only lap bar restraints, no shoulder bars—the centrifugal force of the loops keeps riders glued into their seats. Less remarkable is the Cheetah Chase 🧒 coaster, nothing more than a "wild mouse," carnival-style ride that zips back and forth around a tiny plot of land; it's for families, not hardened thrill seekers. Phoenix is a pirate ship that swings and eventually goes all the way upside-down. The current tenant of the Timbuktu Theater is *Pirates 4-D,* a 3-D movie combined with special effects (such as water sprays) that make you feel like you're part of the action; it's usually on the hour and stars Eric Idle and Leslie Nielsen. (Skip it if you want.) Lots of animals are on view on the way to the next "land," Nairobi, including crocodiles, elephants, and black rhino.

Nairobi

This area *is* the heart of the park, as it's one of the best places to dig into animal learning. Myombe Reserve ✪✪✪ is a spectacular, tropical rainforest walk-through habitat with a three-story waterfall. Inside, a troop of western lowland gorillas dwells behind glass (well, you're behind glass—they're outdoors). Beyond them, a colony of chimpanzees lives in its own habitat. If the animals happen to be hanging out by the windows, staring right back at the tourists and interacting with them, then you could spend a long, happy time in here.

There's usually something happening at the walk-through **Jambo Junction** ★★, where the park's "animal ambassadors" meet the public; on my last visit, a parrot was getting flying practice. Next door, baby animals are raised. Zookeepers bring a new animal onto the surrounding pathways every half-hour (on my last visit: a rescued screech owl).

One of the park's most original attractions is **Rhino Rally** ★★, which starts off like Disney's Kilimanjaro Safaris—passengers board free-wheeled safari vehicles, driven by narrators, for a romp through faux African terrain stocked with elephants, zebras, and (sometimes) rhinos. You won't learn much—the script makes facile reductions such as telling you the Zambezi River is simply "in Africa." But the second half, during which your vehicle stalls on a floating bridge that ends up breaking loose and shooting some river rapids, is unique and is worth the trip. It's also so complex that it often breaks down; then, the experience trims off this climax with a detour. If it's running, seize the moment. You don't have to ride to see elephants; some are in an enclosure visible from the path to Timbuktu.

The other must-do ride is the 2½-mile **Serengeti Railway** ★★★, which may be boarded here for a 40-minute round-trip. At other parks, the choo-choo is the boring thing you take toddlers or grandparents on, but at Busch Gardens, it's the primary way to explore the main animal enclosure, the 65-acre Serengeti Plain, which follows this station stop. The train makes a near-complete revolution of that area, past fields containing roaming giraffe, black and white rhinoceroses, and all sorts of antelope. This leg, which takes 20 minutes, is the best on the circuit. Next, the train stops at Congo (beneath Kumba, near the kids' rides), and then in Stanleyville (beneath SheiKra) before returning here. The walking distance between those last two stations is really only about 2 minutes.

Crown Colony/Egypt

The next two lands are so small they're practically united. Crown Colony is where the **Skyride** ★ one-way bucket gondola alights for its ride over the Serengeti and reboards for its trip to Stanleyville. You can see a few Clydesdale horses doing a lot of nothing in the **Clydesdale Hamlet;** they live here for 6 weeks and then swap with some at SeaWorld. Horse lovers can dash into the tiny **Show Jumping Hall of Fame,** which is located here, of all places. The requisite **Edge of Africa** ★★ is an excellent 16-acre, walk-through collection of habitats themed, exhilaratingly, on meat eaters, including lions, hyena (the rival populations are kept in adjoining pens—and swapped every so often—just to keep their scent detectors sharp), crocodiles, and a bevy of hippopotami visible from below the waterline. In Egypt, the standout ride is the 3-minute **Montu** ★, a smooth-riding "inverted" coaster on which passengers' feet dangle as they're flipped upside-down seven times at up to 65mph. Because this one's located in a distant dogleg of the park, lines don't usually get too daunting.

What the Basics Cost at Busch Gardens Africa

Parking: $10
Single strollers: $12 per day
Double strollers: $19 per day
Wheelchair: $15 per day
ECV: $42 per day
Lockers: $6 per day
Regular soda: $2.60/**Water:** $2.70/**Cup of beer:** $5

WHERE TO EAT AT BUSCH GARDENS AFRICA

Expect prices for a meal to hover around $8.50, not including a drink. Fries can be subbed for coleslaw or potato salad. Although counter-service locations dot the park (the ones in Morocco are $1 more than the mean, for some reason), here are my picks for the most interesting choices, each of which has added entertainment:

Bird Gardens   At press time, the **Hospitality House** sold a few healthy sandwiches and pizza, but conversion to another menu is likely soon.

Stanleyville   The **Zambia Smokehouse** does chicken, ribs, and beef brisket with both indoor and outdoor seating; the latter overlooks SheiKra's dramatic water-sled landing.

Congo (Jungala)   Fish, turkey legs, and club sandwiches at **Bengal Bistro;** chicken strips and wraps at **OrangCafé.** The latter overlooks orangutans.

Timbuktu   The **Desert Grill Restaurant** 🎤 a pseudo-Arabian theater with beer-hall seating, does carvery sandwiches and pastas. Thoughtfully, the park schedules lunchtime entertainment by vocal groups and bands; check the back of your park map for showtimes.

Crown Colony   The **Crown Colony House** 🎤 is a colonial-style counter-service place with some seating overlooking the Serengeti Plain; if you're lucky, animals will come close. Salads cost around $10, sandwiches $9.50. A bowl of clam chowder is $4.50. The top floor is the park's premium restaurant, but prices aren't as steep as you'd think: Family-style dinners including fried chicken and Budweiser batter-dipped fish are $14.75 for adults and $8 for kids—not a bad bargain. The offices upstairs are said by many employees to be haunted by an 8-year-old girl named Wendy, who sometimes appears in a fog or stops the elevator.

7

Beyond the Major Parks

Past the turnstiles, you'll find lots more to do.

WHEN YOU'RE SICK OF PARKING TRAMS, CATTLE-CALL QUEUES, AND THE relentless patronization that comes with theme park "magic," it's time to divert yourself with something new. In many cases, something old—some of these places are among the original attractions that sowed the seeds enabling the area to become the powerhouse it now is. Some are serious, some are downright silly, but when you're on vacation, anything goes.

INTERNATIONAL DRIVE AREA

Although none of the attractions around International Drive are considered first tier, that doesn't mean they're not fun. In many ways, the I-Drive strip north of Sand Lake Road presents the picture of a classic vacation town. Its diversions are mostly inexpensive and it's also the only touristy area in Orlando where a car isn't necessary, not least because the I-Ride Trolley (p. 18) will tote you along, too.

WET 'N WILD

My favorite water park for pound-for-pound thrills, **Wet 'n Wild** ★★★ 🄺 (6200 International Dr., Orlando; ☎ 800/992-9453 or 407/351-1800; www.wetnwild orlando.com; $42 adults, $36 kids 3–9; hours vary, but it generally opens at 9 or 10am and closes at 5pm in winter and as late as 11pm weekends in the summer) is located smack in the middle of the I-Drive area. It's tough to top this, the world's first water theme park, which was opened in 1977 by George Millay, the same guy who started SeaWorld. Other parks far outdo it in landscaping and theming, but Wet 'n Wild is still the purist's paragon—a tightly packed coil of get-to-the-point thrills. There are no cutesy frills at this compact park; the decor consists of steel framework, concrete pathways, and screams. Most water is heated, and bigger rafts are hoisted up the ride scaffolds by conveyors. The prime maintenance period is September to March, when at least one ride at a time will be out of rotation. *Money-saving tip:* It's part of the FlexTicket discount plan (p. 322).

After stashing booty in the multi-entry lockers by the main gates (you can leave your money behind, because RFID-enabled wristbands allow you to make purchases with a wave of your hand—a perk Disney and the newly built Aquatica lack), stake out a beach chair if you want one, because free loungers go fast; parents tend to sit out the slides by hanging at the central, 17,000-square-foot **Surf Lagoon** or in the main kiddie area. You needn't be an excellent swimmer—lifeguards carefully monitor everything, even if most of them are still on Student Council, and riders are dispatched one at a time so there's no competition in the chutes. Most pools are shallow enough to stand in—but a copious supply of waterproof sunblock is a must, and nonslip, waterproof footwear, such as swimming socks, is recommended because you'll be padding around on concrete.

The coolest contraptions include:

- **The Flyer,** a four-rider toboggan run, not unlike a winter luge, through banked turns and speedy straightaway.
- **The Black Hole** ✹, a two-person raft (sorry, soloists) that whisks blindly through a pitch-black tube, pierced momentarily by disorienting strips of lights.
- **The Storm** ✹✹, nicknamed "the Toilet," a gently curving tube that gets your body going and sends it swirling into what might be best called a 30-foot john. You spiral around on your back until you're finally carried to a central drain of sorts and plopped, thoroughly disoriented, into a deep pool. The line can be long for that, depending on whether they're running one or both tubes.
- **Bomb Bay** ✹✹✹, atop the tower to the right of Surf Lagoon, the park's scariest ride. Six stories high, riders step into an enclosed cylinder above a 78-degree chute that drops as close to vertically as physics and lawyers will allow. A sadistic attendant peeks through a window to make sure your arms and legs are crossed, and without warning, hits the release button on a trap door, dropping traumatized riders down the flume below at wedgie speed. The lines for this one aren't as long as you might expect—the wimp-out rate is high.
- **Der Stuka,** Bomb Bay's sister slide and almost as scary, but comes without the torture of the trap door and with a slightly less-vertical incline.
- **Brain Wash** ✹✹, a white-knuckle standout worth waiting for—rafts carrying two or four people are dropped down the wall of a 65-foot-wide funnel that's turned on its side.
- **The Blast,** a soaking ride past colorful broken pipes—making it good for younger kids—and **the Surge,** which sends a family-style round raft down a fun but unspectacular course.

A few of my favorites are rides that you might not realize, at first glance, are as much fun as they are. **Bubba Tub** is a round raft that shoots more or less straight down a humped course—when you get your friends or family on it with you, though, the rushing, hopping journey feels out of control and awfully exhilarating. But the best ride is **Disco H2O** ✹✹✹, in which cloverleaf-shaped rafts (two to four people) are accelerated in a tube and sent spinning around an enclosed chamber where disco music plays and lights spin; eventually, the raft is washed out a chute in the middle. The group of **Mach 5** ✹ flumes is old school, ridden with just a mat. I'll let you in on my speed secret: Only let your elbows and knees touch, reducing drag. You have to tote your own mat to the top for these. The **Lazy River,** a tame floating stream, is uneventful, so don't bother looking for a hard-to-find free inner tube unless you simply *must.*

INDOOR "SKYDIVING"

Across the street, at one of only a few "vertical wind tunnels" in America, the air blowing from beneath the wire-mesh floor is powerful enough to levitate any person, large or small, and for $40, you'll be given a few go-rounds in the simulated

International Drive Area Attractions

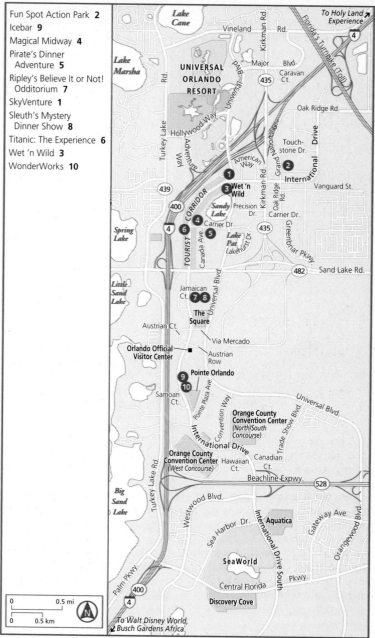

skydive chamber at **SkyVenture** ★★ (6805 Visitor Circle, Orlando; ☎ 407/903-1150; www.skyventureorlando.com; $45 per person; Sun–Thurs 11:30am–9pm, Fri–Sat 11:30am–10pm). You'd swear it was a tourist trap, but surprisingly, there seem to be as many hobby skydivers training as there are curious out-of-towners. The concept approximates the effect of skydiving, except you're never more than a few feet off the ground. Visitors are strapped into jumpsuits and given a short training session on how to walk into the 125mph airflow—mastering the necessary arched-back, splay-legged posture can be tricky, but should you fail, there's a master diver with you to grab you by the sleeve and guide you into a series of adrenaline-fueled climbs and plunges. Or not—you can just hover there, if that's what floats your butt. And it sure beats having to jump out of a plane. A standard ticket is good for two 1-minute rotations in the chamber (wow, they go quickly), plus training; combined, the adventure takes an hour. The owners will e-mail you an $8-off coupon if you fill in a form on the website, and there are deals for lesser discounts in all the tourist publications.

THREE TOURISTY MUSEUMS

Although **Titanic: The Experience** (7324 International Dr., Orlando; ☎ 407/248-1166; www.titanictheexperience.com; $20 adults, $13 kids 3–11; daily 9am–9pm) is not as shallow (if that's the word) as you might expect an incongruous tourist sight like this to be, it also has fewer true artifacts than you might hope. For those interested in the topic, this theatrically presented museum, which walks guests chronologically from boarding to the abbreviated voyage to rediscovery, provides a balanced dossier of the sorry tale. The cases have a few mementos, but upon close inspection, you'll notice that many of them are from her sister ships, the *Olympic* and *Britannia,* and others are props from various movie retellings of the foundering. Everything conflates Hollywood storytelling with history (even the piped-in music evokes James Horner's 1997 movie score), but there's plenty of meat on this hambone. The curators have gone the extra mile by writing informative placards, by inscribing a wall with the names of those lost, and by installing a refrigerated room, complete with ice, that approximates what it might have felt like to stroll down her chilly decks at night. The 8-foot model of what she now looks like on the floor of the North Atlantic is particularly moving.

The museum equivalent of a forwarded e-mail joke, **Ripley's Believe It or Not! Odditorium** (8201 International Dr., Orlando; ☎ 407/363-4418; www.ripleysorlando.com; $19 adults, $12 kids 4–12; daily 9:30am–midnight) is too expensive for the thin, touristy diversion that it delivers. Mostly it consists of wax figures, panels from the old Ripley's comic (does anyone under 45 even remember those?), and the odd coin-operated device—the same as any other Ripley attraction. It has fewer true artifacts than you'll be expecting. Don't set foot in it without at least harvesting coupons from any tourist brochure.

If Mister Wizard had been raised in a carnival, he might have produced **WonderWorks** 🧒 (9067 International Dr., Orlando; ☎ 407/351-8800; www.wonderworksonline.com; daily 9am–midnight; $20 adults, $15 kids 4–12, $5 per game of Lazer Tag), the kind of place you go on a rainy day or if you need to kill an hour or two. The facade looks like someone ripped a mansion out of the ground and turned it upside down—even the FedEx mailbox and the palm trees are upended—but the inverted motif doesn't continue very far into its doors. Instead, you get about 100 hands-on, ad hoc exhibits, not unlike what you'd find at a kids' science museum or an arcade. One booth has kids making bubbles as big as they are, others simulate shuttle landings and fighter jet flights . . . you get the idea. Bring the Purell, because they can get smeary, and bring your patience, because some will be broken. ***Money-saving tips:*** You don't need one of the guidebooks the ticket booth sells. Its website posts $1.50-off coupons, and at night, it puts on the Outta Control magic show (p. 94), one of the cheapest dinnertainment shows in town.

FUN FAIRS

Just south of the big bend on I-Drive—you can't miss the towering apparatus— is **Magical Midway** (7001 International Dr., Orlando; ☎ 407/370-5353; www. magicalmidway.com; $3 per midway ride, unlimited midway rides $16, 3 hr. of Go-Karts $23, unlimited carnival and go-kart rides $28; $2.50-off coupon online; arcade only Mon–Wed 4–10pm, arcade and rides Thurs and Sun 2–10pm, Fri–Sat 2pm–midnight), a small concrete area which by night blares with rock music and heaves with idle youth. The circular swing ride, Star Flyer ($7 a ride), looks tamer than it is because the restraints feel inadequate for the 230-foot height it achieves. The most obvious thrill is the world's tallest **Slingshot** ride ($25, not included on passes), a colossal fork strung with a pod. Two at a time sit inside, are pulled down, and then flung more than 200 feet into the sky. The 90-second adventure is so tense that spectators usually collect nearby. The rest of the small plot is dominated by two thunderous, wooden Go-Kart tracks ($6 each; the Avalanche track has slightly steeper ramps than the Alpine), a few minor rides including cheerless bumper boats, and a dirty arcade thronged with kids. It's the kind of place 11-year-old boys think is the coolest.

While the Magical Midway seduces idle foreign tourists licking ice cream cones and strolling I-Drive, the carnival-style **Fun Spot Action Park** ★ 🐾 🕷 (5551 Del Verde Way, Orlando; ☎ 407/363-3867; www.fun-spot.com; unlimited rides without Go-Karts $35, all rides without Go-Karts $25, each midway ride $3, each Go-Kart ride $6; hours change but are generally Sat–Sun 10am–11pm, Mon–Fri 2–11pm), 2 miles north (you can't miss the Ferris wheel, which appeared in the film *Monster*), is larger, cleaner, better lit, and preferred by local parents. That means parking is a nightmare on weekend nights. There's much more space and selection than at the Midway: four concrete, multilevel Go-Kart tracks (the Quad Helix's stacked figure-eight turns make it my favorite, but I also love Conquest's peaked ramp), a two-level arcade, a scrambler, plenty of snack bars, and a devoted section of kiddie rides (including a teacup ride and a Frog Hopper; passes for them are $15). Don't get me wrong: It's still a cheap carnival.

U.S. 192 AREA

In creating his new breed of amusement park, Walt Disney tried desperately to stamp out the trashy honky-tonk of the American carnival, but it lives on, cotton candy and all, on his doorstep. **Old Town** (5770 W. Irlo Bronson Hwy./U.S. 192, Kissimmee; ☎ 407/396-4888; www.old-town.com; free entry; unlimited rides $25; daily 10am–11pm, rides may remain open later), at Mile Marker 9, is touristy and low-rent—the kind of entertainment center you'd find rusting near a small town somewhere. Old Town, built to look like 4 blocks of a Main Street–style town, is about its beer-soaked ale halls, and its panoply of no-name stores run the gamut from baseball cards to puppets to pins to Western gear. Strung along are a low-rent haunted house and a mechanical bull. The **Human Slingshot** ($25) is 11 feet shorter than the one at Magical Midway (see earlier). The area also has about 18 cheap rides ($2–$6), bumper cars, and **Windstorm,** a skeletal knot of metal tucked at the back of the park. It must be Orlando's least known roller coaster, which is not an injustice. Old Town may not be posh, and some people may even classify it as trashy (Wed night hosts an Elvis impersonator, Thurs night is biker night), but kids love it, international tourists are fascinated by it, and it's a decent place to have a good time for less. And you'll probably eat something fried.

Next door, at the carnival-ride playground of **Fun Spot USA** (2850 Florida Plaza Blvd., Kissimmee; ☎ 321/677-0585; 4 rides $20, unlimited ride armband $35, $2.50-off coupon online; www.funspotusa.tutengraphics.com), there's a selection of basic rides that wouldn't be out of place beside a circus (the Hot Seat swings seated riders on the end of a big stick), and a few multilevel Go-Kart tracks and race car simulators. That skyline-scarring contraption is **SkyCoaster** ★ (2850 Florida Plaza Blvd., Kissimmee; ☎ 407/397-2509; www.skycoaster.cc; $40 a ride; Mon–Fri 2pm–midnight, Sat–Sun 10am–midnight), which harnesses up to three would-be pants-wetters so that they're face-down, hoists them backward, and then drops them to swing back and forth at up to 80mph like wingless hang gliders. Adjacent to that, **Full Speed Race & Golf** (kids) (5720 W. U.S. 192, Kissimmee; ☎ 407/397-7455; www.fullspeed.cc; $10 golf, $10 cars, $15 both; Mon–Fri 2pm–midnight, Sat–Sun noon–midnight) lures gearheads with a line of car simulators that can race and "hit" each other (you'll buck and bump if you do), as well as an 18-hole fluorescent, racing-themed minigolf course under black lights.

I'm sorry, but $21 is too much for a petting zoo unless there's a unicorn. Yet that's the rate, adult or child, at **Green Meadows Petting Farm** (1368 S. Poinciana Blvd., Kissimmee; ☎ 407/846-0770; www.greenmeadowsfarm.com; $21 adults, $15 seniors, free for kids 1 and under; daily 9:30am–5:30pm, last tour at 4pm), and I don't care if that price does include pony rides and the chance to milk a cow. Geese poop has its entertainment limits.

DOWNTOWN ORLANDO

Shaped by evangelicals seeking an increase in values-based entertainment (as if Disney was sleazy), the simplistic **Holy Land Experience** (4655 Vineland Rd., Orlando; ☎ 800/447-7235; www.holylandexperience.com; $35 adults, $20 for children 6–12, $30 for seniors 55 and older, free for children 5 and under, discounts of $5 available online; parking $5; Mon–Sat 10am–5pm) is the world's first theme park dedicated to the Bible. Every day, an actor playing Jesus drags himself to the top of a fake mountain where he's "crucified" by villainous Romans before an appreciative audience. While its owners (the Trinity Broadcasting Network, whose televangelist figureheads are Paul and Jan Crouch) claim they're transporting people back in time to walk through the Bible, I must point out that the recorded voices reading Scripture are always deep, male, vaguely British, and accompanied by a soundtrack of strings and timpani. Ironically for a park devoted

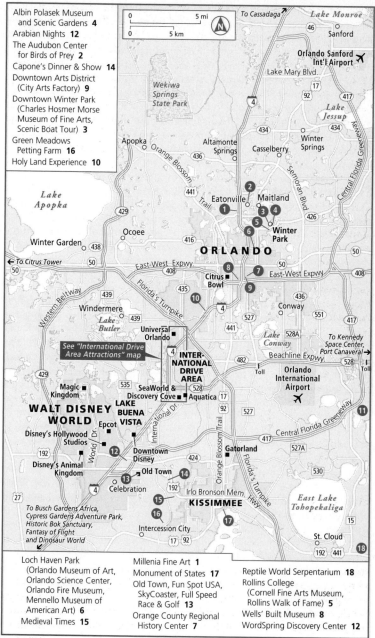

Albin Polasek Museum
  and Scenic Gardens **4**
Arabian Nights **12**
The Audubon Center
  for Birds of Prey **2**
Capone's Dinner & Show **14**
Downtown Arts District
  (City Arts Factory) **9**
Downtown Winter Park
  (Charles Hosmer Morse
  Museum of Fine Arts,
  Scenic Boat Tour) **3**
Green Meadows
  Petting Farm **16**
Holy Land Experience **10**

Loch Haven Park
  (Orlando Museum of Art,
  Orlando Science Center,
  Orlando Fire Museum,
  Mennello Museum of
  American Art) **6**
Medieval Times **15**

Millenia Fine Art **1**
Monument of States **17**
Old Town, Fun Spot USA,
  SkyCoaster, Full Speed
  Race & Golf **13**
Orange County Regional
  History Center **7**

Reptile World Serpentarium **18**
Rollins College
  (Cornell Fine Arts Museum,
  Rollins Walk of Fame) **5**
Wells' Built Museum **8**
WordSpring Discovery Center **12**

to a great book, there are almost no signs—everything is narrated and dumbed down. Having been to the real Holy Land, I think the Holy Land Experience is for people whose understanding of the era comes from Charlton Heston movies.

That's not to say that this park is overtly political; it's not the kind of place that wants your vote—just your tears. Will there ever again be a theme park where a major attraction is the Wilderness Tabernacle, which is essentially 20 minutes of an old man miming his custodial duties in a desert temple while a recorded chorus chants Old Testament verses? The Scriptorium actually contains some impressive specimens of Biblical publishing, including the bloodstained Matthew's Bible from 1537. Even the Scriptorium, though, waxes rhapsodic when discussing the missionary aspect of publishing the Bible, but avoids the stickier, and much more illuminating, historical topics of how some leaders manipulated Biblical translation for personal gain, as well as the specific changes that pioneers such as Martin Luther and John Calvin were actually fighting for.

There are no rides, nor enough attractions to fill an entire day, even though performances and tableaux are spaced out across the clock to pretend there is. It's sad to think that people who could be saving up for a pilgrimage to the real Jerusalem find anything personal in this unsavory one of fake executions and souvenir shops. For me, religion is not a consumer event.

SEVERAL WORTHWHILE MUSEUMS

People who think the culture and history of Central Florida are shallow will have their eyes opened—using such modern museum methods as video and sound portraits—at the elaborate **Orange County Regional History Center** ✪✪✪ (65 E. Central Blvd., Orlando; ☎ 407/836-8500; www.thehistorycenter.org; $9 adults, $6 kids 3–12, $7 seniors over 59; Mon–Sat 10am–5pm, Sun noon–5pm), which is the current occupant of a handsome 1927 Greek Revival courthouse. Head first to its **fourth floor,** where the timeline starts 12,000 years in the past with the native people who lived here, and work your way down. The museum has a wooden canoe, from around A.D. 1000, that was found in lake muck. The Orlando area was the last American refuge for mastodons and mammoths, too, and you'll see a mammoth tooth and jaw found at the nearby Wekiva River (p. 266). As you advance through time, artifacts keep coming: saddles used by the forgotten Florida cowmen (because of the swampy ground, which made meat chewy, they used long whips and didn't dismount their horses the way Western cowboys did), and an amusing loop of vintage commercials for Florida orange juice, including one by the vilified Anita Bryant. The exhibitions are noticeably conflicted about the growth explosion wrought by the theme parks—most Orlando residents are, too, you'll find—but the museum is careful to note that Orlando has experienced other booms (in the 1920s, its population tripled) and that tourism itself is nothing new, because in the late 1800s, the rivers and lakes were crawling with steamship tourist trade. An interesting sidelight is Courtroom B, a former felony court—*Inherit the Wind* could have been set in this woody, rarified space. Its cork floor muffled the shuffling of lawyers, and in 1987, it tried the first case in America in which DNA evidence obtained a conviction. Curious minds could spend a few hours here.

The next four museums are located within a few minutes' walk of each other in **Loch Haven Park,** an area north of downtown that's been set aside for the arts and culture. You can park once, at the covered lot of **Orlando Science Center** kids (777 E. Princeton St., Orlando; ☎ 407/514-2000; www.osc.org; $17 adults, $16 seniors age 55 and over and students with ID, $12 kids 3–11; parking $5; Sun–Fri 10am–6pm, Sat 10am–9pm). The center is an excellent example of its type, but it's still just a science museum, and if you have one in your city, you should probably fill your scarce vacation time with other attractions. That's not to slam what it has: a spectacular atrium-dominated building; a dome that doubles as a movie theater and a planetarium (add about $10 for that); a NatureWorks area stocked with live baby alligators (there's a daily feeding in the early afternoon); an electron microscope; a beehive that feeds outside through a tube; a not-scary dinosaur zone full of reproduction skeletons and sandboxes where kids can dig for simulated fossils. Exhibits are aimed at children and school groups, at the expense of teens and adults who have seen hands-on exhibits in wave-making and conductivity before. Mass-appeal touring exhibitions (Muppets, *Titanic* artifacts) are usually ticketed above and beyond the usual fee. *Tip:* After 4pm, prices are slashed $5.

Also along the southern bank of Lake Estelle, the **Orlando Museum of Art** ✮✮ (2416 N. Mills Ave., Orlando; ☎ 407/896-4231; www.omart.org; $8 adults, $7 college students and seniors over 64, $5 kids 6–18; Tues–Fri 10am–4pm, Sat–Sun noon–4pm) specializes in American art, and it strives to spotlight other cultures through its temporary shows. Among the standout holdings are an 1820 portrait by Joshua Jackson, a rare early African-American artist; a John Singer Sargent portrait of Francis Brooks Chadwick (his gift to the sitter, a classmate); a blue and yellow pile by frenzied glassblower Dale Chihuly (washed in plenty of natural light); Chuck Close's 1982 portrait of his wife, done in fingerprints; and Robert Rauschenberg's haunting *Florida Psalm,* 1997, a collage paean to the state's fading tourism emblems. There are also 21 works by American impressionist Henry Potthast ringing their own gallery. The pompously named Lakeview Salon is a sunny, relaxing nook where you can unwind on leather furniture. The gift shop is pricey (come to think of it, so is the museum, which only takes about an hour to enjoy), but packed with unusual items. On the first Thursday of each month from 6 to 9pm, the **"First Thursday"** event also includes live music, local artworks, and a cash bar; each one has a new theme and costs $10.

Across the lot, the **Orlando Fire Museum** (814 E. Rollins Ave., Orlando; ☎ 407/898-3138; free admission; Thurs–Sat 9am–2pm) is a minor attraction located in a restored 1926 firehouse. It contains a few work vehicles from the early 1900s and may be worth 15 minutes if you're already at Loch Haven Park.

The last, and quirkiest, selection in the park, close to the Science Center, the city-owned **Mennello Museum of American Art** ✮ (900 E. Princeton St., Orlando; ☎ 407/246-4278; www.mennellomuseum.org; $4 adults, $3 seniors over 59, $1 students, kids 11 and under free; Tues–Sat 10:30am–4:30pm, Sun noon–4:30pm) opened in 1998 as a repository for paintings by Earl Cunningham, a folk artist who depicted life through refreshingly naive eyes. Cunningham, who died in 1977 after a life of obscurity running a curio shop in Saint Augustine, is now considered so important that the Smithsonian devoted an exhibition to him. The museums also hosts frequent traveling exhibitions of fine American folk art.

A fascinating glimpse into Orlando's African-American past, the **Wells' Built Museum** ✮ (511 W. South St., Orlando; ☎ 407/245-7535; www.pastinc.org; $5 adults, $3 kids 15 and under; Mon–Fri 9am–5pm) is housed in a rare surviving building constructed as a hotel for the city's illustrious black visitors on the so-called Chitlin Circuit. In its heyday, it served the South Street Casino next door (the home of the hotel's owner was later moved to its plot), and hosted overnight guests including Thurgood Marshall, Ella Fitzgerald, and Jackie Robinson. The 6,000-foot collection is a hodgepodge of civic artifacts (an original Negro League baseball jersey, aging documents, biographies of forgotten individuals who shaped the city—it's starchy). Imagine Orlando before Interstate 4 cleaved it in two; back then, this neighborhood was germane to the downtown area, but its residents decidedly weren't. Central Florida's African-American heritage has a harrowing story. When Disney elected to build, people were still being lynched here in the deep South, and until as late as 1951 in Orlando, black mothers had to give birth in the boiler room of the hospital. Eatonville, 6 miles north of downtown, was America's first municipality founded by black politicians. There's not much to see there except a one-room museum, so start your exploration of the subject here.

THE DOWNTOWN ARTS DISTRICT

Downtown Orlando supports a thriving art scene, the so-called **Downtown Arts District** (www.dadorlando.com). Countless artists decamp to Florida to pursue their muses year-round, so for those moved by contemporary works, a few hours plumbing the galleries would be time well spent. One hub is the **CityArts Factory** (29 S. Orange Ave., Orlando; ☎ 407/648-7060; www.cityartsfactory.org; free admission; Mon–Sat 11am–7pm), housed in a 1917 theater, which holds a few independent galleries, including K/Q Gallery for contemporary works; the Pound Gallery, inspired by the music industry; Kiene/Quigley Community gallery for local items; and **Kelia Glassworks** (☎ 407/590-3902; www.keilaglassworks.com), where, with reservations, the dreadlocked owner, Charles Kelia, will help you make your own colored tumbler for $65 or learn the basics of the craft for $190. Temporary shows crop up in the loftlike performance space, and the on-site **Roho**

The First Black Superstar

I wish someone would build a museum to the great aviation pioneer Bessie Coleman, the first black licensed pilot in history and probably the first black mega-celebrity. After surviving several crashes, she opened a beauty shop in Orlando to fund her dream of starting an aviation academy (not even the librarians at the history center know where it was anymore). Coleman bought the only plane she could afford, and in 1926, died in Jacksonville in 1926, aged 34, after being thrown from it while rehearsing for an exhibition. It's thought a wrench got jammed in the outdated mechanism of her plane. Lesson: Never buy a budget biplane. Ten thousand mourners attended her Chicago funeral, another few thousand here at Mt. Zion Missionary Baptist Church on Washington Street, and tribute Aero Clubs sprang up nationwide—she was a legend in her own time, but today, people have never heard of her. In 1995, she got her own postage stamp.

Art & Coffee (☎ 407/423-4300; www.rohoartandcoffee.com; Mon–Wed 7am–7pm, Thurs–Fri 7am–3pm, Sat 10am–3pm) carefully cultivates Cuban food (coffees, sandwiches) and culture (artwork). Every month, **Gallery at Avalon Island** (39 S. Magnolia Ave., Orlando; ☎ 407/803-6670; www.galleryatavalonisland.com; Tues–Sat 11am–4pm) showcases a new exhibition, particularly Florida artists, on the weathered wood floors of the city's oldest commercial structure, the gorgeous, green Rogers Building (1886). On the third Thursday of the month from 6 to 9pm, there's a free art reception with music. Spendy contemporary art collectors hunt for perfect pieces at the 30,000-square-foot showroom of **Millenia Fine Art** ★ (555 S. Lake Destiny Dr., Orlando; ☎ 407/304-8100; www.milleniafineart.com; free admission; Mon–Fri 10am–6pm, Sat 10am–2pm), northwest of downtown, but before the world's millionaires have slipped that Dale Chihuly glasswork or Marc Chagall painting into their shopping carts, anyone off the street can come in and admire the goodies. The collection is always changing.

SOUTH OF ORLANDO

Diversions thin out as you go south of the city, although two of Central Florida's most authentic reptile parks are roughly between Disney and the airport.

COLD-BLOODED FUN

Recent fatal alligator attacks in Florida, plus a 2006 fire that gutted its main building and rallied the community behind it, have given new immediacy to **Gatorland** ★★★ kids (14501 S. Orange Blossom Trail, Orlando; ☎ 800/393-5297 or 407/855-5496; www.gatorland.com; $23 adults, $15 kids 3–12, $3 off online; daily 9am–5pm), a local landmark known for its 1962 one-story gator-jaw icon out front. The reassuringly hokey nature park has a much more relaxed pace than that at the major parks.

Back in 1949, Gatorland became Orlando's first mass attraction, featuring Seminole Indians wrestling the animals for tourists. Back then, Florida was crawling with alligators—you could see them basking by the sides of the main roads—but these days, the reptiles have been mostly evicted by development, and so sanctuaries like these are the best places to see them in their ornery glory. Birds love it here, too, since the gators don't eat them. Rather than getting more tired with age, Gatorland has gradually become nicer, as concrete pools have been replaced with natural-looking habitats, a sun-seared layout was molded into a pleasing simulated nature walk, and stuff like a **petting zoo, splash playground, aviary,** and **railway** were added. At regular showtimes, rangers, who are clearly buzzed on their own testosterone, wrassle, tickle, and otherwise pester seething gators, and for a few extra bucks, they'll bring your children into the fray—safely, with a wad of rubber bands around the critters' snouts—for snapshots. These guys would be just as comfortable as Broadway actors as gator handlers; every show is staged to contain a near disaster to titillate and thrill tourists. Most of the fun is trawling the 110-acre plot on walkways as the ornery critters teem and breed in murky waters underfoot and wetland birds (such as noodle-necked white American egrets) prance above it all. **Strategy:** The three main shows repeat during the day, so it's easy to get the highlights in 2 or 3 hours. Cap a visit by watching the gators leap for suspended chunks of chicken during the Jumparoo. Bring

Farewell to a Local Legend?

My great-grandfather was a professional photographer from Atlanta. When I was a boy, some of his favorite Kodachrome slides, shot in the 1950s, depicted a group of coquettish women water-skiing across a lake in a pyramid formation, balancing on each others' shoulders. They waved at the camera. What a decadent place! This was **Cypress Gardens** (6000 Cypress Gardens Blvd., Winter Haven; ☎ 863/324-2111; www.cypressgardens.com), an hour south of Orlando, which opened in 1936 and started the world thinking about Central Florida as the seat of a new kind of tourism. Florida's oldest operating tourist attraction is in peril. A procession of owners failed to devise a successful modern identity. Country music concerts couldn't revive trade, nor could a personality as an "adventure park" with carnival-level rides, including a classic wooden coaster rescued from Panama Beach. On a rainy day in November 2008, Cypress Gardens closed its doors for the second time in 4 years, promising to reopen in 2009 after a reorganization removed those rides and the considerable animal exhibits. If that comes to pass, Cypress Gardens will emerge closer to its original form: a low-key horticultural escape (plantings, big banyan trees, pools) where regular shows of water-skiing daredevils entertain. I hope it returns. It's impossible to overestimate its effect on tourism in Florida—it defined the precepts that family park entertainment must be wholesome, fantastic, and celebrate sun and fun.

a fistful of cash if you'd like to partake of extras such as being able to feed tamer animals such as tropical birds. And save a dollar bill for one of its 1960s-era vending machines, which press a miniature alligator out of injected hot wax right before your eyes—it's just one of the many retro Florida souvenirs you can find here. Orlando may be known for citrus, but here, the product is still grade-A cheese.

Snake milking! What other enticement do you need to pay a visit to the **Reptile World Serpentarium** (5705 E. Irlo Bronson Memorial Hwy./U.S. 192, St. Cloud; ☎ 407/892-6905; $5.75 adults, $3.75 kids 3–6; Tues–Sun 9am–5pm; closed most of Sept), which is more of an unassuming biotoxin supply facility—and venom-collection wonderland—than a zoo. Begun in 1972 to collect poison for medical research and to save the lives of bite victims, its location 20 miles east of Disney tempted its operators into joining the ranks of tourist attractions 4 years later, and daily at noon and 3pm, you can thrill (safely behind glass) as staff grab deadly serpents, plant their yawning fangs over the membrane of a venom-collection glass, and get the creatures spitting mad. There are about 55 snakes on display at any one time, but obviously, this one's about the venom show.

AIRPLANES & DINOSAURS
Fantasy of Flight ✦ (1400 Broadway Blvd., Polk City; ☎ 863/984-3500; www.fantasyofflight.com; $29 adults, $15 kids 6–15; daily 10am–5pm), about 20 miles south of Disney on I-4, is a combination hangar farm/airfield dedicated to restoring obsolete aircraft from the dawn of mechanized flight to the 1950s. It's billed

as the only attraction in the world that offers daily aerial demonstrations. More than 45 relics—many rented frequently for Hollywood shoots and all either restored to or destined for flying condition—are on the premises, and guests are shown how they're mended and what it was like to fly them back in the day. For an extra chunk of change, you can hitch a ride in a barnstorming biplane (one from 1929, one from 1942) or a hot air balloon. This elaborate toy shop is a labor of love—its owner, Kermit Weeks, is independently wealthy thanks to a grandfather's oil strike, and he doesn't have to make a penny from the attraction. He just loves planes, and he even pilots many of the demonstrations. Brochures grant $4 off.

An only-in-America attraction, **Dinosaur World** 🧒 (5145 Harvey Tew Rd., at I-4's exit 17, Plant City; ☎ 813/717-9865; www.dinoworld.net; $13 adults, $11 seniors over 59, $9.75 kids 3–12; daily 9am–5pm) is not someplace to spend hours—one will do—but kids like to wander the jungly plot of land, happening upon more than 100 life-size versions of various dinosaurs, some 80 feet long. A labor of love by a Swedish-born man and his family, it's well kept, even if the foam-and-fiberglass models sometimes look more like aliens than reptiles. It's easy to catch on the drive to Busch Gardens Africa.

WINTER PARK & NORTH ORLANDO

The best museum in the Orlando area is unquestionably the **Charles Hosmer Morse Museum of American Art** ★★★ (445 N. Park Ave., Winter Park; ☎ 407/645-5311; www.morsemuseum.org; $3 adults, $1 students, free for kids 11 and under; Tues–Sat 9:30am–4pm, Sun 1–4pm; free for all Fri 4–8pm Sept–Apr). The cache of works here by genius glassblower Louis Comfort Tiffany, from stained glass to vases to lamps, is so sensational that even New York's Metropolitan Museum of Art comes begging to borrow pieces. In fact, the Morse, a graceful space with demure lighting and 11,000 square feet of space, has the best collection of Tiffany glass on the planet, including an entire room reconstructing the master's tour de force chapel, made for the World's Columbian Exposition in 1893. Once face-to-face with the uncanny luminescence of Tiffany's best work, even those who don't care much about decorative arts can't help but come away dazzled. The museum's founders also collected plenty of other top-quality pieces from the Arts and Crafts movement, including prints, but the focus here is definitely Tiffany. Set aside an hour or so, though it's easy to combine a visit here with a stroll through Winter Park's boutiques, as it sits among them.

Yet another fine arts institution in genteel Winter Park, the **Albin Polasek Museum and Sculpture Gardens** (633 Osceola Ave., Winter Park; ☎ 407/647-6294; www.polasek.org; $5 adults, $4 seniors, $3 students 12 and over; Sept–June Tues–Sat 10am–4pm, Sun 1–4pm), called the Polasek, is the former home of the celebrated Czech sculptor; he lived here for the last 15 years of his life. His work, mostly in bronze or plaster, is accomplished and classically literal, unlike the daring forms of other contemporary Eastern European artists. Polasek liked simplicity, and his house reflects it. A 30-minute stop will do.

ON THE CAMPUS OF ROLLINS COLLEGE

Rollins College, whose graduates include Mister Fred Rogers, has long been the university of choice for parents with social aspirations for their children, and so it

Join the Club

Orlando must be one of the world's capitals for miniature golf courses. Ridiculous ones. A flat, green fairway just won't do. Here, you play under waterfalls, through caves, over motorized ramps, and even into volcanoes that "erupt" if you hit your shot. Putter around with one of these. You'll find discounts for all but Disney's courses in the major coupon booklets.

- **Congo River Adventure Golf** ★★★ (5901 International Dr., Orlando, ☎ 407/248-9181; 6312 International Dr., Orlando, ☎ 407/352-0042; 4777 W. Hwy. 192, Kissimmee, ☎ 407/396-6900; www.congoriver. com; 18 holes $11 adults, $9 kids; Sun–Thurs 10am–11pm, Fri–Sat 10am–midnight). One of the best minigolf options, the challenging courses wind through a man-made mountain speared with airplane wreckage. There are live alligators in the pools.
- **Putting Edge** (5250 International Dr., Orlando; ☎ 407/248-0700; www.puttingedge.com; Mon–Thurs 11am–9pm, Fri 11am–11pm, Sat 10am–11pm, Sun 11am–7:30pm; adults $9.35, kids 7–12 $8.35, kids 5–6 and seniors $4.85). An 18-hole glow-in-the-dark course at Festival Bay of fluorescent balls, holes, and decor. Players get glow bracelets.
- **Pirate's Cove** ★★★ (8501 International Dr., Orlando, ☎ 407/352-7378; 12545 S.R. 535, behind the Crossroads shopping center, Lake Buena Vista, ☎ 407/827-1242; www.piratescove.net; $10 adults, $9 kids 11 and under; daily 9am–11:30pm). Navigate wooden ships and falls of blue-ish water. There are two courses: Captain Kidd's Adventure (par 42) and Blackbeard's Challenge (par 47).

makes sense that its star exhibition hall, the **Cornell Fine Arts Museum** ★ (100 Holt Ave., Winter Park; ☎ 407/646-2526; www.rollins.edu/cfam; $5 adults, free for students; Tues–Fri 10am–4pm, Sat–Sun noon–5pm), would be bequeathed with such a fine collection in such a country-club setting. It's too small to showcase its impressive holdings, so even remarkable pieces (such as Vanessa Bell's portrait of Mary St. John Hutchinson) tend to rotate in and out of storage to make way for changing exhibitions, which spotlight a wide range of arresting works, from Rembrandt etchings to Bauhaus paintings. Displays are light on explanations. For example, there's a glass case full of "watch keys," which were once used to wind pocket watches—they aren't individually marked; they're just presented as something pretty. Peaceful, quiet, and usually empty, with a serene backyard gazebo overlooking Winter Park's Lake Virginia, a visit puts one into a contemplative mood. During the academic year, the museum puts on frequent screenings and talks on subjects such as transcendentalism, clown metaphors in French modernism, and the history of the Florida Everglades.

- **Tiki Island Volcano Golf** ✦ (7460 International Dr., Orlando; ☎ 407/248-8180; www.tikiislandvolcanogolf.com; $9.95 adults, $8.95 kids; daily 10am–11:30pm). The 19th hole, a four-story volcano, "erupts" if you hit a hole in one, plus you have waterfalls, caves, life-size dinosaurs, and brontosaurus paddleboats. The two 18-hole courses are so-so, but the grounds look good at night.
- **Disney's Winter Summerland** ✦✦ (outside of Blizzard Beach, Walt Disney World; ☎ 407/939-7529; $12 adults, $10 kids; daily 10am–11pm; 50% discount on the second round). Two cute 18-hole courses themed around Christmas. The Winter side, piled with fake "snow," has more bells and whistles (love that steaming campfire and that squirting snowman). Combine it with Blizzard Beach without moving your car. It's superior to the other Disney course, **Fantasia Gardens** (priced the same), themed to *Fantasia*. Its Fairways has challenging shots; Gardens is sillier. Find it by the Westin Swan hotel.
- **Hawaiian Rumble Adventure Golf** (13529 S. Apopka Vineland Rd., Lake Buena Vista, ☎ 407/239-8300, daily 9am–11pm; 8969 International Dr., Orlando, ☎ 407/351-7733, daily 9am–midnight; both locations 18 holes $10, 36 holes $12). A tropical course threaded with streams and waterfalls that could use upkeep.
- **Bonanza Mini Golf** (7761 W. U.S. 192, Kissimmee; ☎ 407/396-7536; 18 holes $10, 36 holes $12; daily 9am–midnight). Sparsely decorated using an Old West theme (the three-story waterfall adds a lot), it spans two courses; the Gold Nugget is far too easy.

A visit to the Cornell is an ideal time to take a quick 20-minute walking tour of the campus of Rollins College. Built in a Spanish-Italianate idiom more typical of Southern California than of Central Florida, the campus has a lovely lakeside setting of red-tile roofs and swaying Spanish moss. The so-called **Rollins Walk of Fame** (Mills Lawn, www.rollins.edu/walk) is a collection of 526 stones arranged around a green where students like to play touch football and sunbathe. Each tablet is inscribed with the name of a famous person (Louisa May Alcott, Abraham Lincoln, Rameses II of Thebes), and within it is set a rock, brick, or other item purported to come from the luminary's home, tomb, or local church. The effort began in 1929 and seems to have petered out in the last generation, as so many markers are overgrown or eroded that it's tough to make many of them out. I find it the height of selfishness that someone had the ego to chisel a rock from Martin Luther King's house or Dante's tomb just to install it at a minor Floridian liberal arts college, especially considering the project is now as ignored as a cemetery—someone has already stolen Maya Angelou's rock, and Jack London's cannonball has cracked his tablet in two. The decay is depressing.

Towering Dubious Achievements

Why is it that when people the world over want to attract tourists, they build tall things? Central Florida presents these out-of-the-way relics:

Citrus Tower (141 N. Hwy. 27, Clermont, ½ mile north of S.R. 50; ☎ 352/394-4061; www.citrustower.com; $4 adults, $2 kids 3–11; Mon–Sat 9am–5pm). In 1956, when Florida seemed destined to be a powerhouse orange supplier, investors took 5 million pounds of concrete and built this 22-story, 226-foot-tall observation tower over all those groovy groves. Now it's a perch for surveying Spanish-tiled homes priced at $300,000—about what it cost to build this column. Still, some 12,000 ascend each year.

Monument of States (corner of Monument Ave. and Johnston St., Kissimmee). In 1943, the town eccentric wrote to all the state governors and asked them to mail a rock or stone. For the next 22 years, he took his booty, which grew to include bones, teeth, and stuff from 20 foreign countries, embedded it in concrete, and assembled the blocks into a squat tower in a public park. Like the Rollins College's Walk of Fame (see above), it's fallen into macabre disrepair.

Bok Tower (Historic Bok Sanctuary; p. 240). By comparison, this neo-Gothic edifice, a National Historic Landmark, is graceful and elegant, and it signifies what its designer intended—peace.

Florida was once at the edge of civilization and its residents felt compelled to link themselves to the outside world. Now that the world comes to Orlando, the impulse has faded. The 377-seat **Annie Russell Theatre** (1000 Holt Ave., Winter Park; ☎ 407/646-2145; www.rollins.edu/theatre), from 1931, was named for a British acting superstar who created the title role in George Bernard Shaw's *Major Barbara*. She retired to Winter Park and taught at Rollins. The theater is in the Spanish Mediterranean style and is enshrined on the National Register of Historic Places.

BIRDS CONSERVATION

In Maitland, just north of Winter Park, **the Audubon Center for Birds of Prey** ★ (1101 Audubon Way, Maitland; ☎ 407/644-0190; www.audubonofflorida.org; $5 adults, $4 kids 3–12; Tues–Sun 10am–4pm), founded in 1979, rehabilitates more owls, eagles, falcons, hawks, and kites than anywhere else east of the Mississippi. Some 650 birds a year check in for help. The ones who can't be returned to their natural habitats live here, among the walkways and aviaries. Because its mandate is to help animals, not to titillate sticky-fingered tourists, it's a quiet place to visit, but handlers are eager to share their passion for helping these majestic birds.

EAST OF ORLANDO: THE KENNEDY SPACE CENTER

In the late 1960s, Central Florida was the most exciting place on Earth. It had nothing to do with a cartoon mouse—it was because of the moon. As a culture, we're so used to the regularity of space shuttle and rocket launches that they barely seem real. Perhaps that's why the **Kennedy Space Center** ★★★ 🄺🄸🄳🅂 (Rte. 405, east of Titusville; ☎ 321/449-4444; www.kennedyspacecenter.com; $38 adults, $28 kids; daily 9am–5:30pm, Astronaut Hall of Fame until 6:30pm, last bus tour departs 2:15pm), which was established in 1958 and ruled the tourist circuit with Disney in the 1970s, has unfairly been eclipsed by newer attractions. But let me tell you that a visit here is awe inspiring, and even people who arrived on Earth after the moon walks had happened (like me) find the scientific and technological bravura stirring, to say the least.

Start near opening time. A few miles before reaching the actual visitor center, you'll pass the **United States Astronaut Hall of Fame.** Because they see it first, people make it their first stop, but you're going to be getting plenty of similar information on your tour, so only stop here on the way out if you're still yearning for spacemen. Instead, proceed to the Visitor Center proper. There, many are waylaid by the retired rockets, IMAX films, and simulators, but again, that's not the best stuff. You should board the can't-miss **bus tour,** which leaves every 15 minutes until about 2:15pm and takes most people around 4 hours—be warned that the last buses don't leave you enough time to browse. Coaches, which are narrated by both video segments and a live person, zip you around NASA's tightly secured compound. Combined with the nature reserve around it, the area (which guides tell visitors is a fifth the size of Rhode Island) is huge but you'll be making three stops not too far away—still, hope for good weather, since you'll be

---

Be There for Liftoff

Because launches are so often postponed, it would be dangerous to plan a trip to Orlando just to catch one, but then again, if there's a launch when you're in town, it would be a shame to miss it. Kennedy Space Center maintains an updated schedule online at **www.kennedyspacecenter.com**. The general public is not permitted to flood NASA turf during the actual events, but Titusville, a town at the eastern end of S.R. 50, is a good place to get a clear, free view, as you'll be across the wide Indian River from the pad. **Gator Tours** (☎ 800/537-0917; about $100 adults, $80 kids) usually sells Gray Line trips combining transportation from Orlando hotels and seating at the Kennedy Space Center Visitor Center, the closest site available to the public (6 miles from the pad; you can hear the countdown on speakers). The Visitor Center also sometimes sells tickets from $38 adults, $28 kids (☎ 321/449-4400). Even if you can't leave Orlando for a launch, you can still easily see the fire of the rockets ascend the eastern sky from anywhere in town. Night launches are even more spectacular.

in and out of doors. Each stop allows you to disembark, explore, and then catch the next bus. The system can be slow, but it at least lets you linger where you want to. From the first stop, the **LC-39 Observation Gantry,** you'll have a view, across a few miles, of the two launch sites used by the shuttle and by the Apollo moon shots, and you'll receive an intelligent explanation of the preparation that goes into each shuttle launch. Ever wonder why you see a lot of sparks by the shuttle engines during launch, or why water appears to be pouring out the bottom? You'll find out why. (If you'd like to get much closer to the launch pads, you have to pay another $22 adult/$16 kids for the Up Close tour; but that's only for die-hards.)

Back on the bus, you'll buzz by eagles' nests, alligator-rich canals, and the absolutely titanic **Vehicle Assembly Building,** or VAB, where the shuttle—which NASA folk call "the orbiter"—is readied; it's often possible to spy the gleam of its orange solid rocket boosters through the giant doors (which, by the way, are so large the Statue of Liberty could fit through them). If you're incredibly lucky, you'll be on hand when the shuttle makes its slow, 8-hour trip (on tractors that get 42 ft. to the gal.) from the VAB to the launch pad, where it spends its last month before the final countdown. The second bus stop, the **Apollo/Saturn V Center,** begins with a full-scale mock-up of the "firing room" in the throes of commanding Apollo 8's launch, in all its window-rattling, fire-lit drama. The adjoining museum contains a Saturn V rocket, which is larger than you can imagine (the equivalent of 30 stories), and the chance to touch a small moon rock, which looks like polished metal. The presentation in the **Lunar Theatre,** which recounts the big touchdown, is well produced and even includes a video appearance by the reclusive Neil Armstrong. Finally, the bus whisks you past the executive offices (you'll see the building where Larry Hagman worked on *I Dream of Jeannie*—and in the parking lot, notice that even astrophysicists drive Hondas and pickup trucks) and deposits you at the **International Space Station Center.** There, nothing but plate glass divides you from the dust-free clean room where segments of the space station are prepared to be sent into orbit.

Once you've completed the bus tour, it's up to you whether you want to plumb the sillier, kid-geared business at the Visitor's Complex. By this point, much of it will be redundant, and I find the movies pure malarkey, but take the time to check **Launch Status Center,** where current missions are tracked in real time (if there's not a mission on, skip it); the 42-foot-high black granite slab of the **Astronaut Memorial,** commemorating those lost; **Early Space Exploration,** where you'll see the impossibly low-tech Mission Control for the Mercury missions (they used rotary telephones!), plus some authentic spacesuits from the Gemini, Mercury, and Apollo series. The newest addition is the $60-million **Shuttle Launch Experience,** in which 44-person motion-simulator pods mimic a 5-minute launch. For an extra fee, you can try truly professional equipment on the **Astronaut Training Experience (ATX),** described on p. 253.

Because the government commandeers the surrounding land as a buffer, there is nowhere else to eat within a 15-minute drive. The center points out that it uses no public funding for its tourist amenities, but I still think charging $15 for two hot dogs and two drinks is gouging. As the stewards of a precious preserve that belongs to all Americans, Kennedy Space Center should provide refreshment at an earthbound price. Good hospitality isn't rocket science, you know.

Christmas Greetings

Christmas, Florida, on S.R. 50 between Orlando and Titusville, usually isn't much to write home about: Farm supplies, roadkill. Unless, of course, it's the holiday season, when people come from far and wide to give their cards a Christmas postmark from the local post office. You'll find the P.O. near Jungle Adventures Nature Park at 23580 E. Colonial Dr./S.R. 50 (☎ 407/568-2841; Mon–Fri 9am–5pm, Sat 9:30am–noon).

MORE GATORS

Seventeen miles east of Orlando, the 10-acre roadside zoo **Jungle Adventures Nature Park** ★ kids (26205 S.R. 50, Christmas; ☎ 877/424-2867 or 407/568-2885; www.jungleadventures.com; $20 adults, $11 kids 3–11, $17 seniors over 59) is the closest challenger to Gatorland (p. 235). It's even fronted by Swampy, a 200-foot roadside alligator (it was once a house!), the way Gatorland has its famous gator-jaw doorway. Jungle Adventures, which started life more interested in gator wrestling and morphed into an educational park, is a little wilder than Gatorland, but it only takes an hour or two to do, making it a decent stop on the nontoll route to the Kennedy Space Center. Feed black bears through a chute, gawk at the 15-foot-long gator Goliath, take a pontoon ride on the duckweed-clogged "Green Gator River" (a canal containing some 200 alligators), and watch rare Florida panthers from the boardwalk that snakes through the complex. There's also a replica Native American village that amalgamates the lifestyles of the old Timicuan and Calusa tribes, but that part tends to bore kids rigid. Feedings and demonstrations are scheduled throughout the day so that they don't overlap. Souvenirs made of alligator skin, de rigueur in these parts, are on sale.

PORT CANAVERAL

This isn't a book about cruising—for that, you can try *Frommer's Cruises & Ports of Call*—so there's not much point in going in depth about the cruise lines that depart from Port Canaveral, located about an hour east of Orlando.

But for those who didn't know about the option, you should check them out. Almost all of the cruise lines provide bus transportation from Orlando International Airport and back, or even to Orlando hotels, so it's easy to combine a cruise of a few days with a few days at the theme parks. One company, Disney Cruise Line, is active in selling vacation packages that arrange just such a week.

Most cruise passengers will be dumped by their buses at their ships, and that's just as well, because there is nothing to do at the port.

Two casino boats, free to board, also use Port Canaveral as a base for their brief interludes in international waters; see "Boat Tours" in chapter 9 for information on those. Both offer free shuttles to and from Orlando if you've got reservations.

The following major cruise lines go from Port Canaveral, although the ships they send from the port vary depending on the time of year. Prices are per person based on two people sharing a cabin. Food and most entertainment are included:

◆ **Carnival Cruise Lines** (☎ 888/227-64825; www.carnival.com). Considered a low-rent line, it's noisy and twitters with neon and lurid colors like the inside of a pinball machine. It considers Las Vegas an artistic inspiration—yes, there's a casino aboard. Each ship's main pool has a twisting water slide that has also become a line signature. Carnival sails the *Sensation* on 3- and 4-night Bahamas runs under $200, and 7-night western Caribbean cruises on the *Glory*, which is among the line's largest class of ships, from $300. Carnival is popular with families, teens especially like it, and there are few pretensions.

◆ **Disney Cruise Line** (☎ 800/511-9444; www.disneycruise.com). These casino-free ships include character appearances, fireworks at sea, and high-quality entertainment (its musical version of *Toy Story* will reportedly be exported to Disneyland). The hallmark is the kids' program, and I love the way the waiters follow you no matter the restaurant you're in (one of them changes from black and white to full color as you dine). In winter, *Disney Magic* and *Disney Wonder*, both with a 2,400-passenger capacity and little difference between them, do 3-night Bahamas cruises from around $700 per person, and 7-night western Caribbean cruises to either St. Maarten or Cozumel from $1,200. In the summer of 2010, one ship will be in Europe, and beginning in 2011, two additional ships will arrive. Disney packages trips with theme park stays, although that combo won't be the best deal for the Walt Disney World portion.

◆ **Royal Caribbean** (☎ 866/562-7625; www.royalcaribbean.com). It's the line for young couples and teens, with enormous ships and active diversions such as ice-skating rinks, sheet-wave machines, and rock-climbing walls. It hits the sweet spot between the gaudy tackiness of Carnival and the intense branding of Disney. *Monarch of the Seas* and *Freedom of the Seas* do 3- and 4-night Bahamas cruises from $140, and 4-night eastern Caribbean runs from $650.

◆ **Norwegian Cruise Line** (☎ 866/234-7350; www.ncl.com). As of the winter of 2010 to 2011, this middle-ground line, noted for its relaxed dining arrangements, will start sailing its *Norwegian Sun* from the port, heading on 7-day Caribbean cruises to St. Maarten or Guatemala and Belize.

As usual, you won't find many discounts from Disney, although MouseSavers.com tells which departures are going cheap. Quotes from specialty agents are often hundreds lower than those the lines themselves offer. Check **Cruise Brothers** (☎ 800/827-7779; www.cruisebrothers.com), **Cruises Only** (☎ 800/278-4737; www.cruisesonly.com), and **Online Vacation Center** (☎ 800/780-9002; www.onlinevacationcenter.com). Don't quit before you consult a terrific site called **Cruise Compete** (www.cruisecompete.com), on which multiple cruise sellers jockey for your business by offering low bids.

8

The Other Orlando

If you think it's all about T-shirts and coasters, you've got another think coming.

ORLANDO'S TOURIST MECCAS ARE MORE THAN JUST AMUSEMENT PARKS. They are astounding feats of civil planning and engineering. Even people with no interest in cartoon characters or roller coasters will find a great deal to admire and appreciate in the Herculean achievement that each and every theme park represents. When Phase One of Walt Disney World's construction (the Magic Kingdom and three hotels) was undertaken, it represented the largest private construction project on Earth. When Epcot Center was created, it too was the world's biggest project at the time. And today, WDW is the largest single-site employer in the world, with some 58,000 "cast members" pitching in to make the resort run—and that doesn't even count outside contractors, whose ranks are growing every year.

This chapter will introduce you to those people, and to a handful of activities that allow you to peek "behind the curtain." You'll discover that this is a real place inhabited by real people who are trained to cast a spell on you. They operate the one-of-a-kind machines and carry out the peculiar customs that make the world's largest family vacation destination tick. When they go home, they return to a real city with its own identity that is distinct from—and often, at odds with—the hedonistic, secondary world that was imposed upon the landscape beginning in 1971. They return to what could be called the "other" Orlando, while you remain in Fantasyland. To understand the accomplishments behind the theme parks you're seeing, to appreciate how they have come to define the pinnacle of American mass culture, and to be more than just another pacified consumer of these seductive parks, you must peel back the curtain to the "magic," and you also have to find out about the people who make the tricks happen.

HOW ORLANDO WORKS

The major theme parks, ever eager to mine a new revenue stream, discreetly offer those in the know the chance to slip behind the scenes, into restricted areas, and even through the gates before opening time. These out-of-the-ordinary opportunities always happen under the watchful eye of knowledgeable guides whose only job is to teach visitors about the secrets behind the show. Ticket prices are always above and beyond the price of regular admission, which is usually also required (I'll let you know when it isn't), but the added expense is rewarded with unbelievable access and the chance to ask your guide anything and everything you can think of about how it's all done. Even if the pace of these tours is often slow to compensate for the least physically able of your group (which will usually not number more than 10), many visitors—me included—will tell you that their time spent on these insiders' tours ranks among the best they've ever had at the parks. I have yet to meet any fans who said one of these tours ruins the "magic" for them—it only deepens their appreciation. Besides, you look awfully cool when you're ushered behind the velvet ropes.

Reservations are required for all theme park tours, and many of them have age requirements (such as an age minimum of 16 years), although when there's no rule, kids 2 and under are usually free. Most guides won't let you take photos when you're in backstage areas, but you may usually make audio recordings, and many tours are shadowed by park photographers who'll later be only too happy to sell you approved images of your visit.

WALT DISNEY WORLD TOURS

Walt Disney was unquestionably a visionary. When he started out, he was mostly interested in the potential of animation as an art form. But as his fame and resources grew, his dreams became infinite, and by the end of his life, he was obsessed with building a city of his own. In fact, he intended to build that city on a chunk of his Central Florida land. His dream of an Experimental Prototype Community of Tomorrow, or Epcot, in which residents, many of them theme park workers, could try out new forms of corporate-sponsored, minimum-impact technology in the course of their daily lives, emerged 16 years after his death as nothing more than another world's fair, and not the city to save us all. But because the Magic Kingdom was originally shaped by his own hand and by his most trusted designers, it incorporated several key innovations.

One is the **utilidor system.** The bulk of the Magic Kingdom that you see appears to be at ground level. But in fact, you'll be walking about 14 feet above the land. The attractions constitute the second and third stories of a nine-acre network of warehouses and corridors—utilidors—built in part to guard against flooding but mostly so that guests wouldn't be jolted from their fantasy. Cast members make deliveries, take breaks, change costumes, and count money in the windowless, cinder-block catacombs on the true ground floor of the Magic Kingdom, which is accessed through secret entrances and unmarked wormholes scattered around the themed lands. Clean-burning electric vehicles zip through the hallways, some of which are wide enough to accommodate trucks, and all of which are color-coded to indicate which land is directly upstairs. If you're lucky enough to score a ticket to the utilidor system—and yes, I'm about to tell you how you can—you'll have gained entry into the most guarded inner spaces of the Disney World empire.

Among the other engineering feats and innovation that make the Kingdom tick:

- Trash is transported at 60mph to a central collection point by Swedish AVAC pneumatic tubes in the ceiling of the utilidors.
- Fire, power, and water systems are all monitored by a common computer, and the robotics, doors, lighting, sounds, and vehicles on the most complicated attractions are handled by a central server called the Digital Animation Control System (DACS), located roughly underneath Cinderella Castle.
- The Seven Seas Lagoon, in front of the Magic Kingdom, was low, dry land. It was filled to create a new body of water.
- Bay Lake, beside Fort Wilderness, was dredged, and the dirt used to raise the Magic Kingdom site by 14 feet. Underneath the lake bed, white, ancient

sand was discovered, cleaned, and deposited to create the Seven Seas Lagoon's beaches.

♦ Energy is reused whenever possible. The generators' waste heat is used to heat water, and hot water runoff is used for heating, cooking, and absorption chilling for air-conditioning. Waste water is reclaimed for plants and lawns, and sludge is dried for fertilizer. Food scraps are composted on-site. The resort produces enough power to keep things running in case of a temporary outage on the municipal grid. This will keep you up tonight: Disney even has the legal right to build its own nuclear power plant, should it care to.

♦ Some 55 miles of canals were dug on resort property to keep the land from growing sodden. Most of these canals were curved to appear natural.

♦ The resort was the first place to install an all-electronic phone system using underground cable—so guests don't see ugly telephone wires. It was the first telephone company in America to use a 911 emergency system.

♦ In addition to running the largest laundry facility in the world and establishing kitchens to supply the whole resort, by 1970, a year before opening, the park already had its own tree farm with more than 800 varieties of 60,000 plants, and that effort has been greatly expanded to grow nourishment for the many creatures at Animal Kingdom. More than 100,000 trees and two million shrubs have been planted here since 1971.

♦ The rubber-tired monorail system, designed by Disney engineers, now contains nearly 15 miles of track. Walt had intended monorails, and vehicles akin to the Tomorrowland Transit Authority ride, to be the main forms of transportation to and through his Epcot. In 1986, the monorail was named a National Historic Mechanical Engineering Landmark by the American Society of Mechanical Engineers.

Sadly, the Walt Disney Co. of later years has shown little interest in advancing these remarkable innovations. Designs returned to trucks and standard energy methods, which Walt desperately wanted to sideline. Epcot has only a small network of utilidors, located under Innoventions and Spaceship Earth in the center section of Future World, and the other Disney parks were built without them at all, often permitting trash collection and restocking to occur in full guest view. The monorail has not been expanded since 1982, forcing a renewed reliance on buses and cars. The Magic Kingdom, largely because of Walt's lingering influence, is a rare gasp of Utopian idealism put into practice.

Disney is still justifiably proud of many of its accomplishments, though, and it recognizes that for some guests, the sheer size of its operation itself qualifies as a tourist attraction. Cast members eagerly swap trivia about how Imagineers have cleverly manipulated forced perspective and hidden authentic touches to building facades and public spaces. And an entire subculture has grown up around spotting and recording so-called "Hidden Mickeys," which are camouflaged appearances of Mickey Mouse's profile that can appear in carpet designs, on wallpaper, created out of props on rides, and in other unexpected places.

So even if the company's engineers now pay scant attention to developing "Walt's dream"—that Talmudic totem that the company's marketing department invokes to sell DVDs—it will, fortunately, grant a backstage gander at the resort's ingenuity through its **Walt Disney World tours** (☎ 407/939-8687). AAA often discounts some of these tours for its members. There's tons of walking in each.

Resortwide Tours

Backstage Magic ✫✫✫ ($219, including lunch, minimum age 16; Mon–Fri; 7 hr.), the primo prize of Disney explorations, is one of the few tours to require no theme park admission, because you spend all your time exploring the parks' considerable infrastructure. Nearly every minute is fascinating—you start at Epcot, where you go backstage to see the cast building (75 racks of costumes, lots of forbidding signs threatening termination if employees don't do the right thing in the right place) and the mechanized miracle of the American Adventure stage; then, by motorcoach, the 40-odd group goes to Hollywood Studios to have lunch and to see the wardrobe design and sewing shops that the Backlot Tour trams merely pass by (this time, you're on the inside, watching the tram); then it's on to the service area northeast of Epcot where merchandising is handled. At the Magic Kingdom, you thrillingly dip into the utilidor, which for fans is alone worth the tour price. Behind the park, you'll see Central Shops, a 280,000 square-foot facility where ride vehicles are power washed, tweaked, greased, and painted in the blocks-long, 30-foot-tall Assembly Alley, and nearby in the Animation Shop, the famous Audio-Animatronic figures are repaired. When I was there last, skinless elephants from the Jungle Cruise had just arrived for touch-ups.

A good tour is dependent on how snappy your guide is—you have no control over that. They are trained to spout patronizing narration that's at distinct odds with the complexity of what you see (before the florist's workshop: "Imagine you're a flower. What kind of magic am I going to create?"). You also receive a commemorative pin made just for the tour. For fans of theme parks and their design there is no more comprehensive splurge in Orlando, or perhaps anywhere.

Lunch with a Disney Imagineer ✫ (☎ 407/939-3463; $61 adults, $35 kids 3–9; 11:30am Mon, Wed, and Fri) is just what it sounds like: A chance to break bread, over a catered lunch, with one of the folks charged with putting the parks together. Considering Disney's cloistered corporate culture, this gives plebians like us rare access, and a chance to circumvent the company's usually scripted public presentations. Some of them started in writing, some in construction, some in entertainment, and some in engineering—you never know who you'll get, and your experience depends entirely on how polished your Imagineer's raconteur skills are, as well as how forthcoming they're willing to be about Disney secrets and future plans. Have questions ready to get the most out of the meal. Often, your Imagineer will be just as interested in grilling you about your impressions of their handiwork. The lunch is held in a private room at Hollywood Studios' Brown Derby restaurant, and you get a souvenir plate.

Yuletide Fantasy ($79 per person, minimum age 16; Dec. only; 3½ hr.) is the most shallow of the multipark splurges. Much of it is filler: You spend time admiring admittedly lavish Christmas decorations and hearing about holiday traditions. The climax is a stop at the 68,000-square-foot Christmas warehouse, which can also be seen year-round on Backstage Magic. One gift to you, in addition to the special pin: Theme park admission isn't required.

Magic Kingdom

The least expensive way to peek at the utilidors, **Keys to the Kingdom** ✫✫✫ ($65 per person, including lunch; minimum age 16; daily; 4½ hr.) provides a good overview of the Disney design philosophies that will satisfy both newbies and hard-core fans. It includes a long explication of Main Street, the hub, the Castle, and a pass through Frontierland and Adventureland, where the group kills a little time riding one or two rides together, after which your guide (my last one earned his ears in the 1980s) discusses the technology behind them. The real appeal is the brief time spent in forbidden backstage areas: the parade float storage sheds behind Splash Mountain and a quiet cul-de-sac of the utilidors beneath Town Square—the group enters in the Emporium and resurfaces in a parking lot behind eastern Main Street. Lunch is at Liberty Square, and you get a free pin.

Old Walt and his hobby making steam trains are heavily evoked in the **Steam Trains Tour** ★ ($45 per person, minimum age 10; Mon–Tues, Thurs, and Sat; 3 hr.), but once the myth-building is out of the way, train fans will get a trip to the roundhouse, an inspection of one of its four antique engines (which until the 1960s were working machines in the Yucatan) and inside a cab, a spin on one or two trains, and an explanation of procedures. Train fans won't feel shortchanged because Disney's rolling stock is so lovingly maintained. You'll get a free pin.

I consider the next two avoidable because they don't go backstage: On **Mickey's Magical Milestones Tour** ($25 per person, minimum age 10; Mon, Wed, and Fri; 2 hr.), you'll hear a bit about Hidden Mickeys on Main Street; ride the train to Toontown Fair, where everyone draws a picture of Mickey; and then meet Mickey himself. You could do many of those things without paying. You'll get zero dish on **Disney's Family Magic Tour** ($30 per person; daily; 2½ hr.), a bubbly scavenger hunt. In the name of thwarting Captain Hook's evil plans, you'll be skipping and singing (but not riding anything) to a climax attended by Peter Pan. Obviously, it's for little kids. And strange adults.

Epcot

The UnDISCOVERed Future World ★★ ($55 per person, minimum age 16; Mon, Wed, and Fri; 4 hr.) is essentially an overview of Epcot. Depending on your guide and the day, the package includes background on Epcot's original intentions (gently watered down to make the final product seem more like Walt's plan), scant forays into backstage areas (Test Track), maybe a ride (Soarin'), usually a glimpse at one of the VIP rooms laid out for the corporate sponsors of the pavilions, a glowing talk by a temporary cast member from a foreign country, and a walk-through of the cast services building. At the end, you're presented with a special pin and with permission to view that night's IllumiNations spectacle from a VIP area in front of the Italy pavilion (a big reason some people book this one).

Around the World at Epcot ★★★ ($95 per person, minimum age 16 and maximum weight of 250 pounds; daily; 2 hr.) proved to be one of my favorite experiences in years of Disney going. The tour starts in the early morning, before the park opens. For the first hour, guests are taught how to use Segway people movers in a special training facility at Innoventions. That was a treat enough. Once you've got the hang of the vehicles—it's a lot like skiing, and even people with two left feet get the knack within 15 minutes—your two guides lead you outside in single file and you spend the next hour coasting and threading through the international pavilions of the World Showcase, which you'll have all to yourself. Here and there, they'll fill you in about little-noticed details or design triumphs. I slalomed through the columns of the Doge's Palace in Venice, scooted across eyebrow bridges of Japanese gardens, and rode through a biergarten in Germany—all in the warm

Florida morning breeze. You can also do a 2-hour Segway tour of the bucolic trails around Fort Wilderness ($85), but Epcot's more fun.

Because it runs repeatedly, **Behind the Seeds at Epcot** ($16 adults, $10 kids 3–9; daily; 45 min.) is one of the few tours that can be booked on the fly, and one of the only ones that rings with the original altruistic intentions for Epcot. You learn about the research conducted at the Land's experimental greenhouses, insects lab, and fish farm, and guests are filled in on the park's joint efforts with botanists (many from the University of Florida's Horticultural Sciences Dept.) to advance growing technologies. Your guide is likely to be a college student who is studying the very concepts being imparted—how much you learn depends entirely on their mood, so butter 'em up—and little children are usually given ladybugs to release, seeds to plant, or crops to taste. You can book at the desk beside the entrance to Soarin'.

Bring your open-water scuba certification and your swimsuit, and you'll be qualified to swim with the fishes at **Epcot DiveQuest** ($175, including diving gear; minimum age 10; daily; 3 hr.), held in the massive saltwater tank at the Seas with Nemo & Friends—the range of life is unparalleled in the wild. You'll learn a little about the aquarium's upkeep, but the true attraction here is the chance to dive in it for 30 minutes and to wave at your fellow tourists from the business side of the glass. That's a good time, but whether it's $150 worth of a good time is up for debate. **Seas Aqua Tour** ($140, including equipment, T-shirt, and photo; minimum age 8; daily; 2½ hr.) is the alternative for people without scuba certification. If you can snorkel, you can do this—you're equipped with an air tank and with flotation devices that keep you on the surface, where you spend a half-hour swimming face-down above the fake coral in the 5.7 million-gallon aquarium. You wrap up, ironically, with a shower. That's a lot of money for 30 minutes of tank time, but if snorkeling in the wild makes you nervous, or if you've never done it, you might consider the luxury of a safe setting worth it. No theme park admission is required for either, and both come with a free T-shirt.

Perhaps a better name for **Dolphins in Depth** ($175, including T-shirt and photo; minimum age 13; Mon–Fri; 3 hr.) would be Dolphins, Shallowly. The water's only knee-deep, and after preparation and education about Epcot's dolphin rescue program, the interaction lasts only about 20 minutes. The climax: You tentatively hug one of the mammals as your free souvenir photo is snapped. No theme park admission is required. For better dolphin value, try SeaWorld.

Disney's Animal Kingdom

Wild By Design ($60 per person, including a light breakfast; minimum age 14; Thurs–Fri; 3 hr.) is a less rewarding version of Keys of the Kingdom for Animal Kingdom; you learn about how the park was researched and designed, but you spend most of your time in public areas. You'll also learn a bit about how the animal habitats were designed. Here's a shocker: The lions are enticed to maintain their position on their proud viewing rocks using hidden air-conditioning.

Backstage Safari ✭ ($70 per person, minimum age 16; Mon, Wed–Fri; 3 hr.) dwells more on animal care than on the made-up storytelling of the park. It escorts you through the animal-care facilities, including the veterinary hospital. The itinerary may change according to which animals are in social moods and which ones are in the clinic, but white rhinos and elephants are often on the menu. Wear close-toed shoes. The climax is a turn on the Kilimanjaro Safari ride, only with a special narration that gives away the design secrets that keeps animals and humans on their respective sides. Average folks may not care about watching cast members cut up fruit for monkeys. Expect a lot of info about how diets are prepared. Mickey would be sick if he knew which animal the snakes eat.

UNIVERSAL ORLANDO

Universal hasn't established tours that come anywhere near the quality and depth of Disney's. If you want to pry your way into backstage secrets, you pretty much have to spring for the overly expensive **V.I.P. Tour Experience** (☎ 407/363-8295; daily, by arrangement; lasts all day, though you can choose to end it early), on which groups of about 10 guests are assigned a guide who escorts them past the rabble and onto all the rides they want. This method all but guarantees that you'll ride the best stuff (although the shows are skipped), but it isn't cheap: $120 for an adult to see one park ($150 for both), including valet parking, but *not* admission. It does squeak you behind the scenes, briefly, at the awesome Spider-Man ride, where you'll see the control room and the shop in which the Scoop vehicles are repaired—you'll be amazed at how little the cars actually move. Unless you take it upon yourself to interrogate your guide about all the backstage information that your brain can fit, the price won't be right.

SEAWORLD ORLANDO

As a place that prides itself on sharing conservation information—in fact, as a place that keeps animals on display, its reputation depends on it—**SeaWorld** (☎ 800/327-2424, www.seaworldorlando.com) has tours less about touting its vaunted design team, as Disney's are, and more for learning about animals. In fact, they're dubbed "interactions." Because interactions frequently sell out, always reserve—it can be done online—but if you don't, there's a Behind-the-Scenes desk at the entry plaza of the park for last-minute arrangements. Interactions involving swimming include a wetsuit and equipment, and end with a private, hot shower.

Sleeping with the Fishes

Overnight **Sleepovers** (☎ 800/406-2244; www.swbg-adventurecamps.com) at SeaWorld for kids and their parents take place in some of the more interesting pavilions, such as at the Penguin Encounter or in the chilled Wild Arctic habitat with walruses and beluga whales. Families literally lay their sleeping bags (the park doesn't advertise the fact, but it has a limited number for you to borrow—ask for one when you book) beside the windows of the animal habitats. The nights (6pm–9am) come with educational activities, a pizza dinner, and breakfast, and cost $78 per person. For $113, you can include admission to the park in the morning. Registration is imperative. The park also does 6-day summer Adventure Camps for grades 5 and up, should that fit into your schedule and budget.

SeaWorld and Busch Gardens Africa sometimes host talks included in the price of admission. The parks' Terrific Tuesdays seminars for seniors have been slowing down lately, so ask if they're still happening. Also, splitting his time with Busch Gardens, animal expert **Jack Hanna** makes announced appearances every few months; as he does when he's on David Letterman, he trots out animal after exotic animal in his affable way that proves he's not as clueless as he appears.

Educational Tours ($16 adults, $12 kids 3–9; 1 hr.), being short and comparatively inexpensive, are excellent compromises for families that don't want a huge financial or time commitment, but still crave a deeper education. There are four, offered daily: The **Polar Expedition Tour** ✯ dips into the work areas at Wild Arctic, and you're given the chance to touch a live penguin from the habitats, a rarity at any park. You won't pet a polar bear because that would be the last thing you ever did. The **Predators** tour centers on the 600,000-gallon Shark Encounter (the same one caged tourists swim in on Sharks Deep Dive, discussed below), where you don't swim but you touch a shark and learn about their care; you'll also head across the park to see the backstage areas of Shamu Stadium. The **Saving a Species Tour** highlights rare animals in distress, as you visit the veterinary facilities for sea turtles and manatees and hand-feed exotic birds in the park's aviary.

The **Dolphin Spotlight** ✯✯ ($40) is an affordable alternative to Discovery Cove that gives you a capsule education of the bottlenose dolphin and how they are trained and bred. You'll be able to pet the finely muscled mammals—they feel as rubbery as they look. These animals truly have their own personalities, and even 30 minutes is enough to begin to discern them and to begin to fall in love with them. Your time will fly by.

Beluga Interaction Program ✯✯✯ ($179 per person, including souvenir book; minimum age 10; 90 min.) is one of the park's most extravagant choices. Even though it's expensive, opportunities to squeeze into a wet suit and swim for 30 minutes in 55°F saltwater with the beautiful white beluga whales simply don't come often. Participants don't have to be excellent swimmers, but they should be able to tread water, as they'll be maneuvering themselves in a deep tank to stroke and feed the gentle animals. Only about a half-hour is spent in the water; the rest of your visit, you'll become a pocket expert on belugas.

The *ne plus ultra* for a SeaWorld or animal fan is the **Marine Mammal Keeper Experience** ✯✯ ($399, including lunch, T-shirt, book, and a 7-day pass to SeaWorld; minimum age 13; 9 hr.), which starts at 6:30am and leads you through a typical day for an animal keeper. The schedule includes food preparation (get ready for fishy fingers); helping the Animal Rescue and Rehabilitation Team look after manatees; standing over the vets' shoulders as they heal sick animals; and helping trainers interact with and train dolphins, manatees, and beluga whales. This is no put-on for shuffling bus tours; you will have to lift at least 15 pounds of food at one point, and there's a limit of just three people a day. Yes, it's very expensive, but it also gets you unlimited entry to the park for a week. Many people who have done this swear that it's money better spent than a ticket to Discovery Cove; you'll get in the water to care for dolphins and manatees, but you won't grab onto their fins for any gimmicky "swims" with them.

The novelty of **Sharks Deep Dive** ✯✯ ($150 including T-shirt and a booklet on sharks; minimum age 10; 2 hr.) isn't just that you'll be in a tank with some 30 specimens of five varieties of the predators. It's also the newfangled helmet, which enables you to breathe without scuba tanks and even pose questions to an ichthyologist who observes from above the surface. Guests are lowered, two at a time, into a metal cage and pulled slowly across the 125-foot-long habitat while the locals stalk the bars curiously. Meanwhile, your loved ones and park guests watch anxiously from the plastic tunnel that bisects the tank's bottom. You aren't in any danger because sharks are regularly fed and you can swim to the water's surface within the cage at any time, but it makes for a bracing and unique experience. When I did it, I didn't find it at all scary or difficult—I was even able to wear my eyeglasses inside the helmet without so much as a drop of water splashing them. The time allotted underwater is generous, and because the aquarium is also stocked with other types of fish, there's plenty to look at, including the diners in the fancy restaurant through the acrylic walls on the other side of the tank. When you're done, you'll never confuse these fellas with Flipper again.

KENNEDY SPACE CENTER

Every day, the Kennedy Space Center hosts an appearance by a real astronaut, many of whom have retired to the same area where they once worked. Now and then, you'll even see headliners such as Jim Lovell, Story Musgrave, and Wally Schirra making the rounds. Typically, these guys (and a very few women) love basking in fandom and in reliving old tales of glory—and unlike out-to-pasture sportsmen, these old-timers really did risk their lives the way heroes are supposed to—so these half-hour **Astronaut Encounter** ✪✪ (☎ 321/449-4444; www. kennedyspacecenter.com) sessions, which are scheduled throughout the day, are geared toward questions. You will need a ticket to the Space Center to partake of one, but if the session still isn't one-on-one enough for you, you can pay another $41 for adults or $30 for kids to sit down at 12:15pm daily with that week's astronaut and have a catered lunch, at which you can press him about whatever you like.

NASA reaches for the stars, but Kennedy Space Center reaches for the big spenders with its all-day **Astronaut Training Experience** (☎ 321/449-4400; www.kennedyspacecenter.com; $250, minimum age 14; 7 hr.). It dubs the program ATX, but I like to call it Space Daycamp. You'll get a few up-close guided tours of the big launch pads, lunch, and you'll test a few of the pieces of astronaut equipment, such as the multi-axis trainer (which spins your body within a series of interlinked concentric circles to test your equilibrium), a gravity chair, and a spell in a full-scale mock-up of the shuttle. Nothing is as intense as what astronauts experience, but it's still plenty rigorous for most terrestrials, and the facilitators can answer nearly any question you can launch at them. There's also a two-person, 2-day version that includes an overnight hotel ($625).

BUSCH GARDENS AFRICA

Like SeaWorld, Busch Gardens wants its tours (☎ 888/800-5447; www.busch gardens.com) to teach about animals, and they're designed to give guests a sense of learning and some interaction.

As at SeaWorld, its sister park, Busch Gardens hosts occasional **Terrific Tuesdays Seminars** for seniors aged 50 or older. These educational symposiums by animal trainers and other experts are first-come, first-served. Animal expert **Jack Hanna** makes appearances every few months, announced well in advance.

Recognizing that it's enough of a challenge for most people to just make it down to Tampa for a day, I'll list these activities quickly. They're offered daily (try to reserve ahead, or book upon entry at the Adventure Tour desk in Moroccan Village), and while all require park admission, all of them permit plenty of photos.

A few tours get you onto the Serengeti Plain, the park's heart.

+ **Serengeti Safari** ✿ ($34, minimum age 5; 30 min.) puts you on a flatbed truck for a motor out into the middle of the 65-acre animal enclosure, where the resident giraffes—all docile—amble over to wrap their muscular, gooey tongues around any lettuce leaves you proffer. Then you move on to another part of the plain (passing through a wheel wash along the way, to rinse off the smell of rival animals) to feed whatever other animals you can find—usually antelope. Meanwhile, the luckless tourists stuck on the park train watch you jealously from a distance.

+ **Saving a Species** ($45, minimum age 5; 45 min.) is similar, except the post-giraffe portion swings by white and black rhinos, and an emphasis is placed on conservation efforts.

+ **Sundowner Safari** ✿ ($40, minimum age 21; 1 hr.), just like it sounds, happens around sundown. First, you'll imbibe a few Anheuser-Busch lagers, and then you'll venture onto the plain (hold on tight; the ride's bumpy) with some giraffe grub and a cooler full of Bud. It's essentially a sudsy Serengeti Safari.

+ **Serengeti Night Safari** ✿ ($60, minimum age 21; 2 hr.) is different from other animal tours because you tour after nightfall, when creatures are most active. See hippos out of the water for once, and then drive onto the Plain with a few sets of nifty night-vision glasses. There's a short break by a gas-fed campfire for some silly storytelling, more safari, and you finish with coffee and dessert.

Other tours bring you into other park areas. The **Heart of Jungala Tour** ($34; 30 min.) shows off the tigers and orangutans of the new Jungala area and briefly takes you behind the scenes with their keepers. The **Family Friendly Safari** ($34; 45 min.), geared to those with kids 6 and under, is a simplified introduction of animal-rearing concepts held at Nairobi Field Station, which affords the chance to cuddle or touch at least one of the current residents. **Animal Adventure Tour** ✿ ($119; minimum age 5; 2 hr.) combines a short guided walking tour through backstage areas at Nairobi Field Station and the Clydesdale Hamlet with a truck tour across the Serengeti, led by a keeper, for a giraffe feeding.

HOW ORLANDO PLAYS

Sure, lots of locals have season tickets to the parks, but lots more wouldn't set foot in them for fun. Would *you* hang out at work on the weekends? In addition to the usual diversions, the area boasts a few unique pursuits you rarely find elsewhere.

SPRING TRAINING

Baseball is inextricable from Florida's calendar. Way back in 1923, the Cincinnati Reds began spring training in Orlando at Tinker Field. Ever since then, other professional baseball teams have seen the appeal of limbering up in the Florida sunshine before facing the blistering scrutiny of their fans during the season. In the

1930s, the Washington Senators arrived in town, and they stayed for the better part of half a century, finally as the Minnesota Twins (who have decamped to Fort Myers). A few teams in the so-called Grapefruit League (the Arizona trainers are the Cactus League) still call Orlando or its environs their temporary home, and in the preseason you can swing by to watch them practice and to play exhibition games with visiting teams. Unlike at season games, players often mingle with fans—in fact, some teams' facilities were built to cozy proportions (you can leave the binoculars at home), with permanent interaction areas where you can collect autographs of the athletes before or after practice. Sometimes it feels like the spirit of old-time baseball, the one supplanted by high-priced players and colossal arenas, lives on mostly in Little League and at spring training.

Tickets go on sale in early January. Pitchers and catchers report first, in mid-February, and by the end of the month, the whole team's on hand. They play exhibition games with other teams through March before heading to their home parks in early April.

A few more teams (the New York Yankees, the Tampa Bay Devil Rays, the Pittsburgh Pirates, and the Philadelphia Phillies) train around Tampa, and another (the Washington Nationals) near Melbourne, but the 90-minute drive time is beyond the desires of most tourists. In 2009, the Cleveland Indians departed Winter Haven for Arizona after 16 years. For more information, check out **Spring Training Online** (www.springtrainingmagazine.com).

◆ **Atlanta Braves** (Disney's Wide World of Sports, 700 S. Victory Lane, Lake Buena Vista; ☎ 407/939-4263; tickets $15–$23). Since they took up residence in 1997 at Walt Disney World, the Braves can brag about having one of the nicest and largest (9,500 seats) training stadiums under the sun. Tickets for the 18-odd games, which are cheapest ($15) for the bleachers and the lawn, go on sale in early January through Ticketmaster (☎ 407/839-3900; www.ticketmaster.com).

◆ **Houston Astros** ✮✮ (Osceloa County Stadium, 1000 Bill Beck Rd., Kissimmee; ☎ 321/697-3200; tickets $15–$18). The smallest training park in the Grapefruit League (5,200 seats—still hardly tiny) has hosted the Astros since 1985, who make themselves available for fan greetings in their Autograph Alley. Tickets are sold through Ticketmaster (☎ 407/839-3900; www.ticketmaster.com).

◆ **Detroit Tigers** ✮ (Joker Merchant Stadium, Al Kaline Dr., 2301 Lake Hills Rd., Lakeland; ☎ 863/682-5300; tickets $7–$16). Lakeland, between Orlando and Tampa on I-4, has hosted the Tigers since 1934, and the team is such a local institution that their so-called "Tiger Town" training complex, built on the site of a World War II flight academy, has grown up with them.

DRIVE-IN MOVIES

Central Florida is one of the last places on the Eastern seaboard where land values—at least those outside of Orlando proper—are still low enough to allow for that great mid-20th-century American tradition, the drive-in movie. The three most accessible cinemas each have capacity for about 300 cars and are all about an hour's drive from the tourist zone, but they're worth the trip, especially on one of those gloriously warm evenings for which Florida is justifiably famous. Catch them now, while you can, because yesteryear is receding quickly.

Note: Showtimes change according to when the sun sets.

The two-screen **Silver Moon** ✯✯ (4100 Rt. 92 W., Lakeland; ☎ 863/682-0849; www.silvermoondrivein.com; $4 adults, $1 kids 4–9; cash only), **31 miles** southwest of Disney off of I-4, shows first-run films and double features every night. Sound comes over both speakers and FM radio. Considering its opening-night ticket price was 35¢, prices haven't gone up very much since 1948. It even screens those old-fashioned animated enticements to visit the snack bar.

Joy Lan Drive-In ✯ (16414 Hwy. 301, north of Dade City; ☎ 352/567-5085; www.joylandrivein.com; Wed–Sun; adults $3.50, kids 4–9 50¢), over a half-century old and run by the same people behind the Silver Moon, is known for being the cheapest drive-in in America: just $3.50 per person for first-run movies, usually two titles a night. It's 46 miles west of Disney.

CAR RACING

Orlando is only a generation removed from its farming roots, and many of its inhabitants still retain their Main Street traditions, such as showing off their wheels in car races on a Saturday night. NASCAR is no small sport in these parts (Daytona 500, anyone?), and folks take their cars seriously. These automotive traditions have evolved into regular competitions, with the amenities of a carnival and an explosive verve that could put any theme park production to shame. For all the family-friendly trappings, it'll boost the fun if you have grease in your veins.

Amateur drag racers convene and compete in "grudge racing" at the quarter-mile racing surface at **Speed World Dragway** (19442 S.R. 50/E. Colonial Dr., Orlando; ☎ 407/568-5522; www.speedworlddragway.com; $10 adults, kids 11 and under free) on most Wednesdays and Fridays from 6 to 10:30pm for the facility's "Street Drags." Whoever can accelerate off the starting line and reach the finish line fastest—without jumping the gun—is the winner. Speed World bills it as "the largest 'street race' in the world," which may be true, and it's certainly the only track of its kind in the area approved by the National Hot Rod Association (did you even know that existed?). Noisy and spirited, the nights are all about boys and the size of their toys. It's about 20 miles east of I-4, in an undeveloped stretch between Orlando and Titusville. Check the events schedule online first.

Nearby, stock car racing fans turn out to watch their favorites do laps at the oval track at **Orlando Speedworld** (19164 S.R. 50/E. Colonial Dr., Bithlo; ☎ 407/568-1367; www.orlandospeedworld.org; adults $10, kids 11 and under free), about 30 minutes east of downtown Orlando. Racers include superlate models, superstocks, and ministocks, and subscribe to FASCAR (Florida Association of Stock Car Auto Racing) rules. Boisterous Crash-A-Rama derbies ($20 adults, kids 11 and under free) are periodically scheduled. The main season runs March to November, but there are exhibition events in the other months.

Highly touristy is the **Richard Petty Driving Experience** (Walt Disney World Speedway, Lake Buena Vista; ☎ 407/939-0130; www.1800bepetty.com; minimum age 16; daily 9am–4pm). Heaven knows how it secured a matchless location in the Magic Kingdom's parking lot, but there it sits, selling ride-alongs in 600

It's Not on the Tourist Maps

The standard tourist literature won't point them out to you, but pop history happened at these places:

- **1418½ Clouser Ave., in the College Park area.** In July 1957, 9 months before the publication of *On the Road,* writer Jack Kerouac moved in with his mother, and he inhabited a 10×10-foot room with just a cot, a desk, and a bare bulb. Here, he wrote *The Dharma Bums,* an exploration of personal spiritual renewal through a connection with nature. By the time he moved out in the spring of 1958, he was a literary superstar. The Kerouac Project (www.kerouacproject.org) now owns the home and invites up-and-coming writers to live rent-free in it for 3-month tenures.

- **1910 Hotel Plaza Blvd., Lake Buena Vista.** The very first building to be completed on Walt Disney World property was this low-slung glass-and-steel creation, considered painfully modern in January 1970. It was the Walt Disney World Preview Center, on what was then Preview Boulevard. Here, pretty young hostesses guided some one million visitors past artists' renderings, models, and films promoting Phase One of the resort that was being constructed. Naturally, the first souvenir shop at Disney World was also on the premises. The current tenant is a nonprofit promoting sports participation.

- **Disney's Contemporary Resort, Walt Disney World.** It was in a ballroom here where, on November 17, 1973, President Richard Nixon gave his infamous "I'm not a crook" speech to a convention of Associated Press editors, throwing gasoline on the fire of Watergate.

- **839 N. Orlando Ave., Winter Park.** In March 1986, the legendary Canadian rock group The Band was in the midst of a disappointing reunion tour. After playing the Cheek to Cheek Lounge at the Villa Nova Restaurant, which stood here, pianist Richard Manuel, 42, returned to his hotel room at the Quality Inn next door and, when his wife briefly left the room, hanged himself in despair. The lounge site is now a CVS drugstore, and the motel is the Winter Park Inn.

- **Hyland Oaks Drive, off Hiawassee Road, in the Pine Hills area.** The backstory is a mystery, but somebody built this replica of Graceland, down to the musical-note front gates, in a northern suburb of town. It also has a guitar-shaped pool; Elvis didn't have one, but Jerry Lee Lewis's is shaped like a piano. There are no tours.

horsepower Winston Cup–style stock cars on a 1-mile track with 10-degree banking. A mere three laps at 150mph start at $116, but if you want to be behind the wheel, packages zoom up to $450 for eight laps. Petty has 24 other locations around America, so don't feel bad if you miss this one.

HOW ORLANDO LIVES

Idealistic in both design and ideals, **Celebration** ★★ (exits 62 and 63 east of Interstate 4; www.celebrationfl.com) must be seen to be believed. Make a rubber-necked drive-through to break up—and embellish upon—your visits to hyper-designed theme parks.

This modern-day "Stepford" was created and guided by the Walt Disney Company as a model community and makes a consumer real estate product out of Americans' collective Donna Reed fantasies. Walt Disney's personal vision for Epcot strove to solve the transportation and industrial problems of modern cities, but when his company finally got around to building its own city, it chose, in a feat of architectural propaganda, to dote superficially on Walt's affection for small-town insularity. Every facet of the town, which accepted its first residents in 1996 and exploits Disney's specially negotiated right to govern anyone who lives on its property, was intentionally crafted to affirm trite notions of what an American small town should be. Like the Magic Kingdom's Main Street, U.S.A., it's based on a nostalgia for something that never really existed in that form. Property was sold on the merits of a bold plan: Everyone would be within walking distance of the town center, schools would be steered by the finest education experts, and homes would be wired with the latest technologies to enable residents to do anything from call up medical records to consult with kids' teachers via videophone. The town was even given a logo, in which a child rides a bike beneath a maternal, mature tree, chased by a skipping lap dog.

The original idea may have been all-American pie in the sky. The reality, though, turned out to be decidedly different. Instead of solving the problems of modern life, Celebration seems intent on ignoring them. Everything is geared to reassuring residents that they are comfortably well off. Working class trappings are quietly excluded; the town center (along Market and Front sts.) contains pricey boutiques, tea shops, and proud civic buildings by award-winning architects, but nary a hardware store, bookstore, gas station, or grocery. Parking, too, is a pain—it helps to know how to parallel park. What results is a backlot-style community of Plasticine-colored homes—each a pastiche of a bygone style, some even with fake dormer windows painted black—scarcely 10 feet apart. The streets are full of stop signs, the garages full of minivans, and the houses full of white people (in the 2000 census, the black population measured one-quarter of 1 percent).

What's more, many of the hyped innovations simply never materialized. The means of the promised in-home technology has never existed, and bickering among the educators caused many parents to yank their kids out of the schools. After the bulk of its money had been made, Disney divested itself of its interest in the major operations, so under its new stewards, some of the hypocrisies may eventually be fixed. Despite participating in a subtext that I consider a marriage between new urbanism and a cult, prospective buyers respond eagerly to the elitism of the endeavor; two-bedroom condos fetch $500,000 to $900,000.

Take a stroll—you'll feel a twinge of disturbance when you notice many of the white picket fences are made of plastic and its emblematic water tower is just an empty prop. Even the town center, which abuts a lake, is resolutely piped with cheerful music and, a week before Thanksgiving, adorned with assiduously non-religious holiday decorations and dusted with foam "snow" by means of inducing

Pavlov-style merriment. For some free fun, pick up a copy of the widely distributed *Celebration News,* the mouthpiece newspaper for admonishments from the local authorities: "Trash needs to be within 4 feet of the alley or curb before 7am . . ." Parking is scarce, and the residents tend to greet gawkers with suspicious curtain shuffling, which is surprising considering they decided to live in an experiment of willful self-creation.

A CITY THAT TRULY "SEES THE FUTURE"?

Equally good for giving you chills, the lesser known planned community of **Cassadaga** ✦✦✦ (exit 114 from I-4; www.cassadaga.org), about 40 miles northeast of Universal off Interstate 4, is an American original. The anachronistic town, a direct holdover from the Victorian craze for Christian-based spiritualism and séances, is untouched by development, and only accredited mediums may live there. Tree-shaded, whitewashed, and more than slightly creepy, Cassadaga is not unlike one of the intricately themed lands at the theme parks—almost calculatedly rustic and quaint, this 57-acre town is ripe for strolls, yet visitors can't usually shake an anxious feeling they're being watched by unseen eyes. A bastion of metaphysicality in a region otherwise devoted to Christian fundamentalism, Cassadaga makes for a goose-pimply day out.

George P. Colby, who is to Cassadaga what Joseph Smith is to Salt Lake City, was reared in the Midwest by Baptist parents, but incessant visions (and poor health) compelled him south, where in 1875, he came across land that, he said, appeared exactly as it had been shown to him by his spirit guide, Seneca. Soon after that, Colby enticed a group of refugees from Lily Dale, New York—a similar town of spiritualists that still exists on the Cassadaga Lakes outside of Buffalo—to join him in the then-rural wilds of Florida, and the winter "camp" of Cassadaga was born. Nowadays, its residents stay here year-round, where they offer a slate of services, laying on of hands, and readings—all popular among followers of such things.

Before setting out, check the town's website for the full list of events and sessions. The **Cassadaga Camp Bookstore** (1112 Stevens St., Cassadaga; ☎ 386/228-2880; Mon–Sat 10am–5pm, Sun 11:30am–5pm) doubles as an occult supply/gift shop and a de facto visitor center, and everything in town is within a block or two, so park the car here and explore. The best way to wring the most out of a visit is to immediately consult the bulletin board in the back of the store to see which mediums are available to take walk-in clients. And if you find, within the first 5 minutes of a reading, that you and your medium are not making a connection—say, if the medium is spouting nonsense—it's considered good form to politely end the reading and find another medium. Because the rent's so cheap (the land is owned by the governing Southern Cassadaga Spiritualist Camp Meeting Association), services go for a fraction of what they cost in the outside world.

There are public "healing" sessions at the primitive wooden **Colby Memorial Temple** at 7pm Wednesdays, and at 7:30pm, the floor opens up to messages from the other side ($5). The first Monday of the month from October to June is Medium's Night, and anyone can grab a 15-minute reading for $20. Be at the bookstore between 5:30 and 7pm to draw a number; the readings kick off at 7pm. Friday evenings at 7:30pm, "healing" services by candlelight are held; other healing services are held daily at 2pm at the **Caesar Forman Healing Temple.** On

Saturdays, the town indulges the influx of sightseers by offering afternoon **walking tours** ($15) of the historic highlights and evening **photography tours** ($25) to see who can snap a photo of a ghost first. Sundays see a bevy of church services, just like anywhere in America (dress accordingly); at 9:30am in the **Andrew Jackson Davis Building** an "Adult Lyceum" is held to teach the basics of spiritualism, and at 12:30pm, there's a "message service" where visitors can receive word from the other side. A few more psychics operate independently from their apartments on the ground floor of the **Harmony Hall,** usually for around $50 an hour.

There's even a old-fashioned inn: the 1928 **Cassadaga Hotel** (355 Cassadaga Rd., Cassadaga; ☎ 386-228-2323; www.cassadagahotel.net; $55 Sun–Thurs, $70 Fri–Sat, including continental breakfast; no guests 20 or under; MC, V), widely said to be haunted. The long veranda is ideal for watching the living and dead alike pass by. Although some locals grumble that the hotel, woody and homey, is privately owned and not controlled by the town's governing association—a distinction that, you may learn, reveals a schism amongst the residents—visitors shouldn't mind. Besides, its Lost in Time Café is one of the only places in town to grab a bite, and rooms (the cheapest ones don't have TVs or phone) are guaranteed to keep you anxiously listening for bump-in-the-night creaks and groans. I asked the owner if I could take some photos of the time-warp lobby. "Sure, you're welcome to," she said, "but most people get a kind of orb or white light instead." I haven't found those, but my shots *did* come out blurry. I'm just saying.

HOW ORLANDO PRAYS

Central Florida seems to have connections that run just as strongly to the Deep South as they do to the world of fantasy. Christianity is huge here, and in the past generation, churches have grown Texas big, and several innovative missionary projects have started life here. Given that almost all of the Christian endeavors are intensely evangelical in nature, strangers are welcomed in a way they might not be at other religious institutions.

Out past the airport, the state-of-the-art exhibition at **WordSpring Discovery Center** ✫✫ (11221 John Wycliffe Blvd., off Moss Park Rd., Orlando; ☎ 407/852-3626; www.wordspringdiscoverycenter.com; $8 adults, $7 seniors over 54, $6 students, $2 off online; Mon–Fri 9am–4pm) will probably not justify the trip for most visitors, but if you're into linguistics or missionaries, it's good stuff. The Wycliffe Bible Translators' WordSpring project, which operates a 200-acre, 285-employee command center here, hones in on world languages that don't yet have a version of the Bible, and its translators toil years to complete new versions. This explanatory museum, which is very well funded (a $50-million anonymous bequest arrived in 2008), takes about 45 minutes and labors to explain *why* its organizers think Bible translation is important, as well as discussing at length the complexity and multitude of the world's smaller languages (which is pretty fascinating for a wordie like me), but it generally leaves unexplored the enormous political, social, and cultural obstacles that make the undertaking such a challenge, which I find odd. Maybe they don't want to make China angrier by spelling out what they're up to. Visitors can listen to samples of an obscure Mexican language that's whistled; translate their name into Aramaic, hieroglyphics, and Klingon (really!); and consult a database of every known world tongue. But to get the most out of a visit, come by at 1pm, when people with field translating experience explain what they do and tell war stories of their travels, or at 10am, when tours of the offices are granted. The exhibition adjoins an excellent gift shop that sells handicrafts from around the world (like $25 Russian nesting dolls or $15 Peruvian soapstone boxes), as well as some of the more unusual Bible editions, such as the *Da Jesus Book* ($15), written for Hawaii's 600,000 Pidgin speakers. (No, I didn't know they existed, either.)

Nearby is the headquarters for Campus Crusade for Christ. There, a 1979 movie, *Jesus,* is dubbed into myriad obscure tongues and screened worldwide as part of a proselytizing effort. By the organization's (highly optimistic) count, the film has now been seen billions of times. **The *Jesus* Film Project Studio Tour** (100 Lake Hard Dr., Orlando; ☎ 888/225-3787; www.jesusfilm.org; free admission) is a how-they-do-it exhibit; guided tours go Monday through Friday at 10:30am, 1:30, and 3pm. Like WordSpring, it's more interested in the altruistic motives for the propaganda effort than explaining the difficulties in accomplishing it—although you can dub a section of the film for yourself to see how that part works.

Newsweek called the **First Baptist Church of Orlando** (3000 S. John Young Pkwy., Orlando; ☎ 407/425-2555; www.firstorlando.com) "a colossal Wal-Mart of spiritual endeavor." Like many modern megachurches, "First Orlando," with an annual operating budget of $14 million, aims to be all things to all worshipers, which means although the Worship Center seats some 5,500 (that's nearly twice Hard Rock Live's capacity) and the congregation has long since lost track of who their fellow members are, so visitors are welcomed with open arms. To a guy like me who grew up attending neighborhood church, this holy stadium is an impersonal brand of worship. The 9am Sunday service contains classic hymns and a choir, while the 10:45am service is dubbed "contemporary," which means pop singers and a band. The clergy favors a strongly conservative agenda (a recent worship service led everyone in a round of "God Bless America").

Northland Church (530 Dog Track Rd., Longwood; ☎ 407/949-4000; www.northlandchurch.net), which functions as a sort of franchise with four locations—remember what I said about Orlando being a seat for new-idea worship?—has found itself at the center of the culture wars. Its senior pastor, Joel Hunter, has been pulling away from hard-line conservatives. In 2006, he was designated president-elect of the Christian Coalition, but when he said that Jesus Christ would want them to help the needy and steer away from politics, he was forced to reject the position. In 2008, this lightning rod of "New Evangelicanism" prayed by conference call with Barack Obama on the night he was elected president. One of its most accessible locations is in Longwood, about 10 minutes' drive north of Orlando (see the address above); there are three Sunday services from 9am to 6pm.

On the ride to Cassadaga, note the incongruous skyscraper alongside Interstate 4, just north of exit 92 in Altamonte Springs. That 18-story, silolike tower with the arcing roofline is the **Majesty Building,** the so-called "Mistake by the Lake" that broke ground back in 2000 and is slowly being constructed—the completion deadline gets pushed back every year—by a Christian TV station that calls itself SuperChannel and aims to complete the $40-million tower debt-free mostly through donations from viewers. You can't tour this architectural anomaly, but it's proof of how active and powerful the Christian community is in Central Florida.

It may also ultimately be a monument to fiscal foolishness; observers calculate SuperChannel would have saved money on taxes if they had just taken out a loan.

HOW ORLANDO HELPS

You will be surprised to learn that of the 27,000 annual wishes granted by the Make-A-Wish Foundation, *half* of them are to visit Central Florida. Make-A-Wish turns to one entity, the nonprofit **Give Kids the World Village** ✪✪✪ (210 S. Bass Rd., Kissimmee; ☎ 800/995-5437 or 407/396-0770; www.gktw.org), to fulfill those dreams for children aged 3 to 18 with life-threatening illness, which it does for 196 families at a time and some 7,000 international families a year. No one is refused, and each family spends an all-expenses-paid week here (including flights, car, food, and tickets) in their own villa with their parents and siblings, eating as much as they want at the resort premises and playing in a compound that looks like a second Magic Kingdom.

The 70-acre, gated operation is mind-blowingly elaborate, down to the 6-foot rabbit, Mayor Clayton, that serves as the mascot and provides nightly tuck-ins. Perkins Restaurants and Boston Market discreetly support the dining pavilion, which looks like a gingerbread house. Friendly's furnishes an Ice Cream Palace where no child is refused a scoop, ever. Christmas is held every Thursday evening, when there's a parade, holiday lighting, an appearance by Santa, and Hasbro donates a toy for everyone. There's a carousel (the only one in the world that a wheelchair can drive right onto and into a big turtle or snail), horseback riding, a small-gauge train route, miniature golf, a party every evening, and on and on.

As you can imagine, an operation like that depends on volunteers—to the tune of 1,200 slots a week. Volunteers don't have to commit to anything longer than a few hours; all they must do is download the Visiting Volunteer form online and send it back about 2 weeks ahead. They should also be at least 12 years old, although exceptions have been made when families volunteer together.

Mornings or evenings are best, because the kids spend their days at the theme parks (something that should fit nicely with your own schedule). The workload is easy. That includes turning person-size cards at the World's Largest Candy Land game, held Sunday nights on a board measuring 14,400 square feet. You could help at Mayor Clayton's surprise birthday party, thrown every Saturday, or at the "dive-in" movies screened weekly. You can spoon hash browns at breakfast (until about 11am), run the carousel or the train, or serve dinner with a smile (from 6–9:30pm)—the opportunities are virtually boundless and the staff is eager to match your talents and wishes with the right post.

Your mission is not to lavish pity or love, but to simply help families escape from their hard times. You'll be a host, not a nurse, and that makes a few hours here much easier on you. What's more, not every child is sick—their brothers and sisters come, too, and many of them are starved for attention after their siblings' often long illnesses. You'll find that the village is quite a joyous place and that the families are, perhaps briefly, liberated from the burden of their lives.

My favorite part of Give Kids the World is the Castle of Miracles, where the rafters are covered with thousands of golden stars. Each star is affixed by a child on the last night of their stay. Years later, their moms and dads sometimes return and ask to see, one last time, the star that their beloved child put there. I honestly cannot think of a worthier thing to do for a few hours on your vacation than to help another family have their own vacation—one that they will cherish forever.

HELPING THE HOMELESS

Orlando has a surging homeless population. The number of people living on the streets is around 8,500, yet there are only 2,000 beds for them. And how has the government dealt with this issue? By tying the hands of social-service groups in the hope that desperate people will become another city's problem. In 2006, the city declared it illegal to feed homeless people downtown without a permit—and that no group would be granted more than two permits a year. (In the "no feeding zone," tossing food to squirrels and pigeons was still fine.) The ACLU took up the fight, and the heartless law was struck down as unconstitutional in late 2008. Clearly, Fantasyland has a dark side, and the people in this city could use your help. The way for you to do that legally is to go through an established local organization. One of the best portals for meeting and interacting with the city's neediest residents is **Hands On Orlando** (www.handsonorlando.com), a website that matches volunteers with the people who need them most. Your commitment can be as short as a few hours, and no special skills are required. "All we need from you is a smile," says one of the three full-time employees who organize the placements. Opportunities, which change monthly, are posted about a month ahead; you can decide which one most suits your passion and, with a click, sign up to join in. Operating since 1999, Hands On has placed some 125,000 volunteers not only at charities such as Greater Orlando Food Bank (where you might sort donations), but also at noble local institutions such as nursing homes where residents need their days brightened, day-care facilities helping preschool kids learn to read and add, group homes for people with disabilities for Sunday dinners, and the home of elderly seniors who are no longer able to keep up with yard work. In nearly every case, you'll be given the opportunity to meet local volunteers and the people they're helping, to talk with them, and to learn the stories of what brought them to this place in their lives.

Each job posts its own age minimum, although for some simpler assignments, such as sorting food or cleaning donated toys, it's as low as 4 or 6 years old—entire families may sign up to participate together (just use the site's "comment" field to list who's coming, and event organizers can tailor the tasks to your group). Two other websites, part of larger national initiatives to pair volunteers with local charities, also cover Orlando, although they tend to offer fewer single-day opportunities: **Volunteer Match** (www.volunteermatch.com) and **Network for Good** (www.networkforgood.org).

9

Outdoor Orlando

See why Florida is synonymous with natural beauty.

PICTURE AN OLD-FASHIONED STEAMSHIP, NOT UNLIKE THE *AFRICAN QUEEN*, puttering along a narrow river of clear spring-fed water beneath a cool canopy of oak trees. Alongside the vessel swim a few docile manatees that nibble contentedly on the river grass. As the steamship breaks through a curtain of Spanish moss, it enters a wide, warm lake teeming with long-necked birds. The passengers sigh.

It's hard to believe, but that's what Central Florida really is. Well, was. When the area was a nascent vacationland, that was the way it was seen—on multiweek journeys threading through the lakes and rivers once called home by native people, and later by the Spanish. Florida, known as a vast swampland and later as a cattle-driving turf, took weeks to reach from the north, and many more weeks to tour. Although it was a harsh land with arid soil and mosquitoes in flocks, cypress and oak grew along the placid lakes and provided welcome shade. Modern-day developers have cleared away pretty much everything but the lakes, ripping out the thick natural vegetation. (And then people wonder why they feel so hot now.)

People come to Orlando not just because it's where Mickey is. They also come for the weather, which is warm for most of the year, and to enjoy its wide, blue skies chased by billowy, white clouds. They come to swim and for sun. But Central Florida's outdoor activities don't stop there. Botanical gardens, welcome holdovers from the state's years as a wealthy enclave, support a wider array of plants than many others in the country. Their direct descendents, golf courses, comprise one of the area's most popular gaming pastimes. Look around, and you'll find examples of the land's primacy—natural springs that Ponce de Leon once toured, swamps where alligators lurk beneath bladderwort and spatterdock, and marshy preserves thronged with migrating birds. And should all of that scenery bore, you can speed by it on bracing boat tours or observe from the above in a balloon or hang glider.

GARDENS

Botanical gardens seem dull on paper, yet once you find yourself within one, inhaling perfume and being warmed by the sun, you're in no hurry to leave.

So it is with the well-funded, city-owned **Harry P. Leu Gardens** ★★ (1920 N. Forest Ave.; ☎ 407/246-2620; www.leugardens.org; $7 adults, $2 kids, free Mon 9am–noon; daily 9am–5pm), a lakeside escape just north of downtown that gives visitors an inkling of why so many Gilded Age Americans wanted to flee to Florida, where the fresh air and gently rustling trees were a tonic to the maladies inflicted by the industrial North. It's not uncommon to find picnicking families and blissful wedding parties wandering the 50 acres, which include Florida's largest formal rose garden (peaking in Apr); a patch planted with nectar-rich blooms favored by migrating butterflies; a large collection of camellias that bloom in late fall; and the lush Tropical Stream garden, crawling with native lizards and opening onto a dock where freshwater turtles swim and ducks bob. The centerpiece is probably the Leu House Museum, a 19th-century farmhouse that was once the manor house for the property—the old family cemetery is past the vegetable garden—where half-hour tours are offered, for free, from 10am to 3:30pm. The gardens host outdoor movie screenings and storytelling sessions for no extra charge; they're announced on its website's special events page.

About an hour south of Disney, the 250-acre **Historic Bok Sanctuary** ✿✿ (1151 Tower Blvd., Lake Wales; ☎ 863/676-1408; www.boksanctuary.org; $10 adults, $3 kids 5–12, half off Sat 8–9am; daily 8am–6pm, last admission at 5pm) was once one of Central Florida's great tourist attractions, but now its elegant gardens—designed by Frederick Law Olmsted, Jr., who worked on the National Mall and the Jefferson Memorial—are merely a pleasing sideline and not often visited, which is too bad. They're genuinely lovely and among the best surviving remnants of early-20th-century philanthropic privilege. The gardens (don't miss the water lilies, big enough to support a child) and their 205-foot, neo-Gothic Singing Tower were commissioned as a thank-you to the American people by a Dutch-born editor, Edward William Bok, the publisher of *The Ladies' Home Journal* and a pioneer in public sex education. Bok was buried at the tower's base in 1930, the year after its completion and dedication by President Calvin Coolidge. The 57-bell carillon on the tower's sixth level sounds concerts at 1 and 3pm daily, and its 1930s Mediterranean-style Pinewood mansion is open for tours. The sanctuary was enshrined in 1993 as a National Historic Landmark, of which Central Florida has nearly no others.

A very minor attraction, the gloomy **A World of Orchids** (2501 Old Lake Wilson Rd., Kissimmee; ☎ 407/396-1887; free admission; Mon–Sat 9:30am–4:30pm) opened in 1970 and, quite frankly, the bloom is gone. It's in a state of neglect and of interest only to those who want to purchase a flower. I thought you should know since you'll be seeing signs for it.

NATURAL SPRINGS

Bet you never knew this: Florida has some 300 springs, and 27 of them discharge more than 60 million gallons of pure water a day. In fact, Florida has more springs than any other American state. With numbers like that, it's pretty easy to conclude that natural springs are more authentically Floridian than pretty much anything else you might see on a vacation.

Anthropologists have found evidence that people have lived at **DeLeon Springs State Recreation Area** ✿✿✿ 🅺🅸🅳🆂 (601 Ponce de Leon Blvd., Deland; ☎ 386/985-4212; www.floridastateparks.org/deleonsprings; $5 per carload; daily 8am–sundown), a onetime resort an hour northeast of Orlando, for longer than you'd guess—in 1990, a 6,000-year-old dugout canoe was uncovered. The Spanish, Seminoles, and prepresidential Zachary Taylor all fought over this land, and Audubon saw his first limpkin here. (Remember *your* first time?) It's pretty much impossible to overstate the importance of the St. Johns River on the development of Florida—everybody used it—and, like the Nile, it's one of the few world rivers to flow north, not south. Today, on this segment of the river, there are 18,000 acres of lakes and marshes to canoe (boats can be rented by the hour), a concrete-lined spring to swim in, and 6 miles of trails to forge as you try to spot black bears, white tail deer, swamp rabbits, and, of course, 'gators. Forty-five–minute **historical boat tours** run hourly from 10am to 1pm (☎ 386/837-5537; $12; kids 3 and under free). It gets cooler: At its general store–style **Old Spanish Sugar Mill** (☎ 386/985-5644; www.planetdeland.com/sugarmill; Mon-Fri 9am–4pm, Fri–Sat and holidays 8am–4pm), beside the springhead, you can make your own all-you-can-eat pancakes on griddles built into every table ($4.50 per person, but they'll cook you other things, too). When I leave Orlando, this is one of the places I dream about returning to again—if it were closer to town, I'd eat here every morning. Niftier still, the designated swimming area, next to the Griddle House, is in a spring-fed boil—30 feet deep in spots—that remains at a constant 72°F, year-round. Bring your swimsuit. To reach it, take I-4 north, exit for Deland, and 6 miles north of Deland on U.S. 17 turn left onto Ponce DeLeon Boulevard for 1 mile.

There are no pancakes, but you'll have a better chance of seeing manatees at the 2,600-acre **Blue Spring State Park** ✦ (2100 W. French Ave., Orange City; ☎ 386/775-3663; www.floridastateparks.org/bluespring; $5 per car; daily 8am–sundown), especially in the morning on a cold day. Another plus—it's slightly closer to Orlando. The creatures venture up the St. Johns River from the Atlantic Ocean to seek out the springs here, which maintain a constant 72°F temperature, even in the depth of winter. So from mid-November through February, all boating, swimming, and snorkeling are suspended while the big guys (more than 75 were counted in October 2008) are in residence. An exception is made daily at 10am and 1pm, when a **2-hour guided boat tour** (☎ 386/917-0724; www.sjrivercruises.com; $18 adults, $20 seniors, $14 kids 3–12) of the St. Johns River is given, and the park also coughs up a few nature trails and canoe rental. Ask to see the forgotten pilings of the old steamship dock. Find the park from exit 114 off I-4; go south on U.S. Rte. 17-92 to Orange City, and then make a right onto West French Avenue (there are signs).

The closest major spring to Orlando (just 20 min. north, off I-4's exit 94), **Wekiwa Springs State Park** ✦✦✦ 🔆 (1800 Wekiwa Circle, Apopka; ☎ 407/884-2008; www.floridastateparks.org/wekiwasprings; $5 per car; daily 8am–sundown) is, despite its encroachment by suburbs and malls, one of the prettiest preserves in the area. When you think of Florida, you don't normally picture rambling rivers, but the 42-mile Wekiva (yes, spelled differently than the park's name and pronounced "Wek-*eye*-va") is federally designated as "Wild and Scenic," meaning it hasn't been dammed or otherwise despoiled by development, despite the fact it's just northwest of Orlando's sprawl near Apopka. The springhead, fed by two sources, flows briskly and thrillingly over rock and sand, and some people come to fish, but most agree that its canoeing is among the most spectacular in the state. Canoe along; hop out and camp or picnic; snorkel a little in clear, 72°F spring-fed waters; and then canoe some more as the subtropical river makes its way to the St. Johns, Florida's longest river. A shuttle van run by a local company will bring you back to your starting point. To arrange this, call the park's sanctioned rental kiosk, **Wekiwa Springs State Park Nature Adventures** (☎ 407/884-4311; http://canoewekiva.com), which also arranges horseback riding (from $30/hr.) on the park's 8 miles of trails, which were constructed for a railway that was never finished. Developers would love to sink their bulldozers' claws into this paradise; in fact, so much water is being siphoned from it that its flow is expected to diminish by 10% by 2025.

You might consider 90 miles a bit far to go from your hotel, but consider the rewards. The endangered Florida manatee frolics in the constant 72°F temperature of the water at Citrus County's **Homosassa Springs Wildlife State Park** ☆ kids (4150 U.S. Hwy. 19, Homosassa; ☎ 352/628-2311; www.hswsp.com; $9 adults, $5 kids 3–12; daily 9am–5:30pm, last admission at 4pm). Unlike many state parks, rangers keep visitors busy with pontoon boat rides past bird life, plus separate presentations about alligators and manatees. The prime amenity is a 168-ton underwater observatory floating inside the spring, where visitors can watch the lumbering manatees through thick windows. Swimming with the creatures is not permitted, as they're destined to be released back into the wild. Manatee talks are presented three times a day, usually falling between 11:30am and 3:30pm. Should you crave a chance to snorkel with the animals, two local outfitters know where to find wild manatees and arrange regular, 2-hour face-to-fin tours executed with environmental sensitivity: **Crystal River Manatee Tour and Dive** (☎ 888/732-2692 or 352/795-1333; www.manateetouranddive.com; about $50 including equipment rental; 50% discount for kids 9 and under) and **the Plantation Dive Shop** (☎ 352/795-5797; www.crystalriverdivers.com; $30, plus $19 optional suit/snorkel rental), both in nearby Crystal River. The creatures hate noise, so diving is better in early morning.

NATURE RESERVES

Central Florida's development explosion only kicked in a generation ago, and some people were smart enough to rope off some of its land from developers. We're just beginning to understand how important the state's central wetlands are to the ecosystems farther south and how septic runoff in Orlando might affect the drinking water downstate.

On the day you visit the Kennedy Space Center (p. 241), set aside time to visit the northern part of NASA's patch: **Merritt Island National Wildlife Refuge** ☆ (☎ 321/861-0667; http://merrittisland.fws.gov; free admission; sunrise–sunset), reached by driving through Titusville. Astonishingly, these 140,000 acres of quiet marsh contain more species of endangered plants and animals than any other nature reserve in the lower 48 states. I wouldn't call it unspoiled—water management authorities have meddled with the flow—but it's certainly one of the best places for birding anywhere in the state, if not the country (310 species wing through). The Visitor Center (Mon–Fri 8am–4:30pm and Sat 9am–5pm), off S. R. 402 and pretty much next to the space shuttle's Florida landing strip, gives updates on animal sightings. NASA's hulking VAB looms in the distance; the roaring shuttle launches can't help but spook the animals, and even kill a few. In 1987, the dusky seaside sparrow, which lived only within a 25-mile radius of this spot, became extinct. The Visitor Center has a stuffed specimen on display. At Haulover Canal, a 10-minute drive north of the center (go east on S.R. 402, then north on S.R. 3, and then turn right immediately after the drawbridge), manatees congregate in spring and fall near a viewing area. Back in 1994, some 300 manatees were counted around the refuge; that was more than half of all the manatees alive on Florida's east coast at the time. The future of the manatees is in question because as nearby power plants close, the creatures will be deprived of a reliable source of warm water in winter. Scientists aren't confident the animals, now somewhat domesticated, will be able to find new reservoirs of warm water quickly enough to survive.

Just east of the marsh, so close that its border is undistinguishable, the 57,000-acre **Canaveral National Seashore** ✪ (☎ 386/428-3384; www.nps.gov/cana; $3 per car; daily 6am–6pm Nov–Mar, daily 6am–8pm Apr–Oct) is the state's longest undeveloped Atlantic beach, with 24 miles used for breeding by sea turtles. There's almost nowhere else in Florida—or even America—where you can see coastline this unspoiled. It's pretty much as Ponce de Leon found it in 1513. In June and July, rangers bring visitors to the breeding grounds after hours on "Turtle Watch" ($14 per person, reservations required). A museum about the ghost town of Eldora, a onetime citrus village that stood here until it was bypassed by better transportation links, is open Friday to Sunday 10am to 4pm. For other activities, including Sunday guided pontoon boat trips through the park's lagoons ($20), consult the park's website. The easiest way to access both Merritt Island and Canaveral is via S. R. 406, which crosses over the Indian River from the northern end of Titusville. S. R. 50/Colonial Drive and S. R. 528/the Bee Line both reach Titusville from Orlando.

Located more or less between Disney and SeaWorld (in fact, it's incredible it hasn't been turned into a golf course yet), the **Tibet–Butler Preserve** (8777 C.R. 535, Orlando; ☎ 407/876-6696; free admission; call for hours), named for adjoining lakes, is about 5 miles north of the Lake Buena Vista hotel area. The 438-acre, county-run spread is combed by 4 miles of well-maintained trails and boardwalks that will give you a good taste of the cypress swamps and palmetto groves that once dominated this area.

To gain permission to continue developing the swampland it owns, Disney was required by law to set aside some of it. Hence the **Disney Wilderness Preserve** (☎ 407/935-0002; www.nature.org; $3 adults, $2 kids 6–17; Mon–Fri 9am–5pm), which is actually run by the Nature Conservancy. The 12,000 marshy acres, once a ranch, constitute part of the headwaters for the Florida Everglades, and they're scarred by barely more than a 3-mile walking trail through scrub and cypress habitats. It's a shame the businesslike hours keep people from enjoying it.

The Green Swamp is the largest wilderness in Central Florida—some 322,000 acres of pine flats, sandhills, and muck—and lucky you, it's right out the back door of Walt Disney World. (So close, in fact, that the rest areas on Interstate 4 just south of Disney post signs warning, "Caution: Venomous snakes in area.") **Lake Louisa State Park** ✪ (7305 U.S. Hwy. 27, Clermont; ☎ 352/394-3969; www. floridastateparks.org/lakelouisa; $4 per carload; daily 8am–sunset), known for its gopher tortoises and a rolling topography that actually affords views, has six lakes for swimming, short nature trails, and permits fishing and (with permission) hunting. Campsites are $21 a night (at Disney's Fort Wilderness, they're $42–$83), and six-person lakefront cabins with two bedrooms and two bathrooms, air-conditioning, and power are $110 a night. (That's no bargain.) The area gives birth to four important rivers and, as a vital natural reserve, has not been built upon since pioneer days. In fact, during a drought a few years ago,

Florida's Real Natives

- **Manatees:** From the surface, they look like 1-ton potatoes. Sweet and docile, the biggest enemy this marine mammal has is the propeller of a hot-dogger's boat. Experts estimate that only about 2,800 of them are left, and 300 to 425 die each year from boat strikes and red tide infections, so breeding programs are vital.
- **Lizards:** The pigeons of the South. Little kids are fascinated by them, and cats torment them. They can lose a tail and grow it back, but if one dies in your house, it'll stink up the joint and defy discovery.
- **American bald eagles:** Not all of Florida's eagles migrate, so they're here year-round, but the population increases in winter, when the eagles that do migrate show up in "streams," adding to the flock.
- **Alligators:** Poor, misunderstood alligator. We know you'd rather eat small ducks than large people, but sometimes you get hungry and end up in the news. You'll find these reptiles in nearly every body of fresh water, so don't jump into unfamiliar canals. (As if you would.)
- **Florida panthers:** These wily, tan-colored cats weigh up to 130 pounds and feed on deer and hogs. You're not likely to see one, as fewer than 100 remain.
- **Palmetto bugs:** Maddeningly common, these water-loving brown bugs are about 1½ inches long and eat almost anything. They can fly but prefer to scurry, and came from Africa on slave ships. Don't bawl out your hotel if you see one; they're everywhere. Another of its names: American cockroach.

dropping water levels uncovered a World War II plane that went missing during training in 1944. That's remote. Yet it's only about 11 miles west of the Magic Kingdom as the crow flies.

Don't be put off by the fact that **Orlando Wetlands Park** (25155 Wheeler Rd., Christmas; ☎ 407/568-1706; free admission; daily 7am to half-hour before sunset; closed Nov–Feb 1) has only existed in marsh form since the late 1980s (it was farmland before) and it's technically a collection area for reclaimed water, albeit one planted with some two million aquatic plants and 200,000 trees. Nature has quickly reclaimed the 1,650 acres here. Upon arrival, grab a field guide to the birds (including ibis, hawks, vultures, and teal) from a box and walk the 4-mile loop. Or stay in your car and creep through cattails on some 18 miles of roads, conducting your own bird safari. There's more to see in winter, when migration is at its peak. From S. R. 50 in Christmas (about 40 min. east of downtown), head north on C. R. 420, and the turnoff will be a little over 2 miles away.

BOAT TOURS

The real Florida Everglades don't begin in earnest until south of Lake Okeechobee, which is why you'll always hear Central Florida referred to as the *headwaters* of the Florida Everglades. Orlando-area swamps are still home to a wide diversity of life forms, though, a fact several companies vie to show you.

One of those long-running tourist attractions that just won't die, and would diminish the city if it ever did, the Winter Park **Scenic Boat Tour** ✪✪✪ (312 E. Morse Blvd., Winter Park; ☎ 407/644-4056; www.scenicboattours.com; $10 adults, $5 kids 2–11; hourly departures 10am–4pm daily; no credit cards) has been showing visitors the glorious lakeside mansions since 1938, when they were in their heyday of attracting wealthy snowbirds from the North. Three of Winter Park's seven cypress-lined lakes, which are connected by thrillingly narrow, hand-dug canals, are explored in a 1-hour, 12-mile tour narrated by salty old fellas (quipped one about Rollins College students, "Everything is average about those kids except their parents' income") who are usually retired and gigging for extra cash. The lakes, which were crystal clear before fertilizer use mucked them up, are flat and relaxing, with plenty of bird life, and learning about the illustrious lives of moneyed Winter Parkers—to say nothing of ogling their ostentatious Gilded Age winter homes, lawns sloping appealingly to the water's edge—is pretty fascinating. Among the high points are the modest condominium where Mamie Eisenhower spent her waning years, a home inhabited by the most decorated fighter pilot of World War II, and 250-year-old live oaks. Your guide will pay particular attention to the works of James Gamble Rogers II, a virtuosic architect responsible for many of the area's finest homes. The boarding dock feels like it's straight out of a mountain lake resort or *On Golden Pond;* there's a gas pump for boat owners, who idle in the water and trade small talk. You'll find it 3 blocks east of the shops on Park Avenue. Bring sunscreen and sunglasses because the pontoons are exposed.

Airboats use powerful, backward-facing propellers that skip a shallow boat through the bogs, and they're a common form of eco-entertainment in Florida, particularly farther south in the Everglades. **Boggy Creek Airboat Rides** ✪ (kids) (2001 E. Southport Rd., Kissimmee; ☎ 407/344-9550; www.bcairboats.com; half-hour tours $25 adults, $19 kids 3–12; 1-hr. 9pm tours $43 adults, $37 kids 3–12; daily 9am–5:30pm) uses these incredibly loud vehicles (ear mufflers are provided) in southeastern Orlando, adjoining the airport. Though much wildlife is spooked by the din made by boat and plane alike, many water snakes and alligators appear too thickheaded to care, so you should see a few on one of the continuously running 30-minute tours—boat skippers will cut the engine and float near the critters. The boats don't operate in the rain. The wildlife spotting is better in South Florida, but this'll do. There's a $1.50 coupon on its website, or a $1 discount in its leaflet, available at the Orlando Visitor Center.

The **Swan Boats at Lake Eola Park** (☎ 407/232-0111; $12 per half-hour) are a beloved city tradition. They're pedal boats that fit two adults and are simple in most respects—except one: They look like enormous swans. Use one to cruise past the Centennial Fountain (1957), the translucent Plexiglas bulb in the water's center. Find the dock in the park at Robinson Street and Rosalind Avenue.

Animals for Free

One little-known freebie at the otherwise luxury-priced **Gaylord Palms** (6000 W. Osceola Pkwy., Kissimmee; ☎ 407/586-0000; www.gaylordhotels. com) resort is its **alligator feedings.** Gatorland, the venerable gator-raising tourist spot, uses the indoor pools at the Palms as nurseries for young alligators. Most of the time, the animals bask lifelessly under heat lamps, but on Tuesdays and Thursdays around 6:30pm (call for exact times), a zookeeper climbs into their enclosure, rouses them, and even entices a few to jump out of the water to grab hunks of raw chicken. Then he'll carry a littler gator into the waiting crowd for photos and petting, while the more timid children scamper for cover. The whole episode is over in about 20 minutes, but even those not staying at the resort can partake, and seeing it makes for a great excuse to explore the Palms' breathtaking atrium. They want $13 to park, but attendants can be talked out of that.

The **Peabody Orlando** (9801 International Dr., Orlando; ☎ 407/352-4000; www.peabodyorlando.com) can't compete for fearsomeness, but at least its **Duck Parade,** modeled after a tradition at its original property in Memphis, TN, won't scare babies. Each morning at 11am, a Sousa march strikes up, a red carpet unrolls, and a gaggle of five ducks, prodded by their own "Duck Master" in uniform, waddles dutifully from a bank of elevators to their own fountain in the lobby. There, they spend the day bathing and quacking. At 5pm sharp, they're corralled back down their runway to a waiting elevator car. The spectacle is pretty ludicrous for a marble-and-brass hotel like the Peabody, which fancies itself a luxury enclave, but now that I think about it, I can't say it's Orlando's weirdest.

One boat, the 308-foot **SunCruz Casino** (610 Glen Cheek Dr., Cape Canaveral; ☎ 800/474-3423 or 321/799-3511; www.suncruzcasino.com; free admission; Mon–Sat 11am–4pm and 7pm–midnight, Fri–Sat 7pm–1am, Sun 11am–4:30pm and 7pm–midnight), floats into international waters for a few hours so that passengers may legally gamble. Cruises are free (ask to double-check) because it's expected you'll gamble, but you can use the trip to just get out of the city, enjoy the Florida coast, and raise a cocktail. This one has relatively low payouts, free drinks for gamblers, and not much organized entertainment. It operates 35 table games (bets from $5) and has more than 640 slot machines that cost as little as a nickel. Passengers must be at least 21 years old, and free shuttle vans will deliver you from Orlando to the dock (about an hour away).

A similar product is offered by **Las Vegas Casino Lines** (☎ 800/777-8586; www.lasvegascasinolines.com; daily 11:30am–3:30pm, Sun–Thurs 7:30–11:30pm, Fri–Sat 7:30am–12:30am, late Fri–Sat 1:30am–4:30am), a 300-foot vessel that's really a yacht with electronic slots, on which you get free booze as long as you're gambling. This one's distinguished by having a keno game and small bands.

GOLF

Though I am not a golf person, and I personally deplore the damage that building courses does to the water table and the land—especially in such an already precarious ecosystem as Central Florida's—I can't deny that golf is a major attraction in the Orlando area. Many people come to town just for that, and some of the brightest names in golfing, including Tiger Woods, Annika Sorenstam, Ernie Els, and Nick Faldo, maintain homes in Orlando. Every self-respecting resort hotel has a course or three, as do the most luxe condo developments, and when conventions and meetings roll into town, big deals go down in between strokes.

And that's a lot of deal making—there are some 170 courses around town. Most give priority to players who stay in their hotels, either through advantageous tee times or by cheaper fees (Walt Disney World, for example, charges $10 more to players staying off property, and hike prices by $20 Jan–May). Fees at Disney span $89 to $145, and the most exclusive grounds can charge as much as $180, but you'll find most of them charge fees that begin around $60. Prices usually sink to about half the day rate for twilight tee times, which start around midafternoon. Club rentals cost $40 to $60. Reservations are all but required, and most courses have a dress code and even an age minimum, so always ask.

Important tip: Golfing is one of the things that the **Orlando Magicard,** provided for free at www.orlandoinfo.com/magicard, can help discount; many of these courses will knock $10 off their rates if you book with one. (Check the Magicard's ever-changing list of participants.)

Orlando has plenty of award-winning courses that will cost you more than $200 to play, but if you're willing to pay that much, then you probably won't be hearing about them for the first time from me. As you would do before renting a home or a hotel room, go online ahead of time to see what the individual courses are like—whether they're hilly, straightaway, or riddled with sand traps. Golf is such big business here that most courses post maps online.

In addition, Orlando is home to the annual PGA Merchandise Show (www.pgamerchandiseshow.com), held in January at the Convention Center, as well as to the studios of the Golf Channel (which doesn't give tours, but wouldn't that be a good idea?).

For those of us who don't know their handicaps, or know all too well, there's always miniature golf. Orlando excels in that, too. See "Join the Club" in chapter 7 for a roundup.

FANCY DESTINATION COURSES

From pedigrees by well-known designers to clubhouses that operate more like spas, these fashionable courses are selling the fantasy of luxury as much as they're selling good golf. They're the theme parks of the fairway set. I touch upon these pricey greens (around $10 a hole) quickly because they have national reputations:

- ✦ **Villas of Grand Cypress** ✦ (☎ 877/330-7377; www.grandcypress.com/golf; 45 holes). Designer: Jack Nicklaus. In 2006, this club was noted Orlando's best golf resort, and the second best in Florida, by the readers of *Condé Nast Traveler,* who know about such things.
- ✦ **Reunion Resort & Club** (☎ 888/418-9611; www.reunionresort.com; 54 holes). Designers: Jack Nicklaus, Arnold Palmer, Tom Watson, and a golf

school overseen by Annika Sorenstam. It's a 10-minute drive south of Disney.

- ◆ **ChampionsGate Golf Resort** (☎ 407/787-4653; www.championsgategolf. com; 36 holes). Designer: Greg Norman. The headquarters of the David Leadbetter Golf Academy (☎ 888/633-5323; www.davidleadbetter.com). This resort is also 10 minutes south of Disney.

- ◆ **Walt Disney World Golf Courses** ★ (☎ 407/938-4653; www.disneyworld golf.com; 99 holes). Courses include the Lake Buena Vista (the cheapest 18 holes, from $125); Palm; Magnolia; and the most exclusive, Osprey Ridge and Eagle Pines. Oak Trail (9 holes; $38) is the better choice for family outings. Greens fees include golf cart use, when available. All courses opened with the resort in 1971.

- ◆ **Arnold Palmer's Bay Hill Club & Lodge** ★★ (☎ 888/422-9445; www.bay hill.com; 18 holes). Designer: Arnold Palmer, who owns it and also oversees the golf school. This guests-only course regularly receives the most accolades from experts. There's a full map of every hole on its website.

- ◆ **The Ritz-Carlton Golf Club Orlando, Grande Lakes** (☎ 407/393-4900; www.grandelakes.com; 18 holes). Designer: Greg Norman. May through September, there's often a family golf package: 1 adult, 1 child, 1 hr. instruction, a caddie, two sleeves of balls, and 9 holes of play for around $199.

- ◆ **Shingle Creek Golf Club** (☎ 866/996-9933 or 407/996-9933; www.shingle creekgolf.com; 18 holes). Designer: David Harman. There's also a school overseen by Brad Brewer. It's near the Convention Center.

- ◆ **Mystic Dunes Golf Club** (☎ 866/311-1234 or 407/787-5678; www.mystic dunesgolf.com; 18 holes). Designer: Gary Koch. Located just south of Disney, it has steadily won *Golf Digest* praise.

MORE AFFORDABLE COURSES

Unlike the aforementioned courses, these don't have big marketing campaigns and they don't always come attached to celebrity names, but they nevertheless are high-quality courses that you can enjoy at more sensible prices.

- ◆ **Celebration Golf Course** ★ (☎ 888/275-2918 or 407/566-4653; www. celebrationgolf.com; 18 holes). In the Disney-built town next door to the Disney-built world, fees are $99 weekdays, $109 weekends for a course (by English master designer Robert Trent Jones, Sr., and son) pocked with water hazards on 17 of its 18 holes.

- ◆ **Orange County National Golf Center and Lodge** ★★ (☎ 888/727-3672 or 407/656-2626; www.ocngolf.com; 45 holes). At this wide-open complex (922 acres, unspoiled by houses), fees span $69 to $155 for 18 holes, depending on time of year and day of the week (Mon–Thurs are cheapest). "Junior players" 16 and younger pay $10 less. Holes have five sets of tees, allowing you to choose a game that ranges between 7,300 yards and a little over 5,000. It's among the developments north of Walt Disney World.

- ◆ **Highlands Reserve Golf Club** ★★★ (☎ 863/420-1724; www.highlands reserve-golf.com; 18 holes). This highly praised public course, with a fair mix of challenges and cakewalks, is a strong value, charging $44 to $68, and its twilight rates kick in as early as noon. Kids age 15 and under pay $20 to

$25. The course is about 10 minutes' drive southwest of Disney. The clubhouse won't pressure you to rent a cart, either, as they will at many area courses—you will be encouraged to walk the gently rolling hills.

◆ **Errol Estate Country Club** ★★ (☎ 407/886-5000; www.errolestatecc.com; 27 holes). Golf for $28 to $38! The course, mostly through quiet Florida forest with several dogleg-shaped runs and a variety of elevations, is worth more. Its Lake Course is long but easy, while its Grove Course is known for being its trickiest because of dense trees and hills. The club, about 20 miles north of Disney in Apopka, often runs four-for-three deals.

◆ **Royal St. Cloud Golf Links** (☎ 877/891-7010 or 407/891-7010; www.stcloudgolfclub.com; 18 holes). Aiming to recall Scotland's great links—there's even a stone bridge that looks like it was built during the days of William Wallace, not in 2001—this modest club, 25 miles east of Disney, charges $34 to $52 for fees and a cart and is prized as one of the region's most underrated. Its fairways are noted for being wide, well groomed, and firm, and planners promise you'll use "every club in the bag."

◆ **Hawk's Landing Golf Club** (☎ 800/567-2623; www.golfhawkslanding.com; 18 holes). Fees are $109 to $135, depending on the season. Located beneath the Orlando World Center Marriott resort on World Center Drive by Disney, it crawls with convention-goers. Water is in play on 15 of the 18 holes, and the par-72 course carries a slope rating of 134.

◆ **Orange Lake Resort & Country Club** ★ (☎ 800/877-6522 or 407/905-1050; www.orangelake.com; 45 holes). Fees from $30 to $100; it's a few easy miles west of Disney on U.S. 192. Arnold Palmer had a hand in its design. Its Legends course is divided between the exposed Links course, which makes winds a complication, and the Pines, distinguished by heavy tree plantings that eat balls for breakfast. Its Reserve course was rebuilt in 2005, when a lighted driving range was also installed.

◆ **North Shore Golf Club** (☎ 407/277-9277; www.golfatnorthshore.com; 18 holes). Fees are $50 to $80, with kids aged 15 or younger paying half that. Its par-72, 6,900-yard course is divided into 9 wetlands-lined holes recalling links-style golf, and another 9 through an ancient oak grove, which the club calls "Carolina" play. The club is east of the airport.

◆ **Hunter's Creek Golf Course** (☎ 407/240-4653; www.golfhunterscreek.com; 18 holes). Former cattle-grazing land was transformed into a wavy course with a good gimmick: 13 lakes were created as water hazards for 13 of the holes. The fairways are long, so prepare to drive hard. It's $54 to $89 with $5 off online; you'll find it near the airport.

◆ **MetroWest Golf Club** ★ (☎ 407/299-1099; www.metrowestgolf.com; 18 holes). This course is the work of Robert Trent Jones, Sr., famous for tight greens protected on both sides by sand traps, trees, or water. Fees range from $75 to $119, depending on day of week and season, and the design features spring-fed lakes and 100-foot elevation changes, which is unusual for a mostly flat state. The course, a recent qualifying site for both the Champions Tour and the U.S. Open, is less than 3 miles north of Universal Orlando.

◆ **Stoneybrook Golf Club** (☎ 407/384-6888; www.stoneybrookgolf.com; 18 holes). Fees are $54 to $69, $14 to $20 cheaper as the day goes on. The par-72 course has four sets of tees for players of all skill levels, with plenty of water strips where a hole can go wrong. It's located east of downtown.

◆ **Timacuan Golf and Country Club** (☎ 407/321-0010; www.golftimacuan. com; 18 holes). It's located 10 miles north of downtown in Lake Mary and fees are $78 to $88. There are five sets of tees, changing this exceptionally well-groomed course from 7,000 to 5,000 yards, and the designers were careful to leave its handsome Old Florida features (undulating fairways, Spanish moss, wetlands) mostly intact. Only 3 holes are riddled with water, which might make it easier for kids.

HORSEBACK RIDING

For a simple saddle-up, **Horse World Riding Stables** (3705 Poinciana Blvd., Kissimmee; ☎ 407/847-4343; www.horseworldstables.com; trail rides $44–$75, reservations suggested; daily 7am to late afternoon), 12 miles south of U.S. 192, offers three types of guided trails through Central Florida pine forests. The so-called Nature Trail Ride (which is really an unpaved access road) is the simplest, taking about 45 minutes and requiring no experience. Riders 6 years or older get their own horse, and kids 5 or younger share a horse with Mom or Dad. The other two trails, the Intermediate and the Advanced, require more difficult types of maneuvers (trotting or cantering), so they have higher age minimums.

WATER-SKIING

Walt Disney World permits water-skiing, parasailing, tubing, and WaveRunning on the Seven Seas Lagoon and Bay Lake only through **Sammy Duvall's Watersports Centre** (☎ 407/939-0754; www.sammyduvall.com; $95 for parasailing, $85 for 30 min. of tubing or water-skiing). Duvall promises parasailers won't even get wet.

There aren't many of us who follow the exploits of professional water-skiing. Those who do will no doubt treasure the museum at the American Water Ski Education Foundation's **Water Ski Hall of Fame and Experience** (1251 Holy Cow Rd., Polk City; ☎ 863/324-2472; www.waterskihalloffame.com; $5 adults, $4 seniors, $3 kids 6–12; Mon–Fri 10am–5pm), at exit 44 of I-4, about 20 miles west of Disney. On view: the first known pair of water skis, made from pine planks in 1922 by 18-year-old Minnesotan Ralph Samuelson (who also merits a bronze bust), plus assorted ropes, handles, and outboard engines.

HOT-AIR BALLOONING & HANG GLIDING

Florida is well suited to hot-air ballooning for many of the same reasons that it's ideal for golf: flat, even topography and often placid morning weather. Several companies take tourists into the sky over the swamps and groves south of the city. A trip involves a very early start—6am at a central location is common, followed by a trip to the launch site selected for the day based on the day's wind patterns. Each balloon basket carries as many as a dozen people. You'll probably be asked to wear closed-toed shoes and to help unfold and inflate the balloon, and after landing, kids tend to get into the physical exertion of squashing the air back out of it and packing it away. Then you're fed breakfast. You'll be finished by the time the theme parks get cranking. Reservations are required, and each outfit has its own age requirements, although generally speaking, if a child can follow instructions, see over the basket's edge, and not freak out, they'll be welcomed.

Orlando Balloon Rides (☎ 407/894-5040; www.orlandoballoonrides.com; $175 adults, $95 kids 10–15, free for 1 kid 9 or under with each paying adult, additional kids $95 each, $10 less online), which recently merged with Blue Water Balloons, has been in business since 1982 and all its balloons are 2007 models. It meets at a hotel on U.S. 192 near the main Disney entrance.

Magic Sunrise Ballooning (12559 S.R. 535, Orlando; ☎ 866/606-7433; www.magicsunriseballooning.com; $185 per person for 2–4 people, no kids 5 or under) tops off its flight with a champagne toast and an all-you-can-eat breakfast.

Should you crave some more adrenaline with your air time, **Wallaby Ranch** (1805 Deen Still Rd., Davenport; ☎ 863/424-0070 or 800/925-5229; www.wallaby.com; tandem flights $120), about 20 minutes' drive southwest of Disney, arranges hang-gliding flights. In flat Central Florida, where there are no mountains that don't contain roller coasters, daredevils can't leap off cliffs to attain flight. Instead, they're launched by ultralight "aerotugs," to an altitude of 2,000 feet. There is a weight maximum of 240 pounds, and DVDs of your flight are $60.

10 Orlando After Dark—and in the Dark

Fireworks you know about, but where are the clubs and shows?

THE NIGHTLIFE QUANDARY: STAY WITH FELLOW TOURISTS, WHERE THE nightspots are lavish but milquetoast, or go out with the locals, who party a 20-minute drive north? See a show on park property, where the entertainment was devised by committee but is well funded, or try something smaller and smarter in town?

The choice used to be simpler. Years ago, the parks weren't in the nightlife business. Orlando's party drags were downtown, along two intersecting downtown thoroughfares: Church Street and Orange Avenue. But in the late 1980s, the titans devised a way to dominate the evening scene, too. Walt Disney World dropped the ropes on Pleasure Island, a playground of nightclubs located in its Downtown Disney area. Universal Orlando countered with CityWalk, which appeals to a somewhat trendier, younger segment of tourists.

For a while there, downtown Orlando staggered from the double blows. Church Street Station, once a nationally famous nightlife district, was abandoned, and the area degenerated into a jungle of quarter-beer joints and strip contests. In time, though, residents grew weary of the canned experiences at Disney and Universal. Pleasure Island shuttered in 2008, although Disney will replace it with other nightlife options (most likely run by outside companies). Today, downtown has reclaimed some of its cachet, albeit mostly in the under-35 demo. It also still offers the best opportunity to mingle with locals.

The best place to find out what's going on is the events listing of *Orlando Weekly* **magazine** (www.orlandoweekly.com), available for free in newspaper boxes all over Orlando proper but not so much in the theme park universe.

We'll start with the nightlife zones that the parks own and run, and then we'll go farther afield, into the "real" world of Orlando.

THE THEME PARKS' DISTRICTS

After a long day trooping through the parks, my wish list for nightlife begins and ends with a hot bath. But if, once the fireworks fizzle, you've still got beans in your pants, you can shake them out near the amusement giants, which keep the diversion going into the wee hours (1 or 2am most nights). These playgrounds rock on every night, regardless of whether the dance floors are desolate. Much like ongoing wedding receptions, their offerings have been concocted by committee to

After Dark with Kids

Although on some nights, one could argue that the people drinking at the clubs and bars are infantile, you still can't bring your kids to hang out in them. Don't worry—Orlando is a family city, so there's lots for kids to do.

Magic Kingdom parade: Most nights, there are one or two parades through the park. When there are two, the second is less crowded.

Fireworks: The Magic Kingdom is open until 9pm or later on most nights. There's usually an evening parade, and the nightly fireworks display, *Wishes,* happens around Cinderella Castle. Hollywood Studios mounts *Fantasmic!,* a pyrotechnics-and-water display, a few times a week, and Epcot is famous for its *IllumiNations* fireworks-and-electronics show over its lagoon. In summer, when they're open past dusk, Universal Studios does something (fireworks or a spectacle on its lagoon) most nights, as does SeaWorld. Check with each park for showtimes, as they change. Given that they're theme park shows, they're all designed to wow kids, but Magic Kingdom's is the classic.

The Electrical Boat Parade: It's a tradition going back nearly 40 years: A string of 14 40-foot-long illuminated barges floats past the Disney resorts on Seven Seas Lagoon and Bay Lake starting at 9pm, accompanied by music. It's lower key than the fireworks shows. See it for free from any resort hotel in the area or, if your timing is good, from the ferry that goes between the Magic Kingdom and the Ticket and Transportation Center.

Special event evenings: From September through March, the Magic Kingdom schedules irregular special-ticket evenings (Mickey's Not-So-Scary Halloween Party, his Very Merry Christmas Party, and the Pirate and Princess events) for kids with free candy, character meetings, dance parties, and extended hours. The calendar of events can be found on p. 307, online at www.disneyworld.com, or you can call Disney at ☎ 407/934-7639.

Dinnertainment: Every night, there are more than a dozen dinner banquets accompanied by a kid-friendly show. See p. 92.

Character meals: Early bedtime? Very young kids will be sent to sleep dreaming if they meet their favorite character over dinner. See p. 96 for a list.

Orlando Repertory Theatre and the Plaza Theatre: These Orlando-area companies present kids' entertainment (p. 285 and 287).

appeal to as wide a spectrum of visitors as possible, and their playlists and decor alike are designed for the masses, not for aesthetic vanity. True hipsters will probably want to give these milquetoast clubs wide berth, but people who don't mind surrendering to forced folderol are bound to have some fun.

DOWNTOWN DISNEY & DISNEY'S BOARDWALK

Pleasure Island bit the stardust in late 2008. Disney is almost certain to replace it with something else that will divert the masses after dark. As of this writing, though, it hasn't said what that will be. Other diversions remain in the area, although none are stellar.

Other Downtown Disney Entertainment

Downtown Disney (p. 300) comprises nearly a pedestrianized mile of event restaurants and shops along a small lake, away from the major theme parks. Its West Side is home to the DisneyQuest virtual playground (p. 174) and *La Nouba,* the Cirque du Soleil show (see below). To the east, the Marketplace's offerings are dominated by Disney-themed shops of every type. Parking is free, if inadequate.

As for the main nightspot at the West Side, I'm going to say what no one else will about Cirque du Soleil's permanent production at Walt Disney World, *La Nouba* ★★ (Downtown Disney West Side; ☎ 407/939-1298; www.cirquedusoleil. com/lanouba; Tues–Sat at 6 and 9pm; 90 min.): It has special appeal with people who've gotten frisky after a few days of squeaky-clean Disney, and with convention-goers who are far from their spouses. Makes sense. All those taut, athletic bodies, wearing little, flexing and writhing across each other with acrobatic virtuosity—it's as close to sex as Disney's gonna get. That said, it's perfectly acceptable for kids, too—I'm not exaggerating when I say it could end up being the most memorable theatrical experience of a young person's life. The arty, hyper, clownish French-Canadian spectacular, a kaleidoscope of stunts and tricks, overloads senses 10 times a week in a 1,600-seat theater that looks like a postmodern version of a big top. Quality is high, and the talent is extraordinary. So are prices: starting at $53 for adults and $43 for kids aged 3 to 9, up to $117 and $94, depending on where you sit, but don't be afraid to accept the cheapest seat available, since no view is a loser. Get there at least a half-hour early or they'll sell your seat to someone else.

One of the principal nightspots on the West Side is an outpost of the **House of Blues** (Downtown Disney West Side; ☎ 407/934-2583; www.hob.com) chain. Its 2,000-person, theater-style venue (standing space only) hosts regular performers along the lines of B. B. King and Norah Jones (with sometime detours to such acts as Cannibal Corpse). Tickets for those shows start around $20. The Front Porch area (open 4pm) usually hosts a local musician, and you can hang out for free. From Thursday to Saturday, after about 10:30pm, the Blues Kitchen takes over, and a second free stage is born, this one with a wide variety of local and national artists. There are also often live Latin bands at **Bongos Cuban Café** (p. 71), but you'll want to get a drink or dinner (the food is so-so) to see them.

Also on the West Side, you'll easily spot the 30-passenger gas-powered balloon that's safely tethered to Earth. At press time, it was still under construction and

Downtown Disney

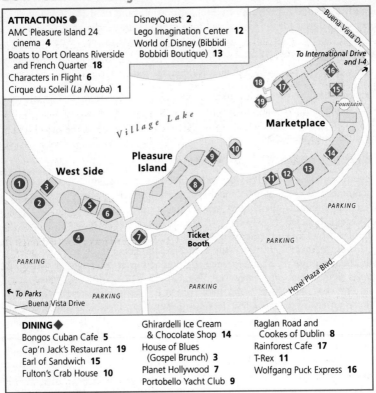

called Characters in Flight. You can bet the fare will be sky high, too. Across the way, there's also **AMC Pleasure Island 24** (☎ 888/262-4386; $10 adults [$8 before 6pm Mon–Thurs and before 4pm Fri–Sun], $7 kids 2–12, $9 seniors, $6 for all before noon Fri–Sun), though I can't imagine having an attention span so short that I'd rather see a movie when Disney World is all around me.

Elsewhere in Walt Disney World

Between the Swan and Dolphin hotels and Epcot, **Disney's BoardWalk** (no admission required) is a lesser entertainment district that is no match for the Downtown Disney area. It can be reached from Epcot's International Gateway side entrance. At the very least, BoardWalk is a scrubbed-down idealization of 1930s Atlantic City that makes for a pleasant backdrop for an evening stroll on the water. Thursday through Saturday evenings, there's a scattering of street entertainers (jugglers and the like), and most visitors grab an ice cream or some candy and stick around for a half-hour or so.

Many a night, I have seen its two clubs thumping along in wretched desolation, although patronage depends greatly on what conventions are staying at the adjoining hotels and if participants are in a party frame of mind. **Atlantic Dance**

Hall (☎ 407/939-2444; minimum age 21; Tues–Sat 9pm to 2am; no cover) is not, alas, a place where they might shoot horses (that concept failed), but a DJ dance club (videos on Tues–Wed and Sat). Its clientele seems to be tipsy trade-show attendees from the Swan and Dolphin hotels, both located next door. Hip it's not, and nostalgic it ain't, which is too bad, because its Art Deco interior holds such promise and its wood floor feels good to dance on. **Jellyrolls** ★ ($10 cover; minimum age 21; daily 7pm–2am), the best option at BoardWalk, is Disney's challenge against the Howl at the Moon Saloon (p. 290): Dueling pianists jam, audiences sing along and try to stump them with requests, and the mood is light. The space usually starts to fill up after 9pm, so arrive earlier for a table. There's no food beyond popcorn and the like.

Another Disney convention hub, Disney's Coronado Springs Resort, recently opened **Rix** (1000 W. Buena Vista Dr., Orlando; ☎ 407/939-3806; www.rix-lounge. com; daily 5pm–2am; AE, DC, DISC, MC, V), a cocktail lounge with an illuminated, amberlike bar, full-wall curtains, and lots of seating nooks. The semisophisticated look gives away the fact it's operated by an outside company. On convention nights, it can turn into quite the scene, and the bar menu isn't great (although the shrimp cocktail served as shots is fun) but it's a welcome break from resort food. Otherwise, the silence verges on death by cosmo glass. I am appalled that any cocktail bar in Florida should serve premixed mojitos by pipe through a tap, as this place does, inexcusably. But Rix is one of the few options.

CITYWALK

CityWalk ★★★ (6000 Universal Blvd., Orlando, exit 75A coming on I-4 from the west, or exit 74B coming from the east; ☎ 407/363-8000; www.citywalkorlando. com; $12 admission to all clubs; daily 11am–2am; parking $12 before 6pm, $3 after 6pm excluding event nights), Universal Orlando's 30-acre nightlife district, takes fewer pains than Disney to present a wholesome face to the public. In fact, there's an upscale tattoo parlor and a cigar bar. Nights here, in the front yard shared by both Universal theme parks, were designed with jellybean colors and rock-concert panache, to be sure, but they attract locals as well as tourists and therefore have a sharper edge. In my opinion, the drinks are stronger, too, but that might be my imagination. The liveliness is bolstered partly by regular concerts at its Hard Rock Live venue.

There is no charge to enter the common area, which is a boon because that allows anyone to tour around before deciding whether they want to pay to enter any clubs. Individual cover charges apply to all the clubs. Buying a $12 **CityWalk Party Pass** from any of the kiosks at the complex grants you unlimited admission to any and all of them on a given night; the clubs usually open after 10pm and are otherwise $7 a pop. Some of them serve food during the day and turn into nightspots late, and others open only in the evening. All Universal park tickets with multiday admission automatically come with one Party Pass. The Party Pass also is available with the addition of a movie ticket at the AMC Universal Cineplex (see later), which is part of the complex. That combo costs $15. Finally, there's a package that buys a prix fixe dinner at eight of CityWalk's restaurants with a ticket to the cineplex for $22. Grab a *Times & Info* guide, which maps the stores and restaurants and lists the current happy hour times and specials.

CityWalk

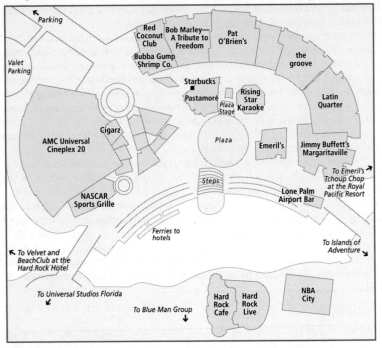

Many clubs, which also serve food, only admit patrons 21 or older because drinking is permitted outdoors anywhere in CityWalk. Every club can be reached via the main CityWalk number, except in the instances noted.

- **Jimmy Buffett's Margaritaville** ✪✪ (☎ 407/224-2155) offers live music nightly in a touristy environment that's first about the cheeseburgers in paradise, secondly about margaritas (there are three bars), and thirdly about island music. You'll get a lot more out of it if you're a Parrothead who knows Buffett's songs, as many of the details are inside jokes pegged to his classic songs. Get there before 10pm, when live bands start inside, to avoid a cover charge of $7. There's often a free singer on the patio at other times. Thursdays grant free admission to locals, so that's a good night to meet Floridians. Kids can come here most nights if their parents are eating.
- **Red Coconut Club** ✪ (☎ 407/224-2425) is Universal's version of an ultralounge, mixing stylish cocktails and one of the more intimate atmospheres at Universal Orlando. Its balcony overlooks the pedestrians thronging CityWalk. Looking down on others is something of a hobby here; it's the district's most upscale venture. Besides a Rat Pack vibe, there are martinis, live music and DJs, and free valet parking from 6 to 8pm with a receipt. It opens at 7pm, and there's a $7 cover after 9pm. Women get in free on Thursdays.
- **Bob Marley—A Tribute to Freedom** (☎ 407/224-3663) often has live music for a $7 cover, but mostly it's an easygoing place to kick back, eat (p. 74),

and listen to recorded reggae. That makes it an antidote to the high-energy clubs around it at CityWalk.

♦ **Pat O'Brien's** ✪✪ (☎ 407/224-3663) is "an authentic reproduction of New Orleans' favorite watering hole," which is cool to see, and its Hurricane rum drinks will make you see it twice. You will see two pianos even if you're sober; its truly talented dueling pianists compete, serenade, and take requests to suit the mood of the crowd. O'Brien's serves good food, but if you can't get a seat (or don't want one), it also sells drinks through a window facing the street. This spot is among the most popular here, and kids can join in.

♦ **CityWalk's Rising Star** (☎ 407/224-2189) is the karaoke joint. Tuesdays through Saturdays, there's a live band, and on Sunday and Monday, music is recorded, but you always get backup singers and a host, and the cover is always $7 (with no charge to sing). Like all karaoke, the more you drink the more ridiculously fun it gets.

♦ **Latin Quarter** (☎ 407/224-3663) is more of a restaurant with music (p. 74). After 9pm, Latin bands play samba, bongos, and other tropical sounds.

♦ **the groove** is sleek and state of the art; this DJ dance club is also middle of the road to appeal to the array of people attending Universal; music skips from the '70s (Tues) to the '80s (Sat) to recent hits. It throws frequent teen-only nights with stringent security. The cover is $7, and it opens at 9pm.

After watching Disney hoard tourists all night, Universal slyly lured the famed **Blue Man Group** ✪✪ (☎ 407/258-3626; www.universalorlando.com; 1hr., 45min.) by building the trio a custom-made theater out the back door of the Hard Rock Cafe. You know their schtick by now, right? Three taciturn, bald, blue guys get into hilarious mischief, play with bizarre homemade toys, and generally make a mess of the theater—get a seat in the first four rows in the so-called "poncho section" (you'll get a plastic cloak) if you think it'd be fun to be splattered with goo. If you've gone to the parks for the day, seeing the Blue Men won't require use of a car or a bus; guests can start drinking cocktails whenever they want and even bring them into the theater, accessible to both CityWalk and Universal Studios (it's practically beneath its new coaster). Shows are $64 to $74 adults and $54 to $64 kids. If you purchase your ticket at the same time as you buy your Universal theme park admission, you can save around $9. Seats in the back and at the extreme side near the front (Tier 2) are $10 less, and you'll save $10 by buying ahead online.

A 3,000-seat, top-of-the-line live-music arena attached to the famous burger joint, **Hard Rock Live** ✪✪ (☎ 407/351-5483; www.hardrock.com/live2) is one of Orlando's primary concert and comedy venues, and it regularly hosts the likes of Keith Urban, Liza Minnelli, Barenaked Ladies, Maroon 5, Jason Mraz, and Simple Plan, which released a live album recorded here—often, concerts are recorded for TV broadcast, too. The second-floor seating is spacious and has commendable sightlines; for some concerts, the first floor is converted to a dance floor or to standing room. You can't miss the theater itself—it's the building that looks like the Roman Coliseum. Check way ahead for what's coming, because ticket availability depends entirely on the popularity of the act.

A 10-minute walk away, at the Hard Rock Hotel, you'll find **Velvet** (☎ 407/503-2000), a laid-back lounge with cushy seating and mood lighting that eschews the clutter of huge CityWalk crowds. The same hotel's **BeachClub** is situated alongside an expansive California-style pool, the largest heated pool in the city, and nonguests can easily pull up a barstool to enjoy the summery atmosphere. The hours there are pegged to the pool area but tend to stretch later in warm weather, so call ahead if you plan to arrive after 10pm or so.

A free 10-minute ferry ride from CityWalk, Universal's lavish **Portofino Bay Hotel** (☎ 407/503-1200) puts on a free nightly show with strolling musicians and opera singers, *Musica della Notte*. It's held, weather permitting, just before sunset on its harbor, so you don't need a room key to enjoy it. There are tables, and waiters will take orders for antipasto and wine by the glass, if you're so inclined.

CityWalk's cinema is the **AMC Universal Cineplex 20** (☎ 407/354-5998; adults $9.50, students $8.50, kids 2–12 $6.50; $5 before noon Fri–Sun).

PROFESSIONAL SPORTS

If you'll be in town during the late winter, check out the section "Spring Training" in chapter 8, "The Other Orlando."

A Florida tradition born, unexpectedly, among the French Basque, jai alai ("hi a-lie") is similar to the New England high school sport of lacrosse, except it's played with Frito-shaped scoops called cestas at a breakneck speed that no varsity coach could condone. Watching the hardened athletes at **Orlando Jai Alai** ★ (6405 S. Hwy. 17-92, at S.R. 436, Fern Park; ☎ 407/339-6221; www.orlandojaialai. com; admission $1; 7pm post time Thurs–Sun Jan–Mar), north of the city, hurl the ball at each other at up to 150mph, knowing that one false move could create a situation beyond the remedy of a mop, is half the fun. The other half is betting (something you can do year-round here), which makes an outing here less family-friendly than it ought to be. Still, delving into the hyper-masculine sport (which took root in Florida, by way of Cuba, as an alternative to horse racing in the 1920s) and watching the terrifying ricochet of the ball in the enclosed court (called a fronton), can make for a gripping night out, if you can slough off its tackier elements. Kids taller than 39 inches are admitted, but one must be at least 18 to wager.

Your one-stop venue for the major league teams should be the indoor **Amway Arena** ★ (☎ 407/849-2001; www.orlandocentroplex.com), which locals call the O-rena or by its previous name, T.D. Waterhouse Centre. Home teams are the **Orlando Magic** (National Basketball Association; www.nba.com/magic; $15 for nosebleed seats behind the basket up to $115 for courtside; Oct–Apr) and the **Orlando Predators** (Arena Football League; ☎ 407/648-4444; www.orlando predators.com; $10 for Upper Bowl end zones, up to $55 for midfield Lower Bowl seats; Mar–June). In 2006, the Predators went all the way to the ArenaBowl in Las Vegas, but were defeated by the Chicago Rush. Major concerts are also held here. Sales are handled by Ticketmaster (☎ 407/839-3900).

THE PERFORMING ARTS

As a place dedicated to showmanship, Orlando fosters a large and diverse talent pool, and when they're not entertaining theme park guests or clowning in dinner shows, some of the city's artists find work at a variety of theater companies and concert halls. Among the celebrities who got their start in Orlando are Wayne Brady, Cheryl Hines, the singers in *NSYNC and the Backstreet Boys, Delta

Burke, and Wesley Snipes. Britney Spears, Justin Timberlake, Ryan Gosling, Keri Russell, and Christina Aguilera began their careers here as Mouseketeers on the early-1990s version of *The Mickey Mouse Show*, which was shot at Disney–MGM Studios. Naturally, with all that talent about, you'll find some excellent performances away from the theme park stages.

THEATER, DANCE & CONCERTS

Orlando, like many American cities, takes its theatrical marching orders from New York City, and although the situation is slowly changing, you're more likely to see a script exported from off Broadway, or an orchestra from another big city, than a true original work by a hometown pen.

There are several things to like about **Mad Cow Theatre Company** ★★★ (105 S. Magnolia Ave., Orlando; ☎ 407/297-8788; www.madcowtheatre.com; tickets $15–$28). The first is that it's ambitious and literate, tackling such tough works as *I Am My Own Wife*, David Mamet's *Glengarry Glen Ross*, and Stephen Sondheim's *Sweeney Todd*. Also attractive is the potential to make a night of it: The downtown space has two comfortably cozy black-box theaters—one with 100 seats and the other with 40 to 60—that are close to the nightclubs for postshow revels. Although it only opened in 1997, its 10-show season, which runs year-round, attracts the city's best talent and is held in high regard by critics. Monday evening shows are the least expensive.

Headquartered at Princeton Street amid the antiques district since the late '80s, **Theatre Downtown** (2113 N. Orange Ave., Orlando; ☎ 407/841-0083; www.theatredowntown.net; tickets $15–$18) produces edgier New York exports such as *Take Me Out* and campy fluff such as *Altar Boyz* and *Little Shop of Horrors*. The thrust stage (one that juts into the audience) is small and so are the budgets, but the company is noted for its big heart.

In the Loch Haven park arts complex north of downtown, **Orlando Shakespeare Theater** ★★ (812 E. Rollins St., Orlando; ☎ 407/447-1700; www.orlandoshakes.org) is one of the city's best-funded and most respected theatrical enterprises, with two major spaces: the 118-seat Goldman, a semi-proscenium space, and the Margeson, a 230-seat thrust stage. While one stage usually has something meaty on (the Bard, of course, or an adaptation of *Crime and Punishment*), another has a children's show up ($10–$12), often only on weekends. The storybook-style posters around the lobby were designed by Sean Simon Ramirez, a former Disney animator who has bestowed a consistently classy look on the company. The complex used to belong to the Orlando Science Center before it built its flashy new HQ next door; the blurry, bouncy acoustics of the dome atop the Patrons' Room, which once served as a planetarium, are fascinating. Most seats are $25 to $38, preview performances cost around $14, students save $5, and the theater schedules regular "senior matinees" that charge older patrons $14. The theater's annual PlayFest series in February mounts 10 days of readings of new works by up-and-coming writers; admission for those are $8.

Across the parking lot, **Orlando Repertory Theatre** ★★ (kids) (1001 E. Princeton St., Orlando; ☎ 407/896-7365; www.orlandorep.com; tickets $11–$17), usually called "The Rep," is the city's preeminent young peoples' theater. Its association with the University of Central Florida's master's program ensures first-rate production values in a modern, two-theater complex, with an intelligent show

Plan-Ahead Performance

These companies don't have year-round schedules, but what they do have is among the best live performance in the state. Check ahead to see what's coming.

Orlando Opera (Bob Carr Performing Arts Centre, Orlando; ☎ 407/426-1700; www.orlandoopera.org; tickets $25–$120) mixes opera standards *(Madama Butterfly)* with popular fare *(The Pirates of Penzance)*, typically in three-performance runs. Although its talent is good, it doesn't land marquee names.

Orlando Ballet (Bob Carr Performing Arts Centre, Orlando; ☎ 407/426-1739; www.orlandoballet.org; tickets $20–$80, $10 kids), the city's only true professional dance company, produces about seven elegant shows a season, running 3 or 4 days each, including the annual *The Nutcracker* (mid-Dec).

Traveling, premium-priced Broadway shows, mostly musicals, tend to put down stakes for 5 nights at a time. Find out what's coming to the Bob Carr Performing Arts Centre through the **Broadway Across America** (☎ 800/448-6322; www.broadwayacrossamerica.com) series. Don't expect a deal.

Orlando Philharmonic Orchestra (812 E. Rollins St., Ste. 300, Orlando; ☎ 407/770-0071; www.orlandophil.org; tickets $16–$60), employing more than 80 musicians, appears in some 125 performances a season. Although its bread and butter is classical music, it also brings in well-known vocalists, and mounts semi-staged musical readings and other lower-brow ticket sellers. Performances are at downtown venues or nearby. Half-price student discounts are available with ID.

---

selection based on adaptations of classic and modern children's literature. Past shows include *Thomas Edison Invents, To Kill a Mockingbird, Tales of a Fourth Grade Nothing, Holes, A Christmas Story,* and the first regional production of Kathie Lee Gifford's musical *Under the Bridge.* The seven-show season runs September to May and includes both afternoon and evening curtains. On occasion, you can use your ticket stub to obtain discounted admission at area museums.

Pinocchio's Marionette Theater ★ 🧒 (Altamonte Mall, Altamonte Springs; ☎ 407/677-8831; www.pinocchios.net; $6.50 adults, $5.50 kids 2–12) may be inside a mall, but its interior is a jewel box of an imitation Italian theater. The expertly executed marionette shows are old-fashioned (mostly retellings of fairy tales), but they're charming. Health problems sidelined the theater's founder and artistic director, David Eaton (a former Bozo the Clown, who worked with legendary stringman Bil Baird), but acolytes are taking up the slack.

The **Festival of Orchestras** (Bob Carr Performing Arts Centre, 401 W. Livingston St., Orlando; ☎ 800/738-8188 or 407/539-0245; www.festivaloforchestras.com) isn't a onetime burp on the calendar but an ongoing program that imports five or more international symphony orchestras a year. It must be expensive to ship in musicians from Brazil, Russia, and the Boston Pops, because the festival won't offer single tickets until it has saturated its base with subscriptions. Even then, prices are high (more than $100 isn't uncommon), though students and active military personnel receive 50% discounts.

Orlando Theatre Project ★ (☎ 407/491-1397; www.otp.cc; $24, $20 students and seniors), or OTP, is an Equity company—meaning its actors are unionized professionals—that takes on, usually quite successfully, challenging modern new plays, including *Proof* and *Souvenir*. Shows are usually performed at the Orlando Repertory Theatre or in Winter Garden for runs of 2 weeks to a month.

The Plaza Theatre (kids) (425 N. Bumby Ave., Orlando; ☎ 407/228-1220; www. theplazatheatre.com; tickets $33–$38), signposted by a Worlds Fair–style marquee tower, opened in 1963 as the city's first two-screen cinema. Now it's a two-theater live performance place with a mandate to serve families. Its slate still attracts area families with mass-appeal, noncontroversial entertainment: well-done small-scale musicals, singing groups, and visiting musical acts and comics. For some shows, students with ID can get $10 discounts.

COMEDY

Orlando's comedy scene has been no laughing matter lately. To wit: the closure of the clubs at Pleasure Island and CityWalk, the shuttering of Orlando Improv on Church Street, and the death of Dottie's Comedy Club (although the jokes had been dying there for years). Besides the big-name shows at Hard Rock Live, that leaves one biggie at the moment, but fortunately, it was always the best choice.

Improv maestro Wayne Brady got his start at **SAK Comedy Lab** ★★ (380 W. Amelia St., Orlando; ☎ 407/648-0001; www.sak.com; Tues–Sat, showtimes vary), and boy, they don't let you forget it. Open since 1991, this 200-seat downtown theater trains improv comics, and you can catch grads in performance on Tuesdays at 9pm for $2; Wednesdays at 9pm for $5; or spring for the elaborate Duel of Fuels improv-off Thursdays, Fridays, and Saturdays at 8pm for $15. Weekend nights often have second shows at 10pm. When comics go blue, a box is put over their heads, and Tootsie Rolls are tossed into the audience to sugar them up. Dave Russell, SAK's artistic director, directed the launch of the Monsters Inc. Laugh Floor (p. 131) for the Magic Kingdom.

DANCE CLUBS, BARS & LIVE MUSIC VENUES

For my taste, Orlando's dance club scene is overpopulated with 20-somethings ordering overpriced bottle service on Daddy's credit card. Deep it ain't, and don't bother looking for trance or community. Downtown, the *strut du jour* is Orange Avenue near Church Street, where lounges, band bars, and dance dens coexist and come on and off the boil at unpredictable intervals. Park the car around there on a weekend night and club-hop, finishing with a giant slice of cake at the Dessert Lady (p. 80). On Wall Street, a few blocks up, frat boy beer bars dominate. Clubs usually open around 8pm, start pumping by 9pm, and start dumping kids back on the street at 2am.

The hot hangouts for theme park workers are always changing. Some workers drink at **Miller's Orlando Ale House** (p. 77). Also near Disney, the much-missed Big Bamboo was a ramshackle, decades-old institution until Hurricane

Screen Gem

The Enzian Theater ★★★ (1300 S. Orlando Ave., Maitland; ☎ 407/629-0054; www.enzian.org; tickets $9 adult, $7 seniors/students), **may be the** only cinema in Florida that actually *feels* like Florida. It would be the envy of any city in America, and I love every visit here. Before the movie, you can kick back and watch the sunset paint the Spanish moss red as you sip a cocktail at the patio bar. It's made of Brazilian walnut, overseen by a mural by animator Bill Plympton inspired by Eden. Should you require a splurge, some of the drinks list comes from the private cellars of the Enzian's founder, the granddaughter of an Austrian princess. The relaxation continues inside at a large single-screen cinema, where a selection of art films and documentaries is shown, plus Hollywood biggies.

Unlike multiplexes, there aren't rows of seats, but four lollipop-colored levels of tables with soft seating. Servers take your order (if you have one—eating's not required) before the movie and once the show is under way, your meal arrives surreptitiously and the cinema is filled with the smells of hot food. We're not talking just popcorn either, although they have that, too; organic mushroom burgers ($10), shaved roast beef sandwiches with fresh-grated horseradish ($14), and 14-inch pizzas (from $12) are served, as are $15 pitchers of interesting organic beers and wines under $20 a bottle. Finish with gooey chocolate-chip cookies ($4) and fresh-made pineapple beignets ($5.50).

The Enzian, just north of Orlando but close, produces six festivals a year, too (including a Jewish festival in Nov and the Florida Film Festival in the spring), and hosts frequent talks; check its website for the schedule. It's located a half-mile north of Lee Road, which has an exit off I-4; on a clear night, it'll take about 20 minutes to drive back to the Disney area.

Charley blew it away in 2004. In late 2008, devotees, including longtime bartender Chaz, resuscitated the scruffy, South Pacific–style boozer. Now "the Boo" is officially reborn as the **Nu Bamboo Lounge** ★★ (4900 W. Irlo Bronson Blvd., Kissimmee; ☎ 407/485-3060; www.nubamboolounge.com; daily 5pm–midnight), cluttered with grass walls and tiki-head goblets and no less professional than its beloved first incarnation—your beer may be served in a Mason jar. Some of the seating was salvaged from old vans, but Disney memorabilia stuck to the walls has carried over. It's friendlier than it looks, and this unkillable dive bar has already started to win back cast members (young and old, gay and straight).

Back when the Backstreet Boys were in high school, you could find them here at **Tabu** ★ (46 N. Orange Ave., Orlando; ☎ 407/648-8363; www.tabunightclub.com; cover $5–$10). It's Orlando's most established dance club, and downtown's largest dance floor, set in the former Beacham Theater, which opened in 1921 and specialized in movies and vaudeville. But despite all the ghosts in its wings, you may miss the boys of O-Town the most. Sniff—Ashley Parker Angel, we hardly knew you! (And if you don't understand any of those references—vaudeville excepted—then perhaps this isn't the place for you.)

A sunken dance floor and video screens usually mark nightspots for banishment from the inner circle. Yet downtown's **Independent Bar** (70 N. Orange Ave., Orlando; ☎ 407/839-0457; www.independentbar.net; cover $5 or less), going since the '80s (and playing plenty from that era), remains popular because its dance-crazed denizens are already retro-minded: Goth, indie, hipsters, and New Wave disciples are welcomed without a second glance, and there's a back patio.

Orlando does South Beach at **Sky60** ★ (64 N. Orange Ave., Orlando; ☎ 407/246-1599; www.sky60.com; cover $5 after 10pm on weekends, free weekdays), a lounge that makes like Miami Beach with billowy fabrics, clubby Moroccan-style cabanas, and DJs too hip for their own good. Fortunately, because it's surrounded by other clubs with size issues, Sky60 survives because its swank gives it a mellowness that other hot spots lack. The prices aren't too bad, the view is terrific, and the clientele isn't wedged too far up their own posteriors.

The Club at Firestone (578 N. Orange Ave., Orlando; ☎ 407/426-0005; www.clubatfirestone.com; cover usually $5) is another big dance megaclub, with the usual trappings: lasers, lights, brand-name DJs, and potentially lethal sound levels. The crowd is diverse, and so is the music (indie, electro, rock).

If you're under 40, presentable, and prepared to find the love of your night, then **Wall Street Plaza** (17 Wall Street Plaza, Orlando; ☎ 407/849-9904; www.wallstplaza.net; no cover), a complex of eight nightspots, is the place for you. Of course, it's also a decent place to unwind after a hard day's work. **The Globe, Waitiki Retro Tiki Lounge,** and the upstairs **Monkey Bar** have seating facing Heritage Square, which makes for fun people-watching—especially as the crowd gets drunker and tries to wrestle with the lifelike alligator sculptures.

I have never seen an American nightclub as spectacular as **Cheyenne Saloon & Opera House** ★★ (128 W. Church St., Orlando; ☎ 407/839-3000; www.cheyenne saloon.net; cover $5), at Church Street Station. It's a cathedral-like, five-leveled vaulted beauty with some 250,000 board-feet of stained golden oak. It took more than 2 years to build it in the early 1980s, when it was a queen of Orlando nightlife. Her set pieces are salvage gold: Huge swaths of $1/8$-inch stained glass, chandeliers from the Philadelphia Mint, and a rosewood billiard table from pre-earthquake San Francisco. Naturally, the thrust of this Western-themed architectural opera is country music, including live acts, but it also does Top 40 and touring bands. The energy doesn't match the opulence; it's truly laid back. There's a cover, but drinks are dead cheap—on Tuesdays before 7pm, they're 50¢ and wings are 25¢. There are free line-dance lessons Thursdays 7 to 9pm, and a few gambling tables prop up the Western theme. You'll find lots of balconies and boxes from which to watch drunk partiers try to boogie or two-step, while the front porch overlooks the nightlife action on the vintage, gaslit stretch of Church Street. The man who built it, Bob Snow, returned in 2008 to restore the Cheyenne's glory. It's not as full as it used to be, but it's breathtaking and merits a look-in.

Icebar (8967 International Dr., Orlando; ☎ 407/426-7555; www.icebarorlando.com; Sun–Wed 4:30pm–midnight, Thurs–Sat 4:30pm–2am) angles for convention business with a terrific, but expensive, gimmick imported from Europe: a bar area made entirely of ice, from chairs down to the cocktail goblets. The size of a hotel room, dotted with ice sculptures, and aglow with eyeball-popping primary colors, the Icebar can only be enjoyed in 45-minute time slots that cost $30, including one medium-strength Grey Goose vodka cocktail. Crowds are kept light and you're loaned gloves and a cape for warmth. Online, it's $5 off.

Another fun gimmick: **Eye Spy** (54 N. Orange St., Orlando; ☎ 407/246-1599; daily 9pm–2am; no cover), a laid-back downtown hideaway, bordering on the spooky, that's outfitted with secret rooms and closet-size booths. When you're in one, cameras broadcast you to the rest of the bar, while two-way mirrors trick trysters into giving free shows. Music is eclectically retro, crowds are thick but the noise isn't, and the photo booth memorializes many tipsy moments.

LIVE MUSIC

Also check out the options at CityWalk (p. 281), since big-name acts head there.

On the last Thursday of every month in the lobby lounge of the Hard Rock Hotel, **Velvet Sessions** ✪ (5800 Universal Blvd., Orlando; www.velvetsessions.com; admission $40 including drinks) brings in a band you remember from your FM dial—Joan Jett, Cheap Trick, Chaka Khan, Eddie Money, among others. Pleasantly, it's not too crowded, and after the civilized show, you can filter over to CityWalk (a smart tactic, since the rush on parking after performances lasts at least an hour). There are free drinks and snacks for 2 hours before the act takes the stage. To hear about gigs, join the mailing list online.

B. B. King's Blues Club ✪ (9101 International Dr., Orlando; ☎ 407/370-4550; www.bbkingclubs.com; AE, MC, V; cover $5 after 7pm, events more) is surprisingly intimate and well laid out for a chain venue, with just three rows of tables encircling the stage. There are usually two shows a night at 7:30 and 10pm; the earlier one is usually the 11-piece house band and the second a visiting artist. The fact there's an outside patio and a smaller mezzanine helps make it more laid back than most blues clubs, but of course, the fact it's smoke-free and not very busy helps, too. Happily, despite its location near convention traffic, the food (mostly barbecue) isn't a rip-off, and the music's a steal for $5.

Part of an 11-strong chain, the huge **Howl at the Moon Saloon** ✪✪ (8815 International Dr., Orlando; ☎ 407/354-5999; www.howlatthemoon.com; Sun–Thurs 7pm–2am, Fri 5pm–2am, Sat 6pm–2am, piano show starts 1 hr. after opening; cover $10, mandatory weekend parking valet $5) caters to folks who want a rough-and-tumble Western-style drinkin' hole without getting rough and without the tumble. It's a saloon delivered as a theme park experience, where dueling pianists outdo each other for laughs and virtuosity (expect to hear "American Pie"), and the patrons, mostly over 35 and white, clap earnestly to the beat.

The city's most respected house for a wide range of touring bands, **the Social** ✪✪ (54 N. Orange Ave., Orlando; ☎ 407/246-1419; www.thesocial.org; opening varies depending on the show, closes at 2am; cover $8–$25, depending on the show, with occasional discounts for advance purchase; minimum age 18)

Good for What Ales Ya

Hidden in an industrial area among concrete makers and scrapyards, the **Orlando Brewing and Taproom** ✪✪✪ (1301 Atlanta Ave., Orlando; ☎ 407/872-1117; www.orlandobrewing.com; Mon–Thurs 3–10pm, Fri–Sat noon–midnight, Sun noon–9pm; DISC, MC, V) doesn't pay much rent, and the neighbors don't care much when the roof gets raised. That's what makes it a casual, off-the-beaten-path hang-out—and a relief in an overly stage-managed city. At least 18 own-label beers (ales, IPAs, stouts—it changes according to how the brewers experiment) are on tap at 42°F and served at a copper-top bar. Double Imperial IPA is the hoppiest, and the Olde Pelican English Ale is also popular. The quick rise of the brewery, which has been certified organic, has been remarkable. Orlando's best hotels (including Disney's) and restaurants now serve it. Mondays through Saturdays at 6pm, the owners grant a free 30-minute tour of the beerworks, where quaffs are made without pasteurization (like the Old World) for sale within 2 weeks of brewing. Other fine beers are also poured—name me another hall where Chimay and Framboise are on draught. The bar area is simple but convivial, like a rec room your dad might have slapped up in the basement, and uncluttered by televisions or pool tables, the way a beer snob would have it. Fridays and Saturdays from 8pm to midnight, there's live, easygoing music outside. Try a flight of beers for $11, or down a pint for $4 ($3 before 6pm). Want food? The bartender will hand you a folder of menus from local delivery joints. Yep, it's that relaxed. Atlanta Avenue is just east of the Kaley Street exit of I-4, exit 81.

---

has a high standing among music fans in part because there's precious little attitude for a club so crammed. The club's historic brick building adds dimension to the scene. Tuesdays are Phat-n-Jazzy parties, for progressive hip-hop. When bands are in, covers are usually $7 to $15, sometimes more.

Always busy despite the fact the local music acts are somewhat chill (acoustic guitars, earnest DJs), **Casey's on Central** (50 E. Central Blvd., Orlando; ☎ 407/648-4218; www.caseysoncentral.com; Mon–Fri 4pm–2am, Sat–Sun 7pm–2am; no cover; minimum age 21) has the atmosphere of a neighborhood bar, especially when compared to the decibel level at other joints, but has been going for so many years that it's really something more important now. The drinks are famously strong, and so are the fumes in the restrooms. One word, Casey: Lysol!

Rebellious college-age kids and alterna-bands that lean into the mic and whine: That's **Backbooth** (37 W. Pine St., Orlando; ☎ 407/999-2570; www.backbooth.com; bands start at 5pm, depending on the schedule, closing time is 2am; cover $4–$20, depending on the band). It's a young, loose scene, and you don't have to worry much about standing on ceremony, although the cramped, dark space means you may end up standing on some UCF sophomore's feet. On many nights, three or four bands—even metal, sometimes—take the stage (the 5pm shows welcome all ages, but later shows may have minimums of 18–21 years).

GAY & LESBIAN ORLANDO

Orlando's gay scene has come a long way since the 1960s, when men had to hide their identities. After a generation of out-and-proud dance clubs, in 2007 the city saw about a third of its venues shut down. Kids today just don't feel the need to self-segregate, and in fact, there's still nowhere you could call a gay neighborhood. The dominant venues are "straight-friendly" clubs where people of all persuasions hang out to have fun. There are still a few places where an upstanding single girl would blush to be seen, but not many.

Going since 1975, there's nothing else in America quite like the **Parliament House** ✩✩✩ (410 N. Orange Blossom Trail, Orlando; ☎ 407/425-7571; www. parliamenthouse.com; cover and hours vary), a Johnson-era, 130-room motel that has been converted into an amusement megacenter for gay folks. It's the nucleus of Orlando gay life. Its rambling size—it's 10 acres, including a sprawling multi-club restaurant area and a beach on a small lake out back—means the Parliament can function as all things to all people and it's easy to blend in, so in fact it tends to be a hangout not only for gay guys, but also for women who love them, women who want to dance without being accosted, and open-minded straight guys. On hot days, people in questionable and puny bathing suits sip drinks around the pool and look like they expect something to happen at any second, and on game days, guys watch sports on the big TVs. Think of it as a gay minimall: There's the Footlight Theater Piano Bar for cabaret and drag shows hosted by resident mistress Darcel Stevens; a diner; Le Club Disco, which gears up around 9pm; the Video Bar; and a scuzzier cubby called Western Bar, for leather-and-jeans-wearing guys who play pool and know how to handle a stick. The scene is unexpected when you consider that its owners are a straight couple with six kids and that Orlando politics are still controlled by conservative Christians. Sundays are for the popular, no-cover T-Dance, which starts at 3pm and lasts the better part of 12 hours. Fridays have no cover until 11pm, and Saturdays are $8. You can stay overnight, too (prices are fab: $64 for a motel room, plus $10 for a microwave and fridge), but you'd better be friendly, because one of the prime activities involves buff fellows peering into your windows to see if you'd like a new friend.

A hip outpost several miles south of downtown, **Pulse** ✩ (1912 S. Orange Ave., Orlando; ☎ 407/649-3888; www.pulseorlando.com; nightly 9pm–2am; cover $5) has a split personality. Its packed front room is pure Space Age, in white decor, yet changes colors as the lights shift. But in back, where lights are less welcome, hot men dance, often shirtless. The combination of upstanding and down low—plus a cabaret space, the Jewel Box, for drag acts and club mixes, starting at 10:30pm—makes this place popular with just about everyone.

Revolution (375 S. Bumby Ave., Orlando; ☎ 407/228-9900; www.revolution orlando.com; daily 4pm–2am; no cover until 11pm) has an easy, good-natured party dance vibe, with three rooms of music including a video bar and a lounge with a small stage (drag is still big here). The week is varied with theme nights from Latin (Mon), karaoke (Fri, and its amateur stripper counterpart on Tues), and a Saturday welcoming lesbians.

Orlando's only bathhouse is **the Club** (450 E. Compton St., Orlando; ☎ 407/ 425-5005; www.the-clubs.com; 24 hr.; $8 membership plus $12 for a locker or $18 for a cubicle), a laid-back, men-only scene with a spacious outdoor pool-and-whirlpool area, a gym, a tanning bed ($5), and movie night Thursdays and free cookouts on Sunday afternoons. Habituees of this style of socializing won't find the atmosphere as sexually charged as other bathhouses are, partly because frisky movies are only permitted to be shown behind closed doors. Customers do more hanging out by the pool than cruising.

I can't say much about **Hank's** (5026 Edgewater Dr., Orlando; ☎ 407/291-2399; daily noon–2am) because this is a family guide book, but I'll just say it's like the '70s all over again. This roadside dive bar is as plain as your dad's workshop in the garage. Signs warn you to buy a drink or leave. But there's pool, and a juke box, and goings-on in the private backyard after dark.

11 Shopping: The Good, the Bad & the Discounted

Even more places where you can part with your cash, from outlet malls to fancy emporia

ORLANDO, AS A CITY SETTLED MOSTLY AFTER THE INVENTION OF THE automobile, is all about malls. The major centers tend to be stocked with the usual brands, so most of the time, there's little surprising or unusual among the offerings. What Orlando does offer is choice—plenty of stores at plenty of malls. International visitors typically set aside an afternoon to scoop up jeans, shoes, and other sundries, but often because their foreign currencies make those things such bargains and not because what's on offer is particularly rare. There's usually a souvenir store at the exit area of every theme park ride, so you will be hardly at a loss for places to buy stuff. Whether your booty will be useful is another question.

The stand-out shopping choices at the big amusement park areas are discussed in the chapters devoted to those parks. This chapter, by comparison, is dedicated to the shopping you'll find outside the parks and Orlando's dirty little secret: You'll always get better buys on almost all of the souvenirs pushed within the park gates, if only you have the discipline to wait until you're off the grounds to buy.

OUTLET MALLS

Like most modern outlet malls (see below), not all of the items you find for sale here will have come from higher-priced "regular" stores; much of the stock has been specially manufactured for the outlet market (although *Consumer Reports* doesn't think the quality is substantially different from retail). You'll usually find outlet prices between 30% and 50% off sales at retail stores, and after the holiday rush, when stores need to ready for the new lines, discounts go deeper. The looks may be a year behind the trends, but honestly, few of us notice. That said, Orlando is a hotbed for outlet activity, partly because the steady flow of international visitors, with their often-superior currencies, foment a buying frenzy among tourists.

At the tippy top end of International Drive, across from Festival Bay, the utterly fantastic and dangerously tempting **Prime Outlets International Orlando** ✹✹ (4951 International Dr., Orlando; ☎ 407/352-9600; www.primeoutlets.com) is the best outlet in the city, and one of the best anywhere. Until recently it was an also-ran asterisk to the shopping scene, but a multimillion-dollar ground-up reinvention resulted in a stupendous 175-store (give or take) open-air village where it is very unlikely you will come away empty-handed. Many times of year, the whole place sings with 40% discounts, luring the tourists by the hordes. Nearly every conceivable brand has a presence here (unlike at many outlet malls, where weird no-name catch-all stores and dumpy novelty carts prevail), but the chief dangers include **Neiman Marcus Last Call**—a clearance center that sells genuine department store castoffs from its namesake stores, Bergdorf Goodman, and the Horchow catalog—**Saks Fifth Avenue Off Fifth, Coach Factory Store, Ann Taylor, Nike, Guess?, Eddie Bauer, Kenneth Cole, Fossil, Reebok Outlet Store, Hugo Boss Factory Store, Calvin Klein, Brooks Brothers Factory Store, Kate Spade, Tumi, Victoria's Secret Outlet,** and **Juicy Couture.** There's a **Disney Character Warehouse** to undercut your souvenir bill, and a few sit-down casual restaurants (such as the Bahamian Kafe Kalik) so you don't have to belly up to the food court (although there's one of those, too). I am a remarkably disciplined shopper, and yet I have shown up here with just a notepad and honorable intentions only to emerge with an unwieldy saucepan from the **Calphalon** cookware store. Weekdays are quietest, and parking is most ample around back, near Saks. The website has print-and-go discount coupons listed by store, and make a point of stopping by Guest Services, in the central courtyard, because spending a few dollars on a discount booklet could save another 20% off a big-ticket item.

Orlando Premium Outlets ★★★ (8200 Vineland Ave., Orlando; ☎ 407/238-7787; www.premiumoutlets.com/orlando) has the added advantage of being just a mile from Disney property, which sends it a lot of business—its owners tout it as the most productive outlet center in America, with sales exceeding $1,000 per square foot. Some 150 stores (40 of them added in 2008) vie for attention, and most of them offer good deals off overstocks. Among the stores: Armani Exchange, Banana Republic, Barney's, Miss Sixty, Versace, and Burberry. Much of this book was researched in a pair of shoes I found for $40 at the Skechers outlet. One popular rare shop because it's so close to the Mouse House is **Disney's Character Premiere,** for cast-off official theme park souvenirs. The food court is well used. Steel yourself if you come during the weekend; the line of traffic snakes for a mile, and the competition for parking approaches Olympian difficulty. It's about 10 minutes from Downtown Disney; the turnoff is just south of I-4's exit 68 on S.R. 535/Apopka Vineland, by Bahama Breeze. The I-Ride trolley (p. 18) touches down here ostensibly every 20 minutes, and the no. 42 city bus also swings here from I-Drive.

Lake Buena Vista Factory Stores ★ (15591 S.R. 535, Orlando; ☎ 407/238-9301; www.lbvfs.com) is a strip mall–style collection of about 50 stores, not all of which are owned by famous brands. The offerings here are not as plush as those at its two rival outlet malls. You will find a bit more diversity of product, though, with fewer clothing boutiques and more choice in jewelry, electronics, and kids' clothes. There are enough names you know (including **Old Navy, Liz Claiborne, Carter's for Kids, Borders, OshKosh B'Gosh,** and **Aéropostale**) to warrant a quick trip. The **Character Outlet** has some Disney bargains (half-price mugs, shirts, toys, and some souvenirs dated from a few years ago), but it can't hold a mouse-shaped candle to the Disney outlets elsewhere. Stop at the mall office for a brochure packed with coupons. The mall provides a free daily shuttle to and from major hotels around Disney and I-Drive; they leave between 9am and 4pm and return in four batches from 12:55 to 7pm.

RETAIL MALLS

Most malls are open 10am to 9pm Monday to Saturday, and 10am to 6 or 7pm Sundays.

One of the few things at the 250-store **Florida Mall** ★★ (8001 S. Orange Blossom Trail, Orlando; ☎ 407/851-6255; www.simon.com) that qualifies as unusual is **M&M's World** (☎ 407/850-4000; www.mmsworld.com), a lavishly decorated emporium dedicated to the famous snack and its voluminous collectible spin-offs. Such stores exist only here, Las Vegas, and Times Square in New York City. The ceiling changes color, pop music blasts, and the staff has the unenviable task of keeping all those little candies off the floor. The merchandise selection is easily as varied as that of the average Disney Store (and as highly priced, charging $25 for a beach towel), except here, the mascots aren't rodents but bulbous sugar pellets. Isn't America weird? M&Ms of wacky shades, such as grey (which they call "silver," but yeah, it's really grey) and light purple (which also looks grey, but I'll give it to them) cost far more than the M&Ms at your local drugstore ($12 a pound), and besides, they're also sold at the biggest candy shops at Disney and Universal. If it's a sugar high you seek, head farther into the mall to the wider inventory of **Dylan's Candy Bar** (☎ 407/812-8955; www.dylans candybar.com), owned by designer Ralph Lauren's daughter.

The mall also has seven anchor stores (including a **Saks Fifth Avenue,** a **Nordstrom,** and a **Dillard's**), an **Apple** store, and a **Lush** soap store. It is worth noting that the gas stations on Orange Blossom Trail, which links the mall to the Beeline (there's no toll between it and I-4), are among the least expensive in the county.

There's usually something drastically on sale at **Festival Bay** (5250 International Dr., across from Prime Outlets, Orlando; ☎ 800/481-1944 or 407/351-7718; www.shopfestivalbaymall.com) because try as it might, this audaciously designed real estate tragedy at the top end of I-Drive hasn't been able to wake from a nightmare that began when it opened in 2001. Big-idea businesses, such as Bill Murray's restaurant based on *Caddyshack* and a Steve & Barry's, open and close in a wink, so a stroll down its peppy but depressingly bleak, half-tenanted corridors can feel at times like a trek through a consumerist's tundra, although because of the light traffic, prices are usually quite low. Even the indoor fountains that flow underfoot to the outdoor pond can't enliven the gloom. The beloved **Ron Jon Surf Shop** (☎ 407/481-2555; www.ronjons.com) from Cocoa Beach runs a giant store here, but its plans for an adjoining playground of man-made waves was a wipeout and died in midconstruction. Ron Jon's presence gives Festival Bay a decidedly athletic slant, as one the mall's other big tenants is a 61,000-square-foot **Vans Skatepark** (☎ 407/351-3881; www.vans.com; $12–$15 to participate, pads $5, board rental $5; daily 10am–10pm), which does for skateboarders and bikers what Ron Jon does for surfers; it's a blast to watch these kids defy physics, and tempt fate, as they soar around the courses. Other anchors at the mall include the camping-and-fishing megastore **Bass Pro Shops Outdoor World** (so gargantuan it must be seen to be believed), **Hilo Hattie** Hawaiian wear store, and **Sheplers** discount Western wear—none of which have other presences in Orlando. For minor entertainment, there's the **Putting Edge** glow-in-the-dark minigolf course, **Monkey Joe's** indoor playground for small children, and the

Stroll & Shop: Winter Park

Seven blocks of Winter Park's Park Avenue, a sleepy Main Street–type thorough-fare canopied by oaks, are known for their shopping. Stores lean toward galleries, chocolatiers, and women's clothes; there's a Pottery Barn installed in a vintage cinema building, and a few pleasant but unremarkable cafes and brunch spots mixed in. I've noticed some high turnover in the past few years, so it's not a place to go in search of a specific item inasmuch as it's a pleasant destination for a stroll in an upscale town. The **Park Avenue Area Association** (www.parkave-winter park.com) tracks the latest tenants. Making an afternoon of it is easy: The incomparable Morse Museum (p. 237) is at the top of the shopping drag, and the campus of Rollins College (p. 237), draped in Spanish moss, is found at the bottom. In the middle, near where the Amtrak rails gently arc into town (a vestige of idealistic early city planning), you can attend the weekly Farmer's Market (Sat 7am–1pm; the best stuff is gone by 9am) and visit the Wine Room (p. 91). Just east, you can break your stroll with a throwback boat tour of the town's lakes and antique mansions (p. 270).

Cricketers Arms British pub (p. 82), which hosts live music. The **Cinemark multiplex** (☎ 407/352-1042; adult $8.25, child and senior $5, student $6.25) is also here; shows before 6pm are $6.25 and Tuesdays are $6.

The most upscale mall in the city is **Mall at Millenia** ★ (I-4, at Conroy Rd., Orlando; ☎ 407/363-3555; www.mallatmillenia.com), opened 2002, where the fanciest brands keep their stores and where fashion runway shows are broadcast on LED screens. Among the wallet-sappers at this 1.3-million-square-foot cathedral to credit: Cartier, Apple, Gucci, Coach, Neiman Marcus, Macy's, Tommy Bahama's, Jimmy Choo, and Tiffany & Co.—none of them are of the outlet variety. Even the restaurants, such as yuppie meat market Blue Martini and the Cheesecake Factory, are a few notches above the standard malls. Even the less expensive stores are hip and stylish, Zara and Urban Outfitters included. The mall, which is ringed by a bunch of useful box-store brands (IKEA, SuperTarget), is a few minutes northeast of Universal and east of I-4's exit 78 (Conroy Rd.). For postcards and packages, there's a post office (☎ 407/363-3555, ext. 242) in the basement.

Pointe Orlando (9101 International Dr., Orlando; ☎ 407/248-2838; www.pointeorlandofl.com) recently underwent an extensive bulldozing and refit, and the results are sparkling. There are a few shopping options (Hollister, Tommy Bahama's Emporium, Kiehl's), but the bigger reason to come is for a night out at its worthy but mostly upscale minichain restaurants, such as the energetic Taverna Opa (p. 83), the Capital Grille, the Grape Wine Bar (www.thegrape.com), and seafood miracle worker the Oceanaire. A few lower-end choices (Hooters, Johnny Rockets, frozen-drink magnet Adobe Gila's) balance the choices. Pointe Orlando is smack dab in the touristy I-Drive area; in fact, you can walk from the Convention Center. The **Regal Cinemas Orlando Stadium 20 & IMAX** (☎ 407/248-9045; adult $10, senior $7, child $6.50, student $8, before 3pm

$7.50, IMAX adult $14, senior $12, child $11) charges adults just $7.50 before 3pm. The mall is just north of the mighty Convention Center, making it a hangout for trade show–goers, many of whom are looking to cut loose and have a good time (hint, hint).

Pick your chin up off the floor after I tell you that when it opened in 1974, **Altamonte Mall** (451 E. Altamonte Dr., Altamonte Springs; ☎ 407/830-4422; www. altamontemall.com), 15 minutes north of Orlando, was the second-largest tourist attraction in the American South, behind Walt Disney World. Steady embellishments have kept it current—some 160 stores—but not trendy. The anchor stores, middle income all, are Sears, Dillard's, Macy's, and JCPenney.

FLEA MARKETS

Back home, you might have a flea market in the parking lot of your church on Saturdays. Orlando, not interested in delicacy, goes over the top. Its flea markets operate day in, day out, in barnlike sheds, mostly in Kissimmee. Tough economic times have emptied many of the stalls of their already struggling proprietors, giving this slouching shopping niche more than a touch of sadness. But bargains can be struck, the deals can exceed those at Wal-Mart, and no one has to know how little you paid for those Donald Duck sunglasses. The best are east of Walt Disney World on U.S. 192.

Five miles east of Disney, the glitzy tourist universe lapses into the more mundane world of Kissimmee, a low-rent town. **192 Flea Market Prices** ✯ (4301 U.S. 192, Kissimmee; ☎ 407/396-4555; www.192fleamarketprices.com; daily 9am–6pm), at Mile Marker 15, is a network of sheds hosting stall after stall (around 450 when all are occupied, which is never) of extremely cheap knockoffs and crafts, many run by hard-working South Asian or Latin immigrants. You'll find rolling luggage for $10, suntan lotion costing $6 for 8 ounces, beach towels for $8 to $12 less than inside the theme parks. You won't just find cheap tourist items, toys, and fragrances either, but also handicrafts and imports, such as $16 Chinese silk pajamas, $9 homemade candles, $2.25 hot dogs and $1.50 churros at the food court, and at the stall of one D. Kioko, woodcarver, a garden of handmade African drums for $15 apiece.

At Mile Marker 10, the **Maingate Flea Market** (5407 W. U.S. Hwy. 192, Kissimmee; ☎ 407/390-1015; daily 10am–8pm) has a similar setup of some 400 interconnected sheds (again, not all of them occupied). Because it's about 3 miles east of Disney's entrance in the thick of U.S. 192's tourist crawl, prices are slightly higher than 192 Flea Market, but they're still dead low.

A further 250 booths are available at the less impressive **Visitors Flea Market** (5811 W. U.S. Hwy. 192, Kissimmee; ☎ 407/396-0114; www.visitorsfleamarket. com; opens at 9:30am daily). It's close to Disney (Mile Marker 9) so it has more souvenirs than some of the other markets.

The quartet of ragamuffin markets on U.S. 192 is completed by the **Osceola Flea and Farmers Market** ✯ (2801 E. Irlo Bronson Hwy., Kissimmee; ☎ 407/846-2811; Fri–Sun 8am–5pm), open 3 days a week. It's in the east end of Kissimmee. Like the other three markets, it could take a thorough browser hours to explore, although the wares will start to repeat themselves as you go. The market also sells food at a savings over most area grocery stores, and there's a live auction (anything goes) Sundays noon to 4pm.

An Amusement Reliquary

Ever wonder what Disney World's overlords do with old ride vehicles, signs, and outdated souvenirs? They send them 45 minutes south of the parks to **Never Never Land** ★★★ (1000 Detour Rd., Haines City; ☎ 863/422-9999; www.mouse surplus.com; Mon–Sat 10am–6pm), Fantasyland's junkyard. For Disney fans, the jumbled warehouse, run by online seller MouseSurplus, is the fire-sale equivalent of the Smithsonian, and they consider a visit to MouseSurplus worthwhile even if they keep their credit cards firmly secure in their wallets. If you have thousands of bucks to burn, parked here are retired vehicles from Epcot's Horizons and World of Motion pavilions, monorail doors, signs from rides, plus giant characters that once stood as props in the parks and at the resorts, but you're most likely to pick from an ever-changing flea market of commonplace stuff from the resorts, hawked by the bin full, including ice cream machines, electronic equipment with mysterious uses, old soft goods (Grand Floridian pillow shams, $10), golf balls ($1), name tags ($2), and dinner plates for $5 apiece, outdated uniforms and souvenirs, and so on. Furniture, too: Recent renovations of Coronado Springs and BoardWalk yielded $24 nightstands, $40 lamps, and $75 easy chairs in a mild, grey Hidden Mickey fabric. MouseSurplus sells online (http://mousesurplus.myshopify.com), although prices are better in person. You'll find similar deals from another Disney Web liquidator, Surplus Kingdom (http://stores.ebay.com/surpluskingdom). To save on shipping, ask if you can pick up the items yourself.

ANTIQUES

Orange Avenue, south of Princeton Street, is known as Antique Row. It's easy to park your car in the vicinity and stroll up and down, but don't do it on Sunday afternoons. Almost everything is closed then, including the traditional way station for weary shoppers, the **White Wolf Café** (1829 N. Orange Ave., Orlando; ☎ 407/895-9911; www.whitewolfcafe.com; Mon 11am–9pm, Tues–Thurs 11am–10pm, Fri–Sat 11am–11pm, Sun 8am–3pm; AE, MC, V), a combination upscale eatery (entrees $9–$20) and antiques store with outdoor and indoor seating. The pickings are in two clusters—one in the 1800s on Orange near Princeton and the other in the 1600s, about 2 blocks south (walkable in about 10 min.). Early each month, the area, known as Ivanhoe Village, mounts **First Fridays Art Stroll** (☎ 407/484-5839; www.ivanhoevillage.org), when stores extend hours from 6:30–10pm, drinks are served, and local artists come to showcase their work. Otherwise, stores keep regular business hours of at least 10am to 5pm.

Shops include:

- ◆ **A+T Antiques** and **Ivanhoe Traders** (1620 N. Orange Ave., Orlando; ☎ 407/896-9831). Large selection of European and wrought-iron furnishings.
- ◆ **Humbugs** (1618 N. Orange Ave., Orlando; ☎ 407/895-6707). Chic '60s swag and fusty midcentury furniture.

- **Déjà Vu** (1825 N. Orange Ave., Orlando; ☎ 407/898-3609). "Vintage clothing and funk."
- **Golden Phoenix Antiques** (1826 N. Orange Ave., Orlando; ☎ 407/895-6006; Thurs–Sat noon–5pm). Upscale selections.
- **Oldies but Goodies** (1827 N. Orange Ave., Orlando; ☎ 407/897-1088). 1960s and 1970s couture.
- **Rock & Roll Heaven** (1814 N. Orange Ave., Orlando; ☎ 407/896-1952; www.rock-n-rollheaven.com). Thousands of CDs and LPs, average price $8.
- **Boom-Art** (1821 N. Orange Ave., Orlando; ☎ 407/281-0246). Eccentric and chatty artist Glenn Rogers recycles old furniture into pop-art curios.

DOWNTOWN DISNEY

Downtown Disney, Walt Disney World's main area for restaurants and shopping, ambles along the shore of Village Lake a few miles east of Epcot. The district has three zones; because of the size, it's helpful to know which one you're heading for because the walk between them can be up to 15 minutes. The busiest and easternmost area is called the Marketplace (it's nearest to the DTS bus stop), and it's for shops and restaurants. The westernmost zone is the West Side, and although it has some shops not listed here (such as **Sosa Family Cigars**), it leans toward nightlife and entertainment, with a Cirque du Soleil show and a 24-screen cinema (p. 280). Between West Side and Marketplace is the zone that was once Pleasure Island but is now under redevelopment (although the **Harley-Davidson** store and the high-end **Curl by Sammy Duvall** surf shop remain). Restaurants abound; for those, see chapter 4.

Shops at the Marketplace (☎ 407/939-3463) are almost pure Mouse, and nearly all of them sell candy, too. Stores are themed for maximum souvenir sales, including one for toys and games (**Once Upon a Toy**—Mr. Potato Head is huge these days), one for Christmas and holiday decorations (**Disney's Days of Christmas),** one for high-end collectibles (**the Art of Disney),** one for kitchen tools (**Mickey's Pantry),** one for athletic wear (**Team Mickey),** one for urban wear (**Tren-D),** one for all things Pooh (**Pooh Corner),** and **Disney's Pin Traders.** There used to be a store selling books about Disney history, but in late 2008 it was converted into a **Design-a-Tee** shop sponsored by Hanes. That should tell you where the modern Disney's values are. There's now not a single place on resort property to browse a healthy range of titles pertaining to Walt and what he accomplished. That's disgraceful.

The sole savings opportunity is the one for rejected souvenirs (that's **Mickey's Mart**) that cost less than $10, such as bags, hats, key chains, and small plush toys. Gee, thanks, Mickey: It's in the only shop that doesn't have air-conditioning.

The Marketplace also has the big kahuna of Disney merch: **World of Disney** ⭐⭐ the largest souvenir department store in the resort, crowned by a giant Stitch burping water onto passersby. It's a rambling cathedral-roofed barn stocked from rug to rafter with every conceivable Disney-branded item, from pin to plush toys. You'll find stuff here you won't find at other Disney stores here or at home.

However, despite its status as the chief Mouse mart, it still may not have what you want. That's because it's the only store that offers annual passholders a discount, which means the most obsessed fans clean the shelves here first. It also may

The Pin Culture

One of the oddest souvenir traditions on Disney turf is the sales of little enamel and cloisonné pins featuring every known character, ride, movie, and promotional event. It's easier to get your hands on a pin than it is to find a bottle of water. They're on sale at carts, at hotels, in souvenir stalls—there's even a pavilion that sells nothing but pins at Downtown Disney. What's going on? A collecting craze that never ends. A standard pin costs $7, and prices scale up as they get more elaborate: $9 for something on two planes, $11 for three-dimensional elements, $13 for limited editions. There are even pins containing tiny snippets of things removed during rehabs (such as circles cut from Madame Leota's crystal ball on the Haunted Mansion). Pins are usually worn not on clothing but on lanyards that hang around the neck. Many cast members wear them, too, but they have to: When workers clock in for their shifts, they replenish their pin supply at a special window in the backstage area—a dozen to a lanyard at all times. The rule is that if a cast member is wearing almost any pin you want (barring their name tag or ones commemorating employment milestones), you're allowed to ask them to trade it for one of your own and they're not allowed to refuse if the pin is legit. Universal sells a fair supply, too, but the craze is fiercest at Disney, where the backings are shaped like a mouse-eared head.

---

not carry items that might be sold at another store at the Marketplace (tree ornaments, for example, or toys). Disney's merchandise distribution is slow; shopkeepers virtually beg superiors for restocking, and even then it can take weeks.

There's something else you should know. Many times, you can buy the same merchandise at home for far less. I have seen the same toys and DVDs for $7 at box stores and online while Walt Disney World wanted $20 or more. Before purchasing, always ask if any item you want is a "park exclusive"—that means it's only available here. Otherwise, you could do a lot better if you got it back home. At least check the real-world price on the Web at the hotel before purchasing.

Only a few stores sell non-Disney plunder. **Ghirardelli Soda Fountain & Chocolate Shop** is one of the few non–San Francisco locations run by the chocolate-making stalwart. It has a pricey sundae shop and a boutique where ½-oz. samples are freely dispensed. Kids can't be separated from the **Lego Imagination Center** store, where there's usually an employee building something elaborate and 36 little stations in pods on the terrace where children can make their own structures for free. Behind the cash-wrap, 4,488 little Lego men are glued in regiments to the wall. **Basin** sells bath products for those teeny hotel room tubs, but the non-Disney goodies at Marketplace pretty much end there. The resort's shopping list has seismically shifted its priorities since the 1970s, when fascinating international goods sold were here when the area was called the Lake Buena Vista Shopping Village.

The **Bibbidi Bobbidi Boutique** 🧒 (Marketplace; ☎ 407/939-7895; www. disneyworld.com/style; daily 9am–7pm; minimum age 3; reservations required) at

Downtown Disney Marketplace gives girls glittery, pink makeovers as princesses (or future Pepto-Bismol spokespeople) for $50 to $250. A kind-hearted "Fairy Godmother-in-Training" oversees your daughter's makeover, which comes with one of three hairstyles from which to choose. The least back-breaking makeover is the Coach Package that does hair and make-up with a sash; add nails for $5; and add a souvenir photo, tiara, and a gown (warning: they are hot and scratchy, so bring a change if the sun is strong) by paying $190 or more. The boutique will also do Hannah Montana looks (wig, cheap microphone headset, guitar-shaped purse, T-shirt) for $110. Staff will try to convince you to add more frills that will cost more money. Boys are mostly blown off, because all they can get is a "Cool Dudes" look of colored hair gel and glitter ($8). Are we teaching our daughters that the ultimate goal should be to find a prince? There's also a salon in the Magic Kingdom beside the Castle, where prices are identical, but you'll need a park ticket.

OTHER INTERESTING STORES

Agra has the Taj Majal and Sydney has its opera house. Orlando has a giant orange. The 60-foot-tall, citrus-imitative roof of **Eli's Orange World** ★★ (5395 W. U.S. Hwy. 192, Kissimmee; ☎ 800/531-3182 or 407/396-1306; www.orange world192.com; daily 8am–9:40pm) has been a city landmark for the generations since it opened. Back when most of this land held orange groves, Florida road-sides used to be full of this kind of souvenir catch-all, stacked high with oranges and grapefruits in their red mesh bags, but as the citrus industry bowed out to make room for the McMansion industry, the state's bumper crop diminished. Now, few visitors associate the area with its fruit values. Here at Orange World, which also ships to most states, a quarter-bushel of oranges is $8, a half is $12, and a box sturdy enough to take on the flight home is $19 full (it'll weigh about 20 lb.). Fruit changes by the season: Fall is for navel oranges, January sees honey-bell tangelos, and February through May sees a procession of oranges, honey tan-gerines, and Valencia oranges; ruby red grapefruit is available year-round. The shelves teeter with the sort of corny Florida souvenirs that time forgot: shellacked alligator heads from $25 to $100, personalized mugs for $4, and 8-ounce jars of papaya or guava butter for $2.50. Sure, there are *lots* of schlocky, fluorescent-lit barns selling junky souvenirs on U.S. 192 and I-Drive—but only the best schlock is good enough for *you*.

The book selection isn't massive, but it's well selected at **Urban Think! Bookstore** ★★ (625 E. Central Blvd., Orlando; ☎ 407/650-8004; www.urban thinkorlando.com; Sun–Mon 11am–6pm, Tues–Sat 11am–9pm), in trendy Thorn-ton Park. Florida topics and authors get extra attention, especially at frequent readings, Signature Series signings, and shows by local artists. Besides being one of the only independent bookstores in the region, on Friday and Saturday evenings, its in-store organic tea bar, which sells wine and beer, often hosts live acoustic music at the store's sidewalk cafe. As for the big-box bookstores, **Borders** (1051 W. Sand Lake Rd., Orlando; ☎ 407/826-8912; Mon–Thurs 10am–10pm, Fri–Sat 10am–11pm, Sun 10am–9pm) can be found near the Florida Mall. There is a smaller Borders at the airport (☎ 407/816-5126). You'll find a **Barnes & Noble** (Venezia Plaza, 7900 W. Sand Lake Rd., Orlando; ☎ 407/345-0900; daily 9am–11pm) among the terrific restaurants of Sand Lake Road west of

I-4 and at the Florida Mall (8358 S. Orange Blossom Trail, Orlando; ☎ 407/ 856-7200; daily 9am–11pm).

A supermarket-size emporium for food and wine (as well as baskets and small furniture) imported from around the world, **World Market** (1744 Sand Lake Rd., Orlando; ☎ 407/240-2064; www.worldmarket.com; Mon–Sat 9am–9pm, Sun 10am–7pm), just west of the Florida Mall, has a presence in 35 states. Foreign visitors load up on flavors from home, including on Arnott's Tim Tam from Australia and Manner wafers from Vienna. I've found 3-pound bags of Haribo gummy bears for just $7. Customers often have the lilting accent of the British north, and they're piling their carts with enough Cadbury bars and HP Sauce to get themselves through 2-week stays at their vacation homes. Or the second Blitz.

I'm not one for the whole **Hard Rock Cafe** (6050 Universal Blvd., Orlando; ☎ 407/351-7625; www.hardrock.com) thing. Its T-shirts were cool in the 1980s, but now wearing one is just a plea for a fashion intervention. Still, people collect them (who are they, exactly?), and because Orlando is home to the company's headquarters, owning one would seem necessary for a collector. The store and restaurant, the largest in the Hard Rock chain, are at Universal's CityWalk. The classic T-shirt is $22 and is sold in a flattened pack, like LPs once were. You can only buy them here; even the Hard Rock Hotel sells a different version.

12 The Essentials of Planning

ORLANDO HOSTS SOME 50 MILLION PEOPLE A YEAR, AND THE PEOPLE WHO run the airports, hotels, and theme parks are specialists in moving tourists from one location to another—the whole system is set up to make it foolproof—so you probably won't get lost in a mire of confusion. You will, however, need to take care of some nitty-gritty details—from flights to transportation. This chapter will fill you in on tricks and strategies to get you on your way—without blowing too much time or money.

WHERE TO FIND TOURIST INFORMATION

Orlando has one of the most responsive and question-friendly visitors' bureaus in America. Its mighty tourism authority is funded by taxes on tourists, who come in such numbers that the organization can afford to spend. Hence, it operates a permanent storefront, **Orlando Official Visitor Center** (8723 International Dr.; ☎ 407/363-5872; www.orlandoinfo.com; daily 8:30am–6:30pm), in a strip mall on the western side of I-Drive not far north of the Pointe Orlando shopping mall, that's stocked from carpet to rafter with free brochures from every hotel, theme restaurant, and amusement you could need. Although many, many other places in town (souvenir stands, mostly) claim to offer "official" tourist information, this is the only truly official place that does. Staff is on hand to answer any questions, and its ticket desk has the inside line on discounts, where they are available.

Kissimmee, the town closest to Walt Disney World and the one where you'll find most of the nearby budget hotels and restaurants, maintains its own tourist office, the **Kissimmee Convention and Visitors Bureau** (1925 E. Irlo Bronson Memorial Hwy./U.S. 192; Kissimmee; ☎ 407/944-2400; www.floridakiss.com; Mon–Fri 8am–5pm). Its website also lists current discounts. The Kissimmee CVB works with the Orlando bureau, so you won't have to make two trips.

For local news, the *Orlando Sentinel* (www.orlandosentinel.com) is one of the best papers in Florida. It maintains two blogs about tourism, Tourism Central and Theme Park Rangers: **http://blogs.orlandosentinel.com**.

When it comes to the theme parks, you'll find that the official websites mostly furnish doctored photographs, meaningless homilies, bandwidth-hogging animation, and a near-total lack of cogent information. Thank goodness, then, that these places inspire fervent followings. Below, you'll find addresses for some of the best of hundreds of websites devoted to tracking every development at the parks, even if it's as minor as a 10¢ rise in pricing at the popcorn stands. Some of these are exhaustive to the point of uselessness—isn't it overplanning to worry about where popcorn costs 10¢ less?—but it's still good to know that truly exhaustive information is out there. Many of these sites have message boards where you can pose questions to other members eager to spread the know.

Mouse Clickers: The Best Websites

Official info:

* **Orlando/Orange County** (www.orlandoinfo.com)
* **Kissimmee** (www.floridakiss.com)

Theme Parks:

* **AllEarsNet** (www.allearsnet.com). Thorough compendium of everything Disney and Universal Orlando, down to the full menus at most restaurants. Indispensable, but very fan oriented.
* **WDW Info** (www.wdwinfo.com) and **WDW Magic** (www.wdwmagic.com). Which rides are closing for rehab? How are the restaurants? These message boards are among the most active.
* **MouseSavers.com** and **TheMouseForLess.com**. These catalog the going Disney deals.
* **MousePlanet** (www.mouseplanet.com). More resort info, opinions.
* **MiceChat** (www.micechat.com). Clear-eyed trip reports and photos.
* **IOACentral** (www.ioacentral.com). A board-based Universal site.
* **Jim Hill** (www.jimhillmedia.com). No one's better at Disney gossip.
* **Laughing Place** (www.laughingplace.com). Strong on backstage news, it publishes a handsome quarterly. The message boards cook.

Active message boards for getting questions answered about Disney include **INTERCOT** (www.intercot.com) and **Sharing Disney Magic** (www.tagrel.com).

Fan sites devoted to single attractions:

* **The Haunted Mansion** (Magic Kingdom): www.doombuggies.com
* **Pirates of the Caribbean** (Magic Kingdom): www.tellnotales.com
* **Country Bear Jamboree** (Magic Kingdom): www.doneinthedark.com
* **Carousel of Progress** (Magic Kingdom): www.carouselofprogress.com
* **JAWS** (Universal Studios): www.amityboattours.com

Park history:

* **Widen Your World** (www.widenyourworld.net) and Walt Dated World (http://waltdatedworld.bravepages.com). Lost WDW stuff.
* **Walt Disney World:** A History in Postcards (www.bigbrian-nc.com/pctoc.htm). Classic images.
* **Waltopia** (www.waltopia.com). Walt's dreams for Epcot.
* **Extinct Attractions Club** (www.extinct-attractions-club.com). It sells ride documentaries culled from interviews and vacation videos.
* **EPCOT Central** (http://epcot82.blogspot.com). A critique of Epcot.

WHEN TO VISIT

One of the principal reasons Orlando is such an attractive destination is that it's in Florida. Summers are hot and winters aren't frigid, at least by most Northerners' standards, and although winter morning frosts occur, they're not the norm.

The city culture cranks year-round, although theater and concerts tend to be scheduled outside of the summer months. The main consideration when it comes to selecting a date for your visit is balancing good weather with thin crowds. When you choose to go to Orlando will determine to a large degree how many days it will take you to see everything you want. In the peak season (such as spring break or the week after Christmas), the Magic Kingdom's turnstiles are spinning like propellers—on December 27, 2006, three Disney parks reached capacity and briefly sealed gates against further guests. You can end up riding only a half-dozen attractions in a 10-hour period. Come back in September, one of my favorite times, and you can do nearly everything in a day, enjoying your vacation more.

So when are the **peak seasons?** Put simply: When American kids are out of school. That means midspring, summer, and the holidays. Not only will it take longer to see what you want, but hotel prices will be higher then, too. If you want to **save cash,** early January, early May, late August, all of September, and the first half of December are prime. For a more defined calendar of the low season, turn to chapter 3, where you'll find the pricing schedule that Walt Disney World uses.

The flipside of low season is that the theme parks tend to trim services when it's quieter. More food service locations are shuttered, and more rides are closed for maintenance—and no, admission won't be discounted. January is a particularly tough month for missing out on rides due to rehabs. The ones that are open, such as roller coasters, may have fewer cars running.

And especially in the winter months, you may find it too chilly to enjoy the rides that get you wet. Same goes for the water parks. They're open year-round (although each Disney water park closes in turn for 2 months in the winter) and Wet 'n Wild has heated water, but you have to get out of the pool *sometime*.

June to September is the heaviest season for rain. It seems like every afternoon, like clockwork, another heavy storm rolls in. Those storms usually roll out within an hour, just as reliably, but in the meantime, you'll see torrents and lightning fiercer than you ever have at home. During those tropical seasons, bring along a cheap poncho from home. You'll also sweat a lot more, but that's to be expected.

Central Florida suffers more lightning strikes than any other American locale. Much rain falls, but even more water is used—some 786 million gallons are consumed in the pursuit of daily life, and you have to assume a goodly portion of that is coursing through the flumes at Typhoon Lagoon. You will notice that tap water has a distinct mineral taste. Your hotel's pipes are not to blame. Rather, think of Orlando as a giant island floating over a cushion of water. Most of the city's lakes started, in fact, as sinkholes that permitted the water table to flood upward. The drinking water is drawn from underground, hence the specific flavor and odor.

Orlando Average Temperature & Rainfall & Disney's Lowest Hotel Prices

	Jan	Feb	Mar	Apr	May	June	July	Aug	Sept	Oct	Nov	Dec
Hi/Low Daily Temps (°F)	72/ 49	73/ 50	78/ 55	84/ 60	88/ 66	91/ 71	92/ 73	92/ 73	90/ 73	84/ 65	78/ 57	73/ 51
Hi/Low Daily Temps (°C)	22/ 10	23/ 10	26/ 13	29/ 16	31/ 19	33/ 22	33/ 23	33/ 23	32/ 23	29/ 19	26/ 14	23/ 11
Inches of Precipitation	2.25	2.82	3.32	2.43	3.30	7.13	7.27	6.88	6.53	3.16	1.98	2.25
Hotel Room Cost*	$82	$82–$125	$125	$105–$135	$105–$115	$105–$115	$115	$82–$115	$82	$82–$105	$105–$115	$82–$145

The price for a Value-class Disney room with two double beds; the lowest off-property prices start at just over half this rate.

Orlando's Visit-Worthy Events

There's usually so much going on in Orlando (both the city itself and the theme parks), that I list only the highlights; check the special events pages at the theme park websites to see if any themed weekends or smaller events are in the works. In addition, the events listings in *Orlando Weekly* magazine (www.orlandoweekly.com) and the *Orlando Sentinel* newspaper (www.orlandosentinel.com) are excellent starting places; they're useful to check even while you're on vacation, as many of their announcements are for the short term. You will also find a few listings at *Orlando* magazine (www.orlandomagazine.com).

January

Capital One Bowl (www.fcsports.com): It used to be called the Citrus Bowl—can *anyone* keep track of the square-dancing corporate naming rights anymore? Held New Year's Day at the Florida Citrus Bowl Stadium, it pits the second-ranked teams from the Big Ten and SEC conferences against one another. Tickets are $80.

Zora Neale Hurston Festival of the Arts and Humanities/ZORA! Festival (☎ 407/647-3307; www.zorafestival.com): The great folklorist and writer (1891–1960) was from Eatonville (a 30-min. drive north of Orlando), the country's oldest incorporated African-American town. This weeklong event includes lectures and a 2-day public art fair.

February

Winter Park Bach Festival (☎ 407/646-2182; www.bachfestivalflorida.org): This annual event at Rollins College began in 1935 and has evolved into one of the country's better choral fests. Although it has stretched to include other composers and guest artists (Handel, P.D.Q. Bach), at least one concert is devoted to Johann. It takes place mid-February to early March, with scattered one-off guest performances throughout the year.

Silver Spurs Rodeo of Champions (1875 Silver Spur Lane, Kissimmee; ☎ 407/677-6336; www.silverspursrodeo.com; $15): Lest you doubt Central Florida is far removed from the American Deep South, it hosts the largest rodeo east of the Mississippi (with bareback broncs, racing barrel horses, rodeo clowns, and athletes drawn from the cowboy circuit) over 3 days in mid-February in an indoor arena off U.S. 192.

Mardi Gras at Universal Studios (☎ 407/224-2691; www.universalorlando.com/mardigras): On Saturday nights, Universal books major acts

(Bonnie Raitt, Hall & Oates, LL Cool J) and mounts a parade complete with stilt-walkers, jazz bands, Louisiana-made floats, and bead tossing—although here, what it takes to win a set of beads is considerably less risqué than it is in the Big Easy. It's included with admission.

SeaWorld's Bud & BBQ (www.budand barbecue.com): Free with admission to SeaWorld, this lineup of country music and classic rock (Styx, Sugarland) is followed by a paid barbecue serving lots of beer made by the park's parent company. It's held Saturdays from late February into March.

Mickey's Pirate & Princess Party (☎ 407/934-7639; www.disneyworld. com): The Mouse found a good way to pump up sales in off months: Throw a special after-hours event that can double paid attendance in a day. Like the Halloween and holiday events that spun it off, this effort is an evening at Magic Kingdom, separately ticketed ($44 adult and $38 kids if bought in advance), where candy is freely distributed, a special parade is launched, and kids come dressed in their gender-dictated dream gear—boys are taught how to be pirates by the dubious role model of Jack Sparrow, and girls turn to one of the princesses for, presumably, advice on catching a prince. It takes place on various nights from late February to through early June, and most of the major attractions are open. It's $4 more at the gate. Some years, it doesn't run.

Spring Training: See p. 254 for a rundown of which Major League Baseball teams play where. It lasts mid-February through March.

March
Florida Film Festival (☎ 407/644-5625; www.floridafilmfestival.com): Produced by the Enzian Theater (p. 288), this respected event showcases films by Florida artists and has featured past appearances by the likes of Oliver Stone,

William H. Macy, Christopher Walken, and Dennis Hopper. Admission is $10 per film. The Theater's Brouhaha Film & Video Showcase, in December, is a proving ground for entries.

April
Epcot's International Flower & Garden Festival (☎ 407/934-7639; www.disney world.com): This spring event, which lasts from March to May, transforms the park with some 30 million flowers, some 70 topiaries, a screened-in butterfly garden, presentations by noted horticulturalists, a French fragrance garden, and a steady lineup of concerts (Davy Jones, Petula Clark). It's free with standard entry.

Grad Nites (www.disneygradnite.com): Held weekends in April, these special Disney events for high school seniors ($50 admission) are a beloved ritual for nearly every kid raised in the southeast United States. Hollywood Studios closes around 7pm to regular folk and turns into an all-night romp for America's Future before closing at 4am. Acts like Fall Out Boy and Britney Spears perform on scattered stages, and when they're not making out in the restrooms, kids hit every ride. Universal does its own $43 version, **Grad Bash** (www.universalorlando.com/gradbash), with equally cool acts (Rihanna, Akon).

May
Orlando International Fringe Festival (☎ 407/648-0077; www.orlandofringe. org): This theatrical smorgasbord was created in the image of the anyone's-welcome fest held in Edinburgh, Scotland. It spends 10 days mounting some 500 newly written, experimental performances by artists from Florida and around the world.

Florida Music Festival (www.florida musicfestival.com): Less expansive than the Fringe Festival, it takes 3 days and limits itself to up-and-coming musicians, although it crams about 250 bands into that brief window. Prices are $10 for a day of shows, or $25 for all 3 days.

June

Gay Days (www.gaydays.com): What started as a single day for gay and lesbian visitors has mushroomed into a full week of some 40 events managed by a host of promoters. It's said that attendance goes as high as 135,000—it's become one of the biggest annual events in Florida. Held around the first Saturday in June, Gay Days are a blowout party for outgoing gay and lesbians, with unofficial group visits to each of Disney's parks, plus an ongoing pool bash at the Regal Sun Hotel. Most participants come because they love the atmosphere, and they keep the ribald behavior behind closed doors—but they do wear red shirts as a statement of equality. All a Gay Day participant needs is a regular ticket to the parks, but parties cost extra. Dance events—including the Beach Ball at a Disney water park and Magic Journeys, an all-night, after-hours dance party at Arabian Nights—are sold through www.onemightyweekend.com.

Star Wars **Weekends** (www.disney world.com/starwars): Hollywood Studios' major annual do, held over 3 weeks in June, sees actors from the franchise arrive for signings, parades, Q&As, and brief workshops. Warwick Davis, who once squeezed into an Ewok costume, has made a career out of these events. It's not just for kids—the finer points of the Lucas catechism are discussed. A regular ticket gets you in.

July

Independence Day: All the theme parks go patriotism-mad—Disney in particular, followed by SeaWorld—with extra fireworks, concerts, and longer opening hours.

September

Night of Joy (☎ 877/648-3569; www.nightofjoy.com): It's actually a long-running pair of nights of outdoor Contemporary Christian concerts—eight or nine acts—spread throughout Hollywood Studios, which stays open late just for the occasion. Rides run all night, and the event usually sells out. The party continues around the same time for **Rock the Universe** (www.rocktheuniverse. com), a weekend festival of top-flight Christian rock bands who perform on stages around one of the Universal parks. Rides and performances continue past midnight, after regular patrons have gone home. Tickets to both events must be purchased separately from tickets good for regular operating hours.

October

Epcot's International Food & Wine Festival (☎ 407/939-3378; www.disney world.com/foodandwine): The World Showcase makes amends with the countries it ignores by installing nearly 30 temporary booths serving tapas-size servings of foods and wines ($2–$5) from many nations. New Zealand brings lamb sliders, South Africa makes *bobotie* pie, and Australia brings enough wine to choke a kangaroo. It also often brings kangaroo. In the usually abandoned Wonders of Life pavilion, there are chef demonstrations and seminars, and in World Showcase, expect regular concerts by known acts (Kool and the Gang, David Cassidy), and tastings by at least 100 wineries. A few of the more extravagant events are charged, but most talks are free. The festival lasts through mid-November and the hotly awaited details are posted by Disney in the summer.

Mickey's Not-So-Scary Halloween Party (☎ 407/934-7639; www.disney world.com): Another one of the Magic Kingdom's separately ticketed evening events, this one costs $56 for adults and $50 for kids, and for that you get a special Halloween-themed parade (I like the gravediggers who pound their shovels on the ground in time to the music), a few special shows, a few locations for dance parties with costumed characters, a fireworks display with notably more orange than usual, and—the part I like most, and what makes it a safe alternative to the suburban trick-or-treat tradition—stations where you can pick up bagsful of free candy. Lots of kids even show up in costume, although it's not required. Some nights offer advance-purchase discounts of about $6. The event happens on scattered evenings from mid-September through the end of October. Halloween sells out early. Target audience: People who like lollipops.

Halloween Horror Nights (www. halloweenhorrornights.com; $70): Unquestionably Universal's biggest event, HHN is the equivalent of a whole new theme park that's designed and built for a month's run. After dark on selected nights, the Studios park is overtaken by grotesque "scareactors" who terrorize crowds with chain saws, gross-out shows, and eight big, walk-through haunted houses that are made from scratch each year. The mayhem lasts into the wee hours. Wimps need not apply; children are discouraged by the absence of kids' ticket prices. A bawdy revue based on the Bill and Ted movie characters skewers the year in pop culture and draws huge, enthusiastic crowds of tipsy young people. On top of all this, most of the rides remain open, so it's like getting two theme parks for the price of one. Fridays and Saturdays are hellishly crowded. HHN has legions of fans who slavishly follow it. Target audience: People who like to poop themselves in fright. (Busch Gardens' Howl-o-Scream event's scariness is somewhere between Universal's and Disney's.)

SeaWorld's Halloween Spooktacular (www.seaworldspooktacular.com): SeaWorld throws a sweet, toddler-approved weekend Halloween event of its own, with trick-or-treating (kids dress up), a few encounters with sea fairies and bubbles, and a *Sesame Street* stage show. It's included in admission on weekends.

Orlando Film Festival (☎ 407/843-0801; www.orlandofilmfest.com): Like all festivals worth their salt, this one presents mostly mainstream and independent films in advance of their wider release dates. It's a new program and lasts only a few days in mid-October or early November, screening at various downtown venues.

Children's Miracle Network Golf Classic (☎ 407/824-2250; www. childrensmiraclenetworkclassic.com): For avid spectators, many top PGA touring names, including Tiger Woods (who has a home in Orlando), come out to play on the Disney courses for 4 days in October of November, just as they have done since the grass was planted in 1971; Jack Nicklaus swept the first three. Tickets start at $20 and it's not usually crowded.

November

Ice! (☎ 407/586-4423; www.gaylord palms.com/ice): It debuted in 2003 at the Gaylord Palms hotel and has quickly become a holiday perennial. The hotel brings in nearly 2 million pounds of ice, sculpts it into a walk-through city, keeps it chilled to 9°F, and issues winter coats to visitors. Add Christmas and synchronized light shows and you've got an event that charges $10 to $25 for entry—and sells out.

The Osborne Family Spectacle of Dancing Lights (www.disneyworld. com): No, not Ozzy and Sharon, but Jennings, Paul, Mitzi, and Breezy (I swear I'm not making this up), whose preposterously overdone Christmas display at their Little Rock house was deemed so vulgar that neighbors went to the Arkansas Supreme Court to shut it down. Enter Disney, which installs their millions of lights each year on Hollywood Studio's Streets of America. Every 15 minutes, it twitters and "dances" to Christmas carols, all as foam "snow" gently wafts from above. The city is barely mopping up from Halloween when it's mounted around Thanksgiving. It lasts until the first week of January.

December

Mickey's Very Merry Christmas Party (☎ 407/934-7639; www.disneyworld. com): This miserably crowded Christmas event, which occurs on various nights starting even before Thanksgiving—the Orlando calendar skips right from Halloween to the holidays, no gratitude included—is probably Disney's most popular special annual event. It requires a separate ticket (as much as $56 adults, $50 kids) from regular admission. What you get is a tree-lighting ceremony, a few special holiday-themed shows, a special fireworks display (more green and red), an appearance by Santa Claus, and a special parade. Throughout the park, you'll find stations serving free hot cocoa and cookies. Not everything is open; outdoor rides involving boat trips, for one, are usually shut down, and the same Christmas decorations will be up during normal-priced operating hours, too, so don't feel too compelled. Meanwhile, the Disney hotels deck the halls: the Grand Floridian erects a life-size house made of gingerbread in its lobby.

Epcot Presents Holidays Around the World (www.disneyworld.com): This one features a daily tree lighting led by Mickey Mouse and a host of costumed storytellers, but its real showpiece is the thrice-daily, 40-minute candlelight processional, a retelling of the Christmas Nativity story by a celebrity narrator (recent names have included Steven Curtis Chapman, Rita Moreno, Mario Lopez, Phil Donahue, and Neil Patrick Harris) accompanied by a 50-piece orchestra and a full Mass choir. The processional is a WDW tradition going back to its earliest days—Cary Grant did it!

Grinchmas and Macy's Holiday Parade at Universal Orlando Resort (www. universalorlando.com): Usual holiday traditions include a musical version of "How the Grinch Stole Christmas" and daily parades by Macy's, which brings balloons and floats to the resort when Thanksgiving is over. That's included in the ticket price.

SeaWorld's Holiday Celebration (www.seaworldorlando.com): Befitting SeaWord's laid-back attitude, its holiday attractions are not nearly as bombastic as Disney's. Expect lots of decorations, carolers at the Waterfront; a Christmas-themed overlay on its evening Shamu, Makahiki Luau, and Clyde and Seamore shows; and a *Polar Express* theme for its Wild Arctic pavilion. Everything's included in the regular admission price. Bayside Ski Jam and Mistify, two water spectaculars, are also mounted during holiday week; they're normally only shown in the summer.

Champs Sports Bowl (www.fcsports. com): An ACC team battles a Big Ten team, usually a few days before New Year's and always at the Florida Citrus Bowl Stadium. Tickets are $60.

New Year's Eve: Yahoo.com reports that Orlando regularly makes its list of top five most-searched New Year's Eve destinations. There's no shortage of places to party. At the parks: **CityWalk** ($119) lures top acts (in 2007, it got Cyndi Lauper, and in 2008, the Doobie Brothers) for its bash, which serves gourmet appetizers. Three of **Disney's parks**, minus Animal Kingdom, stay open until the wee hours. **SeaWorld** brings in big-band music or jazz, plus fireworks.

INFORMATION FOR INTERNATIONAL VISITORS

Be sure to check with your local U.S. embassy or consulate for the very latest in entry requirements, as these continue to shift. Full information can be found at the **U.S. State Department**'s website, www.travel.state.gov.

ENTRY REQUIREMENTS

VISAS Citizens of western and central Europe, Australia, New Zealand, and Singapore need only a valid machine-readable passport and a round-trip air ticket or cruise ticket to enter the United States for stays of up to 90 days. Canadian citizens can also enter without a visa as long as they show proof of residence.

Citizens of all other countries will need to obtain a tourist visa from the U.S. consulate. Depending on your country of origin, there may or may not be a charge attached (and you may or may not have to apply in person). You'll need to complete an application and submit a 1½-inch square photo, and your passport will need to be valid for at least 6 months past the scheduled end of your U.S. visit. If an interview isn't mandated, it's usually possible to obtain a visa within 24 hours, except during holiday periods or the summer rush.

PASSPORTS To enter the United States, international visitors must have a valid passport that expires at least 6 months later than the scheduled end of their visit.

MEDICAL REQUIREMENTS No inoculations or vaccinations are required to enter the United States unless you're arriving from an area that is suffering from an epidemic (cholera or yellow fever, in particular). A valid, signed prescription is required for those travelers in need of **syringe-administered medications** or medical treatment that involves **narcotics.** It is extremely important to obtain the correct documentation in these cases, as your medications could be confiscated; and if you are found to be carrying an illegal substance, security officials tend to lock you up first and ask questions later. You could be subject to significant penalties. Those who are **HIV positive** may also need a special waiver in order to enter the country; however, that restriction is soon to be eliminated. The best thing to do is contact **AIDSinfo** (☎ 800/448-0440; www.aidsinfo.nih.gov) for up-to-date information.

CUSTOMS REGULATIONS

Strict regulations govern what can and can't be brought into the United States—and what you can take back home with you. The rules mostly concern restricted substances such as booze or tobacco, so I wouldn't get too worried, unless fresh citrus was part of your plan. Fortunately, there are no bans on Mouse-ear caps.

WHAT YOU CAN BRING INTO ORLANDO Every visitor over 21 years of age may bring in, free of duty, the following: 1 liter of wine or hard liquor; 200 cigarettes, 100 cigars (but not from Cuba), or 3 pounds of smoking tobacco; and $100 worth of gifts. These exemptions are offered to travelers who spend at least 72 hours in the United States and who have not claimed them within the preceding 6 months. It is forbidden to bring foodstuffs (particularly fruit, cooked meats, and canned goods) and plants (vegetables, seeds, tropical plants, and the like). Foreign tourists may carry in or out up to $10,000 in U.S. or foreign currency with no formalities; larger sums must be declared to U.S. Customs on entering or leaving, which includes filing form CM 4790. For details regarding U.S. Customs and Border Protection, consult your nearest U.S. embassy or consulate, or **U.S. Customs** (☎ 202/927-1770; www.cbp.gov).

WHAT YOU CAN TAKE HOME FROM ORLANDO For a clear summary of **Canadian** rules, write for the booklet *I Declare,* issued as publication number RC4044 by the **Canada Border Services Agency** (☎ 800/461-9999 in Canada, or 506/636-5064; www.cbsa-asfc.gc.ca).

For information, **U.K. citizens** should contact **HM Customs & Excise** at ☎ 0845/010-9000 (outside the U.K. ☎ 2920/501-261) or www.hmce.gov.uk.

Australians should consult **Australian Customs Service** at ☎ 1300/363-263 (outside Australia ☎ 2/6275-666) or on www.customs.gov.au.

New Zealand rules are laid out through **New Zealand Customs,** the Customhouse, 17–21 Whitmore St., Box 2218, Wellington (☎ 0800/428-786; from outside New Zealand 9/300-5399; www.customs.govt.nz).

GETTING TO ORLANDO

Orlando is served by lots of airlines, so thankfully, airfares are among the lowest on the East Coast. Nearly 35 million people fly in or out of Orlando International Airport (MCO) each year, or nearly 100,000 a day, meaning competition is fierce and prices can be under $100 each way. Strategies for finding a good airfare include:

♦ **Look at the low-fare carriers.** Airlines such as **JetBlue, Southwest, USA3000, AirTran, America West Airlines, Frontier, CanJet, WestJet, Spirit Airlines, Sun Country** flit in and out of MCO like bees at a hive, and they will sometimes have better fares than the larger airlines, but they may not be searched if you go to a site such as Expedia. So use a search tool such as **SideStep** (www.sidestep.com), **Kayak** (www.kayak.com), or **Momondo** (www.momondo.com), which search airline sites directly, adding no service charges and often finding fares that the larger travel sites miss. If you have kids, booking an airline with seatback TV sets makes the journey go faster. If you're flying from Europe into the United States, take a look at the fares from British Airways, American, Continental, Delta, United, Virgin Atlantic, Lufthansa, Icelandair, Martinair, and Iberia, as these carriers tend to have the lowest rates for international travel. **Mobissimo** (www.mobissimo.com) and **CheapFlights.co.uk** are good for fares that don't originate in the U.S.

♦ **Watch for sales.** They happen a lot. Sites such as **Trip Watcher** on Hotwire (www.hotwire.com), **Airfarewatchdog.com,** and **Farecast** (www.farecast. com) will send you e-mail alerts when airfare to your city drops below a certain threshold; the last one even graphs historic prices over time to give you a feel for the best timing. Helpfully, Orlando's own airport lists online low-fare alerts of running specials for flights to it (at **www.orlandoairports.net**). Monitor such sites as Frommers.com and SmarterTravel.com for fare sales.

♦ **Fly when others don't, and take an itinerary other travelers don't want.** Those who fly midweek and midday, and who stay over a Saturday night, generally pay far less on the standard carriers than those who fly at more popular times. If you jigger your days and you're still finding that prices are high, then perhaps a cruise ship is coming or going from Port Canaveral on the day you want, increasing air traffic.

♦ **Book at the right time.** Sounds odd, but you can often save money by booking between 3 and 4 months in advance and on a Tuesday or

Wednesday. Airline sales are announced on Mondays and matched by competitors on Tuesdays; hitting them right, therefore, helps garner you a lower-priced seat. And those who book too far in advance are rarely able to take advantage of sales (the same can usually be said of last-minute bookings, though the current economic downturn has produced more last-minute sales than were normal in 2006 and 2007).

Plenty of companies provide packages that lump airfare with discounted hotel rooms. See p. 35 for a discussion of those, because the deals can be ripe.

Amtrak's (☎ 800/872-7245; www.amtrak.com) Silver Service/Palmetto route serves Orlando and Kissimmee. Trains go direct to New York City, Washington, D.C., Charleston, Savannah, and Miami, which isn't a bad lineup if you're on a whistle-stop tour of great American cities. One-way trips from New York, as an example, take a little less than 24 hours (in theory—Amtrak, the national train line, is in a deplorable state of benign neglect and trains are often delayed) and start around $117 for a coach seat. The carrier's Auto Train service will tote your car along starting at an add-on of $198; it departs from Lorton, VA, in the Washington, D.C., area, and finishes in Sanford, which is north of Orlando but close enough to do the job. Lastly, the Sunset Limited train used to run from Orlando to Los Angeles via New Orleans, but Hurricane Katrina in 2005 suspended the section east of New Orleans. Check to see if it's up and running; a more circuitous route is available.

ARRIVING OR DEPARTING BY AIR IN ORLANDO

The main airport, **Orlando International Airport** (www.orlandoairports.net), is a pleasure. The airport, 25 miles east of Walt Disney World, was originally built during World War II as McCoy Air Force Base, which closed in the early 1970s but bequeathed the airport with its deceptive code, MCO. I don't know how they do it, but the late-departure rate of 19% is among the lowest in the country, even though the airport is America's 14th largest (and the 24th largest in the world). The airport serves 96 cities around the world. Flight delays occur most often after 11pm, and the fewest delays occur before lunch. The busiest days are when the cruise ships at nearby Port Canaveral are loading or unloading, but it's tough to predict when that will happen because there are so many 4-day cruise runs. Saturdays can be hairy for incoming traffic, and midmornings and midafternoons can be crowded for outgoing passengers. Flights late at night may also be delayed.

Killing time at MCO isn't painful; it's a relatively pleasant environment and the shopping is particularly good. If, on the way home, you realize you neglected to buy any park-related souvenirs, fear not, because Disney, SeaWorld, Kennedy Space Center, and Universal all maintain lavish stores (located *before* the security checkpoint, so budget enough time). When I first arrive in town, I frequently kill the few minutes during which my luggage is catching up with me by stopping by the food court, where there's an outpost of the delicious Southern fast-food chain Chick-fil-A.

Interestingly, Orlando was one of the first American airports to offer a special express lane for paying members who have been pre-vetted by the Transportation Security Administration. **Clear** (☎ 866/848-2415; www.flyclear.com; $200 a year) isn't for average tourists, but it's a harbinger of how, soon, the time you wait at airports will have a lot to do with how much money you make. Awful, right?

When you first arrive at MCO, you'll have to hop a free elevated tram to the main terminal building to claim your bags and rent your car. Kids go goggle-eyed at this twist, thinking they're on their first ride. The main terminal is divided into two sides, A and B, so if you can't find the desk for your airline or transportation service open on one side, it may be on the other side. Transportation desks are on the lower level, beneath baggage claim. Then you just head across the road to the parking garage structure, where their lots are located. The system works well.

Other airports in the region are used much less frequently. **Orlando Sanford International Airport** (www.orlandosanfordairport.com), or SFB, 18 miles northeast of downtown, is served mostly by international charters, plus Icelandair, Allegiant Air, and Flyglobespan. It's connected to the Disney area by the Central Florida GreeneWay, or S. R. 417—the trip takes about 40 minutes and there are tolls, so foreign visitors should have American dollars before leaving the airport. If you have a choice, go with MCO instead, which is closer. Some people, particularly European visitors on long-haul trips, might fly into **Tampa International Airport** (www.tampaairport.com), or TPA, 90 minutes southwest.

TRANSPORTATION TO & FROM MCO
Rental Cars

Having a car ensures you can experience the "real" Florida and it will noticeably improve your ability to see and do more things, so I strongly recommend renting one. Be alert as you drive out of the airport, though—very soon, you will have to decide whether to use the south exit (marked for Walt Disney World) or the north exit (for SeaWorld, Universal, the Convention Center, and downtown Orlando). If you accidentally take the wrong one, don't worry, as they both eventually hook up with Interstate 4 where you can correct your mistake. The city planners have the system rigged, though. Whichever route you take, you will pay about $2.75 in accumulated tolls, so have loose change ready. The north exit is the cheaper one. Whichever path you choose, stay on the right, where the cash-only toll booths are.

In my experience, **Alamo** and **Dollar** are among the least expensive car-rental companies (economy cars start around $20–$25 a day), and **Avis** and **National** are the highest priced. But test the waters at a site such as Orbitz (www.orbitz.com), Travelocity (www.travelocity.com), or Kayak (www.kayak.com), which compare multiple renters with one click. At times when those sites quoted prices around $23 a day, I have been able to snag deals from Priceline for as little as $15 a day.

For those who insist on staying on Disney turf, a budget-saving solution is to rent a car for only the days you'd like to venture off property. To that end, **Alamo** (☎ 800/462-5266; www.alamo.com) operates satellite agencies within the Walt Disney World Resort: one at the Dolphin hotel, one at the Car Care Center near the parking lot of the Magic Kingdom, and one at the Buena Vista Palace Hotel east of Downtown Disney. In my experience, renting a car for, say, a 2-day stint is cheaper if you pick up and return to Alamo's airport location. The same rental costs about $10 more a day if you pick your car up within Disney (but not always, so poke around). Renting at Disney and dropping off at the airport is another option that doesn't incur a scary surcharge. A similar pricing pattern is true at most of the area hotels that have small rental-car desks (and there are many).

Using Priceline, you might be able to obtain quotes as low as $17 a day in the off season, and about $27 when business is more average. Renting away from the airport incurs taxes of around half of those charged by renting (or even merely returning) a car at the airport, where they're over 20%. For longer stays, that might make it worth the hassle to take the Magical Express or Mears and rent at Disney.

Money-saving tip: Always fill up your car before driving back to the airport. Gas stations near the airport's entrance have been nabbed for gouging. You might be surprised to learn that the Hess stations inside Walt Disney World charge a competitive price. Prices are best, though, well away from the tourist zone.

The legal age minimum in Florida for a rental driver is 21. Agencies will usually slap those aged 21 to 25 with a surcharge of $25 a day, regardless of how trustworthy you look. Enterprise charges lower surcharges ($15), depending on the office (such as at the airport). **Continental Rent-a-Car** (☎ 800/656-4223; www.continentalcar.com), a privately owned outfit located 4 miles from the airport by shuttle bus, also charges $15 a day. So does the little-known Hertz outfit **Simply Wheelz** (☎ 888/999-9078; www.simplywheelz.com), which operates one of its six simplified, touch-screen rental locations at the airport. On the flip side of generosity, National has been known to charge up to $50, so watch out and ask what the fee is before committing. Most companies won't rent to anyone older than 85. The following rental car agencies have lots in the airport's parking garage, meaning you shouldn't have to board a bus to claim your car: Alamo, Avis, Budget, Dollar, National, and L&M. Brands requiring use of a shuttle are Enterprise, Hertz, Payless, and Thrifty. Another shuttle brand, **Sunshine Rent A Car** (☎ 888/786-7446; www.sunshinerentacar.com; $15 underage fee), may charge as little as $10 a day when it's quiet.

Shuttles, Coaches & Taxis

Mears Transportation (☎ 407/423-5566; www.mearstransportation.com) is the 800-pound gorilla of Orlando shuttles and taxis; it sends air-conditioned vans bouncing to area hotels every 15 to 20 minutes. Round-trip fares for adults are $28 ($21 for kids 4–11, kids 3 and under free) to the International Drive area, or $32/$24 to Walt Disney World/U.S. 192/Lake Buena Vista. You'll probably have to make several stops because the vans are shared by other passengers.

If you have more than four or five people, it's usually more economical to reserve a car service (do it at least 24 hr. ahead) and split the lump fee. **Tiffany Towncar** (☎ 888/838-2161 or 407/370-2196; www.tiffanytowncar.com) charges about $110 round-trip to the Disney-area hotels and $80 round-trip for SeaWorld/Universal/I-Drive, all for up to four people. It also runs vans seating up to seven people for $70 one-way and $125 round-trip for Disney, and $65 to $70 round-trip for SeaWorld/Universal/I-Drive. A similar service and price come from **Quicksilver Tours** (☎ 888/468-6939 or 407/299-1434; www.quicksilver-tours.com), which will also throw in a free 30-minute stop at a grocery store for round-trips so you can stock up on supplies. So will **Happy Limo** (☎ 888/394-4277; www.happylimo.com). All town-car services take the four big credit cards.

If you have a reservation at a Disney-owned hotel, you have the right to take the company's airport motorcoaches (also known as **Disney's Magical Express**) to the resort for free. By offering the perk, the Mouse makes it seem simple by sending you tags for your luggage, which you affix before leaving home, and telling you everything will be taken care of from there. And yes, Disney employees will pick up your luggage at baggage claim while you check in for the Magical Express ride. But by the time you board the bus to the resort, you'll already have waited in two long lines—the first of many, many lines you'll endure during your visit, so get used to it—and then you'll stop at up to five other hotels before reaching your own. Your bags, which must weigh less than 50 pounds, may not meet up with you for 6 to 8 hours, so hitting a park right away may be difficult without coordinating your carry-ons. When you depart for home, you'll have to be ready for the coach 3 to 4 hours before your flight; the extra time, again, accounts for all the undisclosed stops you'll be making. It's free, which is terrific. But the Magical Express route costs you in time. It also lulls you into not renting a car, which means you'll probably never leave Disney property again and you'll have to rely on the park's slow buses for your entire vacation. That has huge opportunity costs. Don't let the promise of a free ride lure you onto the sticky trap of Orlando without a car.

Taxis are not the best bargain. The going rate is $2 for the first ⅖ of a mile or the first 80 seconds of waiting time, followed by 25¢ for each ⅛ of a mile and 25¢ for each additional 40 seconds of waiting. Airport trips incur a 50¢ surcharge. Taxis carry five passengers. It'll be about $70 to the Disney hotels, $60 to Universal, not including a tip, which is still cheaper than a town car.

TRAVEL INSURANCE—DO YOU NEED IT?

Yes, you do, principally because you're traveling. Should something unpleasant befall you, you may need to be flown back home on a stretcher, and no matter how much you beg, you can't save money by coming home as cargo. At the very least, you may need to cancel your trip before you leave, and travel insurance can buffer you from a large financial loss.

But does that mean you need to buy some? Not necessarily—you may already have it. Your existing medical coverage may include a safety net; ask so you're sure. The credit card you use to make reservations may cover you for cancellation, lost luggage, or trip interruption; again, the only way to be sure is to ask your issuer. Most hotels will issue refunds with enough notice, but a few of the cheap ones won't.

So what else may you want to insure? If your medical coverage and credit cards don't lend a hand, you may want special coverage for **villa stays,** especially if you've plunked down a deposit, and any **valuables,** since airlines are only required to pay up to $2,500 for lost luggage domestically, less for foreign travel, and not every hotel provides in-room safes.

If you do decide on insurance, you can easily compare available policies by visiting **InsureMyTrip.com**. Or contact one of the following reputable companies:

Access America (☎ 866/807-3982; www.accessamerica.com)
CSA Travel Protection (☎ 800/873-9844; www.csatravelprotection.com)
MEDEX (☎ 800/732-5309; www.medexassist.com)
Travel Guard International (☎ 800/807-3982; www.travelguard.com)
Travelex (☎ 800/228-9792; www.travelex-insurance.com)

TRAVELING FROM ORLANDO TO OTHER PARTS OF AMERICA

Many international visitors combine visits to Orlando with other stops in famous American locations such as the Grand Canyon, New York City, and San Francisco. Orlando, while not an important air hub, is well connected to the cities that are, particularly New York and Chicago. For advice on how to find cheap airfare to any domestic American city, see "Getting to Orlando," earlier in this chapter.

The **USA Rail Pass** is the American equivalent of the Eurail Pass in Europe—although our national rail system, **Amtrak** (☎ 800/872-7245 or 215/856-7953; www.amtrak.com), hardly compares to the European system. The pass allows travel within the U.S. for one set (and fairly reasonable) rate. The passes, which are not valid on the Auto Train, cannot be purchased on trains and are good for 15, 30, and 45 days of travel. The cheapest pass is a 15-day pass, which grants eight trips ($195); the most expensive offers 45 days of travel over 18 trips throughout the U.S. ($750). Those on a grand tour of America may benefit from those rates compared to flying.

From late January through June, many major car renters redistribute their inventory by offering "drive-out" deals for one-way rentals that originate in Orlando and drop off elsewhere in the country. Since per-day rates can be as low as $1, it pays to ask if there's a special available that fits your plans.

For bus travel, an International Discovery Pass for foreign visitors is offered by **Greyhound** (☎ 800/231-2222; www.discoverypass.com). The company's prices, both for individual trips and for the passes, are equivalent to what you'll find at Amtrak (from $329 for 7 days). Bus travel in the United States is usually a purgatorial experience, and I recommend you look at train and air options first.

MONEY MATTERS

This town lives to make money, and consequently it places few obstacles between you and the loss of it.

Most **ATMs** that you'll find are run by third parties, not your bank, which means that you'll be slapped with fees of around $2.50 per withdrawal (around $5 for international visitors). But the good news is that $2.50 is still cheaper than the fees you'd be charged to draw traveler's checks, and machines accept pretty much anything you can stick into them; Walt Disney World's, for example, take Visa, Plus, MasterCard, Cirrus, American Express, and Discover/Novus. If you're staying near the parks, you won't stumble across a branch of your local bank unless you do advance research, and even then you'll probably discover that your bank is too far away, in the "real" Orlando, to bother. The Presto! machines at widespread Publix supermarkets waive the fee for members of 1,500 member banks; visit www.publix.com and search for "presto" to see if your bank's included. Citibank customers can avoid the usage fee by using the fancy Citibank machines located at most 7-Eleven convenience stores in the area. International visitors should make advance arrangements with their banks to ensure their cards will function in the United States.

Credit cards are nearly universally accepted. You could strut off the plane with just a Visa, MasterCard, or American Express card and live in style for your entire trip. In fact, you *must* have one to rent a car. Your only problem would be how to

What Things Cost in & out of the Parks

Orlando's cost of living is creeping upward, as it is in so many cities. Things are even more expensive at the theme parks, because the corporations that run them know they've got a captive market.

Bus ride	$2
Theme park admission	$75 for a 1-day ticket
Theme park parking	$12
Counter-service meal at a theme park, without drink	$7
Regular Coke at a theme park	$2.50
Bottle of water at a theme park or Disney hotel	$2.75
20 oz. bottle of Coke	$2.50 (Disney hotel), $1.30 (7-Eleven)
Big Mac	$2.69
Evening movie ticket	$9
8 oz. of SPF 15 sun lotion	$8 (Walgreens), $12.25 (Disney)
4 oz. of SPF 45 sun lotion	$8 (Universal)
Rain poncho	99¢ (Walgreens), $7 (Disney)
Huggies Little Swimmers swim pants	$8.50 for 12 (Walgreens), $1.60 per pair (Disney)
27-exposure Kodak camera	2 for $18 (CVS), $18.50 (Disney)
27-exposure Kodak waterproof camera	$15 (Walgreens), $20 (Disney)
Beach towel	$10 (CVS), $15 (Walgreens), $20 (Disney)
4 AA Duracell batteries	$2.80 (Walgreens), $6 (Universal), $5 (Disney)
Water shoes	$16 (Disney), $18 (Aquatica)
ATM fee	$2 (standard)
Budget motel room at Disney	From $82
Budget motel room outside of Disney	From $45

pay the highway tolls. The majority of places accept the Big Four: American Express, MasterCard, Visa, and Discover. A few places add Diners Club to the mix, and some smaller family-owned businesses subtract American Express because of the pain of dealing with the company.

Before you leave home, let your credit card issuer know that you're about to go on vacation. Many of them, guarding against potential fraud, get antsy when they see unexpectedly large charges start appearing so far from your home, and sometimes they freeze your account in response. With warning, they won't.

Not only will Orlando clerks almost always neglect to check the purchaser's identification, but also, in the high-volume world of the theme park restaurants, credit card charges under $25 often don't even require signatures. You just swipe and go. That means you need to be doubly sure to keep your cards safe.

Try not to use credit cards to withdraw cash. You'll be charged interest from the moment your money leaves the slot. If your credit card allows for online bill paying through links with your bank account, set up that capability before you leave—at the very least, you can pay off your withdrawals within hours, cutting your losses. Using an ATM card linked to a liquid bank account, like a debit card, is far less expensive. *Tip:* There is an exception that the resorts don't sanction, but I certainly do: Instead of using your credit card to draw cash from an ATM, use it to buy Disney Dollars or Universal Dollars. They're private scrip (sold at big shops and most guest services desks), valued precisely like U.S. dollars. But they are charged as a purchase, *not* as a cash withdrawal, so there are no additional fees. You can spend them like cash within the respective resorts. Pretty sneaky, sis!

Traveler's checks are also widely accepted, but they are slipping from favor outside of the theme parks and you should not rely on them as your primary source of funds. Because redeeming them can involve time-consuming paper-work, you may hear exasperated sighs from people in line behind you. They can deal.

Traveler's check cards, also called **prepaid cards,** which are essentially debit cards encoded with the amount of money you elect to put on them, may be more useful. They're not linked to your personal bank accounts, they work in ATMs, and should you lose one, you can get your cash back in a matter of hours. If you spend all the money on them, you can call a number and reload the card using your bank account information. The main traveler's check card is **Visa TravelMoney** (www.visa.com), sold through AAA offices in the United States (☎ 866/339-3378); it costs $10 and keeps a little over 1% of everything you load onto it, plus any foreign transaction fees. It's not ideal, but it's a relatively safe way to travel with money.

Like traveler's checks, **exchanging cash** is on the outs, and good riddance, as exchange rates are usurious. Because ATM withdrawals give better deals, old-fashioned exchange desks are few and far between, although you'll still find a few at the airport and at large hotels. If you need to change money, take advantage of the better rates offered by banks during regular banking hours (Mon–Fri 9:30am–4pm).

Finding a bank isn't difficult in the "real" world of Orlando around SeaWorld and Universal, but at Walt Disney World, you could use a hand. The nearest bank is the **SunTrust** (1675 Buena Vista Dr., across from Downtown Disney Marketplace; ☎ 407/828-6106; Mon–Fri 9am–4pm, until 6pm on Thurs).

HEALTH & SAFETY

Disney may advertise itself as "the Happiest Place on Earth," but it's still on Earth. That means bad things can happen.

Pickpockets are virtually unheard of, but that doesn't mean they don't exist—you just don't hear about them. Be vigilant about bags, too, such as waist packs and backpacks; you're going to be bumped and jostled many times while you wait in line—one of those bumps could be a nimble-fingered thief taking your cash, and you're unlikely to feel it.

Stuff You Never Thought to Bring (But Should)

Besides the usual toiletries, recharging cords, and drugs, you might not have realized that it'd be good to bring these things from home, too:

- **Earplugs.** Flights to and from Orlando are jumping with kids going insane with excitement. If you plan to sleep, stuff your ears.
- **Hand purifier.** Turnstiles. Safety bars. Handrails. Furry mascots. You're going to be touching a lot of dirty things. Carry a little bottle of sanitizer for before you eat or absent-mindedly chew your fingernails.
- **Dark-colored shorts or pants.** On almost all boat or flume rides, the seating doubles as a step, so you're bound to plant your butt in a slightly muddy puddle. Dark clothes hide spots.
- **Sandals that fasten.** Whoever designed Tevas should be Velcroed into shackles in the fashion-crimes dungeon, but I own a pair to wear at the parks because I know the water-based rides soak regular shoes and cause pruning. Flip-flops won't do because they fall off and you can't wear them on some roller coasters.
- **Skin-tight underwear.** Long, moist days at the parks can cause chafing even in people who rarely experience it, making walking excruciating for the rest of your vacation. Wearing a skin-tight undergarment, such as Under Armour (there's a store at the Prime Outlets, p. 294), or nonpadded bicycle shorts, is a smart precaution.
- **Sunscreen, a hat, and sunglasses.** Okay, so you probably thought of these, but it bears repeating. People forget that many attraction queues will strand them, baking, in the Florida sunlight for long periods (especially the ones at Disney).
- **Cellphones.** Split parties can use them to stay connected in the parks. They're not perfect—the system frequently gets overloaded and text messages have a way of arriving late—but they'll do.
- **A superabsorbent shammy.** For lenses and wet children.
- **Pocket-size games.** People talk about the rides, but they neglect to mention the hour you'll spend in line before those exciting 3 minutes. Orlando *is* lines. The fun you have depends on your ability to kill time with the people in your group. If you don't bring diversions, at least bring conversation topics and a gratitude for togetherness.

If you are traveling with kids, train them to approach the nearest park employee in case of **separation.** For older children, pick a landmark at which you can meet. Never dress your kids in clothing that reveals their name, address, or hometown. Also, unless it's a travel day, remove any luggage tags where this information will be visible. Think about it: If people can read your address off a backpack tag while you're in line at Jurassic Park, then they they'll know you're not at home; an unscrupulous person could do some damage with that information.

Your biggest concern will be **sun,** which can burn you even through grey skies on cloudy days. You will be spending a lot more time outdoors than you might suspect—rides take 3 minutes, but some of their lines will have you waiting outside for an hour first. Also have a hat, if you're susceptible to burning, and make sure that infants, especially, will be completely covered.

Stay off the road during **extreme downpours.** Florida's cloudbursts can overwhelm even people used to rain, and the quick volume of water also increases the potential for hydroplaning. Rain tends to pass or abate quickly in Florida.

PACKING

For the latest rules on how to pack and what you will be permitted to bring as a carry-on, consult your airline or the **Transportation Security Administration** (www.tsa.gov). Also be sure to find out from your airline what your checked-baggage weight limits will be. Even airlines that previously were lax with the limits, such as JetBlue, now impose maximums of around 50 pounds per suitcase. Anything heavier will incur a fee.

There's nothing you can't buy in Orlando. It's hardly Timbuktu. But to save yourself a hassle, bring the basics for sunshine (lotion of at least 30 SPF, wide-brimmed hat, bathing suit, sunglasses), for rain (a compact umbrella or a poncho, which costs $7 inside the parks), for walking (good shoes, sandals for wet days or pool wear), and for memories (camera, film or storage cards, chargers).

If you plan to visit a water park, don't bring swimsuits with rivets or buckles, as they'll scratch the slides and they're forbidden.

GETTING ATTRACTION DISCOUNTS

For a full breakdown of Disney's ticketing system, how it works, and how to ward against overspending on it, see p. 99.

One of the true discounted programs is the **FlexTicket,** which is sold by both Universal Orlando and the Anheuser-Busch parks (SeaWorld Orlando and Busch Gardens Africa). For admission to five parks (Universal's pair, SeaWorld, Aquatica, Wet 'n Wild), you want the Orlando FlexTicket ($235 adults, $215 kids 3–9), which grants unlimited admission to all of the parks for a full 2 weeks. Tack on Busch Gardens for $45 adults or kids. Considering 1-day admission to Busch Gardens alone is $68 adults and $58 kids, you don't have to get near a calculator to see the savings. Once you've paid for parking at your first theme park ($12 is the going rate—incredible when you consider that in 2001 it was just $6), you can keep your ticket and avoid paying it again. Many hotel closed-circuit TV programs promise $10 off, so when you're buying a FlexTicket in person, claim you learned about it from your in-room programming and ask for the deal. FlexTickets are sold online, too (www.worldsofdiscovery.com and www.universal orlando.com).

SeaWorld and Busch Gardens package their parks, too. A **2 Park Unlimited Admission Ticket** that gets you into both for as many times as you want for 14 days, plus a free round-trip bus ride from Orlando to Busch Gardens, is $100 adults and $90 kids. Adding Aquatica will save you $20 off buying it separately.

Either before leaving home or once you arrive, ask for the free **Orlando Magicard,** which grants discounts to heaps of attractions, meals, vacation home rentals, and hotels. It's essentially just a marketing tool for the Convention and

Buyer Beware!

Before Magic Your Way made ticket expiration standard, pretty much every Disney ticket was good forever. That means there are a lot of unused days floating around out there. It's illegal to sell them, but that doesn't stop many people. When you see a sign on the side of U.S. 192 promising discounted tickets, that may be what's for sale. Buying a ticket like this is a gamble, particularly if you don't have the expertise to recognize a fake. Often, there's not even a way to tell by looking whether unused days really remain on a ticket; only a magnetic scan can tell.

Other organizations, such as timeshare developers, do indeed offer legit tickets to theme parks and dinner shows, but to get them, you will have to endure heavy-duty sales presentations that last several hours. The requirements for attendance can be tight: Married couples must attend together (gay couples are usually excluded entirely), you both must swear your combined annual income is above a certain amount ($50,000, for example, for Westgate branded resorts), that you are in a given age range (23–65 is common), and that you commit to staying for at least 90 minutes, although as long as 4 hours is also common. At that point, you'll be rigorously and relentlessly pitched property. That's when many people begin to grow uncomfortable. Even if you're fearless about parrying sales pitches, I think that an entire morning out of your hard-earned vacation time is worth a lot more than whatever discount is being provided. After all, how many days of working did it take for you to accrue those 4 or 5 hours? You also may not arrive at the parks until lunchtime, missing (in some cases) a third of the opening hours. Don't be so cheap and discount-obsessed that you throw away your time.

One more item to be wary of: the **Go Orlando Card** (☎ 866/628-9036; www.goorlandocard.com). This paid card purports to offer discounts on secondary attractions (no major theme parks). Try as I might to make the math work, I can't do it without springing for the option that includes an exhausting Miami day tour. Rare is the person who can visit enough places to make the price (a 1-day card is $59, 2 days is $45, 3 days is $159) pay off, even with the 20% discounts frequently offered on its website. Do serious calculations based on the prices in this book before buying.

Visitors Bureau's many members, but considering just about everyone in town is on board and almost everyone offers snappy deals through this card, it's a gimmick that works. Its hotel discounts aren't much different from what the free coupon circulars promise, but they're still a good bargaining chip in terms of knowing the going rate and negotiating for something ever better. The Magicard is downloadable from the Orlando CVB website (www.orlandoinfo.com), where you can preview the discounts on offer, or you can pick one up at the Visitor Center.

A few outfits such sell discounted tickets. **Maple Leaf Tickets** (☎ 800/841-2837; www.mapleleaftickets.com) and **the Official Ticket Center** (☎ 877/406-4836; www.officialticketcenter.com) are both in good standing with the Better Business Bureau. Secondary options include **Undercover Tourist** (☎ 800/846-1302; www.undercovertourist.com) and **Ticket Momma** (☎ 866/996-7508; www.ticketmomma.com). Make sure you calculate tax before comparing prices. No Disney deals are ever deep enough to offset shipping fees or the hassle of picking up your tickets at their offices; however, the math behind multiple purchases as well as for third-tier diversions such as dinner shows ($10–$15 off) may work out for you. Tickets are nontransferable. A desk at the Orlando Official Visitor Center (p. 304) furnishes similar discounts on tickets you can trust.

You will also find coupons available through **Orlando Coupons** (www.orlandocoupons.com) and the statewide hotel discount circulars **Roomsaver.com** and **HotelCoupons.com**. Not all of the motels offering deals in those brochures are of good quality.

SPECIALIZED TRAVEL RESOURCES

If you have a wallet, Orlando wants you. Few tourist sponges are more adept at rolling out the red carpet for people of all needs. No matter who you are, Orlando has a system for dealing with you.

ADVICE FOR FAMILY TRAVELERS

The theme parks were built to make money off you. I mean, this is a place where kids are charged the full adult price once they turn 10! Although a very few minor attractions, mostly off resort grounds, sell "family tickets" that allow for everyone in your group to enter on one discounted pass, there aren't many breaks.

Think carefully about whether your child is *ready* for the theme parks. Too many parents consider an Orlando vacation such a rite of passage that they rush into it too early, without considering whether their child will find the experience overwhelming, or heck, even if they'll *remember* it. I agree with many parenting experts who say that about 3 years old is the minimum age. I can also say, from experience, that even that may be too young; as an adult, I still bear the pain of being turned away from Space Mountain for years because I was too short to meet the ride requirements. That kind of rejection *hurts,* man.

Also think about whether *you're* ready to bring your kids. Having little ones with you means you won't be able to do lots of the things you might otherwise have wanted to. If you get right up to the Tower of Terror only to find you can't do it with the rugrats, the last thing you want is to take your frustration out on your kids. I've witnessed many an ugly family meltdown at the parks, and although no one wants to admit it, I bet that half the time, it's because the *adults* can't have their way, not the kids. Note, however, that at every park, the scarier rides are capable of what's called a **child swap.** That provides an area where one parent or guardian can wait with a child while their partner rides and then switch off so the other gets a chance. Many rides also have a bypass corridor where chickens can do their chicken-out thing after waiting with their group. Ask staffers about it.

I suggest you let your kids take an active role in planning your vacation. Believe me, they'll be more than eager to fantasize about all the things there are to do, and their excitement will only make your investment pay off. Kid-directed planning will help *you*, too—if only because sorting the must-sees out ahead of time will keep your family from quarreling later, and it will keep expectations in check. The Walt Disney World website provides interactive online maps of its four parks, which you can use to highlight a must-see list according to your tastes. With 3 weeks' notice, the resort will print a color version of your customized maps and mail them for free to your house to get you jazzed up for your trip.

Strollers will not be allowed inside most attractions, and they will not be attended in their parking sections, so make sure you never leave anything valuable in them. Come prepared with a system for unloading your valuables every time you enter an attraction. Also have something with which to cover the seat, as most stroller parking is exposed, and like parked cars, they get sizzling hot in the Florida sun. Finally, you might want to tie some identifying marker (like a colorful bandana) to yours so you can identify it amidst the sea of clones.

A few other things to think about:

- **Familiarize yourself with the height restrictions for all rides,** which are posted at the parks' websites and listed on the maps. Universal also keeps physical gauges in front of both its parks. Everything is measured in inches, so if your child is usually measured in centimeters, multiply by 0.393.
- **Bring supplies to kid-proof your hotel room.**
- **Slather your kids in sun lotion.** Young skin burns easily.
- **Some hotels offer "kids eat free" programs**—you pay, they don't. Ask.
- **The theme parks' strollers are easy, but basic;** they don't recline, and they are not adequately secure for kids younger than toddlers. Folding strollers have distinct advantages. They make getting onto parking trams, monorails, and into other tight spaces so much easier.
- **Bring a current picture of your child** or keep one on your mobile phone. Should your kid get lost, this will help the people who try to find him or her.

ADVICE FOR TRAVELERS WITH DISABILITIES

The theme parks are way ahead when it comes to making life easier for guests with special needs. Nearly everything is accessible. This excellent customer service predates the Americans with Disabilities Act of 1990; as multigenerational attractions, the parks have always worked to be inclusive, and in response, guests with mobility issues have long embraced them.

There was a time when guests in **wheelchairs** and **ECVs** were given special treatment and ushered to the front of lines, but now, with so many guests on wheels for reasons including obesity, Disney (with the exception of Make-A-Wish Foundation kids and other special groups, by prior arrangement) feeds everyone into the same attraction queues. Once you're near the end, there will usually be a place for you to wait for the special wheelchair-ready ride vehicle to come around. Often, this translates into longer waits, as the special vehicles can be in high demand. The park maps carefully indicate which rides will require you to leave your personal vehicle. A very few, pre-ADA attractions, such as Tom Sawyer Island and the Swiss Family Treehouse, require you to be ambulatory. Those are marked, too, but the vast majority of things to see are accessible to all.

Hotels in Florida are required by law to have at least one room equipped for wheelchairs, and because guests with mobility issues are big business, most of them have more than one such room. At Disney, the best locations for wheelchair guests are probably Coronado Springs Resort, which has 99 equipped rooms; and the deluxe-level Polynesian and Grand Floridian resorts, which are connected to the Magic Kingdom and Epcot by easy transfers to the monorail. (The Contemporary, another monorail hotel, is perhaps too escalator ridden.) You might consider tackling the issue by renting a house, which provides much more room; most of the home-rental companies also comply with ADA requirements, so any request for an equipped condo or villa rental should not be beyond them.

In addition, every show has at least one **sign language–interpreted** performance daily, and many more are equipped with subtitles, projected in reverse on the back wall, that can be viewed with a Disney-issued device. Narrated rides provide interpreters and handheld devices; let them know you're coming at least 2 weeks in advance. For more information, call the sign language coordinator at ☎ 407/824-5217 or the Devices for the Deaf coordinator at 407/827-5141 (a TDD/TTY number).

All the theme parks produce **brochures concerning accessibility** that can be downloaded or picked up at in-park guest services desks. Disney's hotline is ☎ 407/824-4321 or 407/824-5141 [TTY]; Universal Orlando can be reached at ☎ 888/519-4899 [TTY] or 407/224-5929 [voice] (www.universalorlando.com); SeaWorld Orlando's number is ☎ 407/363-2414 or 407/464-2400 (www.seaworld.com); Kennedy Space Center is at ☎ 321/454-4198 [TDD] (www.kennedyspacecenter.com). Most parks can arrange sign language interpreters with at least 2 weeks' notice; all furnish assisted listening devices or scripts for some, but not all, of the biggest attractions.

Medical Travel, Inc. (☎ 800/308-2503 or 407/438-8010; www.medicaltravel.org) is a local company that specializes in the rental of mobility equipment, ramp vans, and supplies such as oxygen tanks (be aware that many rides do not allow tanks). Electric scooters and wheelchairs can be rented and delivered to your hotel room or villa through these established companies: **Buena Vista Scooters** (☎ 866/484-4797 or 407/938-0349; www.buenavistascooters.com), **Scootaround** (☎ 888/441-7575; www.scootaround.com), **Care Medical Equipment** (☎ 407/856-2273; www.caremedicalequipment.com), and **Walker Medical & Mobility Products** (☎ 888/726-6837 or 407/518-6000; www.walkermobility.com). All the theme parks, except the water parks, also rent ECVs for about $45 a day and wheelchairs for about $10 a day. If your own wheelchair is wider than about 25 inches, you might think about switching to the model rented at each park, as those are guaranteed to navigate tight squeezes such as hairpin queue turns.

Organizations that offer assistance to travelers with disabilities include the **American Federation for the Blind** (☎ 800/232-5463; www.afb.org) and **Society for Accessible Travel & Hospitality** (☎ 212/447-7284; www.sath.org).

ADVICE FOR SENIORS

Although just about every secondary attraction offers a special price for seniors, the major theme parks offer precious little in the way of special deals or amenities aside from the odd ticket discount. If you're over 50, you can join **AARP** (601 E. Street NW, Washington, DC 24009; ☎ 888/687-2277; www.aarp.org) to find out what's being offered in terms of discounts for hotels, airfare, and car rentals. Disney has been known to give small discounts on souvenirs, too. Before you bite, be sure that the AARP discount you are offered actually undercuts others that are out there (at a standard 10% off the usual rates, sometimes they don't). The well-respected **Elderhostel** (☎ 800/454-5768; www.elderhostel.org) runs many classes and programs, both inside the theme parks and around the Orlando area, designed to authentically delve into literature, history, the arts, and music. Packages last from a day to a week and include lodging, tours, and meals. Some are even multigenerational; bring the grandkids.

ADVICE FOR GAY & LESBIAN TRAVELERS

Orlando still has a conservative streak, but an influx of different types of people from across America, as well as the steady influence of the theme parks (which employ tens of thousands of gay people), have fostered a city in which two ideologically opposed communities coexist. Especially among the younger generation, the two communities mix and play together. See p. 292 for some of the biggest gay and lesbian hangouts in town, including the Parliament House, said to be the largest gay entertainment complex in the world.

Although it's not an official event, Walt Disney World is secretly proud to host Gay Days events (p. 309) in June—after all, many cast members are gay, too. With some 125,000 participants, it's one of the largest annual events in town.

As a consequence of all this mainstream visibility, most visitors to Orlando simply won't need any special resources or assistance. Most hotels aren't troubled in the least by gay couples, and gay people can be themselves anyplace. The most intolerant attitudes will come from other guests at the theme parks, who, of course, mostly aren't from Orlando—public displays of affection there are not likely to be attacked by families sharing the park with you, but don't expect a warm reception, either. Use your intuition—and your common sense.

Should you still worry about possible harassment, the **International Gay and Lesbian Travel Association** (☎ 954/630-1637; www.iglta.org) can connect you with gay-friendly hotels and businesses, but the list is a short one. Most of the Orlando-based gay groups deal mostly with residents' issues. The **Gay, Lesbian & Bisexual Community Center of Central Florida** (946 N. Mills Ave., Orlando; ☎ 407/228-8272; www.glbcc.org) offers the usual support, such as counseling and social groups in an environment where those who seek help are likely to be understood. **Gay Orlando Network** (www.gayorlando.com) lists events, but they're more likely to be resident-oriented (bowling nights or youth alliances) than tourist-oriented, although it does announce Sunday worship services.

A few publications may give you ideas of places to go, including nightlife journal *411* (www.the411mag.com), *Watermark* (www.watermarkonline.com) for state issues, and *Gay Parent* magazine (www.gayparentmag.com), which is sensitive to the issues faced by kids and their same-sex parents. As many kids of same-sex couples will tell you, their biggest problems often come from people who claim to care the most about their welfare.

STAYING WIRED

Getting online isn't hard with your own laptop. Most hotels will have access—sometimes in common areas, sometimes in guest rooms, and sometimes in both places. Strangely, it's the least expensive properties that seem to offer this service for free. Walt Disney World's hotels, for example, charge $10 a day, a pretty standard price. Bring your own Ethernet cable in case your hotel can't produce one. Many home rentals also come with Internet-connected computers, and a large number have Wi-Fi, too. Almost all of the offices of the major home rental agencies maintain computers for guest use, and countless cafes and restaurants have Wi-Fi now.

Those whose hotels don't have access have been known to crib free use by trawling the parking lots of the budget hotels on International Drive or U.S. 192. Many establishments don't password-protect their Wi-Fi signals.

You can also find access at Starbucks (www.starbucks.com), FedEx Office (www.fedex.com), Panera Bread bakeries (www.panerabread.com), and the Apple Stores at Mall at Millenia (p. 297) and Florida Mall (p. 296).

Those without laptops can usually find at least one taxi computer at their hotel, sometimes for a nominal fee ($2–$5 for 10 min. of access). Because of this, and the fact that few tourists need to check their e-mail who haven't also brought the means to do it, there are no dedicated Internet cafes.

Alternatively, locations of the **Orange County Library** (101 E. Central Blvd., Orlando; ☎ 407/835-7323; www.ocls.info) have terminals for public use, although they often require a library card to operate. Use these as a last resort, because you may have to do some sweet-talking.

RECOMMENDED BOOKS & FILMS

Surprisingly, for a city that is so emblematic of American culture and ideals, it's hard to find books that are interested in providing an honest retelling of Orlando's history and its character. Hyperion, a Disney imprint, tends to publish love letters, but it grants extraordinary access to its writers. These works, some of which are out of print, will give you a sense of the city as a place as well as a product:

BOOKS

- *Walt Disney: The Triumph of the American Imagination,* by Neal Gabler. Troubled, distant, driven, brilliant. A portrait of the real man and his business.
- *Since the World Began,* by Jeff Kurtti. One of the few Disney-produced books on park history that doesn't go all misty eyed and mealy mouthed.
- *Their Eyes Were Watching God,* by Zora Neale Hurston. Set in Eatonville, 6 miles north of Orlando, this classic novel is about African-American life in Florida at the turn of the last century.
- *Celebration, U.S.A.,* by Douglas Frantz and Catherine Collins. Two journalists are among the first to move into Disney's model community.
- *Inside the Mouse: Work and Play at Disney World,* by the Project on Disney. High-minded academics wander the World and muse on its rhetoric.
- *Vinyl Leaves,* by Stephen M. Fjellman. A professor examines the urban planning tenets and ideological messages at work in the Disney resorts.
- *30 Eco-Trips in Florida,* by Holly Ambrose. The best book for getting to know the real state of the state.
- *Florida, My Eden,* by Frederic B. Stresau. A classic on Florida horticulture.
- The Kingdom Keeper series, by Ridley Pearson. Juvenile adventure series in which teens romp, video-game style, through the Magic Kingdom on quests.

FILM & TV

- ◆ *Marvin's Room* (1996). As a sign of faith to Miramax, Disney allowed it to be the first movie to shoot in the Magic Kingdom, despite the unpleasant scene.
- ◆ *From the Earth to the Moon* (1998). Not only does the HBO miniseries retell the wonders of NASA's missions, it was also shot at Disney–MGM Studios.
- ◆ *Jaws 3-D* (1983). Shot at SeaWorld and on land that became Universal.
- ◆ *Moon over Miami* (1941) and *Easy to Love* (1953). Shot at Cypress Gardens.

The ABCs of Orlando

Area Codes The area code for the Orlando area is **407** (if you're dialing locally, a preceding 1 is not necessary, but the 407 is), although you may encounter the less common **321** code, which is also used on the Atlantic Coast. The **863** area code governs the land between Orlando and Tampa, and the Tampa area uses **813** and **727**. The region west of Orlando uses **352**.

ATMs and Currency Exchange See "Money Matters," earlier in this chapter.

Business Hours Offices are generally open weekdays between 9am and 5pm, while banks tend to close at 4pm. Typically, stores open between 9 and 10am and close between 6 and 7pm Monday through Saturday, except malls, which stay open until 9pm. On Sunday, stores generally open at 11am and close by 7pm.

Drinking Laws The legal age for the purchase and consumption of alcohol is 21. Proof of age is almost always requested, even if you look older, so carry photo ID. It's illegal to carry open containers of alcohol in any public area that isn't zoned for alcohol consumption (as CityWalk is), and the police may ticket you on the spot.

Electricity The United States uses 110 to 120 volts AC (60 cycles), compared to the 220 to 240 volts AC (50 cycles) that is standard in Europe, Australia, and New Zealand. If your small appliances use 220 to 240 volts, buy an adaptor and voltage converter before you leave home, as these are very difficult to find in Orlando.

Embassies & Consulates The nearest embassies are located in the nation's capital, Washington, D.C. Some consulates are located in major U.S. cities, and most nations have a mission to the United Nations in New York City. If your country isn't listed below, call for directory information in Washington, D.C. (☎ 202/555-1212) or log on to www.embassy.org/embassies.

The embassy of Australia is at 1601 Massachusetts Ave. NW, Washington, DC 20036 (☎ 202/797-3000; www.austemb.org). There are consulates in New York, Honolulu, Houston, Los Angeles, and San Francisco.

The embassy of Canada is at 501 Pennsylvania Ave. NW, Washington, DC 20001 (☎ 202/682-1740; www.canadianembassy.org). Other Canadian consulates are in Buffalo, Detroit, Los Angeles, New York, and Seattle.

The embassy of Ireland is at 2234 Massachusetts Ave. NW, Washington, DC 20008 (☎ 202/462-3939; www.irelandemb.org). Irish consulates are in Boston, Chicago, New York, San Francisco, and other cities.

The embassy of New Zealand is at 37 Observatory Circle NW, Washington, DC 20008 (☎ 202/328-4800; www.nzembassy.com). New Zealand consulates are in Los Angeles, Salt Lake City, San Francisco, and Seattle.

The embassy of the United Kingdom is at 3100 Massachusetts Ave. NW, Washington, DC 20008 (☎ 202/588-7800; www.britainusa.com). Other British consulates are in Atlanta, Boston,

Chicago, Cleveland, Houston, Los Angeles, New York, San Francisco, and Seattle.

Emergencies Call ☎ **911** for the police, to report a fire, or to get an ambulance. If you have a medical emergency that does not require an ambulance, you should be able to walk into the nearest hospital emergency room (see "Hospitals," below).

Holidays Banks close on the following holidays: January 1 (New Year's), the third Monday in January (Martin Luther King, Jr., Day), the third Monday in February (Presidents' Day), the last Monday in May (Memorial Day), July 4 (Independence Day), the first Monday in September (Labor Day), the second Monday in October (Veterans Day), the fourth Thursday in November (Thanksgiving Day), and December 25. The theme parks are open every day of the year.

Hospitals Dr. P Phillips Hospital (9400 Turkey Lake Rd., Orlando; ☎ 407/351-8500) is a short drive north up Palm Parkway from Lake Buena Vista. To get to **Florida Hospital Celebration Health** (400 Celebration Place, Celebration; ☎ 407/303-4000), from I-4, take the U.S. 192 exit; then at the first traffic light, turn right onto Celebration Avenue, and at the first stop sign, make another right. Clinics: **Centra Care Walk-In Urgent Care** in Lake Buena Vista (12500 Apopka-Vineland Rd., ☎ 407/934-2273; Mon–Fri 8am–midnight, Sat–Sun 8am–8pm); near the vacation homes south of Disney (7848 W. U.S. 192, Kissimmee; ☎ 407/397-7032; Mon–Fri 8am–8pm, Sat–Sun 8am–5pm); and by Universal (6001 Vineland Rd.; ☎ 407/351-6682; Mon–Fri 7am–7pm, Sat–Sun 8am–6pm). In addition, each theme park has its own infirmary capable of handling a range of medical emergencies. If you don't have a car, **EastCoast Medical Network** (☎ 407/648-5252; www.themedical concierge.com) makes house calls to area resorts for $150 to $275 for most ailments. It's available at all hours and brings a portable pharmacy, although prescriptions cost more.

Mail At press time, domestic postage rates were 27¢ for a postcard and 44¢ for a letter. For international mail, a first-class letter of up to 1 ounce costs 98¢ (75¢ to Canada, 79¢ to Mexico); a first-class postcard costs the same as a letter. For more information go to **www.usps.com** and click on "Calculate Postage."

There's a post office at the Mall of Millenia (4200 Conroy Rd., Orlando; ☎ 407/363-3555; Mon–Fri 9am–5pm, Sat 10am–1pm) and at Lake Buena Vista, north of the Downtown Disney area (12133 S. Apopka Vineland Rd., Orlando; ☎ 407/238-0223; Mon–Fri 9am–4pm, Sat 9am–noon). Ask at the theme park Guest Relations desks if mailing your items there will entitle you to a themed postmark.

Newspapers & Magazines Most hotels distribute that shallow McNewspaper, *USA Today,* to use as your morning door-mat. The local paper, the *Orlando Sentinel* (www.orlandosentinel.com), is less widely available but much better for discovering local happenings. *Orlando Magazine* (www.orlandomagazine.com) is a glossy that covers trends and upscale restaurants. Also see the box on amateur-run websites covering the theme parks on p. 305; you can usually find more information on those than in professional publications.

Pharmacies As much as I wish there were such a thing as a "local" pharmacy, the tourist area hosts mostly national chains. **Walgreens** (7650 W. Sand Lake Rd. at Dr. Phillips Blvd., Orlando; ☎ 407/370-6742), which has a round-the-clock pharmacy, could, at a stretch, be deemed an outfit with local roots; back in the day, Mr. Walgreen spent the cold months in Winter Park. **Turner Drugs** (12500 Apopka Vineland Rd., Lake Buena Vista; ☎ 407/828-8125) is not a 24-hour pharmacy, but it delivers prescriptions to most Disney-area accommodations.

Smoking Smoking is generally prohibited in all public indoor spaces, including offices, bars, restaurants, hotel lobbies, and most shops. In general, if you need to smoke, you'll have to go outside into the open air, and in the theme parks there are strictly enforced designated areas.

Taxes A 6.5% to 7% sales tax is charged on all goods with the exception of most edible grocery items and medicines. Hotels add another 2% to 5% in a resort tax, so the total tax on accommodations can run up to 12%. The United States has no value-added tax, but the custom is to not list prices with tax, so the final amount that you pay will be slightly higher than the posted price.

Telephone Generally, hotel surcharges on long-distance and local calls are astronomical, so you're better off using your **cellphone** or a **public pay telephone.** Many convenience groceries and packaging services sell **prepaid calling cards** in denominations from $10 to $50; for international visitors these can be the least expensive way to call home. Many public phones at airports now accept American Express, MasterCard, and Visa credit cards. **Local calls** made from public pay phones in most locales cost either 35¢ or 50¢. Pay phones do not accept pennies, and few will take anything larger than a quarter. Make sure you have roaming turned on for your cellphone account.

If you will have high-speed Internet access in your room, you can save on calls by using **Skype** (www.skype.com) or another Web-based calling program, as calls between members cost nothing.

Most long-distance and international calls can be dialed directly from any phone. **For calls within the United States and to Canada,** dial 1 followed by the area code and the seven-digit number. **For other international calls,** first dial 011, then the country code, and then proceed with the number, dropping any leading zeroes.

Calls to area codes **800, 888, 877,** and **866** are toll-free. However, calls to area codes **700** and **900** (chat lines, bulletin boards, "dating" services, and so on) can be very expensive—usually a charge of 95¢ to $3 or more per minute, and they sometimes have minimum charges that can run as high as $15 or more.

For **reversed-charge or collect calls,** and for person-to-person calls, dial the number 0, then the area code and number. An operator will come on the line, and you should specify whether you are calling collect, person to person, or both. If your operator-assisted call is international, ask for the overseas operator.

For **local directory assistance** ("information"), dial ☎ 411; for long-distance information, dial 1, then the appropriate area code and 555-1212.

Time The continental United States is divided into four time zones: Eastern Standard Time (EST), Central Standard Time (CST), Mountain Standard Time (MST), and Pacific Standard Time (PST). Orlando is on Eastern Standard Time, so when it's noon in Orlando, it's 11am in Chicago (CST), 10am in Denver (MST), and 9am in Los Angeles (PST). Daylight saving moves the clock 1 hour ahead of standard time. Clocks change the second Sunday in March and the first Sunday in November.

Tipping Tips are customary and should be factored into your budget. Waiters should receive 15% to 20% of the cost of the meal (depending on the quality of the service), bellhops get $1 per bag, chambermaids get $1 to $2 per day for straightening your room (although many people don't do this), and cab drivers should get 15% of the fare. Don't be offended if you are reminded about tipping—waitstaff are used to dealing with international visitors who don't participate in the custom back home.

Toilets Each theme park has dozens of clean restrooms. Outside of the parks, every fast-food place—and there are hundreds—should have a restroom you can use. Barring those, many large hotel lobbies also have some.

Index

See also Accommodations and Restaurant indexes, below.

338   Index

ACCOMMODATIONS

RESTAURANTS